Mediamerica, Mediaworld

Form, Content, and Consequence
of Mass Communication

D0082158

Edward Jay Whetmore California State University

Mediamerica, Mediaworld:

Form, Content, and
Consequence of
Mass Communication
Updated Fifth Edition

Edward Jay Whetmore
California State University
at Dominguez Hills

Wadsworth Publishing Company

™ An International Thomson Publishing Company

Belmont • Albany • Bonn • Boston • Cincinnati • Detroit • London • Madrid • Melbourne •
Mexico City • New York • Paris • San Francisco • Singapore • Tokyo • Toronto • Washington

Editor: Katherine Hartlove
Communications Editor: Todd R. Armstrong
Editorial Assistant: Janet Hansen
Production Services Coordinator: Debby Kramer
Production Editor: Merrill Peterson, Matrix Productions
Print Buyer: Barbara Britton
Art Editor and Technical Illustrator: Nancy Spellman
Permissions Editor: Robert Kauser
Interior and Cover Designer: Cloyce Wall
Copy Editor: Margaret Moore
Photo Researcher: Monica Suder
Compositor: ColorType
Printer: R. R. Donnelley/Crawfordsville
Credits continue on page 492

 The ITP logo is a trademark under license.

Printed in the United States of America

1 2 3 4 5 6 7 8 9 10—01 00 99 98 97 96 95

For more information, contact Wadsworth Publishing Company:

Wadsworth Publishing Company
10 Davis Drive
Belmont, California 94002, USA

International Thomson Publishing Europe
Berkshire House 168-173
High Holborn
London, WC1V 7AA, England

Thomas Nelson Australia
102 Dodds Street
South Melbourne 3205
Victoria, Australia

Nelson Canada
1120 Birchmount Road
Scarborough, Ontario
Canada M1K 5G4

International Thomson Editores
Campos Eliseos 385, Piso 7
Col. Polanco
11560 México D.F. México

International Thomson Publishing GmbH
Königswinterer Strasse 418
53227 Bonn, Germany

International Thomson Publishing Asia
221 Henderson Road
#05-10 Henderson Building
Singapore 0315

International Thomson Publishing Japan
Hirakawacho Kyowa Building, 3F
2-2-1 Hirakawacho
Chiyoda-ku, Tokyo 102, Japan

Library of Congress Cataloging-in-Publication Data

Whetmore, Edward Jay.
  Mediamerica, mediaworld: form, content, and consequence / Edward
Jay Whetmore. — Updated 5th ed.
       p.   cm. — (Wadsworth series in mass communication and
journalism)
     Includes bibliographical references and index.
     ISBN: 0-534-25818-2
     1. Mass media — United States.   2. Mass media.   3. Popular culture —
United States.   I. Title.   II. Series.
     P92.U5W48   1995   94-45388
     302.23'0973 — dc20

This book is dedicated to the memory of my mother, Phyllis JoAnn Armstrong (1923–1970), who was an amazing lady and who continues to be a guiding spirit in my life. It was she who first helped me understand the beauty and excitement of life in Mediamerica and Mediaworld.

Brief Contents

Detailed Contents

two   Electronic Media: Edison Came to Stay

three

Beyond the Media:
The Phenomena of Mass Communication

About the Author   Edward Jay Whetmore
(Ph.D., University of Oregon) lives and works in
southern California where he has sold feature
screenplays to Warner Brothers and LTL
Entertainment. His articles on the media have
appeared in magazines as diverse as *Emmy* and
Soap Opera Digest.

Edd is currently associate professor of
communications at California State University,
Dominguez Hills, where he is also faculty adviser
to the campus newspaper. Though he awakens
every day to a view of the Pacific Ocean, he does
not own a surfboard. He has, however, frequently
been known to "channel surf" across his cable
television landscape.

Preface

Like so many creative projects, *Mediamerica, Mediaworld* was born of frustration. For years I looked in vain for a text that communicated the excitement media can generate — a book that went beyond facts and figures to uncover the heart and soul of mass communication. Finding none, I decided to write my own. With the help of Senior Editor Rebecca Hayden and the excellent staff at Wadsworth, the first edition appeared in 1979 and was followed by new editions in 1982, 1985, 1989, and 1993. This text has been used in hundreds of colleges and universities by hundreds of thousands of students. Many have commented that they enjoyed reading a "different" kind of media book.

This updated fifth edition includes dozens of revised paragraphs as well as new time-line material designed to provide up-to-the-minute coverage of topics as diverse as the media significance of the O. J. Simpson case and the success of "Melrose Place." *Mediamerica* has become *Mediamerica/Mediaworld*. Today's media environment is best described in global terms. Worldwide satellite distribution has revolutionized the television industry, and international investors now control many Hollywood film studios. American newspapers and magazines, once fiercely independent, are increasingly run by massive corporate interests. We have tried our best to explore these changes while maintaining the "user friendly" approach that has made *Mediamerica* one of the most successful texts of its kind.

You'll find updated time lines, conceived to give the reader a sense of how crucial historical events have led us to where we are today. We've updated our visual package, selecting examples that convey the material effectively while maintaining those that readers felt worked best in previous editions. You'll also find the feature inserts, guest essays from media experts, and topical up-to-the-minute references that have long characterized *Mediamerica*.

New to the edition are separate, expanded chapters on advertising and public relations. The advertising industry has been particularly hard hit by the recession, and we've got the story. Public relations practitioners have evolved from publicists to information specialists, and we'll take a look at their new roles in corporate Mediamerica.

My collaborator Alfred P. Kielwasser has contributed completely revised chapters covering ethics ("Morality and the Media") and international media practices ("Mass Communication in the Global Village"). I think you'll find the ethics chapter provides an exciting and solid historical context for the examination of many of our current and most crucial media controversies.

More than ever before, any understanding of mass communication must extend far beyond the borders of Mediamerica. With that in mind the new international chapter provides an around-the-world tour of mass communication practices. In addition, you'll also find new information covering the global marketplace throughout the book.

Like most texts, *Mediamerica, Mediaworld* provides names, places, and statistics, but because history is more relevant when it relates to what is happening *now*, this text continues to emphasize not only what has happened but also what *is* happening, exploring the whys as well as the whats. Why did *Beverly Hills, 90210* and *Roseanne* become such hits? Why has MTV become such a phenomenal global success story? Why has the Super Bowl come to dominate the American sports scene? All *mediated* phenomena offer clues about our-selves and our culture.

I have noticed that many authors of other media texts prefer not to acknowledge the existence of the *National Enquirer,* soap operas, and rock and roll; if they do, it is often in a condescending manner. I have included at least some discussion of each of these phenomena because, for better or worse, they are part of our culture. To ignore them is to ignore many of the most important manifestations of Mediamerica and Mediaworld. So we'll deal with David Letterman, R.E.M., and *Mad* magazine along with more traditional topics, because they all play an important part in our mass communication system. You may not be completely happy with the content of mass media; no one is. But if we are going to try to change it, we must first examine *what* it is and *why* it is.

When I was in college, my instructors seemed to have largely negative opinions about mass media. We students read texts and listened to lectures about how bad newspapers, magazines, radio, and especially television were. I'd be the first to admit that mass media have many problems, but I just cannot accept an antimedia perspective, perhaps because I find the form and content of mass media so endlessly fascinating. Nevertheless, I don't think that my enjoyment of the subject inhibits me from helping you develop a critical perspective as a media consumer.

During the last 20 years, I have worked professionally as a freelance writer, teacher, disc jockey, and advertising executive. Currently I can be found making the rounds of the film and television production studios in southern California "pitching" feature film and TV series concepts. I've included a few of these personal media experiences. This is a textbook, of course, not an autobiography, but I hope that my own background as a producer and consumer of mass information will help you understand your own experiences. The forces of mass communication are so overwhelming that whether we like it or not we are all involved. In the last analysis Mediaworld is our world after all.

As you turn the page and begin your own journey through Mediamerica and Mediaworld, you go where many have gone before. Yet your trip will remain uniquely yours, for such is the nature of all mass communication. With that in mind, I hope to hear from you and your instructors about your reactions to the book. When we sit down to construct the sixth edition, we'll begin by reviewing your comments. Just use the postage-paid form you'll find at the back of the book and let us know how we're doing. I'll be glad to respond to any questions or comments you have.

Acknowledgments

In a project of this size it is difficult to thank all of those who have contributed, but there are several people that I especially want to acknowledge. Alfred P. Kielwasser's contributions extend far beyond his authorship of chapters 13 and 15. He is also responsible for the Queries and Concepts and the Readings and References sections throughout the book. He is a gifted media scholar and I have been fortunate to have his assistance.

Editor Katherine Hartlove and Production Editor Jerilyn Emori have suffered extensively at the hands of my chaotic work habits. My apologies. Art Editor Nancy Spellman and Designer Cloyce Wall are responsible for most of the new photos and visual material included in this edition. Their care and personal concern are greatly appreciated.

I have never met Peter Pringle of the University of Tennessee, Chattanooga, but his incredible attention to detail helped make this the most thorough and accurate edition of the book to date. My special thanks.

Thanks also to the legion of reviewers: Susan Caudill, University of Tennessee, Knoxville; Gerald Flannery, University of Southwestern Louisiana; Mary-Lou Galician, Arizona State University; Bruce Hann, Des Moines Area Community College; Jack F. Holgate, University of Southern Mississippi; Jim Mattimore, Suffolk Community College; Maclyn H. McClary, Humboldt State University; David H. Mould, Ohio University; Alfred Owens, Youngstown State University; Peter K. Pringle, University of Tennessee, Chattanooga; Michelle J. Stanton, California State University, Northridge; Douglas P. Starr, Texas A&M University; Joseph O. Tabarlet, Wesleyan College; Jan Whitt, University of Colorado, Boulder; and Laurie J. Wilson, Brigham Young University. Each of them has contributed directly to the new edition. Thanks also to all of those who labored on previous editions.

The staff at Wadsworth continues to impress me with their professionalism. Kudos to Editorial Assistant Janet Hansen, Print Buyer Barbara Britton, and Permissions Editor Robert Kauser, in addition to those already named.

Finally, I would like to thank those unsung heroes and heroines; the Wadsworth sales representatives. They believed in this book from the beginning and managed to get it in the hands of professors, convincing them to give it a try. Without their support, *Mediamerica, Mediaworld* could never have grown to become what it is today.

Edd Whetmore

Welcome to Mediamerica and Mediaworld! You're about to discover some of the ways in which today's global environment is constantly being reshaped by the form, content, and consequence of mass communication. In the process, we are continually reinventing ourselves as well.

It's been over 550 years since Gutenberg came up with the idea of a mass-produced form of communication. What changes we've been through since then! It wasn't so long ago that ships crisscrossed the Atlantic Ocean bringing with them "the latest" news from Europe to an information-starved American public. Since the first communications satellite was launched in 1962, we've been busily exchanging billions of bits of information instantaneously with others all over the world.

Gutenberg could hardly have known he was setting such a revolution in motion, yet his early efforts represented the first step in the attempt to disseminate information "to the masses." What's more, despite intense competition from the electronic media, print communication continues to exert a tremendous influence on our social and cultural development here in America and around the world.

In Part One, I have devoted one chapter each to books and magazines and two chapters to newspapers. This is not to say that any one medium is more important than another. But, for many, newspapers seem to be a basis of comparison, the yardstick for all mass media. Even defining what constitutes a newspaper can be troublesome. Is the *National Enquirer* a newspaper or a magazine? Think about it, then turn to Chapter 4 for the answer. Can you name the only major American humor magazine that accepts *no* advertising? You'll find out all about it in Chapter 5.

The most frustrating thing about writing a general text is space limitation. I would have liked to devote a dozen chapters to each medium, but of course that would make for a very long semester. I hope that the queries and source material at the end of each chapter will lead you to the further exploration so necessary to developing a real understanding of each medium.

one

Print:
The Gutenberg
Gallery

Welcome to Mediamerica, Mediaworld

There's something happening here

What it is ain't exactly clear . . .

I think it's time to stop

Hey, what's that sound

Everybody look what's going down . . .

Stephen Stills

"Four . . . Three . . . Two . . . One . . . Zero . . . Lift off!" At 3:35 on the morning of Tuesday, July 10, 1962, a three-stage Thor-Delta rocket blasts off in a swirl of smoke at Cape Canaveral, Florida. The rocket's payload is a small spherical satellite just 34½ inches in diameter.

As the *Telstar* satellite enters its predetermined orbit, engineers begin to relay sound and pictures directly to it. The signals are amplified about 10 billion times before they reach their destination in France. What the French see is a giant dome containing AT&T's antenna and a 50-star American flag flapping in the breeze. What they hear is a recording of "America the Beautiful." In an instant, Mediamerica has become Mediaworld.

Hailed as a communications breakthrough as significant as the invention of the printing press, satellite communication has lived up to the hype by revolutionizing the ways in which the citizens of the world learn about one another. Whether it's war in the Persian Gulf or political upheaval in the Soviet Union, we see it all live, via satellite. As extraordinary as this is, it's still the electronic extension of a revolution that began in Germany over 550 years ago.

1.1

Telstar, the first communications satellite, ushers in a new era of instantaneous global communication.

The Birth of Mass Communication

In 1436 Johannes Gutenberg was asking all of his friends for money, despite the fact that he had moved from his native Mainz to Strasbourg with servants and plenty of capital. His sudden need for funds sprung from a desire to develop what he called a "secret art."

Before long he was able to find several partners who were interested in this mysterious new art. Among them was Andreas Dritzehen, who mortgaged his property and borrowed on his inheritance to invest in Gutenberg's idea. He boasted to a friend that the project "will not fail us; before a year is passed we shall have our capital again." Such candor was rare among the investors in Gutenberg's project. When asked about their investment, they avoided mentioning printing specifically, instead speaking vaguely of "the work" or "the adventure and art."

Historians now know that the art involved a set of molds that could be arranged and rearranged to print virtually any message. Gutenberg's secret was a new kind of printing press using movable type, which would greatly expand the dissemination of the printed word (see 1.2). No longer would printers have to carve a new set of molds for each page.

The invention of the Gutenberg press with its movable type made possible mass literacy and constituted the birth of what we call "mass communication." The term *mass* is of critical importance. In earlier days, the masses could communicate only by using the oral, or story, form because most books were handwritten and very expensive. Gutenberg's press changed all of that. Culture, history, and religion, preserved on the pages of books, could now conceivably be made available to everyone. It was also the beginning of mass culture. (See Chapter 14.)

During its first 200 years, the publishing business was usually the tool of the church and state. Early books and pamphlets encouraged readers to accept the doctrine of the ruling elite. But mass literacy brought with it more sophisticated and curious citizens. Eventually, many people, encouraged by their new literacy, began to question the divine right of rule and authority. It is no accident that the rise of printed literature coincided with the Renaissance and the Reformation. Sometimes great ideas bring with them more than even their inventors can imagine.

Defining Communication

What we know about the form and content of mass media is part of a larger field of study we call *communication.* Communication researcher Frank E. X. Dance offers 15 separate definitions of communication. One says:

The connecting thread appears to be the idea of something being transferred from one person to another. We use the word communication sometimes to refer to what is so transferred, sometimes to the means by which it is transferred, and sometimes to the whole process.

We refer to what is being transferred as the *content*. For example, so far the content of this chapter can be summarized as:

1 The launching of *Telstar*
2 A brief historical sketch of how the Gutenberg press came into being
3 A brief discussion of the significance of Gutenberg's invention
4 One definition of *communication*

So the message of this book is the content of its communication. *Form* involves how a message is being transferred. There are many ways to send a message. We can whisper, shout, write, dance, or paint. We might also choose to use any number of technological devices.

The model found in 1.4 by Shannon and Weaver is a simple representation of how communication works. Such a model can be used to represent all three of the major types, or

1.2

Gutenberg demonstrates his new movable type to investors.

modes, of communication: intrapersonal, interpersonal, and mass.

Intrapersonal communication involves the messages we send to ourselves. You are reading this book in the library when suddenly you realize you are hungry. You put the book down and go off to a vending machine. Through a complex series of cybernetics, your internal system has motivated you to seek food, even in the form of stale potato chips. A countless number of such messages happen within you every day. One part of your system acts as the

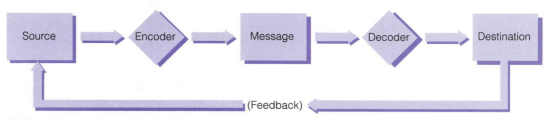

1.4

This chart traces the path of communication according to the Shannon-Weaver model of the communication process.

From Wilbur Schramm and Donald F. Roberts, eds., The Process and Effects of Mass Communication. Copyright 1972, University of Illinois Press. Used by permission.

1436 Gutenberg's "secret art" is a printing press with movable type, mass communication begins.

1877 Thomas Edison creates the "talking machine," dubbing it a "phonograph."

1400

1450–1500 An estimated 30,000 new book titles are printed. Most popular are law and religious books.

1600

1640 Stephen Day is commissioned to typeset *The Whole Booke of Psalms*, one of the first books printed in the new world.

1690 *Publick Occurrences Both Forreign and Domestick* is the first U.S. newspaper.

1700

1733 Benjamin Franklin's *Poor Richard's Almanack*, a collection of tide tables, proverbs, and harvest suggestions, is all the rage. Franklin also begins the new world's first subscription library.

1741 Franklin and Andrew Bradford each begin publication of the first regular American magazines. Both fail.

1783 *The Pennsylvania Evening Post and Daily Advertiser* is America's first daily newspaper.

1.3 Milestones in the Evolution of Mass Communication

1927

The *Jazz Singer* is the first sound motion picture.

1990s

"Virtual reality" technology promises to revolutionize mass communication practices.

1800   1900

1841 Volney Palmer organizes the first American advertising agency.

1884 Ottmar Mergenthaler's Linotype machine creates "instant" movable type, greatly speeding production of books, newspapers, and magazines.

1888 Thomas Edison and William Dickson develop the first workable motion picture camera.

1901 Guglielmo Marconi sends the first "wireless" signals across the Atlantic Ocean.

1903 *The Great Train Robbery* is the first "feature film."

1906 Lee de Forest's audio grid makes wireless voice transmission possible.

1923 *Crystallizing Public Opinion* is Edward L. Bernays' ground-breaking book on the emerging role of public relations. He teaches the first college course in PR the same year.

1927 Philo Farnsworth applies for a patent on the first "electronic television system."

1933 Edwin Armstrong harnesses frequency modulation (FM), a new kind of radio service is born.

1940 RCA demonstrates the first color TV system library.

1940s The appearance of the paperback book revolutionizes the industry.

1962 *Telstar* is the first communications satellite.

1969 Live TV coverage of the first moon landing.

1975 Sony introduces the first home video recording system.

1981 IBM markets its first personal computer.

1995 The Clinton administration pushes for expansion of the nation's fledgling "information superhighway."

source: It encodes the message "I am hungry" and sends it to your brain, where it is decoded on arrival. When the message reaches its final destination, you put down the book and act on it.

Interpersonal communication happens when two or more beings are involved. Assuming that you are no longer hungry, you return to the library and begin to read again. Suddenly a friend comes in, sees you, and says "What's happening?" At this point, he or she becomes the source, encoding the message "What's happening?" and then saying those words. Through a complex process involving language as well as nonverbal cues, you decode the message and it arrives at its destination, namely you. What's really "happening" is interpersonal communication.

In *mass* communication, the source may be one person, but more often it is a group of people. In print, there are writers, editors, typesetters, distributors, and many more. In electronic media, there are scriptwriters, actors, producers, directors, and others. Each group becomes a source. The encoding process involves a media form such as a book, radio, or television set. The message is then decoded by the media consumer, who may or may not offer some form of feedback to the source. The question of *delayed* feedback is of special interest in mass communication because it may be at the heart of a number of crucial political and economic decisions. The government agency that sends health-care books to a remote South American village where the people can't read has not communicated successfully.

Accuracy is another factor essential to the success of a particular act of communication. In *Speech Communication, Concepts and Behavior,* authors Frank E. X. Dance and Carl E. Larson define accuracy in each of the three communication modes:

In very general terms we may say that intrapersonal communication is accurate to the extent that what an indi-vidual tells himself approximates "reality." On the interpersonal level, we may say that communication is accurate to the extent that one person understands another's sentiments, preferences, values and so on. On the person to persons (or mass) level . . . accuracy is often viewed (as) the extent to which information transmitted by a source has been acquired and retained by members of an "audience."

Communication researcher Harold Lasswell contended that the basic components of the communication process could be identified in one question: *Who* says *what,* on which *channel,* to *whom,* with what *effect?*

Consequences, or effects, involve every step of the process. Form involves *how* the message is communicated; content involves *what* is communicated. A consequence can be the result of either or of both. But to understand effects fully, we need to examine all components of the communication process.

Another way of looking at the consequences or effects of communication in each of the three communication modes can be found in the Whetmore Grid for Understanding Communication Relationships (see 1.5). In this model, the intrapersonal mode is described as internal reality, the interpersonal as external reality, and the mass as mediated reality. Each dimension has unique characteristics described in several different ways. From a psychosocial point of view, we use intrapersonal communication to perceive the world. Meanwhile our communication with others helps us relate to what we perceive in a meaningful way. Mass communication brings about a linking process that enables us to feel connected to everyone in our Mediaworld.

From a psychological point of view, we begin with our internal instincts and habits. These often come under scrutiny when we take them into the "real world," where the interpersonal mode frequently provides an an-

Reality Level	Reality Dimension	Communication Mode	Psychosocial Mode	Philosophical Mode
Internal reality	Inside dimension	Intrapersonal communication	Perceiving	Thesis
External reality	Outside dimension	Interpersonal communication	Relating	Antithesis
Mediated reality	Collective dimension	Mass communication	Linking	Synthesis

1.5

The Whetmore grid for understanding communication relationships.

tithesis. How often have you found your ideas or beliefs challenged in a classroom discussion or even a casual conversation with a friend? Mediated reality often acts to bring about a synthesis. A close examination of the values espoused in TV's prime-time programs, for example, yields the fact that we all hold pretty much the same set of values: Crime doesn't pay, love conquers all, good deeds are rewarded, illegal behavior is punished, and so on. Whether these things are true or not, most of us like to believe that they are. In many ways, mediated reality provides us with reinforcement of those beliefs.

Consider the prime-time soap "Melrose Place." Heather Locklear's character always seems to be willing to bend the rules to make sure she gets what (or who!) she wants. At first her devious schemes seem to succeed, but in the end they always backfire. Why?

Like other villainous soap characters (remember J. R. Ewing of "Dallas"?), her actions run counter to acceptable societal codes of conduct. As a result she is constantly being "punished" by script writers by having all

manner of disastrous things happen to her. Such is the nature of mass communication.

Form: Mass Media

We call a medium a "mass medium" if it meets two requirements:

1 *It must reach many people.* Gutenberg's press made books a mass medium. Later came other media: newspapers, magazines, radio, and television, to name a few. All are mass media because they can reach hundreds, thousands, or even millions of people simultaneously.

2 *It requires the use of some technological device, located between source and destination.* Let me illustrate by using this book as an example of how mass media fit the Shannon-Weaver model. The thoughts you're reading now come from me, the source. I encode them using the English language and my computer. From here they go by

messenger to my publisher, where they occasionally arrive on time. Then they are edited, more changes are made, and finally they go to the printer. The technological device used by these modern-day Gutenbergs represents the medium. It comes after encoding and before decoding. The technological device is the printing press, the result is *the book*.

Now you go to the bookstore and wait in line. Wait in line a little longer. Finally you buy the book and open it to the first page. There you begin *decoding* my message by reading it. Finally my thoughts have reached you, their destination. As the Grateful Dead's Jerry Garcia says, "What a long strange trip it's been."

So this book qualifies as a mass medium because it is designed to reach many people and employs a technological device between source and receiver.

Content: Mass Message

Controversial communication researcher Marshall McLuhan's favorite slogan was "The medium is the message." (For more on McLuhan, see Chapter 14.) He believed that because all mass messages pass through a technological device, they are no longer the same message at all but have been radically changed. His slogan is an exaggerated plea for examining the form of mass messages as well as their content.

From the very beginning of the process, mass messages are different from interpersonal ones. A source who designs a mass message realizes that it will be altered by the medium. Imagine R.E.M.'s Michael Stipe in your living room. You are talking about your homework. Suddenly he blurts out, "That's me in the corner. That's me in the spotlight, losing my religion. Trying to keep up with you, and I don't know if I can. . . ." It might seem a little strange. (But since he's famous you'd probably humor him.) The point is that "Losing my Religion,"

which was transmitted from the source to the receiver via radio, cassette, and CD, was one of the more successful messages in the recent history of mass communication!

Consequence: Mass Culture

A good deal of mass communication research involves mass culture. We use the term *mass culture* to identify the *effects* of mass media. In the Michael Stipe example, the media were radio and recordings. But you would not be familiar with "Losing my Religion," or even with R.E.M., unless you were a participant in mass culture. Mass culture involves a body of knowledge that you *share* with others in your environment.

Communication researcher Alex Gode points out that all communication "makes common to two or several what was the monopoly of one or some." In other words, a central purpose of communication is to establish some common ground between people. Mass culture in Mediaworld, made possible by global mass communication, is shared by virtually everyone. This sharing process opens up many possibilities, and not all of them are pleasant. For example, critics worry about the possible effects of TV violence on the nation's children. Will children's beliefs and attitudes about violence be affected by their endless diet of cops and robbers? Are we becoming so mesmerized by the *mediated* world of commercial products that we forget that material goods are not everything in life? Have we forgotten "quality art" and its importance in a world filled with the popular art found in mass media?

Other critics worry that the mass audience is too easily swayed, that the era of the individual is over. On the one hand, we may be trading our individualism for a more collective, tribal identity we don't yet completely understand. On the other hand, we may simply be on the verge of a new kind of individualism. Futurist Alvin Toffler was one of the first to predict that products like home video and audio recorders would bring about more diverse media and "un-mass" the mass media. In either case, there can be no doubt that this is a time of transition. No person or nation can afford to be self-oriented as in the past. In the Mediaworld of instantaneous communication, everything we do affects everyone else all the time. And that is what mass culture is all about.

The Technological Embrace

Can you imagine a world without mass communication? There would be no newspapers, radios, television sets, or McDonald's golden arches. Before Gutenberg the myths, proverbs, and fairy tales that were used to pass wisdom from one generation to the next were limited by their channel capacity. *Channel capacity* is the term communication researcher Wilbur Schramm and others use to describe the ability of a particular medium to transfer a message successfully.

Remember the parlor game in which each person whispers a story to the next? The end version is usually quite different from the original. Obviously, verbal exchange is not necessarily the best way to transfer a story. We cannot remember long messages exactly, and we tend to embellish or exaggerate some details and omit others. Naturally, the ability to remember exact words differs for every individual. Gutenberg's printing offered everyone a *precise* method of exchanging information. You can still go back and read the original Gutenberg Bibles, if you can read Latin. They haven't changed. Nor have the handwritten books from before Gutenberg's time, but those books could reach only one reader at a time.

Chaucer's *Canterbury Tales* offers an example of a series of folktales that became part of the mass culture thanks to the printing press. Though they were written some 80 years before Gutenberg's invention, once they were set in type, they became standard literature for the information-hungry mass audience. The tales remain intact and are still literary standards in our society. More recent examples of the same basic phenomenon are Arnold Schwarzenegger, Mr. Spock, Elvis Presley, Garth Brooks, Boris Yeltsin, Nike, Bill Clinton, and the Sex Pistols — all brought to us in whole or in part via mass communication. How have we changed as a result of these mass communication experiences?

McLuhan contended that we now live in a "global village" where we share our hopes, dreams, and fears in a "worldpool" of information. He said that in the global village (or Mediaworld), the old social, racial, and ethnic barriers of the past will break down, and media will eventually help us achieve world peace and harmony. Others disagree, citing a host of problems from the social unrest in the 1960s to the North Korea nuclear controversy in the 90s as examples of problems created and nurtured, at least in part, by mass media. Just about everyone agrees that mass media have altered our evolution and destiny, but no one is quite sure how.

Competing Technologies in Mass Communication

One of the most intriguing theories about how mass media affect our lives involves competing communication technologies. In certain time periods, one particular medium seems to dominate. Thus, we speak of the pre-Gutenberg oral or folk period, the rise of print, the golden age of radio, and so on.

Most of us spend more time watching television than reading. This shift of our attention away from books has disturbed many people. What effect might it have on our attitudes and beliefs? To cite one example, our decisions in the voting booth probably are influenced heavily by the 30-second campaign commercials we see on TV. Do these commercials give candidates enough time to discuss the complex issues of our society, or do they reduce the political arena to a world of meaningless slogans and redundant clichés? In the 1960s, newscaster David Brinkley gave his reaction to surveys showing that most Americans relied almost solely on television news: "Then they're getting damn little news."

One thing is certain: In many ways, print and electronic media compete with each other. Their form and content represent different approaches to delivering entertainment, reporting the news, and distributing vital information.

A book is something we experience alone, often in a quiet, isolated environment. Remember the last time you sat next to someone who was whispering in the library? It probably distracted you. Yet loud audience reaction is common in most movie theaters, especially when action vehicles like *Terminator 2* are showing. Even when the audience is silent, the film is a shared event. We can experience radio and television equally well alone or with others. Rivalry between media is a rivalry of diverse *forms*. The form of a mass medium directly affects what the message will be, how we perceive and understand the message, and how that message affects us.

The Cone Effect: Understanding Mediated Reality

The *cone effect,* named after the two cones that make up its design (see 1.6), is another way of examining the effects of mass media on our lives. It involves the relationship between *mediated reality* and real life. In 1.6 we see that everything begins in the circle labeled "real life." Real life represents all life experiences that do not *directly* involve a mass medium. For example, we may take a walk in the park on a sunny day and eat a sandwich. People had these kinds of real-life experiences long before there were any mass media.

Certain aspects of real-life experience are then used by a communicator to form *constructed mediated reality* (CMR). CMR may consist of a TV show, magazine ad, or any other media message. It's important to remember that, even though CMR is taken from real life, there are many differences between the two. Basically, CMR tends to be funnier, sexier, more intense, more colorful, and more violent than real life. After all, nobody ever wrote a song about an ordinary relationship. Songs are written about special relationships, ones that have a great degree of intensity. On "Married . . . With Children," dozens of funny and entertaining things happen every half hour, but in real life we are lucky if one funny thing happens to us in an average day. Even novels and short stories are usually written about larger-than-life people, those who have special qualities.

Because CMR is real life "blown up," the mere fact that something appears as part of CMR triggers audience expectations about its larger-than-life qualities. We *expect* CMR to offer us things that are out of the ordinary. If it didn't, there would be no reason to suspend real life long enough to experience mediated reality.

In many ways, this book is really a study of various mass media and their competing CMRs. You'll learn something about how and why these are constructed as they are. In our society, many mass media vie for the consumer's attention. More often than not, CMR is designed in such a way so as to attract and hold the largest possible portion of the mass audience.

Once CMR is completed, it is transmitted via a mass medium to the audience. We call the audience perception of this information *perceived mediated reality* (PMR). We perceive mediated reality in many ways. We can listen intently to a song on the radio (foreground), or we can use the mediated reality of a radio station as background while we concentrate on other tasks. A magazine advertisement can be studied closely or simply glanced at as we turn the page.

Whatever the case, our perception of mediated reality takes up a great part of our waking hours. With the average TV set on about 7 hours every day and our radios and CD players going constantly, it's obvious that we're exchanging an increasing amount of our real life for various PMRs.

It should be noted that PMR is a highly *selective* process. We start to select what we wish to perceive by choosing our medium. Once connected with the source, we also choose what to retain. We may regard something as memorable and pay close attention to it, even taking notes or recording it for later review. Or we can disregard it. How many times has someone asked you about a particular TV show or movie you saw recently, but try as you might, you simply could not remember the details?

The final step in the process involves the relationship between PMR and real life. We often take information gleaned from mediated reality and apply it to our real lives. Sometimes this process can be disappointing. After all, how many people do we meet who are as attractive as those on "Beverly Hills, 90210"? How often do we have a love affair that is as dramatic as those depicted in romance novels or in the songs that are routinely played on the radio? The fact is that real life seldom measures up to the more glamorous and intense world of mediated reality.

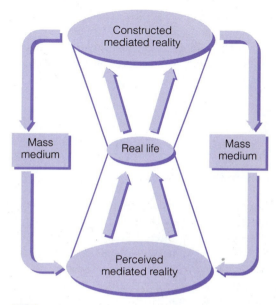

1.6

The cone effect is one way to represent the processes involved in bringing you mass messages. Note that the information must pass from real life to the constructed mediated reality and then through a mass medium to the audience. The consumers make it part of their perceived mediated reality and eventually incorporate it into their own lives.

Perhaps the single most important thing to remember about the cone effect—and mass media in general—is that mediated reality and real life are indeed worlds apart. Mediated reality will always remain a place where significant and exciting things are constantly happening. As long as we understand why this is, media can provide us with a world of fascinating, informative, and entertaining stimuli. However, the confusion between mediated reality and real life can lead to serious consequences. You can't expect every doctor to treat you with the tender loving care of one found on "General Hospital" or every wealthy person to be as flamboyant and mysterious as *The Great Gatsby*.

The cone effect applies equally to all mass media. In books, newspapers, magazines, radio, films, and TV, there is always a mediated reality exerting some degree of influence on the mass audience.

Media Education and Research

Relationships between the mass audience and mediated reality with its form, content, and consequence are often difficult to understand. So much is happening so quickly that traditional approaches are often obsolete. Many college and university departments have begun to erase established boundaries and experiment with multidisciplinary approaches to understanding communications. The word *communicology* is appearing more often. Communicology is the study of intrapersonal, interpersonal, and mass communication processes under what is called the "communication umbrella." The umbrella has many supportive ribs, including journalism, theater arts, speech and rhetoric, technical writing, advertising, radio and television, film, public relations, and popular culture.

Most educators now agree that technology is reshaping our environment so quickly that teaching specific vocational skills to communication students is only part of the job. The study of communication also involves teaching students how to land on their feet in unforeseen communication situations. We can train students to operate today's television cameras, but tomorrow's cameras will be different. Today's hot marketing strategy may have burned itself out before you graduate. Cable and satellite communication altered forever the commercial TV "broadcast" system that I was instructed to study so carefully when I was in college.

Mediamerica, Mediaworld, and You

Even if you never become directly involved in the production of mass media messages, you will always be a message consumer. Directly or indirectly, you will have a hand in deciding the future of the mass media and the way they shape your life.

This book is part historical and part exploratory. It offers historical information as a backdrop to how we got here. In addition it explores what is happening now and speculates on what is to come. This is not an encyclopedia of mass communication, nor could it be. But I hope it will be a catalyst that encourages you to think more about mass communication. You don't have to think very hard to come up with ways the media *directly* affect your life. Examples are everywhere.

There are many possible *contexts* or approaches to studying and understanding Mediamerica and Mediaworld. For example, one can examine media strictly from an economic point of view, focusing on the interrelationships among the corporations that own so many media outlets or the revenues generated by each medium. A political context might involve how power is wielded in various communications industries, or the relationships that exist between the media and our elected representatives. A social context would offer studies regarding the *impact* of the media on our opinions about and relationships with one another. A vocational context would concentrate on the various employment possibilities in each medium and perhaps cover the organizational aspects of media businesses in detail.

All of these contexts provide useful ways to examine the media, and all are included to some extent here. However, I would be remiss if I did not tell you up front that an introductory text simply cannot cover each of these contexts with the kind of depth it deserves. What is hoped is that you will discover which of these contexts most interest you and then spend some time exploring them in future classes and on your own as well. In addition you may find a few new contexts of your own! Just remember that there are many ways to explore the media of Mediamerica and Mediaworld. With that in mind, here is the way this text approaches the information landscape.

Part One covers the print media. They have a rich history, and you'll meet some of the more important contributors to their 500-year history. Of course, print started with books, the "permanent press," and books are still the most revered of all mass media.

Separate chapters deal with historical and contemporary newspaper practices. In recent years, the functions of the newspaper have changed. Readers' needs have been affected by the appearance of other mass media. Serious questions about the newspaper's relationships with government and the public have arisen. America's concept of freedom of the press has changed as well. The discussion of these issues at the end of Chapter 4 focuses on newspapers but is applicable to all mass media.

Magazines are the most rapidly changing of all print media. Their trends often provide early clues to changes in the characteristics of the mass audience. Dozens of new magazines appear each year, and dozens of others disappear.

Part Two, "Electronic Media: Edison Came to Stay," is about all the media that rely on electric power to get their message to you. No one invented electricity, of course, and several people had a hand in harnessing it, but Edison's contribution in coupling it with message delivery was unprecedented.

First came record players and films, but in the beginning these were regarded as mere amusement. Radio became the first mass medium to link the source and the destination simultaneously, and immediately began to play an important part in our social and political development. A separate chapter deals with the recording industry and music itself. Contemporary music enjoys a unique relationship with the youth culture and dominates radio's entertainment programming.

Two chapters deal with television. The structure of the medium is analyzed to help you understand how our commercial television system has developed. You'll also learn about peoplemeters and those troublesome Nielsen ratings that so influence TV decision makers.

Often when we think of television, we think of the programs that led former Federal Communications Commission (FCC) Chairman Newton Minow to call the medium "the vast wasteland." Writer Horace Newcomb, among others, has a different perspective. He feels that television is an art form, the nation's most popular and meaningful experience.

Film, like television, is an audiovisual medium, but it delivers larger-than-life people and has been described as the "American dream machine." Since it has been around longer than any other electronic medium, we have developed a more serious attitude about its status. The motion picture industry also provides an excellent example of the international market for America's media output.

In Part Three, "Beyond the Media: The Phenomena of Mass Communication," we consider some areas related to the growing power of the mass media. Advertising and public relations are mass communication's two biggest growth industries. We'll take a look at each, and at the specialists who manage and disseminate information, with an eye toward discovering why their skills are in such demand.

Virtually all of those who work in mass communication eventually encounter situations that test their moral convictions. In this context, a number of ethical questions need to be considered. Chapter 13 raises some of them and examines them in the context of traditional ethical principles as well as the events of recent years.

Popular culture is not an industry but a social and global by-product of mass media. Virtually everything we see, touch, smell, hear, and taste has something to do with mass media. These mass-mediated experiences make up our life styles and culture, here and around the world.

The relationships between Mediamerica and Mediaworld have become more powerful and increasingly complex in recent years. In Chapter 15 we'll look at the emerging international focus of mass communication and discover how American information products and programming are competing in the ever-changing global marketplace. In addition we'll learn how some other nations manage their own domestic mass communication systems and how those strategies contrast with our own.

In Chapter 16, "Mass Communication Research: A Beginner's Guide," we examine several research studies that address crucial media issues. You'll discover how research is conducted and what it can and can't tell us.

Finally, we'll look into the mediated future. How will new technologies change society? In the world of mass communication, some of yesterday's dreams included:

- A wire service that would give the small-town newspaper a reporter in every news capital on the globe

- A radio news network that would enable all Americans to hear a speech by their president at the time it was being given

- A communication device that would bring sound and pictures simultaneously into every American home

- A way in which the sights and sounds of newsworthy events anywhere in the world would be transmitted live to its inhabitants

These dreams are now realities. New predictions for Mediaworld's mass communication — its form, content, and consequence — challenge the imagination.

Queries and Concepts

1 If you had to give up all mass media, which one would you miss the *most*? Which one would you miss the *least*? Why?

2 List five questions about a mass medium you would like to have answered. Which involve form? Content? Consequence?

3 Conduct an informal poll among three of your friends, and ask them to define "communication" and "mass communication." What do the definitions have in common? How do they differ? Did your respondents seem to have an easy time defining these terms?

4 Using the Shannon-Weaver model in 1.4, define how each component could be applied to a newspaper, magazine article, radio program, television program, and movie. Does the model work more effectively for some media than for others?

5 Many attempts have been made to diagram the complex process of communication. Drawing on information in this chapter, develop your own communication model. Remember, your model must be able to account for intrapersonal, interpersonal, *and* mass communication.

6 Using the Whetmore grid in 1.5, can you think of specific examples where mass communication content has performed the linking and synthesis functions? Are some media more adept at these tasks than others?

7 Use the cone effect to examine the experience you had the last time you listened to
a popular song or watched a television
program. Be as specific as possible, and
be sure to apply each component of the
cone effect to your personal experience.

Readings and References

The Birth of Mass Communication

Elizabeth Geck
Johannes Gutenberg: From Lead Letter to the Computer. Bad Godesberg, Germany: Inter Natione Books, 1968.

An interesting account of Gutenberg's life and his influence on the rise of mass communication. Easy to read and comprehensive enough for everyone.

Wilbur Schramm
The Story of Human Communication: From Cave Painting to Microchip. New York: Harper & Row, 1988.

A broad and interesting overview that manages to capture the full sweep of our communication history. The author pioneered media education and research in the United States.

Defining Communication; Form, Content, Consequence

Frank E. X. Dance
"The 'Concept' of Communication." *Journal of Communication,* June 1970, pp. 201–10.

Every definition of communication you ever wanted, along with a bibliography of original sources. The article might be tough to read, but the definitions will make you stop and think.

Dennis McQuail
Sven Windhal
Communication Models. New York: Longman, 1980.

A comprehensive yet concise introduction to many of the major attempts that have been made to diagram the complex process of communication.

Werner J. Severin
James W. Tankard
Communication Theories: Origins, Methods, Uses. 2d ed. New York: Longman, 1988.

This primer examines a number of important theories, models, and definitions of the process and effects of mass communication. Written with beginning students in mind.

The Technological Embrace; The Cone Effect; Media Education and Research

Edward Jay Whetmore
American Electric: Introduction to Telecommunications and Electronic Media. New York: McGraw-Hill, 1992.

This overview includes material on media research, mass culture, and new technologies. The author's style is engaging . . . and strangely familiar.

Stan Le Roy Wilson
Mass Media/Media Culture. 2d ed. New York: McGraw-Hill, 1992.

This introductory book examines the mass media from a cultural studies perspective and also makes use of the cone effect in the process.

See also Chapters 14, "Popular Culture and Mass Communication" and 16, "Mass Communication Research: A Beginner's Guide," and the readings and references at the ends of those chapters.

Books: The Permanent Press

**He had grown up to a thousand books,
a thousand lies; he had listened eagerly
to people who pretended to know, who
knew nothing. . . .**

F. Scott Fitzgerald

Hundreds of colleges and universities used the first four editions of this book. Hundreds of thousands of students have read it. Since 1979 I have received countless letters, phone calls, and feedback sheets from students just like you. They've come from all over Mediamerica and the English-speaking portions of Mediaworld as well. (You'll find your own postage-free feedback sheet at the end of the book. Please take a moment to fill it out and let us know how we are doing.)

Needless to say, I am gratified by all this reaction, but it pales in comparison to other successful texts in many fields. It is estimated that one popular psychology text has reached millions of students in the past two decades.

And a successful novel or exercise book might sell millions of copies in a single year.

Marshall McLuhan (see Chapter 14) said that writing "has the power to translate man from the tribal to the civilized sphere." What we think of as a civilized society cannot exist without reading and writing. If it's important, it's in print.

The Permanent Press

Binding adds respectability to print. Despite the occasional factual error, the hardback book is considered the ultimate reliable source, followed in descending order by the

If your product needs a reflective audience, a selective audience PRINT IT!

If the purchase requires deliberation—or liberation from the accepted way of doing things, nothing performs like print.

Print it. Print is for keeps.

Shirley Polykoff
Copywriter
and President
Shirley Polykoff
Advertising, Inc.

Magazine Publishers Association, Inc. 575 Lexington Avenue, New York, N.Y. 10022

2.1

Print is for keeps. Magazine publishers naturally chose print for their message, an implied disparagement of the electronic media.

paperback book, the magazine, and finally the newspaper. The better the binding, the greater the credibility! All of these print forms are often perceived as superior to the electronic media, which seem fleeting and unstable by comparison. Print is for keeps! (see 2.1).

Print is the keeper of records, great literature, and all accomplishments. It is the medium that, more than all others, daily dictates the fortunes and failures of men and women. Professors who publish flourish; those who don't, perish. Students who read the right books are said to be those who go to the head of the class, meet the right people, and go on to the right jobs.

If we want to know who is the best at a particular activity, we consult *The Guinness*

Book of World Records. From the pages of books flows truth, the answer to any conceivable question. Books are permanent and durable and offer information retrieval with the greatest of ease. What's more, they are the mass medium most geared to the *individual*. Books are the "Supreme Court," the ultimate arbiter, of our culture. When we say we are doing it "by the book," we mean we are doing it in a civilized, correct, coherent, logical manner.

For most of the history of mass communication, the book was the only readily accessible means of storing information and retrieving it at will. Of course, the proliferation of computer data banks, microfilm, microfiche, and even "paperless" and electronic books is changing that. Nevertheless, the dominance of the book in our culture as a means of storing and retrieving information is undeniable.

We do not only *what* books tell us, but *how* they tell us to do it. We perform most activities the same way we read, in a *linear* fashion. *Linear* (from *line*) means one thing at a time, one job at a time, one spouse at a time. This seems quite normal; in fact, we are so conditioned to doing things one at a time that any other way seems absurd. Yet in preliterate cultures, people tended to do many things simultaneously. Hawaiians had no written language until the missionaries came in the 19th century. Perhaps that is why things on the islands are still done according to "Hawaiian time," involving hours of delay. If you are to meet some friends at one o'clock, it may be two or later before they show up.

McLuhan predicted that as literate societies spend less time with books and more time with electronic media, they will return to this preliterate state. He said, "Ours is a brand new world of all-at-once-ness, time has ceased, space has vanished." Our concepts of time and space are influenced by the *form* of our dominant media. The real message of the book medium may not be *what* it says, but *how* it says it. Whereas books deliver their messages one topic at a time, one thought at a time, the electronic media use a kind of simultaneous approach, delivering many kinds of information in a rapid-fire manner. These differences have had important consequences in Mediamerica and Mediaworld. Yet despite McLuhan's observations, in many ways we are still a print-oriented culture.

The Gutenberg Legacy

When Gutenberg's movable type ushered in the new era of mass communication, he was totally unaware of it. He was more interested in deriving some creative pleasure from the experience and turning a profit for his investors. What happened was of considerably greater consequence.

We are all numb to our changing environment, much too preoccupied with day-to-day problems to get "the big picture." Look around the room where you are right now. Take a good look. You are at home, in a classroom, in a library. No doubt you've been here many times before. Yet have you ever noticed the pattern on the ceiling? The small holes in the wall? The plaster chips on the floor? The linoleum design? The trademark on the desk in front of you? By stopping and looking at these things, you are really seeing them for the first time, getting a glimpse of the "invisible environment" always surrounding you.

Our information environment, created by books and other mass media, is very much like that. It surrounds us constantly, yet we are completely oblivious to it. We think that if we're not reading at the moment, books have no influence on us.

We human beings have always had the urge to keep records of ourselves, our friends, and our dreams. Inside each of us is a secret archivist; we like to collect things that prove our accomplishments are of lasting value. Books perform a different function than the newspapers and magazines we chew up and recycle daily: They provide a permanent record.

No one really knows how long books have been around, but the earliest records show that clay tablets were used in Babylonia about 4,500 years ago. Chinese scholars may have invented the first books, a series of bamboo strips tied together. But bamboo, clay, and stone were impractical and not easily transported. According to most accounts, the Chinese were the first to invent paper, but the earliest inexpensive writing materials were made by Egyptians from the papyrus plants growing along the Nile River.

Some early forms of paper appeared in Italy and Spain in the 12th century. At that time, books were handwritten, primarily on vellum or parchment (both made from lambskin or calfskin), and that practice continued into the 15th century. In fact, in some parts of Europe, vellum and parchment are still used today. In the middle of the 15th century, Gutenberg used paper along with movable type and an old wine press to print his first book, a Bible.

An estimated 30,000 titles were printed in the first 50 years of mass-produced books (1450–1500). Today approximately 45,000 new titles are printed annually in America alone. Early works were law books, Bibles, and other religious publications. Later came folklore, stories, and verse, such as *The Canterbury Tales*. The costly hand-copied manuscripts that had been the exclusive property of the ruling elite gave way to the more accessible mass-produced works. This encouraged literacy among the general populace. In fact, it can be argued that books were the first mass-produced "product" and the forerunners of the industrial age.

The mechanical procedures of printing changed very little during the first 350 years. All type had to be set by hand and each sheet pressed separately. About 1800 the French invented a machine that made paper in one continuous roll. In England the first successful iron press replaced the old wooden ones. In 1810 a steam-powered press replaced earlier, hand-operated models. In 1884 Ottmar

Early printing presses were labor intensive, requiring the efforts of many workers.

Mergenthaler, a German-born American, invented the Linotype. Now movable type could be created instantly by the new machine, greatly speeding production.

In recent years, a number of technological developments have sped up the printing process. Some print experts would contend that computer typesetting has had a much greater impact than the Linotype did on the distribution of the printed word. Computer technology used in conjunction with the CD-ROM disc promises to revolutionize our very concept of what constitutes a book (see Chapter 17).

The Permanent Press in America

Books landed at Plymouth Rock with the Pilgrims in 1620. Twenty years later, Stephen Day was commissioned to print one of the first books published in the New World, *The Whole Booke of Psalms*. Just as in Europe, most early books in America were about law or religion. The Bible was the most popular of all.

Benjamin Franklin's *Poor Richard's Almanack*, a collection of tide tables, harvest suggestions, and proverbs like "Early to bed and early

to rise makes a man healthy, wealthy, and wise," was the rage from 1733 to 1758. Franklin also started the first subscription library in the colonies. In many ways, his was the first American mass communication success story.

Until 1800 the price of books kept them out of the hands of many U.S. citizens. Books cost a dollar or more, which amounted to a week's pay for the average wage earner. During the next 50 years, many cities started compulsory public schools, and a new generation grew up hungry for the printed word. Heavy demand for books plus technological innovation helped lower the price. Though many successful publishers were upper-class Americans, printing was not entirely controlled by the ruling elite, because the new nation had established freedom of the press in its Bill of Rights. Education of the masses posed no threat to a nation that had already rejected a king.

By the mid-1800s, the price of some books was down to 10 cents and the era of the "dime novel" was in full swing. Horatio Alger and other authors of this era stressed action, romance, adventure, and the puritan ethic of honesty and hard work (see 2.2). The message of these inexpensive novels was indelibly woven into the fabric of American culture. People across the country shared the same romantic notions, fears, hopes and dreams through the pages of the books they read.

By 1900 nine out of every ten Americans could read, and read they did. Naturally, not all of the social and political events of that day were triggered by books, but the medium's influence was great. Just as *Uncle Tom's Cabin,* by Harriet Beecher Stowe, had aided the cause of freedom for slaves before the Civil War, Upton Sinclair's *Jungle* exposed the wretched conditions of Chicago's meat-packing plants at the turn of the century. During the 1930s, John Steinbeck's *Grapes of Wrath* sensitized many to the plight of those who had fled the Dust Bowl during the Depression. All of these books had a lasting impact on the conscience and the consciousness of the nation.

Horatio Alger and the American Dream

Perhaps the most successful of all the 19th-century novelists was Horatio Alger (1834–1899). Though the literary merit of his work was subject to criticism, his writings were both abundant and widely read. His 120 titles sold about 30 million copies. The name Horatio Alger became synonymous with the American struggle for upward social mobility. Here's the philosophy of the Alger novel in a nutshell, taken from his first book, *Ragged Dick:* "'I hope, my lad,' Mr. Whitney said, 'you will prosper and rise in this world. You know in this free country poverty is no bar to a man's advancement.'"

Alger's belief in piety, purity, frugality, and hard work was a legacy from his conservative father, a Unitarian minister in Revere, Massachusetts. For a time Horatio thought he too would have a career as a minister. He graduated from Harvard Divinity School before his success with *Ragged Dick*.

Alger eventually moved to New York and became some-

what of a celebrity, lending his name to a number of reform and antivice crusades, including the New York Society for the Suppression of Vice.

All the Alger novels celebrated the self-made man. The hero was "a bright-looking boy with brown hair, a ruddy complexion, and dark blue eyes, who looked, and was, frank and manly." The villain was often another boy, son of a rich but corrupt family. He often had a "slender form and sallow complexion, and dressed with more pretension than taste." Inevitably, the hero triumphed.

Alger's own life story mirrored the success of his heroes. Though his books brought him fame and fortune, he did know sorrow. Alger's father talked him out of marrying his "one true love" at 17 because he was too young. Some biographers have contended that Alger was gay. Whatever the case, he said on a number of occasions that he longed to write "one great book," to be applauded by the critics who scoffed at his "boys' stories." That book was never written, though he once chose a title: *Tomorrow.*

The important cultural contribution of the Alger novel had nothing to do with literary quality. Popular media reflect the emotions and ideologies of their times. Alger's ideas were already in the thoughts and feelings of Americans. Although his medium and message may no longer dominate the social landscape, the implications of Alger's work have helped form our cultural legacy. His millions of readers have grown up and passed that legacy along to succeeding generations.

The Paperback Revolution

In the 1940s, paperbacks changed the role of books in America. First popular more than 100 years ago, paperbacks have enjoyed escalating sales since World War II. According to *Publishers Weekly,* paperbacks now account for 20,000 new titles or editions annually, almost half of all those published. And they no longer deal only with "lighter" material. Virtually all the world's literature, from Shakespeare to Saul Bellow, now appears in paperback. Even that once stalwart hardback, the textbook, has yielded. The evidence is in your hands.

For many years, paperbacks were largely reprints of material already available in hardback, but costs for the rights to reprint hardback materials have now escalated astoundingly.

Ethics and Economics: Behind the Used-Text Wars

Isn't it amazing how much textbooks cost these days? Think back to the day you bought this book, probably a couple of weeks ago. Were both new and used copies available? The used copies cost a little bit less, and if you were on a tight budget you probably bought one. Or maybe only new books were available, but you purchased used texts for some of your other classes.

The question of used texts is the hottest controversy in textbook publishing just now. It is an American microcosm involving ethics, economics, and serious questions about the nature of the free enterprise system.

For virtually the entire history of modern textbook publishing, college bookstores have bought back books that students did not want to keep, then resold them at a profit to the next group of students. Publishers and authors complained such practices cheated them, because no royalties are paid on used sales. Bookstores said they needed the extra income to stay in business. Publishers adjusted to the practice by charging a higher price for new texts.

That's pretty much where things stood until a new element was added to the equation. Someone figured out that unwanted texts could be bought from one college bookstore and sold to another where they were needed, at a profit. This practice became commonplace. Used-text companies, aided by computer systems, keep track of what is needed where. As a result, when professors request a text, many college bookstores don't order them from publishers but opt instead for large quantities of used books ordered directly from used-text companies. This means that more used copies find their way onto the shelves. Publishers say they must once again raise prices to retain a reasonable profit margin.

When the paperback rights to Judith Krantz's hardback best-seller *Princess Daisy* were auctioned off, the bidding was brisk. Eventually they brought $3.2 million.

Many bookstores now derive half or more of their gross revenue from paperback books, while used-book stores have given over shelf after shelf to paperbacks. The average mass market paperback cost $4.57 in 1990 compared to 50 cents during the 1950s. Still, most magazines cost around $3, and paperbacks have a much longer life.

Speedy production of paperbacks has made possible the "instant book," which appears soon after a news event hits the headlines. Such was the case in 1991, when several paperbacks were produced within weeks of the start of the Gulf War. These included eyewitness accounts and photographs. Though some of these books were credited to one author, most were actually the work of special staffs put together by major paperback companies.

The Business of Books

Media analyst Charles Madison lists four major eras in American book publishing. *The colonial era* lasted from the 17th century until about 1865. Early colonial publishers in Philadelphia, New York, and Boston tended to come from the upper classes. Men like Matthew Carey, Charles Wiley, and James Monroe were well-educated aristocrats who thought the books they published should offer something of lasting value. Periodicals, they believed, catered to the desire for instant gratification that might be harmful to the masses. In those days, publishing was something of a private club; publishers were so few that most knew each other by their first names.

The Gilded Age (1865–1900) brought an abrupt change. The number of publishers mushroomed, and with the arrival of the dime novel, publishing became big business. George P. Munro was a $6-a-week clerk when

Some college bookstores resist ordering from the used-text companies. They maintain that although they need to buy used books from their own students to stay in business, buying from the companies constitutes a breach of ethics, because it denies the author and publisher a fair return for their efforts. Professors on those campuses, many of whom are authors themselves, often help influence bookstore policy.

Still other professors have exacerbated the situation by selling what are known as "examination copies," free copies sent to them by publishers in an attempt to interest them in adopting the book for their course. Every semester, representatives of the used-text companies can be found making the rounds of professors' offices, offering to buy "unwanted" examination copies. Those are then sold to bookstores across the country, where they are marked "used" and eventually wind up in the hands of students.

Writing in the *Chronicle of Higher Education,* Professor Karl J. Smith reports that a new math text he wrote came out just a few weeks before the semester began. No other college had adopted it for that semester.

When I walked into my classroom the first day, however, more than 50 percent of the books on the students' desks were marked "used." In a three-week period, the brand-new textbook had made the trip from publisher to professor to used-book dealer to college bookstore to my students.

Smith maintains that "we need a solution that will protect the free enterprise system, provide access to new knowledge, and at the same time be fair to authors and publishers." Indeed we do. In the meantime, the controversy continues, and you end up paying the escalating costs of the used-text wars.

---

he persuaded his employer's brother to publish cheap reprints of pirated editions of popular fiction. Thirty years later he left an estate valued at more than $10 million. The Munro story was typical of this era, when publishing experienced its most rapid growth. The dime novel also represented a coming-of-age for the book as a mass medium. For the first time, it became commonplace for ordinary citizens to own books.

The commercialization of literature (1900–45) was a period of great technological advance. The antiquated printing practices of the 18th and 19th centuries were replaced by streamlined commercial procedures more in keeping with the Industrial Revolution. Book selling, as well as publishing, had become big business.

Famous authors found publishers less willing to meet their financial demands as competition increased and publishing costs skyrocketed. The unknown author was having an increasingly difficult time breaking into print. A new, untested book required substantial financial commitment. Most publishing companies were cutting back and trying to ensure success with the books they did publish.

The era of *publishing goes public* (1945–present) encompasses the greatest change in business practices in publishing's history. The post–World War II era brought another boom in the demand for books as veterans flocked into American classrooms. The textbook business flourished. Older, family-owned publishing houses sold stock and became corporations.

Gross annual sales for all books exceeded $3 billion for the first time in the early 1970s. Of these books, nearly half were educational, including textbooks and legal, medical, and other professional works (see 2.3). Millions of copies of popular paperbacks were also sold as required reading in college courses.

Book clubs still account for about 10% of the total, offering highly touted selections to members at discount prices. Authors know that selection as a "Book of the Month" can mean instant success.

The goal of commercial publishers is to get their titles on the influential best-seller lists, particularly the one published in the *New York Times*. Yet sources inside the industry reveal that such lists are inaccurate at best. One bookseller said, "If George Gallup conducted his political polls the same way, we'd have Harold Stassen, Mary Tyler Moore, Al Capone, and Rin Tin Tin as America's favorite candidates for the presidency." Best-seller lists never include books like *The Living Bible,* for example, despite the fact that it sold more copies than any other book one year. Also missing are dictionaries, cookbooks, and titles that sell well in rural locations, which are seldom polled. Most confusion could be cleared up if publishing houses were willing to disclose sales figures, but most don't want the competition to know exactly how they're doing.

Some writers are now receiving more royalties from the sale of film rights than from the books themselves. Sometimes the film is made first and a book is then based on the film. One of the first was *Love Story,* written by Erich Segal, a Yale professor. It was originally a screenplay and was later marketed as a novel. Both versions enjoyed tremendous success. *Time* magazine has labeled this film-to-book process the "bovie." More recent examples of successful bovies include *Robin Hood, Prince of Thieves* and *Another 48 Hours.*

Despite the paperback boom and increasing total book sales, America's love affair with books may be going sour. In 1990 there were 44,218 new titles published, a drop of 17.2% from the previous year. According to *Library Trends,* although 78% of Americans 18 years and older read a newspaper every day, fewer than one in five can answer yes to the question "Do you happen to be reading any books or novels at the present?" A Gallup survey reveals about one in four adults is a hard-core book reader. A little less than half the adults in the survey reported they "read occasionally — perhaps at the rate of one book a year." Only one in four possessed a library card.

Critics are disturbed by this trend, particularly those in the academic community whose business it is to assess the impact of mass media. Many decry the time Americans spend with electronic media. If we spent more time reading, they say, we would be much improved. Usually the argument stops there, for it is always assumed that books are far more worthwhile than other mass media.

The more we learn about all mass media, the more we know that each medium delivers certain kinds of information and entertainment more effectively than others. Media forms may compete with one another, but they also have a potential *symbiosis,* or mutually beneficial relationship.

Eventually we may discover which medium performs which tasks most effectively. Considerably more empirical research needs to be done, however, before we can assume that any single medium will enable us to be "much improved."

Book Publishing in the 1990s

As competition for the consumer book dollar continues to heat up, publishing companies are increasingly becoming the targets of corporate takeovers and mergers. The result is a number of changes in the way publishers do business. *Time* writer Richard Zoglin observes that "the book industry increasingly bears more resemblance to Hollywood's high-rolling studios than to the decorous literary houses of yore. Most large publishers are now part of corporate conglomerates that are looking for blockbuster subjects to attract new audiences."

Not long ago Random House paid $6.5 million for the rights to General Colin Powell's memoirs, a lot of money to be sure, but still only the second highest price ever paid for the rights to a nonfiction book. Ronald Reagan received a whopping $7 million for his memoirs. Writing in the *New Republic*, Jacob Weisberg charged that today's high-powered book editors are "not judged by the quality of the books they acquire" but instead "by the dollar amount of the contracts they sign."

One way publishers are gearing up to pay for all of this is by streamlining the ways in which books are produced. In 1991 Macmillan Computer Publishing produced the first "paperless book." *The Best Book of Auto-CAD*, a computer text, was produced only one month after the author handed it to the publisher. The process normally takes a year or more. The 600-page, two-color text with nearly one piece of art work per page went from author to publisher to printer as a single shiny silver-toned magneto-optical disc. Paper was never used until the first copy rolled off the press.

Another technological breakthrough dubbed the "electronic book" may ultimately force us to rethink our very definition of the book itself. According to *Publisher's Weekly,* instead of old-fashioned forest-consuming books, we may all soon own something called the Bookmark reader. It looks like a miniature laptop computer, has an 8×10-inch screen, and weighs about 2 pounds. When we want a "book" we'll take the computer to a library or bookstore and, utilizing CD-ROM disc technology, simply "plug in" and retrieve the information. Buttons will turn pages while a search window identifies chapter headings. The technology is already in place to do all of this. But wait, there's more. Also included will be color graphics and a built-in sound option that can play music or read the information directly to us. A serial port will allow us to print out individual pages if we so desire.

Issues and Answers: Purity in Print

All the new technology in the world will not solve one problem long associated with print. As long as there have been books, there has been censorship. King Henry VIII of England issued a list of prohibited books in 1529, and for the next 170 years each English monarch issued a similar list. Those caught reading or circulating prohibited works were subject to fines and imprisonment. Thousands of titles were in print in Europe by 1600. As literacy and information spread, the threat of revolution swept Europe. Books sparked increasing demands for social, religious, and political reform. The ruling elite were losing the battle for control of the printing presses.

Many people feel the days of book banning have passed. Ray Bradbury's 1954 science fiction novel *Fahrenheit 451* (the title refers to the temperature at which paper catches fire), about a society where all books were burned, shocked and dismayed many readers. While it was a science fiction story, the implications remain ominous even today.

The banning and burning of books have been commonplace in America. Historian Paul Boyer has speculated on the reasons. His theory is that as America developed a unified identity after the Civil War, it also developed a unified conscience. This new collective conscience encouraged certain religious and social groups to feel they should have the power to decide what was and was not appropriate reading material for everyone.

In 1873 Anthony Comstock founded a nonprofit social organization known as the New York Society for the Suppression of Vice (see 2.4). He headed that controversial group for 40 years. According to Boyer, the vice-society movement

was in response to the deep-seated fears about the drift of urban life in

Anthony Comstock and the Suppression of Vice

Anthony Comstock arrived in New York, "the wickedest city in the world," in 1867, shortly after the Civil War. He had been born in 1844 to devout Connecticut parents.

According to his biographers, he worked in a dry-goods store until 1872, when he noticed that "shocking" literature was being passed around by other employees. Until then there was little or no enforcement of the antismut laws in New York City, but Comstock brought suit and

had a fellow employee arrested for distributing such material. As it turned out, that was only the beginning. Comstock's Society for the Suppression of Vice was backed by most of the New York aristocracy, and Comstock became legendary in his self-appointed task of "cleaning the filth out of this town."

Sporting thick muttonchop sideburns, a pot belly, thick neck, and jutting jaw, he railed against what he called the "base villains" of pornography and their "pathetic and awful" cases. In 1893 he greeted a roomful of reporters with an im-

promptu belly dance to graphically illustrate the evils of the Chicago World's Fair. It must have been quite a sight!

the post–Civil War years. The origin of Comstock's society, the first of its kind in America, is illustrative. Throughout the nineteenth century, as today, New York City possessed a magnetic attraction for ambitious and restless young men from other parts of the country. The metropolis which held so much promise for these youths, however, was also somehow threatening. The familiar sources of guidance and support — family, church, close-knit community — had been left behind, and often it seemed that the city offered nothing in their place.

Book censorship represented a paternalistic approach. The reader was to be protected from falling into the depths of depravity. The problem, then as now, was figuring out exactly what constitutes the "depths," or even "depravity." The Supreme Court has never successfully defined obscenity.

During the 1920s, the term *banned in Boston* described literature of "questionable taste." Authors whose works were banned in Boston included H. G. Wells, John Dos Passos, Theodore Dreiser, Sinclair Lewis, Upton Sinclair, Ernest Hemingway, and Robert W. Service. Sinclair didn't seem to mind; he mused, "We authors are using America as our sales territory and Boston as our advertising department." The mass audience has always expressed a pronounced curiosity about forbidden literature, and this curiosity can lead to increased sales.

The Nazi book burnings of the 1930s and the Soviet suppression of books prior to glasnost may seem far removed from American society. Yet in 1953, more than 100 titles were banished from the worldwide libraries of the United States Information Service after "exposure" by Senator Joseph McCarthy's congressional subcommittee. Among them were the works of American patriot Thomas Paine. McCarthy contended the books were "procommunist," and several public book burnings were held. *Saturday Review* editor Norman Cousins moaned, "What do we do about the charge that a nation that became great because of a free flow of ideas has itself become frightened of ideas?"

In March 1976, several members of the Island Trees School District Board of Education in New York entered a high school library and confiscated 60 books they later said were "anti-American, anti-Semitic, anti-Christian, and just plain filthy." Removed were Pulitzer Prize winners *The Fixer* and *Laughing Boy.* Also banned were Kurt Vonnegut Jr.'s *Slaughterhouse-Five,* Desmond Morris's *Naked Ape,* and *Go Ask Alice,* which makes a strong statement against the use of drugs by teenagers.

The board's action stirred an uproar in the small Long Island town. Eventually New York's WCBS radio aired an editorial condemning such actions as "prejudgments of the worst kind. . . . The idea of students getting off on this forbidden literature suits us just fine!"

The president of the school board went on the air to reply, contending that "what is taught in schools should reflect local values" and that "one of the purposes of a board of education is to see that local control is maintained and that the will of the majority prevails." He also emphasized: "Education is supposed to be an uplifting experience, but if you have to get down into the gutter to do it, then it is just not worth it. For as the twig is bent, so grows the tree." The New York Civil Liberties Union filed a class-action suit demanding that the books be returned to the library and arguing that no board of education had the right to go over the heads of administrators to blacklist certain works.

After a long series of delays, the case wound up before the U.S. Supreme Court, and in a 5–4 decision in 1982, the Court held that "local boards may not remove books from library shelves simply because they dislike the ideas contained in those books and seek by

The Nazi book burnings of the 1930s added an unwelcome chapter to the history of book censorship. Nazi youth groups were particularly active in the movement. Throughout history, many books have been banned under the auspices of "protecting" young people from inflammatory ideas.

their removal to prescribe what shall be orthodox in politics, nationalism, religion or matters of opinion."

Despite that decision, the censorship of school books continues. In 1991 the annual survey by the liberal group People for the American Way counted 229 incidents of attempted censorship of school books, up 20% from the previous year. Arthur J. Kropp, the group's president, called it "the single worst year for school censorship" since the surveys began in 1982. He concluded that "the 1990's are shaping up to be the decade of the censor, and unfortunately our public schools have not been spared." Among those works in question: J. D. Salinger's *Catcher in the Rye,* Mark Twain's *Huckleberry Finn,* John Steinbeck's *Of Mice and Men,* and a "Preventing Teen Pregnancy" video series.

Sexual behavior and pornography are often involved in censorship attempts. Community and national standards change from day to day. *Ulysses* (1922), the famous novel by James Joyce, was once banned in this country. *Lolita, Tropic of Cancer, Fanny Hill, Candy,* and other novels that seem tame by today's standards were also banned.

During the 1950s, the liberal Earl Warren Supreme Court struck down most state obscenity laws as being too vague and subjective. The more conservative Warren Burger Court of the 1970s reversed the Warren rulings, and in *Miller v. California* it struck down all national standards, reestablishing the right of local juries to apply local community standards in judging obscenity.

In 1986 the Meese Commission on Obscenity and Pornography issued a voluminous report that added fuel to the controversy. The report concluded that obscenity was on the upswing and that the government should do something to stem the flow of magazines and books judged to be pornographic.

In 1987's *Pope v. Illinois* decision, the Supreme Court ruled that the social value of the material must be assessed from the standpoint of a "reasonable person," rather than on the basis of community standards.

Utilizing these standards, local governments are once again arresting editors and publishers, and there have been some convictions by local juries. Some of these cases are on appeal, and it will be many years before all the results are in. In fact, the results probably will never be "all in." The war between the government and "obscene" publishers seems to be a never-ending one.

Queries and Concepts

1 Imagine what our culture might be like if we weren't "doing it by the book." What if we were doing it by TV or by radio? What would happen to our relationships with government? With one another?

2 A survey project: Poll 10 people by posing the age-old cliché, "Read any good books lately?" How many have they read in the past 6 months? How many are of the "pop" variety?

3 What is the single book that has had the greatest influence on *your* life? Why?

4 Reread this chapter's discussion of the four eras in American book publishing. Predict a fifth era.

5 The qualities that make America unique are embodied in American myths and stories like those of Horatio Alger. Examine a current best-selling book. Does that book embody any myths that seem to be a vital part of the American character?

Examine any book that you read as a child, and answer this same question.

6 Can you think of any sentence, words, or phrases that should not be allowed in print? Should there be an age limit on the freedom to read any kind of information? If so, draw up some guidelines. If not, what about books on how to make bombs and set them off by remote control? Do you want your local terrorist to have that information?

7 Which would you prefer for use in your college classes, regular "old fashioned" textbooks or electronic books? Which would you prefer for your leisure reading? Why?

8 Does your campus bookstore have any policies in regard to the purchase and sale of used textbooks? If so, what are they? If not, what (if any) policies do you think the store should adopt?

The Permanent Press; The Gutenberg Legacy

Marshall McLuhan
The Gutenberg Galaxy: The Making of Typographic Man. New York: Signet/New American Library, 1962.

"Schizophrenia may be a necessary consequence of literacy," argues Marshall McLuhan as he takes us on a wild tour of the consequences of the printing press, linear thinking, and life in our "book culture." McLuhan's "mosaic" writing style can be tough for new students (and even for not-so-new professors!), but the effort seldom fails to produce a rewarding insight or two.

Walter J. Ong
Orality and Literacy: The Technologizing of the Word. New York: Methuen, 1982.

Ong believes that the nature of human consciousness is determined, to a great extent, by the dominant technologies of communication. In this book, he explores some of the significant differences between oral and literate (print) cultures. Provocative reading.

The Permanent Press in America

John Cawelti
The Six-Gun Mystique. 2d ed. Bowling Green, OH: The Popular Press, 1973.

In the second edition of this classic study, the author explores the western genre. Despite the somewhat narrow focus, however, this study is really a broad-ranging treatise on the nature of formula fiction and its impact on our culture.

Kenneth Davis
Two-Bit Culture: The Paperbacking of America. Boston: Houghton Mifflin, 1984.

A good overview of the paperback revolution. For current industry trends, you'll need to consult the periodicals and reference books listed below.

John Tebbel
Between the Covers: The Rise and Transformation of American Book Publishing. New York: Oxford University Press, 1987.

A serious history of the permanent press in the United States. Covers "The Rise of Modern Publishing," "The Age of Expansion," "The Golden Age Between Two Wars," and "The Great Change."

Lawrence C. Wroth
The Colonial Printer. Charlottesville: University Press of Virginia, 1964.

This book describes printing in the pre–Revolutionary War period, including discussions of Franklin, Day, and others. A thorough, in-depth look at the colonial printer.

The Business of Books

Lewis A. Coser
Charles Kadushin
Walter W. Powell
Books: The Culture and Commerce of Publishing. New York: Basic Books, 1982.

Covers the entire book and publishing landscape, including sections on history, economics, how publishing companies are organized, channels of distribution, women in book publishing, and virtually every other important aspect of the industry.

Elizabeth A. Geiser, ed.
The Business of Book Publishing. Boulder, Colo.: Westview Press, 1985.

Subtitled "Papers by Practitioners," this book is a handy compendium of essays that cover all major aspects of book publishing: editorial, production, design, and marketing.

David Shaw
"Book Business Best Sellers: Are They Really?" *Los Angeles Times* News Service, Oct. 24, 1976.

Useful periodicals that deal with the phenomena of books include *Publisher's Weekly* and *Library Journal. Writer's Market* (see Chapter 5) and *Literary Market Place* list the kinds of books each major house publishes and the number of titles each produces yearly. Industry trends, including discussions of new technological developments, are highlighted in *The Book Publishing Annual. Books In Print,* a weighty index found in most library reference rooms, is a guide to the vast array of books currently in publication. Various perspectives on the cultural and social impact of books and literacy can be found in these journals: *Journal of Popular Culture, Journal of Popular Literature,* and *Written Communication.*

Issues and Answers: Purity in Print

Paul S. Boyer
Purity in Print: The Vice Society Movement and Book Censorship in America. New York: Charles Scribner's, 1968.

This historical overview is both lively and thorough. Boyer is a scholar with a sense of humor who delivers the problems of book censorship with gusto. The author brings out details about historical figures that make them come alive.

Louis Edward Ingelhart
Press Freedoms: A Descriptive Calendar of Concepts, Interpretations, Events, and Court Actions, From 4000 B.C. to the Present. New York: Greenwood Press, 1987.

Sometimes you *can* judge a book by its cover; in this case, the title says it all! This reference book is an impressive, accessible, year-by-year description that touches on just about everything: Gutenberg, the arrival of printing presses in England, the 14th Amendment, attacks on vice, and more. Includes a selected bibliography.

Walter Kendrick
The Secret Museum: Pornography in Modern Culture. New York: Viking Books, 1987.

A challenging history of the struggle to regulate or eliminate pornography. Plenty of material on Anthony Comstock is included in Chapter 5, "The American Obscene." Chapter 8 covers the 1970 report of the Obscenity Commission and the emergent feminist debate over pornography. The author comes down firmly on the side of a free, uninhibited press.

Thomas L. Tedford
Freedom of Speech in the United States. New York: Random House, 1985.

This popular textbook is considered one of the "standards" in this area. Well illustrated and comprehensive enough for any student. Recommended.

Commission on Pornography Report. Washington, D.C.: U.S. Government Printing Office, 1986.

Report of the Commission on Obscenity and Pornography. Washington, D.C.: U.S. Government Printing Office, 1970.

These two government reports on pornography and obscenity, one issued in 1970 and the other completed in 1986, are worth comparing. Their sharp differences might suggest more about our changing political climate than our understanding of these complex issues.

Newspapers, Part One: The Evolution of American Journalism

Fairly soon the press began to sense that news was not only to be reported but also gathered, and, indeed, to be made. What went into the press was news. The rest was not news.

Marshall McLuhan

In the fall of 1982, *USA Today* began to appear on America's newsstands. Subscriptions weren't available, but anyone who wanted a copy needed only to deposit some coins in one of the high-tech boxes emblazoned with the *USA Today* logo and the words *by satellite*.

Those who did were treated to a newspaper that bore only a slight resemblance to their hometown paper. *USA Today* stories, brief and breezy, were dressed up with splashy graphics, full color in every section, and a motley array of charts and graphs to simplify the day's events for the reader.

The decision to attempt a national newspaper had been made late in 1981 by the board of directors of Gannett, one of the country's most successful publishing conglomerates. (Circulation for all Gannett papers at that point was around 3.5 million nationwide — by 1993 it was around 6 million.)

As with most new publishing ventures, there was red ink at first. Yet Gannett continued to pour its resources into *USA Today,* and thanks to aggressive advertising and marketing, "McPaper," as it came to be called by its critics, soon became a familiar part of Mediamerica's print landscape.

By 1993 *USA Today*'s Monday–Thursday circulation was 1.8 million while Friday's edition topped 2.2 million. The weekly baseball edition first appeared in 1991, about the time that *The National* sports daily failed. Meanwhile *USA Weekend,* a kind of national Sunday magazine, continues to appear in selected markets each weekend.

Those who had predicted failure for the new paper were astonished. In 1977 the *National Observer,* a weekly national newspaper, had folded after 15 consecutive years in the red. In 1981 alone, 45 daily newspapers, many in America's largest markets, had gone under. Facing such overwhelming odds, how did *USA Today* succeed?

Gannett research had indicated that 15% of all U.S. households bought a paper that was not produced in their county. This meant that many people in rural areas were buying a major metropolitan paper to get something the local paper wasn't providing. Gannett board chairman Allen Neuharth stressed that *USA Today* would be a "second buy" for many newspaper readers, one that would supplement the information they were getting from their local paper.

The technology that makes *USA Today* possible is almost as flashy as the color features of the paper itself. Assembled in a suburb of Washington, D.C., the final copy, ads and all, is transmitted by satellite to 15 locations across the country, where it is automatically turned into printing plates. Then the presses roll.

This process was relatively easy for Gannett to implement because it owns more newspapers (many with printing facilities) than any other newspaper chain — more than 100 in all. Many of the Gannett papers are published in the afternoon, leaving the presses free for an early-morning run.

Such a huge undertaking was not entirely without problems. When Gannett announced plans to attempt a national daily, its stock tumbled to a 12-month low. In areas where Gannett didn't own a paper, it was forced to rent press facilities, often at inflated costs. Publishers in each of the initial target markets vigorously resisted the new competition. In Los Angeles, Tom Johnson, publisher of the *Los Angeles Times,* vowed to "go rack for rack" with *USA Today*'s ambitious marketing strategies. Everywhere the paper appeared, the competition was forced to take note.

Whatever the ultimate fate of *USA Today,* it has certainly shaken the journalism establishment. Criticism has been heavy, especially concerning the perceived "frivolous" nature of its content. Readers get a lot of information about the activities of singer Michael Jackson and baseball's José Canseco but decidedly fewer details about world events. News of the day is capsulized in the "Newsline" section, in the left-hand column of the front page. Also on the front page is "USA Snapshots," a graphics display of "the statistics that shape our lives." According to *Business Week, USA Today*'s "emphasis on color photos, sports, and business appeals to a generation hooked on TV" (see 3.1).

At least one publisher has admitted to stealing the idea of *USA Today*'s color weather map (see 3.2). In addition, many newspapers have moved toward more color graphics and color photos and are imitating *USA Today*'s use of blue throughout. According to *Newsweek,* the *Akron Beacon Journal,* the *Houston Chronicle,* and Gannett's own *Tennessean* are among the latest converts to *USA Today*'s reliance on brief punchy stories and slick graphics to help attract new and younger readers.

For all of its success, *USA Today* simply capitalized on a growing newspaper trend, that of emphasizing "soft news," entertain-

3.1

Highly colorful, highly visual, and highly innovative, *USA Today* is an American success story. The publishers, however, might find that description unusual, because the word *America* never appears in *USA Today.* It's always life "in the USA."
© *1994 USA Today. Reprinted with permission.*

BASEBALL SWIRLING CLOSER TO THE DRAIN

PLAYERS FILL TIME WITHOUT WORK AS OWNERS COUNT 48 HOURS TO SAVE THE '94 SEASON 1C

By Charles Tasnadi, AP
BUD SELIG: Says Friday is cutoff day, 1C
▶ BASEBALL REPORT, 9,10C

USA TODAY

NO. 1 IN THE USA . . . FIRST IN DAILY READERS

WEDNESDAY

SEX BIAS IN SCHOOLS TOUGH ISSUE FOR TEENS

APPLICANTS FOR OUR PANEL HAVE NO CLEAR ANSWERS TO ISSUE ADULTS DEBATE, 1D

1958 QUIZ SHOW SCANDAL: WHERE ARE THEY NOW?
FILM OPENS SEPT. 14, 10D

By Dennis Magee, AP
JENNIFER TYUS: Boys treated more harshly, 1D

WEDNESDAY, SEPTEMBER 7, 1994

NEWSLINE

A QUICK READ ON THE NEWS

WALL STREET: Dow Jones industrial average rises 13.13 points to 3898.70; NASDAQ index inches up to 759.48; 30-year Treasury bond yield climbs to 7.53%. 1,4B.

JEWELRY HEIST: Tiffany's opens on schedule Tuesday after two thieves swiped $1.25 million in jewelry from the New York store Sunday; police have few leads. 3A.

BOUNCING BACK: Marion Barry, fallen former Washington, D.C., mayor, has a chance to move closer to another term as leader of the nation's capital. 3A.

MARLON'S MEMOIRS: Much-hyped autobiography, *Brando: Songs My Mother Taught Me*, for which actor Marlon Brando, left, was paid a reported $5 million, leaves many questions unanswered. Review. 1D.

By Jim Smeal, Galella Ltd.
BRANDO: "Writing this book for money"

IRELAND: Prime minister and leader of IRA's political wing make pledge for "equitable and lasting" peace. 6A.

CUBAN REFUGEES: About 100 Cubans are flown to Panama, launching transfer of many being held at Guantanamo Bay Naval Base. 6A.

CHIPPING IN: President Clinton could wrap up vacation without realizing wish of breaking 80 in golf. 6A.

ENVIRONMENT: In southeast Alaska, Fish and Wildlife Service considers status of two Tongass National Forest species, as logging industry hangs in balance. 2A.

GLOBAL LEADER: USA is first among 41 industrial nations in new World Competitiveness Report. 1B.

CAR SAFETY: Dr. Ricardo Martinez, trauma surgeon, is new National Highway Traffic Safety Administration chief. Martinez champions the seat belt, but favors safety education more than regulation. 3B.

GRADING SCHOOLS: U.S. gets C+ for education reforms, says report from past GOP education officials. 1D.

TODAY'S DEBATE: Fighting fires. In USA TODAY's opinion, "Proposals to subvert dying trees could increase fire risks, not reduce them." 10A.

▶ "We either spend (money) to reduce fuels and get our forests back into balance, where fires are frequent but small, or we will surely spend the money fighting huge, devastating fires," says Wally Herger. 10A.

MONEY: Tennis champions try to give game a lift. 1B.
▶ Demand for cars and trucks jumps in August. 1B.
▶ American Express has credit card with grace period. 3B.

SPORTS: Jerry Rice, greatest receiver ever? 1,4C.
▶ Greed is motivator in horse insurance fraud. 12C.

LIFE: Tiffany-Amber Thiessen moves to 90210. 1D.
▶ Fall brings a bunch of jazz and R&B recordings. 7D.

COMING TOMORROW

MTV AWARDS: Previewing the MTV Music Video Awards Thursday night at Radio City Music Hall in New York, with a report from rehearsals.

By John O. Buckley

Inside USA TODAY   4 SECTIONS

Classified   7-8D
Crossword   8D
Editorial/Opinion   10-11A
Lotteries   8D
State-by-state   4A
Stocks   5-9B

© COPYRIGHT 1994 USA TODAY, a division of Gannett Co.

USA SNAPSHOTS®

A look at statistics that shape the nation

Remembering Nixon

People in each age group who say Richard Nixon, who resigned the presidency 20 years ago, will be remembered as a great president

Age	
18-24	15%
25-34	30%
35-49	25%
50-64	27%
65 & over	37%

Source: Bruskin/Goldring Research poll

By John Riley and Marcia Staimer, USA TODAY

Peruvian runs tired Sampras out of Open

By Doug Smith
USA TODAY

Graf, Agassi in action today, 1,3,8C

NEW YORK — Little-known Jaime Yzaga cut down Pete Sampras, the men's reigning giant, Tuesday at the U.S. Open.

Peruvian Yzaga (EE-ah-ga) outlasted Sampras 3-6, 6-3, 4-6, 7-6, 7-5 in 3 hours, 38 minutes.

Sampras had heart, but lacked hustle, to stay in contention for his third U.S. Open title.

"I'm just not in great shape. Both feet are sore, my whole body was sore," says Sampras,

who was sidelined for six weeks with a sore left ankle.

"I just hit the wall."

Sampras took a breather whenever he could; his clothes were soaked with sweat.

The elimination of No. 1 Sampras means that for the first time since 1927, the top three seeds have been ousted before the quarterfinals.

Sampras picks unseeded Andre Agassi to win the crown.

He "has a really good shot," Sampras says of Agassi, who plays Thomas Muster tonight.

Sampras had lost only one set in his first three matches.

But Yzaga ignored the Sampras-is-Superman headlines, and tried to move him around.

"Everybody was saying he

was unbeatable," Yzaga, 26, says. "He's the best . . . (but) everybody is beatable."

The stadium crowd of 21,533 cheered every point.

"It was kind of tough at the end," Yzaga says. "I kept hearing the people and they were pulling for him."

Sampras would agree. "I was going on adrenalin and was determined to go the distance. The crowd was awesome, it just got me going. I wish I could have pulled out a win for them."

By Eileen Blass, USA TODAY
YZAGA: Celebrates victory

BATTLING BARRIERS

Hispanic leaders in Denver are calling for a citywide school walkout Sept. 16 to demonstrate concern over the continuing high dropout rates of Hispanic students.

By David Zalubowski, AP
ASPIRING SCHOLARS: Jose Saucedo, left, and Nereida Barron work in their kindergarten at Denver's Smedley Elementary School. At that age, officials work to avoid future dropouts.

High school completion rate

	Hispanics	Whites	Blacks
1972	51.9%	81.7%	66.7%
1992	57.3%	83.3%	74.6%

Source: U.S. Census
USA TODAY

COVER STORY

Pope cancels Sarajevo trip; truce cracks

By Tom Squitieri
USA TODAY

Pope John Paul II's "pilgrimage of peace" to Sarajevo was called off Tuesday out of concern for the safety of the city's besieged residents.

The decision came after leaders of the Bosnian Serbs — renewing attacks on Sarajevo — refused to guarantee the safety of the pope or the 25,000 expected at a Thursday Mass.

They said Muslims may attack him and blame Serbs.

Tuesday, Serbs fired 11 artillery rounds within Sarajevo's weapons-free zone. Small arms fire hit two U.N. planes.

The Vatican said the pope will hold the Mass "as soon as circumstances permitted."

His bulletproof "popemobile" arrived in Sarajevo just before the cancellation.

Workers preparing the Mass site, Zetra Stadium — used in the 1984 Winter Olympics — were sniper targets until U.N. peacekeepers fired back.

Posters just went up for the Mass with the pope's picture and the message, "You are not abandoned, we are with you."

The cease-fire that has prevailed in Sarajevo since March crumbled over the weekend.

Muslims were partly to blame. Monday, U.N. officials said an investigation found Muslims carried out an Aug. 18 mortar attack on the airport.

John Paul still will visit Zagreb, Croatia, this weekend to mark the archdiocese's 900th anniversary. A visit to Serbia's capital, Belgrade, was denied.

Hispanics in Denver give schools an F

Expert says the approach to Hispanic kids often 'is sink or swim, and they sink'

By John Ritter
USA TODAY

DENVER — In 1969, Hispanics clashed with police over demands a teacher who uttered a racial slur be fired.

That "West High Blowout" ignited a push for higher Hispanic achievement and cultural sensitivity in city schools — a battle, Hispanic leaders say, that has made scant progress.

Now, furious over chronically high dropout rates and poor performance, Hispanic leaders have called a citywide school walkout and protest march Sept. 16 — Mexican independence day — to dramatize their impatience.

"The issues haven't changed since '69," says Nita Gonzalez, head of Denver's Latino Education Coalition. "Here I am, 25 years later, and nothing's been done. The district has to know we can't tolerate that anymore."

In Denver and school systems across the nation, officials

Please see COVER STORY next page ▶

Jesus loses place of 30 years

A picture of Jesus hanging in a Michigan public high school hallway for 30 years must come down, a federal appeals court panel ruled Tuesday.

The 2-by-3-foot print at Bloomingdale High violates the Constitution and "entangles" government in religion, it said.

"It's frustrating the court seems to be so far apart from public opinion," says school board head James Dickerson.

Eric Pensinger, 19, a senior when he sued in 1992, says he's

agnostic and the picture made him feel like an outcast.

"A lot of the townspeople were pretty ticked off at me. I was called a devil-worshiper. I was told I was going to hell."

U.S. District Judge Benjamin Gibson last year rejected a compromise to add pictures of Abraham Lincoln and Martin Luther King Jr. "This is not a fender-bender where you can split the difference," he said.

— *Carrie Dowling*

Crime spree suspects found asleep

By Carol J. Castaneda
USA TODAY

Police say a deadly weeklong crime spree ended with the arrest of two suspects, one only 16, asleep under a bridge.

The two were charged in Albuquerque Tuesday with kidnapping, burglary and unlawful flight.

Eric Elliott, 16, and Lewis Gilbert, 22, of Newcomerstown, Ohio, were held pending identity hearings Thursday.

Tipped by a motorist who gave them a ride Monday, police found them sleeping early Tuesday under a bridge near Santa Fe. Two rifles, a shotgun and a pistol lay nearby.

"Because of the element of surprise . . . nothing bad happened," said John Denko, New Mexico state police chief.

Elliott and Gilbert are suspects in a trail of burglaries, killings and car thefts that began a week ago in Ohio.

Robert and Judy Elliott, Eric's father and stepmother, spoke with him and said they don't think he willingly took part in the crime spree.

"I think he might have been afraid for his own life," said Robert Elliott.

"We told him we loved him and that we were here for him," said Judy Elliott.

Wearing gray jeans, a green shirt and sneakers, the teenager said nothing as he was led to court, his hands in chains.

Gilbert, also in manacles, wore a black T-shirt, black jeans and sneakers.

Officials say they met Aug. 15 when Gilbert was released from prison after serving 18 months for stealing a bus.

Elliott was awaiting trial on charges of breaking into a bowling alley.

They are suspects in:
▶ Last week's disappearance of Ruth Loader, 79, of Port Washington, Ohio.
▶ The deaths of William Brewer, 86, and his wife, Floris, 74, of Fulton, Mo.
▶ The killing of Rosie Ruddel, 37, near Oklahoma City.

▶ The crime list, 3A

Abortion deal close in Cairo

By Ellen Hale
Gannett News Service

CAIRO, Egypt — Delegates to a U.N. conference today are expected to accept a compromise on abortion in the plan to limit population growth.

The compromise would leave regulation of abortion up to each nation, while emphasizing concern that unsafe abortions are a worldwide problem.

"We're well on our way to a consensus," says Vice President Gore.

But a fight looms today as delegates decide whether to change the definition of reproductive health care. As drafted, the U.N. document calls on countries to make available by 2015 a range of reproductive services — including abortion.

But it goes on to emphasize eliminating abortion through better family planning.

Key language in the compromise: "In no case should abortion be promoted as a method of family planning."

That alleviates the Vatican's major concern: that the conference would proclaim an international right to safe abortion.

But Gore says the Vatican remains unlikely to sign regardless of the compromise.

A sovereignty clause on abortion also may ease conservative Muslims' concerns the plan encourages homosexuality and promiscuity.

Although abortion has gotten the most attention, it is only a small part of the proposal, which seeks to limit world population growth by making family planning universally available, raising women's status and reducing infant mortality.

▶ Vatican's position, 5A

Manhunt ends in N.M.

By Murrae Haynes, AP
CAPTURED: Lewis Gilbert, one of two crime spree suspects, is taken from New Mexico state police headquarters in Santa Fe.

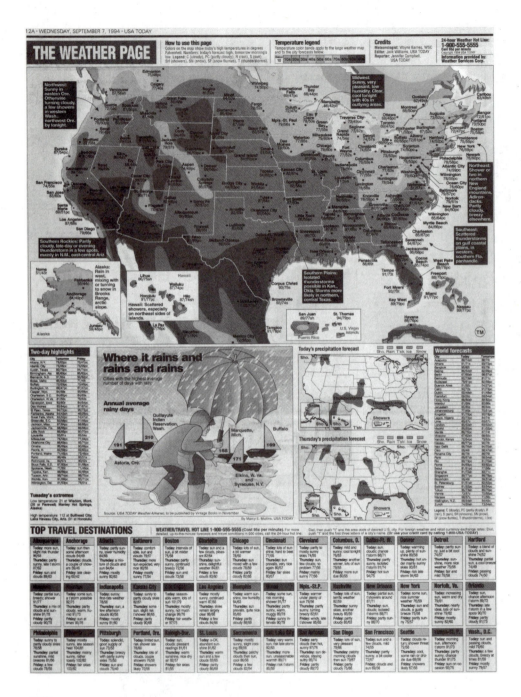

3.2

In *USA Today*, even the weather is subject to splashy graphics and alliteration.
© *1994, USA Today. Reprinted with permission.*

THE WALL STREET JOURNAL.

© 1994 Dow Jones & Company, Inc. All Rights Reserved.

VOL. CXXXI NO. 47 ★★★ WESTERN EDITION WEDNESDAY, SEPTEMBER 7, 1994 RIVERSIDE, CALIFORNIA .... 75 CENTS

On the Defense

Lawyer's Fast Work On Death Cases Raises Doubts About System

Mr. Cannon's Style in Court Has Fans on the Bench But Not on Death Row

'A Mockery of the Process'

By PAUL M. BARRETT
Staff Reporter of THE WALL STREET JOURNAL

HOUSTON – Joe Frank Cannon defends people charged with murder, some facing the death penalty if convicted. His strategy for these capital-punishment cases is simple: Work fast.

"Juries don't like a lot of questioning, all these jack-in-the-box objections, going into every detail, so I've never done it," explains the veteran criminal lawyer. He boasts of hurrying through trials "like greased lightning."

Some judges and juries may like Mr. Cannon's speedy approach, but it isn't clear that it benefits his clients. Acting as a court-appointed attorney, Mr. Cannon has defended eight men who are currently awaiting execution. Of two others who were sentenced to death, one has already been executed by lethal injection, and the other was killed by a fellow prisoner. In Texas, which executes more people than any other state, Mr. Cannon's collection of 10 death sentences is one of the largest among active lawyers.

Joe Frank Cannon

Millions of Americans are watching Los Angeles attorney Robert Shapiro lead the expensive, meticulous capital-murder defense of O.J. Simpson. But for many ordinary capital defendants who must rely on court-appointed counsel, the "greased-lightning" approach extolled by Mr. Cannon may be all that is available. Critics in Houston legal circles say he is an extreme example of a breed of publicly paid lawyers who handle death-penalty trials in the rushed manner of traffic-court disputes.

What's News—

Business and Finance

JOHNSON & JOHNSON agreed to buy Eastman Kodak's clinical diagnostics unit for $1.01 billion, making J&J the No. 3 firm in the medical-testing industry. Like its offer last month for beauty-products concern Neutrogena, J&J's foray into clinical diagnostics is an attempt to diversify beyond pharmaceuticals, where managed-care institutions are exerting tremendous pressure on drug prices.

(Article on Page A3)

* * *

Kidder Peabody's former head of government-bond trading, Joseph Jett, is accusing the brokerage firm of stonewalling his request for documents for an arbitration case he has brought against Kidder.

Kidder named Michael Madden, an executive managing director, to the newly created post of chief origination officer, putting him in line to assume the president's post at the firm.

(Articles on Page C1)

* * *

Mexican financier Carlos Cabal Peniche, who controls a sprawling fresh-produce and banking empire valued at about $2 billion, was accused of obtaining funds through illegal loans to himself from his bank.

(Article in Column 6)

* * *

The U.S. has replaced Japan as the world's most competitive economy for the first time since 1985, but middle-income Americans have paid a stiff price in the process, according to an annual global study.

Japanese business sentiment at major manufacturers has improved sharply, a survey showed. The results are the clearest sign yet that the nation's economy is recovering.

(Articles on Pages A3 and A2)

* * *

Michael Steinhardt is preparing for Steinhardt Management to settle expected federal antitrust charges stemming from an April 1991 Treasury-note squeeze, people close to the

World-Wide

SOME CUBAN REFUGEES BEGAN leaving Guantanamo for Panama.

The first refugees to be moved out of the overflowing tent city at the Guantanamo naval base in Cuba were put aboard planes and taken to Panama. All 100 were volunteers. Many said they were optimistic that conditions in Panama would be better than in Guantanamo. Meanwhile, two U.S. soldiers were injured during a disturbance involving the Cuban refugees at Guantanamo. Cuban and U.S. negotiators met briefly in New York for talks on the refugee influx.

Four campsites are being built in Panama to accommodate up to 10,000 Cubans. Panama has agreed to shelter the refugees for six months.

* * *

Pope John Paul II called off his trip to Sarajevo after failing to win guarantees of safety for residents of Bosnia's besieged capital. The decision to cancel tomorrow's visit coincided with heavy gunfire around the city's airport and a Serb artillery attack east of the city. The pontiff will leave Saturday for a two-day trip to Croatia.

* * *

The Vatican ruled out concessions in its standoff with the U.S. over abortion, as delegates at a U.N. population conference tried to revise parts of a draft paper referring to abortion. Though the Holy See said it won't compromise on moral issues, a Vatican aide said, "We are on the road to getting something we could eventually sign."

* * *

Ireland's Prime Minister Reynolds held his first face-to-face meeting with the head of the Irish Republican Army's political wing, Gerry Adams, and the two made a joint commitment to peace in Northern Ireland. British Prime Minister Major cut off an angry session with Protestant politician Ian Paisley about Northern Ireland.

* * *

A Haitian lawyer was shot and killed not far from an army barracks in Port-au-Prince, and police authorities said they had no details on the slaying. Separately, the Clinton administration failed to persuade Canada to join a proposed U.S.-led military invasion to restore democracy in Haiti, Ottawa officials announced.

* * *

German parliamentarians are accusing each other of having close ties to Communists ahead of Oct. 16 legislative elections. Kohl has repeatedly said Social Democrats are soft on communism, and a Social

Help-Wanted Advertising

Seasonally adjusted, 1967=100

THE HELP-WANTED ADVERTISING index rose in July to 121, up from 117 in June, the Conference Board reports.

Is Hikmet Kotsch Only 'Schuhputzer' In All of Germany?

* * *

The Shoeshining Profession Is Beneath People There, The Bureaucrats Believe

By DANIEL BENJAMIN
Staff Reporter of THE WALL STREET JOURNAL

BERLIN – With a long, curved brush in his polish-stained hand, Hikmet Kotsch is a shining example of resistance to change.

Mr. Kotsch delicately applies brown goo to an outstretched shoe. Around him, in the corridor of a downtown mall, a familiar sequence of events begins: Passersby rubberneck, crowds gather to gawk, jaws slacken in amazement.

A shoeshine in progress may not sound so outlandish. But, then, Mr. Kotsch is proffering the sole legally sanctioned professional shine in Berlin and, probably in all of Germany, a country with roughly 81 million pairs of shoes in daily use.

Hikmet Kotsch

Officials aren't absolutely sure about Mr. Kotsch's uniqueness, since they refuse to recognize shining shoes as a legitimate occupation and thus keep no statistics on other exceptional cases.

The 67-year-old Turkish-born Mr. Kotsch, a naturalized citizen who has lived here in Germany for three decades, is

Tax Report

A Special Summary and Forecast Of Federal and State Tax Developments

CONFUSION GROWS about whether companies may deduct loan fees for LBOs.

Courts this summer issue conflicting opinions on this high-stakes question. In June, the U.S. Appeals Court in San Francisco said Kroy Inc., a Scottsdale, Ariz., maker of labeling products, may deduct loan fees paid in a leveraged buyout. But now the Tax Court takes the opposite view in a case involving Fort Howard Corp., a Green Bay, Wis., maker of paper products.

The law generally bars companies from deducting costs, except for interest, paid in connection with the redemption of their own stock. Figuring whether deductions are "in connection with" a redemption can be tricky. In the Fort Howard case, Tax Court Judge Ruwe specifically rejects the Kroy ruling. A dozen other Tax Court judges agree, but two dissent. "We're probably heading to the Supreme Court" over this, says Robert Willens of Lehman Brothers.

The issue affects many companies because "it extends to any debt-financed buyback of shares," not just those associated with LBOs, Mr. Willens says.

THE MYSTERY DEEPENS: Why aren't more people filing tax returns?

The IRS received about 112.6 million individual returns as of Aug. 19. That was up from 112 million a year earlier but down from 113.1 million the year before that. "Something is wrong here," says Donald C. Alexander, a former IRS commissioner and now a Washington lawyer at Akin Gump. "The population is growing, the economy is expanding and more people are working, but the IRS is getting even fewer returns than two years ago."

Some analysts attribute the problem to mind-numbing tax laws. But others also blame George Bush's 1992 move to cut withholding, which meant fewer people got refunds. IRS analysts agree but cite other factors, too. For example, they point to their direct-mail efforts to tell many low-income people that they were filing returns unnecessarily. An IRS spokesman also says lower 1993 interest rates meant less interest income for some, pushing them below the minimum required for filing.

THE IRS STUDIES the idea of regulating commercial tax-return preparers.

The IRS has no rules governing who may hang a shingle as a professional tax preparer. But that may change. The IRS and several private tax specialists are analyzing proposals to regulate and register pre-

Fast Finance

Mexican Accusations Reveal the Workings Of a Rising 'Grupo'

Loans From Its Bank Are Said To Be Used Improperly In Cabal's Acquisitions

Plucking Pieces of Del Monte

By CRAIG TORRES and DIANNE SOLIS
Staff Reporters of THE WALL STREET JOURNAL

MEXICO CITY – In a restaurant, a prominent economist earlier this year speculated on the wealth of Mexican financier Carlos Cabal Peniche. Leaning over a plate of buttered snails, his eyes darting cautiously around the room, the man whispered, "*El Vaticano.*"

For his part, Mr. Cabal said in a rare interview about two months ago: "In Mexico, with any new group with money, they say it's politicians backing them. If that doesn't work, they say it's drugs. And if that doesn't work they say it's the Vatican."

But now, Mexico's Finance Ministry says it has the answer to how Mr. Cabal came up with the money to control a sprawling fresh-produce and banking empire, Grupo Cabal, valued at about $2 billion: A large chunk of the money came from illegal loans made from Mr. Cabal's bank to himself to invest in various businesses.

Carlos Cabal Peniche

In a move that could have serious implications for the Mexican economy, Finance Minister Pedro Aspe on Monday accused Mr. Cabal of funneling between $200 million and $700 million to himself through a series of direct loans or through loans made through shell companies.

The ministry issued an arrest warrant for criminal charges against the 37-year-old banker and several associates, and it seized control of Mr. Cabal's banking group, Grupo Financiero Cremi-Union SA, the eighth-largest banking group in Mexico. The action put bank stocks under selling pressure on the Mexican stock

3.3

With the highest daily circulation of any national newspaper, the *Wall Street Journal* has lived up to its billing as the "daily diary of the American Dream."

ment, and feature stories to gain new readers and entertain those they already have. At a time when the economics of daily newspaper publishing has never been more precarious, *USA Today* has become a unique success story.

The Wizards of Wall Street

Another American journalism success story has a decidedly different angle. It is hard to imagine any newspaper more different from *USA Today* than the *Wall Street Journal.* Where *USA Today* is graphically exuberant, the *Journal's* format is staid and sedate (see 3.3). Yet in maintaining a circulation of about 2 million for the past 5 years it has become, according to *Newsweek,* "the best business newspaper and one of the best newspapers of any kind."

The *Journal* was founded by Dow Jones and Company in 1889. Its growth over the past decade has clearly reflected America's increasing interest in the complexities of business and the stock market. At the same time, the paper has broadened its coverage to include many late-breaking stories and augmented its regular columns with news stories that are not directly related to business.

According to managing editor Norman Pearlstine, "We're not going to double our news hole and drown the reader . . . but business has changed and we have to reflect that change." Today's *Journal*, which includes a Leisure and Arts section, appears to reflect the philosophy that business is concerned with everything, but vice-president and associate publisher Peter Kann insists that "we'd be bats to try and turn this paper into a general newspaper."

Some might argue that such a move would only be fair, considering that the national edition of the *New York Times* boasts an expanded business section and has gone directly after the *Journal*'s traditional market. *USA Today*'s business section, though obviously thin and breezy by comparison, still provides some of the same basic information in a much more colorful and upbeat format.

An embarrassing turn of events for the *Journal* came in 1983, when reporter R. Foster Winans secretly agreed to leak the contents of his "Heard on the Street" column to Peter N. Brant, a stockbroker friend. For several months, Brant invested heavily in stocks just before they were spotlighted in the column. His advance inside information allowed him to accumulate hundreds of thousands of dollars in profits, which he split with Winans.

The Securities and Exchange Commission investigated, and the scheme soon unraveled. Winans was promptly fired from the *Journal* and was eventually sentenced to 18 months in prison for his role as an inside trader, even though the inside information was simply the contents of his own columns.

The case was appealed to the Supreme Court. In 1987 its decision upheld the lower court's ruling sentencing Winans and several others involved to prison. The legal precedents in the case were complicated, but the essence of the Court's decision was that information contained in "Heard on the Street" was the property of the *Journal* and that Winans' improper use of the information "amounted to theft."

Through it all, however, the *Wall Street Journal* has lived up to its own advertising as "the diary of the American Dream." Its columns reflect that dream on a daily basis, and the prosperity of the paper itself makes it one of America's journalism giants.

Whether the emphasis is soft news and splashy graphics or hard news and traditional journalism, the newsstand always has something for everyone. The battle between hard and soft news remains at the very heart of the history of American journalism.

Hard and Soft News

In theory, hard news is timely, factual accounting; soft news is background information. A report on the mayor's heart attack is hard news; an interview with her husband in the hospital corridor is soft news. Hard news is facts and statistics: temperatures, box scores, the number of votes cast for a candidate. Soft news is opinion and color: columns, comics, editorials, and "Dear Abby." *Time*'s Thomas Griffith puts it this way:

> The truth is that there are two kinds of news, the important and the interesting, and most readers . . . feel entitled to both. In fact, the simplest way to judge the coverage of any newspaper . . . is to measure which kind of news it accents the most, the important or the interesting.

The *New York Times* carries a preponderance of hard news, the *New York Post* very little. Each has cultivated an audience that expects the balance between fact and feature found there.

Mass and Special-Interest Audiences

Most media deal with two constituencies: the mass audience and the special-interest audience. When newspapers run general-interest stories, their appeal is similar to magazines like *Reader's Digest,* which draw a large readership of people from diverse age groups and various educational, social, and cultural backgrounds. When sports, stocks, and other features are emphasized, newspapers are catering to the special-interest audience. Communication authors John Merrill and Ralph Lowenstein call this approach "internal specialization."

The approach of each editorial staff can be found in their newspaper's format, which sets an information *agenda,* grading events according to how important or interesting they may be to the reader. Perhaps this function was best described by media researcher Bernard Cohen in his book *The Press and Foreign Policy:* "The press may not be successful much of the time in telling people what to think, but it is stunningly successful in telling its readers what to think about."

In most newspapers, important stories are displayed prominently on or near the front page. The lead story, at the top of the page, is supposed to be the day's most significant event. Inside the paper, the special-interest reader finds information in neatly divided sections: sports, editorial, family, entertainment, and business. These divisions help readers set their own agendas. Some may read their horoscope first, then work the crossword puzzle, and never get around to the front page. A stockbroker may go straight to the business section.

Of course, sometimes special-interest news makes it to the front page. So many people have become fans that sports is sometimes front-page news. On "Black Monday," October 19, 1987 (or on the day after, in morning papers), we all read about the worst stock market crash since 1929. But on a normal day, only the special-interest audience will pore over the day's stock quotations.

What's News?

How do those who present "the news" to us make their decisions about exactly what it is? To some extent, reporters find news *where the editors tell them to look.* Thus the news is often institutional, predictable, and likely to come from the same sources day in and day out.

Experienced news editors know that a story must have certain attributes to qualify as news. These attributes are not always what you might imagine. There is more to be asked than "Is it important to the reader?" Actually, that might be one of the last considerations at some papers. Instead, editors decide what goes in the paper using the following time-honored criteria:

Newsmakers Some people make news no matter what they do. The president of the United States, Elizabeth Taylor, a controversial Arab leader, or Princess Diana always seem to be worthy of a story. (In fact, a controversial Arab leader's relationship *with* Princess Diana would make a terrific story!) These newsmakers seem to parade endlessly across the pages of our daily newspapers.

Regional or local interest Readers want to know about an event because *it happened here.* If a bridge collapses and two are killed in Paris, it doesn't "play in Peoria." If the Peoria bridge goes out, it's on the front page of the Peoria newspaper and the lead story on the Peoria evening news.

Rewards The late Wilbur Schramm, perhaps the best known of all communication researchers, once said that news stories have either *immediate* or *delayed* rewards that satisfy a need. We all need to feel informed, and immediate-reward news stories provide instant satisfaction. We can laugh, cry, sympathize, or become angry about them right away. Stories concerning disaster, crime, sports, and social events all give us immediate rewards. Delayed-reward news stories may be about public affairs, business, finance, or other complex matters. There are exceptions of course. The Clarence Thomas confirmation hearings were a public affairs story that captivated millions. A failed savings and loan institution is of vital interest to those who have deposits there. Yet generally these types of stories don't carry any immediate relevance to our lives, and increasingly, editors are finding less room for them.

Human interest These stories are becoming more common on the nation's news pages. They're often heart-tuggers: the "miracle baby" who grew outside the womb, the disabled man who rises to an important government position. The unusual, the unique, the sensational—this is the stuff of soft news. Editors are finding that an increasing number of readers want the "human side" of the day's events. Perhaps this reflects a general feeling of disaffiliation from government and world affairs.

Good News Is No News

Despite the trend toward uplifting human-interest stories, one of the most frequent complaints an editor hears is, "How come you never run any *good* news?" It's true that reporters can't and don't seek out stories about murders that did not happen. Perhaps this is human nature. We don't usually go out of our way to tell people how *good* we feel, but if something is bothering us, we let them know.

Chet Huntley, co-anchor with David Brinkley on NBC news in the 1960s, once said flatly, "Journalists were never intended to be the cheerleaders of society." This is particularly true for print journalists. Reporters often see themselves as the thin buffer between the people and their government. The relationship can be a difficult one (see Chapter 4). When the United States invaded the tiny island of Grenada in 1983, the press was virtually barred from the scene. Reporters protested that they were prevented from doing their jobs.

The situation was repeated during the 1991 Gulf War. Shortly after war broke out, veteran newsman Walter Cronkite observed that "the greatest mistake of the military so far is to attempt to control coverage. . . . The fact that the military apparently feels that there is something it must hide, can only eventually lead to a breakdown in home-front confidence."

Most reporters believe that their duty is to report governmental failures. Implicit is the hope that if these wrongs are reported, they may eventually be righted. Journalists also defend their actions on the basis of truth. "If we neglect to report some news because we think suppression is in the public interest," they might insist, "we'll lose our credibility as impartial news reporters." That impartiality may already be suspect, given the criteria for news selection, but the point is well taken nonetheless.

Five Eras of American Newspaper Journalism

Historians differ about the best way to divide the history of newspaper journalism. The five-way division in 3.4 appeared for the first time in earlier editions of this book and merits some explanation. The eras alternate between an emphasis on objective, or factual, reporting and on subjective, or advocacy, reporting. The early, yellow, and new-journalism eras are dominated by the subjective opinions of reporters, editors, and owners. The penny press and objective eras are characterized by more dispassionate attempts to report the news.

Some would argue that today's tabloids have ushered in a new era of subjective reporting. Any division suffers to some degree from over-simplification, but this one does point to a continuing historical cycle.

The Early Years

During the first years of American newspapers, the opinions of the owner-editors were paramount in deciding how a story was to be played. In fact, sometimes those opinions *were* the story. Several small papers were published in each metropolitan area, and each reflected a particular point of view. The question of political independence was obviously a major topic during the revolutionary period. Owner-editors usually printed stories to appeal to the faithful and bring new subscribers into the fold. Newspapers crusaded for political causes and decried political injustice. Editorial opinion did not appear on a special page but was given within a story, often in the lead paragraph, sometimes in italics. Because editors and reporters were advocates for a point of view, we refer to this period as the beginning of *advocacy journalism.*

The most heated debates appeared in the letters-to-the-editor column. Historian Frank Luther Mott notes that letters were often contributed by editors as well as readers. After the Revolution, debate centered on the adoption of a federal constitution, taxes, the treaty with England, and problems with the French.

Did newspapers in the new nation really have freedom of the press? Massachusetts adopted a tax on newspapers, and later on newspaper advertising, that smacked of state control. Fledgling printers, often strapped for cash, were susceptible to promises of lucrative government printing or post office contracts.

In 1798 Congress passed the Sedition Act, which provided that "any person . . . writing, printing or uttering any false, scandalous or malicious statement against the Government of the United States . . . should be imprisoned not over two years and pay a fine not exceeding $2,000." This was interpreted by most editors as direct censorship, because those most likely to be punished were the ones who disagreed with the powerful Federalist Party.

Several trials were held under the act, and a few prominent printers were fined and sent to prison. When Thomas Jefferson was elected president in 1800, he pardoned the prisoners, and the House Judiciary Committee denounced the Sedition Act as unconstitutional. All fines collected were returned with interest.

The first 30 years of the 19th century have been called the dark ages of partisan journalism. The profession was rife with corruption, and attacks on political leaders grew increasingly vicious. The personal lives of prominent figures were considered fair game, and Jefferson probably suffered the most. Andrew Jackson was never a favorite of journalists either, but he knew how to use the press to his own advantage (see Chapter 12). In 1830 he endowed the *Washington Globe* with a federal printing contract, and it became the official organ of the Jackson administration.

The Penny Press

Until 1833 newspapers had generally been sold by yearly subscription, although several publishers (including Horace Greeley) tried unsuccessfully to publish a cheap daily paper that could be sold on the streets for as little as 2 cents a copy. Still, the going price for most dailies was 6 cents. In 1833, thanks to technical improvements that sped production and distribution, Benjamin Day was able to launch the *New York Sun* at just a penny a copy.

Advocacy journalism did not magically disappear in 1833, but the "penny press" was the beginning of a different kind of newspaper and provided an important step forward in what has been called the "massification" of the newspaper. The *New York Sun* offered to "lay

1783

The Early Years

1600   1700   1800

1690 *Publick Occurrences Both Foreign and Domestick* is the first U.S. newspaper; it folds after one issue.

1721 James and Benjamin Franklin are early colonial printers. James starts the *New England Courant.*

1735 John Peter Zenger is acquitted of charges of seditious libel, setting a precedent for truth as defense in libel cases.

1767 John Dickinson writes his series of "Letters from a Farmer in Pennsylvania" in the *Pennsylvania Chronicle*, characterizing the political nature of early papers.

1798 The Sedition Act is the first effort to suppress the young nation's free press. It is abolished 2 years later.

1808 First on-the-spot correspondents in Washington D.C., report political news for the papers back home.

1820s A colorful era for an information-starved public. Seacoast city papers hire boats to meet incoming ships carrying news. Pony express riders race each other from Washington to Boston and New York to carry congressional news.

3.4 Five Eras of American Newspaper Journalism

1844

Samuel Morse invents the telegraph, wires are strung between major cities, and news now travels instantaneously.

1887

William Randolph Hearst is put in charge of the *San Francisco Examiner*. Long an admirer of Pulitzer, he imitates *World* style and the *Examiner* prospers.

The Penny Press

Yellow Journalism

1850

1833 Bejamin Day begins the *New York Sun*. Now everyone can afford a daily paper. His success is soon imitated by dozens of others.

1835 James Gordon Bennett launches the *New York Herald*.

1841 Horace Greeley starts the *New York Tribune*, the first newspaper to develop the editorial page as we know it today. Nine years later it is the first major newspaper to come out for the abolition of slavery.

1848 The Associated Press is founded. It serves papers of many political persuasions and encourages reporters to write stories more objectively.

1865 After the Civil War, industrialization invades the press room and newspapers become increasingly mechanized.

1878 Joseph Pulitzer founds the *St. Louis Post-Dispatch*.

1883 Pulitzer's *New York World* brings what is eventually called yellow journalism to America's largest city.

1886 The *World* tops 250,000 in circulation and surpasses the *Daily News* as New York's most widely read newpaper.

1889 The *Wall Street Journal* begins publication.

1895 Hearst comes to New York, buys the *New York Journal*, and hires away many *World* Staffers.

1896 Circulation war between the *Journal* and *World*. Within 12 months, the *Journal* is tops in circulation.

1896–1898 Stories in the yellow press whip up public sentiment for a war with Spain.

1900

1900 One-third of all metropolitan dailies practice yellow journalism. President McKinley is assassinated. The Hearst papers are blamed for inspiring the murderer.

1900–1910 Circulation of most yellow papers falls and yellow journalism disappears.

1914

The *New York Times* begins a policy of publishing important documents in their entirety.

Objective Journalism

The New Journalism

1900

1950

1896 Adolph Ochs takes over the *New York Times*.

1900 The Associated Press expands, moves to New York.

1907 United Press founded.

1923 The Canons of Journalism adopted by the American Society of Newspaper Editors stress the responsibility of newspapers and reporters to report the news "fairly."

1933 The American Newspaper Guild is founded as the first union for newspeople.

1941 The *Wall Street Journal* is taken over by Bernard Kilgore. Circulation soars as the *Journal* practices detached reporting with emphasis on financial news and detailed analyses of economic events.

1942 Voluntary "Code of Wartime Practices for the American Press" is issued by government; the press is willing to cooperate.

1947 Hutchins Commission report is critical of press practices. It argues for tighter regulation of print journalism.

1958 United Press and International News Service combine to form United Press International.

1958 Both major wire services begin running more "interpretive" articles and columns.

1960 The *New York Herald Tribune* begins using a magazine-style layout—more pictures and a lighter writing style.

1960s American metros lose circulation in many cities. Many combine to save press and circulation expenses. Many dailies in business for 60 years or more fold.

1962 Tom Wolfe, founding father of the new journalism, joins the staff of the *New York Herald Tribune*.

3.4 (continued)

1972

Bob Woodward and Carl Bernstein's *Washington Post* articles expose Watergate scandals.

1980s

Journalists fear the worst as U.S. Supreme Court decisions appear to narrow the constitutional definitions of freedom of the press

---

1963 Sportswriter Jimmy Breslin begins column for the *Herald Tribune,* using writing techniques borrowed from fiction.

1968 Some Democratic convention reporters find they need more than objectivity to tell the story. Domestic violence and increasing hostility over the Vietnam War make objective reporting difficult.

1968–1969 Underground newspapers like the *Los Angeles Free Press* and the *Village Voice* experience rapid circulation increases.

1971 President Nixon temporarily blocks *New York Times, Washingrton Post,* and *Boston Globe* pubication of Pentagon Papers.

1972 Hunter Thompson's *Fear and Loathing: On the Campaign Trail 1972* appears as a series of articles in *Rolling Stone.*

1974 President Nixon resigns.

1978 Over 60% of U.S. dailies are owned by large chains. Daily circulation of the 1,764 English-language dailies nears 62 million.

1983 Just 1 year after its inception, *USA Today* circulation tops 1 million.

1986 *Editor & Publisher* reports that the trend toward morning distribution continues, afternoon dailies struggle to survive.

1987 Scandals dominate the nation's headlines. Press coverage of the Gary Hart and Iran-Contra affairs raises serious questions regarding journalistic ethics.

1989 The *Los Angeles Herald Examiner* folds, a casualty of the metro circulation wars.

1991 Reporters chafe under military restrictions designed to control press coverage of the Gulf War.

1994 *New York Times* reports that 8 of the 10 largest U.S. dailies have declining circulation over last year.

1995 Weekly newspaper circulation nears 60 million, could surpass that of dailies for first time by the end of the decade.

Independence Day at the *New York Sun*

"Police Office" was one of the most popular columns in the Sun. *This sample is from the July 4, 1834, issue as reproduced in Frank Luther Mott's* American Journalism. *Note the occasional editorial quip.*

Police Office

Margaret Thomas was drunk in the street—said she never would get drunk again "upon her honor." Committed, "upon honor."

William Luvoy got drunk because yesterday was so devilish warm. Drank 9 glasses of brandy and water and said he would be more cursed if he wouldn't drink 9 more as quick as he could raise the money to buy it with. He would like to know what right the magistrate had to interfere with his private affairs. Fined $1—forgot his pocketbook, and was sent over to Bridewell.

Bridget McMunn got drunk and threw a pitcher at Mr. Ellis, of 53 Ludlow st. Bridget said she was the mother of 3 little orphans—God bless their dear souls—and if she went to prison they would choke to death for the want of something to eat. Committed.

Catharine McBride was brought in for stealing a frock. Catharine said she had just served out 6 months on Blackwell's Island, and she wouldn't be sent back again, for the best glass of punch that ever was made. Her husband, when she last left the penitentiary, took her to a boarding house in Essex st., but the rascal got mad at her, pulled her hair, pinched her arm, and kicked her out of bed. She was determined not to bear such treatment as this, and so got drunk and stole the frock out of pure spite. Committed.

Bill Doty got drunk because he had the horrors so bad he couldn't keep sober. Committed.

Patrick Ludwick was sent up by his wife, who testified that she had supported him for several years in idleness and drunkenness. Abandoning all hopes of a reformation in her husband, she bought him a suit of clothes a fortnight since and told him to go about his business, for she would not live with him any longer. Last night he came home in a state of intoxication, broke into his wife's bedroom, pulled her out of bed, pulled her hair, and stamped on her. She called a watchman and sent him up. Pat exerted all his powers of eloquence in endeavoring to excite his wife's sympathy, but to no purpose. As every sensible woman ought to do who is cursed with a drunken husband, she refused to have anything to do with him hereafter—and he was sent to the penitentiary.

From Frank Luther Mott, American Journalism, A History, 1690–1960. 3d ed. *Copyright 1962 Macmillan Publishing Company, Inc.*

---

before the public, at a price well within the means of everyone, all the news of the day." In contrast to the advocacy journals, the *Sun* was apolitical. It offered very little political news, reporting short, breezy items about local people and domestic events. One of the most popular features was the "Police Office" report, which carried a long list of local people who had been arrested for drunkenness and rowdy behavior (see 3.5).

Within a few months, the *Sun*'s circulation surpassed all others in New York. Because the paper did not depend on any one political constituency, it tended to present the news impartially to all. Its overnight success prompted a number of imitators, including the *New York Herald* and the *New York Tribune*. All sold for a penny, and all were successful.

The *Herald* was the brainchild of James Gordon Bennett, who pioneered in the organization of the modern newsroom and was the first to send reporters out on "beats" to gather news for information-hungry readers.

Soon the penny press appeared in Philadelphia and Baltimore. Penny-press owners seldom had an ax to grind; their purpose was to provide the public with the news at the cheapest possible price and, of course, to turn a profit.

This is not to say the penny papers did not take editorial positions. Horace Greeley's *New York Tribune* printed his famous articles on the suffering in the New York slums. Greeley called his paper "the great moral organ," claiming it was on a much higher ethical plane than competing penny papers. The *Tribune* did much to convince religious and community leaders that the cheap newspaper could be an instrument for good and that journalism was not the exclusive bailiwick of sensation-seeking commercial publishers. However, none of Greeley's opinion articles appeared on the news pages. In fact, the *New York Tribune* was the first paper to develop the editorial page as we know it today.

Mott credits the penny press with changing the concept of news. Newspapers of the early era had emphasized politics and events in Europe. The penny press shifted attention to hometown events, particularly those involving crime and sex. There was also the human-interest story—forerunner of today's soft news. Obviously a strong audience appetite for sensational stories remains even today.

Another blow to advocacy journalism came in 1844 with the invention of the telegraph and the founding of the Associated Press (AP) 4 years later. The AP plan was to provide news stories to editors for a fee, but what about the political slant? It was decided that events would be reported as neutrally as possible, so as not to offend any subscriber. Organized as a cooperative and owned by its member publications, the AP offered its service to newspapers of every political persuasion.

Yellow Journalism

The slavery issue and the threat of civil war heated up political debate in the late 1850s. More and more penny-press space was given over to political news. Later, battles between the Yankee and rebel armies were reported in detail. After the war, a young ex-soldier named Joseph Pulitzer arrived in St. Louis to seek his fortune (see 3.6). Almost immediately he became involved in local politics and, to everyone's surprise, was elected to the state legislature. There he became an ardent spokesman for the common people while fighting graft and corruption.

In 1878 Pulitzer bought the *St. Louis Dispatch* at a sheriff's auction and combined it with the *Post*. The new *Post-Dispatch* enlivened its columns with crusades against lotteries, tax evasion, and the corrupt city administration.

Buoyed by his success, Pulitzer moved east and acquired the *New York World,* which had been losing $40,000 a year. Pulitzer promptly announced that the *World,* under his leadership, would "expose all fraud and sham, fight all public evils and abuses . . . and battle for the people in earnest sincerity." It is that spirit which is embodied in the most coveted of all journalism awards, the Pulitzer Prize. For reporters and photographers, it represents the ultimate recognition.

The phenomenal success of the Pulitzer formula changed journalism forever. The news reporter searched for an "unusual" slant to the story; stunts and "people's crusades" were launched. One reporter feigned insanity to be admitted to a state asylum and then exposed conditions there. *World* crusades against telephone and railroad monopolies were incessant. Most articles featured diagrams, illustrations, and, later, photographs. The *World* also made daring use of the editorial cartoon.

Pulitzer's fiercest rival was William Randolph Hearst, who bought the competing *New York Journal* in 1895. In 2 years the *Journal*

Profile: Joseph Pulitzer

Every year on his birthday Joseph Pulitzer gave each of his friends a little gift and passed out cigars to his top executives. This reverse of the usual practice guaranteed that no one forgot his birthday, but it also said something about the paradoxical nature of one of history's most influential journalists.

His was a Horatio Alger story. He started out penniless, worked hard, and saved his money. He turned the *St. Louis Post-Dispatch* into one of the best-known newspapers in America in less than 5 years. Then he moved on to New York, where he boosted the *New York World*'s circulation from 20,000 to more than 250,000.

Though what he did was amazing, the way he did it was even more so. Both of his papers were examples of yellow journalism. The "yellows" had a lively and uncompromising style that included emotion as well as fact. No political party or candidate felt safe from the sting of the *World*.

Pulitzer was careful to distinguish his brand of advocacy journalism from Hearst's. The Hearst papers, he explained, were simply "malicious and hateful." In all fairness, Hearst's own political ambitions may have sparked his most vicious attacks, while Pulitzer's worst ulterior motive was to increase circulation. But contemporary critics see very little difference between the practices of the two yellow-journalism giants.

A colorful character in his own right, Pulitzer was often cantankerous and arbitrary, demanding superhuman performance from his workers, who often put in 16-hour days. Ironically, the once penniless trustbuster became part of the

surpassed the *World*'s circulation. Money was no object, and Hearst hired the best writers and illustrators away from his competition. Like Pulitzer's, his paper embarked on large-scale crusades, but none more extravagant than the publicity Hearst bought for the *Journal* itself: full-page ads in other publications and giant billboards and notices plastered everywhere. Through it all, Hearst maintained that profits were secondary. His was a mission to defend "the average person" (see 3.7).

Like Pulitzer, Hearst was not above using stunts in the pursuit of circulation and even of news itself. According to legend, Hearst sent an illustrator to Havana to document atrocities and cover the war that was soon to break out there.

The illustrator cabled:

> EVERYTHING IS QUIET. THERE IS NO TROUBLE HERE. THERE WILL BE NO WAR. WISH TO RETURN.

To which Hearst replied:

> PLEASE REMAIN. YOU FURNISH THE PICTURES AND I'LL FURNISH THE WAR.

No one knows whether the story is true. But it is true that the Hearst papers helped convince Americans that their pride and freedom were threatened. Before long, America was at war with Spain.

In 1895 the Hearst-Pulitzer battle centered on the Sunday editions. The *World* was the undisputed leader in that area. Sunday supplements were costly to produce but very profitable. They featured large, sensational articles and drawings about science or pseudo-science, along with crime, sports, society news, and color comics.

Most renowned of all *World* cartoonists was Richard Outcault, whose *Yellow Kid* comic strip depicted local scenes and situations and soon became the city's favorite. Hearst hired Outcault away from Pulitzer and featured the

capitalistic establishment he criticized with such vehemence; his profits from the *World* helped buy a yacht and hire personal servants. But his paper never wavered from the original editorial commitments that had been made when Pulitzer took command in 1883. It continued to crusade for social and economic equality.

During the final 20 years of his life, Pulitzer was virtually blind and seldom came to the *World* offices, gaining a reputation as an eccentric recluse. The reputation was well deserved. During the summer of 1911 he mused, "From the day

on which I first consulted the oculist up to the present time I have only been three times in the *World* building. Most people think I'm dead." Before the end of the year, he was.

strip in his competing Sunday *Journal.* Pulitzer claimed he had sole rights and hired another artist to draw his own version of the strip. For a while New York had two *Yellow Kids.* So famous was the character, the strip, and the story of the competing journalists that critics began to call both "yellow papers." Eventually the term *yellow journalism* was used to describe this style of American news reporting.

Objective Journalism

Not everyone was happy with yellow journalism. Some readers boycotted the *Journal* and *World,* and some libraries and clergymen canceled their subscriptions. They believed the exploitation of sex and crime news was a public menace. Critics cited Hearst's involvement in the Spanish-American War as one of the dangers of yellow journalism.

But other things were also happening in New York. In 1896 Adolph Ochs rescued the

New York Times from bankruptcy. Within a few years, he made it one of the country's most successful newspapers without the help of yellow journalism. By 1914 the *Times* had a policy of printing speeches, treaties, and government documents *in full,* the ultimate expression of objectivity.

Reporters were professional observers whose role was limited to reporting "just the facts." The period after 1900 saw journalism move from a vocation to a profession. Journalism schools began springing up across the country.

In 1923 the American Society of Newspaper Editors stated explicitly what was already the credo of most major American newspapers: "A journalist who uses his power for any selfish or otherwise unworthy purpose is faithless to a high trust." This "selfishness" included slanting stories to accommodate a particular political perspective.

The approach most journalism schools continue to teach as "proper reporting" is

Citizen Kane and His Declaration of Principles

The office is dark except for the dim light from a gas lamp. Charles Foster Kane has taken over the *New York Inquirer* and moved into the office, bag and baggage, reminding a befuddled editor that "the news goes on 24 hours a day and I want to be here for all of it." In his first 24 hours he has fired that editor, dropped the price of the *Inquirer* from 3 cents to 2, and remade the front page four times. He is joined by his business manager, Mr. Bernstein, and his best friend, Jed Leland:

Bernstein You just made the paper over four times tonight, Mr. Kane — that's all.

Kane I've changed the front page a little, Mr. Bernstein. That's not enough — there's something I've got to get into this paper besides pictures and print — I've got to make the *New York Inquirer* as important to New York as the gas in that light.

Leland What're you going to do, Charlie?

Kane My Declaration of Principles — don't smile, Jed. (Getting the idea) Take dictation, Mr. Bernstein.

Bernstein I can't write shorthand, Mr. Kane.

Kane I'll write it myself. (Kane grabs a piece of rough paper and a grease crayon. Sitting down on the bed next to Bernstein, he starts to write.)

Bernstein (Looking over his shoulder) You don't wanta make any promises, Mr. Kane, you don't wanta keep.

Kane (As he writes) These'll be kept. (Stops and reads what he has written) I'll provide the people of this city with a daily paper that will tell all the news honestly. (Starts to write again, reading as he writes) I will also provide them . . .

Leland That's the second sentence you've started with "I."

Kane (Looking up) People are going to know who's responsible. And they're going to get the news — the true news — quickly and simply and entertainingly. (With real conviction) And no special interests will be allowed to interfere with the truth of that news. (Writes again, reading as he writes) I will also provide them with a fighting and tireless champion of their rights as citizens and human beings — Signed — Charles Foster Kane.

Leland Charlie . . . (Kane looks up)

Leland (continuing): Can I have that?

Kane I'm going to print it. (Calls) Mike!

Mike Yes, Mr. Kane.

Kane Here's an editorial. I want to run it in a box on the front page.

Mike (Very wearily) Today's front page, Mr. Kane?

Kane That's right. We'll have to remake again — better go down and let them know.

---

perhaps summarized best in George Fox Mott's *New Survey of Journalism* (1958). According to Mott, the beginning reporter should realize at the outset that

> there is little or no opportunity in the reporting of news for the writer to give rein to his innermost thoughts, however high, or his deepest feelings, however subtle . . . reporting the news, even the hot news, is a coldly impersonal job. The editor wants to find the facts in the story and not the writer's personal impressions or emotions. He has learned from long experience that effective news-writing must be objective.

Not all journalists would agree that slanted reporting disappeared entirely during this period. *Time* magazine often came in for criticism from those who felt it presented a conservative political bias, particularly during the period just after World War II. Until its demise in 1971, the liberal *I. F. Stone's Weekly* followed

Mike   All right, Mr. Kane. (He starts away)

Leland   Just a minute, Mike. (Mike turns)

Leland   (continuing): When you're done with that, I'd like to have it back. (Mike registers that this, in his opinion, is another screwball and leaves. Kane looks at Leland.)

Leland   (continuing): I'd just like to keep that particular piece of paper myself. I've got a hunch it might turn out to be one of the important papers — of our time. (A little ashamed of his ardor) A document — like the Declaration of Independence — and the Constitution — and my first report card at school. (Kane smiles back at him, but they are both serious. The voices of the newsboys fill the air.)

That scene, from perhaps the greatest American film ever made, *Citizen Kane,* is fiction, of course. But it captures precisely the image of the crusading editor that we all carry around in our heads. The editor who fights for the public's rights "as citizens and human beings" is part of the folklore of American journalism and is based on the real-life stories of men like Hearst (who served as the obvious model for *Citizen Kane*) and Pulitzer. Though journalism has changed in many ways since the beginning of the century, most of us still think of newspaper work as romantic, glamorous, and socially vital. Films like *Citizen Kane* (the crusading publisher) and *All the President's Men* (the crusading reporters) reinforce that image.

earlier traditions of advocacy journalism. Still, most editors insisted on objectivity and got it. Objectivity became synonymous with good journalism, and few challenged it. Papers still conducted crusades, of course, but journalists were careful to print both sides of an issue wherever possible, and they generally bent over backward to double-check facts and figures before printing them.

Modern journalistic business methods reinforce the practice of objective reporting. Local ownership of the metropolitan daily has rapidly become a thing of the past. Large chains like Newhouse and Gannett have bought up dozens of major newspapers. In many cases, one chain owns both major newspapers in a city. In addition, competing papers in the same market may attempt to save money by signing a Joint Operating Agreement that allows them to share office space, printing facilities and all noneditorial activities.

Today's large newspaper corporations may also be less concerned with local political issues since top management is often thousands

Journalism on Campus: New Voices on the Right

As you read this chapter and consider the issues confronting journalists today, it all may seem a bit abstract if you're not on the staff of your campus newspaper. If you are, you know that the questions surrounding exactly what constitutes "real" journalism are considered on a daily basis by the thousands of students who publish campus newspapers across the country.

Campus newspapers have generally been ideologically liberal, reflecting the tendency for college-age men and women to be more politically liberal than other age groups. But that changed with the election of Ronald Reagan in 1980. In his reelection campaign in 1984, the popular president drew support from 56% of all college students.

The result has been a shift in the political leanings of campus newspapers and a flurry of new alternative conservative campus papers. Publications such as the *Wisconsin Review* and the *Michigan Review* reflect this growing conservative student trend. Many of them are funded in part by the Washington-based Institute for Educational Affairs (IEA), which specializes in granting seed money to such efforts. In addition, the IEA began a "collegiate network" in 1986 to pitch the papers as a group to national advertisers.

IEA president Leslie Lenkowsy says that the major emphasis in his organization is shifting away from national politics and toward helping students improve journalistic standards while becoming financially self-supporting. Yet the ideological base of IEA-supported publications remains intact.

Writing in the *New Republic,* Jeffrey L. Pasley noted: "Although IEA doesn't tell its editors what to print, it does bring them into contact with the network of conservative think tanks, publications, schools and youth organizations that developed in the Reagan era." Currently the IEA supports an estimated 35 conservative student newspapers nationwide.

---

of miles away and does not wish to get involved. Of course, most papers do take sides on local and national issues on the editorial pages, and local editors and reporters do have a stake in the community. But the kind of all-out pressure that comes from an owner-publisher or owner-editor on the scene is missing.

The New Journalism

Not all would agree that objective journalism is a blessing. Some believe, for example, that having to present all sides to every story may have prevented journalists from doing what print does best, describing the complexities of an issue or event. According to Marshall McLuhan:

> The old (objective) journalism tried to give an objective picture of the situation by giving the pro and the con. It was strangely assumed that

there were two sides to every case. It never occurred to them that there might be 40 sides, 1,000 sides . . . no, only two sides.

During the McCarthy hearings of the early 1950s, the press was careful to maintain its objectivity. Senator Joseph McCarthy from Wisconsin was making serious allegations about Communists in the United States (see 3.9). Most journalists disagreed with McCarthy and his methods but feared taking him on directly in their stories. Only a few did not. The *New York Times* editorialized against McCarthy. Columnist Drew Pearson and broadcast journalist Edward R. Murrow were among those who vehemently denounced McCarthy's tactics. Murrow's famous *See It Now* broadcast, using clips from the senator's own speeches, seemed to help turn the public tide against the Wisconsin senator.

The prototype for these new publications was the *Dartmouth Review,* founded in 1980. The *Review* came to the forefront of public attention in 1984 when Teresa Polenz, then a Dartmouth freshman, attended a meeting of the Dartmouth Gay Students Association and secretly tape-recorded the proceedings. Her subsequent story set off a political furor. At one point the New Hampshire attorney general moved to prosecute her under a New Hampshire wiretapping statute. Eventually the case was dismissed but not before Polenz had become something of a heroine to conservative students. At the same time, her actions were condemned in a special resolution by the faculty. Ironically, she was supported through her legal struggles by the usually liberal American Civil Liberties Union. The ACLU was interested in the freedom of the press issues involved.

The *Review* became embroiled in another controversy in 1991 when it ran an anti-Semitic quote from Hitler's *Mein Kampf* alongside its logo. Boston Lawyer Richard Glovsky of the Anti-Defamation League headed up a study of the paper and concluded that it had continually succeeded in getting the attention of the national press "by intentionally inflaming certain controversial issues and . . . engaging in highly confrontational and offensive conduct."

Another interesting development came from the University of Wisconsin-Madison, where the *Badger Herald* surpassed the official campus newspaper in circulation in 1986 and became the first daily alternative conservative student newspaper in the country.

The IEA project has been such a success that the liberal Center for National Policy has begun funding alternative liberal campus newspapers. Their first project was the *Harvard Perspective,* whose editor, Peter Robertson, says that he wants to "make it OK to say 'I'm a liberal.'"

At this point, the press began to seriously reexamine the reporter's role. Perhaps facts alone weren't enough. The public had a right to get *more* than the facts. Veteran reporters were in a position to make value judgments about the facts as well as report them.

In 1958 both the Associated Press and the new United Press International (UPI) began running more interpretative articles and columns on their wires. The use of large pictures and more visually attractive magazine-style layouts became common practice in most metros. A band of renegade journalists began experimenting with the *new journalism,* a subjective, no-holds-barred reporting style. Objectivity, they said, had been a sacred cow long enough — truth was best reported by those who let their emotions become *part* of the story.

In the 1960s, dozens of underground newspapers like the *East Village Other, Los Angeles Free Press,* and *Berkeley Barb* appeared.

They had a definite left-of-center political viewpoint, and their bias showed in almost every article. The underground press was irreverent, funny, frank, and often outrageous. It was also very popular. Apparently, there was an audience for subjective journalism.

The new journalism is still more at home in underground newspapers and magazines like *Mother Jones* than on the front pages of metros. Those who predicted that "new j" would revolutionize mainstream journalism practices overstated their case. Nevertheless the underground press left its mark on those "above ground." Newspapers now devote more space to soft news and new-journalism stories than ever before, and reporters are not as timid about expressing their points of view. Today, every issue of the *Los Angeles Times* carries a soft news-analysis story on the front page.

In 1991 the *New York Times* shook up the journalism establishment with its explicit

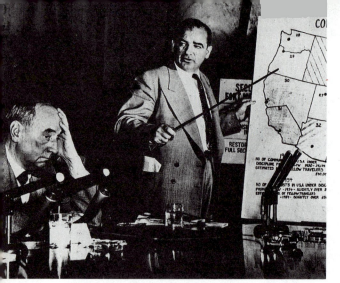

3.9

Army Counsel Joseph Welch (left) and Wisconsin's Senator Joseph McCarthy during the 1954 hearings that were McCarthy's final turn in the spotlight.

coverage of the William Kennedy Smith Palm Beach rape scandal. The *Times* released the name of the alleged female victim, in violation of its longstanding policy of withholding the names of sex-crime victims. Ironically, all the competing New York tabloids and even the *National Enquirer* withheld the name. *Enquirer* Editor Dan Schwartz told *Time* magazine, "I think we took a more ethical stand than they did."

The *Times* eventually ran an apology, but the damage was done. *Times* staffer Richard LaCayo observed that the *Times'* woes "appear to be the result of tension between its reputation for prudence and cautious news judgement and its recent attempt to develop a more with-it image." LaCayo contends that since executive editor Max Frankel took charge in 1986 he "has tried to liven up the 140-year-old paper with more flavorful writing and beefed-up coverage of sports and city news." Everette Dennis, executive director of the Gannett Media Center, chimed in: "The *Times* has been ahead of the pack recently in bringing more soft news and how-to stories, plus adding a touch of tabloid sensationalism."

The Evolution of American Journalism

Each of the five eras of American journalism had its own distinct flavor. Each contributed to and reflected the social order.

Early newspapers were formed in a new society, still seeking a political and social direction. They were chaotic and sometimes bitter, and so were their readers. The penny press resulted from advances in technology and mechanization. Penny papers may have served the first real popular desire for equality and honest government. Their zeal in this pursuit reflects the zeal of the times. The objective years may have been a necessary consequence of yellow journalism. The more sophisticated reader expected something less sensational. It is probably too early to pass judgment on the new journalism, but it was born of the social and political ferment of the 1960s and is still changing modern news practices. Critics worry that readers spotting a bias in a story may grow to distrust newspapers and reporters as much as they now distrust the politicians the stories are often about.

Yet newspaper messages remain vital clues to the social norms and behaviors of their times. The newspaper, like all mass media, contributes to and amplifies those behaviors. In every case, an important part of this contribution involves *how* a subject is presented as well as *what* is presented, *form* as well as *content, medium* as well as *message.*

Business Trends in Newspaper Publishing

According to the trade magazine *Editor & Publisher,* approximately 1,625 daily newspapers and about 7,600 nondailies are currently published in the United States. Total daily circulation has remained stable at about 63 million while weekly circulation has climbed from 40 million in 1980 to about 55 million today. According to *Forbes* magazine, weeklies represent one of the few economic bright spots in an otherwise depressed newspaper economy:

> Today most people get most of their international and national daily news from TV, and so younger people have never developed the daily newspaper habit. Weeklies, by contrast, tend to concentrate on local sports, school issues, zoning and property taxes—news too narrow for TV and for broad-based dailies. In short, weeklies have a unique marketing niche.

While most dailies are owned by large chains, about 2,500 of the weeklies, a third of the total, are independently owned. Nationally, weeklies produce about $4.5 billion in annual revenues while daily revenues run around $32 billion each year.

The average daily newspaper runs almost 60 pages. More than half that space is devoted to advertising, however, while editorial content—the stuff we call the news—averages around 40,000 words and appears on about 25 pages.

Staff sizes vary tremendously from one newspaper to the next. The typical large daily newspaper employs a full-time editorial staff of 75 to 100 people. Major dailies like the *Washington Post* may have several hundred editorial staffers. Small rural weeklies are often "mom and pop" operations run entirely by one family or (in some cases) one person.

Of the dailies, about 150 are in metropolitan areas. In many major cities, the number of "metros" has been steadily decreasing. For example, 14 English-language dailies were published in New York City in 1900. Today only 5 remain. One of them, the *New York Daily News*, was about to go under in 1991 until British media mogul Robert Maxwell stepped in with an 11th-hour bid. Since his death, the paper's future is again in doubt. It's been a long way down for the *Daily News,* which was once the proud owner of America's largest circulation.

The metros have been particularly hard hit by rising labor costs. Printing-plant workers have joined truck drivers and construction workers as the most highly paid blue-collar employees in America. Maxwell's deal eliminated 800 of 2,600 union jobs at the *Daily News.*

Another problem is the skyrocketing cost of newsprint. In 1940 newsprint cost about $50 per short ton; by 1988 the cost had climbed to more than $400. By 1992 the list price (without volume discount) was $580. Though prices have fallen a bit in recent years, 20 cents worth of paper is still used for every 100 newspaper pages. Add the cost of ink (about 3 cents per 100 pages), and the raw materials of your newspaper alone may equal the actual purchase price.

One way the metros have dealt with rising production costs has been to raise the selling price of the paper. In the past 10 years, the street price of most papers has risen from 10 cents to 35 cents or more. The cost of advertising has also increased.

Most newspapers get about 75% of their revenue from advertising, which means that the paper you buy for 35 cents probably costs over a dollar to produce, once raw materials, overhead, salaries, and distribution costs are accounted for.

It may surprise you to learn that production of the day's newspaper begins in the advertising department. The ads are placed first, the news must then fit *around* them in the space that's left, often referred to as the *newshole*. In addition, advertisers may specify stories that they do or don't want to run with their advertising. An airline might prohibit plane crash stories on the same page with its ad. A real estate advertiser may be promised a related news story on the real estate market in the same section with its display ad.

Another problem facing metros involves circulation. Although the total circulation of most metros continues to rise, it is not keeping up with population growth. Metro owners have paid for exhaustive marketing studies to find out why interest in their product is waning.

They found that some age groups (20–29, for example) and ethnic groups (e.g., blacks and Hispanics) often feel there is nothing for them in the paper.

Metros are also threatened by the suburban dailies, whose numbers have increased in recent years. As city dwellers move to the suburbs, they come to prefer the smaller dailies that focus on information particularly relevant to their communities. The smaller local newspaper is one of the few forums where citizens can exchange information with one another on a community-wide basis. Suburban dailies can also deal directly with community issues that metros cannot or will not cover. Classified and local advertisers reach their target market at considerably less cost.

Some metros have moved to minimize this competition by publishing "zoned editions" that concentrate more on relevant local news in a particular geographic area in the greater metropolitan region. Morning papers have countered afternoon papers by publishing later editions with up-to-date sports results. Afternoon papers are publishing morning editions specifically aimed at suburban markets.

Any discussion of the decline of the metros is incomplete without mentioning the impact of electronic media, which deliver the up-to-the-minute kind of news once covered by the extra newspaper edition. In the early 1970s, a Roper poll reported that 49% of the population thought that television was the most believable news source; 20% cited newspapers. A 1980 Roper poll asked, "Where do you usually get most of the news about what's going on in the world today?" People were allowed to respond in multiple categories; 64% cited TV, 44% newspapers, 18% radio, 5% magazines, and 4% "talking to people."

Other studies have found that Americans get more news from newspapers than they actually think they do. A Simmons Market Research/Roper study conducted in 1982 indicated that many Americans get more news from newspapers than from TV, despite what they might *perceive* they're getting. Despite this, a 1991 study by the American Society of Newspaper Editors concluded that "45% of the American population no longer reads newspapers, or is considering stopping, and that . . . the TV generation is not turning to print as it reaches 30."

It is often assumed that any decrease in the number of newspapers or in their circulation translates into a less-informed public. But a symbiosis may be at work here, too: Newspapers provide a wide range of news, opinion, and interpretation, radio a quick summary of the headlines, and television a brief eyewitness account of the day's events. All perform different news-related functions while covering the same events. The consumer receiving information from all media probably is better informed than the one who insists that a single medium is the "best" way to get the news. For that matter, researcher Leo Bogart determined that most people who watched TV news found that it increased their desire to read the newspaper. Newspapers can provide details missing from 22-minute TV newscasts.

The newspaper format is not fixed and frozen. The success of *USA Today* indicates that newspapers can and will adjust to changing consumer tastes. Changes may come from any of the departments or individuals who contribute to the final product.

The Newspaper You Never See

We all have a picture of the investigative reporter in our mind. We know about the crusading editor or publisher. But, as with all media, these people represent only the tip of the iceberg. There are dozens of lesser-known personnel, and many less-glamorous departments offer a recent graduate the opportunity to break into the business (see 3.10). Staff positions are generally broken down into three

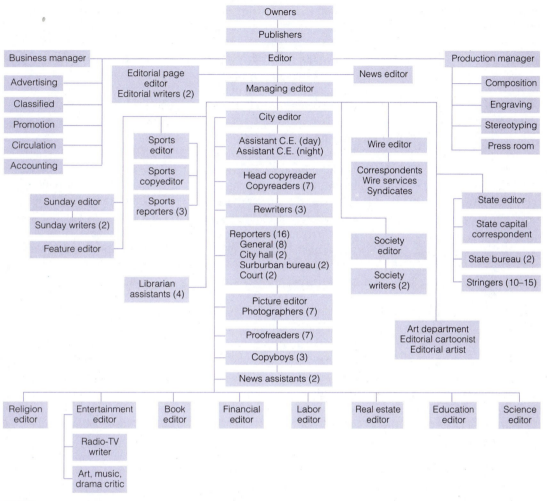

Owners
Publishers
Editor

Business manager
Advertising
Classified
Promotion
Circulation
Accounting

Editorial page editor
Editorial writers (2)

Managing editor

News editor

Production manager
Composition
Engraving
Stereotyping
Press room

City editor

Sunday editor
Sunday writers (2)
Feature editor

Sports editor
Sports copyeditor
Sports reporters (3)

Assistant C.E. (day)
Assistant C.E. (night)

Head copyreader
Copyreaders (7)

Rewriters (3)

Wire editor

Correspondents
Wire services
Syndicates

State editor
State capital correspondent
State bureau (2)
Stringers (10–15)

Reporters (16)
General (8)
City hall (2)
Surburban bureau (2)
Court (2)

Society editor

Society writers (2)

Librarian assistants (4)

Picture editor
Photographers (7)

Proofreaders (7)

Copyboys (3)

News assistants (2)

Art department
Editorial cartoonist
Editorial artist

Religion editor
Entertainment editor
Radio-TV writer
Art, music, drama critic
Book editor
Financial editor
Labor editor
Real estate editor
Education editor
Science editor

3.10
This organization chart offers a glimpse at many of the unsung departments and staff positions that exist on an average-size daily newspaper.
Courtesy: ANPA Research Bulletin.

areas: business, editorial, and production. All are vital to getting the paper out on time. In an average metropolitan daily, the major roles break down this way:

Owner-Publisher

This can be one person or many. Usually the owner and publisher are two different people. The *Kansas City Star* was even owned by its own employees until they sold the paper in 1977. The publisher hires the editors and fills key editorial positions.

Editors

The editor-in-chief is in charge of all editorial functions but delegates the power of review to individual specialized editors in all but the most extraordinary cases. These specialized

How Journalism Really Works

Dave Barry is a humor writer for Knight News Service.

As a professional journalist, I find that when I attend social functions I am often peppered by questions from members of the public who are eager to learn more about how the "news game" works, questions such as:

"You work for a newspaper?"

"Hey! This guy works for a newspaper!"

"GET HIM!!"

"(Punch punch punch kick spit.)"

Thanks to my journalism training, I have been able to detect, underlying this curiosity, a certain amount of pub-lic skepticism and, yes even hostility toward the press. . . .

Anyway, today I thought I'd explain how journalism works, in hopes that you will gain a better understanding of why you skip straight to the comics.

It Begins with News

The newsgathering process begins, of course, with the out-break of the news event itself. Generally there will not be any journalists present unless the event occurs inside a news-paper building, which is where we modern journalists must spend all our time so that we can remain linked, via our computer terminals, to a so-phisticated worldwide elec-tronic information network, which we use to transmit late-breaking developments to each other. For example, if a journalist finds out from one of his "sources" about an impor-tant new joke, such as the one about the man who walked into the bar with a parrot on his head, he (the journalist) can use advanced microchip tech-nology to transmit this joke, instantaneously, to literally THOUSANDS of other journal-ists, who can respond at nearly the speed of light with the one about the man who tells his wife that he was at a bar with solid-gold urinals. How, then, do we obtain our actual news? We get the vast bulk of it from the "wire services," such as the Associated Press and United Press International. You would assume, judging from their names, that these are vast om-niscient information-gathering machines, but in fact they con-sist mostly of caffeine-crazed

editors include the managing editor, city edi-tor, news editor, wire editor, and editors of var-ious sections, including sports, editorial, fi-nancial, education, science, religion, and life style. Many of these specialists make decisions about which reporters will cover a story and where it will be placed.

Business Manager

This person, who ranks equally with the edi-tor-in-chief, is in charge of advertising, pro-motion, circulation, and accounting. A busi-ness manager monitors revenues and expenses to determine if the paper is earning a profit. She or he may report directly to the owner-publisher or to the editor-in-chief.

Production Manager

This person is in charge of paste-up as well as the workers and equipment needed to print the paper. The production manager may re-port directly to the owner-publisher or to the editor-in-chief.

Reporters and Photographers

These people work under the city editor or are assigned to an editor in a special department. A crew of 75 has about 15 reporters, so they represent only 20% of the total editorial staff. However, like radio disc jockeys, they are the staff members best known to the average reader, due primarily to the appearance of their by-lines each day. General-assignment

individuals sitting at computer terminals and hastily rewriting stories out of their local newspapers.

So to summarize the basic journalism system: The newspapers get almost all of their information from the wire services and the wire services get almost all of their information from the newspapers. The result is that certain news stories go around and around, gaining momentum each time. A good example is the Middle East. Many years ago, archaeologists now believe, some kind of news event occurred there—it was "Jordan rejects talks with Syria, Lebanon" or "Lebanon rejects Jordan, talks with Syria," or "Lebanon, Syria, Jordan talk about rejection," something like that—and the story got caught up in the wire service/newspaper circuit and now has attained a state of Eternal Media Life.

Then There's "Thin Air"

Another important source of news is Thin Air. This is where we professional journalists obtain our information about Trends, which are enormously important societal changes. An excellent example was the cover story in *Newsweek* magazine a few years back headlined: "The '80s Are Over." This was a wonderful piece of journalism, taking dozens of smaller trends such as yuppies, nouvelle cuisine, "couch potatoes," Madonna, "cocooning," etc.—all of which exist primarily in the minds of journalists—and forming them into a gigantic Death Star of a trend—"The '80s Are Over!"— spinning somewhere out in Deep Journalism Hyperspace, invisible to millions of normal Earth people, who continue to do pretty much the same stuff they've been doing since before *Newsweek* officially declared that the '80s had begun (probably around 1973).

Well, I hope that this brief discussion has given you a deeper appreciation for modern journalism, and the kind of intensive effort that goes on "behind the scenes" from the moment that a terse news bulletin flashes over the wire ("Syria rejects Gary Hart and Donna Rice") to the moment, just hours later, when your delivery person hurls your newspaper into your neighbor's child's scum-filled wading pool.

---

reporters cover a number of diverse areas. Other reporters have special beats, such as city hall or the courts. In large labor towns like Detroit and San Francisco, a labor editor and a staff of reporters cover the union beat. Photographers work with reporters and are also assigned on their own to events that don't merit a story but offer good "picture possibilities."

Copyeditors

These are the unsung champions of the newsroom. Without them, articles would read strangely. No reporter hands in a story with every word spelled correctly, every punctuation mark in place, every fact expressed clearly. Copyeditors clean up stories before they are set in type. This job is absolutely vital, because readership studies indicate that spelling mistakes and grammatical errors detract from a story's credibility. The content may be correct, but if form is poor the reader is skeptical. Copyeditors usually write all the headlines and photo captions as well.

Stringers

Many newspapers employ a shadow staff of occasional contributors. Many of them are young journalists still in school or those working full time in other jobs and who hope to break in as full-time reporters. Stringers are sometimes paid by the column inch. In journalism lore, the word originated from the old practice of measuring their copy with a piece of string or of keeping track of the number of stories used by tying knots in a string. A newspaper with a full-time editorial staff of 75 people may use 15 to 20 stringers.

Naturally, no two newspaper staffs are exactly alike; all functions vary according to individual editorial needs and staff abilities. Most major dailies have a separate art department with editorial cartoonists and illustrators. Many have special correspondents at the state and federal levels to give the "local angle" to regional and national news.

Straight from the Wires

The shifting priorities of local newspapers mean that they have had to rely more than ever on the wire services for their regional, national, and international news-gathering functions. Wire services were so named because they sent their stories to subscribers via telephone (formerly telegraph) wires. Today, satellite delivery is the norm. The price of these services represents a huge chunk of many papers' budgets, but hiring their own reporters to cover global events would be far more costly.

A glance through your local daily newspaper will reveal that many global and national stories now begin with the familiar AP or UPI logo. Even big-budget dailies like the *Washington Post* and the *Los Angeles Times,* with their own foreign and national correspondents, rely heavily on wire copy.

It all began back in 1848 at the *New York Sun,* where a number of New York newspaper publishers met to form a cooperative news-gathering association called the Associated Press. The idea was simple: Each newspaper would receive stories from its fellow member newspapers, and some of the wasteful duplication caused by intense competition for "scoops" would be eliminated. The telegraph, which came into common use shortly after the AP formed, meant that newspapers all over the

country could receive news instantaneously. Thus the day's important stories were disseminated rapidly. Readers now had access to information that had once taken weeks or even months to reach them.

The United Press was formed in 1907 as a combination of several smaller news services that had tried to compete with the AP. In 1958 the UP merged with the International News Service and became United Press International. While the AP was the leading service for many years, UPI was first to recognize that service to broadcasters would become big business, and it got a head start. UPI was also first to provide radio stations with wire "actualities," or tapes recorded on the scene at important news events. The AP lagged behind in this area until finally launching its own AP audio wire in 1974. Despite its pioneering efforts in some areas, UPI has been in financial trouble since the mid-1980s. In 1992 it was sold to a Middle Eastern news service based in London.

The two wire services are by far the nation's largest news-gathering agencies, with offices in each major city and reporters on every important beat around the world. So dependent have local newspapers become on the wires that they often wait for wire reports on major events in their own cities just to be sure they have all the background material and other information necessary for in-depth coverage.

In addition to the two major wires, hundreds of foreign and specialty wire services supply an endless array of copy. The largest of these is Reuters, a British news service that also specializes in financial information. On the other end of the spectrum, The Lumber Instant News carries prices and other information of special interest to lumber companies as well as to newspapers in "Twin Peaks" type areas where lumber is big business. Grain Information News and Poultry and Egg News are examples of other special-interest wire services.

Large newspapers like the *Los Angeles Times, Washington Post,* and *New York Times* operate their own news services, as do newspaper chains such as Gannett and Knight-Ridder.

Americans have an insatiable appetite for printed news. They feel they need to know what's happening. There is also a feeling that it hasn't really happened unless it has appeared in the paper. Why read the full newspaper account of the baseball or football game you saw yesterday? You want to match your perceptions with those of a professional observer who was on the scene.

The event described in a newspaper story is not the original event at all, but a constructed mediated reality. Newspaper stories are selective, condensed versions of the real thing. A quote standing alone, for example, with no explanation of events preceding or following it, may appear absurd or sensational. Politicians are often irritated when they see themselves quoted in the morning paper. Their immediate response is that their words were "taken out of context."

In a sense, all speeches are taken out of context, because they have been taken from one medium (interpersonal speech) and put into another (print). Tape-record a conversation at random. Then transcribe the first several sentences. What you write on paper will seem very different from what you overheard. If it were printed, the difference would be greater still. We don't *talk* the way we *read*. Talk, as they say, is cheap. But print has a finality, a permanence about it that can change the meaning of events and messages, making them appear different from the original.

In addition, reporters bring their own perspective to a story. No matter how hard they try to remain objective, they inevitably develop opinions about a newsmaker. Whether reporters are aware of it or not, personal bias can play a major role in how they "see" and report a news event.

Nor is the reporter the only person who influences the news. Along the way a story must pass through the hands of various gatekeepers before it appears in print. *Gatekeeping* is a term often used by media professionals and researchers to describe the various processes information must undergo before it reaches the public. News editors decide which stories will run and where they'll be placed. Layout editors decide how long each story will be and whether it will be accompanied by a photo. Copy editors correct errors, rewrite for easier comprehension, and create headlines. Perhaps a photographer assigned to a story turns in a picture that tells a "different" story from one the reporter wrote.

In conclusion, the efforts of many people go into the production of your newspaper. Crucial decisions are made on a daily basis. Generally, newspaper staffers do the best they can to keep readers informed. By increasing your awareness of the process, you'll be better able to make the many political, economic, and personal decisions that are based, at least in part, on the information you find there each day.

Queries and Concepts

1   Delve into your own local newspaper, sifting the hard news from the soft. What is the balance of the front section in numbers of stories? How many total column inches are devoted to each?

2   How many people in your class read at least one story from a newspaper every day? Which section do they prefer and why?

3   Pick your favorite character from the history of American journalism and find a biography. Write a brief portrait along the lines of the story on Pulitzer in this chapter.

4   Citizen Kane's crusade and the Watergate reporters are two images we have of journalism as a career. Can you think of others? Where did they come from?

5   Should newspapers print the names of rape victims? Why or why not? Call or write your local paper and ask if they have a policy on this issue. How does that policy compare with your own position?

6   Most libraries maintain current and back issues of the *New York Times* and the *Wall Street Journal*. Compare the form and content of the front pages of one of these papers in issues published on each of these three dates: 50 years before today's date, on the day you were born, and today. What topics are front page news? Do you notice any differences in reporting styles? Layout?

7   Does the same company control all print news outlets in your city? Do your local news outlets have any interests in the broadcast media?

8   Make up your own list of criteria defining "what's news." How does it differ from the list included in this chapter? How would newspapers be improved if they followed your list?

Readings and References

Hard and Soft News

Lee B. Becker
Jeffrey W. Fruit
Susan L. Caudill
The Training and Hiring of Journalists. Norwood, N.J.: Ablex, 1987.

This book examines the relationship between formal U.S. education in journalism and the "real world" of practicing journalists. Some interesting conclusions. Offers alternatives to the U.S. system.

James M. Cain
60 Years of Journalism. Bowling Green, Ohio: Popular Press, 1985.

The author traces the development of contemporary journalism from the Mencken era of the 1920s to the early 1980s. Popular, easy-to-read history. Recommended.

Curtis D. MacDougall
Interpretative Reporting. 8th ed. New York: Macmillan, 1982.

The author's career spans the history of journalism in this century; the first edition of this standard introduction for journalism students was published in 1932. Of course, it has been substantially rewritten since then, but all the basics of reporting and writing are still covered.

Marshall McLuhan
Understanding Media. 2d ed. New York: McGraw-Hill, 1964. (Also available in paperback from New American Library, 1973.)

Much of McLuhan's work deals with the permanence of print and the unique characteristics of the newspaper form. See especially Chapters 9 ("The Written Word: An Eye for an Ear"), 16 ("The Print: How to Dig It"), 18 ("The Printed Word: Architect of Nationalism"), and 21 ("The Press: Government by News Leak").

George Fox Mott, Jr.
New Survey of Journalism. 4th rev. ed. New York: Barnes & Noble, 1958.

Doug Newsom
James A. Wollert
Media Writing: Preparing Information for the Mass Media. 2d ed. Belmont, Calif.: Wadsworth, 1988.

This is a comprehensive, contemporary, and holistic approach to journalistic writing. The authors deal with news writing for newspapers, as well as for radio and television. Also covered are such areas as videotex and teletext, technical writing, editorials, depth reporting, public relations, advertising, and more.

Michael Schudson
Discovering the News: A Social History of American Newspapers. New York: Basic Books, 1978.

The author deals explicitly with the various definitions of objectivity throughout journalism's history. The book is a series of essays covering the range of that history, but the most telling analyses of the objectivity question come in the section on the 20th century. Recommended.

What's News?

For a number of articles groping with definitions for news, see the special section "What Is News?" *Journal of Communication,* Autumn 1976. Most introductory journalism textbooks also deal with this fundamental question.

Five Eras of American Newspaper Journalism

Journalists are preoccupied with their history. Hundreds, likely thousands of books have been published on the subject. Those selected here are included for their comprehensiveness and readability. Use their bibliographies to pursue specific historical eras or personalities if you wish. See also the readings and references in Chapter 4.

J. Herbert Altschull
From Milton to McLuhan: The Ideas Behind American Journalism. New York: Longman, 1990.

This unique history attempts to uncover the philosophical traditions that shape American journalism. Covers key thinkers and historical events, including the penny press, yellow journalism, muckraking. Written for the undergraduate reader.

David A. Armstrong
A Trumpet to Arms: Alternative Media in America. Los Angeles: Tarcher, 1981.

Many journalism histories still give short shrift to alternative media, such as the underground press. This books fills an important gap.

Perry Ashley, ed.
Dictionary of Literary Biography: Volume 29, American Newspaper Journalists 1926–1950. Detroit: Gale Research Co., 1984.

Fifty biographies of some of the most important figures in 20th-century journalism. Includes a number of photographs, as well.

Edwin Emery
Michael Emery
The Press and America: An Interpretative History of Journalism. 6th ed. Englewood Cliffs, N.J.: Prentice-Hall, 1988.

A respected, thorough, and comprehensive history of journalism in the United States. Events are given more or less in chronological order. Nicely illustrated; includes an extensive bibliography. Dozens of chapters, hundreds of pages, everything you always wanted to know. . . .

Frank Luther Mott
American Journalism: A History, 1690–1960. 3d ed. New York: MacMillan, 1962.

Obviously, this book is not up-to-date. It is, however, a widely read history of American journalism, very popular among journalists and journalism teachers. Considered a classic.

Karen Rothmyer
Winning Pulitzers: The Stories Behind Some of the Best News Coverage of Our Time. New York: Columbia University Press, 1991.

For many journalists (and aspiring journalists), the ultimate in professional success is still the Pulitzer Prize. In this book, Rothmyer takes us behind the scenes as she digs into the history of Pulitzer Prize–winning stories.

W. A. Swanberg

Citizen Hearst. New York: Charles Scribner's, 1961.

Pulitzer. New York: Charles Scribner's, 1972.

Swanberg is a biographer who makes his subjects come alive, and both volumes illuminate these men in a way few others do. As interesting as any biographies you will find, each of these books has a useful bibliography and index.

Business Trends in Newspaper Publishing

Editor & Publisher. New York: Editor & Publisher, annual.

As far as facts and figures are concerned, this is the bible of newspaper publishing. Available in most libraries.

"Why Weeklies Are Hot," *Forbes,* Feb. 5, 1990, pp. 100–106.

Issues and Answers: Is It Real, or Is It Newspaper?

Questions about objectivity and bias, news definition, gatekeeping decisions, and the like are asked (if not answered) in most journalism textbooks, including those listed above. These issues regularly fill the pages of magazines like the *Columbia Journalism Review,* the *Washington Journalism Review,* and the *Quill.* See also the readings and references listed for Chapter 13.

Newspapers, Part Two: Contemporary American Journalism

The New York Times slogan, "all the news that's fit to print," advertises the fact that news is actually fiction.

Marshall McLuhan

In 1919 Joseph Patterson decided New York City was ripe for a new kind of newspaper. For a number of years, staid papers like the *New York Times* had been tops in circulation, and Patterson thought the city was ready for a no-holds-barred journal more in the tradition of the yellow papers of the 1890s. His *Illustrated Daily News* (later simply the *New York Daily News*) sported a tabloid format with a strong emphasis on photography. On some days the entire front page consisted of a masthead, photograph, and caption.

This caught the eye of New Yorkers who had not been daily newspaper readers. While the circulation of most city papers remained the same, the *Daily News* became, for a time, the largest-selling daily in the country. Sensational weeklies like the *National Enquirer* later copied the layout formula and prospered as a result.

Patterson's was a new kind of publication that seemed to typify the jazz age of the 1920s and the style became known as "jazz journalism." While jazz journalism consisted of much more than visual appeal, layout was a factor in the phenomenal success of the *Daily News*. Since that time, all newspapers have become more aware of how necessary graphics are to hold the reader's attention. Considerable research is done to determine reader preferences for various typefaces. Editors have found that most readers prefer bigger pictures, larger headlines, and more eye-catching material. *Form* as well as *content* is crucial in getting and holding a large readership.

The average 60-page newspaper is read in just less than half an hour. That's about two pages per minute. Readers make critical decisions about what they will read by glancing at a headline or photograph and by focusing their attention on favored sections of the paper. An awareness of this process has led to increasing specialization in most daily newspapers.

In the future, your newspaper may be quite different from the one delivered to your neighbor, though both come off the same press. If your neighbors are executives, they may get a larger business section. The technology is not quite here yet, but newspaper people know they must help readers find the news they want in a hurry.

Special magazines, inserts, and advertising supplements are now produced for individual areas of interest. When rock artists like the Rolling Stones or Bruce Springsteen go on tour, local dailies mark the occasion with 8- or 12-page advertising supplements. In addition, more advice columns, soft news, and how-to and where-to news appear in the daily paper than ever before.

Editors and Readers: A New Social Contract

Two different perceptions of what constitutes news in newspapers were very evident in a study commissioned several years ago by the American Society of Newspaper Editors. It describes the problem in detail:

> There is indeed a serious gap between editors and readers, and it is much more than a simple difference of opinion between what editors think is new and interesting and what people want in their newspapers. It is a failure of

communication and therefore of basic understanding.

What is happening, according to the study, is the emergence of a new "social contract," which readers seem to understand fully but which editors may be a little slower in coming to grips with. The social contract contains a number of needs that readers feel should be addressed by their local papers. Paramount among these is the need for self-fulfillment, for a "focus on self." One reader put it this way: "Editors live in one world, I live in another. They're worried about the Middle East and I'm worried about meeting my bills." Articles that emphasize self-help in one form or another are designed to address these needs.

Readers questioned in the study also expressed a deep, if subconscious, desire for a more *personal* type of journalism.

> In a television age when personalities dominate and credibility depends on the chemistry between anchor and viewer, it is not surprising that readers want to know who is speaking to them through their newspapers! "How can I believe you if I don't know who you are?" they ask.

The popularity of local columnists and feature reporters is yet another indication of this need for communication on a one-to-one level.

Readers also said that they want more local coverage and less emphasis on national and international affairs. "Whatever the importance of national news, strong local coverage still produces the strongest ties between readers and editors." It is these ties that bring about a stable circulation base for many newspapers.

The study concluded that readers still demand some hard news, but it must be accompanied by features — and a lot of them. They find features easier to read than news, partly because they are written in a personal and conversational style, but mostly because they are often aimed at the individual interests of the "me" generation: health, diet, money management, and self-improvement.

A related complaint was that far too much emphasis is given to negative news, perhaps because standard fare such as the police beat is keyed to trouble. Readers pleaded for more positive news about their communities, more personal coverage through human-interest reporting and local columnists, and more service information to help them in their daily lives.

While the message of the study was loud and clear, editors reacted with varying degrees of concern. The *New Yorker* magazine deplored the study, saying that if editors heeded it, newspaper content would become simply stories about readers and reporters and that "what used to be called the news" would be shut out.

Despite this warning, one glance at your local newspaper probably will reveal an increasing amount of soft news and other materials speaking to the needs articulated in the study. Once it was up to the editor to decide what was news, and the readers could take it or leave it. Now, readers' priorities surface in marketing studies and must be taken into account, largely because of the fiscal realities of running a newspaper. Newspapers are, after all, a business.

The recession that gripped the nation in the early 1990s spotlighted these concerns. Covering a 1991 convention of the American Society of Newspaper Editors, *Los Angeles Times* reporter Thomas Rosenstiel saw it this way: "While the problem of declining readership is as old as the 6 o'clock news, editors acknowledge that they gave it too little attention during the advertising boom years of the 1980s." He went on to cite a MORI Research report that identified reader concerns and articulated their feelings about the inadequacies of their daily papers. Among their requests:

- Stories should not be so long that they need to jump from one page to another.
- In place of stories, newspapers should run more briefs or summaries, more calendars of upcoming events, more listings of places to buy things.

- Papers should run more material that is "entertaining to read" and should focus more on people rather than events.

Paradoxically, some readers requested more "in-depth" coverage and more "explanations of complex issues." It's no wonder that editors are confused and frustrated. Yet ultimately their ability to deliver what readers want will determine if their newspapers are to survive in the precarious economic times that lie ahead.

Supermarket Sensationalism

Our desire to read about other people may help explain the success of the largest-selling newspaper in America, the *National Enquirer* (see 4.1), and its imitators such as the *Star,* and the *National Examiner.* Such publications can usually be found at grocery checkout counters, hence the tag "supermarket journalism." In many ways they are the direct descendants of yellow journalism (see Chapter 3).

While their location guarantees enormous exposure, the subject matter, too, is designed to appeal to the largest possible audience. Gossip about Hollywood stars and other national and international celebrities is prominently displayed. In addition there are weekly stories about cancer and arthritis breakthroughs and common but overlooked diseases "you can diagnose by taking a simple test right in the privacy of your own home."

Bill Burt, editor of the *National Examiner,* says that his publication is not interested in sex per se ("You can't do that when you sell in the supermarkets") but that it is "mightily interested in the unusually unusual." In an interview with *Maclean's* magazine, Burt explains: "What we go for is the stuff you look at and say 'Hard to believe.' And the harder it is to believe, the better it is, because that's what our readers are looking for."

The tabloids offer stories involving UFOs ("The Russian military has revealed that they

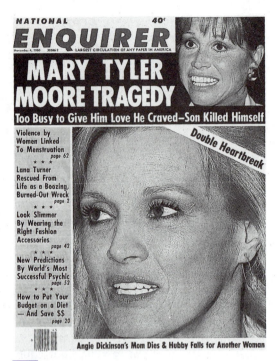

4.1

This 1980 front page shows that bold headlines and close-up pictures of the stars have long characterized the National Enquirer's brand of "supermarket journalism." The Enquirer's approach to reporting "intimate secrets" of celebrities took a severe blow in 1981 when a Los Angeles jury awarded Carol Burnett $1.6 million in damages for a 1976 item that reported her drunk and disorderly in a Washington restaurant. The libel suit has blazed the trail for other stars who have suits pending against the Enquirer. Like Burnett, they claim that the tabloid fabricates stories about them which damage their reputation. As a result, the Enquirer has begun to shy away from gossip, concentrating instead on other types of stories.

had a shoot-out with alien beings in Siberia in 1944") and unusual animals ("Chicken Is 1⅛ Inches Tall"; "Parrot Is Reincarnation of Woman's Husband"; "Junkie Dog Kills Masters for Fix"). The unusual is a staple: "'Send crooks into outer space' says doc who plans orbiting prison." Faith healers who routinely perform miracles are also recurring subjects. Every subject is chosen for its popular appeal. The

National Tattler calls it "people-to-people journalism."

When publisher Generoso Pope paid $75,000 for the *National Enquirer* in 1952, its circulation was only 17,000. Right away the paper began offering up massive helpings of sex and gore (headlines screamed "I Cut Out Her Heart and Stomped on It"; "Mom Boiled Her Baby and Ate Her"), and in time, circulation rose to just over 1 million, where it stalled. Then, in a stroke of marketing genius, Pope "cleaned up" the *Enquirer* in 1968. Though he eventually sold his interest in the paper, circulation has been climbing ever since. Today, "America's liveliest newspaper" sells over 4 million copies each week.

Pope accounted for his success by saying the *Enquirer* gives people what they want. "What you see on page 1 of the *New York Times* does not really interest most people, and interest is our only real rule." As for the critics, he said, "I don't care if other media respect us or not; a Pulitzer Prize ain't going to win us two readers."

According to spokeswoman Jane Bartnett, the *Enquirer* these days is aimed at "a 'pink collar market' — high-school-educated working women, married, with kids, in their 20s, 30s, and 40s."

Supermarket journalism seldom lets the reporter become part of the story. Instead, reporters try to "help" subjects tell it in their own words. One memo from Pope's office told writers to "prod, push and probe the main characters in your stories, help them frame their answers. Ask leading questions like, 'Do you ever go into the corner and cry?'" In fact, like the yellow papers, the *Enquirer* will do anything to get a story. Pope admitted a certain affection for the stunts of the old Hearst-Pulitzer days and paid writers up to $50,000 a year to dream them up.

While writers may appear to approach their subjects with some degree of objectivity, *Enquirer* stories have a definite point of view. The *Enquirer*'s world is one of modest heroes, brutal killers, brilliant astrologers, and sophisticated superstars. Consider the following headlines from a recent issue:

- Space-Age "Greenhouse Gang" Are Members of a Bizarre Cult
- Why John Lennon Believed in UFOs — and Thought He'd Been Abducted by Space Aliens
- Your Favorite Snack Tells a lot About You
- The Day Death Came to Lunch
- Commuter Risks Life to Save Woman from Speeding Train
- Look Out, Terminator! Here Comes Cher
- Hollywood's Secret Hell of Sexual Harassment

These are the stories that most intrigue the consumers of supermarket journalism. Like all successful media, the *National Enquirer* anticipates trends in popular tastes and provides gratification for the mass audience. The object, of course, is enormous circulation, and the formula has paid off handsomely.

The *Enquirer* also delivers dozens of moral lessons that reflect popular myths and beliefs. *Enquirer* stories satisfy the hopes of their readers and justify their view of the world: The policewoman in New York teaches blind children to read in her spare time; the disabled mother of six refuses welfare.

But there's a dark side too — government officials are crooks living off the sweat of the working people. Meanwhile, the courts set criminals free to roam the streets and prey on their unsuspecting victims, who are often *Enquirer* readers. For better or worse, these beliefs are held by many, and the *National Enquirer* offers proof for only 99 cents.

Sorting Out the Soft News

How different is your local daily newspaper from the *National Enquirer?* If you asked daily staffers, they probably would maintain that the *Enquirer* contains no hard news and that its only goal is financial profit, whereas the local daily provides important hard news and supplies readers with vital local coverage while operating within a strict set of journalistic ethics.

Yet the overwhelming majority of news in the local paper is most certainly in the soft category: features, syndicated material, and columns. Even front-page stories are not all hard news. Often a big photograph, colorful description, or human-interest piece takes up a large part of page 1. After the first few pages, news-section content typically includes a detailed story about a recent lottery winner or a plea for the paper's latest crusade to send needy children to summer camp.

The editorial section is filled with interpretative and passionate pronouncements on the issues of the day from both editor and reader. Most papers now run an *op-ed* page (literally "opposite the editorial page"). First-person narratives, stories about "interesting" important people, and detailed discussions of cultural trends appear as well.

The sports section of many newspapers now rivals the news section in terms of size and advertising volume. In fact, many young male readers report it is the only section of the paper they read regularly.

Meanwhile, the real estate section contains large ads for new housing projects next to "news" stories about those same projects. The entertainment section is filled with advertising for TV shows and feature films plus reviews of those same TV shows and films.

The family section is chock full of helpful household hints. Here you'll find columns by Erma Bombeck, Ann Landers (see 4.2), and syndicated gossip columnists. Many dailies now include a midweek food section with recipes, restaurant and wine reviews, and, of course, the inevitable supermarket and restaurant ads. Life-style features teach readers how to balance their checkbooks in new and creative ways. Consumer features advise which

Ask Ann Landers

She is the most widely read newspaperwoman in the world. Her column runs in more than 1,000 newspapers worldwide, and according to a poll taken by United Press International, she is considered one of the world's 10 most influential women. Each day her mailbox is stuffed with about 1,000 letters from readers, most pleading for advice. She is Ann Landers, queen of the advice columnists.

Ironically, the closest competition comes from her twin sister, Abigail ("Dear Abby") Van Buren. Raised in Sioux City, Iowa, both were taught the old-fashioned American virtues of hard work, honesty, and sexual restraint. Though Ann turned 74 in 1992, she has given no sign that she is about to retire. She brags she can "run rings around" her secretaries, primarily because they smoke and/or drink. Ann does neither.

Unabashedly she exclaims, "How do I feel about being a square? . . . Why, I think that's just fine. . . . I am a square and

that squareness has paid off in ways that are very important to me." To teenagers contemplating premarital sex, she has her "three commandments": (1) four feet on the floor, (2) all hands on deck, and (3) no fair sitting in the dark.

For years her own nuptial bliss served as an example to those who thought marriage might be an outmoded institution. But after 36 years with Jules Lederer (founder of the Budget Rent-a-Car chain), she was divorced in 1975. She announced the news to readers in a special column, and more than 30,000 wrote to express their sympathy.

In all, she has received about 10 million letters since the column began in 1955. One of the most famous, regarding nuclear weapons, came in 1981 from none other than Ronald Reagan. A reader had requested that Ann speak out against war, and she did so, urging readers who agreed with her to send a copy of the column to the president. His response, published in the column, ended with a suggestion that readers send the Reagan

Ann Landers

Dear Ann Landers:
You stated in your column recently that the executive who exposed himself to two neighborhood females was "mentally ill." Will you please explain?
Does this mean that all people who have the desire to display their bodies are ill in the same way? What about the folks who frequent nudist camps? And the ones who like swimming in the nude? And the nude dancers—both male and female?
Are these people sick? If so, where can they get help? Please print this letter, Ann. It is very important that I get answers to these questions, and there is nowhere I can go but to you.—Wondering in U.S.A.

Dear U.S.A.:
The executive who exposed himself to the neighborhood girls is indeed sick. The poor fellow needs psychiatric help. This illness is called exhibitionism. The man is intensely insecure about his sexuality and gets his jollies from the startled reactions of females who come upon the sight of him unexpectedly. It reassures him that he is male.
Nudists and strippers and people who enjoy swimming in the buff run the gamut from free spirits to nature-lovers. They may be a little far-out, but they are not necessarily in need of a head doctor. There's a big difference between showing off a good body and flashing one's genitals.

letter to the Soviet secretary-general. There were no reports on how many took that step, but you can bet many tried. Glasnost was sure to follow. After all, when Ann Landers speaks, people listen!

---

type of car, food processor, or word processor may offer the best value.

In other words, except for obituaries, tide tables, weather information, and a few stories in the front section, most daily newspapers deal primarily in soft news. This is often the reason readers subscribe in the first place. In this respect, the hard/soft news ratio of your

local newspaper probably is not very far from that of the *National Enquirer*, though the treatment of subject matter is obviously different.

Journalists who still think of newspapers primarily as purveyors of hard news are clearly mistaken. However, many editors do understand that their hard-news stories are written for a minority of thoughtful and analytical readers. Most readers seek personalities, not politics; simple explanations, not exhaustive analyses. Faced with losses in circulation, newspaper editors have been forced to give readers more of what they want and less of what editors think they *should* have. After all, news is also entertainment, and it has been since the days of the penny press.

Comics: You're Significant, Charlie Brown!

Among the most beloved of all newspaper features is the comic strip. Arthur Asa Berger, who teaches at San Francisco State University, points out that comic strips and comic books have long been part of the American imagination and contends that it is strange that so little academic attention has been given them. There is much to be learned from studying this unique medium and its audience. Some comics appeal to almost all of us ("Garfield"), whereas some may appeal to special groups ("Single Slices"), but in each case a special relationship forms between reader and strip.

The forerunners of American comic strip artists were the great British caricaturists of the 18th and 19th centuries. James Gillray, Thomas Rowlandson, and George Cruikshank pioneered in telling stories with a series of pictures. Rowlandson was among the first to use speech balloons to give his characters a voice. Most of these early strips dealt exclusively with politics. By the end of the 19th century, American comic pioneer Richard Outcault was drawing a regular humorous strip for the *New York World*. Rudolph Dirks's "Katzenjammer Kids" were pulling tricks on the captain as early as 1897 in the *New York Journal*. Names like "Oliver's Adventures," "The Yellow Kid," "The Gungles," and "Dixie Dugan" will ring no bells unless you are a real old-time comic buff. On the other hand, many strips that started as

early as the 1930s and 1940s or even earlier are still with us today. These include Chic Young's (now Dean Young's) "Blondie" (which first appeared in 1930—she married Dagwood later that same year), "Mary Worth," "Little Orphan Annie," and a host of others.

Most of us tend to think of comic strips as either humorous or serious. Certainly "Calvin and Hobbes," "Garfield," and "Cathy" are humorous, whereas "Rex Morgan, M.D.," "Mary Worth," and "Apartment 3G" are more soap opera than strip. But what do we do with strips like "Feiffer" and "Doonesbury" (see 4.3)? Perhaps these "social" comics need a category of their own.

Another category might include the action-adventure strips like "Teenage Mutant Ninja Turtles" and "The Amazing Spiderman," but these are seen less and less often on newspaper comic pages. Action-adventure heroes seem to survive with greater dignity in other media. Superman, Batman, and Captain Marvel still have a faithful audience who follow their adventures in comic books. Superheroes like the Incredible Hulk sometimes turn up on television in their own series.

Many comic strips faithfully depict real-life characters in more or less realistic situations ("Rex Morgan, M.D.," "Mary Worth"). Others caricature human facial or body features in a distinctive way ("Cathy," "Dennis the Menace"). Some strips allow us to enter a world where animals (even stuffed animals!) talk and think in human terms ("Calvin and Hobbes," "Shoe").

For many years most leading cartoonists were men. But in the 1970s, women became more prominent on the comic pages just as they did in all other areas of media. Cathy Guisewite's "Cathy" provides realistic and humorous glimpses into the world of the working woman. In "For Better or for Worse," Lynn Johnston depicts home and family problems as grist for humor, from the wife-and-mother point of view.

"New wave" cartoons like Gary Larson's "Far Side" and Piraro's "Bizarro" represent a

Doonesbury and His Heritage

In 1968, the *Yale Daily News* began running an occasional comic strip by undergraduate Garry Trudeau. Initially, it depicted the antics of B.D., the mythical star quarterback of the Yale football team. The student audience quickly connected B.D. with Brian Dowling, who was, in fact, the captain of the Yale football team. Before long, Trudeau was adding new characters: Mike Doonesbury, the make-out king who never quite made out; Bernie, the science major who revealed casually that he had been weird since age 4 when he ate an entire outboard motor; and Megaphone Mark, the campus radical.

The strip was picked up by Universal Press Syndicate in 1970, and Trudeau began to add noncampus characters like Joanie Caucus, the "liberated" ex-housewife; Phred the Terrorist, a lovable North Vietnamese soldier; and Uncle Duke, a drug-crazed reporter for *Rolling Stone.*

Almost immediately, "Doonesbury" became the most talked-about strip since "Peanuts." It was earthy, contemporary, political, and funny. Real-life characters began making appearances in the strip: Dan Rather speaking from Zonker's television set and Richard Nixon, Gerald Ford, Jimmy Carter, Ronald Reagan, and George Bush from inside the White House. A series of strips on Watergate won Trudeau the first Pulitzer Prize for editorial cartooning ever given to a daily comic-strip artist.

Trudeau's insistence on delving into political issues has not been totally without consequence for the strip. During the Watergate affair, a number of newspapers refused to run strips they deemed too controversial. Others shifted "Doonesbury" to the editorial page, and some have left it there. Similar responses came when the strip discussed the political fortunes of the "invisible" George Bush in 1988. Dan Quayle was a favorite Trudeau target. Through it all, the artist has remained stoic and enigmatic, choosing to let the strip do his talking for him.

In 1982 "Doonesbury" fans were shocked when Trudeau announced he would be taking a "sabbatical" at the end of the year to work on other projects and that the strip would not be appearing again for at least 2 years. Trudeau claimed that the break was necessary to give him time to help his characters make the transition from

type of offbeat, some might say "sick" humor appreciated by many adults and puzzling to many children. Come to think of it, it is puzzling to many adults as well! Most of the new-wave cartoonists trace their lineage to Charles Addams and his "Addams Family" cartoons, which first appeared in the *New Yorker* in 1938. (A television show based on those cartoons aired on ABC from 1964–66 and can still be seen in syndication. A feature film appeared in 1991.)

Why do most of us devote a part of our day to these cartoon fantasies? Because they are a source of diversion and escape, and for many they supply the heroes and heroines that are all too rare in real life. They also give us a chance to become morally involved. When Mary Worth dispenses folksy common sense to ease the troubled lives of her fellow characters, thousands write to agree or disagree with her advice.

The comic pages are replete with perennial losers. Charlie Brown and Dagwood cannot win no matter how hard they try. Often they are rejected by their friends for reasons beyond their control. We sit helplessly by and watch it happen, but perhaps we chuckle. We have been in similar situations, and it's good to see somebody else lose for a change. We can identify because we've all been rejected, lonely, or frustrated.

It is no secret that most of us derive a certain pleasure from vicarious experience. We like to look in on other people's lives, to share

DOONESBURY By Garry Trudeau

"draft beer and mixers to co-caine and herpes." The strip reappeared in September 1984 with all its old sting still intact. In his first year back, Trudeau's favorite targets were then Vice-president George Bush (as-serting his political "manhood") and Frank Sinatra (who was shown cozying up to a Mafia chieftain).

But there was a softer side, too, as many "Doonesbury" characters dealt with the onset of middle age. During the re-cession of the early 1990s, Mike Doonesbury, like many other Americans, found him-self unemployed. Meanwhile Zonker Harris, like other impov-erished baby boomers, be-came living proof of the "boom-erang effect" when he moved back in with his parents.

Whatever happens from here, "Doonesbury" has left its mark on the evolution of the American cartoon strip. Tru-deau's willingness to comment on social issues has brought a new dimension to the genre and paved the way for more "offbeat" approaches like those employed by Gary Lar-son's popular "The Far Side." The "funny papers" will never be quite the same again.

---

in their victories and defeats. Comic strips afford us that opportunity in a safe and com-fortable way, in direct contrast to the harsh re-alities of the daily news. For many readers, the comics provide the most appealing and com-forting "news" of all!

A Delicate Balance: Press, Public, and Government

From comic strips and gossip columns to war coverage and the latest from Washington, Me-diamerica's newspapers continue to provide us with a nonstop barrage of print information.

Like other media, newspapers are part of the invisible web of mediated reality that envelops us each day (see Chapter 1). For this reason we often take them for granted, though it's hard to imagine just what our world would be like without them.

Fortunately, those who founded our coun-try were keenly aware of the key role that a free and unencumbered press could play. Emerg-ing from the censorship and oppression of British rule, they wisely decided to ensure that the young country would have many diverse sources of information available to its citizens. After extended debate, a Bill of Rights was passed that guaranteed freedom of the press.

Like all freedoms, the freedom of the press must be tempered by certain responsibilities.

For example, freedom of speech does not include the right to yell "fire" in a crowded theater. Any examination of the role the press plays in our lives would be incomplete without an introduction to the delicate relationships between press, public, and government that help shape the news we see and hear each day. ("Press" in this section applies to news gatherers in all the media, not just those who work on newspapers.)

Each of these three entities has certain rights guaranteed under the Constitution. The public has a "right to know," and thus the press has a constitutional right to gather information and print it for public consumption. But the public can also include one or more parties accused of a crime. The accused also have a number of rights under the Constitution, such as the right to a trial by an impartial jury of their peers.

Because the news media play such a large role in determining what potential jurors might hear about a case, the press's right to obtain and print information and the rights of the accused to a fair trial often conflict. Obviously, if everyone in town reads all about the "guilt" of an accused person before he or she is brought to trial, finding 12 unbiased peers to serve on a jury would be difficult, if not impossible.

In a larger context, the duties of various branches of the government can conflict with the duty of the press to report information to the public. When conflict arises between the press and the government, as when a reporter declines to name a source to an investigating government agency, such as a grand jury, it generally is resolved through the courts. When the police want access to a reporter's notes regarding, say, an investigation of a crime, the reporter might refuse and once again the matter must be decided by the courts.

In recent decades, a number of key Supreme Court decisions have spoken to these issues. These decisions are particularly crucial because the Court interprets the Constitution and makes the final decision in selected cases. These rulings are then *interpreted* by lower courts. Thus one Supreme Court decision might eventually affect hundreds of cases in the lower courts.

In general, Supreme Court decisions made in the 1960s tended to favor the press, offering journalists a much broader protection from government interference than had been true earlier. But during the 1970s and 1980s, the Court handed down a number of decisions that were seen as severely limiting the freedom of the press where it conflicts with the duties of the various branches of federal, state, and local governments.

A number of rulings involved reporters' access to court proceedings and the trials of accused persons. The court is interested in protecting the rights of the accused and ensuring a fair trial. Reporters are interested in preserving the public's right to know by reporting all aspects of the case to them.

Two of the more controversial cases were *Gannett Co., Inc. v. DePasquale* (1979) and *Richmond Newspapers, Inc. v. Virginia* (1980). In *Gannett* the Court ruled 5–4 that a pretrial suppression-of-evidence hearing in a murder case could be closed to the public and the press. What worried journalists most was the language of the majority decision. Writing in the *Columbia Journalism Review* (September–October 1980), Bruce Sanford said that the language of the decision "suggests that even trials may be closed to the public and the press whenever the defendant and the judge agree to do so."

A year later, however, a 7–1 majority ruled in the *Richmond Newspapers* case that "absent an overriding interest articulated in findings, the trial of a criminal case must be open to the public and the press." Chief Justice Warren Burger said that "people in an open society do not demand infallibility from their institutions, but it is difficult for them to accept what they are prohibited from observing." This opinion seemed in marked contrast to *Gannett*,

but the Court was careful to distinguish between pretrial hearings and actual trials. Although journalists could take some comfort from *Richmond Newspapers,* many contended that it did not completely undo the damage done to the news-gathering process by *Gannett.* What mattered most, of course, was how the lower courts used this decision to bar the press from judicial proceedings (see 4.4).

When it comes to protecting their sources, however, journalists have had little to rejoice about in recent years. A number of decisions in the late 1970s seemed to deeply undercut the traditional right of reporters to maintain the confidentiality of their sources. In *Zurcher v. Stanford Daily* (1978), the Court upheld the right of the Santa Clara County Sheriff's Department, armed with a search warrant, to "rummage through" the files of the Stanford University paper in a search for "criminal evidence." At issue were photographs taken during a campus demonstration. The Sheriff's Department contended that because the paper had covered the demonstration and because a number of photographs had been taken but not published, deputies should be allowed to inspect any and all files in the *Stanford Daily*'s newsroom to look for the pictures. The idea was that the photos *might* reveal some wrongdoing on the part of the demonstrators. The department persuaded a judge to issue a search warrant and spent several days searching the newsroom. Ironically, the officers found nothing they wanted.

The newspaper contended that this search was a violation of the First Amendment, which prohibits government infringement of freedom of the press, because:

1   The presence of the police in the newsroom disrupted the paper's editorial processes.
2   Reporters' confidential notes and other materials covering unrelated matters would be examined by the police. Hence reporters

could no longer guarantee confidentiality to their sources.

The Court disagreed, ruling that where the rights of the government to conduct a "good-faith" investigation of criminal activity and the rights of the press to keep a newsroom off limits to police came into conflict, the press must give way. In a dissenting opinion, the late Justice Potter Stewart suggested that such materials should be obtained by issuing a court subpoena rather than a search warrant. A subpoena directs that specific materials be submitted for inspection. A newspaper would also have the right to petition the court and argue its side of the story before giving up the disputed documents. Thus both sides would be represented at a hearing, and a judge would make a final determination based on the facts in that specific case.

Press reaction to the *Stanford Daily* decision was swift and decidedly negative. Paul Davis, then president-elect of the Radio-Television News Directors Association, said, "I am convinced that we will see more newsroom search warrants in the near future and that sometimes unintentionally, sometimes intentionally, abuse will come as quickly." Jack C. Landau, of the Reporters Committee for Freedom of the Press, noted that "the fabric of journalism on a daily basis is so intertwined with obtaining information of a confidential nature that permitting police to search through a newsroom jeopardizes the relationships of every reporter in the newsroom."

Journalists' reactions to the decision were also heard in Washington, where Senator Birch Bayh, an Indiana Democrat, introduced a bill during the 1980 session that restricted surprise police searches of newsrooms. A modified version of that bill became law in 1981.

Other Supreme Court decisions seem to have further eroded reporters' relationships with confidential sources. The *Reporters Committee for Freedom of the Press v. American Telephone & Telegraph Co. et al.* decision (1979) found that the telephone company's routine

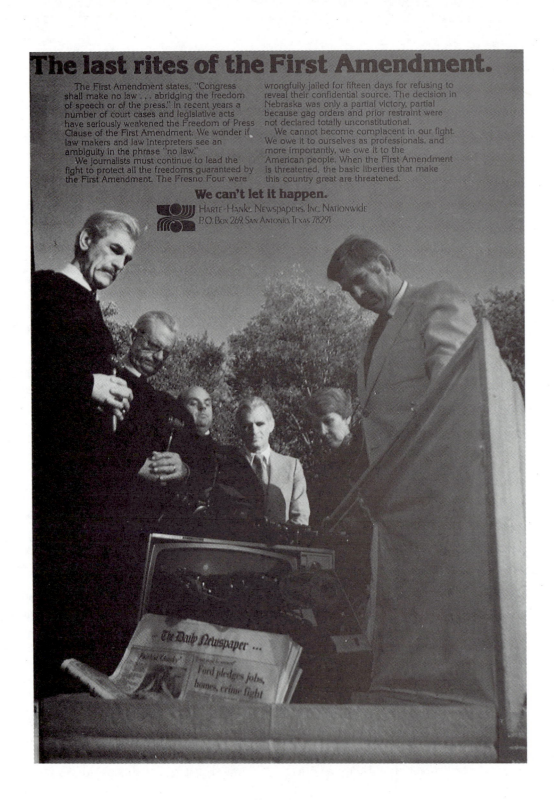

The last rites of the First Amendment.

The First Amendment states, "Congress shall make no law . . . abridging the freedom of speech or of the press." In recent years a number of court cases and legislative acts have seriously weakened the Freedom of Press Clause of the First Amendment. We wonder if law makers and law interpreters see an ambiguity in the phrase "no law."

We journalists must continue to lead the fight to protect all the freedoms guaranteed by the First Amendment. The Fresno Four were wrongfully jailed for fifteen days for refusing to reveal their confidential source. The decision in Nebraska was only a partial victory, partial because gag orders and prior restraint were not declared totally unconstitutional.

We cannot become complacent in our fight. We owe it to ourselves as professionals, and more importantly, we owe it to the American people. When the First Amendment is threatened, the basic liberties that make this country great are threatened.

We can't let it happen.

HARTE-HANKS NEWSPAPERS, INC. Nationwide
P.O. Box 269, San Antonio, Texas 78291

practice of supplying various government investigative agencies with the telephone records of certain journalists was indeed constitutional and did not significantly abridge the freedom of the press to gather information. The Court again held that government interests in the process of conducting "good-faith felony investigations always override a journalist's interests in protecting his source." The Court said further that "in our view, plaintiff's position is based on erroneous propositions. First, the so-called right of journalists to gather information from secret sources does not include a right to maintain the secrecy of sources in the face of good-faith felony investigations."

Phone records were again the subject of a 1991 case in which the giant Procter and Gamble corporation persuaded Cincinnati law-enforcement officials to provide phone records of some 803,000 Cincinnati Bell customers in an attempt to find out who had leaked sensitive inside corporate information to a reporter for the *Wall Street Journal*. Widely criticized in the press, P&G eventually said they made "an error in judgement" but maintained they had "a legal right" to request the information. Especially vexing was the fact that neither the reporter, nor the *Journal*, was notified before the fact. Hence there was not even the protection of a judicial review, as was employed in the AT&T case.

Perhaps the most controversial of all the decisions involving the protection of journalists' confidential sources came in the matter of *New York Times Co. v. New Jersey* (1978). Myron Farber, a reporter for the *Times*, wrote a series of articles in 1976 investigating "mysterious deaths" at a hospital in New Jersey. The stories were widely read and reprinted and eventually led to the 1976 indictment of Dr. Mario E. Jascalevich on charges of poisoning five patients. In the pretrial hearing, Jascalevich's lawyers asked the court to subpoena the reporter's notes and other related materials to examine them for potential use in defending their client. When Farber refused to give them up, the judge found him and the *Times* guilty of contempt of court and sentenced the reporter to 6 months in jail with the sentence to begin *after* he gave up the notes. Meanwhile, Farber was ordered to jail and held there without bail. In addition, the *Times* was ordered to pay a fine of $100,000 plus $5,000 for each day that passed until the notes were surrendered.

The case went through the courts, and finally the Supreme Court upheld the lower-court actions, again ordering Farber to jail. While the case was still pending, the *Times* commented in an editorial: "The loss of this case on the merits would be a serious blow to all news-gathering. The present trial by nights in jail is itself a dangerous infringement on the right to publish." What was particularly disturbing to journalists was that the case was tried in New Jersey, a state that has one of the toughest "shield laws" in the nation. In recent years many states have passed such laws, which are intended specifically to protect reporters' confidential notes and sources. By letting the lower-court decision stand, the Supreme Court said that when a shield law and a defendant's rights under the U.S. Constitution collide, the shield law must yield. The lower court further questioned certain aspects of the shield law and concluded that they might violate existing citizen guarantees as granted under the United States and New Jersey constitutions.

In recent years, the courts have usually found against the press in matters concerning reporter access to criminal proceedings, government access to reporters' confidential notes and sources, and press responsibility for potentially libelous stories (see below). Many journalists believe that the current Supreme Court has a decidedly antipress sentiment and that this is, in part, a reflection of the beliefs of justices appointed by Presidents Nixon, Reagan, and Bush.

Whatever the reason, it is clear that the Court's decisions over the past 15 years may have seriously hindered journalists in their work and may indeed be narrowing our concept of freedom of the press. How seriously these decisions will hamper reporters in the future, and the extent to which the public's right to know will be diminished, remains to be seen.

Whatever the outcome, it is clear that the balance of power between press, public, and government is in a constant state of flux. During the colonial years, the King of England determined what colonists could read. The new nation established freedom of the press as a cornerstone of its democracy with the First Amendment, which flatly declared that "Congress shall make no law . . . abridging the freedom of speech, or of the press . . . ," but unrestricted press freedom posed some problems. The balance of power has continuously shifted to reflect current social and political trends.

The excesses of the early years and yellow journalism prompted reform movements within newspapers themselves. Competing publishers stepped in and changed news practices in response to public demand. The government has, for the most part, stayed out of the business of reforming the press. But as mass media have grown in power and status, there have been calls for the government to "do something."

Way back in 1947, the Hutchins Commission on Freedom of the Press concluded: "It becomes an imperative question whether the performance of the press can any longer be left to the unregulated initiative of the few who manage it." The commission's skepticism reflected the growing power of mass media to determine our political and social attitudes and beliefs. For example, press coverage of a political candidate may mean the difference between victory and defeat. Thus the delicate balance that exists between the power of the press to determine the outcome of an election and its obligation to report the hard facts surrounding that election remains a volatile issue today.

Many books have been written about these press-public-government relationships; this has been a very simple overview. I hope it will start you thinking about these issues and encourage you to do additional reading. A good starting point is the references at the end of this chapter.

Issues and Answers: Love, Law, and Libel

The *National Enquirer*'s recent shift away from certain types of celebrity gossip resulted directly from fears regarding libel suits. Libel laws were designed to give the individual recourse against damaging statements in the press, and the issue provides another example of the public-press-government relationship at work. Because all parties may not agree on what is fair and unfair, the courts have handed down three guidelines for reporters anxious to avoid libel suits:

1   Is it true?

2   Is it privileged?

3   Is it fair comment and criticism?

Truth was established as a defense of libel in 1735. That landmark decision acquitted New York printer John Peter Zenger of libel charges brought by the Royal Governor, who had often been a target of criticism from Zenger's press. Though existing law forbade such criticism, Zenger's lawyer argued that the statements were true and therefore not libelous.

Privileged information includes charges or statements made as part of the official record during court trials or legislative sessions. If one senator calls another a crook during a speech on the floor of the Senate, a newspaper may print it without fear of libel. If the senator does so outside in the hallway, newspapers publishing it *could* be subject to a libel suit, even though they are quoting a source.

The standard for "fair comment and criticism" rests on the question of intent and whether the offending material is an expression of *opinion* or an expression of *fact*. In *New York Times Co. v. Sullivan* (1964), the Supreme Court held that the Constitution "prohibits a public official from recovering damages for a defamatory falsehood relating to his official conduct unless he proves the statement was made with actual malice." The Court believed that newspaper reporters were bound to make some errors in reporting the facts. Even if charges as printed were eventually proved false, the plaintiff must prove that the reporter knew they were false and wrote the story with "malicious intent."

New York Times Co. v. Sullivan started a trend of giving the press every benefit of the doubt in potentially libelous situations. This decision wiped out almost any chance for public officials to recover damages in libel suits and granted the press wide latitude in covering those officials. During the decade immediately following *Sullivan,* the courts interpreted "public officials" to include not only those in government but all public figures in all matters of public interest. This drastically reduced the number of libel suits filed against the press each year. The more liberal Supreme Court

justices, many of whom have died or retired in recent years, have said flatly that libel laws, as they relate to the press, should be completely abolished. The late Justice Hugo Black once wrote: "The First Amendment [guaranteeing freedom of the press] was intended to leave the press free from the harassment of libel judgments."

When being interviewed by David Frost, former president Richard Nixon cited *New York Times Co. v. Sullivan* as the reason he could not sue *Washington Post* reporters Bob Woodward and Carl Bernstein for what he called "factual errors" in their book *The Final Days.* Nixon and the press have never been fond of one another.

Two other notable decisions were *Hutchinson v. Proxmire* (1979) and *Wolston v. Reader's Digest Association, Inc.* (1979). In both instances, the Court narrowed significantly the broad definition of what constitutes a "public figure." In *Wolston,* the Court found that the mere accusation of criminal activity does not make one a "public figure." This decision severely limits newspapers' attempts to report on criminal proceedings, because it forces them to write their stories with an eye toward being sued for libel by the defendant, whether or not she or he is eventually found guilty.

Two additional libel lawsuits were resolved in 1985 and have helped shape the public's perception of the libel process. General William Westmoreland sued CBS as a result of a documentary that accused him of allowing officers under his command to exaggerate enemy casualty figures during the Vietnam War. Westmoreland withdrew his suit just days before it was set to go to trial, but legal costs on both sides were already into the millions.

In another highly publicized case, Israeli General Ariel Sharon sued *Time* magazine for its reports that he had a role in a 1982 massacre of Palestinian refugees in Beirut. Both sides claimed victory when the jury reported that *Time*'s coverage was "false and defamatory . . . though not technically libelous" because the magazine had not acted with "actual malice."

The bottom line is that suing a print or electronic news organization for libel is increasingly costly and time-consuming. Cases typically take several years to go to court. According to Washington attorney Bruce Sanford, juries often find for the plaintiff despite laws that clearly indicate a finding for the defendant is in order because "libel law gives an enormous protection to the media which, when it's explained to people, they don't much like." Often awards are reversed or reduced in the appeals process as judges examine the evidence with less emotion than that of the jury.

At the same time, the potential costs of successful libel suits to defending media outlets can be astronomical. In 1986 Dallas television station WFAA ran a 10-part investigative series on the activities of McLennan County District Attorney Victor Feazell, concluding that he "improperly dismissed certain drunk driving charges." Feazell sued for libel, and in 1990 the jury awarded him a record $58 million. A year later, with the case bogged down in the appeals process, WFAA's owners eventually settled out of court for an undisclosed sum.

According to the Libel Defense Resource Center, of some 30 awards in excess of a million dollars between 1980 and 1990, all were eventually reduced by at least half. Some of the decisions were reversed altogether.

In the last analysis, there is no easy solution to the libel problem. Anyone who has been defamed in the press should be able to seek a remedy, yet the First Amendment and the *Sullivan* decision offer the media a broad blanket of protection. Writing in *Time,* William A. Henry III concludes that "like other mechanisms in American society that balance one set of rights against another, libel law probably must remain fluid, never satisfying anyone's Platonic ideal."

Queries and Concepts

1   Get a copy of the *National Enquirer* and examine story content. Do most stories have a particular point of view? Is it direct or implied?

2   Now use that same copy of the *Enquirer* and compare story categories (crime, health, occult, celebrity profiles, and others) with story categories in your local daily newspaper. What are the major differences? Similarities?

3   What is your favorite comic strip? Would it fall into any of the categories defined in the text? Do you identify in any direct way with any of the characters? What is it about them that you enjoy?

4   Examine and clip the comics page from today's newspaper. Then, visit your library and photocopy the comics page from a newspaper published 50 years ago. Compare and contrast the two. What categories of comics predominate in each period? What sorts of characters and themes are depicted? Are there any significant differences in terms of *form?*

5   Clip an article about a crime from your local newspaper. Examine any ways that this news coverage might impact decisions made by a jury deciding the case in question.

6   Can you find at least one article in your local paper that might contain some libel? Apply the three criteria from the text.

7   You're the editor of a major newspaper and you've been approached by a source who claims she can deliver the "authentic" diaries of John Lennon. What do you do?

Editors and Readers: A New Social Contract

Leo Bogart
Press and Public: Who Reads What, When, Where, and Why in American Newspapers. Hillsdale, N.J.: Lawrence Erlbaum, 1981.

This detailed study of newspaper reading habits might shed some light on your own use of the newspaper. Useful in conjunction with the study by Clark, listed below.

Ruth Clark
Changing Needs of Changing Readers: A Qualitative Study of the New Social Contract Between Newspaper Editors and Readers. Reston, Va.: American Society of Newspaper Editors, 1979.

This is the complete report, cited in this chapter. The American Society of Newspaper Editors (ASNE) publishes a wealth of information on trends both inside and outside of the news room. Many of these reports are available for a nominal fee. Write for a publications list: ASNE Foundation, P.O. Box 17004, Washington, DC 20041.

Doris A. Graber
Processing the News: How People Tame the Information Tide. 2d ed. New York: Longman, 1988.

A fascinating, exhaustive look at how individuals interpret, make use of, and are affected by the news media. Graber focuses on the consequences of the "information tide," the virtual downpour of news that flows from a seemingly endless array of sources in our society.

Supermarket Sensationalism

"From Worse to Bad." *Newsweek,* Sept. 8, 1969, p. 75.

Tom Goldstein
The News at Any Cost: How Journalists Compromise Their Ethics to Shape the News. New York: Simon & Schuster, 1985.

A controversial, close-up examination of the techniques and attitudes of working reporters. Includes chapters on such topics as lost credibility, when journalists *become* the story, and journalists who masquerade to get a story. See also the readings and references listed for Chapter 13.

"Goodbye to Gore." *Time,* Feb. 21, 1972, pp. 64–65.

Elizabeth Peer
William Schmidt
"The Enquirer: Up From Smut." *Newsweek,* April 21, 1975, p. 62.

Sorting Out the Soft News

Marian Christy
Invasions of Privacy: Notes From a Celebrity Journalist. Reading, Mass.: Addison-Wesley, 1984.

Christy worked for 18 years at the *Boston Globe,* where she covered the rich and the famous. In this book, she dissects her own techniques for getting the scoop on the private lives of public figures, a soft-news staple.

Harry F. Waters
Martin Weston
"Don't Ask Ann." *Newsweek,* July 14, 1975, pp. 53–55.

Linda Witt
"Ann Landers: 'Let's Hear It for Us Squares.'" *Today's Health,* Jan. 1974, pp. 38–41.

Comics: You're Significant, Charlie Brown!

Arthur Asa Berger
The Comic-Stripped American: What Dick Tracy, Blondie, Daddy Warbucks and Charlie Brown Tell Us About Ourselves. New York: Penguin Books, 1974.

The sociological end of the comic-strip phenomenon. Berger examines some mainstream comic figures and explores audience identi- fication with each. The context is popular cul- ture. Chapters on Blondie, Dick Tracy, Buck Rogers, underground comics, and more. In paperback; no bibliography or index.

Berke Breathed
Bloom County: Loose Tails. New York: Little, Brown, 1983.

The first collection of "Bloom County" strips traces the development of many now-familiar characters.

Reinhold C. Reitberger
Wolfgang J. Fuchs
Comics: Anatomy of a Mass Medium. Boston: Little, Brown, 1972.

First published in Germany, this text remains a comprehensive *historical* portrait of the comic strip and the comic book. Most major strips are covered. Useful index and reading list.

Garry Trudeau
The Doonesbury Chronicles. New York: Holt, Rinehart & Winston, 1975.

The ultimate collection of "Doonesbury" car- toons from the early days at Yale to 1975, some in color. A short but interesting introduction and discussion of the significance of "Doones- bury" as a new force in the comic world.

The People's Doonesbury. New York: Holt, Rinehart & Winston, 1981.

The final "large format" collection before the sabbatical period, this covers strips that ap- peared in 1978–80. Includes a widely pub- licized "annotated conversation with the au- thor." (Trudeau rarely grants interviews.)

A Delicate Balance: Press, Public, and Government

Free Speech Yearbook. Annandale, Va.: Speech Communication Association, annual.

A most-useful collection of essays are regularly included in volumes of this annual publica- tion. Both contemporary and historical issues are covered, and plenty of resources and re- views are provided. If your library does not have copies, you can contact the Speech Com- munication Association for subscription and back-issue information: SCA, 5105 Backlick Road, #E, Annandale, VA 22003.

Nat Hentoff
The First Freedom. New York: Dell, 1980.

Hentoff is a leading commentator on freedom of expression. This paperback book provides a comprehensive, highly readable account of many important events in the history of the First Amendment. Recommended.

Kent R. Middleton
Bill F. Chamberlin
The Law of Public Communication. New York: Longman, 1988.

One of the most comprehensive introductions to this area. Includes an excellent overview of the workings of the American legal system. Recommended.

Don R. Pember
Mass Media Law. 4th ed. Dubuque, Iowa: Wm. C. Brown, 1987.

This textbook is considered one of the main- stays in the area of media law and regulation. Covers all the important court cases affecting relationships among the press, the public, and the government.

John D. Stevens
Shaping the First Amendment: The Development of Free Expression. Beverly Hills, Calif.: Sage, 1982.

This slim volume provides a concise, easy-to- follow history of one of our most important legal concepts.

The *Columbia Journalism Review* is an excellent source of interpretative articles dealing with court actions affecting newspapers and report- ing. Some of the material in this section was drawn from the following review articles:

Bruce W. Sanford
"No Quarter from This Court," Sept.–Oct. 1979, pp. 59–63. "The Press and the Courts:

Is News Gathering Shielded by the First Amendment?" Nov.–Dec. 1978, pp. 43–50. "Richmond Newspapers: End of a Zigzag Trail?" Sept.–Oct. 1980, pp. 46–47.

Issues and Answers: Love, Law, and Libel

John J. Watkins
Mass Media and the Law. Englewood Cliffs, N.J.: Prentice-Hall, 1990.

A comprehensive and current survey, this book is written for prospective media professionals. Libel is among the many standard topics covered. Includes a useful glossary of legal terms and a broad overview of the American legal system.

For more recent cases, see the *Reader's Guide to Periodical Literature*. There are usually a few major libel cases each year, and court rulings constantly reinterpret existing libel laws. Also, the Stylebook of the Associated Press includes a concise "libel manual," invaluable to working reporters. If your library does not have a copy of a recent AP Stylebook, write the Associated Press, 50 Rockefeller Plaza, New York, NY 10020.

Magazines: The Variety Store

The word *magazine* means variety store.
It should have something for everyone.

Christopher Hitchens

Where were you the last time you were looking for that special magazine? You stood there, gazing at row after shiny row of covers, a seemingly endless array of bright, colorful magazines. Perhaps it was at a newsstand, bookstore, drugstore, or supermarket. Whatever the store, its function duplicated that of magazines themselves. Grocery stores and drugstores contain a lot more than groceries and drugs these days, and modern magazines are "storehouses" that contain "something for everyone" and "everything for someone."

Without a mass audience, few magazines would survive. Yet they are also among the most specialized of the mass media, dramatically demonstrating that today's mass audience is becoming increasingly selective. The study of magazines affords us insights into how we spend our leisure time while a survey of the ups and downs of the magazine industry provides a microcosm of life in Mediamerica.

Shopping at the Variety Store

Ninety-four percent of Americans 18 years of age and older read magazines during an average month. Each of us reads an average of 11.6 different magazine copies per month. Eighteen magazines have circulations of over 3 million

Mediamerica's magazines are literary and visual variety stores, containing something for everyone.

copies per issue (see 5.1). Thus it is safe to conclude that we have a voracious appetite for magazines and the unique and specialized information we find in them.

Relationships between magazines and readers reveal changing trends and patterns in social behavior. Like all commercial mass media, magazines create and reflect popular beliefs and tastes. The success—and profits—of a magazine depend on how well it can anticipate those tastes and deliver an information package the audience will buy.

Magazines can generally be broken down into two categories: *general interest* and *special interest*. General-interest magazines such as *Reader's Digest* and *TV Guide* (see 5.2) try to appeal to the largest possible readership by providing information virtually anyone can re-

late to. Special-interest magazines like *Road and Track* and *PC Computing* focus more narrowly, appealing to a particular group of readers with common interests.

However, general-interest magazines still specialize, often by targeting certain key *demographics* (age, sex, ethnic background, and other composition factors) of the general population. *Atlantic* aims for affluent, college-educated readers. *Modern Maturity* and *New Choices* go directly after older readers (currently America's fasting-growing demographic group), while *Sassy* targets female teens and *Chickadee Magazine* is designed for younger children.

Writer's Market, a guide for freelance writers, classifies all magazines as either *consumer publications* or *trade/technical/professional journals.* The consumer category includes both general-interest and special-interest magazines that do not relate directly to a particular business. The second category includes magazines generally read by those in a particular industry to learn about their trade.

The use of the word *magazine* to mean "periodical publication" actually stems from its use in 18th-century books that collected literary works or information about a single subject. These books were a "storehouse" in the same way that the term *magazine* still means a place where ammunition is kept. For over 250 years, American magazines have been firing their ammunition of information directly at their target audiences.

The Good Old Days

The earliest American magazines were local journals of political opinion. None circulated far beyond its geographic origin; most were monthlies. In 1741 Andrew Bradford's *American Magazine* was the first to appear in the colonies, beating Benjamin Franklin's *General Magazine and Historical Chronicle* by 3 days (see 5.3). Both folded within 6 months.

National Circulation of Leading U.S. Magazines

This table lists all U.S. magazines that charge for subscriptions and single copies and have a total national circulation of 3 million or more according to the Audit Bureau of Circulation. It does not include publications such as *Modern Maturity* (no single-copy sales) or *American Legion Magazine* (given away to those paying a membership fee).

The Magazine Publishers Association estimates that the average copy of a magazine is read, in part, by 3.8 people. (Think of all those old magazines in dentists' offices and auto repair waiting rooms!) If they are right, then the actual readership of these magazines is about four times the number indicated.

Also note that the Audit Bureau of Circulation considers the *National Enquirer* and *Star* to be magazines, but I have chosen to include them as tabloid newspapers in Chapter 4. The debate about their proper category continues.

Magazine	Total Paid Circulation (in millions)	Magazine	Total Paid Circulation (in millions)
Reader's Digest	15,231,649	Time	4,188,303
TV Guide	14,266,020	Redbook	3,253,746
National Geographic	9,367,954	National Enquirer	3,230,283
Better Homes and Gardens	7,615,315	Playboy	3,421,496
Family Circle	5,004,635	Newsweek	3,171,827
McCall's	4,636,022	Sports Illustrated	3,464,674
Good Housekeeping	5,056,700	People	3,557,926
Ladies' Home Journal	5,036,495	The Star	2,805,075
Woman's Day	4,508,333	Prevention	3,367,550

Based on Audit Bureau of Circulations' FAS-FAX Report for 6 months ending June 30, 1994. Used by permission.

For the next 130 years, magazines came and went. All were aimed at the local audience; most sold advertising and were published monthly. In 1879 Congress lowered the postal rates for periodicals to encourage literacy via a broader distribution of magazines and newspapers.

In 1893 S. S. McClure founded *McClure's* magazine and priced it at 15 cents for those who could not afford the usual 25 or 30 cents. His strategy was simple: Deliver an entertaining, easy-to-read magazine to the masses. Thus armed with a large circulation, the magazine could charge higher advertising rates.

McClure's also gained fame through a journalistic practice known as *muckraking*. Muckraking stories generally exposed political or social injustices. Two early exposés in *McClure's* that helped the magazine gain notoriety were Ida M. Tarbell's "History of the Standard Oil Company" and Lincoln Steffens's "Shame of the Cities."

The chief competitor of *McClure's* was Frank Munsey's magazine *Munsey's*, which dropped its price to 10 cents in 1893. Like the newspaper yellow journalists, Munsey stopped at nothing to increase circulation.

Taking on *TV Guide*: A Brief Bright Star on the Video Horizon

In April 1983, Time Inc. mailed the first issue of *TV-Cable Week* to 150,000 subscribers in five test markets. At stake was $100 million, the largest sum ever spent to launch a magazine. But the rewards might have been equally great, as *TV-Cable Week* aimed for a piece of the $240 million in annual advertising revenues then enjoyed by *TV Guide*.

TV Guide began life as a national publication in 1953 with 1.5 million subscribers. Its circulation is now over 16 million, though it has dipped from its all-time high of 19 million in 1980. In 1974 *TV Guide* had became the largest-selling magazine in America, briefly replacing *Reader's Digest* in that coveted position.

But the people at Time Inc. thought *TV Guide* had been too slow to respond to the video revolution. Many cable subscribers found they could not readily identify all of their channel choices using *TV Guide*'s regular listings. By catering specifically to the cable subscriber, *TV-Cable Week*

hoped to slowly gather a large, loyal readership.

Of course, *TV Guide* did not take this lying down. In 1982, $40 million was spent to expand its cable listings; soon beneath the familiar *TV Guide* logo were the words "Local, Network and Cable/Pay Listings." All of this was accomplished before the first issue of *TV-Cable Week* was in the mail. Nevertheless, the new publication offered a more complete picture of the myriad choices confronting the cable subscriber.

When the first issue of *TV-Cable Week* came out, *TV Guide* editorial director Merrill Panitt didn't seem too worried. He told *Newsweek,* "Competition is fine, it wakes everybody

up!" Indeed, it appeared that the impending arrival of new competition had woken up the folks at *TV Guide*. With their new cable-listings section in place, they were able to do a successful end run around Time's marketing strategies.

In September 1983, just 5 months after its debut, *TV-Cable Week* published its final issue. The 250 staff members were laid off. The still unfinished offices in New York were closed. Total 1983 losses had been close to $50 million. Many reasons were given for the failure of *TV-Cable Week,* but in the end it was yet another victim of the fierce competition in the variety store of the magazine marketplace.

When he died in 1925, one critic wrote: "Frank Munsey contributed to the journalism of his day the talent of a meat packer, the morals of a money changer, and the manner of an undertaker." While other publishers made

speeches about getting quality reading to the masses, Munsey was primarily concerned with making money.

The muckrakers of this period helped establish a tradition of investigative journalism in America. Only a few magazines carry on this tradition today, however. Among them is *Mother Jones,* which began publication in 1976 and achieved national recognition for its 1977 articles charging that some Ford Pintos posed a fire hazard. With a circulation of 200,000, Editor Doug Foster calls it "the largest magazine of political opinion in the United States."

In 1897 Cyrus Curtis bought the floundering *Saturday Evening Post* for $1,000. That year its circulation was 2,200, and advertising revenues were just under $7,000. *Printer's Ink,* a trade paper, described the investment as "an impossible venture." But Curtis developed just the right combination of fact, fiction, and folk story. Within 5 years, circulation had risen to more than 300,000, and ad revenues to $360,000. By 1912 circulation neared 2 million, and ad revenues soared accordingly.

McClure's, Munsey's, the *Saturday Evening Post,* and many more ushered in the era of the mass-circulation magazine. Readers regularly supplemented news from their daily paper with the in-depth articles and fiction of their favorite magazines.

During the 1930s, many successful magazines ran quality fiction to boost sales. The *Saturday Evening Post, Esquire,* and even *Look* and *Life* were showcases for the shorter fiction of writers like Ernest Hemingway and F. Scott Fitzgerald. Technical developments in photography and typography also increased their appeal.

From 1900 to 1950, the number of "magazine families" subscribing to one or more periodicals rose from 200,000 to more than 32 million. This magazine boom came in spite of the introduction of film, radio, television, and the paperback book.

After World War I, new magazines appeared by the hundreds. *Time* presented a capsulized version of the week's news. Within a year after its first issue, it was turning a profit. Even more successful was *Life.* It appeared in 1936, offering bold, imaginative photography and tremendous visual impact for just 10 cents a copy.

By the beginning of World War II, most of the earlier mass-circulation magazines had died, including *Munsey's* and *McClure's.* Some, like the *Saturday Evening Post, Collier's, Cosmopolitan,* and *McCall's,* remained, but many were in financial trouble. Publishers had used profits from successful magazines to finance less prosperous new ones. Because magazines are among the freest of the free-market enterprises, those that command adequate circulation and attract advertisers survive. Those that don't, perish.

These Days: Magazines Since 1950

Nostalgia buffs would have us believe that the "good old days" of magazines are gone forever. They wail that there will never be another *Look* or *Collier's.* Their reverence for the old has prompted special "nostalgia" issues of magazines like *Liberty* and the *Saturday Evening Post.*

What happened to these magazines? The world of mass communication is one of mass change. Public tastes and information needs shift over the years; some magazines couldn't or wouldn't shift with them.

For better or worse, the economic and social history of magazines since the middle of the century has certainly been influenced by television. *Life,* for example, which had provided its audience with pictures from around the world, was clearly upstaged by the new medium.

Other economic problems included increased postal rates, paper costs, salaries, and other production costs as well as poor management. The loss of advertising revenue to other media played a key role. By 1960 advertisers were wondering why they should pay almost $8 to reach 1,000 *Life* readers when a minute of television time could be had for about $4 per 1,000 viewers.

1824 Author Edgar Allan Poe predicts, "This is the age of magazines; the whole tendency of this age is magazineward."

1700 1800

1710 Several American printers collect essays and print them in newspaper format.

1741 Andrew Bradford's *American Magazine* and Benjamin Franklin's *General Magazine and Historical Chronicle* are the first regularly published magazines in America; neither is financially successful.

1821 The *Saturday Evening Post* is founded, appealing to both women and men.

1857 *Harper's Weekly* begins publication and offers engravings that add visual depth to stories; it immediately becomes the country's largest-selling magazine.

1865 Beginning of the first magazine boom. In the next 20 years the number of periodicals increases from 700 to 3,300.

1865 E. L. Godkin founds the *Nation*, a journal of news and a forerunner of magazines like *Time* and *Newsweek*.

1879 The federal government decreases postal rates for magazines and other publications to encourage wider circulation.

1880s Women's magazines like *Ladies' Home Journal* and *Good Housekeeping* begin to have major market impact.

1893 *McClure's*, at 15 cents a copy, is the first inexpensive mass-circulation magazine.

1893 *Munsey's* magazine cuts its price from 25 cents to 10 cents to compete with *McClure's*.

1897 Cyrus Curtis takes charge of the *Saturday Evening Post*.

5.3 The History of American Magazines

1922

DeWitt Wallace founds *Reader's Digest*. His idea: Take the best articles from other magazines and reprint them in condensed form. Articles must be "constructive, of lasting value, and applicable to readers."

1940s

The heyday of the big general-interest magazines. *Life*, *Look*, *Saturday Evening Post*, *Reader's Digest*, and *Collier's* show healthy profits while expanding; black and white format is replaced with new color format.

1900   1925

1903 Magazine muckraking era begins. Writers expose unethical practices in business and government.

1907 The *Saturday Evening Post* is one of the first magazines to top $1 million in annual advertising revenues.

1918 William Randolph Hearst hires Ray Long to edit *Cosmopolitan*. Long becomes the highest-paid editor of the era and gains a reputation for his uncanny ability to predict public reading tastes.

1920 Gross annual revenues in magazine advertising top $129 million.

1923 Henry Luce and Briton Hadden found *Time* magazine, an overnight success.

1925 The *New Yorker* begins publication and becomes the most successful metropolitan magazine.

1925 Many magazines shift emphasis from subscription to newsstand sales to increase profits.

1929 *Business Week* magazine is founded.

1930 Gross annual revenues in magazine advertising peak near $200 million, then fall to less than $100 million in 1933.

1930s Magazine circulation greatly increases from sales in grocery stores.

1933 *Esquire's* first issue appears, and at 50 cents a copy it is the most expensive of its day.

1936 *Vanity Fair*, perhaps the most elite and "cultural" mass-circulation magazine of its era, ceases publication after 22 years.

1936 Time Inc. founds *Life* magazine; first issue sells for 10 cents.

1937 *Look* magazine appears, a frank imitator of *Life*.

1947 *Reader's Digest* becomes the first magazine to boast a circulation of more than 9 million.

1948 *TV Guide* founded for New York viewers; later exp to national publication.

1970

Cosmopolitan leads the way to more explicit magazines for women. Burt Reynolds is the first centerfold.

1950

1951 Gross annual revenues in magazine advertising exceed $500 million.

1952 William Gaines starts *Mad* magazine.

1953 Hugh Hefner founds *Playboy*; Marilyn Monroe is the first centerfold.

1954 Time Inc. founds *Sports Illustrated*.

1955 Rising production costs force *Reader's Digest* to accept advertising for the first time.

1956 *Collier's* is the first modern mass-circulation, general-interest magazine to go bankrupt and cease publication.

1967 *Look* publishes its first "demographic" edition in an attempt to reach various special-interest readers and advertisers.

1971 *Look* ceases publication.

1972 *Life* magazine prints its final regular issue.

1972 *Ms.* magazine is published, devoted to women's rights and the women's movement.

1974 Time Inc. founds *People* magazine, a smaller, livelier, and more "show biz" version of *Life*. It thrives.

1975

1978 Time Inc. announces that *Life* will begin publication again—as a monthly.

1980s Demographics is "the name of the game" as magazine content and marketing strategies are aimed at the special-interest audience.

1983 After a 47-year absence, *Vanity Fair* is revived as a contemporary monthly. After a slow start, it once again becomes a trend-setter.

1983 Time Inc. launches *TV–Cable Week* in April to compete with *TV Guide*, but it ceases publication in September.

1987

Jessica Hahn sells her story to *Playboy* for a reported $1 million.

1988

Frances Lear uses $25 million of her divorce settlement to begin *Lear's*. First issue headlines proclaim: "At Last! A Magazine for the Woman Who Wasn't Born Yesterday."

1987 Longtime *New Yorker* editor William Shawn is unceremoniously replaced by Robert Gottlieb as new owner Sam Newhouse attempts to inject new life into one of America's most cherished journalism institutions.

1990 Gross magazine revenues reach an all-time high of $14 billion.

1991 Family Media Inc. publisher of *Discover* and *Health* is first major group to cease operation in the wake of the recession. *Psychology Today* publishes its final issue.

1992 New York magazine establishment shudders, as controversial *Vanity Fair* editor Tina Brown is named editor of the staid *New Yorker*.

1993 *Omni Magazine Online* is first computer service to offer readers a forum for interactive response to issues raised in the magazine.

1994 *Lear's* ceases publication, a victim of the economy and magazine circulation wars.

1995 Industry watchers Hal Riney and Partners cite recovering economy and stress that the "future of magazines is bright" in new era to be dominated by digital communications.

Beyond the Brown Shadow: Prosperity at *Vanity Fair*

"The culture is changing constantly," enthuses Tina Brown, "and we have to change with it." Sounds like a simple formula for prosperity, and these days hardly anyone in the magazine industry can match the success of Tina Brown. A former reporter for *The Times of London,* Brown was relatively inexperienced when she took over as editor-in-chief of *Vanity Fair* in 1984. Nevertheless she promised her boss, Condé Naste Chairman S. I. Newhouse, a magazine that would be "frothy, exciting, literate, romantic, funny — and solvent." Brown has delivered on all counts, and become one of the world's best-known magazine editors in the process.

Everyone in the industry seems to have something to say about *Vanity Fair.* Michael Kinsley, former editor of *Harper's,* relates, "*Vanity Fair* makes you feel glamorous. It's vulgar and shallow, but that goes with the territory." A former art director called the magazine "a glorified *People.*"

Indeed, celebrity profiles and other gossipy fare are the magazine's stock in trade, for which Brown makes no apologies. "Part of the magazine's identity is the electric, modern, alive feeling that a celebrity cover gives it." Profiled on "60 Minutes," she acknowledges that "*Vanity Fair* sells illicit pleasure. My job is one of seduction. I'm about entrapping the reader."

Sometimes it's hard to know just where Brown ends and the magazine begins. She tells one reporter flatly, "If you don't like my identity, you won't like the magazine." New York media critic Edwin Diamond agrees. "Any successful magazine is the shadow cast by its editor. The question is how long people will find Tina Brown's shadow interesting enough to ponder month after month."

These days, there appears to be no end in sight. *Vanity Fair* printed over a million copies for the first time in August 1991. The now-famous cover featured a very nude, very pregnant Demi Moore, and set off a storm of controversy. In a profile of Brown for *Los Angeles Times Magazine* (the source for many of the quotes reprinted here), writer Bill Thomas explains, "The real aim . . . was to startle, to stimulate, and to sell magazines, three things that Brown has managed to do with uncanny consistency, no matter what her identity is."

When Brown was named editor of the conservative *New Yorker* magazine in 1992, the New York magazine establishment was shocked. "I think too many times editors are cowed by the conservatism of the industry," she declares. "My philosophy is when in doubt, take the risk. At least you'll never be boring."

Of course, not all the older magazines died. Among those still doing well are *National Geographic, Better Homes and Gardens,* and *Ladies' Home Journal.* And if some former giants have departed, hundreds of new magazines have sprung up to take at least a part of their place or establish new niches of their own (see 5.1). *People* magazine (a spinoff of *Time's* popular "People" section) has competed successfully with the supermarket tabloids since its inception in 1974. More recent success stories such as *Vanity Fair* (see 5.4) prove that while magazines are not dying, reader needs are changing and modern magazines must respond to those changes.

Figures alone don't tell the survival story in the variety store. Magazines are people: owners, editors, writers, and readers. These people represent a coalition of the diverse interests that make a magazine live.

Two of the biggest magazine stories since 1950 have been the rise of *Playboy* and the death of *Life*. The *Playboy* story is one of manners, morals, and ingenuity. (See the guest essay by John Brady on page 96.) Even though *Playboy*'s fortunes have declined a bit in recent years, the evolution of the magazine and the personality of founder Hugh Hefner still make for interesting reading. Like *Playboy*, *Life*'s story begins with a founder's vision.

A Portrait: The Death (?) of *Life*

To see life; to see the world; to eyewitness great events . . . to see strange things — machines, armies, multitudes, shadows in the jungle and on the moon; to see man's work — his paintings, towers, and discoveries; to see things thousands of miles away, things hidden behind walls and within rooms, things dangerous to come to; the women that men love and many children; to see and take pleasure in seeing; to see and be amazed; to see and be instructed. Thus to see, and to be shown, is now the will and new expectancy of half mankind.
Henry R. Luce, 1936

Henry Luce, cofounder of Time Inc., shared this vision for a new magazine with potential advertisers and financial backers in 1936 (see 5.5). The nation was still in an economic depression, but Luce sensed that technological development had made possible a new kind of journalism. Paper was cheap, and photographs were increasingly appealing to readers. Why not a magazine that would provide a weekly "window on the world" for a mass audience starved for visual information?

Life's initial success was so overwhelming that it nearly killed the magazine. Luce had contracted with advertisers, anticipating a circulation of 250,000 for the first year. To his delight and dismay, circulation was twice that

5.5

Henry R. Luce, founder of *Life,* chats at a banquet with Elsa Maxwell, the songwriter, radio star, and syndicated columnist.

almost immediately. This meant double production costs without higher advertising rates. *Life* lost $6 million before appropriate adjustments could be made. Luce should have learned a lesson from *Munsey's* and *McClure's;* both magazines had experienced the same problem 40 years earlier.

In its early years, *Life* was often controversial. A 1938 issue featured a photo essay (the term itself was a *Life* invention) on the birth of a baby. Some readers were shocked, and the magazine was banned in 33 cities. Though Luce maintained that *Life*'s photo essays would "begin in delight and end in wisdom," some critics disagreed. One described the *Life* photo formula as "equal parts of the decapitated Chinaman, the flogged Negro, and the rapidly slipping chemise." As years went by, *Life* did provide a certain amount of sex appeal, and pinup pictures of actress Rita Hayworth and others often created a stir.

Life was also a news magazine. During the Spanish Civil War, World War II, and the Korean War, readers depended on *Life* to be there,

The Nude Journalism

John Brady is a former editor of Writer's Digest *and author of* The Craft of Interviewing. *This is excerpted from an article that first appeared in the* Journal of Popular Culture *in 1974. Today the* Playboy *legacy is carried on by Hefner's adult daughter, Christie, while the magazine's founder has become the husband of a former Playmate and father of two young children.*

For the past 20 years a gaunt, pipe-smoking, Pepsi-swigging man in Chicago has edited a magazine that was never intended for female chauvinist sows or for the little old ladies of Dubuque. Along the way he has been called — among lesser delicacies — "the Crusader Rabbit of Sex," "the Norman Vincent Peale of Erotica," and "the man who started the loosening of sexual attitudes in America." If, as Emerson suggested, "an institution is the lengthened shadow of one man," *Playboy* magazine is surely one Hugh Marston Hefner.

Hefner's success is even more remarkable because it came at a time when American magazine journalism was, at best, risky. The period, in fact, is a mausoleum for once-successful publications — *Collier's, Saturday Evening Post, Look,* and *Life* — while hundreds of lesser magazines slipped quietly into unmarked graves.

Yet *Playboy* prospered. The Hefnerian secret? "I invented sex," the publisher wryly observed on a recent TV talk show. And, to an extent, it's true — at least insofar as publishers are concerned. Hefner led the way. He gave popular culture a sex life. The Nude Journalism. But of course!

No other magazine in America has had an impact to match *Playboy's*. "*Playboy* is probably the most influential publication of my lifetime," says Gay Talese.

Whether the magazine fostered the revolution or the revolution nurtured the magazine is debatable. "*Playboy* came at the right time, when the United States was experiencing a sexual revolution," says Hefner. "My naked girls became a symbol of disobedience, a triumph of sexuality, an end of puritanism." It seems safe to conclude, however, that *Playboy* at least helped bring about a cultural change in our society much more rapidly than would have occurred otherwise. Hefner's magazine became the foremost chronicler of sexual change throughout this period. Thus, following closely on the heels of Dr. Kinsey, and paralleling the development of The Pill, *Playboy* served as midwife while the age of sexual candor was born unto the popular press in America.

In 1952, only two major publications could be called general magazines for men — *Esquire* and the now-defunct *Gentry.* Other magazines that featured female nudity were a pretty seamy lot in general. The remaining men's magazines emphasized the great outdoors. Hefner found them "asexual at best, and maybe homosexual. With the outdoor and hunting and adventure things in which the place for the woman was in the kitchen while you hung out with the guys and played poker or went out on a hunting trip to chase the abominable snowman."

The first issue of *Playboy* was put together with paste pot and scissors on a bridge table in Hefner's kitchen. The publisher's personal investment was $600, which he obtained by mortgaging furniture and borrowing from friends. He also sold $10,000 in stock to random social acquaintances.

"I'm sitting in my studio one day and in comes this skinny, intense, wild-eyed guy," recalls Arthur Paul, then a young Chicago freelance artist. "He showed me this magazine he had put together. He had done all the artwork by himself, and it was awful. But he looked at my work and asked me to redesign his magazine." Of course, Hefner had no money. "I took on the job," adds Paul, "accepting private shares of stock in the company he was founding, instead of salary" — and it was probably the best thing that ever happened to him.

Sales mushroomed. By the end of 1954, monthly circulation was 104,189; one year later that figure had more than tripled, and by 1956, sales averaged 795,965 monthly.

Each month the book became thicker and slicker as profits were plowed back into the product. Not until 1956, though, did *Playboy* attract advertisers in large numbers — partly because conservative accounts were reluctant to be associated with a "skin" magazine, but mostly because Hefner rejected some 80 percent of the advertising submitted for publication, including ads for firearms, weight reducers, acne and baldness cures, correspondence courses, trusses, athlete's foot powder, sex manuals, "life-like" inflatable dolls, vibrators, and whatnot.

"Right from the start, he knew it would be fatal in the long run to carry the kind of schlock ads that usually go in pinup magazines," says a longtime associate of the publisher. "It was the best decision he ever made." *Playboy*'s former advertising director Howard Lederer added: "We create a euphoria and we want nothing to spoil it. We don't want a reader to come suddenly on an ad that says he has bad breath. We don't want him to be reminded of the fact, though it may be true, that he is going bald."

Now that the field suddenly belonged to *Playboy*, the magazine began to change. "I've always edited on the assump-

tion that my tastes are pretty much like those of our readers," said Hefner in 1955. "As I develop, so will the magazine." One of the first things to develop was the centerfold. Although the feature had begun with Marilyn Monroe as "Sweetheart of the Month" ("Playmate" did not appear until the second issue), subsequent centerfolds were nameless. "In the early days, when it was hard to get a decent girl to pose in the nude," observed J. Anthony Lukas, "a few of the Playmates looked as though they might feel at home on a barstool."

Critic Benjamin DeMott pointed out that the [later] Playmate, generally chosen from a middle-income background, could be *any* girl with an attractive figure. *Playboy,* he said, undertakes "to establish that the nude in Nassau and the stenotypist in Schenectady — the sex-bomb and the 'ordinary girl' — are actually one creature. Essential Woman." Today, of course, when one passes the men's-magazine section of a newsstand, *Playboy* is pictorially tame compared with publications that seem to have staff gynecologists rather than art directors. "*Playboy* has become part of the Establishment," says Bob Guccione, editor of *Penthouse,* a younger, more virile *Playboy.*

Whether *Playboy* has gone "establishment" is debatable, but clearly many of the causes the magazine once fought

have either been won or forgotten. The magazine's circulation, which once flirted with 7 million, has fallen back to some 5 million monthly — mostly because *Playboy* has fallen behind in the commodity its publisher invented: sex. [1992 circulation was 3.5 million.] Despite the criticism, the competition, and the awareness that the *Playboy* phenomenon has probably peaked, Hugh Marston Hefner's place as a journalist of distinction and of influence is rather secure. "All history," said Emerson, "resolves itself very easily into the biography of a few stout and earnest persons." In the annals of popular culture and The Nude Journalism, Hefner is surely the publisher who led the change. "I'm sure that I will be remembered as one significant part of our time," Hefner told an interviewer a few years ago. "We live in a period of rapid sociological change, and I am on the side of the angels."

to help them witness these important world events in a way no other medium could. In 1969 *Life* brought the Vietnam War home by running the pictures of 217 Americans killed during a single week of combat.

But *Life* was more than news and photographs. Some of the world's first-rate authors published original stories there, including Ernest Hemingway, Graham Greene, Norman Mailer, and James Dickey. *Life* carried the memoirs of Winston Churchill, Harry S Truman, Charles de Gaulle, Dwight Eisenhower, and Nikita Khrushchev.

A generation that had grown up with the institution called *Life* was dismayed when Time Inc. announced abruptly that *Life*'s 1972 year-end issue would be its last. Many *Life* staffers were no less surprised, though rumors had been circulating for some time. *Look* had stopped publishing in 1971, and many had said that *Life* would soon follow.

What really killed *Life*? *Life* writer and longtime staffer Tommy Thompson said: "We lost our focus, we didn't know who we were writing to. We continued to try to put out a mass magazine when America was not a *mass* any more, but divergent groups of specialized interests." Perhaps the needs of the "mass" audience were now better served by television. In 1952, when *Life* published color pictures of the coronation of Elizabeth II in only 10 days, readers were amazed; a few years later, television was bringing viewers similar events instantaneously. Of course, television is not exactly photojournalism, nor can it replace it. *Life*'s pictures captured a unique moment and could be enjoyed again and again.

Columnist Shana Alexander rejected the doomsday theories of those who felt *Life*'s demise foretold shifting trends in American taste: "Photojournalism is not dead, and the American people have not stopped reading, nor have they lost interest in the world around them. What died at *Life* was an appropriate and responsible relationship between editors and management."

During its final 3 years, *Life* swam in a sea of red ink, losing some $30 million. A conservative management rejected numerous plans from editors and other staffers to "save" the magazine. *Life* could have gone to a smaller format (its large size made postal rate increases disastrous) or shifted its balance between photo and story content. It could have trimmed from its circulation list those whom demographers did not consider prime targets for potential advertisers, thereby cutting circulation costs and increasing advertiser appeal. But this would have meant a major shift in editorial policy and in the very concept of the magazine as well. In the end, *Life* did nothing, and died.

In death it was remembered as a social force of unparalleled magnitude. William Shawn, then managing editor of the *New Yorker,* said: "*Life* invented a great new form of journalism. It contributed much to the American community that was valuable, often reaching moments of brilliance and beauty." Poet James Dickey noted, "I can't begin to calculate all of the things I have learned from *Life*. I'm not quite the same person I was because of what I read and saw in its pages." Indeed, hundreds of millions of *Life* readers had their lives transformed in some way.

For 36 years, *Life* was an information source that expanded its readers' vision of the world around them. It continued that mission through a number of special issues during the mid-1970s. The success of those issues prompted an announcement by Time Inc. in 1978 that *Life* would return as a monthly. Perhaps reports of the death of *Life* had been greatly exaggerated after all!

The new monthly *Life* has become solidly entrenched in the current magazine scene, and *Life* still sets the standard for excellence in photojournalism. During the Gulf War there were even rumors that it might become a weekly again. Whatever happens, it's hard to imagine a magazine with quite the impact the "window on the world" once had on its readers. *Life* is a monument to an era of magazine journalism that may never come again.

Specialization and Marketing Trends

While general-interest magazines like *Life* target the mass audience, special-interest publications are aimed at a very specific readership. *Onion World* and *Soybean Digest* are destined to remain anonymous to all but those in the onion and soybean trade. Meanwhile, *Sinsemilla Tips, Domestic Marijuana Journal* advises freelance writers that by-lines are given but "Some writers desire to be anonymous for obvious reasons."

Writer's Market lists more than 100 magazines that deal with farming, soil management (*Tobacco Reporter*), dairy farming (*Butter-Fat*), and rural life (*Maine Organic Farmer and Gardener*). There is even an Ohio publication called *Gleanings in Bee Culture*. Such magazines provide examples of special-interest publications, which account for more than 90% of the total number of magazine titles being published today.

Other vocations have their magazines as well. There is *Firehouse Magazine, Police Times, Compressed Air, Florida Underwriter*, and *Canadian Jeweller*. Many periodicals appeal to readers' ethnic backgrounds (*Ebony, Southern Jewish Weekly*) and their religious preferences (*Gospel Carrier, Catholic Digest*). Numerous publications reflect unique geographic locations (*Golden Gate North, Gulfshore Life, Nashville!*) and hobbies (*Biker/Hiker*). There is even *Lefthander Magazine*, featuring interviews with famous southpaws and "exposés on discrimination against lefthanders in the work world."

Not surprisingly, the fortunes of magazines come and go according to shifting economic, demographic, and reader-interest patterns. In the mid-1980s, there was a sudden glut of magazines devoted to video games and personal computers. *Byte* is still with us, but *Personal Computing* and *The Macintosh Buyer's Guide* have ceased publication. In the early 1990s, the recession led to a plethora of "how-to-survive with less" articles and diminished circulation for nearly every mass-circulation magazine.

While mass-circulation magazines give us a sense of global participation, special-interest publications allow us to share our individual concerns with people more like ourselves. Special-interest magazines have flourished, partly as a result of the success of their general-interest big brothers and sisters. Because mass-circulation magazines print millions of copies, they must charge extremely high advertising rates. Only a handful of advertisers can afford to pay up to $100,000 for a full page in a mass-circulation magazine. As a result, many smaller companies have turned to less expensive, special-interest publications, where their ads will be seen by fewer but perhaps more receptive readers.

Of course, general-interest magazines have not calmly stood by and watched their revenues evaporate. Magazines such as *Time* offer local companies reduced rates for regional "breakouts"—ads that will appear only in copies sent to a specific geographic region. This gives smaller companies a chance to appear in a national magazine at a rate they can afford. *People* magazine has experimented with different covers for different geographic regions, because impulse buys account for such a large portion of their sales and nothing triggers an impulse to buy like an interesting cover.

But geography is only one of the special-interest trends in magazine marketing. *Time* offers advertisers the opportunity to reach subscribers who are doctors, members of top management, students or educators, or even those who live in special high-income ZIP code areas (see 5.6). This trend toward demographic breakouts began in 1967 when *Look* published its first *demo-edition* and continues today.

TIME NATIONAL 4.0

The world's leading weekly newsmagazine in circulation, newsstand sales, advertising revenue and pages. Available weekly.

Rate Base: 4,000,000	Black & White	Black & 1 Color	4 Color
Page	$ 91,000	$113,700	$134,400
Fourth Cover	NA	NA	172,200
2 Columns	68,300	85,300	107,500
1/2 Page Horizontal*	54,600	68,200	87,400
1/2 Page Horizontal Spread*	109,200	136,400	174,700
1 Column	36,400	45,500	60,500
1/2 Column	22,800	28,400	NA

* Subject to limited availability.

TIME NATIONAL 2.5

Offers national distribution to the same subscribers with the same geographic and demographic characteristics as TIME National 4.0 and includes all newsstand copies. Available every other week.

Rate Base: 2,500,000	Black & White	Black & 1 Color	4 Color
Page	$ 56,900	$ 71,100	$ 84,000

TIME 50 MAJOR METROS

Concentrates circulation in 50 major U.S. ADIs accounting for 67% of U.S. population and 71% of effective buying income. Includes all TIME Group I and II Spot Market Editions. Available every other week.

Rate Base: 3,100,000	Black & White	Black & 1 Color	4 Color
Page	$ 77,500	$ 97,000	$114,700
2 Columns	58,100	72,800	91,800
1/2 Page Horizontal Spread*	108,500	135,800	160,600
1 Column	31,000	38,800	51,600
1/2 Column	19,400	24,300	NA

* Subject to limited availability.

TIME TOP ZIPS

Provides national circulation exclusively to the highest-income postal ZIP Codes as ranked by estimated average household income. Available every other week.

Rates are based on subscription circulation only.

Rate Base: 1,300,000	Black & White	Black & 1 Color	4 Color
Page	$ 52,800	$ 65,900	$ 78,000

TIME BUSINESS

Offers the largest all-business circulation of any magazine in the United States. All TIME Business subscriber households are qualified by job title, verified by the ABC. Provides in-depth reach to top, middle and technical management and professionals in all 50 states. Available every other week.

Rates are based on subscription circulation only.

Rate Base: 1,635,000	Black & White	Black & 1 Color	4 Color
Page	$ 56,900	$ 71,100	$ 84,100
2 Columns	42,700	53,300	67,300
1/2 Page Horizontal Spread*	79,700	99,500	117,700
1 Column	22,800	28,400	37,800
1/2 Column	20,700	24,900	NA

* Subject to limited availability.
See page 17 for TIME Business Bonus Plan Discount.

TIME TOP MANAGEMENT

Circulation exclusively to owners, partners, directors, board chairpersons, company presidents, other titled officers and department heads. Subscriber households are 100% qualified by job title, verified by the ABC. Provides highly refined reach targeted to top management nationwide. Available every other week.

Rates are based on subscription circulation only.

Rate Base: 600,000	Black & White	Black & 1 Color	4 Color
Page	$ 31,300	$ 38,700	$ 46,200
2 Columns	23,500	29,000	37,000
1 Column	12,500	15,500	20,900
1/2 Column	7,800	9,700	NA

TIME INQUIRY PROGRAM

TIP is a direct-response service that helps generate top-quality sales leads from TIME's highly selective audience. Advertisers in TIME National 4.0 or TIME Business may participate in the TIME Inquiry Program at no additional charge.

Available in 1992 issues dated March 2, April 13, May 11, September 14, October 12, and November 9. More TIP information is available on request.

NOTE: See page 16 for Discount Schedules.
See page 22 for Calendar/Closings.
Bleed Charge: add 15% to above rates.

5.6

This special rate card is distributed to agencies and potential advertisers to give them an idea of how much it will cost to reach various portions of the *Time* readership. For example, 600,000 top-management people can be reached with a full-page, four-color ad for $46,200 on a one-time basis. The same ad in all U.S. editions of *Time* would cost more than $155,000.

Courtesy Time Inc. Used by permission.

The Variety Store in the '90s

Looking ahead, increasing audience specialization seems a certainty. The day may not be far away when magazines can promise an advertiser that its message will reach, for example, only scotch-drinking readers. Demographic breakouts and other strategies designed to reach selected readers are also effective because they're easy for agencies to sell to their advertiser clients; it is as if a special service is being performed just for them.

In their unending quest for more advertising revenues, many magazines employ promotion specialists who assist sales staffers in convincing media buyers that their magazine is a "must-buy." In today's competitive environment, such specialists are more in demand than ever, especially when they can find innovative ways to contribute to the bottom line. (See the guest essay by Amy Krakow on page 102.)

An intriguing development in the specialization saga came in 1988 when Whittle Communications announced a series of entirely new publications called *Special Reports*. The only "subscribers" to these slick quarterly magazines were doctors who agreed to put them in their waiting rooms and not to subscribe to more than two additional magazines for such use. The result is that patients in 15,000 offices in 125 cities would be virtually assured of reading *Special Reports*. Advertisers were guaranteed that competing ads would not be placed in the same issue.

All of this shook up the magazine establishment, and lawyers were soon put to work to check out the legality of the Whittle plan. According to *U.S. News and World Report*, "Medical waiting rooms are traditionally an important source of new subscribers, [and provide] the largest share of 'out of home' readers for some." Recently, Whittle has consolidated the six *Reports* to three, and *Adweek* now reports that they are considering merging them into one, "to make them more effective for both readers and advertisers." Whatever the outcome, Whittle has clearly broken new ground and given the competition a lot to think about.

No overview of the current state of the art of magazine publishing would be complete without considering the impact of the recession of the early 90s. While the effect was felt by all communications media, the magazine industry was particularly hard hit. The Publisher's Information Bureau reported that the number of advertising pages in the $14 billion magazine industry dropped 10.3% for the first 8 months of 1991 while revenues dipped almost 5%. This came on the heels of a 3.7% page drop in 1990.

Family Media Inc., publishers of *Discover, Health*, and five other magazines, closed its doors in 1991. Time-Warner Publishing laid off 105 editorial and 500 business employees at its six magazines. Magazines such as *Esquire, Redbook*, and *Connoisseur* contributed to a total of some 1,200 job losses in one 2-month period alone.

Life continues to be very competitive in the variety store. According to the industry magazine *Folio*, the introduction of 789 new magazines in 1993 generated about a 10% increase in sales. As they see it, the general-interest monthly and bimonthly publications operate in a overcrowded field, while there are good opportunities for new magazines that focus on "sports, sex and home service." (Perhaps riches can be yours if you come up with a new magazine format that covers all three!)

Folio also predicts a "slow and steady recovery" for the industry amidst signs that the economy is picking up again.

What, No Advertising?

While the fortunes of advertising-supported magazines rise and fall, what about those that survive without advertising? Once upon a time, there were a number of these magazines.

Magazine Promotion . . . Art *and* Science

Amy Krakow is president of A. G. Krakow, a New York company specializing in media marketing & promotion. During her career, she has worked with and for a number of leading magazines including U.S. News and World Report, Popular Mechanics, Road and Track, Soap Opera Digest, Lear's, Bon Appetit, *and* Travel and Leisure.

An indefatigable "conceptualizer" and problem solver, Krakow has acquired a reputation in New York media circles for being "brilliant . . . and very irreverent." Among her unique promotional campaigns are several that have become widely regarded as industry standards.

Magazine promotion is both art and science — but the single word that best describes it might be "diversity." To most people, promoting a magazine means increasing circulation. But if you were hired for an entry level position in magazine promotion you'd soon discover there is much more involved.

Foremost is sales promotion — creating and producing business to business advertising that helps boost magazine revenues by increasing the number of advertising pages.

That's where diversity comes in. In my 15 years of magazine promotion and marketing I've written ads, booklets, and brochures. I've also hired (and fired) a lot of art directors whose job it is to design those same ads, booklets, and brochures.

Like other magazine promotion specialists, I work with writers and editors to help them translate their vision of the publication into a form that advertisers can grasp. Sometimes this involves sending staffers to lunches and dinners where they can tell advertisers directly about their editorial product. Usually it involves organizing and hosting these affairs as well.

Yes, parties are a big (and fun!) part of the business. I've coordinated everything from huge events at places like New York's Hard Rock Cafe to intimate cocktail parties and dinners for 12 in suites at the exclusive Waldorf towers.

Every assignment is different and presents a series of creative choices. I've created laser light shows for liquor advertisers and fashion shows to introduce new cars as well as new fashions. I've sent leprechauns on St. Patrick's Day deliveries and produced "personals" seminars — evenings filled with tips on how to write and answer personals ads. All of these events had one thing in common, they were designed to increase magazine advertising pages and/or support a schedule of ads for an important client.

Magazine readers are fiercely loyal to their favorite publications. Advertisers can and do use that devotion to sell their products to those readers. In the "good old days" it was enough to show advertisers how many readers your magazine had, how much they bought, and how much they liked the publication. Now advertisers demand "added value" — they want more than just a simple ad. Often this means events, mailings and other promotional devices designed to increase store traffic and move products.

They were able to make enough from subscriptions and newsstand sales to cover production costs and still make a profit. In recent years, however, skyrocketing production costs have made this all but impossible.

Reader's Digest resisted selling advertising for more than 30 years until rising costs finally forced it to give in; *Mad* magazine, unique in a number of ways, now stands alone as the only large-circulation entertainment-oriented magazine that refuses to accept advertising (see 5.7).

Like newspapers, most magazines have suffered heavily from inflation in recent years. And no wonder — magazine production is a

In today's world of magazine promotion, you need to have a fix on the "art" of permitting the advertiser to use the good name of the magazine. But there are also budgets, demographics, and a lot of other numbers to deal with. That's where the "science" comes in.

I also provide magazine sales staffs with collateral materials; booklets, brochures, mailers, kits, and presentations which describe in detail why the magazine is a "must-buy" for advertisers. Collateral materials today also include multimedia presentations, slide shows, and video displays as well as advertising campaigns that appear in trade publications aimed at—you guessed it—advertisers.

Once the materials are assembled, magazine sales people go to agencies on client sales calls. Sometimes we need to create something charming or funny for them to leave behind. Over the years I've produced cute teddy bears in tee-shirts emblazoned with the magazine's logo, personalized Raggedy Ann Dolls, cakes, cookies, and chocolate

bars that not only replicate a magazine cover but taste pretty good too. It's hard to go wrong with chocolate!

After 15 years of staff jobs, I now have my own business, working as a promotion consultant. That means it's my job to find new sources of revenue for my clients. One successful strategy has been to tie publications into major events. For the *Village Voice,* I created and produced an annual Festival of Street Entertainers. Sponsors paid a fee and received pages in the *Voice* for weeks before the festival. At the festival itself they had signs and banners with their names and logos prominently displayed. In cases like this, there are benefits for the reader, the advertiser, and the publication. The Street Entertainer's festival led to *Voice* publicity from many New York newspapers and television stations. "Entertainment Tonight" and CNN were there, and our entertainers actually appeared on the Johnny Carson show. What's more, 75,000 happy New Yorkers had a great day of free entertainment, courtesy of the *Voice* and other sponsors.

If all this sounds like fun, it is. After all, how often in business do you have the opportunity to be wildly creative *and* contribute significantly to the bottom line? On the other hand, magazine promotion can be a hard and demanding way to make a living. The hours are long, and the pay is rarely high. Still, if you love magazines and advertising it's a natural fit. And if it's diversity you crave, the art and science of magazine promotion might just be the career for you.

very costly business that is getting more expensive all the time. The paper must be of better quality than newsprint. In order to remain competitive, virtually all general-interest and many special-interest magazines must feature color photographs.

Recent technological innovations such as

the use of computers in the editorial and typesetting processes have reduced production costs to some extent. But a glance at the price of your favorite magazine now as compared with 5 years ago should be enough to convince you that the price of magazines, like most other things, continues to rise.

MAD Magazine: "What, Me Worry?"

The late William Gaines' *Mad* magazine is, perhaps, the most widely read journal of satire in America today. Though it started as a comic-book-size publication in 1952, it soon grew to its present format. *Mad*'s success reflects its unique ability to satirize the very products others rely on for advertising revenues. *Mad* gleefully attacks drug, automotive, and household products. Other frequent targets are movies, television commercials, and other magazines. *Mad* has even been known to satirize itself. These "attacks" are not malicious, but they point out the absurdity of our heavy reliance on advertising and the products it promotes. Ironically, the offices of *Mad* are on Madison Avenue, giving staffers a bird's-eye view of the advertising industry.

During the 1950s, the "sick humor" of *Mad* was attacked by many parent and teacher groups. But what was once counterculture has now become a part of the mainstream, and *Mad* seems harmless, if frivolous, to most parents. For them, more radical humor magazines like the *National Lampoon* pose a greater threat. *Mad*'s readers, once almost exclusively teenagers, now include people of all ages.

One target of *Mad*'s satire was those big expensive glossy gift books: "You're supposed to buy one as a gift to impress a friend, who will then put it on his coffee table to impress his friends," they explained. Nevertheless, *Completely Mad*, a big, slick "coffee table" compilation of *Mad* material appeared in 1991.

Alfred E. Neuman, the fictitious publisher of *Mad,* has become so widely recognized that he is a cult hero. His motto, "What, me worry?" aptly describes the *Mad* approach to the complexities of the technological and materialistic American culture that the magazine satirizes so successfully. *Mad* celebrated its 40th year of publication in 1992.

Writing for Magazines

If you've ever read a magazine article about something that interests you and thought you could do a better job, you're not alone. Despite tough economic times, magazines still offer unpublished writers the best opportunity to see their work in print. Before you rush right out and start writing, however, here are a few facts about the industry you should consider.

A local newspaper will always have some loyal readers simply because it covers events in a given geographic area. For the national magazine, the "local area" is the entire country. To attract readers, each magazine develops a "formula" for the type of material it publishes.

This formula is passed along to staff writers and to the freelancers (independent writers paid per article), who write the majority of magazine stories.

Most beginning freelancers shoot for the mass-circulation magazines, which, they assume, will pay well for their stories. Some do. *Reader's Digest* and *Playboy* pay about $3,500 per story; *TV Guide*, however, may pay as little as $500. More likely markets for the beginner are the special-interest magazines, which pay anywhere from nothing to $250. Regional and local magazines also use a tremendous amount of freelance material.

Any would-be contributor should pick up a copy of *Writer's Digest* or *The Writer,* monthly magazines devoted to the business of freelancing. *Writer's Market,* published yearly, is available in most libraries. Even if you have no writing aspirations, you will find it fascinating. It lists more than 4,000 markets for freelancers, and editors describe the exact formula for their magazine, as in 5.8. These descriptions are often interesting, amusing, and even shocking to the uninitiated.

Unfortunately, there is much more to freelance writing than sending in a story and waiting for the check. Editors are highly selective about what they buy. Big-name magazines may receive more than 100,000 unsolicited manuscripts every year. That's an average of almost 300 a day! This year fewer than 1,000 writers will have their work published in mass-circulation magazines. About 30,000 will be rejected. Only a few hundred will be able to live solely on their freelancing incomes.

Acceptance of an article is only the beginning. Editors carefully read the stories, altering them to conform to the magazine's style. Graphic designers and photographers supply artwork. Art directors choose typefaces and plan layouts.

Writers are often unhappy with these processes, which so vitally affect the finished product. But unless you are Norman Mailer or Tom Wolfe, you will have very little control over the story as it finally appears. Yet in all fairness, the editor is often in a much better position to know what will appeal to the magazine's readers. Writers are often too personally involved with their material and feel that each word is inviolable. Good editing remains essential to the quality of the finished product.

Issues and Answers: Professional Print — The Curious Collective

Because editors, writers, and others all work on magazine stories, what we finally read is the result of a collective, or collaborative, effort. Yet reading is something we do alone. You can't simultaneously share a magazine with someone else the way you can share a film or a television program. Often the most successful stories are those in which the reader vicariously shares the writer's personal experiences. Yet this one-to-one communication is really a myth.

Virtually all the print we consume daily is edited, rewritten, and recycled many times before it reaches us. Take this book, for example. It may be different from other texts you've read because I am speaking directly to you, just as I would if you were in my office. Occasionally I share personal experiences with you and hope they will help you recall your own media experiences. Despite this, the words you are reading now are not all mine. Some belong to my editors, others to colleagues who have read earlier drafts and offered suggestions. Students

have read many chapters and suggested that I add or delete material. In short, virtually all books, magazines, and newspapers are written "by committee," even though they are perceived by the reader as being written by individuals.

For many years, *Time* magazine used this one-to-one illusion to its advantage. In the beginning, *Time* presented the news as if it were written *by* one person *for* one person. Founder Henry Luce's formula was considered a key ingredient in the magazine's success, and *Time* staffers never received a byline. Current editor Henry Muller has dismantled Luce's "single voice" system and showcases more byline essays and interpretive writing by *Time* staffers.

True-confession stories are almost always written in the first-person singular to enhance the emotional impact of a "this-happened-to-me" experience. On the other hand, the "Talk of the Town" section of the *New Yorker* is always written with a collective *we,* even when it is obviously the experience of a single person:

Writer's Market: A Peek Behind the Editor's Desk

For more than half a century, Writer's Market *has provided descriptions of magazine formulas for the freelance writer in the editors' own words. Some examples:*

Bronze Thrills, Lexington Library Inc., 355 Lexington Ave., New York, NY 10017. Editor: D. Boyd. 100% freelance written. Eager to work with new/unpublished writers. A bimonthly magazine covering romance and love. Pays on publication. Buys all rights. Pays $75–100.

Fiction: "Stories can be a bit more extraordinary and uninhibited than in our other magazines, but still have to be romantic. For example, we might buy a story about a woman who finds out her husband is a transsexual in *Bronze Thrills,* but not for *Jive* (our younger magazine). The stories for this magazine tend to have a harder, more adult edge of reality than the others."

Compressed Air, 253 E. Washington Ave., Washington, NJ 07882. Editor/Publications Manager: S. M. Parkhill. 75% freelance written. Emphasizes applied technology and industrial management subjects for engineers and managers. Circulation 150,000. Buys 56 manuscripts/year. Pays negotiable fee.

Nonfiction: "Articles must be reviewed by experts in the field. We are presently seeking freelancers with a track record in industrial/technology/management writing. The magazine's name does not reflect its contents. We suggest writers request sample copies."

The Wine Spectator, M. Shanken Communications, Inc., 387 Park Ave. South, New York, NY 10016. Managing Editor: Jim Gordon. 20% freelance written. Twice-monthly consumer news magazine covering wine. Length: 100–2,000 words. Pays $75–$1000.

Nonfiction: General interest (news about wine or wine events); interview/profile (of wine, vintners, wineries); opinion; and photo features. No "winery promotional pieces or articles by writers who lack sufficient knowledge to write below just surface data."

Though most of its space is devoted to magazines, Writer's Market *also lists greeting-card companies that buy lines of verse, along with poetry publications, regional newspapers, book publishers, and foreign markets. Special sections also cover markets for plays, scripts, and short stories.*

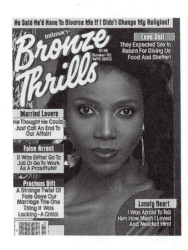

"We picked up our hat and umbrella and headed out into the mist."

Academic texts often use the impersonal *one*, as in "One need only read this." The idea is that *one* will bring a kind of detachment from the subject. What may result is a detachment from the text. In my view, the purpose of any text should be to get the student involved with subject matter.

This is not to say that all textbooks, magazines, newspapers, and printed material should be written the same way. Authors and editors must still make decisions based on what they think is best in a given situation. Still, decisions made on the basis of tradition alone are often blind to the real needs of the reader. The final result is poor communication.

Queries and Concepts

1 Visit your local newsstand or bookstore and browse through the magazine offerings. Select one that appeals to a highly specialized segment of the mass audience. Read through the magazine, and based on the magazine's content (including any advertisements), prepare a description of the publication's "typical reader." Give specific examples to justify your generalizations.

2 What does your favorite magazine supply you with that you can't find anywhere else? Examine a copy of *Writer's Market* (available in most libraries) and look up the listing for that magazine. Do you fit the editor's description of a typical reader?

3 Libraries have bound and microfilm copies of many magazines like *Look* and *Liberty* that have quit publishing. Pick one and read a few issues. Venture some guesses as to why it failed.

4 Is *Playboy* a legitimate magazine or still a "skin" mag? What about *Playgirl?* Does your local library carry either of these? Does your school library? Should it?

5 Pick up the latest copy of *Reader's Digest* and select an article that interests you. Now go to the library to read the original version (most *Digest* articles are severely edited). What parts were omitted? Any guesses as to why? Does this say anything about the editors' perception of the typical *Reader's Digest* subscriber?

6 To which of the top 10 magazines in 5.1 does your school library subscribe? Write a letter asking it to subscribe to one it now overlooks. Justify your choice.

7 Can you think of a particular segment of the mass audience that could be served by a magazine but doesn't seem to be? Describe that audience and the sort of magazine that would appeal to this collection of readers. Prepare a mock-up of the cover for your new magazine. Who knows—you just might have a real moneymaker on your hands!

Readings and References

The Good Old Days

A number of magazine histories have been published. Though many were written 20 or more years ago, each of these books offers a comprehensive look at the early history and development of the magazine during "the good old days":

Frank L. Mott
A History of American Magazines. 5 vols.
Cambridge, Mass.: Harvard University Press,
1957.

Theodore Peterson
Magazines in the Twentieth Century. 2d ed.
Urbana: University of Illinois Press, 1964.

John Tebbel
The American Magazine: A Compact History.
New York: Hawthorn Books, 1969.

Roland Wolseley
Understanding Magazines. Ames: Iowa State
University Press, 1965.

The Changing Magazine. New York: Hastings
House, 1973.

James P. Wood
Magazines in the United States. 3d ed. New
York: Ronald Press, 1971.

These Days:
Magazines Since 1950

J. W. Click
Russel Baird
Magazine Editing and Production. 4th ed.
Dubuque, Iowa: W. C. Brown, 1986.

An overview of the process by which magazines are created. Fairly current and comprehensive. Useful in conjunction with the text by
Friedlander and Lee, listed under "Writing for
Magazines."

Michael Emery
Edwin Emery
The Press and America. 6th ed. Englewood
Cliffs, N.J.: Prentice-Hall, 1988.

The latter chapters of this textbook cover the
rise of many prominent magazines. Excellent
bibliography will lead you to even more
resources.

H. R. Mayes
The Magazine Maze. New York: Doubleday,
1980.

William Taft
American Magazines for the 1980s. New York:
Hastings House, 1982.

For current information, you'll want to check
the *Reader's Guide to Periodical Literature.* Also
indispensible is *Folio: The Magazine for Magazine Management.*

Specialization and Marketing
Trends; The Variety Store
in the 90s

Arthur Asa Berger, ed.
Media U.S.A.: Process and Effect. New York:
Longman, 1988.

This collection of short essays includes a little
something about each of the mass media. Five
chapters on magazines cover everything from
Playboy and *Ms.* to the development of the special-interest audience.

Benjamin Compaine
"The Magazine Industry: Developing the Special Interest Audience." *Journal of Communication,* 1980, vol. 30, no. 2, pp. 98–103.

The best single source for up-to-the-minute
information on magazine marketing, advertising, and readership trends is *Magazines: A
Newsletter of Research.* It is published monthly
by the Magazine Publishers Association, 575
Lexington Avenue, New York, NY 10022. Back
issues are available.

Magazine Industry Market Place (annually published by R. R. Bowker) can be found in the
reference rooms of most libraries. MIMP, as it
is known in the trade, lists all magazines published in the United States by subject matter
and type of publication. In addition, you'll
find information on magazine organizations,
awards, photography, artists and art services,
printing services, and more.

What, No Advertising?

Vincent P. Norris
"*Mad* Economics: An Analysis of an Adless

Magazine." *Journal of Communication,* vol. 34, no. 1, pp. 44–61.

A detailed economic analysis of how *Mad* bucked the system and managed to thrive while spurning advertising support.

Writing for Magazines

Edward Jay Friedlander
John Lee
Feature Writing for Newspapers and Magazines. New York: Harper & Row, 1988.

Writer's Market. Cincinnati: Writer's Digest, annual.

Issues and Answers: Professional Print — The Curious Collective

Robert T. Elson
Time, Inc.: The Intimate History of a Publishing Enterprise, 1923–1941. New York: Atheneum, 1968.

The World of Time Inc.: The Intimate History of a Publishing Enterprise, 1941–1960. New York: Atheneum, 1973.

Elson draws heavily on the *Time* success formula to explain the most popular news magazine of the 20th century. Includes a lot of background on the founders of *Time.* Keep in mind that this project was undertaken under company auspices. Comprehensive index.

James Thurber
The Years with Ross. Boston: Little, Brown, 1959.

James Thurber, one of America's renowned humorists, recalls his years with the *New Yorker* and its founding editor, Harold W. Ross. Until his death in 1951, Ross dominated the magazine. Thurber's insights into that particular "curious collective" are entertaining as well as informative.

Electronic Media:
Edison Came to Stay

Imagine a world without electricity: no lights, no computers, no microwave ovens; no TVs, VCRs, or CD players, not a fax machine or laser printer in sight! Electric circuitry has become more than a convenience; it has re-created our environment and radically altered our life styles. When the electricity failed in New York City in 1965, thousands of incidents of vandalism and looting were reported. Electricity seems to have become part of that thin veneer of civilization that keeps some of us from reverting to our primal selves. From the stock ticker to the coffeemaker, we have come to rely on electricity in virtually every facet of our day-to-day activities.

Electronic media information is not print in electronic form but a brand-new kind of data we are only beginning to understand. In an instant we can find out what the weather will be like this afternoon or what is happening in the Mideast. Mediamerica continues to become Mediaworld. Increasingly we are plugged into a giant worldwide information network that is all-encompassing and all-pervasive.

In this section, the first chapter is devoted to radio. From the early days of "wireless" to its current role as a conveyor belt of pop tunes full of angst and emotion, radio has retained a special, personal relationship with its listeners. As you will see, it has earned its title as "the magic medium."

Chapter 7 is devoted exclusively to "the sound of music." From the earliest phonograph to the latest CD technology, American popular music is a subject largely ignored in most other texts. Like television, popular music is a part of our lives whether we listen or not. So many people are listening that we cannot help being affected. What's more, popular music has become big business, a multi-million-dollar media industry in its own right.

The discussion of television is divided into two chapters: one for the structure of TV in Mediamerica, another for programming. I have devoted a relatively large amount of space to analyzing prime-time commercial television, with the hope that it will help you become a more critical consumer of what you find there each evening.

In Chapter 10 we'll explore the world of feature films. We do not often think of film as an electronic medium, but film does rely on electricity to operate. What's more, the film medium has much in common with television in its use of visual imagery and its consequences in our mass-mediated environment.

Just as Gutenberg is not responsible for all that has happened since the invention of movable type, Edison cannot be held responsible for all the developments since the invention of the light bulb and the phonograph. But he really started something. In that sense, Edison came to stay.

6

Radio: The Magic Medium

Radio affects most people intimately, person to person, offering a world of unspoken communication between writer-speaker and listener.

Marshall McLuhan

The summer I left San Francisco I was determined to make a fresh start and leave the Haight-Ashbury craziness behind. I enrolled as a journalism major at a southern California college. An engineer in a broadcast journalism course tipped me to a copywriting job at KYMS, the local "underground" station. The next morning I was at its door. The station manager was playing the guitar as I entered his office: "Oh — you're the guy about the copywriting job. Got any experience?"

"Sure, I've written a novel, and a lot of poems and short stories. I'm a journalism major and . . ."

He interrupted me. "Is this the easiest job you ever got?"

I gulped — I was actually in radio.

The salary of $250 a month wasn't much, but the job was supposed to be only part-time. Before long I was working 10 to 12 hours a day and juggling classes in between. The only thing I could think about was getting on the air. The thought dominated my mind night and day — I practiced in the car, in bed before I went to sleep at night: "This is *Edward Jay* on KYMS-FM . . . *This* is Edward Jay on KYMS-FM . . . This *is* Edward Jay . . ."

Finally, the big break came: We had been scheduled to go off the air for maintenance between midnight and five, but the engineer was busy; nobody else was available — the program director I had been bugging for months finally

113

came through. Was I ready to give it a try? I'd practiced for 6 months in the production room, but this was the real thing—on the air. Thousands (well, maybe dozens) of people would be listening, and I would be sailing them away on a magic carpet of music, *my* music.

The last thing I needed to worry about was falling asleep. I was so wired all night that I couldn't stop: push a cart here—cue a record there—don't forget the ID on the half hour—not too close to the mike—answer the phone—somebody wants to hear Cream—somebody wants to hear Neil Young—somebody wants to hear Grateful Dead—Jefferson Airplane—Rolling Stones. . . .

By the time morning came, I was both exhausted and jubilant. I don't think there is any way to describe that incredible night. I've done thousands of radio shows since then, but I can recall that one for you record by record, mistake by mistake. Radio is that kind of thing—it's magic.

That adrenalin rush still surges today whenever I go into a radio studio to cut a commercial or do an air shift. There is so much to do, so much to remember; and in the true McLuhan spirit, everything happens all at once, all the time, because sound surrounds you. You see only what's in front of you, but you *hear* all around you. Of course, disc jockeys are only a small part of what makes radio work, but they *are* radio for the listener. The deejay represents that real-life link with radio, the magic medium.

Pioneers and Programmers

Several 19th-century inventors paved the way, but credit for the invention of radio is generally given to Lee de Forest (see 6.1 and 6.2). In 1906 he invented a special grid that enabled a vacuum tube to function as an amplifier. This formed the basis for the amplification needed

6.1

Lee de Forest, the father of radio, lived long enough to see his cultural vision for the medium replaced by the commercial system we have today.

to make voice transmission possible via "wireless." The tube itself was the product of the work of Thomas Edison and British inventor John Ambrose Fleming. (Of course, none of this would have been possible had not Guglielmo Marconi successfully sent "wireless" dot and dash signals across the Atlantic Ocean in 1901.)

Surprisingly, at first there was little interest in radio as a commercial vehicle. Most early broadcasters were hobbyists who built their own equipment. When Congress finally passed some radio regulations in 1912, it was to keep private operators from interfering with government communication channels. The American Marconi Company set up several huge sending and receiving stations and successfully transmitted wireless signals across the Atlantic. By the time World War I came along, wireless was well established, and it played an important part in the American victory.

In 1919, after a long series of costly court battles to protect its patents, American Marconi was sold. Its assets became the property of the new Radio Corporation of America (RCA). This gave RCA dominance in the infant industry. Today, RCA is a subsidiary of General Electric, one of the world's largest electronics companies. GE owns the NBC network and TV stations in most of the nation's top markets.

In 1920 Westinghouse obtained a broadcast license and its KDKA went on the air in Pittsburgh. The first broadcast, on November 2, 1920, covered the Harding-Cox election returns. The next day KDKA began offering listeners regularly scheduled programs. Soon many people began to show interest in the new medium; yet, to many more, radio still seemed like a fad, and almost everyone agreed that if any money was to be made in radio, it was in the sale of radio receivers.

American Telephone and Telegraph (AT&T) had a better idea. When AT&T opened its radio station WEAF in New York in the summer of 1922, someone decided that radio was really an extension of the telephone. AT&T charged for telephone calls, so why not charge people to talk on the radio? A Long Island real-estate firm bought 10 minutes of air time to tell listeners about available properties, and the response was said to be good. Radio advertising was born. By the end of the decade, WEAF was grossing almost $1 million a year in "toll charges." It didn't take other stations long to get the message. Soon the airwaves were flooded with advertisements for everything from gasoline to hair oil. It's been that way ever since.

In 1922 AT&T had also began to experimentally link up stations for simultaneous broadcasting. Suddenly a *network* was possible. This development had a tremendous impact on advertising practices and on the listening habits of Americans. More important, it paved the way for the coast-to-coast broadcasting system that followed.

The Golden Age of Radio (1926–48)

In 1922 RCA's David Sarnoff (see 6.3) wrote a memo to his staff arguing that the novelty of radio was wearing off; to persuade people to keep buying radio sets, better programs would have to be offered. Sarnoff's idea was a revolutionary one. Why not a "specialized organization with a competent staff capable of meeting the task of entertaining the nation"?

In 1926 RCA formed the National Broadcasting Company (NBC) "to provide the best programs available for broadcasting in the United States." It was so successful that NBC formed a second network a year later to accommodate increasing listener demand. The two "chains" were identified by the color of pens used to trace their paths in stockholders' meetings, the *red* and *blue* networks. Initially they linked only the Midwest and the eastern seaboard, but by the end of 1927 NBC had leased a transcontinental wire to bring its programs to the West Coast. Simultaneous coast-to-coast broadcasting was a reality.

Young Bill Paley, the 26-year-old heir to the Congress Cigar Company, was fascinated by the way radio advertising had boosted his father's cigar business. In 1928 he bought a controlling interest in the Columbia Phonograph Broadcasting System, a 16-station "network" that then dared to challenge the mighty NBC. The number of affiliates grew to 47 by the end of the year. Nevertheless, despite Paley's efforts during the 1920s and 1930s, NBC's two networks aired the most popular radio shows. During that time, a number of other small networks tried to challenge NBC's dominance, but none was entirely successful. After CBS, the Mutual Broadcasting System probably came closest, thanks largely to several popular shows, including "The Lone Ranger."

1906

Lee de Forest adds his "audion" grid, which makes the vacuum tube function as an amplifier. Voice transmission is now possible over wireless.

1925

President Coolidge's inauguration is heard coast to coast through a 21-station hookup.

1900   **1920**

1901 Marconi is successful in sending "wireless" signals across the Atlantic Ocean.

1919 Radio Corporation of America (RCA) is formed.

1920 Westinghouse obtains a license for KDKA, Pittsburgh, the first radio station to offer continuous, regularly scheduled programs. KDKA covers the presidential election.

1922 WEAF, New York, begins selling air time to advertisers, opening the door for advertiser-supported electronic media.

1926 AT&T sells out its radio interest; NBC eventually gains control.

1927 The Radio Act of 1927 is passed, and the Federal Radio Commission (FRC) is established.

1927 The United Independent Broadcasters radio network, later named CBS, airs its first broadcast; it is heard from Boston to St. Louis.

1928 *Amos 'n' Andy* begins, eventually becomes the first successful radio situation comedy.

6.2 The History of American Radio

1949

Todd Storz buys Omaha's ailing KOWH and develops the first "Top 40" radio format.

1930

1931 The FRC refuses to renew the license of KFKB in Milford, Kansas, citing dishonest programming as the reason.

1932 Al Jarvis' "Make-Believe Ballroom" on KFWB, Los Angeles, becomes the first successful deejay show.

1933 President Franklin D. Roosevelt begins his radio fireside chats, speaking directly to the American people.

1933 Edwin Armstrong, the father of FM radio, applies for patents for "frequency modulation," and a new kind of radio service is born.

1934 The Communications Act of 1934 includes provisions for a new seven-member Federal Communications Commission (FCC) to regulate radio, television, and telephone communication.

1935 Martin Block's version of the "Make-Believe Ballroom" is a big success at New York's WNEW.

1937 Herb Morrison's recording of the *Hindenberg* airship disaster becomes one of the most dramatic events in radio history.

1938 Orson Welles' fictional "War of the Worlds" creates panic among thousands of radio listeners; a government investigation follows.

1939 First experimental FM station goes on the air in New Jersey.

1940

1940 A federal court of appeals rules that records purchased by radio stations may be played on the air with no prior consent from record companies or artists.

1943 NBC sells its second network, which eventually becomes ABC, the third major network.

1945 The FCC encourages the development of television, to the detriment of FM radio.

1948 Radio's biggest money year; from here on, television begins to take a larger share of advertising revenues.

1949 The FCC allows licensees to present editorials as part of regular programming and requires time for opposing views.

1955

Bill Haley and Comets' "Rock Around the Clock" becomes the first rock 'n' roll hit to make it to number one. The rock era of radio begins.

1970

The FCC issues a statement warning that broadcasters are liable for obscene or drug-related lyrics in songs they air.

1950

1951 Hundreds of radio stations switch to the deejay format and scramble to make up for lost revenues as network feeds diminish.

1959 With the payola scandal uncovered, deejays admit receiving money to "plug" certain records. The rise of the program director follows.

1960

1966 KSAN-FM in San Francisco and KPPC-FM in Los Angeles become the first "underground" FM stations, playing album cuts. Deejays are again given power to select music.

1968 ABC radio successfully breaks into various "networks" with news, information, and entertainment designed for specialized audiences.

1970

1972 All-news formats are successful in New York, Washington, and Los Angeles.

1975 Don Imus, controversial and often abusive New York deejay, snares top ratings in the nation's most competitive radio market.

1978 Pressure for a new Communications Act mounts in Congress, but most broadcasters are reluctant.

6.2 (continued)

1981

The FCC "deregulates" radio, allowing stations to discontinue public-service programming and exceed 18 commercial minutes per hour if they choose.

1980

1980 The FCC creates a furor when it proposes to restructure the AM and FM bands and to allow many new stations on the air.

1982 More and more AM stations switch to talk as FM dominates music programming.

1984 MTV (Music Television) plays an increasingly larger role in determining FM music playlists.

1986 Seventy percent of all radio listeners are tuned to FM. As recently as 1973, the AM band had 70% of the listeners.

1987 The FCC issues new guidelines regarding the airing of sexually explicit material.

1988 The new-age format is the latest radio trend, appealing to upscale yuppie listeners.

1989 The FCC revokes the license of a New York radio station when the owner is found to be practicing blatant racial discrimination.

1990

1990 Modern rock replaces "new music" as the latest label for cutting-edge rock and roll radio.

1992 The nation-wide recession sends radio ad revenues spiraling downward.

1994 Record-breaking network radio revenues top $46 million, signal end of recession.

1995 Music from the 70s is a hit all over again, thanks to outlets such as New York's WPLJ-FM. Nationwide, over 100 stations now offer the 70s' format. Meanwhile, national Arbitron figures indicate Top 40 is also making a comeback.

David Sarnoff Broadcasts the Disaster of the Decade, or Does He?

As legend has it, young David Sarnoff, one of Marconi's most capable operators, was on duty in a New York store called Wanamaker's the fateful night of April 14, 1912. Suddenly, a faint message came through from the S.S. *Olympic,* a ship some 1,400 miles away: "S.S. *Titanic* ran into iceberg. Sinking fast."

Sarnoff, so the story goes, alerted the press and kept listening for more details. For 3 days and nights he received and transmitted messages. There was little time for food or sleep. The first reports included names of survivors. Later came the long list of casualties. Sarnoff's wireless became the nation's information link with the disaster of the decade.

The *Titanic* was the pride of British shipbuilders, who thought her unsinkable. This made the news all the more amazing, and word of the disaster spread quickly. Many amateur radio transmitters were soon trying to make contact with the sinking ship. Never before had the country been so completely dependent on electronic technology. Eventually, new regulations would be passed to make sure that all ships were equipped with proper wireless devices and that an operator was on duty at all times.

Fifteen hundred lives were lost on the *Titanic,* but ironically, of all those important people, few are remembered today. What is remembered is the way America found out about the disaster. The power of radio was suddenly evident. Newspapers took their information directly from radio. Many years later Sarnoff recalled, "The *Titanic* disaster brought radio to the front . . . and incidentally me." Interestingly, when the remains of the *Titanic* were finally located in 1987, they became the basis for a syndicated television special, "Return to the Titanic."

Though the impact of wireless on the reporting of the sinking is undisputed, the extent of Sarnoff's role has been debated. For years every historical account of the incident portrayed Sarnoff's role as pivotal. However, in his 1986 biography of Sarnoff, *The General,* Kenneth Bilby reveals that it was Sarnoff himself who had originated the tale of his 72-hour vigil. In fact, Wanamaker's had been closed when the *Titanic* went down and neither the *New York Times* nor the *Herald Tribune* mentioned Sarnoff's name in their exhaustive accounts of the details surrounding the disaster.

Perhaps we will never know the whole truth of the matter. But one thing is certain. The lesson of the *Titanic* was not lost on the young David Sarnoff. The 21-year-old who was there when the importance of wireless was first dramatized to the nation went on to become the driving force behind RCA and the National Broadcasting Company.

NBC's greatest hit in the early days was "Amos 'n' Andy." It was a situation comedy of sorts, featuring the adventures of a group of black workers, one of whom owned the Fresh Air Taxicab Company. The show was loaded with black stereotypes. Ironically, the voices of Amos and Andy were those of two white men.

Probably the most popular genres of radio entertainment during the golden age were the mystery and action-adventure series. Among the most successful were "Gangbusters," "Calling All Cars," "Ellery Queen," "The Fat Man," "Sam Spade," "The FBI in Peace and War," and "The Green Hornet." The action-adventure format has been carried on by TV shows like "Hunter" and "Sweating Bullets."

Like daytime TV today, daytime radio had its soap operas, including "Our Gal Sunday," "The Romance of Helen Trent," and "Pepper Young's Family." For the kids there were "Jack

Armstrong, the All-American Boy," "Superman," "Uncle Don," and of course, "The Lone Ranger." There were quiz and talk shows as well. If all of these formats sound familiar, it's because television borrowed heavily from radio. In fact, virtually every format that would appear later on television was developed on radio during this fertile period.

Radio was the magic medium, and everybody loved it. Listeners from coast to coast could hear symphonic music (and fill in the visual picture with their imagination) from the great concert halls in Boston, or they could be transported to the Grand Ballroom at the Waldorf-Astoria Hotel in New York City, where the big bands performed. For those who lived in rural isolation, radio provided a link with the outside world. The magic medium brought everyone into the cultural and social mainstream of Mediamerica.

Of course, entertainment was not the only way radio served the American people. It continued to be what it had been since KDKA broadcast the 1920 election returns, a way to keep people informed. President Franklin Roosevelt made the most of the medium in the early 1930s, speaking directly to his constituents and urging them to support his new and controversial programs (see 6.4). His "fireside chats" gathered most Americans around the radio.

Radio also made Americans acutely aware of current events in Europe in the late 1930s and early 1940s. Broadcasters like Eric Sevareid and Edward R. Murrow were on the scene, bringing listeners the sounds of war as they happened. Murrow's reports from London during the bombing were the ultimate in believability—bombs exploded in the background as he reported the latest war news. Those pre–Pearl Harbor broadcasts by Murrow prepared Americans for the war to come. Sentiment shifted rapidly from neutrality to a full commitment to the United Kingdom by 1941. Somehow, the war did not seem very far away, and radio was the reason.

6.4

President Franklin Delano Roosevelt often spoke on the air to bring his message to the people.

The significance of radio as an arbiter of the national mood was brought home to many in 1938 when the "Mercury Theater on the Air" broadcast its anxiety-provoking "War of the Worlds" production (see 6.5).

NBC's reign as king of network radio suffered a serious blow in 1941 when the FCC moved to ban the operation of two networks by one company. A 1943 Supreme Court decision upheld the FCC's position, and NBC sold its blue network for $7 million to Edward Noble, who renamed it the American Broadcasting Company.

NBC radio stars began to defect to CBS in the 1940s, lured away by "Bill Paley's checkbook." The CBS president offered big-money contracts to Jack Benny, George Burns and

War of the Worlds and World War

October 30, 1938, was a rainy night over most of America. In Europe, Hitler was invading Czechoslovakia and turning his eyes toward Poland. There was a definite tension in the air. Millions of Americans tuned in their radios to CBS' "Mercury Theater on the Air." Instead, they heard a late news bulletin: Aliens had landed in New Jersey—America was being invaded by men from Mars!

Thousands of calls poured in to newspapers and radio stations—was it true? Were there really men from Mars? Army personnel were called back to their bases—this could be serious.

Orson Welles' production of H. G. Wells' "War of the Worlds" set off a genuine panic. There were traffic jams near the "landing site," and many people reported spotting the aliens. Public reaction was overwhelming. Some listeners had tuned in late—many had a habit of listening to the opening dialogue between ventriloquist Edgar Bergen and dummy Charlie McCarthy on NBC before tuning in to the play. This added to the confusion. Welles attempted to avert disaster by broadcasting repeated warnings that this fictional radio play was not to be taken seriously; it was only *entertainment*.

That broadcast has been called the most famous of all radio entertainment programs, and perhaps it was. It is certainly the one that had the greatest *immediate* impact on its listeners. The FCC investigated, and new regulations were passed: There would be no more fictional news bulletins.

In a larger context, *War of the Worlds* demonstrated the awesome power of radio. No newspaper or magazine had the ability to evoke such immediate emotional response. Radio was an infant medium, but many people began to wonder—this could be more than just an entertainment device after all.

Gracie Allen, Ozzie and Harriet Nelson, Red Skelton, Bing Crosby, and others, establishing CBS as the top network in the late 1940s and forming a nucleus of talent for its new television network as well.

The Big Change: Radio After Television

When television arrived, comedienne Gracie Allen observed that "it seems like nobody watches radio anymore." Many new TV stations were put on the air by the owners of newspapers and lucrative radio stations. Radio lost a tremendous amount of revenue to the newer broadcast medium.

Just as many people think the "good old days" of magazines are gone forever, some contend that radio will never be what it was during the golden age. In a way, they're right—though some remnants of the golden age still linger (see 6.6). The magic medium spins a different kind of spell today. It has undergone tremendous change.

By the mid-1950s, television had captured many radio programs and radio stars. An industry-wide panic took hold in radio. In their heyday, national radio networks provided programs from 9:00 A.M. to 11:00 P.M. Local stations simply pulled the switch and raked in the profits. As network offerings declined, the locals looked for the least expensive format that would allow them to stay on the air and sell advertising time. The day of the deejay had arrived.

Of course, music had been played on radio since the beginning, and as early as 1932, Los Angeles radio personality Al Jarvis began play-

Garrison Keillor: Lake Wobegon's Tall Tale Teller

For 13 years, until June 1987, each Saturday at 5:00 P.M. midwestern time, some 2 million listeners gathered round their radios, much as they had half a century before, to catch the latest from the mythical town of Lake Wobegon. This Minnesota community was described as a place where "all the women are strong, all the men are good-looking, and all the children are above average." If this seemed like unlikely stuff for a 1980s hit radio show, it was, but if you ever got a chance to listen to American Public Radio's "Prairie Home Companion," perhaps you understand.

Sponsored by the mythical Powdermilk Biscuits ("Heavens, they're tasty!"), "A Prairie Home Companion" created the effect of being in a time capsule. You see, Lake Wobegon was "the place that time forgot and the decades cannot improve." Its creator, 46-year-old Garrison Keillor, is a shy, soft-spoken Minnesotan whose rambling monologues have earned him comparisons to other notable American humorists like Mark Twain, James

Thurber, and E. B. White. His 1985 book *Lake Wobegon Days* became the publishing sensation of the year. A second book of Lake Wobegon tales, *Leaving Home,* also enjoyed success.

As to the exact location of Lake Wobegon, Keillor explains that early surveyors "mapped Minnesota in quadrants and when it turned out that there was some overlap, the State Legislature dealt with this by canceling the overlap, which happened to include Lake Wobegon."

Raised in a fundamentalist sect that "abhorred dancing . . . and went to church twice on Sundays," Keillor knew well the small-town life he described each Saturday evening, and he talked fondly of the family storyteller who kept everyone enthralled with tales of turn-of-the-century Minnesota: "I remember Uncle Lew's stories not coming to a point really, but to a point of rest, a point of contemplation."

Striding onto the stage in St. Paul where he did the show live each week, this six-foot-four farm boy became the unlikely hero to a generation of listeners who felt they knew

Lake Wobegon as well as they knew their own neighborhood. Though Keillor ended the show in 1987 "to resume the life of a shy person," its impact lingered. Eventually he agreed to return to public radio, where his new show "The American Radio Company" can be heard each week.

Keillor admits that the role of caretaker of an American time and place long since vanished is one he relished. In a rare serious moment he once remarked, "For children who have a great deal of curiosity about what happened before they came along, I'm willing to work hard."

---

ing a few records from a tiny studio at KFWB that he called "The World's Largest Make-Believe Ballroom." KFWB library assistant Martin Block noted the success of the show, moved to New York, and presented the idea to his skeptical bosses at WNEW. When they balked, he arranged sponsorship for the show himself.

By 1935 it was on the air at WNEW and enjoying good ratings.

A key ingredient in the "make-believe ballroom" formula was the personality of the disc jockey. Prior to this time, announcers simply read the names of records like they read poetry or news, in detached pear-shaped tones. Jarvis

Entertainment Radio in the 1950s: More Than an Afterglow of the Golden Age

While many radio stations bailed out of entertainment programming and got into music via the deejay after TV arrived, a number of network radio offerings in the 1950s carried on the golden-age tradition. Huber Ellingsworth believes that the golden age and the modern format systems were not as incompatible as some would have us believe. Dr. Ellingsworth is currently a professor of communication at the University of Tulsa.

The decade of 1950–1960 was unique in American broadcasting because it offered the public a choice between network entertainment programming on radio and television. There was in no sense a fair competition for audiences, because the networks had already announced that they would close

down entertainment radio as soon as possible, and they undertook extensive print advertising to lure listeners to the new visual medium. New radio programs were not publicized and promoted, and it became increasingly difficult to find program schedules. But a determined group of network radio executives, producers, advertisers, and listeners kept "foreground radio" alive until Black Thursday (Thanksgiving Day, 1960), when the last programs were arbitrarily terminated amid a storm of protest.

In the interim, radio networks offered a full programming schedule that included many new programs of remarkable quality, variety, and originality. These supplemented long-running series continued from the so-called Golden Age (1926–1948). The new burst of creativity came about for a variety of reasons. The development of audiotape meant shows could be easily edited, and there were newer, more

sophisticated sound mixing and dubbing techniques. The loosening of artistic control by national sponsors was another factor. In addition, there was more local sponsorship, and a change from a mass one-medium audience to smaller, more discerning groups of listeners composed mostly of adults. All these factors combined to generate opportunities never before available. So entertainment radio reached its maturity at the wrong time, for many of the wrong reasons.

The genres of the adult Western and the police detective show were explored, and became the basis for later exploitation in television. Certainly the best adult Western, and perhaps the most artistically superior radio series ever produced, was "Gunsmoke." Marshal Dillon (William Conrad) stayed alive by shooting first and talking later. And when he rode into Dodge after days on the trail and growled,

and Block were far more animated, injecting their own personalities into the process.

Though the format proved successful, there were also problems. Performers fought airing of their songs on radio, fearing it would dilute the product and make record purchases unnecessary. In 1940, however, a federal appeals court ruled that broadcasters who had bought a record could play it on the air without obtaining prior permission from the artist, though some compensation had to be paid.

The idea of mixing records, personality, chatter, and commercials was just what radio

stations needed in the early 1950s. Before long, the local disc-jockey format had replaced network programs as radio's most common commodity.

During the mid-1950s, the transistor reduced the size and price of the portable radio. Now it was truly the medium that "goes where you go." What's more, Americans *were* on the go. A record number of cars were sold during the period, and most of them were equipped with radios. The most popular deejays appeared in "drive time" from 6:00 to 9:00 A.M. and from 3:00 to 6:00 P.M., keeping com-

"Where's Kitty?", listeners knew why he was asking. Kitty (Georgia Ellis) ran a tough saloon, the Long Branch, with rooms upstairs definitely not operated by Sheraton. Life was hard and violent and people died of wounds, starvation, freezing, and childbirth, sometimes aided by hard-drinking Doc Adams. A later TV version of this program portrayed Dillon as a gun-toting frontier psychiatrist who brought order and mental health to the snow-capped mountain region of central Kansas. The TV Dillon hung out at the Long Branch YMCA, which inexplicably served liquor but was kept respectable by housemother Miss Kitty.

The long tradition of radio drama was continued and enhanced by a number of BBC imports, including Shakespeare plays and a Sherlock Holmes series. Documentaries and public-service programs included "Capitol Cloakroom," "Meet the Press," and an ambitious series of hour-long "Biographies in Sound." Light entertainment came from "What's My Line," "College Quiz Bowl," and Groucho Marx's "You Bet Your Life." There was news analysis by Edward R. Murrow, Howard K. Smith, and Lowell Thomas.

Comedy, one of the brightest spots, was generated by Bob and Ray, who were heard throughout the decade on NBC, CBS, and Mutual. "The Goon Show," a BBC import with Peter Sellers, Terry-Thomas, and Spike Milligan, was carried on NBC, as well as an occasional Stan Freberg special.

The sharpest contrast with current TV and radio programming philosophy was the richness of programming for the classical-music audience. To counter NBC's live broadcasts of the New York Philharmonic, CBS created its own symphony orchestra, while ABC carried Metropolitan Opera performances live.

Perhaps the fullest realization of entertainment radio's unique capabilities was in NBC's weekend "Monitor," which began in 1954. It was an easy mix of live and recorded music, comedy, reviews, interviews, commentary, news, and weather (sultry-voiced Miss Monitor always began with "In Atlanta, the temperature is . . ."). Mike Wallace was one of several New York anchors, and there were segments from six major cities. Comedy was the chief attraction, based around Bob and Ray, with sketches by Bob Newhart, Mike Nichols and Elaine May, Bill Cosby, Stan Freberg, and others. It did require listening, but it was easy listening; stations and listeners could drop in and out.

For ten years listeners had a choice, and enough of them chose radio that it was still producing a tidy financial profit at the end. Some of what it supplied has never been replaced, and American society is the poorer for it.

muters company to and from work. Drive time became radio's prime time and gave the medium a much-needed financial boost. The deejays — colorful, provocative, and eccentric — were largely responsible for keeping radio alive.

Meet the Deejay

Though I have had professional experience in many areas of mass media, it is my years as a Los Angeles deejay that seem to provoke the most questions from students. What are deejays really like?

Real-life deejays are sometimes the proud possessors of giant egos. At the risk of generalizing, many of the male deejays I've known were 5 or 6 inches shorter than the norm and had three things in common. They were generally insecure, usually divorced, and almost always hyperactive.

One Los Angeles disc jockey refuses to take a vacation. He works 52 weeks a year because each of his last three vacations cost him his job. Program directors slotted in a newer, younger, and lower-paid deejay in his place. When the listeners liked the new voice, the old one was off to the unemployment line. Being on the air is a risky business, because there is always someone willing to do your job for less, or even for nothing.

One reason disc jockeys are often divorced is that many stations are swarming with "groupies." The deejay, whether male or female, is likely to be accosted by these warm and loving creatures at any moment. The groupie is usually young and is always caught up in the magic of the music and the people who play it on the radio.

My father did a radio show in Portland, Oregon, during the late 1930s, and I once asked him whether there were groupies even then. He confirmed that there were, smiled quietly, and got a faraway look in his eyes. Finally he added that most of them wanted to be vocalists with a band but would settle for a love affair with a disc jockey.

Hyperactivity, the third professional trait, is a necessity. Deejays must be able to play a cart (a tape cartridge with a commercial or pre-recorded message), cue up a CD, give the time and temperature, and answer the phone—all at the same time. They must do it smoothly so that the listener never senses the frenzy (see 6.7). As far as the listeners know, the deejay is listening to the music right along with them. TV viewers of "WKRP in Cincinnati" are often given a fairly accurate picture of how hectic things can get in the control room.

In the early 1950s, disc jockeys programmed their own shows, selecting the records and planning whatever additional material they wanted. In recent years, the program directors and format consultants have taken over, dictating the content of the show right down to the last supposed ad-lib. The rise of the program director came in response to the payola scandal of the late 1950s. Once record companies discovered that air play boosted record sales, they started sending disc jockeys cases of liquor, free passes to concerts and films, and finally lump cash sums (or payola)

to "promote" a song. Eventually a 1959 government investigation led to a brief rift in the public's love affair with the deejay.

Though it has diminished, the payola problem still exists. One record industry executive admitted privately to me, "It's a lot cheaper to get to one program director than to get to half a dozen jocks." "Drug-ola"—the exchange of drugs for preferential treatment of a song—is not unknown in major markets.

The authoritarian rule of the program director was challenged briefly by the appearance of the "underground" FM stations in the late 1960s. These stations played longer album cuts instead of singles, and control by a program director did not fit with their "loose and free" image. For a short time, these disc jockeys were given back the freedom to select the songs they aired. The program director's role was limited to riding herd on the often erratic deejays, who would sometimes forget a commercial or swear on the air. The commercial success of some underground formats led to the similar but slicker and more organized so-called progressive stations, which reinstated the program director's power to select the music.

Of course, all markets are different. At many small stations the deejay may pick all the music, and there may not even be a program director. But even this is changing as small-market owners increasingly rely on pre-recorded or satellite-transmitted syndicated shows. Such programming is often cheaper than hiring live deejays. Deejays, themselves a product of a big change, are finding that recent changes in radio technology are drastically altering their role in radio programming.

The People You Never Hear

To most listeners, the commercial radio world consists of the disc jockey and the newscaster. But the real world of radio is quite different.

The on-the-air people may represent only 10–15% of the total staff of most stations. In metro markets they may make up less than 10% (see 6.8). Who are the rest of the people?

Management personnel are at the top of the ladder. Each station has an owner or owners and a general manager (GM), who supervises all station activities. The GM's word is law. Under the GM are the heads of the major departments.

Programming is the first department you might think of. The program director (PD) keeps track of air personnel, schedules shifts, and is responsible for all on-air content. It is the PD's job to make sure that air personalities are slotted in at the proper times to elicit maximum audience response. If the ratings for the entire station are poor, the format may be changed and the PD is likely to go.

Sales is often the most financially rewarding of all station jobs. Usually, salespeople have a small guaranteed salary, but they make up the difference by selling air time on commission. If they don't sell, they don't eat. A sales director or sales manager who reports directly to the GM is usually in charge. Major markets may have a few highly paid on-air stars, but at most stations it is the salespeople who take home the biggest paychecks.

Traffic is the department least known to the average radio listener. The traffic staff must schedule all the commercials. Station policy usually dictates a fixed number each hour, and competing products must not be placed back to back. It wouldn't be good business to play a spot urging listeners to "buy a Chevrolet today" right after one that said "Ford has a better idea!" Traffic people devise the program logs, minute-by-minute lists of all commercials and other nonmusic materials. Air staff and engineers follow these logs exactly.

Engineers are usually found poking around with screwdrivers and soldering irons, repairing broken equipment. Most stations have a chief engineer who reports directly to the GM. Engineers are responsible for the operation of the transmitter and must make sure the sta-

6.7

Life on the air can be frantic, but the best deejays make it look easy.

tion's signal conforms to various FCC regulations. They can often be heard muttering (with some justification) that nobody notices them "until something goes wrong."

The *production* department is vital to the overall "sound" of the station. Copywriters and on-air "talent" produce the jingles, IDs, promos, and most important, local commercials. A salesperson will sell time to a local merchant and then order a spot for production. A copywriter works with information supplied by the salesperson. The talent goes into the studio and reads the spot. Larger stations have an engineer who works exclusively in production. At a smaller station the copywriter, talent, and engineer may be the same person. At a very small station, that person may do the selling as well.

Large metro stations have separate departments for editorials, publicity or promotion, public relations, and so on. Still, most of the 11,000 or so radio stations in America have fewer than 50 employees—and there never seems to be enough people to get all the work done.

As with other media outlets, the atmosphere of most radio stations is frantic. From morning to night, everyone is on the go, writing commercials and getting things on the air at the last minute. Coffee is the precious fuel

The people you never hear can sometimes be found even in the control room.

that makes radio work; I've never been in a radio station that didn't have a gigantic coffeepot in need of constant refilling. Chaos just seems to be the nature of the medium. Almost everyone who works in radio complains about it, but no one would really have it any other way.

In direct contrast are the "automated" stations, where all music and talk is selected by a computer. Today such formats may be linked to a satellite feed. The atmosphere in the automated stations is more like that of a library or a museum.

Music Formats

In previous chapters, we have seen that each mass medium presents a constructed mediated reality (CMR) that is quite different from real-life experience. The specific CMR is the reason we are attracted to a particular medium. For most radio stations, music dominates that CMR.

Although no two radio stations are exactly alike, a number of basic formulas exist. These formulas, or *formats*, involve a specific blend of certain types of music and talk designed to attract a large, desirable audience to the station. Radio formats are not permanent things but are constantly being adjusted as management perception of audience needs evolves.

Nevertheless, programming constraints often leave commercial radio ignorant of the cutting edge of musical trends. It always takes some time for new styles to catch on with the mass audience. When they do, you can be sure some innovative radio programmers somewhere will find a way to fit them into current programming.

Disco music was quite popular in the mid-1970s, but it took several years before disco formats began to appear. Ironically, by the time "all-disco" radio had gotten under way, the disco craze had cooled. A similar cycle occurred with the coming of rap music in the 1980s. NWA and 2 Live Crew may generate large retail sales, but their music is rarely heard on commercial radio.

Another example involved punk and new-wave music. Punk pioneers like the Sex Pistols and the Ramones were played little, if at all, by established rock stations in the mid- and late 1970s. Today, while former counterculture groups like Metallica may enjoy mainstream airplay and MTV exposure, the darker sounds of heavy-metal groups such as Megadeath, Slayer, and Prong are largely excluded from mainstream rock formats.

Occasionally a commercial station will follow the lead of a college station. KUSF-FM, the station licensed to the University of San Francisco, offered punk and new-wave music in the late 1970s. By 1982 a new-wave format had emerged along with a large and loyal audience. Finally the city's commercial KQAK adopted a similar format, and soon several other commercial rock stations began adding more new music to their playlists. However, KQAK ultimately failed, as did many commercial "new music" format stations across the country during this period. There were simply not enough new-music fans to sustain the format.

The basic formats of radio cover a wide spectrum of listener needs and tastes. Some, like classical, are tried and true and have been around since the beginning of broadcasting. Others, like new age, are relatively recent and experimental. In each case, the goal is to get and hold as many listeners as possible, particularly those with desirable demographics, or audience characteristics. With that in mind, here are the formats reflecting the radio trends of the 1990s.

CHR: Contemporary Hit Radio

Hot hits, CHR, Top 40—by any name this jukebox method of radio programming has seen its ups and downs over the years. Credit for the creation of the format is generally given to Todd Storz, who convinced his father to purchase Omaha's ailing KOWH in 1949. While sitting in a restaurant one afternoon he observed the patrons putting money into a jukebox to listen to the same songs over and over. "Why can't radio be like a jukebox?" he asked himself. At that moment "Top 40" radio was born. Success came swiftly and soon young Storz was running a string of Top 40 stations all over the Midwest.

Top 40 reigned supreme on the airwaves from the mid-1950s until album-oriented rock found success in the early 1970s. It appeared that Top 40 would die with the decrease in AM listeners in the 1970s, but a new, less cluttered version appeared on FM in the early 1980s. Dubbed CHR or hot hits, this "new" format became the rage on the FM dial and by the mid-1980s was enjoying healthy ratings in New York (WPLJ), Los Angeles (KIIS), Chicago (WLS), and many other markets.

The Top 40 genre spawned some giants. Bill Drake's success came in the early 1960s with KHJ, a Los Angeles Top 40 station. While sitting by his pool at Malibu Beach, he picked the songs that were to be played on his station. His method was simple: Play only the very top singles, and play them more often than anyone else.

Another giant is Casey Kasem, who helped form Watermark Productions to begin his syndicated "American Top 40" in 1970. Kasem got his hits from the number one authority in the industry, *Billboard* magazine. Every week he "counted 'em down in order" for millions of listeners in hundreds of cities from New York to Newberg, Oregon. Kasem's show was also heard in Europe and Asia. His trademark was airing little-known facts about stars, along with his final advice to listeners each week: "Keep your feet on the ground, and keep reaching for the stars."

Kasem parted company with "AT40" in a contract dispute in 1988 and was replaced by Shadoe Stevens. The show survived, but before long there was some new, yet familiar competition. Today "Casey's Top 40" reaches some 8 million listeners worldwide and is the premiere countdown show in an industry that *Newsweek* estimates generates about $50 million in annual ad revenues. There are other countdown shows of course, from country to Hispanic to R&B. Even trivia buff Dr. Demento offers a countdown of the week's "most demented tunes." Nevertheless, there remains only one Casey Kasem "counting 'em down in order" for his loyal listeners around the world.

Album-Oriented Rock

Album-oriented rock began in the late 1960s when it became evident that a growing number of rock enthusiasts were tired of the limitations of Top 40. Rebellious deejays contended that the more innovative rock music was not getting on the air because songs were often too long or too controversial to fit on tight Top 40 playlists.

The founding father of AOR is generally acknowledged to be Tom "Big Daddy" Donahue, a dissatisfied Top 40 deejay who left a successful job at San Francisco's KYA to start a new kind of radio, first at that city's KMPX-FM and later at KSAN-FM. Donahue and his irrepressible (some would say irresponsible) deejays would play anything that struck their fancy, and that was a lot. In the early days, it was not unusual to hear a 15-minute "home tape" of the Grateful Dead sandwiched between an esoteric sitar piece by Ravi Shankar and a song by the Jefferson Airplane extolling the virtues of an illegal drug. Because the music and the deejays' comments often centered on counter-culture themes, the format was initially dubbed "underground radio."

At first, most underground stations struggled for listeners, advertising dollars, and respectability. What's more, many stations were found on the then less-popular FM dial. Corporate owners responded by bringing in more conservative program directors who fired radical deejays and instituted mainstream-oriented playlists. The result was dubbed "progressive" radio for a time, and its popularity was buoyed by the rise of FM. Progressive radio eventually evolved into album-oriented rock in the 1970s.

Many AOR stations still feature heavy-duty rock, but as the counterculture generation aged, its music tastes mellowed. Elton John seems right at home in most of today's AOR stations, yet listeners can also hear everything from Stevie Wonder to Def Leppard and Neil Young to U2.

"Mellow rock," an oxymoron of sorts, began making inroads in the mid-1970s. Sometimes called "easy rock," mellow-rock stations feature music from the softer side of the rock spectrum by such artists as the Beatles, Elton John, Lionel Richie, Dan Fogelberg, James Taylor, and Phil Collins.

"Classic rock" is yet another version of AOR. Highly popular with the baby-boomer crowd, this AOR variant prominently features the 60s-oriented sounds of the Beatles, the Rolling Stones, and Jimi Hendrix, deftly blended with more current boomer favorites like Bob Seger, U2, and Tom Petty. Whatever the permutation, AOR remains rock's most popular musical format.

New Music/Modern Rock

A recent and innovative rock format is *new music*, or *modern rock*, generally found on FM. The distinctions between these and AOR stations are sometimes difficult to discern. How-

ever, the emergence of punk, new-wave, and new-music songs in the late 1970s and early 1980s generated a tremendous interest in and enthusiasm for rock that had not been seen since the 1960s (see Chapter 7). A few stations, mostly in major markets, responded to this interest by featuring what they called "new music" exclusively.

Arbitron research suggests that modern rock, featuring everything from mainstream artists like U2 and R.E.M. to the more esoteric sounds of Smashing Pumpkins and the Red Hot Chili Peppers, appeals primarily to a younger audience. About three quarters of the listeners are in the coveted 18-to-34 age bracket. Once confined primarily to the college stations, modern rock can now be found on about 75 commercial outlets, offering advertisers an excellent chance to tap into the elusive youth market.

Modern rock also appears to be capturing disaffected album rock listeners. One 1994 Arbitron survey indicated that while the national share of album rock listeners had dropped from 9.5 to 8.9%, modern rock had increased its share from 1.0 to 1.8%

Currently, the Honolulu and San Diego markets each boast two competing modern rock stations, with both earning respectable audience shares.

Urban Contemporary

In the early 1980s, the term *urban contemporary* became commonplace in many markets around the country. The format is often found on CHR-type stations on the AM dial that program a large amount of dance music and upbeat hits to appeal to the black and inner-city audience. Often this audience is heavily populated with teens and young adults.

Many urban contemporary formats evolved from the soul or R&B stations of the 1960s, which appealed predominantly to the black audience, though they were often owned and listened to by nonblacks. San Francisco's KSOL was so successful with urban contemporary that it was, for a time, the city's top-rated music station. There are numerous examples in the Midwest and East Coast as well. Acts such as Hammer, Boyz II Men, and Ice-T currently dominate their playlists.

"Urbancontemp" has been a boon to many AM stations in their ongoing battle with FM competition and is credited with helping the AM band survive. But success breeds imitation in radio, and in markets where the format succeeded it was not too long before one or more FM stations adopted it. As with all music formats, listeners tend to prefer FM over AM because it offers stereo and clearer, static-free reception.

Middle of the Road

MOR radio began as "chicken rock" in the 1950s. Stations afraid of playing the hard-driving sounds of upstarts like Elvis Presley would lean toward the softer love ballads of then-contemporary artists and blend them with songs by the standard crooners like Bing Crosby and Frank Sinatra. As MOR evolved, the idea was to get some young listeners without alienating the older crowd who found the more raucous rock tunes unacceptable. Unlike Top 40 deejays, MOR personalities feature a continual patter between songs in an effort to entertain the audience with their words as well as the music.

Adult Contemporary

Adult contemporary is a blend of MOR and AOR programming. In the 1970s, MOR programmers found their audience growing older and thus less desirable to many advertisers. They spiced up their playlist with soft-rock songs, particularly those that had been popular in the late 1960s and early 1970s, in an attempt to reach the 18- to 34-year-old audience. Most major markets have several stations that call themselves adult contemporary (see 6.9).

Country

Country stations employ what is probably America's most commercially successful radio format. Though rock, with all of its permutations, is the most popular format in Mediamerica, it is the numerous country stations that tend to be most profitable. More than 50% of all popular-music radio stations play some country music. Every major metropolitan market has at least one country station, and the format is common in the rural western states. In the Deep South, it competes with Top 40 and AOR for the highest ratings.

For years it was easy to separate country music from Top 40, but the recent country influence on rock groups has made the distinction less clear. In addition, many country singers have found success on the Top 40 charts. The result has been an introduction to country music for many listeners. Several stations now follow a "pop-corn" formula, alternating rock and country hits, hoping to attract listeners from both camps. Country-music artists like Garth Brooks enjoy huge record sales that rival those of Michael Jackson and Guns N' Roses.

Beautiful Music

Originally called "easy listening" or "good music" by its fans, beautiful music is one of today's most popular radio formats. The music of such artists as Henry Mancini and Mantovani forms the basis for this format, but more adventurous beautiful-music stations may occasionally program a soft vocal track by the Carpenters or Neil Diamond. This trend has become more noticeable of late, because beautiful music, like MOR, appeals to an audience that is growing older.

The secret of the success of beautiful music lies in the nature of radio itself. Often, radio is something we listen to while we're doing something else. It provides a kind of backdrop or sound track for our daily activities.

KABL 98.1 FM 960 AM

A SOUND THAT WORKS!

KABL: Lifestyle Radio

Today's radio listeners have many choices: Bay Area airwaves are full of stations "narrowcasting" to a defined niche in the spectrum of music and/or talk. But KABL has developed a different strategy. Over the years, KABL has established a very special relationship with Bay Area listeners who demand more from a radio station than just music or talk. KABL has developed a unique mixture of personalities, humor, topical information and music that reflects the diversity and richness of life and musical preferences in the Bay Area. Tastes and lifestyles of 25-54 adults in the Bay Area have changed over the years, and so has KABL. But one thing has been constant: KABL has remained firmly rooted in the special flavor of life around the Bay. We know our listeners, and they know KABL as the thoughtful, upbeat, intelligent alternative. What was true 30 years ago is true today; KABL is in touch with the Bay Area.

The Popular Sound Of KABL

KABL has developed a signature sound to achieve a broad musical appeal: a unique mixture of familiar songs whose popularity has been proven over the years through constant research and audience testing. It's no accident: listeners tune to KABL to find all of their favorite artists, from the ones they grew up with to the hit-makers of today.

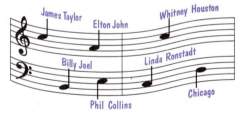

KABL–Radio You Can Live With

No station puts it all together like KABL. KABL plays the Bay Area's favorite music, blended with up-to-the-minute information, intelligent humor, and a long tradition of community service and involvement. It's no wonder that the familiar sound of KABL RINGS THE BELL for Bay Area listeners at home, work or play.

1025 BATTERY • SAN FRANCISCO, CA 94111 • 415/788-5225 • FAX 415/981-2930

Represented Nationally by CHRISTAL COMPANY

A SHAMROCK BROADCASTING COMPANY

Drawing by R. Chast; © 1987 The New Yorker Magazine, Inc.

Beautiful-music programming is perfectly suited to this background function.

Beautiful-music fans see their stations as an oasis amid the "noise" of the other outlets. The announcers display little emotion or personality, but simply and softly announce the songs. News and commercials (when possible) are done in the same soft-spoken way. The idea is never to violate the listener's trust by starting to sound like "those other stations." Beautiful-music formats are usually automated or prerecorded, with the computer selecting programming elements according to a formula (three instrumentals, one vocal, two commercials, and so on).

The competition among beautiful-music stations is fiercer than the name might suggest. Although fans are as devoted to their format as are any radio listeners, they also tend to be less tolerant of commercials. Typically, a new beautiful-music station will enter a market with few sponsors. As the ratings grow, so does the number of commercials. Soon, listeners are tuning elsewhere.

The more conservative strains of beautiful music are often piped into dentists' and doctors' offices. Sometimes these offices pay to re-

6.9

The programming promotion sheet for San Francisco's KABL touts the typical advantages of an adult contemporary format.

ceive a closed-circuit broadcast of such music, such as the one called Muzak. The Muzak format is the easy listeners' dream — no commercials, no disc jockey, no interruptions, just music. Critics contend that Muzak isn't music at all, but simply a pleasant, mindless noise.

Jazz

In a few urban markets, the jazz format still receives a comfortable chunk of the ratings. Jazz stations were once quite popular, but enthusiasm dwindled in the 1960s. Those fans that remained were hard-core, however, and went to great lengths to find a station that offered what they wanted. Now there is some indication that young people are becoming interested in jazz again. Pop performers like Joni Mitchell and Sting are combining traditional and experimental jazz sounds with rock.

New Age

New age is radio's newest format, featuring light jazz and classical-like instrumentals from labels such as Windham Hill and ECM. Artists like George Benson, Michael Franks, Pat Metheny, and Kitaro are new-age favorites. Critics often refer to this format as "Muzak for yuppies," and the much sought-after 18–39 young urban professionals do indeed form the core of its audience. New-age stations such as Los Angeles' KTWV–"The Wave" have not enjoyed overpowering ratings to date, but the desirable demographics of those listeners they do attract have helped them keep their heads above water while they attempt to build a larger audience.

Ethnic

In a Mediamerica composed of many diverse subcultures, it's no surprise that ethnic stations are flourishing as never before. Programming is targeted largely to one ethnic group, often in a foreign language. Today it is the Spanish-speaking stations that are most suc-cessful. In fact, in markets as unique as Los Angeles and San Antonio, Spanish-language radio stations are currently rated number one.

Because ethnic programming appeals to a specialized audience, its impact can be overlooked. Found around the clock on commercial powerhouses or at odd hours on local college outlets, native-language programming provides a vital cultural lifeline for many Americans.

Classical

The commercial classical station, once a firmly established format, is now virtually extinct. About 20 full-time commercial classical stations remain today, down from more than 50 in 1965. Classical music may be alive and well, but teaming it with the financial realities of commercial radio seems an impossible task. Often classical stations are subsidized by listeners or survive because a wealthy owner writes off station losses at tax time.

Classical fans now find themselves drawn primarily to the noncommercial stations. Many of them broadcast from colleges and can be found between 88 and 92 on the FM dial. Many noncommercial National Public Radio (NPR) stations offer classical music along with other fine-arts and information programming.

Big Band

One solution for some struggling AM stations has been to switch to a nostalgia–big band format. Big band was most popular during the 1940s; hence the format appeals to older demographic groups. These listeners generally support news and talk stations and would not otherwise listen to music radio.

Music Radio Today

You've now been briefed on the basic music formats that make up the constructed mediated reality of radio today. Many stations offer a combination of two or more formats in an attempt to "fine-tune" the station's audience demographics. Thus it is difficult to know exactly where CHR ends and urban contemporary begins or what the differences are between more progressive AOR formats and those that feature modern rock. Even stations that do admit to following an established format have program directors who claim that their sound is "one-of-a-kind" in order to convince advertisers that they are buying something unique.

Yet the truth is that most stations stay within the boundaries of established formats. These confines, initially set up in the 1950s and refined for decades, have spelled success for many stations. Although station programmers always think that they should be allowed to experiment, station owners are usually more concerned with the bottom line. If the station is making money, let's keep it the way it is; if it's not, *then* we can talk about change.

According to *Broadcasting* magazine, more commercial music stations report losses than profits each year, but those figures can be misleading. Owners often pay excessive salaries to themselves or their top executives to avoid heavy profit taxes at the end of the year. Actually, as soon as a station is a real money-loser, it will change formats, go up for sale, or both.

Despite incessant competition from MTV and numerous other audio and video sources, music radio continues to be a vital force in the music industry. From the big-band sounds of "Make-Believe Ballroom" to the big blare of Metallica it remains the cornerstone of commercial radio in Mediamerica.

And Now the News . . .

Flipped around the AM dial lately? You probably encountered lots of talk and a lot less music. Though there are formats of every conceivable description, today's most successful AM

stations are those that offer some variation of news and news-talk.

This is an interesting turn of events, given the fact that during the early 1920s, radio broadcasters were not very interested in news. There were no radio reporters; most news came directly from newspapers and sounded rather dull on the air. Advertisers expressed little enthusiasm for sponsoring news broadcasts, preferring to back more popular entertainment and music shows. Yet some news events seemed designed for radio coverage.

The Hoover-Smith presidential race of 1928 was fully covered by the new medium. The three wire services (AP, UP, and INS) supplied radio with details of the campaign and official election results. Listeners found that they could get the returns without having to wait for the next morning's newspaper. The candidates themselves spent almost $1 million on radio advertising. The age of radio news and public affairs had arrived. By the time the Depression began in 1929, some stations had as many as 10 reporters whose sole job was covering the news.

Newspapers were among the first to feel the economic pinch of the Depression, and they were not about to sit by and lose advertisers to radio. They reasoned that radio was supposed to provide entertainment, but real news coverage should remain exclusively the job of print. In 1933 a majority of Associated Press members fired the first volley of the press-radio war by refusing to provide wire-service information to radio networks. This forced newscasters to go to the early editions of newspapers for their news, but the AP soon went to court to stop even that practice. NBC and CBS responded by setting up their own news-gathering bureaus.

A compromise was tried: In exchange for the networks' dropping their plans to expand radio news coverage, a newly created "Press-Radio Bureau" would supply two 5-minute newscasts daily, culled from wire-service stories. But that wasn't enough. Radio stations

Edward R. Murrow: Patron Saint of Broadcast Journalism

The voice that so many Americans came to trust during World War II was that of Edward R. Murrow. Christened Egbert Murrow in 1908, he was the youngest of three sons born to Scottish immigrant parents. Though they began American life in Kentucky, the Murrows soon moved to a small town in Washington State.

Egbert's education began at home; with his mother's patient tutoring he had a head start on his classmates. Young Egbert always liked school. Mrs. Murrow also instilled in her son the firm belief in a solid day's work. Later, he was to admit that he would feel "miserable" if he didn't work and that he was not "equipped for fun."

After high school, Murrow briefly attended the University of Virginia before returning to enroll at Washington State. There he came under the influence of Ida Lou Anderson, an instructor in speech. She taught him speech, diction, and presence. Always a debate enthusiast, Murrow worked hard and was regarded by Anderson as her most promising pupil. It was she who suggested later that Murrow pause after the first word of his introduction to his London broadcasts. Thus, "This is London" became "This . . . is London," the phrasing that became a Murrow trademark.

After working briefly in several radio-related jobs, Murrow joined the CBS radio network in 1935 as "director of talks" through the recommendation of an old friend, Fred Willis, who was then special assistant to CBS president William Paley. Murrow soon proved his worth.

The talks director set a precedent for CBS by hiring reporters, rather than announcers, to broadcast the news in Europe. Some of these, like Walter Cronkite and Robert Trout, would go on to become famous television journalists. Murrow expected superhuman effort from his staffers, but he was no less dedicated himself. During one crisis, he anchored 35 broadcasts in less than 3 weeks and arranged for 116 others from 18 points in Europe.

After returning from Europe in 1946, his name now a household word, the still young (38) Murrow was named CBS vice president in charge of news, education, and discussion programs. He was joined a year later by his lifetime friend and mentor, Fred Friendly. Together they produced the popular radio news show "Hear It Now." The program was unusual in that it blended straight, or

and listeners demanded more. In no time half a dozen competing radio news services had sprung up.

Radio bypassed traditional news channels to bring listeners the events leading to World War II. Edward R. Murrow organized a series of broadcasts for CBS from the capitals of Europe (see 6.10). As Hitler's demands became more preposterous, listeners heard reporters describe the tense situation. And in Murrow's 1940 broadcasts from London, while bombs burst all around him, he told the poignant tale of Great Britain's struggle to survive the war. This sense of immediacy and involvement would not soon be forgotten by the millions of Americans glued to their radios. Radio had won the press-radio struggle and achieved its rightful place in news reporting.

The Commentators

Over the years, many radio commentators developed a unique voice or delivery—a recognizable "byline." The brief listing that follows highlights a few newscasters who pioneered a new brand of radio journalism.

Paul Harvey is still going strong. His delivery includes long pauses that drive the point

hard, news stories with the interpretative reports Murrow dubbed "think pieces."

In 1951 "Hear It Now" became "See It Now," and the face that went with the famous voice was introduced to American television viewers. Critic Gilbert Seldes called "See It Now" the most important show on the air—"not only for the solutions it found to some problems but also for the problems it tackled without finding the right answers."

Murrow was to narrate many famous broadcasts, including a courageous and successful attack on Senator Joseph McCarthy in 1954 and a famous CBS documentary, "Harvest of Shame," which explored the tragic conditions of American migrant farm workers. All of this was not without its consequences.

Though originally a Murrow admirer, Paley eventually grew disenchanted with Murrow and

"See It Now." The controversy, he said, upset his stomach. This precipitated a falling-out of sorts between Murrow and CBS. There was an extended sabbatical, and finally Murrow left the network to head the United States Information Agency under the Kennedy administration. According to one biographer, the last straw involved Murrow's being denied his usual "instant access" to Paley.

Ironically, "See It Now" was the first television program to openly discuss the possibility that cigarette smoking might lead to lung cancer. For years, Murrow's trademark had been his endless chain of cigarettes with smoke curling across the screen. In 1965, after a long battle with lung cancer, he assembled his family for a last on-air appearance, a public-service announcement urging Americans to quit smoking. He died in April of that year.

Perhaps his accomplishments were best summed up by Friendly: "He laid down a standard of responsibility for radio and television broadcast journalists, a standard lacking before his time and seldom measured up to since."

From Edward Jay Whetmore, The Magic Medium: An Introduction to Radio in America. © 1981 by Wadsworth, Inc.

home. Seldom does Harvey have to spell out for his audience how he feels about a subject. His tone tells all. Harvey has said: "The cold hard facts have to be salted and peppered to make them palatable. Since objectivity is impossible, I make no pretense of it—I just let it all hang out."

His daily newscasts seem to strike a particularly responsive chord in small-town and rural America. Stories include the big news of the day as well as the item about the couple who have been married "68 years today . . . and still holding." His trademark sign-off is punctuated by 5 seconds of silence. "This is Paul Harvey. . . . Good day."

Gabriel Heatter had a flair for the emotion-packed human-interest story while with the Mutual network during the 1930s. He was one of the first to be strongly identified by voice and broadcast style; his name became a household word. Along with Fulton Lewis, Jr., and Elmer Davis, he pioneered the 15-minute "news commentary" format.

H. V. Kaltenborn started broadcasting in 1922 and joined CBS 8 years later. He probably was the best-known radio commentator of his day, reaching the height of his fame during a 20-day crisis in 1938 when Hitler made a number of demands on Czechoslovakia. Europe appeared on the brink of war, and Kalten-

Walter Winchell taps out his famous "Morse code" signature in 1943 on the NBC blue network.

born set up a cot in his famous "Studio Nine" to give listeners all the latest. During those 3 weeks, he did more than 80 broadcasts, including a number of long commentaries. Never had Americans heard so much news and comment.

Lowell Thomas began at Pittsburgh's KDKA in 1925 and worked until his death in 1981. Thomas had a unique, brash, but sincere delivery that caught on with the public. His era of reporting stretched from the Great Depression to the Vietnam War. Thomas' trademark was his introduction: "From Moscow to the Suez Canal [the day's top datelines] comes today's news. Good evening everybody, this is Lowell Thomas for CBS news."

Walter Winchell, who may be best remembered as the machine-gun staccato voice that introduced the old "Untouchables" TV series, was a New York newspaper columnist who got into radio as a sideline. Unlike his radio colleagues, Winchell was strictly in the entertainment business, supplying humorous tidbits and personal "secrets" (see 6.11). His popularity among peers faded somewhat in the 1950s. He once accused Lucille Ball of being a Communist and sided with Senator Mc-

Carthy against Murrow in their famous 1954 TV battle.

Armed with a plethora of politically incorrect pronouncements, conservative commentator **Rush Limbaugh** is probably Mediamerica's best known radio pundit. Thanks to an impromptu network of over 500 radio stations, Limbaugh's faithful followers, known as "dittoheads," hang out in restaurant "Rush Rooms" and cheer on the portly commentator's every acerbic political observation.

News and News-Talk: Information Exchange in the 1990s

Despite an exciting beginning, radio news made few major advances after World War II. No sooner had radio established news personalities like Edward R. Murrow and Eric Sevareid than television came along and offered them a more exciting challenge. Most radio networks were forced to cut back on expensive news operations when radio began losing lucrative entertainment advertising dollars to TV.

But in 1961 Gordon McLendon, a pioneer of Top 40 radio in the 1950s, came up with another winning idea. He signed on as program consultant for XTRA, a Mexican station just across the border from California that could be heard plainly in the competitive Los Angeles market. Under his guidance, XTRA became the first all-news radio station, giving Los Angeles commuters and others an up-to-the-minute account of what was going on in international and national affairs. XTRA's early coverage was limited mostly to wire-service copy, because it had no budget for local reporters. But before long, the success of XTRA had sparked competition, and a number of all-news stations went on the air in most major markets.

All-news programming has some unusual implications. Traditionally, programmers hope to persuade the listener to tune to their station and stay with it. All-news asks only that you tune in every once in a while to get an idea of what's going on in the world. In Los Angeles, KFWB typifies this philosophy with its slogan "Give us 20 minutes, and we'll give you the world."

The startling success of all-news radio has been attributed to a number of factors. The competition from stereo-equipped FM stations has left AM music stations looking for alternatives. And it appears that the more information we get, the more we want. An increasingly large audience needs to feel it is in tune with up-to-the-minute events (hence the proliferation of TV "news breaks").

Prompted by the increase in popularity of all the all-news and news-talk formats (see 6.12), the Cable News Network (CNN) made a 24-hour all-news service available to radio stations nationwide in 1982. CNN radio, like CNN TV, was the brainchild of Atlanta's TV "superstation" owner Ted Turner. It offers potential affiliates the possibility of becoming all-news at the push of a button.

Most all-news stations draw their largest audience during morning and late-afternoon drive-time hours. In the early 1970s, some stations began to experiment with attempts to attract the predominantly female daytime audience with cooking shows and other feature items designed to appeal primarily to women. The all-news format was also a logical home for weekend and evening coverage of major sporting events, which draw a primarily male audience.

Many all-news stations soon found that audiences wanted to be entertained as well as informed, to have the news explained and discussed as well as reported. Two-way talk shows address these needs, while providing listeners with a vehicle for sounding off about political and social events. The successful marriage of news and two-way talk produced the hybrid *news-talk*. News-talk stations are now number one in the ratings in many major markets.

In addition, many music stations, particularly those on AM, now offer substantial por-

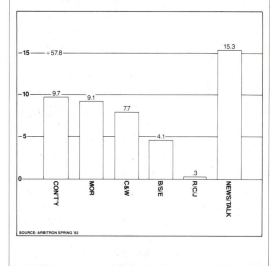

AVERAGE REACH PER FORMAT IN TOP 10 MARKETS

In the top 10 markets, the average News/Information/ Talk station can reach 57.8% more adults 18+ than the average contemporary radio station; 68.1% more than MOR; 98.7% more than C&W. News/Information/Talk reaches an average of 42.7% of adults 18+.

SOURCE: ARBITRON SPRING '82

6.12

This chart reflects the widespread audience interest in the information/talk format in most major markets. It was used by Turner Broadcasting to help market its CNN format.
Turner Broadcasting Systems, Inc., 1982. Used by permission.

tions of news and especially news-talk in an effort to bolster sagging ratings.

Historically, syndicated news-talk programs such as "The Larry King Show" found listeners, even during the early-morning hours. King pioneered radio satellite distribution with his show in 1977, though his CNN TV duties finally forced him to discontinue his radio efforts in 1994.

Today the AM airwaves are full of nationally distributed satellite fare. Among the most popular is ESPN radio, another example of the successful merger of TV and radio programming.

Meanwhile, news-talk has gone through several evolutions. Originally designed to give listeners a chance to air their opinions about the news topics of the day, the format now includes discussions of such subjects as medicine and health, finance, and law, together with human-interest stories and celebrity interviews. ABC-FM radio affiliates now feature "Soap Talk" twice every weekday; programs such as "Sextalk" spotlight frank discussions of sex-related matters between psychologists and listeners. Perhaps the most popular of these shows are found in New York, where Dr. Judith Kuriansky is WABC's resident therapist and Dr. Ruth Westheimer can be heard Sunday nights on WYNY. Westheimer's show is also syndicated nationally. Kuriansky reports that she receives as many as 600 calls each night from listeners with a wide range of sexual problems they want to discuss on the air.

Sexually related material can also be found in abundance on "The Howard Stern Show." Once fired for an on-air sketch called "Bestiality Dial-A-Date," Stern has nevertheless reigned as the king of New York morning radio since 1985. No longer content in his Big Apple confines, "shock jock" Stern is slowly making his presence felt in Los Angeles, Cleveland, and Philadelphia as well as a number of other major markets where his nonstop morning simulcast talk-fests have found an appreciative audience. Numerous complaints have also been filed by irate listeners.

The only thing that Stern and conservative commentator Rush Limbaugh have in common is that they are both on the radio and have a knack for making a lot of people angry. Limbaugh's vitriolic commentary on the day's events has endeared him to a loyal audience that, like Stern's, is continually growing as his show is heard in more cities across the country.

AM Versus FM: The Battle of the Bands

The concept of FM was developed by Edwin Armstrong, who first applied for patents for this new type of radio service in 1933. FM, or *frequency modulation,* was more than just another radio band. In fact, it was a whole new way of broadcasting, one that eliminated the static and interference so common on the AM dial.

The chief difference between AM and FM involves the method of modulation of the signal. AM stands for *amplitude modulation.* Television utilizes both of these systems, AM for the picture and FM for the sound. According to author Sydney Head:

> Modulation means imposing a meaningful pattern of variations on an otherwise unvaried stream of energy. . . . Because amplitude modulation depends on *amount* of energy received, its signals are vulnerable to electrical interference. . . . FM carriers, relying on frequency rather than amplitude patterns, are relatively immune to electrical interference. Unwanted amplitude variations of the modulated carrier can be clipped off the wave peaks without disturbing the essential pattern.

When he had a working FM model, Armstrong approached RCA's Sarnoff, an old friend, and offered to let RCA develop it. Though Sarnoff was properly impressed, it soon became evident that RCA was not about to introduce an entirely new radio service when the old one was paying off so handsomely. Eventually, friction between Armstrong and Sarnoff over the future of FM increased, and in time they became bitter enemies. Armstrong took his idea to others, and in 1939, with some financial backing, his W2XMN in Alpine, New Jersey, became the first successful FM station.

Just as it appeared that FM would finally get off the ground, along came World War II, and development of the medium stalled. Armstrong also made FM available to the armed forces free of charge. It was used extensively, particularly by the Navy, where it proved ideal for short-range transmissions.

After the war, the FCC decreed that FM broadcasting would have to move to another part of the spectrum, thus making all existing FM receivers obsolete. Adding insult to injury, the commission also ruled that part of the FM spectrum would now be allocated for TV sound.

In 1964 Congress and the FCC, bowing to pressure from UHF (ultra-high frequency) television stations, forced manufacturers of TV sets to include both VHF (very high frequency) and UHF capability on all sets sold in this country. Naturally, FM radio stations were anxious for the same sort of boost, but it never came. For years FM floundered while TV boomed. Finally, in the 1960s the underground movement in radio found a home on FM. By then, owning an FM set was getting less costly, and soon FM became commonplace in homes and cars all over the country.

By 1993, FM stations accounted for 75% of all radio listeners and 60% of all radio advertising revenues. According to *Broadcasting* magazine, AM radio has become a "band on the run." As revenues have declined, the asking prices of many AM stations up for sale have declined as well. Edwin Armstrong's vision of FM as a superior alternative to AM has finally come true. Unfortunately, he did not live to see it happen. In 1954, a broken and bitter man, he jumped to his death from the 13th floor of his New York apartment house.

The Numbers Game: Ratings and Radio

Most of you probably have heard of the famous Nielsen ratings, the audience estimates that determine whether your favorite TV show lives or dies (see Chapter 8). In radio, the equivalent of the Nielsens is the Arbitron "book." Although several smaller companies compete with Arbitron, it is the Arbitron ratings that generally determine how a commercial radio station is doing in its unrelenting quest for listeners (see 6.13).

An Arbitron book can run to 300 pages or more. It is filled with thousands of numbers estimating how many and what kind of listeners are tuned in to a given station at a specific time of day. Major markets are served with up to four Arbitron books each year; smaller markets might be surveyed only once a year.

Basically, the Arbitron book acts as a guide for advertisers, who want to know which stations offer the greatest potential audience for their product or service. As with magazine readers (see Chapter 5), "demos," or demographic breakdowns of listeners, provide valuable data. For example, if you are selling a women's shampoo, you want to buy time on a station with a large female audience. You also want to make sure your spot is aired at a time of day when it will reach the maximum number of potential buyers.

Another important demo involves the age characteristics of a station's audience. Advertisers found long ago that if a station's listeners are too young (12 to 17), they do not have the kind of ready cash available to invest in a new sports car. Of course, soft-drink manufacturers and music stores may want to reach exactly this audience. A station that primarily attracts listeners 35 and above is at a disadvantage because people of this age group can be more easily and economically reached through television. Hence, it is the 18- to 34-year-old age group that is most desirable for many advertisers, and many formats such as AOR and adult contemporary are geared to reach precisely this group.

The Arbitron book delivers data in two broad categories, called *quarter-hour estimates* and *cume estimates*. Quarter-hour figures indicate how many people are listening at any given moment, whereas cume (cumulative) estimates indicate the total number of people who have tuned in during a specific period (for example, on Saturdays and Sundays from 6:00 A.M. to midnight).

Armed with such a diversity of information, it is not unusual for half a dozen stations

A Rating or a Share?

Most of the confusion people have about radio and television ratings arises from the difference between a rating and a share. These two numbers dominate discussion of the ratings race in both media. Actually, it's quite simple.

A rating represents a percentage of an entire population. Let's say a radio station has a rating of 3.0. That means 3 of every 100 people who live in that market were listening to that station during the period described.

A *share* represents a percentage of the population in question *that had their radios (or televisions) turned on* during the period in question. Let's say that one quarter of the population had their radios turned on. The station with a 3.0 rating would have a 12.0 share because 12 of every 100 persons who had their radios turned on were listening to our mythical station.

Share numbers are always larger than ratings because there is never a time when everyone in a given population has his or her radio turned on. Were that to happen sometime, the two numbers would be equal.

---

to claim that they are number one in a market. There are many ways to interpret the book, and naturally station salespeople want their station to be put in the best possible light.

The biggest complaint about Arbitron—and indeed about all ratings services—is that they can tell us only what people are tuned to, not what they really want to hear. Thus, commercial programmers are a bit like a dog chasing its tail. They know where listeners have been and maybe even where they are now, but not where they would like to go.

The pressures of our commercial radio system, with the all-important ratings books, probably contribute to the tendency of commercial stations to program more of the same. This is a tendency many critics and listeners find disturbing. Perhaps you are one of them.

Educational and Public Radio

Away from the din of the marketplace and the ratings wars, educational and public radio stations provide alternative programming for those weary of the commercial stations. The first educational station is generally acknowledged to have been WHA, licensed to the University of Wisconsin at Madison. Under the designation 9XM, it began experimental broadcasts in 1917. The early educational stations were the first step toward the kind of radio that early inventors had envisioned, one that could "educate and illuminate the general public."

However, it was not easy going for educational radio in the early years. According to *Educational Telecommunications,* by Donald N. Wood and Donald G. Wylie, "By the mid-1920s only half of the educational institutions that held broadcast licenses actually had stations on the air." Although many institutions were quick to obtain licenses, persuading college and university administrators to pay for such stations was another matter. Funding has continued to be a problem for virtually all noncommercial stations.

In 1934 the National Association of Educational Broadcasters (NAEB) was formed. This association included not only educational institutions that had their own studios but also those that used existing commercial facilities. The NAEB has continued to be a strong voice for educational broadcasting through the years.

As late as 1948 only 50 on-air radio stations were licensed to colleges and universities. Today there are about 130 such stations. In addition to offering fine-arts and educational programming, these facilities provide an excellent opportunity for students enrolled in radio courses (see 6.14). Many of today's most successful radio entertainers and executives got their first break and valuable experience in educational radio.

Since the 1960s, most educational radio stations have relied heavily on government funds. In 1967 the nonprofit Corporation for Public Broadcasting (CPB) was formed to disburse those funds to various noncommercial stations. The CPB established the noncommercial radio network, National Public Radio (NPR), in 1970. By 1976 NPR boasted 160 affiliates. The public network produces and distributes radio programs to member stations. Among the most popular is "All Things Considered," a news and feature program that gives in-depth coverage to stories that most commercial stations might handle in a few seconds. "All Things Considered" and NPR's "Morning Edition" reach a combined estimated audience of some 2 million people each day. What's more, those who do listen constitute a special audience that includes some of the nation's top political and economic opinion leaders. It is estimated that some 300,000 people listen each week in the Washington, D.C., area alone.

NPR's programming, though generally acclaimed, has not been without its critics. Writing in the *New Republic,* Fred Barnes contends that "news coverage is palpably slanted. . . . When NPR goes beyond breaking news, as it does in lengthy background pieces, cultural reports, interviews by anchors and commentaries, the left wing agenda dominates." Barnes says that "all this would be fine if NPR were entirely funded by its listeners and didn't

6.14

College radio provides many students with their first on-air experience.

claim to present balanced news." At the heart of this issue is the question of exactly what public radio should be.

When the term *public* was chosen for National Public Radio, an important distinction was being made. Many broadcasters believed it was necessary to recognize that "educational" radio was only a part of the noncommercial picture. Indeed, a large number of noncommercial radio stations are licensed to private foundations rather than educational institutions. The idea behind public broadcasting is that these stations not only educate but also offer programming not available on their commercial counterparts. For example, as we have seen, the classical-music format survives largely on noncommercial stations. Virtually all noncommercial stations can be found between 88 and 92 megahertz on the FM dial, the space the FCC has reserved exclusively for such outlets.

Despite the excellent record that educational and public stations have established, their existence seemed jeopardized in 1981 when the Reagan administration announced plans for phasing out the CPB. If this vital source of funding were lost, the future would be bleak for many noncommercial stations.

The administration's lack of support for CPB was part of the "marketplace" philosophy that seemed to dominate the politics of this period. According to *Broadcasting* magazine, the Reagan administration felt that "stations should generate revenue by soliciting contributions from the public and corporations. If the stations can find enough support in the marketplace, they'll survive. If the marketplace won't support them, obviously some stations will die."

Responding to government cutbacks and what they considered unworkable NPR policies, a group of public stations banded together to form American Public Radio (APR) in 1982. APR does not rely on government funding, but on dues paid by its members. A loose-knit coalition, the purpose of the network is to acquire and distribute programs among all member stations. It was APR that was responsible for the highly successful "A Prairie Home Companion" show, hosted by Garrison Keillor.

Whither Radio?

From early experimental stations run by devoted amateurs to the computerized programming of today, radio has undergone a number of metamorphoses. It is a tremendously fluid medium, able to adapt almost immediately to the desires and needs of its audience. In the 1950s, when television was stealing radio stars and programs, radio rediscovered music, and business boomed. When MTV came on the scene in 1981, some predicted it was the beginning of the end for music radio. Yet today music radio keeps rolling (and rocking!) along.

Whether AM or FM, commercial or non-commercial, most radio stations fight to survive in today's crowded mass-media marketplace. Mark Twain once quipped, "The reports of my death are greatly exaggerated." The same is true of radio. The death of radio was predicted at the end of the golden age in the late 1940s, when rock music took over in the 1950s, and in the wake of extensive commercialization in the 1960s and 1970s. But like the famous watch, radio seems to be able to "take a licking and keep on ticking."

More than 11,500 radio stations are now operating in America. Of these, only about 1,400 are noncommercial. Radio ad revenues are currently about $8.5 billion yearly. There are more than 500 million radios in America—about 2 for every man, woman, and child in the country. As we have seen, today's radio offers an ever-expanding array of music, news, and talk formats. Digital audio technology has already brought sweeping change to the medium, and industry watchers predict a radio future filled with diversity and growth.

In addition, an increasing number of adjunct industries have sprung up to service the radio industry. Program syndicators, music services, ratings services, and research specialists have all found a place in the radio spectrum. Those seeking radio-related employment now have possibilities that extend far beyond the stations themselves.

As radio faces the challenges of the 1990s, it seems certain that the medium's inherent flexibility and ability to adapt to constantly shifting economic realities and audience trends will ensure its continuing and very vocal presence in the years to come.

We have seen how many ways radio has changed over the years. This mercurial quality has posed a problem for those who are charged with regulating the medium. By 1927 more than 700 private radio stations were in operation. Until that time, licensing procedures had been rather loose, and stations could go on and off the air at will. This practice was detrimental to both listeners and other stations, so Congress passed the Radio Act of 1927, which created a five-person Federal Radio Commission (FRC) to oversee licensing of radio stations. Each station was given permission to broadcast for 3 years and was assigned a specific frequency.

Almost everyone agreed that some form of regulation was needed at that time. Stations were springing up at an astounding rate, and signals were interfering with one another. In many populated areas, the poor befuddled listener could pick up little more than a jumbled cacophony.

The act established a policy that no one had a "right" to broadcast in the same way that there is a "right" to print. The supply of paper and ink is seemingly unlimited, but the airwaves contain only a certain number of channels. These channels cannot belong in perpetuity to any individual; like some lands and minerals, they are a national resource that must be operated in the "public interest, convenience, and necessity." Thus the FRC's power to make decisions about who could and could not broadcast was clearly established. These laws remain essentially intact today, despite technological innovations like cable and fiber optics, which may eventually mean that an unlimited number of channels will be available.

The FRC decided to include the quality of programming as one criterion in making license decisions. Though it was not always a major determinant, some licenses were awarded to those who promised the highest-quality programs.

"Aha!" you exclaim. "Then what happened to radio? Why don't we have better programs?" The problem is, what is quality programming for you may not be quality for someone else. Some people would like to banish rock music from the face of the earth. Others couldn't live without it. The FRC didn't help much; it never defined quality. In fact, we still don't have a real working definition for it, and perhaps we never will.

An important precedent was set in 1931 when the FRC refused to renew the license of KFKB in Milford, Kansas. The station had been selling patent medicines over the air, and a doctor had been telling would-be patients about "miracle" cures. KFKB took the FRC to court, contending that it had the right to broadcast anything it liked and that the FRC could not restrict the content of radio programs. KFKB lost the case. The courts ruled that the "public interest, convenience, and necessity" clause gave the FRC the right to control certain kinds of programs.

A few years later Congress passed the Communications Act of 1934, which included provisions for telephone, telegraph, and television as well as radio. To administer it, the seven-person FCC replaced the FRC. The FCC commissioners were given 7-year terms. Each year one retired and a new one was appointed by the president and approved by the Senate. FCC decisions are often split, because FCC commissioners reflect the political philosophy of their party. During the cost-conscious Reagan administration, the FCC was trimmed back from seven members to five. By law, no more than three members can belong to the same political party.

FCC appointments are among the most important a president can make, because an FCC commissioner has the potential to influence every piece of information we receive from radio and television.

However, that potential is seldom realized. Traditionally, FCC commissioners exercise little power over broadcasters. Of the 60,000 applicants for broadcast licenses and license renewals reviewed since 1954, only about 100 have been rejected or given less than a complete renewal. Of these, just a handful have been revoked. One recent case involved an AM station in New York. In 1989 the FCC ruled that the owner was guilty of blatant racial discrimination. It was the first outright revocation in 5 years. More recently, the FCC has revoked licenses held by those convicted of drug-related charges.

Why is the FCC so reluctant to act? One reason is that the commissioners are under tremendous pressure from the media industry. Another reason is that radio stations do their best to behave themselves. Owning a TV station has been called a license to print money, and ownership of most radio stations is also quite lucrative. Obviously nobody wants to lose such a valuable license. Licensees do everything they can to ensure that the FCC will not be displeased.

This compliance can be both good and bad for the public. The FCC, as an agent of the government and the people, can ensure that phony patent medicines are not sold over the air. But the five FCC commissioners, who are often advanced in years and sometimes out of step with the tastes of the general public, can also heavily influence programming. Broadcasters often overreact to FCC "suggestions" and bend over backward to provide dull, noncontroversial content. For example, during the early 1970s when the FCC attempted to crack down on stations playing songs with drug-related lyrics, Peter, Paul and Mary's "Puff the Magic Dragon" was banned on many stations. Station owners thought "Puff" might be about marijuana, and they weren't taking any chances.

At about the same time, Los Angeles deejay Bill Balance was pioneering a new kind of radio talk show. His "Feminine Forum" invited female listeners to call in and talk about their most intimate sexual problems. Immediately popular, "Feminine Forum" and its imitators

spread to every major radio market. The FCC soon made it clear that there might be an obscenity action if the content was not moderated. Balance was issued a set of guidelines by his bosses, and the more extreme topics were deleted. He complained on the air that his freedom of speech was being violated, but to no avail. No matter how popular the show, the station simply did not want to risk the wrath of the FCC.

In a 1975 case, the FCC placed a sanction against WBAI-FM in New York for airing a George Carlin monologue that contained seven four-letter words "that you could never say on the air." Previous court decisions had ruled that it was not the commission's place to set obscenity standards for broadcasters, but this didn't seem to deter the FCC. In 1978 the U.S. Supreme Court upheld the FCC action in the WBAI case.

A more recent FCC action has reopened the debate regarding obscenity and broadcasting. In 1987 the FCC issued new guidelines on "indecent" programming, indicating that radio and TV stations wishing to air sexually explicit material could do so between the hours of midnight and 6:00 A.M. without fear of reprisal. They reasoned that at those hours children were least likely to be part of the audience.

In 1988 Congress reacted swiftly and passed a law enacting an around-the-clock ban on broadcast indecency. An appeals court ruled that legislation illegal, and in 1992 the U.S. Supreme Court let the ruling stand. In essence we are back where we were before 1988, with the FCC under the gun to find a daypart where few children are tuning in and stations may broadcast without fear of FCC sanctions.

It can be argued that any FCC standards may not be in the best interests of the majority of listeners or viewers. After all, there is such an abundance of radio and TV stations and formats that what may be appropriate for one station's audience may be inappropriate for another's. It is difficult to outline one set of standards for all stations to follow.

Occasionally, the commission moves to try to increase diversity. In 1980 it announced that it was looking into the possibility of major alterations in the FM band. Basically, technical refinements of recent years have reduced the chance for one station to interfere with the signals of another nearby station. The basic allocation decisions were made more than 50 years earlier, so a change might be possible. By requiring power and antenna alterations in some existing stations, new laws could open up the airwaves for many (some said 100 or more) new FM stations.

At the same time, some commission actions seem destined to reduce the availability of certain kinds of information on radio. In 1981 the FCC voted 6–1 to "deregulate" radio. Detailed program logs would no longer have to be kept. Before 1981 the FCC had strongly suggested that no station should carry more than 18 minutes of commercials an hour. That restriction has now been lifted. Nonentertainment functions of commercial radio stations were now to be governed by "marketplace forces." This meant a reduction of public-affairs programming at most commercial stations. The deregulation of radio has had a tremendous impact on radio programming practices — and not all of it is for the better, as far as the listening audience is concerned.

As you can see, the FCC has followed a zig-zag trail with respect to the regulation of broadcasting and the encouragement of diverse points of view. Creative new solutions must be found to nagging long-term problems. Some argue that a complete overhaul of the Communications Act of 1934 would be a good start. Ideally, the new act would incorporate a realistic view of contemporary public tastes and modern station practices. It might not solve all the problems facing broadcasting today, but it would be a beginning.

Queries and Concepts

1 Music videos have had a tremendous impact on rock radio programming. Can you think of at least five ways our *perception* of music (PMR) might change as a result of *seeing* songs on TV rather than only hearing them on the radio? How might buying patterns change? How about our awareness of the song itself? The singer(s)?

2 Interview some people older than 55 about radio's golden age. Design a questionnaire to measure their attitudes about how early radio programs compare with today's TV and radio programs.

3 Identify five radio stations in your market. Write a two-paragraph description of the format each employs.

4 Come up with your own list of *must* items for quality radio programs. Compare with others in the class. Are there any items that *everyone* considers essential for quality?

5 What percentage of radio stations in your market are primarily music oriented? Why do you think music plays such an important part in radio programming?

6 Write a brief history of radio from the perspective of someone living in the year 2093. What has happened to the magic medium over the past century? Be imaginative, but try to ground your predictions in the material provided in this chapter.

7 Listen to a radio station for at least 2 hours, and take careful notes on what you hear. Can you identify what sort of audience this station is trying to target? Try to identify such factors as the age group the station appeals to, which consumer habits are addressed, and so on.

Marshall McLuhan
Understanding Media: The Extensions of Man.
New York: McGraw-Hill, 1964.

McLuhan offers some unique explanations of the magic in the magic medium. See Chapter 30, "The Tribal Drum."

Pioneers and Programmers

Erik Barnouw
A History of Broadcasting in the United States,
3 vols. Vol. 1, *A Tower in Babel: To 1933.* New York: Oxford University Press, 1966.

Vol. 2, *The Golden Web: 1933 to 1953.* New York: Oxford University Press, 1968.

A classic and comprehensive historical account of the rise of radio in North America from an amateur toy to a dynamic social institution. The first two books in this trilogy can be tough going in places but are full of radio lore and legend that keep the reader interested. A definitive bibliography and index.

Orrin E. Dunlap
Radio's 100 Men of Science. New York: Harper and Brothers, 1944.

The earliest radio pioneers were not programmers or businesspersons, but scientists. This book introduces you to an ample number of them.

Allan Havig, ed.
"Radio." Special issue of the *Journal of Popular Culture,* vol. 12, no. 2, 1979.

Includes 13 articles on radio, most covering historical material. Women radio pioneers, radio drama, daytime radio, and radio's debt to vaudeville are some of the topics explored.

Russell Nye
The Unembarrassed Muse: The Popular Arts in America. New York: Dial, 1970.

This concise, yet comprehensive history deals with the development of radio in the United States. The author's unique approach grounds historical research within the context of popular culture.

Christopher H. Sterling
John M. Kittross
Stay Tuned: A Concise History of Broadcasting in the United States. 2d ed. Belmont, Calif.: Wadsworth, 1990.

Offers a chronological look at the development and evolution of radio and television in the United States. Covers all important aspects of broadcast history in a readable format; topical, well illustrated, and up to date. Excellent index. Recommended.

The Golden Age of Radio (1926–48)

Frank Buxton
Bill Owen
The Big Broadcast: 1920–1950. New York: Viking Press, 1972.

A catalog of programs and stars from radio's golden age, complete with a short synopsis of each program.

Hadley Cantril
The Invasion from Mars: A Study in the Psychology of Panic. Princeton, N.J.: Princeton University Press, 1940.

This study is considered one of the classic milestones in mass media research. Cantril's analysis of the consequences of the "war" broadcast includes interesting data from listeners.

Alexander Kendrick
Prime Time: The Life of Edward R. Murrow. New York: Avon Books, 1970.

This biography features an excellent account of the war years and the part radio played. See especially Chapters 5 and 6, "Hello America

. . . Hitler Is Here" and "London Is Burning, London Is Burning."

J. Fred MacDonald
Don't Touch That Dial!: Radio Programming in American Life from 1920 to 1960. Chicago: Nelson-Hall, 1979.

A thorough history of radio's golden age. Well indexed; includes a concise bibliography.

Irving Settel
A Pictorial History of Radio. New York: Grosset & Dunlap, 1967.

An entertaining visual exploration of the people who made radio during the early years. Radio's history is neatly broken down decade by decade. A must for old-time-radio buffs, the book includes particularly thorough coverage of the 1930s and 1940s.

Anthony Slide, ed.
Selected Radio and Television Criticism. Metuchen, N.J.: Scarecrow Press, 1987.

A compendium of reviews of early radio and television shows and stars. Must reading for all golden-age-radio fans. Includes segments on Jack Benny, "The Lone Ranger," Edgar Bergen (you know, Murphy Brown's father!), and much more.

Glenhall Taylor
Before Television: The Radio Years. Cranbury, N.J.: A. S. Barnes, 1979.

A good account of entertainment radio during the golden years. The emphasis is on the great network giants who made a name for themselves in the era. Lots of pictures.

The Big Change: Radio After Television; Meet the Deejay; The People You Never Hear

Broadcasting Yearbook. Washington, D.C.: Broadcasting Publications, annual.

The primary reference book for professional broadcasters. Data of every conceivable kind are found here, including ownership, person-nel, format, and other information for every radio and TV station in the country. Available in the reference rooms of most libraries.

Diane Foxhill Carothers
Radio Broadcasting from 1920 to 1990: An Annotated Bibliography. New York: Garland, 1991.

This reference book will lead you to a wealth of information about radio, past and present. Especially useful for term papers and the like!

Lewis B. O'Donnell
Carl Hausman
Philip Benoit
Radio Station Operations: Management and Employee Perspectives. Belmont, Calif.: Wadsworth, 1989.

A comprehensive, current introduction to modern radio. All the basics are well covered, including programming, history, operations, business, management, and more. Useful glossary and suggested readings. Recommended.

U.S. Radio Directory. Burbank, Calif.: Parrot Communications, published quarterly.

Lists addresses, personnel, top radio stations. This relatively expensive publication is best obtained through your library.

Edward Jay Whetmore
The Magic Medium: An Introduction to Radio in America. Belmont, Calif.: Wadsworth, 1981.

This textbook covers all the major aspects of radio. It includes chapters on history, contemporary programming, popular music, ratings and research, employment opportunities, production and evaluation, and the future of radio. An obvious favorite.

American Electric: Introduction to Telecommunications and Electronic Media. New York: McGraw-Hill, 1992.

Radio is covered throughout this textbook. Chapter 2 covers radio history. Chapter 3 explores the contemporary radio scene. For some reason, I love this book.

Music Formats

James T. Lull
Lawrence Johnson
Carol Sweeny
"Audiences for Contemporary Radio Formats." *Journal of Communication,* vol. 22, no. 4, 1979, pp. 439–453.

Edd Routt
James B. McGrath
Fredric A. Weiss
The Radio Format Conundrum. New York: Hastings House, 1978.

The first book to accurately detail radio programming format by format. The authors offer interviews with a number of notable programmers and include a good analysis of each of the major format types. Of course, the book has become somewhat dated (for example, beautiful music is referred to as "good music," and you won't find any mention of new music or the new-age format), but it is still well worth reading. Chapter 3 of the O'Donnell, Hausman, and Benoit text (see page 149) provides a format update.

Music Radio Today

For information on the latest developments in music formats, you'll need to read the following trade magazines: *Billboard, Broadcasting, Cashbox, Electronic Media, The Gavin Report, Radio & Records (R&R).*

Most radio stations will furnish you with some of their own handouts, booklets, and promotional material. Call these stations and make your request to the receptionist or someone in the research or sales departments. Typically, radio stations offer coverage maps, rate cards, DJ photos and biographies, and playlists.

The Commentators

You'll find an interesting discussion of Paul Harvey and his influence in William L. Rivers's *Mass Media,* 2d ed. (New York: Harper & Row, 1975). See also *CBS: Reflections in a Bloodshot Eye* by Rovert Metz (New York: New American Library, 1976) for the inside story of early CBS radio and TV commentators and stars.

News and News-Talk: Information Exchange in the 1990s

Cameron B. Armstrong
Alan M. Rubin
"Talk Radio as Interpersonal Communication." *Journal of Communication,* vol. 39, no. 2., 1989, pp. 84–94.

Ted White
Adrian J. Meppen
Steve Young
Broadcast News Writing, Reporting and Production. New York: Macmillan, 1984.

This is a practical introduction to news writing; plenty of useful examples are provided.

AM Versus FM: The Battle of the Bands

Sydney W. Head
Broadcasting in America, Cambridge, Mass.: Riverside Press, 1956.

There are numerous updated versions of this solid, comprehensive overview of the broadcast media. The cited modulation material appeared in the first edition.

The Numbers Game: Ratings and Radio

Susan Tyler Eastman
Sydney W. Head
Lewis Klein
Broadcast/Cable Programming Strategies and Practices. 4th ed. Belmont, Calif.: Wadsworth, 1989.

Parts One and Four of this highly recommended textbook deal with contemporary radio formatting. The chapter on "Program and Audience Research" offers an excellent overview of the "numbers game." The chapter includes plenty of examples and a bibliography.

Educational and Public Radio

Alfred P. Kielwasser
"The Alternatives: From Noncommercial to Nonbroadcast Telecommunications." Chapter 7 (pp. 197–224) of E. J. Whetmore, *American Electric: Introduction to Telecommunications and Electronic Media.* New York: McGraw-Hill, 1992.

Historical material can be found in many of the radio-history books listed elsewhere in this section. See also Chapter 19 ("Public Radio Programming") of the Eastman, Head, and Klein's *Broadcast/Cable Programming,* cited above.

Issues and Answers: The Regulation of Broadcasting — The Zigzag Trail

Marvin R. Bensman
Broadcast Regulation: Selected Cases and Decisions. Lanham, Mass.: University Press of America, 1985.

Barry Cole
Mel Oettinger
Reluctant Regulators: The FCC and the Broadcast Audience. Reading, Mass.: Addison-Wesley, 1978.

Don R. Pember
Mass Media Law. 4th ed. Dubuque, Iowa: Wm. C. Brown, 1987.

Chapter 12 covers broadcast regulation, the Radio and Communication Acts, the FCC.

The very latest issues in broadcast regulation (and deregulation) are followed intently by *Broadcasting* magazine, which is a favorite of station owners and employees alike.

The *Federal Register,* available in many libraries, lists all "Notices of Inquiry and Proposed Rulemaking" currently issued by the Federal Communications Commission. The FCC will provide you with handouts describing FCC structure and operations, as well as lists of current FCC publications. Write: Consumer Assistance and Small Business Division, Office of Congressional and Public Affairs, Federal Communications Commission, 1919 M Street, NW, Washington, DC 20554.

7

The Sound of Music

The effect that pop music has on society is incredible. . . . It concerns far more than 20-year-olds. It's lasted too long. It concerns everybody now.

Peter Townshend

Where were you on the night of July 13, 1985? In London and Philadelphia more than 60 music acts paraded across two stages in a once-in-a-lifetime rock 'n' roll event known as Live Aid. David Bowie, Elvis Costello, Elton John, Julian Lennon, Sade, Sting, Dire Straits, Paul McCartney (performing live for the first time in 7 years), and the Who (reunited for the occasion) all performed in London.

Rock fans hardly had time to catch their breath when the USA contingent, headed up by Bryan Adams, the Cars, Bob Dylan, Eric Clapton, Tears for Fears, Rod Stewart, and Tina Turner began to play. Phil Collins caught a quick jet and became the only performer to sing at *both* locations.

The broadcast, bouncing off 16 satellites, reached some 1.5 billion people in 150 countries. *Newsweek* called it "MTV meets Woodstock," but it was much more than that. Rock had spoken out against hunger in Africa.

Popular music is a global language all its own that leaves a personal and permanent impression. With little effort you can probably think of many songs that have a very special meaning for you. One represents a summer romance. Another reminds you of someone far away. Perhaps there's a song you still can't listen to because you associate it with an unpleasant experience. Or one that never fails to bring a smile.

Recorded music represents a mediated reality we can enjoy alone or with others. Special songs seem to grow and take on new depth and meaning as we become more familiar with them. When we share that experience, we seem to enjoy it even more. There is a unique pleasure in playing a favorite CD for someone who is hearing it for the first time. You want so much for that person to hear what you hear and share your enthusiasm.

If live concerts are like motion pictures, then records, cassettes, and CDs are like still photos that we can return to again and again. We may join Hammer or Garth Brooks at any time, simply by pushing a button. Thus an album can become literally a "record" of our thoughts and feelings.

For the generations that have grown up after World War II, popular music seems to have an extraordinary meaning. Many of those they admire most—from Buddy Holly and Elvis Presley to Bob Dylan, John Lennon, and Joni Mitchell—are, or were, recording artists. During the 1980s, Sting and Bruce Springsteen had enormous influence on millions of fans. So did Jim Morrison and Jimi Hendrix, even though they died long before the decade began. Today there are those who hang on the latest rap from Ice-T and each new release from George Michael, Michael Jackson, or Guns N' Roses. Meanwhile, bands like R.E.M. go their own way but somehow seem part of the rock 'n' roll continuum that began in the revolutionary 1960s.

Whatever the song, whoever the singer, popular-music lyrics convey everything from eternal truth to cultural cliché while the irresistible beat seems inexplicably in synch with our own lives.

"And the beat goes on."

Scientific American, Dec. 22, 1877

7.1

Edison's original phonograph as it appeared in 1877.

The Fabulous Phonograph

In 1877 Thomas Edison's carbon transmitter had greatly improved Alexander Graham Bell's telephone and given the young Edison ample funds to experiment with a "talking machine." Edison's talking machine used a metal cylinder with a spiral groove (helix) impressed on it (see 7.1). A piece of tin foil—the record—was wrapped around the cylinder. The first words ever recorded were "Mary had a little lamb." When Edison played them back, he recognized his own voice and it startled him (see 7.2).

No time was lost exploiting this marvelous new invention. By 1878 the Edison Speaking Phonograph Company was formed to conduct exhibitions of this new device all over the country. As a curiosity, the phonograph was a success. In June 1878, Edison predicted 10 uses of the phonograph that would benefit humanity. These predictions proved remarkably accurate:

1 Letter writing and all kinds of dictation without the aid of the stenographer.
2 Phonographic books, which will speak to blind people without effort on their part.
3 The teaching of elocution.
4 Reproduction of music.
5 The "Family Record"—a register of sayings, reminiscences, etc., by members of a family in their own voices, and of the last words of dying persons.
6 Music-boxes and toys.
7 Clocks that should announce in articulate speech the time for going home, going to meals, etc.
8 The preservation of languages by exact reproduction of the manner of pronouncing.
9 Educational purposes, such as preserving the explanations made by a teacher, so that the pupil can refer to them at any moment, and spelling or other lessons placed upon the phonograph for convenience in committing to memory.
10 Connection with the telephone, so as to make that instrument an auxiliary in the transmission of permanent and invaluable records, instead of being the recipient of momentary and fleeting communication.

By the turn of the century, home phonographs were being marketed with great enthusiasm. They were crude by today's standards, with large hornlike protrusions to amplify the sounds. Still, the early cylinder records contained some great music, and the well-to-do family had to have one. Prices started at $25, a lot of money in those days. There were no plug-in models, of course; all phonographs had to be "wound up" by hand.

Enrico Caruso, a famous opera singer at the turn of the century, lent prestige to the new invention by allowing his performances to be

7.2

Thomas Edison works with an early phonograph.

recorded. These recordings were enormously successful. In the two decades following his first recording session in 1902, Caruso earned more than $2 million (an astronomical fortune at that time, and still a lot of money today!) from record sales.

The Victor Talking Machine Company developed and promoted the flat disc (forerunner of today's record), which eventually made the cylinder obsolete. At first, cylinders were of far superior quality, but the disc was more portable and easier to use. Were it not for the rise of the disc, today's radio announcers would be cylinder jockeys!

After World War I, some of the early Edison patents ran out, and the record field became more competitive. More than 200 phonograph manufacturers were in business by 1920, up from just 18 before the war. The heyday of the phonograph record had begun, and that heyday coincided with what was known as "the jazz age." Jazz was really the first popular music to gain status with the aid of the new medium. The record industry boomed; 100 million records were sold in 1927.

An important technological barrier was overcome in 1931 when Leopold Stokowski's Philadelphia Orchestra recorded Beethoven's entire Fifth Symphony on a single record without a break. Music fans could look forward to the day when their favorite operas and symphonies would no longer be cut up to fit on 4-minute records.

But the Depression and the rise of radio's popularity in the 1930s seemed to cripple the growing phonograph industry. By 1932 record sales had dropped to 6 million, and magazine writers wrote of the "rise and fall of the phonograph." Record collectors were akin to antique dealers. Few people thought there was a future in the phonograph record.

Popular Music in the 1940s

In 1939 big-band leader Harry James went to the Rustic Cabin in Teaneck, New Jersey, and happened to hear a new singer. James liked what he heard and hired Francis Albert Sinatra to sing with his band for $75 a week. Within a year Sinatra had left and signed with Tommy Dorsey's orchestra. He was described by one critic as "a skinny kid — not much to look at — but he really had a sound."

By 1943 Sinatra was the most familiar vocalist in America. His national fame came when thousands of "bobby soxers" mobbed New York's Paramount Theatre to see him. His was dubbed "the voice that thrills millions." Fans were actually screaming and passing out during Sinatra's performances. No one had ever seen anything like it. But not everyone could be in New York or afford to see the singer in person. Record prices had dropped,

and mass production kept them down to about a dollar each, so now the whole country began listening to Sinatra on their phonographs.

There had been other popular recording vocalists, among them Al Jolson and Rudy Vallee. But Vallee had been the "megaphone man," whereas Sinatra's intimate style seemed more suited to the microphone. He was exclusively the product of a new technology, a new electric sound.

Not too much is made of it now, but Sinatra was also a social hero to young people of his day. He made a documentary film attacking racial prejudice even though his business managers warned him it could cost him the support of some influential newspaper columnists. The film alienated some critics but won the hearts of young people everywhere. Sinatra didn't need the newspapers, the magazines, or even the radio. His records were instant hits.

Bobby soxers and other young people took over the record market. They seemed to prefer the big swing bands of Benny Goodman, Glenn Miller, and Duke Ellington and the hot jazz of Louis Armstrong. These teenage record buyers were not as interested in *songs* as they were in *artists*. "Do you have the latest Sinatra record?" became the request at the record store.

During the 1940s a number of popular vocalists enjoyed success, including Frankie Laine, Perry Como, Mel Torme, Dick Haymes, Vic Damone, Peggy Lee, Doris Day, Jo Stafford, and Dinah Shore. Their records were ballads, love songs mostly. Boy meets girl, boy falls in love with girl, boy can't live without girl, you get the picture. But you could always understand the words, and most lyrics seemed to make sense.

An interesting technological achievement came in 1947 when CBS engineer Peter Goldmark invented the long-playing 33⅓ rpm (revolutions per minute) record. The larger record had superior sound quality and enabled consumers to listen to 23 minutes of uninterrupted music, perfect for long classical compositions. The problem was there were no machines that could play them!

CBS approached RCA, then a leading record-player manufacturer, with an offer to exploit the invention together. RCA chief David Sarnoff was impressed but said he was committed to the 45 rpm format. The result was two different kinds of record players. Consumer confusion reigned, and record sales slowed.

Eventually, conductor Arturo Toscanini persuaded Sarnoff to relent and a deal was struck. CBS would issue their popular songs on 45 while classical recordings would use the new format. RCA and other record players soon offered the two new speeds along with the traditional 78.

The Birth of Rock

In some ways, the origin of rock 'n' roll can be traced to a rivalry between two organizations in the music industry: ASCAP and BMI. The American Society of Composers, Authors, and Publishers was formed in 1914 to guarantee that its members received a fee for the use of their songs. ASCAP charged each station a blanket amount to use the material, and its right to collect that fee stood one court test after another. In 1941 ASCAP announced a 100% fee increase. Radio stations refused to go along, and as a result all songs protected by ASCAP were taken off the air. Most popular songwriters of the time were ASCAP artists, and radio stations were left with very little music to play. The dispute was settled, at least temporarily, toward the end of 1941, but by that time radio stations had begun to rely on music provided by a new source.

Broadcast Music, Incorporated (BMI) was formed to scout for fresh talent who could provide radio stations with music. This became increasingly important as more stations switched to the deejay format. BMI was looking for a new sound. The sound they found was rock 'n' roll. By the mid-1950s, BMI was a powerful force, and so was the new sound.

In 1956 the antitrust subcommittee of the House Judiciary Committee investigated BMI's domination of the recording industry. Songwriter Billy Rose, an ASCAP member, outlined BMI's role in the rise of rock 'n' roll:

> Not only are most of the BMI songs junk, but in many cases they are obscene junk pretty much on a level with dirty comic magazines. . . . It is the current climate on radio and TV which makes Elvis Presley and his animal posturings possible. . . .
>
> When ASCAP's songwriters were permitted to be heard, Al Jolson, Nora Bayes, and Eddie Cantor were all big salesmen of songs. Today it is a set of untalented twitchers and twisters whose appeal is largely to the zoot-suiter and the juvenile delinquent.

But of course there was much more to it than that. Rock had come at a time when young people were finding it difficult to relate to the likes of Doris Day and Patti Page. There had been too many "adult" bands, too many tired crooners. Youth now wanted a sound of its own—something new, different, and vital.

Rock was actually a blend of country music and the rhythm and blues (R&B) records that were popular among black people during the early 1950s. But in a still-segregated America, record producers suspected that national white audiences would never idolize a black popular singer, no matter how much they liked the R&B beat.

Sam Phillips, the lawyer and former disc jockey who formed Sun Records in Memphis in the early 1950s, was a tireless promoter. He drove all over the South looking for new talent and promoting his records. "What I need," he said unabashedly, "is a white boy who can sing colored." In 1954 he found him. Elvis Presley recorded "That's Alright Mama," and the song enjoyed moderate success on the country-music

Elvis Presley's hound dog may never have caught a rabbit, but he helped launch the career of "The King." Popular music would never be the same.

charts. Within 2 years, Presley became the Sinatra of the 1950s, and by the end of the decade the older generation was explaining to the young that Sinatra had been the Elvis of the 1940s.

The father of rock 'n' roll was Cleveland deejay Alan Freed, who had started mixing R&B songs with Al Martino and Sinatra records as early as 1951 on WJW. It was he who coined the term *rock 'n' roll* in an effort to make R&B palatable to his white audience. In 1954 Freed moved to WINS in New York, where his "Moondog's Rock and Roll Party" was an instant success. WINS was soon the number one station in New York. Freed helped introduce Bill Haley's "Rock Around the Clock," the first rock 'n' roll single to reach the top of the charts.

Blackboard Jungle, a film about juvenile delinquency, featured "Rock Around the Clock" as part of its soundtrack. It became the best-selling song of 1955. The pulsating, uninhibited new sound was linked with restless, rebellious youth. Young people flocked to that film and others like it. Radio, movies, and print media all contributed to the rise of rock as the dominant form of popular music.

In 1956 Elvis Presley had 5 of the year's 16 best sellers, including the number one and number two records: "Don't Be Cruel" and "Heartbreak Hotel." Dick Clark's TV show "American Bandstand" (a sort of early version of Club-MTV) sent the latest songs out to millions of America's teenagers. Watching the show each weekday afternoon became a ritual of adolescence. Like MTV today, "Bandstand's" influence on fashion and even language could be felt far and wide.

Artists such as Frankie Avalon, Fabian, Paul Anka, Bobby Darin, and Bobby Rydell used the dance show as a steppingstone in their careers. Every one of them was a teenage idol in the mold of Sinatra and Presley; all made millions of dollars and were adulated wherever they went. But none surpassed Presley; he remained "The King." Though he died in 1977, his music and the impact it had on American youth will continue to be felt for decades to come.

If you saw the film *La Bamba,* you were treated to an interesting glimpse of rock's early years. Ritchie Valens was one of many overnight sensations during this period, but his music had an enduring quality and enjoyed somewhat of a renaissance when the film was released in 1987. If you remember your rock history, you may recall that Valens was not alone when he died in that plane crash. Singing star the Big Bopper died with him, and so did rock legend Buddy Holly. Holly was the most popular of the three, and rock critics still consider him the most influential and revered rock star of his era. Many of Holly's hits such as "Maybe Baby," "That'll Be the Day," and "Peggy Sue" represented new directions in popular music.

Another change during the 1950s was the disappearance of the 78 rpm discs that had taken over from Edison's cylinders. The 78s were too large and fragile and were soon replaced by the smaller, more durable 45s. Teenagers could pick up a couple of dozen of these and take them to a "sock hop." This portability helped records become an important part of the youth culture. Popular music also found its way to the 33⅓ format with collections of songs from the hottest artists of the day. The LP album was born.

Despite the anguished pleas of the older generation and of songwriters like Billy Rose, rock 'n' roll was here to stay. Danny and the Juniors, a popular rock group, sang it this way in 1958:

Rock 'n' roll is here to stay
I'll dig it to the end.
It'll go down in history,
Just you wait, my friend.
I don't care what people say
Rock 'n' roll is here to stay.

The British Are Coming!

By 1964 rock music had topped the charts for almost a decade, solidifying its position as the most important new sound in popular music. But was it still new? How long would Mediamerica youth stay enchanted with the same old rock 'n' roll?

If the fickle pop audience was looking for something new, they found it in the Liverpool sound. The Beatles led the "British invasion" of American popular music. On April 4, 1964, the top five singles in the nation were:

1	"Twist and Shout"	*The Beatles*
2	"Can't Buy Me Love"	*The Beatles*
3	"Please Please Me"	*The Beatles*
4	"She Loves You"	*The Beatles*
5	"I Want to Hold Your Hand"	*The Beatles*

No musical artists had ever so completely dominated the hit parade. Dressed in Edwardian suits and sporting similar "mop-top" haircuts, the "fab four" stirred up tremendous excitement among America's teens (see 7.3). Ed Sullivan featured them on his Sunday night TV variety show just as he had featured Presley a decade before.

Why the sudden Beatlemania? Perhaps rock fans needed new love objects or idols, or maybe it was the appeal of a "foreign" culture. The older generation greeted the Beatles with the same hostility they had earlier reserved for Presley. Fundamentalist preachers urged their congregations to burn Beatle records; they considered the new music a sacrilege. But Beatle fans were too engrossed in the sound to worry.

The first Beatle tours in America brought back memories of Presley and Sinatra. Young women screamed, mobbed the stage, and fainted at the sight of the quartet. Young men adopted Beatle haircuts. But the Beatles were not the only British invaders. Herman's Hermits, the Dave Clark Five, and Peter and Gordon all had Top 10 hits that year.

While the singers got the glory, the technicians behind the scenes had a great influence on the music. Legendary among them was Phil Spector. Spector's wizardry took place in the control room. During the early 1960s he produced over a dozen top hits, mostly by all-female singing groups like the Ronettes. In fact, he married the lead singer of that group. You may remember seeing Ronnie Spector in the Eddie Money video of "Take Me Home

Masters of the Mersey Beat

It all began in a strip joint in Germany in 1962. Brian Epstein, a London music promoter, found four young men playing there. Their music was just loud enough to be heard over the din. "Their act was ragged, their clothes were a mess," he said. "And yet I sensed at once that something was there."

That something was called the "Mersey Beat" (named after the Mersey River in Liverpool), a new sound that was sweeping Britain. The American press found the Beatles curious. *Newsweek* said, "The sound of their music is one of the most persistent noises heard over England since the air raid sirens were dismantled. . . . Beatle music is high pitched, loud beyond reason, and stupefyingly repetitive."

The Beatles in 1963, from left to right: Paul McCartney, John Lennon, Ringo Starr, and George Harrison.

Time predicted flatly that the Beatles stood little chance of making it with the American audience: "Though Americans may find the Beatles achingly familiar (their songs consist mainly of Yeh! screamed to the accompaniment of three guitars and a thunderous drum), they are apparently irresistible to the English."

Irresistible indeed. "Beatlemania" was already part of the English vocabulary in 1963. That was over 30 years ago, and we know now that it was only the beginning.

Tonight." She also sang the chorus, reprising her group's hit "Be My Baby."

Spector utilized multiple-channel dubbing techniques, putting together layer upon layer of music until the listener was overcome by what became known as the "wall of sound." Spector's lush, highly polished productions made him the most sought-after record producer in the business during these years.

I call the period from the birth of rock in 1955 to the end of 1964 the Age of Innocence because on the whole, rock music was just plain fun then. The conflicts addressed in rock lyrics were not the conflicts of the world but those between boy and girl, those simple yet intense moments filled with love, anxiety, and angst.

The Rock Renaissance

At the end of 1964, one fan magazine held a contest among readers to decide which of the new British groups would be most likely to remain popular for the next decade. The readers chose the Beatles, but the Dave Clark Five finished a close second. That seems absurd now, but one of the reasons the Dave Clark Five were not able to sustain their initial frantic following was because their music remained the same. The Beatles, on the other hand, dared to change. They saw that rock was growing up, and they grew with it. Even if the Beatles didn't last 10 years as a group (they disbanded in 1970), Paul, George, and Ringo are still active.

(John Lennon was murdered in 1980.) And they haven't stopped changing.

When I moved to southern California in the summer of 1965, I tuned in Top 40 radio and heard a new kind of song lyric. Rock artists were attempting to go beyond traditional clichés to communicate something meaningful with their songs. The Rolling Stones sang of social discontent and alienation in "Satisfaction." The Byrds' "Mr. Tambourine Man" (written by Bob Dylan) was a strange lyrical journey with heavy spiritual overtones. Barry McGuire's "Eve of Destruction" was an angry protest ballad that urged the young audience to

> Look at all the hate
> There is in Red China,
> Then take a look around, to Selma,
> Alabama.
> You may leave here for four days in
> space
> But when you return it's the same old
> place.

In September, Dylan's "Like a Rolling Stone" hit number one on the charts. It was an extraordinary, long, and cryptic song. Attempting to understand the lyrics was like trying to put together the pieces of a mysterious puzzle. Dylan, a wandering poet from Hibbing, Minnesota, by way of New York's Greenwich Village, clearly had a message that was unlike any other in pop music history.

In 1966 Simon and Garfunkel's songs of quiet social protest and personal bitterness also hit the top of the charts. The Beatles joined this movement with their *Revolver* album. One song urged listeners to "turn off your mind, relax, and float downstream." In 1967 the Jefferson Airplane's *Surrealistic Pillow* pointed the way toward San Francisco. Haight-Ashbury was the gathering place for a generation looking for a better way. Scott McKenzie sang, "If you're going to San Francisco, be sure to wear some flowers in your hair." Eric Burdon and the Animals advertised those "warm San Francisco nights."

Beatlemania was at its peak in 1964 when these British fans welcomed the "fab four" home after their triumphant American tour.

This was the Rock Renaissance. During the period from 1965 to 1970, rock came of age. Lyrics dealt with the grim realities of war, hatred, racism, and the infinite complexities of interpersonal relationships. To be sure, the simplistic lyrics of old were still around, but all over the country people began to take rock seriously for the first time. Perhaps the new music had something to say after all.

The Diffusion of Rock

Of course, if people actually counted on rock to solve the world's problems, they were in for a big disappointment. Despite antiwar protest ballads of the 1960s, the war in Vietnam dragged on into the 1970s. And as rock continued to develop, it didn't stay preoccupied with complex social problems. Even the great crusader, Dylan, brought out an album of simple country ballads aptly titled *Nashville Skyline*.

The early 1970s saw a trend toward a gentler rock style, with musicians such as James Taylor, Gordon Lightfoot, and Crosby, Stills, Nash, and Young becoming big stars. Their music was often soft and melodic, and the words were usually simple, soothing. The success of Joni Mitchell, Carly Simon, Carole King, and Linda Ronstadt in the 1970s gave women more of a voice in popular music than they had enjoyed since the 1940s. These women rode the crest of the softer rock, which purists claimed was not rock at all but some sort of new folk music set to an electric beat.

Not all the music that came from female artists was on the soft side, however. Artists like Grace Slick (with Starship as well as in solo efforts) and Heart carried on with straight-ahead rock 'n' roll, often with a hard edge.

"Soft rock" had hardly arrived when Alice Cooper, Kiss, and David Bowie appeared on the scene. Cooper's favorite stage antics included cutting off the heads of live chickens, something that did not endear him to critics who had decided rock had grown up. But the success of these groups points out that rock is flexible enough to offer something for everyone in the pop audience. If rock gets a little too staid, there is always a new group to set it on its ear.

The mid-1970s brought disco, perhaps the antithesis of the lyrically complex music of the late 1960s. Disco music was listened to strictly for the beat. It revived dancing, which had been very popular during the early 1960s, when the Twist, the Fly, and the Loco-motion were the rage. One enthusiast reported turning down a college basketball scholarship to continue his daily ritual of sleeping all day and dancing all night. "I'd rather disco," he said. "If it wasn't for the music, I wouldn't want to be in the world."

No real unifying trend marked the rock of the 1970s. Those who had gyrated to "Rock Around the Clock" were now in their 30s or 40s. Many of them preferred to sink nostalgically back into the "good old" rock 'n' roll of the 1950s, and that too enjoyed a revival.

From the innovative instrumentation of Stevie Wonder to the urban angst of Paul Simon, the 1970s brought rock enough for everyone. As the rock audience had grown in numbers, its needs had diversified. In the best traditions of commercial mass media, there was a rock product to fit every need.

New Music and Modern Rock

A fourth era of rock burst onto the scene on the heels of disco in the late 1970s. Though it has already been through a number of changes and has been labeled everything from punk to new wave to techno-pop to modern rock, we'll refer to it here simply as *new music*.

The first successful punk group is generally acknowledged to have been the Sex Pistols, an erratic and uninhibited band from England. Their first (and only) American tour was hailed as a breakthrough by many critics. On the heels of punk came slightly more melodic and far more accessible new-wave artists like Elvis Costello, the Ramones, and R.E.M. Mainstream artists like Linda Ronstadt and Billy Joel even released new wave–like albums, though Joel pointed out in one song that, no matter what the trend, "It's still rock 'n' roll to me."

The 1980s brought a flood of new music. Though it may still be too recent to be categorized and identified definitively, some clear trends have emerged.

The term *techno-pop* (derived from the use of synthesizers and other high-tech instruments) was generally associated with groups that incorporated a new-music sound but seemed to be more accessible to the average listener. Their music was also content oriented, with lyrics that were fairly recognizable to the mass audience. Among these were Culture Club, Duran Duran, Human League, Men at Work, A Flock of Seagulls, and especially the Police.

A number of new-music bands, a bit outside the mainstream, developed a cult following. These groups tended to be more form oriented, with nontraditional lyrics and a heavy dose of computerized effects. Among those heard most often in the 80s were the Fixx, Orchestral Maneuvers in the Dark (OMD), the Cure, and Berlin. Talking Heads continues to produce quirky and innovative material and always seems to be perpetually perched on rock's cutting edge.

In 1987 U2's "With or Without You" finally brought them international acclaim, though they are still listed in *Billboard*'s cutting edge "Modern Rock Tracks" section as well as on the pop charts. Along with R.E.M., U2 has been at the forefront of rock's renewed interest in social and political change.

Of course, assigning any group to a specific category can be risky business. The pop-music scene goes through so many changes that today's "artsy" cult band might be tomorrow's mainstream idols. Duran Duran was generally regarded as a cult band until "Hungry Like a Wolf" became a rock-video classic. Until they broke up, they enjoyed wide audience appeal. The Police developed a cult following for several years and had a couple of alternative/college radio successes until their 1983 LP *Synchronicity* placed them squarely in the mainstream.

Former Police songwriter and lead singer Sting (see 7.4) deserves a category of his own. His solo efforts not only have had tremendous audience appeal but have been critically acclaimed as well. In *Dream of the Blue Turtles*, he incorporated jazz, blues, and other musical forms into a thoroughly original work. The 1987 release of *Nothing Like the Sun* was another landmark, with several tracks reflecting a unique Latin flavor.

Of interest also is the work of Thomas Dolby, a synthesizer expert whose music enjoys a cult following and seems to help define what the new music is about. Perhaps more than any other artist, Dolby's music work reflects a combination of esoteric lyrics and newly created musical forms. Any analysis of

7.4

Sting emerged as one of the true innovators in rock, thanks to his solo efforts after leaving the Police.

the impact of the new music would not be complete without considering the marriage of the computer/synthesizer to more traditional instrumentation.

Laurie Anderson is an artist/performer who experiments with various musical forms, breath techniques, and studio effects. Much of her work is characterized by a sense of satire and humor.

In 1995 modern-rock charts and playlists featured the work of Counting Crows, the Red Hot Chili Peppers, and Pearl Jam. Nirvana still enjoyed a huge following, despite the untimely death of lead singer Kurt Cobain. By definition modern rock and new music are always about what's new, yet some artists seem to be able to provide consistently fresh material while resisting the temptation to produce "the next hit album." Familiar sources for some of 1995's crop of modern-rock material included such familiar yet innovative groups as R.E.M. and U2.

Rock and Rote: The Themes of Rock Music

To a generation raised in the golden age of radio, rock remains a mystery. What is it all about? How does it work? Bob Dylan's words "You know something is happening here but you don't know what it is, do you, Mr. Jones?" come to mind. I vividly recall my father's description of his first brush with rock. Though he was a professional musician most of his life, the music of the 1950s baffled him; he dubbed it "pots and pans . . . because it sounds like pots and pans banging together." After that I could expect to hear, "Edward, turn down the pots and pans!" whenever my radio was at top volume.

When critics complain that rock 'n' roll "all sounds the same," they mean the *form* sounds the same. To the untrained or uninterested ear, all rock songs do sound very similar. This makes examination of content even more important, because the lyrics contain a rich diversity of ideas that parallel the social and emotional concerns of youth culture. Such an examination may often turn up controversial as well as culturally significant material. This was the case when a group of influential "Washington wives" condemned rock lyrics (see 7.5).

Rock lyrics are learned by rote—that is, through repetition. Lyrics that may be barely discernible the first time around usually become quite clear by the 10th, 20th, or 200th time. Rock stations tend to play relatively few songs, most of them by just a handful of superstars. Thus we hear the same songs over and over again, and we can't help learning the words. Millions of Mediamericans share the same words and ideas simultaneously.

Love to Love You Baby

Though rock from the Age of Innocence is championed by some, both the musical form and the content were often pretty elementary. Songs fell into predictable categories. Lyrics tended to repeat phrases such as "I love my baby," "I lost my baby," "I need my baby," or later, "My baby got run over by a train."

Rock has grown up since the 1950s, and examination of its content yields some interesting patterns that help unravel what rock is about. Many rock songs still revolve around love. But then, most songs do. What else have we been singing about since the beginning of civilization?

Pop songs from the 60s and 70s described the process of discovering that someone cares about you and that you feel the same way (Paul McCartney's "Maybe I'm Amazed"); someone special who's left (Hall and Oates' "She's Gone"); love affairs gone wrong (Paul Simon's "April Come She Will," "Dangling Conversation," and "50 Ways to Leave Your Lover"). Simon is of particular interest, because his lyrics use traditional literary tools like allegory and metaphor. He weaves these carefully into the music to give it a depth rarely matched in rock music.

A different kind of love song came in 1970 when David Crosby's "Triad" suggested to two women who love him, "Why can't we go on as three?" Another topic frequently discussed in rock lyrics is homosexuality. Lou Reed's "Walk on the Wild Side" painted a graphic picture of the transvestite jungle of New York City. A more recent rap version describes an urban jungle beset by gang violence.

The Kinks' "Lola" told the story of a guy who took home a gal and found out she was really another guy. With a touch of naiveté he

Warning: Rock 'n' Roll May Be Hazardous to Your Emotional Health!

The chairman of the Senate Commerce Committee rapped his gavel and called the meeting to order. Among those scheduled to testify: Frank Zappa, John Denver, and Twisted Sister's Dee Snider. The issue: Have rock lyrics gone too far?

Though this may sound like a plot line for a rock video, it really did happen in September 1985. Several influential Washington women—including Tipper Gore and Susan Baker (wives of Senator Albert Gore and Treasury Secretary James Baker)—had formed the Parents' Music Resource Center (PMRC), which lobbied successfully to have hearings held on the "proliferation of songs glorifying rape, sadomasochism, incest, the occult, and suicide." The PMRC demanded legislation that would force record companies to label controversial lyrics as such. They also suggested that such albums be declared off-limits to minors.

Frank Zappa testified that "the complete list of PMRC demands reads like an instruction manual for some sinister kind of toilet-training program to housebreak all composers and performers." Dee Snider said he thought that "the only sadomasochism present was in Tipper Gore's mind." John Denver left early. In an interview with *Time,* David Geffen of Geffen Records said, "I have no intention of carrying a warning label on my records. It's censorship. They'd have to pass a law before I would do it."

Geffen's stand was not universally accepted by record companies. A casual trip to the record store today will reveal that many controversial albums carry warning labels of some kind, and there seem to be more of them every day, thanks in part to the controversial lyrics of artists like 2 Live Crew, N.W.A., and Public Enemy.

Whatever the outcome of this latest chapter in rock's irreverent history, the hearings themselves were immortalized in a 12-minute rap song by Zappa that actually includes recorded comments of those present. Perhaps *Time* reporter Jay Cocks summed it up best when he said, "Whatever their political effects, the hearings were certainly high on entertainment value." As it turned out, the political effects were of no small consequence either. PMRC activities were in the news again when Tipper Gore's husband became Bill Clinton's running mate in 1992.

---

notes that it's a "mixed-up, jumbled-up, shook-up world." In the latter 1970s, a new-wave group called the Vapors released a single called "Turning Japanese," which extolled the virtues of masturbation. And of course who could forget Divinyls' 1991 hit "I Touch Myself," released on the Virgin label?

In the 80s, George Michael stirred up quite a controversy with his hit "I Want Your Sex," which he insisted was "not a song condoning casual sexual relationships." The theme of Color Me Badd's "I Wanna Sex You Up" was pretty obvious, but Amy Grant's 1992 hit "Baby Baby" wasn't about relationships at all. In fact it was about . . . a baby!

Social Issues

The lyrics of Bob Dylan, one of the first rock poets, were complex where others had been simple, mysterious where others had been transparent, socially significant where others had been narcissistic. Many of the Dylan songs from the mid-1960s were scathing indictments of society. They had something to say about war ("Blowin' in the Wind," "A Hard Rain's

The Image of Women in Contemporary Music

Deborah Gordon is a graduate of the American studies program at the University of Maryland, where she helped teach a course about popular music in American culture. Here she reviews the images of women most often found in the lyrics to popular songs from rock 'n' roll's early years and suggests that the problem is still with us today.

The history of popular music has been, and continues to be, dominated by men singing about men's lives. The overwhelming majority of the writers, producers, and executives in the music industry are men. Because of this, much of popular music has either distorted women's life experiences or omitted a female perspective on those experiences.

Early rock-and-roll themes of romantic love presented images of women like that of "Earth Angel." "Earth angels" derived their power and influence over men's lives through their sexuality and femininity. Those women who failed to meet the feminine standards set in the music were made to feel inadequate. Those who did fit the image were viewed as sex objects, as portrayed in the lyrics of songs like "What Is Love?" The answer? Someone who "sways with a wiggle when she walks."

The early 1960s saw a continuance of traditional sex roles. The sex double standard could be seen in the double messages of Dion's hits "Runaround Sue" and "The Wanderer." Dion warned, "Keep away from Runaround Sue" but glorified himself as the "type of guy who'll never settle down." If you were a female and "ran around," you were wicked—someone to be avoided, but if you were a male who did the same, you were popular.

Female singers in the early 1960s made hits by singing songs idolizing men. The central message of Connie Francis' "Where the Boys Are" was the same as that of the fairy tale *Sleeping Beauty*. She sang of a boy somewhere waiting to find her, and she pledged, "Till he finds me I'll be waiting patiently." Like the passive Sleeping Beauty, the woman of this song is seen as dreaming and waiting for a man to give her life. Little Peggy March sang "I Will Follow Him," which was one of the few active interests a young woman could pursue. Like the images of women and men from Stone Age myths, Joanie Sommers begged Johnny to get angry and "give me the biggest lecture I've ever had." She claimed that she wanted "a brave man . . . a cave man."

The Beatles sang traditional themes of boy meets girl, boy gets girl, and boy gets hurt by girl. Females were portrayed as teases in songs like "Day Tripper," in which they sang, "She's a big teaser." Much of the early Beatles music was filled with images of men and women in traditional sex roles. Boys were active and girls were passive, as seen in the lyrics of songs like "I Saw Her Standing There." . . .

When the second wave of the British invasion hit America, the Rolling Stones challenged the Beatles as the most popular musical group in the country. The Stones' music expressed more blatant hostility and contempt toward women than the earlier British music. Mick Jagger sang "Under My Thumb" about a girl "who does just what she's told." In "Time Is on My Side," the Stones mocked the dependence of a woman, telling her she'd come running back "like you did so many times before, to me."

Along with the more overt objectification of women, violence against women appeared more and more frequently in the music of the late 1960s and 1970s. In the Rolling Stones' version of "Midnight Rambler," Albert De Salvo, the notorious Boston Strangler who killed a number of women, is celebrated as a hero.

Despite the generally negative images of women in popular music during this period, some songs achieving popularity suggested that women's roles were in a state of transition. In the early 1960s when female singers were worshiping "Johnny Angel" and "The Leader of the Pack," Lesley Gore sang "You Don't Own Me," in which she told a man not to tell her what to do or say. In "Different Drum," Linda Ronstadt sang that she was "not in the market for a boy who wants to love only me," and Aretha Franklin asked for "respect" for herself. The rigid sex roles of the 1950s, with women seen as appendages of men without identities of their own, were directly challenged in songs like these.

Some popular music has reflected the growing consciousness of feminism. Helen Reddy's "I Am Woman" was perhaps the song most widely associated with the women's movement of the 1970s. In it Reddy sang, "I am woman, hear me roar in numbers too big to ignore," proclaiming that women were determined to change their position within the culture.

Carly Simon's "You're So Vain" portrayed a man's narcissism with bitterness and anger. Loretta Lynn sang "The Pill," a hit on country and western charts, in which she told her husband, "There's gonna be some changes made right here on Nurs'ry Hill." Women were less inclined to subordinate their own needs to those of men, and they protested about poor treatment they received from men.

By 1975 a new genre of music was offering an alternative to popular music for feminist listeners. "Women's," or "feminist," music was part of a larger consciousness within the feminist movement, which produced creative expressions of women's experiences as well as the social problems they faced.

As part of the sexual revolution of the 1960s, another image of women in popular music became that of a sex bomb, who projected liberation through good sex. Donna Summer's "Love to Love You Baby" aimed moans and groans, imitating sexual excitement, at the male listener. But it covertly spoke to women, reinforcing their role as sex object.

The 1970s brought an ever-increasing amount of violence aimed at women in the music of punk-rock groups like the Ramones, who sang "You're Gonna Kill That Girl."

With an antifeminist backlash emerging, feminists began mobilizing against the music industry. They protested against what they felt were violent and pornographic images of women on album covers and promotional materials. In Los Angeles, feminists protested against an advertising billboard for the Rolling Stones' album Black and Blue. On the billboard was a picture of a woman beaten and tied up; the caption read "I'm black and blue from the Rolling Stones,

and I love it." Those protesting the billboard attempted to get it taken down through legal channels; when those efforts didn't work, they painted across it, "This is a crime against women." The billboard was then taken down.

In November 1979, feminists won a victory over Warner/Atlantic/Elektra/Asylum Records, which they had been boycotting and protesting against for two and a half years. The record company issued a statement saying that it opposed violence against women or men depicted on album covers and promotional materials. Of course, sometimes an individual artist or group may have final control over album-cover design, so it is not easy to say what kind of impact this statement will actually have. Still, it is significant that there was enough pressure by feminists to move the company to respond.

Today, the different messages of a number of genres of music do not give us a simple, clear-cut picture of what future images of women will be. There is ambiguity in cultural definitions of male-female relationships and changing sex roles and politics. On the one hand, there is a growing amount of violence against women depicted in punk rock and new wave. On the other hand, the 1970s brought a growing number of female

Continued on next page

musicians who portrayed images of women that show human complexity and a break with traditional beliefs. The ambiguity of the 1970s suggests that the 1980s will go down in history as a turning point for women and their relationship with the media. Feminist recording companies and businesses like Olivia Records face an economic situation that may not allow them to continue operating as autonomous structures countering the larger recording companies. . . . Thus what the image of women in popular music is to become in the 1990s remains to be seen.

Used with permission of Deborah Gordon.

Gonna Fall," "Talking World War III Blues") and racial injustice ("Oxford Town"). Dylan's intensely personal and politically charged lyrics, coupled with his unwillingness to be packaged, promoted, or even interviewed, seemed to contribute to his success.

A concern for the environment is evident in the hundreds of rock and country songs that offered an escape from the city ("Goin' up the Country," "Thank God I'm a Country Boy," "Rocky Mountain High").

The new-music era was characterized by lyrics that point up a number of social concerns. The deceptively simple lyrics of the Clash, for example, were clearly about the freedom of the individual in society. Neil Young's 1983 *Trans* LP was a dissertation on what might happen to human beings in the computer age.

More familiar social concerns were found in the lyrics of U2. In "Sunday Bloody Sunday," from the *War* album, they sang:

Broken bottles under children's feet
Bodies strewn across the dead end streets
But I won't heed the battle call
It puts my back against the wall

Lyrics like these catapulted U2 to the forefront of rock's conscience. Their phenomenally successful 1987 tour solidified their position as one of the most universally acclaimed rock groups of the decade.

But the heir apparent to Bob Dylan's mantle of social concern and personal introspection in popular music is Bruce Springsteen. "The Boss" continues to use his personal success as a forum for bringing to our attention the plight of the unemployed and homeless. Portions of the proceeds from his concert tours are always donated to local charities benefiting these causes.

The socially relevant lyrics of R.E.M. led to seven 1992 Grammy nominations for the Georgia-based band. R.E.M.'s music reminds us all that popular music can prompt us to think while we dance and be informed while we are being entertained.

The Artist and Society

In 1972 Don McLean's "Vincent" described the tortured world of Vincent van Gogh, and Joni Mitchell's "Judgment of the Moon and Stars," subtitled "Ludwig's Tune," was a portrait of the agony Beethoven felt as he was going deaf.

In developing the theme of the artist's alienation, rock artists often describe their own situation. Hence we have rock songs that describe what it's like to be a rock star or a would-be star. That star is a product of the jet age, often doing concerts all over the world in the same month. There are moments of loneliness ("Holiday Inn," "Come Monday," "Turn the Page") and ever-present groupies ("Superstar," "Guitar Man," "Blonde in the Bleachers"). In an age when artists are bought and sold in a maze of recording contracts and highly promoted concert dates, they sometimes feel like prisoners of the system. Joni Mitchell's "For Free" laments the plight of a musician who couldn't attract an audience because "they knew he'd never been on their TV so they passed his music by." James Taylor tells an unbelieving patron in a café, "Hey, mister, that's me up on the jukebox."

More recently, Peter Gabriel satirized the star-making process and the artist's role in society in "Big Time," from the *So* album. In the song, we hear from the upcoming rock star who says unequivocally "I'm on the way to making it. . . . Big time . . . so much larger than life. . . . My car's getting bigger. . . . My house's getting bigger. . . ." Joe Walsh's "Life's Been Good to Me So Far" is another classic in this genre.

Country Music

Though rock has been the most listened-to popular music of the last three decades, that period has also brought an amazing growth in country music. In 1961 only 81 radio stations were playing it, but by 1980 more than 1,000 stations played country full time, and 1,500 more played at least 3 hours of it daily. Country fans claimed 1991 as the biggest year ever for their music, and sales figures backed them up. Garth Brooks's *Ropin' the Wind* album *entered* the Billboard chart at number one, and "Hot Country Nights" proved successful for NBC in prime time.

Meanwhile, in Nashville, home of the Grand Ole Opry and center of the country-music business, residents could boast of the most sophisticated recording studios in the nation. More songs are now recorded in Nashville than in New York City, Los Angeles, and Detroit combined. In fact, over *half* of all the music recorded in America is recorded in Nashville. Robert Altman's film *Nashville,* an overwhelming critical success in the mid-1970s, familiarized many with the city and its

music. Nevertheless, in recent years Nashville's prominence has been challenged by a new country-music mecca: Branson, Missouri.

The country sound has come a long way from the days of the hillbilly fiddle and banjo. Country artists now often record with full orchestras, and their sound is as elaborate as that of rock. Indeed, during the 1970s many country tunes, such as Charley Rich's "Behind Closed Doors" and C. W. McCall's "Convoy," hit the top of the pop charts. "Underground country," a synthesis of rock and C&W sung by stars like Waylon Jennings and Kris Kristofferson, combines acoustic sound with electric instruments and Moog synthesizers. Often these sophisticated recording techniques have sophisticated lyrics to match.

More than any other artist, Kenny Rogers typifies the successful "country crossover" phenomenon with his pop-country renditions of songs like "Ruby, Don't Take Your Love to Town" and "The Gambler." Other popular rock artists like the Eagles and Lynyrd Skynyrd forged unique syntheses of rock and country that met with enthusiastic acceptance from both AOR and country-music listeners. The genius of Lynyrd Skynyrd ended abruptly and tragically when several members of the band were killed in a plane crash in 1977.

More recently, the pronounced country influence in the rock albums of John Mellencamp has helped keep rock's country roots current. Garth Brooks won *Billboard*'s 1991 album artist of the year award and was named top country-album artist as well. His "No Fences" was the top-selling country album that year and was a clear crossover success. Billy Ray Cyrus was 1992's country crossover sensation.

Why the rush to the country? John Colley, who teaches English literature at Yale University, puts it this way: "Country music is becoming the *soul* music of white middle- and working-class people. It reminds them of quieter and more peaceful times and it describes

Billboard HOT 100 SINGLES

FOR WEEK ENDING AUGUST 1, 1992

COMPILED FROM A NATIONAL SAMPLE OF TOP 40 RADIO AIRPLAY MONITORED BY BROADCAST DATA SYSTEMS, TOP 40 RADIO PLAYLISTS, AND RETAIL AND RACK SINGLES SALES COLLECTED, COMPILED, AND PROVIDED BY SoundScan

THIS WEEK	LAST WEEK	2 WKS AGO	WKS ON CHART	TITLE (PRODUCER/SONGWRITER) — LABEL & NUMBER/DISTRIBUTING LABEL	ARTIST
				★★★ NO. 1 ★★★	
1	1	1	17	BABY GOT BACK ▲ — 5 weeks at No. 1 — (C) (T) (X) DEF AMERICAN 18947/REPRISE	◆ SIR MIX-A-LOT
2	2	7	13	THIS USED TO BE MY PLAYGROUND — (C) (V) SIRE 18822/WARNER BROS.	◆ MADONNA
3	3	5	13	BABY-BABY-BABY — (C) LAFACE 4-2028/ARISTA	◆ TLC
4	4	4	13	ACHY BREAKY HEART ▲ — (C) (V) MERCURY 866 522	◆ BILLY RAY CYRUS
5	6	10	16	JUST ANOTHER DAY — (C) (D) SBK 07383/ERG	◆ JON SECADA
6	5	6	10	NOVEMBER RAIN — (C) (V) GEFFEN 19067	◆ GUNS N' ROSES
7	7	11	12	LIFE IS A HIGHWAY — (C) (V) CAPITOL 44815	◆ TOM COCHRANE
8	32	53	3	END OF THE ROAD (FROM "BOOMERANG") — (C) MOTOWN 2178	◆ BOYZ II MEN
9	16	21	9	GIVING HIM SOMETHING HE CAN FEEL — (C) (D) (X) ATCO EASTWEST 98560	◆ EN VOGUE
10	9	9	10	WISHING ON A STAR — (C) (T) (V) EPIC 74343	◆ THE COVER GIRLS
11	5	10	11	I'LL BE THERE — (C) (V) COLUMBIA 74330	◆ MARIAH CAREY
12	12	13	8	TOO FUNKY — (C) (M) (T) (V) (X) COLUMBIA 74353	◆ GEORGE MICHAEL
13	14	16	9	WARM IT UP — (C) (M) (T) (V) RUFFHOUSE 74376/COLUMBIA	◆ KRIS KROSS
14	10	8	15	IF YOU ASKED ME TO — (C) (V) EPIC 74277	◆ CELINE DION
15	8	3	18	UNDER THE BRIDGE ● — (C) (V) WARNER BROS. 18978	◆ RED HOT CHILI PEPPERS
16	18	18	8	COME & TALK TO ME ● — (C) (V) (X) UPTOWN 54175/MCA	◆ JODECI
17	15	14	10	THE BEST THINGS IN LIFE ARE FREE — (C) (V) PERSPECTIVE 0010/A&M	◆ LUTHER VANDROSS AND JANET JACKSON
18	21	22	11	KEEP ON WALKIN' — (C) (M) (T) A&M 1598	◆ CECE PENISTON
19	19	19	8	FRIDAY I'M IN LOVE — (C) (X) FICTION 64742/ELEKTRA	◆ THE CURE
20	13	6	12	TENNESSEE — (C) (T) CHRYSALIS 23829/ERG	◆ ARRESTED DEVELOPMENT
21	24	26	6	MOVE THIS — (C) SBK 50400/ERG	◆ TECHNOTRONIC FEATURING YA KID K
22	26	26	8	THE ONE — (C) (V) (X) MCA 54423	◆ ELTON JOHN
23	23	27	8	TAKE THIS HEART — (C) (V) CAPITOL 44782	◆ RICHARD MARX
24	17	12	12	DAMN I WISH I WAS YOUR LOVER — (C) (V) COLUMBIA 74164	◆ SOPHIE B. HAWKINS
25	20	20	20	MY LOVIN' (YOU'RE NEVER GONNA GET IT) ● — (C) (M) (T) (X) ATCO EASTWEST 98586	◆ EN VOGUE
				★★★ POWER PICK/AIRPLAY ★★★	
26	33	50	5	STAY — (C) (X) LONDON 869 730/PLG	◆ SHAKESPEAR'S SISTER
27	31	35	4	JAM — (C) (T) (V) EPIC 74333	◆ MICHAEL JACKSON
28	29	29	7	GOOD STUFF — (C) (V) REPRISE 18895	◆ THE B-52'S
29	22	15	18	JUMP ▲ — (C) (M) (T) (V) (X) RUFFHOUSE 74197/COLUMBIA	◆ KRIS KROSS
30	28	25	13	THEY WANT EFX ● — (C) (M) (T) (X) ATCO EASTWEST 96206	◆ DAS EFX
31	27	28	11	JUST FOR TONIGHT — (C) (V) WING 865 888/MERCURY	◆ VANESSA WILLIAMS
32	25	23	14	HOLD ON MY HEART — (C) (V) ATLANTIC 87481	◆ GENESIS
33	30	24	13	SLOW MOTION — (C) (V) (X) GIANT 18908	◆ COLOR ME BADD
34	35	43	6	ALL I WANT — (C) (D) COLUMBIA 74355	◆ TOAD THE WET SPROCKET
35	41	46	7	YOU REMIND ME (FROM "STRICTLY BUSINESS") — (C) (M) (T) UPTOWN 54327/MCA	◆ MARY J. BLIGE
36	39	49	6	JUMP AROUND — (C) (M) (T) (V) TOMMY BOY 526	◆ HOUSE OF PAIN
37	40	42	6	EVERYBODY'S FREE (TO FEEL GOOD) — (C) EPIC 74388	◆ ROZALLA
38	36	36	6	MAKE LOVE LIKE A MAN — (C) (V) MERCURY 864 038	◆ DEF LEPPARD
39	34	32	15	I WILL REMEMBER YOU — (C) A&M 1600	◆ AMY GRANT
40	46	45	8	MR. LOVERMAN (FROM "DEEP COVER") — (C) (M) (T) EPIC 74257	◆ SHABBA RANKS
41	51	59	7	PLEASE DON'T GO — (C) (M) (T) (X) NEXT PLATEAU 339	◆ K.W.S.
42	48	52	4	EVEN BETTER THAN THE REAL THING — (C) (T) (X) ISLAND 866 977/PLG	◆ U2
43	37	31	21	LIVE AND LEARN — (C) (M) (T) COLUMBIA 74012	◆ JOE PUBLIC
44	45	39	11	HONEY LOVE ● — (C) (V) JIVE 42031	◆ R. KELLY & PUBLIC ANNOUNCEMENT
45	38	34	12	WHY — (C) (V) ARISTA 1-2419	◆ ANNIE LENNOX
46	44	38	26	TEARS IN HEAVEN ● — (C) (V) REPRISE 19038	◆ ERIC CLAPTON
47	43	37	27	SAVE THE BEST FOR LAST ● — (C) (V) (X) WING 865 136/MERCURY	◆ VANESSA WILLIAMS
48	50	61	4	BACK TO THE HOTEL — (C) (T) PROFILE 5367	◆ N2DEEP
49	47	47	13	SOMETIMES I RHYME SLOW — (C) (M) (T) RAL 74167/COLUMBIA	◆ NICE & SMOOTH
50	42	33	14	DO IT TO ME — (C) (D) MOTOWN 2160	◆ LIONEL RICHIE
51	49	40	17	JUST TAKE MY HEART — (C) (D) (V) ATLANTIC 87509	◆ MR. BIG
52	52	58	7	SLOWLY — (C) (D) RCA 62271	◆ STACY EARL
53	57	60	8	TWILIGHT ZONE — (C) (M) (T) (X) RADIKAL 15486/CRITIQUE	◆ 2 UNLIMITED
				★★★ POWER PICK/SALES ★★★	
54	78	87	4	WE WILL ROCK YOU/WE ARE THE CHAMPIONS — (C) (M) (V) (X) HOLLYWOOD 64725	◆ QUEEN
55	71	—	2	GIVE U MY HEART — (C) (T) LAFACE 4-2026/ARISTA	◆ BABYFACE (FEATURING TONI BRAXTON)
56	62	79	4	I WANNA LOVE YOU — (C) GIANT 18950	◆ JADE
57	61	70	5	I MISS YOU — (C) (M) (T) COLUMBIA 74321	◆ JOE PUBLIC
58	82	—	2	CROSSOVER — (C) (M) (T) (X) RAL 74173/CHAOS	◆ EPMD
				★★★ HOT SHOT DEBUT ★★★	
59	NEW ▶		1	JESUS HE KNOWS ME — (C) ATLANTIC 87454	◆ GENESIS
60	63	78	4	RESTLESS HEART — (C) (V) WARNER BROS. 18897	◆ PETER CETERA
61	58	63	6	THEY REMINISCE OVER YOU (T.R.O.Y.) — (C) (T) ELEKTRA 64773	◆ PETE ROCK & C.L. SMOOTH
62	73	—	2	JUS LYKE COMPTON — (C) (T) (V) PROFILE 5372	◆ DJ QUIK
63	69	82	3	MONEY CAN'T BUY YOU LOVE — (C) PERSPECTIVE 0011/A&M	◆ RALPH TRESVANT
64	64	76	5	THE WAY I FEEL — (C) SCOTTI BROS. 75315	◆ TAG
65	56	44	15	IN THE CLOSET — (C) (M) (T) (V) (X) EPIC 74266	◆ MICHAEL JACKSON
66	59	57	9	SCENARIO — (C) (M) (T) JIVE 42056*	◆ A TRIBE CALLED QUEST
67	NEW ▶		1	SHE'S PLAYING HARD TO GET — (C) (D) (V) JIVE 42067	◆ HI-FIVE
68	53	41	13	YOU WON'T SEE ME CRY — (C) (V) SBK 07385/ERG	◆ WILSON PHILLIPS
69	70	80	4	TEQUILA — (C) (T) ATCO EASTWEST 96161*	◆ A.L.T. AND THE LOST CIVILIZATION
70	60	54	8	REMEDY — (C) (V) DEF AMERICAN 18877/REPRISE	◆ THE BLACK CROWES
71	68	68	16	JAMES BROWN IS DEAD — (C) (V) ARISTA 1-2387*	◆ L.A. STYLE
72	NEW ▶		1	DO I HAVE TO SAY THE WORDS? — (C) A&M 1611	◆ BRYAN ADAMS
73	66	—	2	SEXY MF — (C) (V) PAISLEY PARK 18817/WARNER BROS.	◆ PRINCE AND THE N.P.G.
74	67	62	18	EVERYTHING ABOUT YOU — (C) (V) STARDOG 866 632/MERCURY	◆ UGLY KID JOE
75	72	75	18	PLEASE DON'T GO — (C) (M) (T) MOTOWN 2155	◆ BOYZ II MEN
76	72	75	3	BOOT SCOOTIN' BOOGIE — (C) (V) ARISTA 1-2440	◆ BROOKS & DUNN
77	65	64	16	HELLUVA — (C) (M) (T) GASOLINE ALLEY 54350/MCA	◆ BROTHERHOOD CREED
78	75	71	13	NEVER SATISFIED — (C) (T) GIANT 18981	◆ GIANT
79	77	69	5	BRAINSTORMING — (C) (M) (T) MOTOWN 2170	◆ M.C. BRAINS
80	74	—	2	SILENT PRAYER — (C) (M) (T) MOTOWN 2165	◆ SHANICE
81	88	97	3	ANOTHER MINUTE — (C) (T) (X) SRC 14036/ZOO	◆ CAUSE & EFFECT
82	96	—	8	GIVE IT AWAY — (C) (T) (X) WARNER BROS. 19147	◆ RED HOT CHILI PEPPERS
83	80	92	5	STROBELITE HONEY — (C) (M) (T) MERCURY 866 868	◆ BLACK SHEEP
84	100	98	5	TAKE ME IN YOUR ARMS — (M) (T) HIGH POWER 1005/WARLOCK	◆ LIL SUZY
85	86	83	17	LET'S GET ROCKED — (C) (V) MERCURY 866 568	◆ DEF LEPPARD
86	91	95	3	WHEREVER I MAY ROAM — (C) (V) ELEKTRA 64741	◆ METALLICA
87	71	56	9	STRAWBERRY LETTER 23 — (C) QWEST 18919/WARNER BROS.	◆ TEVIN CAMPBELL
88	91	77	11	VICTIM OF THE GHETTO — (C) (T) (V) VIRGIN 98635	◆ THE COLLEGE BOYZ
89	NEW ▶		1	CONSTANT CRAVING — (C) SIRE 18942/WARNER BROS.	◆ K.D. LANG
90	79	73	18	MARIA — (C) (T) (V) (X) TOMMY BOY 987	◆ TKA
91	99	—	2	I'VE GOT MINE — (C) (D) MCA 54429	◆ GLENN FREY
92	92	85	7	FOREVER IN YOUR EYES — (C) PERSPECTIVE 0009/A&M	◆ MINT CONDITION
93	65	65	13	T.L.C. — (C) (D) ATLANTIC 87484	◆ LINEAR
94	NEW ▶		1	THE HITMAN — (C) (M) (T) INTERSCOPE 98506	◆ AB LOGIC
95	83	84	5	REACH FOR THE SKY — (C) EPIC 74335	◆ FIREHOUSE
96	84	74	17	WHY ME BABY? — (C) (M) ELEKTRA 64777	◆ KEITH SWEAT
97	93	93	5	SO WHAT'CHA WANT — (M) (T) (X) CAPITOL 15847*	◆ BEASTIE BOYS
98	NEW ▶		1	NOTHING BROKEN BUT MY HEART — (C) EPIC 74336	◆ CELINE DION
99	90	91	16	NOT THE ONLY ONE — (C) (V) (X) CAPITOL 44764	◆ BONNIE RAITT
100	97	99	4	WHO'S GOT YOUR LOVE — (M) (T) MICMAC 2572*	◆ NYASIA

BILLBOARD   AUGUST 1, 1992

7.6

The *Billboard* "Hot 100" are watched closely by artists, record executives, and everyone else in the recording industry.

7.7

Whitney Houston was one of several female artists to leave an indelible mark on popular music in the 1980s.

their everyday life as they see it—as an epic adventure, full of dangers, tragedies, and triumphs."

Rhythm and Blues: Soul Music for the 90s

Like rock and country, soul music seems to have as many definitions as there are those who sing it, although all agree that soul is associated with blacks. The term *soul* was first popularized in the 1960s, at a time when black pride and black power were first recognized as a strong social force. White folk music and the complex arrangements by the Beatles and Dylan were then receiving wide critical acclaim and public acceptance, and there seemed to be a need for a term to describe the more fundamental beat practiced by artists like Otis Redding and James Brown.

Soul grew out of rhythm and blues, a traditional black sound that was rearranged by white musicians like Carl Perkins and Elvis Presley during the early development of rock 'n' roll. But soul was something different — different from R&B and different from rock.

Soul was far more than a kind of music. Little Richard explained: "To me, soul is when a man sings from his heart and it reaches another heart. When you sing with feeling and you really feel what you are singing, that's soul." Black artists were fed up with trying to imitate whites or reach the white audience; instead, they sang what they felt. Nearly everyone agreed that if you had to *explain* soul to someone, he or she didn't have it.

Whatever soul music is, it has been tremendously popular, and not only with the black audience. Many songs crossed over from *Billboard* R&B charts to the Hot 100 (see 7.6). During the 1950s and 1960s, artists like Ray Charles and the Platters were prime examples of this phenomenon. Then came the "Motown sound" led by black superstars like Diana Ross and the Supremes and Stevie Wonder. The appeal of these artists was and continues to be universal.

Despite his recent problems, Michael Jackson's music continues to have strong crossover appeal and remains widely accepted by the entire popular-music audience. Jackson's 1983 album *Thriller* became the best-selling record in history. To date it has sold some 50 million copies. His 1987 *Bad* sold 25 million. Even the gloved one's *Dangerous* enjoyed a long stay at number one on the album charts.

Jackson's sister Janet, Whitney Houston (see 7.7), Mariah Carey, and C&C Music Factory enjoy wide success on both the R&B and pop charts. Today's R&B charts afford a broad

The Politics of Rap

I got my 12-gauge sawed off
I got my headlights turned off
I'm 'bout to bust some shots off
I'm 'bout to dust some cops off

Ice-T, "Cop Killer"

When Ice-T's "Cop Killer" became a focal flashpoint for political debate during the 1992 presidential race, politicians stood in line to condemn the song.

Meanwhile, rapper Ice-T (whose real name is Tracy Mar-row) told the *Los Angeles Times* that he didn't see what all the fuss was about. "After all, don't these politicians realize that the country was founded on the kind of revolutionary political thought expressed in my song? I mean haven't they ever listened to the national anthem? Anybody knows that the 'Star Spangled Banner' is really just a song about a shoot-out between us and the police."

The Ice-T controversy was just one of a number of incidents along the campaign trail that pointed to the fundamental schism between the political establishment and the politics of rap. Bill Clinton condemned Sister Souljah (Lisa Williamson) when she told a *Washington Post* reporter that the L.A. riots were really quite easy to understand. "If black people kill black people every day, why not take a week and kill white people?"

Tipper Gore, wife of Clinton running mate Al Gore, came under fire for her work in promoting the use of warning labels on music products, though she was careful to point out that she never advocated censorship.

Dan Quayle was adamant: "Time-Warner is making money, a lot of it, off a record that's

---

spectrum of sound from the innovative offerings of Prince to the smooth ballads of Peabo Bryson. There is also room for the intense and controversial lyrics of Ice Cube, N.W.A., and Ice-T (see 7.8). In short, there is R&B for just about every musical taste with a lot of it crossing over successfully to the pop charts.

Popular Music in the 90s

Will the 1990s simply provide a continuation of trends begun in the 1980s, or will an entirely new form of popular music emerge? Clearly the new music of the 80s was the work of a number of creative artists who expanded the vocabulary of rock in a way that hadn't been attempted since the 1960s.

A list of women performers who left their mark on the 80s would certainly include Madonna, Whitney Houston, and Suzanne Vega, though none of them could be considered modern rock. Madonna parlayed a string of hits and a streetwise demeanor into one of the more intriguing personas of the decade. Along the way she provided grist for the gossip mill with her on-again off-again relationships and the acclaimed "Truth or Dare" concert film.

Whitney Houston's electrifying delivery adds a special touch to everything she records. Her debut album was the most successful first album ever—selling over 6 million copies. Suzanne Vega first came to national attention with her 1987 hit "Luka," a song about an abused woman. Vega's fragile voice combined with the richness and depth of her lyrics made her one of the most innovative popular-music artists of the decade.

Early in the 80s many credited the new music and rock videos with saving the sagging record industry, but perhaps they overstated their case. The music business, like many

suggesting that it's all right to kill cops." When stores refused to sell Ice-T's music, mega-corporation Time-Warner stood squarely behind their "gangsta rapper" and accused the outlets of censorship. Eventually Ice-T asked Time-Warner to recall all CDs and cassettes containing "Cop Killer."

Love it or leave it, rap today is a $700 million a year growth industry. Interestingly, about three fourths of all rap records are purchased by white listeners, most of them in their teens. Is rap a revolutionary vehicle for the expression of social injustice or simply an irresponsible commer-

cial vehicle that encourages hatred?

Music critics are sharply divided. Stanley Crouch of *The Village Voice* says flatly: "All they are is just third-rate street thugs and would-be thugs, who have rhymed doggerel on a third-grade level with no literary content."

Music journalist Chuck Phillips observed that "the debate over rap really goes beyond the presidential race and looks to music's place in today's cultural framework." Nova University law professor Bruce Rogow concludes simply that "our leaders need to listen, not chide or censor these artists."

What's clear is that rap, once an obscure cutting-edge genre, has moved into the mainstream and generated a lot of attention along the way. USC journalism professor Sherrie Mazingo feels that it's high time we all paid attention. "These artists . . . have become the pioneers in the new frontier of black political awareness and action," she insists. Like the rock 'n' roll controversies that preceded it, the politics of rap promises to be one of those musical debates that will continue for some years to come.

American industries, experienced an economic decline during the late 1970s and again in the early 1990s. Home taping and a lack of creative music that excited consumers were the reasons given in the 70s — the sluggish economy is generally thought to be the more recent culprit. Home taping has continued to be a problem for the industry, with no solution in sight. No amount of fresh music appears to be able to solve that problem.

New Technology: The CD Boom

As we have seen, the old metal cylinders of Edison's day were eventually replaced by 78 rpm vinyl records. These in turn gave way to 45s and eventually to 33s. Ask anyone over 40 and they will tell you that once upon a time

there were 4 track — then 8 track — prerecorded tapes. These quickly gave way to recordable cassette tapes.

The music industry's latest technological triumph is the compact disc, or CD. Introduced in 1985, the CD continues to increase its share of recording industry profits each year. CD technology has virtually obliterated the vinyl "record," and some feel it will do the same to the cassette. A 1991 survey revealed that, for the first time, the wholesale dollar value of CD sales surpassed that of cassettes.

Ironically, the very features that prompted skyrocketing CD sales pose an increasing problem for CD manufacturers. Because CDs hardly ever wear out, used CDs are indistinguishable from new ones. As a result, used-CD stores have been springing up everywhere and represent an increasingly larger share of retail CD sales (see Issues and Answers, p. 174). Meanwhile, Sony has announced plans for a recordable CD about half the size of the current disc while Phillips has plans for a digital compact cassette (DCC) system that would allow consumers to tape music while maintaining digital quality.

Rock 'n' Roll Is Here to Pay!

Like all media industries, the recording industry faces uncertain economic times in the years ahead. A related problem that developed in the early 90s involved the megastar deals landed by top pop artists. Despite numerous layoffs and cutbacks, major record labels found enough cash to offer Michael Jackson $60 million (Sony), Janet Jackson $40 million (Virgin), and Motley Crew $35 million (Elektra). The Rolling Stones signed with Virgin for $40 million while the durable Aerosmith was awarded $25 million for returning to Sony. Superstar royalties, now in the 17–25% range, also guarantee to take a big bite out of future record-company profits.

With megastar deals, new music, and new technology, the last decade will definitely go down in history as a period of extensive change for the recording industry—and for the consumers who support it. Yet no matter what the format, it is rock 'n' roll that continues to thrive and dominate the industry. And part of its charm will always be in its unpredictability. Neil Young's "Hey Hey, My My (Into the Black)" offers this succinct observation:

Hey hey, my my
Rock and roll will never die
There's more to the picture, than meets
the eye
Hey hey, my my

Issues and Answers: CD Technology: The Double-Edged Sword

Durability and indestructibility were touted as key selling points when the CD was introduced. Now the editors of *Billboard* say that the shiny discs may come back to haunt the industry in ways no one anticipated.

When the compact disc first appeared, its manufacturers proudly cited the durability and relative indestructibility of the CD as two of its key selling points. Those claims have, by and large, proved to be true. But, unexpectedly, they have come back to haunt the record companies in the form of used CDs.

Traditional retailers have lately been sounding the alarm about the spread of used-CD stores—and some have even accused Sony Music of encouraging the practice by not accepting returns of opened CDs. Sony has denied this, claiming that its policy is aimed at reducing the used-CD problem. Meanwhile, used-CD retailers are delighted over the growth of their business, and some new-product retailers are also threatening to get into used CDs rather than be undersold by the competition.

Like cassette tapes, which spawned the plague of home taping, the CD technology itself contains the seeds of this dilemma. Because of its durability, a used CD generally sounds as good as it did when it was first played; in fact, even the jewel-box packaging conspires to preserve the artwork. Thus the very elements that make a new CD a "keeper" for the consumer also make a used CD an attractive product, especially at a much lower price.

The industry debate over the level of front-line CD pricing has raged for years. Some retailers believe a reduction in such pricing would significantly reduce the problem of used CDs. The record companies, on the other hand, do not think CD prices are too high. They tend to believe setting limits on returns of opened CDs—an approach rejected by most retailers—is one way to combat the used-CD threat.

While this rhetoric flows without any meeting of minds, the used-CD problem continues to worsen. Not having anticipated it to begin with, the industry is in a catch-up position. The best thing all parties can now do is to admit the seriousness of the situation and figure out how to address it.

If the used-CD phenomenon is not dealt with, it will certainly do further harm to consumers' perception of the value of new CDs. And, by draining sales dollars from new product, it could reduce the manufacturers' cash flow to the point where they would not be able to record, promote, and market as many new acts as they do now. Eventually, that would affect everyone's business—including that of the used-CD merchants.

As wonderful and as profitable as it has been, the CD technology must be regarded as a double-edged sword. If its uses are not better controlled, its abuses could lead to grave consequences for the industry.

Queries and Concepts

1 How many songs can you name that mark a special place or time for you? Can you remember the *first* time you heard them? The *last* time you heard them? Why do you think that we tend to associate particular songs with specific events in our lives? Why does popular music seem to fulfill this function in a way other media do not?

2 Check *Billboard* for the Top 10 songs of today. Can any of them be traced logically to the roots of early rock? How do the lyrics compare with those of the 1956–60 era of the birth of rock? Other eras?

3 Do a content analysis of those same Top 10 songs. What kinds of issues and emotions do the lyrics deal with? Are they largely interpersonal or political? How many deal exclusively with love relationships? Compare your findings with others'. Are there any significant disagreements over the interpretation of any lyrics?

4 Again, using those same songs, examine what images of women they suggest. How about images of men? Of other groups? As an alternative activity, select one song from each of the rock eras and explore its portrayal of women (or any other group). Are there any changes across eras? Any consistent themes?

5 What's your position on record labeling? Does the system endorsed by the PMRC go too far? Not far enough? Do you think that certain "offensive" lyrics should *not* be played on the radio? Any "offensive" images that should *not* be shown on MTV? Explain.

6 Can you think of any creative solutions to the problems posed by the used-CD dilemma? Remember to consider all points of view: the music industry, the retailer, the artist, and the consumer.

The Fabulous Phonograph

Ronald Gelatt
The Fabulous Phonograph: 1877–1977. 3d ed. New York: Macmillan, 1977.

The phonograph—and the vinyl records it plays—is quickly fading into the past. This book covers the development of the record player from Edison to stereo with many personal stories about the men and women who made it happen. Particularly good chapters on the early years.

Popular Music in the 1940s

Timothy Scheurer, ed.
American Popular Music: Vol. 1 — The Nineteenth Century and Tin Pan Alley. Bowling Green, Ohio: Popular Press, 1990.

An examination of music culture *before* the advent of rock 'n' roll. Also useful is the second volume, which picks up where this leaves off, tracing rock from its roots to the 1980s: *American Popular Music: Vol. 2 — The Age of Rock* (Bowling Green, Ohio: Popular Press, 1990).

Ian Whitcomb
After the Ball. Rev. ed. New York: Simon & Schuster, 1986.

You might recognize the author's name. He's a former rock star who took to writing about music after his fall from the charts. This is a panorama of popular music from rag to rock, written in an entertaining style. The book has sections on ragtime, jazz, and Tin Pan Alley. Recommended.

The Birth of Rock; The British Are Coming!

Carl Belz
The Story of Rock. 2d ed. New York: Oxford University Press, 1972. (Available in paperback from Harper & Row).

I prefer this to Charlie Gillett's *Sound of the City: The Rise of Rock and Roll* (New York: Dutton, 1970), though both do an admirable job of chronicling the evolution of rock from rhythm and blues to the age of the superstars. Belz is the more meticulous writer with his cautious assessment of the contributions of many "sacred cows," including Bill Haley, Chuck Berry, and Elvis Presley. Excellent annotated bibliography.

Jim Curtis
Rock Eras: Interpretations of Music and Society, 1954–1984. Bowling Green, Ohio: Popular Press, 1987.

This history gives particular attention to the relationship of rock music to culture.

J. Miller, ed.
The Rolling Stone Illustrated History of Rock & Roll. New York: Random House, 1981.

An encyclopedic look at the evolution of rock, with a focus on key artists. Most important groups are covered, and the artists' hit songs are listed along with their best showing on the charts.

H. Kandy Rohde, ed.
The Gold of Rock and Roll, 1955–1967. New York: Arbor House, 1970.

A year-by-year account of *Billboard's* top songs. Included are the Top 10 for each week during the 13 years covered as well as the Top 50 songs (in retail sales) from each year. There is also a brief introduction and some commentary for each year.

The Rock Renaissance

Richard Goldstein, ed.
The Poetry of Rock. New York: Bantam Books, 1969.

A good anthology of significant rock lyrics. This kind of book is rare because artists often demand an arm and a leg for reprint rights to lyrics of their songs. Includes some interesting illustrations.

See Alan Aldrige, ed., *The Beatles' Illustrated Lyrics*, 2 vols., (New York: Dell, 1980), and Bob Dylan's *Writings and Drawings* (Westminster, Md.: Knopf, 1973) for the complete works of the two most influential rock forces in the 1960s.

The Diffusion of Rock; New Music and Modern Rock

R. Serge Denisoff
Solid Gold: The Popular Record Industry. New Brunswick, N.J.: Transaction Books, 1981.

This book is best when describing how the record industry has worked, how a record becomes a hit, and other such processes. Particularly informative regarding the business end, its history, and trends in the late 70s.

Dick Hebdige
Subculture: The Meaning of Style. New York: Methuen, 1979.

Youth subcultures and popular music are intractably linked. In this small book, Hebdige delves into the worlds of the rockers, skinheads, and punks, as well as the subcultures that have emerged around ska and reggae music.

Dick Hebdige, ed.
Hiding in the Light: On Images and Things. London: Comedia, 1988.

This collection of beautifully written essays covers a lot of (pop) cultural ground. Among the offerings: A fascinating study of the Talking Heads and an insightful piece of Sid Vicious and the birth (and death) of punk. Recommended.

Adam White, ed.
Inside the Recording Industry: An Introduction to America's Music Business. Washington, D.C.: Recording Industry of America, 1988.

Covers much the same territory as Denisoff's book (listed above), though from a more contemporary perspective.

"Why Country Music Is Suddenly Big Business." *U.S. News & World Report,* July 29, 1974, pp. 58–60.

Rock and Rote: The Themes of Rock Music

Theodor W. Adorno
Introduction to the Sociology of Music. New York: Continuum, 1976.

This collection of Adorno's lectures is a scathing indictment of the phenomenon of popular music. A number of Marxist-oriented scholars of what is called the Frankfurt School have charged rather eloquently that popular music—in fact all popular media—is at least tacitly in league with the capitalist forces that keep "the masses" enslaved. Popular music here is seen to promise "permanent gaiety" yet deliver "inner emptiness."

B. Lee Cooper
Popular Music Perspectives: Ideas, Themes, and Patterns in Contemporary Lyrics. Bowling Green, Ohio: Popular Press, 1991.

Lee—a history professor—probes a wide range of recorded material, looking for the ideas and themes that permeate American popular music. The author examines rock as well as a number of other popular-music forms. Includes a bibliography and an index.

R. Serge Denisoff
Sing a Song of Social Significance. 2d ed. Bowling Green, Ohio: Popular Press, 1983.

An interesting and illuminating examination of protest songs, from a sociological perspective.

Simon Frith
Sound Effects: Youth, Leisure, and the Politics of Rock 'n' Roll. New York: Pantheon Books, 1982.

Divided into three sections: Rock Meanings (rock roots, rock and mass culture), Rock Production (making music, records, and most important, money), and Rock Consumption (youth, music, sexuality, and leisure). This book is an excellent sociological look at the consequences of rock. Traces closely the relationship between rock music and the mass audience.

Simon Frith
Andrew Goodwin, eds.
On Record: Rock, Pop, and the Written Word.
New York: Pantheon, 1990.

A wide range of essays delve into various popular-music phenomena. Sexuality, artists and businesses, meaning, group images, pop genres, social aspects — it's all here. One of the best anthologies on pop ever assembled. Highly recommended.

James Lull, ed.
Popular Music and Communication. 2d ed.
Beverly Hills, Calif.: Sage, 1992.

One of the first anthologies to collect serious academic research on popular music. Useful in conjunction with the Frith and Goodwin anthology listed above.

Popular Music and Society is a most-useful journal dedicated to scholarly research into popular music. The journal is edited by R. Serge Denisoff and has been published quarterly for 14 years. Back issues are available. For information, contact: Bowling Green State University, Popular Press, Bowling Green, OH 43403.

Rhythm and Blues: Soul Music for the 90s

"The Uncivil War." *Calendar, Los Angeles Times,* July 19, 1992, pp. 6–7.

Writer Chuck Phillips examines the rap controversy in the context of the 1992 presidential race and beyond.

New Technology: The CD Boom; Issues and Answers: CD Technology — The Double-Edged Sword

Steve Jones
Rock Formation: Music, Technology and Mass Communication. Newbury Park, Calif.: Sage, 1992.

Jones, a veteran of the pop-music industry, takes a hard look at how technology influences — and often dictates — creativity. While a number of books explore pop-music content and audiences, this is the only one I know of that focuses on the influence of recording technology — on the consequences of *form.*

Again, to keep up with current trends in popular music, including new technological developments, you'll need to read these trade magazines: *Billboard, Broadcasting, Cashbox, Electronic Media,* and *Variety.* Also useful for current material on popular music are *Downbeat, Rolling Stone,* and *Spin.* See also the readings and references listed for Chapter 17, "New Technologies and the Future of Mass Communication."

8

Structures and Strategies: The Business of Television

The networks used to be run by showmen, by real broadcasters with a real vision of what the future of the medium could be, and I don't see that any more.

Steven Bochco

Imagine, if you will, a world without MTV, HBO, ESPN, TBS, or any other satellite-delivered premium channels or superstations. There is no Fox network. No Oprah Winfrey, Phil Donahue, "Wheel of Fortune," or "Jeopardy." Imagine, too, that there are no VCRs or TV remote-control devices. No backyard satellite dishes or 50-channel cable systems. The average household receives seven television channels, but on any given night over 90% of all viewers are tuned to just three. Got the picture?

What you've just imagined is the "prehistoric" television landscape of 1975. ABC, CBS, and NBC ruled the airwaves and raked in an-nual double-digit profits, thanks to advertisers who had nowhere else to go in their quest for a national audience. With no VCRs or "zapping" capability, viewers were pretty much the captives of the networks and a few independent stations. All of that was about to change. But, then, technology has a way of changing things. It always has.

Pioneers

The technical devices that made TV possible were developed long before the new medium was "discovered" by viewers. In 1923 Vladimir

Philo T. Farnsworth was dubbed the "forgotten inventor of television."

Zworykin invented the iconoscope tube, which made the transmission of TV possible (see 8.1).

By 1930 Zworykin had become the head of a group of 40 engineers working at the RCA laboratory in Camden, New Jersey. The group had been the result of a merger of the ongoing TV research programs of Westinghouse, General Electric, and RCA. Over the next 9 years they solved most of the technical problems that had been associated with early transmissions, including weak picture resolution, image size, and brightness difficulties. They had even placed some sets in homes on an experimental basis.

Zworykin had applied for patents for an all-inclusive television system as early as 1923, but years of litigation ensued as other inventors' claims and counterclaims were investigated. Philo T. Farnsworth had come up with the same idea at the age of 14 in 1922. A startled high school teacher who had seen the boy's early schematic drawings for an "electronic television system" kept one of them, and this formed the basis for Farnsworth's lawsuits against Zworykin and RCA. Eventually RCA settled, and Farnsworth was paid $1 million for his patents.

Farnsworth is often referred to as the "forgotten inventor" of television. His widow reveals that in his later years "he felt it was such a shame that they didn't make better use of the air time to bring something more meaningful to the people." The inventor did live long enough to see the televised moon landing, however, and said that "this makes it all worthwhile." He died in 1971.

Another inventor, Allen B. Dumont, was responsible for the receiving, or "picture," tube. Old-timers will remember the Dumont name; many of the early TV sets were "Dumonts," and once there was even a Dumont Network.

But it was RCA that possessed the resources to bring the new invention to the public. By 1939 the Camden Group had convinced RCA they were ready, and modern television got its first American public demonstration at the World's Fair in New York City. The demonstration was a success, and within 2 years the FCC had adopted the universal standards for TV broadcasting suggested by the National Television Systems Committee, which represented all the major electronics companies. At last the stage was set for the new medium.

In the beginning, most agreed that TV could never replace radio because radio was the "theater of the imagination." During the late 1930s, the experimental broadcasts of major political and sports events began to make more people aware of the tremendous potential of TV. By 1939 a Milwaukee newspaper had applied for the first ever *commercial* TV license. The application was granted in 1941, along with licenses for nine other stations.

But radio was in its heyday, films were doing better than ever, and suddenly Americans had a war to worry about. Only six of the original applicants for TV licenses were left by 1945. Nevertheless, the FCC was convinced that TV was here to stay and allocated band space for 12 VHF, or very high frequency, channels. This move involved cutting back space that had been allotted to FM radio, and it made existing FM receivers obsolete. While CBS was experimenting with TV, they had invested heavily in new equipment for FM — and were badly hurt by the decision. Thus the technical advantage was given to RCA and its subsidiary NBC in the new business of television.

In fact, the FCC decision to go primarily with the VHF band helped lead to the domination of television by the networks because most cities could have only a handful of stations. Had the UHF, or ultra-high frequency, band been utilized as the primary TV broadcast band, each market could have had dozens of channels in just a few years.

The Growth of Television

By 1948 the FCC was deluged with applications and decided to freeze the granting of licenses until it had more time for study. When the freeze was lifted in 1952, one third of all American families had bought a TV set and were happily involved with Ed Sullivan, Milton Berle, and "I Love Lucy." The transition from radio to television was brief. Many radio stars fell by the wayside, many switched over to the new medium, and dozens of new television stars were born overnight. When the freeze ended, hundreds of license applications were pending. By the mid-1960s more than 600 stations were on the air. By 1992 there were almost 1,500.

The numbers describing television's hold on the top spot in the media business boggle the mind. According to figures released by the A. C. Nielsen Co., Mediamerica's "television fixation" reached an all-time high in 1983, when average daily TV viewing per household surpassed the 7-hour mark for the first time. Over the 24-hour broadcast day, on the average, about 30% of all households had at least one set turned on at any given moment.

In 1984 and 1985, television viewing continued to increase, but the numbers dipped slightly for the first time during the 1986–87 season. Nielsen reported that during that season American households watched an average of 49 hours and 48 minutes of TV each week, down 28 minutes from the previous year. In 1992 America's 93 million TV households still watched an average of 6 hours and 55 minutes each day.

By the time most American children enter kindergarten, they have already spent more hours watching TV than they will spend in college classrooms getting a degree. Those hours come when the child is considerably more open to new impressions and ideas than the average college student. (What's more, information presented on television is designed to keep the "learner" constantly involved and entertained, something I rarely see in college classrooms.)

The FCC set the same evaluation standards for television that it did for radio. Licensees were supposed to be broadcasting in the "public interest, convenience, and necessity." Critics are quick to point out that TV stations more often broadcast in their own self-interest. Prime-time programs are aimed at the "lowest common denominator," with the idea that if everyone can understand a show, everyone will watch it. With a large audience come better ratings and more advertising revenues.

Some critics argue that TV programmers should be concerned with improving programming quality. The fact is that they aren't (for the most part), and they won't be until it becomes financially rewarding.

Those who criticize these practices forget that the average newspaper is written at an eighth-grade vocabulary level; even the *New York Times* never prints a word the average

1922

Fifteen-year-old Philo Farnsworth sketches the first schematics for an "electronic television system."

1940

First demonstrations of color television by CBS and NBC.

1900

1907	The word *television* is first used in *Scientific American*.
1923	Vladimir Zworykin invents the iconoscope tube.
1927	Philo Farnsworth applies for his first patent.
1936	Regularly scheduled TV begins in Great Britain.
1939	RCA demonstrates television at the New York World's Fair.

1939	The Journal Company of Milwaukee (now the owner of WTMJ-TV) applies for the first commercial television broadcasting license.
1944	Sponsors begin to buy TV time.
1945	FCC moves FM radio to another place on the spectrum, giving part of the FM band to TV.
1948	FCC freezes the granting of new TV broadcasting licenses.

1950

1951	Movie attendance declines in many cities that have TV.
1951	NBC "Today" show begins; CBS airs "See It Now."
1953	First noncommercial TV programming, in Houston, Texas.
1954	The Army-McCarthy hearings are shown on TV; Edward R. Murrow challenges McCarthy on "See It Now."
1955	"The $64,000 Question" begins, the first successful big-money TV quiz show.

8.1 The History of American Television

1963

The assassination of John Kennedy brings the nation together in a communal electronic experience.

1960

1956 The Eisenhower-Stevenson presidential campaign is covered extensively by all networks.

1959 Westerns, including "Gunsmoke," "Have Gun, Will Travel," "The Rifleman," "Maverick," and "Wyatt Earp," dominate the ratings.

1959 Quiz-show scandals sweep TV, and networks become more responsible for programs. Sponsors have less to say.

1960 Nixon-Kennedy debate is the first of TV's presidential "Great Debates."

1961 FCC Chairman Newton Minow describes TV as a "vast wasteland."

1962 "The Beverly Hillbillies" is the latest rage.

1966 FCC assumes control over cable television in a precedent-setting decision.

1966 "Bonanza" is the number one prime-time show; it stresses traditional American values.

1968 "Rowan and Martin's Laugh-In" pioneers a new kind of made-for-TV comedy.

1968 The Robert Kennedy and Martin Luther King assassinations and funerals are covered by TV.

1968 Unprecedented viewer protests bring the original "Star Trek" back for a third season.

1969 CBS cancels "The Smothers Brothers Comedy Hour," deeming its political satire too controversial.

1969 Live TV coverage of the first moon landing.

1971

"All in the Family" is the first of Norman Lear's controversial but successful sitcoms.

1984

In a 5–4 decision, the Supreme Court rules that the videotaping of television programs for private use does *not* violate the copyright law.

1970

1970 "The Mary Tyler Moore Show" premieres.

1972 Television is blamed for the death of *Life* magazine.

1973 Televised hearings of the Watergate affair give Mediamerica a chance to see the cast of characters.

1973 "Upstairs, Downstairs" is first aired on PBS.

1974 Televised impeachment hearings of the House Judiciary Committee again focus the nation's attention on Watergate.

1975 Ninety percent of all prime-time viewers are tuned in to one of the big three.

1976 HBO becomes the first satellite network.

1977 "Roots," a special eight-part ABC made-for-TV movie, becomes the most watched mini-series of all time. Its success prompts dozens of multiple-part specials to compete with regular weekly shows.

1978 Controversial programmer Fred Silverman takes over as president of NBC. He is fired in 1981.

1980

1980 An episode of "Dallas" becomes the most-watched series installment ever with a 53.3 Nielsen rating and a 76% share of the audience. Everyone finds out who shot J.R.

1982 After sweeping the Emmy awards, NBC's "Hill Street Blues" becomes one of prime time's top-rated shows.

1983 Mobil creates a temporary network for the showing of "Nicholas Nickleby."

1984 FCC votes to deregulate television along the lines of the 1981 deregulation of radio.

8.1 (continued)

1992

CBS dethrones long-time prime-time ratings champ NBC with an eclectic mixture of sports, movies, and special programming.

1990

1985–1986 The Fox network goes on the air while the "big three" undergo tremendous upheaval. ABC and NBC are sold. Leows buys 25% of CBS.

1987 ABC's "thirtysomething" debuts, first television show with desirable demographics conveniently located in the title.

1987 At $1.3 million per episode, "Star Trek: The Next Generation" premieres as the most expensive ever first-run syndicated program.

1988 The success of "thirtysomething" and "L.A. Law" leads to acute network awareness of crucial audience demographic data.

1991 The message of zapping spells an uncertain future for TV's one-hour dramas.

1991 CNN becomes Mediamerica and Mediaworld's premiere TV news source, achieving recognition for its around-the-clock Gulf War coverage. Viewer awareness of CNN in Europe goes from 15% to 80% during the war.

1993 Fox ratings are boosted by youth-oriented shows, "Beverly Hills, 90210" and "The Simpsons."

1994 Fox's "Melrose Place" finds a willing audience among key youth demographics, while ABC's controversial hit "NYPD Blue" breaks new barriers in network programming practices.

1995 History is made as rising TV ad revenues surpass magazine income totals for the first time.

high school graduate can't understand. Newspapers, radio, and television are all designed to be consumed by a *mass* audience, composed of everything from Ph.D.s to high school dropouts and children to senior citizens. Commercial network practices still prohibit catering to any narrow segment of the audience, though that too is changing as the viewing audience becomes increasingly fragmented and diffused thanks to cable and satellite delivery systems and a mind-boggling array of new viewer choices.

Advertisers, who currently spend over $20 billion annually on television, are becoming increasingly concerned with the demographics of the mass audience as well as its size. Age, social and ethnic background, and income are factors that determine how receptive a given viewer might be to the sponsor's message.

This trend became especially pronounced in 1981 with the arrival of "Hill Street Blues." NBC research found the award-winning show appealed to precisely those upscale viewers most advertisers wanted to reach. As a result it was able to institute a "premium program" surcharge of 10% for commercials aired during the show. Currently such shows as "60 Minutes," "Sienfeld," and "Northern Exposure" are considered premium programs and thus represent additional revenues to the networks. ABC capitalized on this appeal in 1987 with the debut of "thirtysomething," a show about the lives of a group of friends in their 30s. It was the first TV show in history whose title actually incorporated desirable demographics. Interestingly, "thirtysomething" also turned out to be a hit with older viewers until the novelty wore off. It was canceled in 1991.

Programs and Producers

The men and women who produce television programming must overcome tremendous odds to get their shows on the air. Their work can range from info-mercials to prime-time quality drama. Everything you watch must be produced by somebody. Whether it's a game show, soap opera, or network mini-series, it is the producers who choose the content of their programs. A mini-series producer may employ hundreds of people whereas a small local or cable show may have a staff of three or four.

For many years the FCC financial interest and syndication rules (FIN-SYN) prohibited the "big three" from producing or sharing in the revenues from most of the shows they air. With the exception of news, sports, and information programs, ABC, CBS, and NBC had to purchase their programming from independent producers.

Though a 1991 FCC decision relaxed these rules somewhat, the networks are still unable to produce the bulk of their own prime-time programming. (Fox is able to own some of its shows, as they are technically still under the 15-hour-per-week definition of what constitutes a "network.")

The result of all this is that the most glamorous positions and greatest financial rewards are reserved for those who successfully produce hit prime-time network series. Among the most successful are Steven Bochco ("L.A. Law," "Doogie Howser," "Civil Wars"), Witt/Thomas/Harris Productions ("The Golden Girls," "Empty Nest," "Beauty and the Beast," "Blossom"), Bloodworth/Thomason ("Designing Women," "Evening Shade"), and the Carsey-Werner Company ("The Cosby Show," "A Different World," "Roseanne.")

But the road to producer riches can be a bumpy one. The networks pay a license fee for each episode they order, but typically that covers only about 75–80% of production costs. The balance, known as the *deficit*, must be borrowed by the producer from banks and other lending sources. This can amount to a considerable sum. In 1992, for instance, "L.A. Law" cost $1.3 million per episode while NBC paid a license fee of $1,050,000 per episode. Thus, Bochco had to come up with $250,000 per episode, or over $5 million for the season.

Producers recoup (and occasionally become multi-millionaires) by syndicating the show, that is, selling rerun rights to individual stations or other non-network sources. All of this can take time, and meanwhile the interest mounts up. Syndication normally begins after about 100 episodes are in the can. Of course, if a show is canceled before 100 episodes can be made, as the vast majority are . . . well, you get the picture.

In addition to the financial risks, the pressure of producing a weekly series can take a tremendous toll. Ron Cowen learned all about it when he and his partner put "Sisters" on the air at NBC:

> This is our first series and I must say that I have new found and enormous respect for anyone who does a series. Even to keep a bad series going is a monumental effort. To do a good one is beyond comprehension. It's not a question of talent or of caring, there's just so many hours each day and eventually you get tired. You have to sleep, you have to eat, you have to take a break from it. And time is a terrible enemy when you're doing a series. The hour shows just kill you.

The Networks

The basic function of a television network is relatively simple. It involves buying a product (program) from a source (producer), providing the means to distribute that product (local affiliates), and making a profit by selling commercial time to national advertisers. Of course, if the networks pay too much for a program, or if ratings are lower than expected, they cannot hope to make a profit.

Programming costs have skyrocketed in recent years, and this, along with several other factors, has determined network fortunes. As recently as 1968, the average cost for a 30-minute situation comedy was about $70,000 per episode. In 1992 NBC paid a record license fee of $2,850,000 per episode of "Cheers," even though each cost about a million dollars to produce.

According to *Variety*, the 1-hour show on the 1991–92 schedule that was least expensive to produce was CBS' own "60 Minutes," at about $600,000 an episode, up from $140,000 in 1980. The most expensive was Lorimar's (see 8.2) "Knots Landing" with a $1,375,000 budget per episode, all of which was covered by the license fee paid by CBS. (Soap operas traditionally have very little syndication value.)

When it was launched, Paramount's "Star Trek: The Next Generation" became the most expensive first-run syndication show ever, with a budget of $1.3 million an episode. Network made-for-TV movies generally run about $2.6 million each. At the other end of the spectrum, Fox's reality-based "Cops" manages to get by on a meager $325,000 every week.

Nevertheless, each of the big three networks spends about $40 million a week for first-run programming. The inevitable result is steeper rates for advertisers. According to *The Broadcast Yearbook*, buying 30 seconds of prime-time network television now costs $100,000 while a 30-second spot on the Super Bowl runs about $800,000.

The proliferation of cable and syndicated programming and increased competition from Fox, independent stations, and superstations has cut deeply into the big three's share of the audience in recent years. As we have seen, the three-network share of prime-time viewers was over 90% in 1975. Today that figure is about 60%, and it continues to spiral downward. The average home now receives 33 channels, and 7 of 10 homes have VCRs.

What's worse, basic and premium cable channels tend to siphon off the most desirable (that is, the most affluent) segments of the TV audience. According to *Newsweek*, ". . . cable has penetrated urban areas with more upscale viewers like DINKS (double income, no kids) and OINKS (one income, no kids) and the standard-issue yuppie."

Inside Lorimar: The Business of TV Production

You may have first encountered the Lorimar Productions logo back in the 1970s if you watched "The Waltons." Since then, Lorimar has been responsible for a number of TV's best-known shows, including "Dallas" and "Falcon Crest." Despite its successes, Lorimar ran into economic hard times in the 1980s, and the reasons were indicative of a number of industry and business trends.

In 1985 Lorimar merged with Telepictures Corporation into a $750-million-a-year company. In addition, $200 million was spent acquiring the Bozell Jacobs agency, as well as several radio and television stations. CEO Merv Adelson dreamed of creating the next "Hollywood powerhouse," but his dream began to take on the aspects of a nightmare.

Almost immediately the new Lorimar-Telepictures Corporation was in financial hot water. According to *Business Week,* Lorimar "lost $37 million on syndicated programs sold to financially troubled independent TV stations, produced a series of box office failures (do you remember "The Boy Who Could Fly" or "The Morning After"?), and released three of its top video executives over alleged conflicts of interest."

In addition, the troubled company lost money when a home shopping show, "Valuevision," had to be scrapped after its ratings plummeted. The net result of these disasters was a $59 million loss in fiscal 1987, which came on top of a $19.2 million loss in fiscal 1986.

Adelson responded by putting three of the company's six television stations up for sale while the rest were sold to an investor group. His goal was to raise $300 million to keep the company afloat. These moves, according to Adelson, would enable Lorimar to "get back to what we do best, make television programs, motion pictures, and videocassettes."

In fact, it was the successful TV programs that kept Lorimar from going under, at least for a while. By 1992, 13 Lorimar programs were on the network schedules, including "Knots Landing," "Homefront," "I'll Fly Away," and "Reasonable Doubts." A year later most were off the air, and the company merged once again, this time with Warner Brothers Television. For the first time since "The Waltons," no network shows would bear the familiar Lorimar logo. Lorimar had gone from being TV's most prolific production company to a mere video memory. Such is the volatile nature of the TV production business.

With their audience and revenues diminishing, it's no wonder that all three networks have experienced management crises. It all came to a head in the mid-1980s. Capital Cities bought ABC. NBC and its parent company, RCA, were purchased by General Electric. Meanwhile, CBS successfully fended off two hostile takeover attempts, thanks to an infusion of cash from the Loews Corporation. Loews now owns 25% of the eye network. All of this led to one round of cost cutting after another with no end in sight and ever-increasing pressure on network executives to come up with the next hit show.

The Quest for Hits

Despite all the upheaval at the networks, one thing hasn't changed. It is still the hit series that seems to make or break a network's ratings. Given the economic realities of the business and the incessant pressure from advertisers for high-rated shows, it's no wonder that network programming executives stay up nights trying to decide which of the many proposed new series should appear on the fall schedule.

Former NBC president Fred Silverman, perhaps the most controversial network decision maker in the history of the medium, estimated that in any one season each network receives about 1,200 series submissions. These can range from an outline of a few pages to a complete script. Past practice had the network funding an average of 135 completed scripts each year, of which about a third, say 40 to 50, would be made into a *pilot,* or single episode, to test on potential audiences.

Recent budget constraints have forced the networks to cut back to some extent on the number of these projects, but the process still essentially works the same way. The completed pilots then compete for the dozen or so slots that might be available in the network's schedule. Silverman has said with some justification, "I don't think there is any more competitiveness anywhere than that involved in getting a show on the air."

The mortality rate of those that do make it is also high. Only about 1 in 10 shows will be back for a second season. Thus the odds of the original submission becoming a hit series are in the neighborhood of 1,000 to 1. Yet, as has been pointed out, one hit series can often make the difference between being the number one and number two network. Multiple millions of dollars ride on the outcome.

As a viewer, you may think that the quality of many new shows—and even some hits—is questionable. In an ABC interview, Hollywood producer Aaron Spelling ("The Love Boat," "Beverly Hills, 90210," "Melrose Place") said, "We try to anticipate what the audience wants to see, and of course we have to anticipate what the networks will buy too." Recently Spelling offered his own candid assessment of current network fare in an interview with the *Los Angeles Times:* "I don't think the networks are giving people what they want. They need escapism. That's what "The Love Boat," "Fantasy Island," and "Dynasty" gave — escape from the harshness of day-to-day life."

Meanwhile, network programming executives are constantly scrambling to try to fill holes in their schedules and come up with as many hit series as possible (see 8.3). This is not an easy task. Why are there so many mediocre shows? Many blame producers like Spelling; ultimately, however, it comes back to the public. Spelling points out that "you can be a marvelous shoe salesman, but it's the customer that buys the shoes."

To predict public reaction to new pilots, networks have become increasingly involved in audience research. In Los Angeles at an institution known as the Preview House, pilots for new series and freshly minted commercials are aired on a regular basis. Volunteers are wired to electronic machines that measure physiological reactions indicating emotional response. They watch program after program and feed millions of bits of data into a computer.

Some believe that the industry-wide trend toward more empirical research has produced an increase of lowest-common-denominator programs, those that offend no one yet please no one. While no one can blame the networks for trying to find out what people want to watch, many industry insiders question the ability of research to provide empirical answers to questions that involve the creative process. "Sisters" producer Ron Cowen is not convinced that research is the answer:

> It's hard to get people to watch. I agree with that. But why? I think that's the question. I don't have the answer. The networks don't have the answer. If all their research was truly valid and really working — then how come every network doesn't have 10 shows in the top 10? . . . They're trying to predict and control what's unpredictable and uncontrollable — and that's an audience response.

Ted Harbert, executive vice-president of ABC Entertainment, explains that current TV audience research practices are part of a larger historical continuum:

Time Period Estimates

STATION BREAK AVERAGES

DAY AND TIME / STATION PROGRAM	ADI RTG TN 12-17	ADI RTG CHILD 2-11	ADI RTG CHILD 6-11	TSA TV HH	PERSONS 18+	PERSONS 12-34	WOMEN 18+	WOMEN 18-34	WOMEN 18-49	WOMEN 25-49	WOMEN 25-54	WKG WOM	MEN 18+	MEN 18-34	MEN 18-49	MEN 25-49	MEN 25-54	TNS 12-17	CHILD 2-11	CHILD 6-11	TIME ADI TV HH RTG	TIME MET TV HH RTG	TSA IN 000's TV HH	TSA IN 000's WOM 18+	TSA IN 000's MEN 18+
	36	37	38	39	42	41	45	46	47	48	49	50	51	52	53	54	55	56	57	58	5	8	39	45	51
▲ RELATIVE STD-ERR THRESHOLDS (1σ) 25%	5	5	7	88	58	61	42	46	45	42	41	42	47	58	51	45	45	54	89	69	2	3	88	42	47
50%	1	1	1	22	14	15	10	11	11	10	10	10	11	14	13	11	11	14	22	17	-	-	22	10	11
MONDAY																									
8:30P- 9:00P																					8:30P				
KCBS MAJOR DAD	1	2	2	497	713	120	454	59	171	163	212	133	259	48	123	108	126	13	51	28	9	8	467	425	246
KNBC BLOSSOM	16	7	5	440	521	430	354	167	299	227	243	147	167	76	128	97	108	187	167	69					
NBC MON MOV	17	4	5	455	592	461	358	127	247	203	236	100	235	134	180	126	132	201	86	65					
--4 WK AVG--	17	6	5	448	556	445	356	147	273	215	240	124	201	105	154	112	120	194	127	67	10	10	507	407	251
KTLA CH5 MOVIE	13	7	7	546	873	499	453	181	327	248	276	123	419	160	301	253	282	158	159	103	10	10	551	453	424
KABC AMER DETCTVE	2	3	5	552	856	317	430	158	281	197	252	170	426	130	273	245	270	29	76	60					
FMLY MTTR SP	18	23	11	495	647	427	475	216	369	300	348	133	171		90	90	118	211	518	136					
--4 WK AVG--	6	8	6	538	804	345	442	173	303	223	276	161	362	98	227	207	232	74	187	79	10	10	471	395	301
KCAL PRME 9 NWS 8	1	1	1	199	269	69	146	28	56	52	62	28	123	29	50	42	43	12	15	8	5	5	227	165	149
KTTV MARRD CH-S 2	9	11	10	367	653	367	345	114	319	319	321	123	309	149	167	167	187	104	247	124					
SMPSN SPC MO	21	22	30	724	998	809	470	230	355	238	291	279	529	327	470	347	390	252	490	379					
FOX NGHT MOV	11	9	8	327	286	405	160	160	160	135	135	32	126	108	126	86	86	137	212	110					
FOX NT AT MV	10	9	11	306	408	417	158	113	158	89	89	62	250	174	226	106	108	130	203	155					
--4 WK AVG--	13	13	15	431	586	499	283	154	248	196	209	124	303	190	247	176	193	156	288	192	8	8	404	264	283
KCOP 8 OCLOCK MOV	5	3	3	376	508	274	181	74	138	123	136	96	327	137	282	242	256	62	68	45					
CLIPPRS PLYF	2	2	3	256	392	229	160	56	117	87	87	37	232	144	212	143	149	30	36	36					
--4 WK AVG--	4	2	3	346	479	263	176	69	133	114	124	81	303	139	264	217	229	54	60	43	6	7	334	178	284
KWHY ABUELO Y YO	1	3	4	56	114	77	49	28	44	26	29	3	65	39	65	57	57	10	74	52	1	1	51	43	63
KMEX ATRAPADA	2	2	3	170	327	263	155	98	116	57	61	45	172	142	156	134	134	23	51	42					
MUCHACHITAS	2	7	10	248	509	339	279	170	246	192	192	45	230	144	212	191	200	25	162	126					
--4 WK AVG--	2	5	7	209	418	301	217	134	181	124	127	45	201	143	184	162	167	24	107	84	4	5	211	220	200
KVEA VELO NEGRO			1	51	56	33	30	17	29	22	22	16	26	13	20	11	14	3	8	8	1	1	45	24	21
KDOC HOGAN HERO 2				34																					
BODY PLUS																									
RCG HLYWD MG				9																					
PAID PROGRAM																									
--4 WK AVG--				11																		1	21	3	5
KCET PTV				133	188	30	87	7	24	24	28	26	101	23	49	48	52				2	3	128	81	95
KOCE PTV				8	8		3				2		5		3	3	5						9	5	4
HUT/PVT/TOT	55	40	43	3473	5064	2681	2696	997	1789	1407	1607	864	2368	987	1687	1396	1520	698	1076	664	68	67	3426	2663	2326
9:00P- 9:30P																					9:00P				
KCBS MURPHY BROWN	9	3	3	842	1258	493	769	225	459	400	471	294	489	166	325	289	323	102	69	43	13	12	658	600	366
KNBC NBC MON MOV	6	2	2	445	690	307	404	118	246	202	232	117	286	115	180	147	163	74	49	23	9	9	444	380	239
KTLA CH5 MOVIE	12	7	8	479	771	463	407	178	292	224	250	94	364	144	249	211	241	142	158	107	9	10	514	432	391
KABC ABC MN NT MV	4	2	3	461	713	238	432	145	285	220	251	143	281	50	172	155	175	43	54	36	11	11	516	449	336
KCAL PRME 9 NWS 9	1		1	206	293	59	142	19	48	48	71	27	151	25	67	63	65	15	11	10	4	4	195	142	127
KTTV AM MST WANTD	5	2	2	328	542	203	288	86	205	160	160	133	255	63	144	144	169	54	37	27					
B HL90210 MO	39	7	10	671	641	925	384	274	355	196	209	138	257	182	237	182	182	468	153	125					
FOX NGHT MOV	9	1	1	379	430	433	223	165	218	179	185	65	207	158	184	121	121	111	18	18					
FOX NT AT MV	15	7	13	444	626	562	242	163	242	167	167	128	384	220	309	167	169	179	171	171					
--4 WK AVG--	17	4	6	455	560	531	284	172	255	175	180	116	276	156	219	154	160	203	95	86	9	9	440	282	285
KCOP 8 OCLOCK MOV	5	3	4	391	510	259	176	67	116	99	110	80	334	127	285	259	272	65	61	51					
CLIPPRS PLYF	2	1	2	225	402	212	153	48	110	96	96	31	249	142	207	150	156	22	31	31					
--4 WK AVG--	4	2	4	350	483	247	170	62	115	99	107	67	313	131	265	232	243	54	54	46	6	7	339	166	301
KWHY ANABEL	1			25	32	28	12	6	12	6	6		20	13	20	10	10	10	2	2	1	1	43	36	48
KMEX EL DESPRECIO		2	3	125	189	139	112	73	89	59	60	36	77	66	69	62	62		35	32	3	4	170	167	140
KVEA CINE MILLONR	1	2	2	125	261	178	108	77	100	58	62	18	154	86	129	100	115	15	41	26	2	2	89	64	91
KDOC COMBAT				9	9	1	3		1	1	1		5		2	2	2	1	1	1			10	1	1
KCET PTV				117	188	41	81	14	29	20	28	17	107	27	52	43	53				2	3	122	83	104
KOCE PTV				8	5		3		3	3	3		3		3	3	3						7	2	4
HUT/PVT/TOT	49	24	29	3647	5452	2725	2927	1089	1934	1515	1722	929	2526	979	1752	1471	1615	659	569	412	69	69	3547	2804	2433
9:30P-10:00P																					9:30P				
KCBS DESIGNG WOMN	3	3	3	647	835	293	531	168	303	269	324	205	305	85	187	164	194	40	61	39					
EVE SHDE 930	1			703	1188	283	726	158	361	307	400	160	462	109	281	273	305	16	8	8					
--4 WK AVG--	3	2	2	661	923	291	579	166	318	279	343	194	344	91	211	191	222	34	48	31	15	15	779	702	435
KNBC NBC MON MOV	6	2	2	441	677	282	401	114	243	205	236	123	276	99	163	138	155	68	36	25	9	8	438	397	279
KTLA CH5 MOVIE	13	7	8	529	848	512	436	189	309	243	278	104	412	172	283	236	270	152	161	117	9	9	493	411	378
KABC ABC MN NT MV	4	3	4	456	692	238	424	136	274	225	258	134	268	50	158	137	158	52	69	47	9	10	465	435	276
KCAL PRME 9 NWS 9	1			183	244	52	123	19	45	44	65	27	121	24	62	58	59	9	6	4	4	4	196	132	143
KTTV AM MST WANTD	4	2	4	371	585	271	318	126	233	163	163	111	267	99	175	175	201	46	47	47					
B HL90210 MO	36	8	12	660	700	879	450	309	420	235	245	174	250	145	226	170	170	424	181	148					
FOX NGHT MOV	10	1	1	357	413	437	231	165	220	180	191	63	182	158	158	94	94	113	18	18					
FOX NT AT MV	12	6	11	344	502	467	179	109	179	149	149	66	323	212	285	150	152	145	136	136					
--4 WK AVG--	15	4	7	433	550	513	295	177	263	182	187	104	255	154	211	147	154	182	95	87	9	9	456	297	270
KCOP 8 OCLOCK MOV	6	3	4	421	539	273	182	61	122	104	114	85	357	145	304	272	287	67	63	53					
CLIPPRS PLYF	2	2	3	309	551	264	212	63	139	121	121	76	339	173	270	181	189	28	40	40					
--4 WK AVG--	5	2	4	393	542	271	190	62	126	108	116	83	352	152	295	249	263	57	57	50	7	8	361	180	328
KWHY ANABEL	1	1		24	42	33	17	12	17	11	11		24	13	24	14	14	8	18	4		1	21	10	13
KMEX EL DESPRECIO		1	1	124	161	109	99	59	74	46	47	30	62	51	54	47	47		18	16	2	3	120	104	70
KVEA CINE MILLONR	2	2	2	149	336	242	150	116	142	83	88	28	185	107	158	119	137	18	37	24	3	3	141	136	171
KDOC COMBAT				10	4		2						2										7	3	5
KCET PTV				122	192	53	82	20	29	13	18	13	110	33	57	39	44				2	3	121	83	106
KOCE PTV				11	5		3		3	3	3		3		3	3	3						11	3	3
HUT/PVT/TOT	42	22	27	3536	5216	2596	2801	1070	1843	1442	1650	840	2414	946	1679	1378	1526	580	545	405	70	70	3609	2893	2477
	36	37	38	39	42	41	45	46	47	48	49	50	51	52	53	54	55	56	57	58	5	8	39	45	51

MAY 1992 TIME PERIOD AVERAGES 60 MONDAY LOS ANGELES

Daily

8.3

This compilation of figures from a 1992 Arbitron ratings book for Los Angeles covers programs appearing in prime time on Monday nights.

As soon as American industry was able to research consumer preferences they did so. Every move that Procter and Gamble and General Motors makes is based on some empirical or scientific method that predicts how the public is going to react. Television is no different. We use research as a tool. We weigh it along with gut feelings and other factors.

One research study that did make the industry sit up and take notice came in 1987 when the J. Walter Thompson advertising agency found that "58 million viewers — one third of the total audience — are perpetual 'flippers' who use remote control devices not only to zap commercials, but also to roam the airwaves in the midst of shows, sometimes watching two or more at once." Industry expert Roger Percy agrees: "We have a generation of younger people who watch TV differently."

In 1991 ABC Entertainment chief Robert Iger made headlines when he released a study indicating viewers were more prone than ever toward "zapping." In a recent interview, he reaffirmed his view that "the remote control device has truly changed the way we watch TV," and "one-hour dramas are uniquely susceptible to zapping." Indeed, there was some feeling that the one-hour drama, long the hallmark of quality network television, was on the way out. Industry reaction was decidedly negative.

ABC's Harbert characterized hostile industry reaction to Iger's message as "unfair and naive. The remote control device has had a profound effect on the viewing habits of the audience, especially the men. They are simply less likely to watch a one-hour show from start to finish. We can sit here and hope and pray they will but wishing doesn't make it so. Iger's point is that we've got to put on more compelling programs that don't allow you to zap away from them. That's our job, and it's not easy."

Bryce Zabel, whose writing credits include the highly regarded one-hour dramas "L.A. Law" and "Equal Justice," agrees. "If you pro-

vide interesting material they'll stop all their zapping. Rather than fighting zapping you need to understand zapping. All during the night you have to have something worth *stopping* on. What's dead are the days when you had a strong 8 o'clock show and you had crap at 9 and 10 and people just left the TV on that channel and watched."

Harbert says ABC still supports the one-hour drama, despite the message of zapping. "There are wonderful writers, producers and directors making one-hour dramas, and we have more than our fair share of them. It's not a program problem, it's an audience problem."

Despite the success of such ABC dramas as "NYPD Blue," Harbert sees a big difference in today's viewing habits. "A decade ago the audience would quickly find a show they liked and they would stay with it. Now, you may have to wait a couple of years . . . it puts us in the impossible dilemma of coming in third in a time period while we wait for the audience to come and sit in front of their TVs and watch a one-hour drama."

With increasing production costs, zipping and zapping, the public's continuous clamoring for quality shows, and intense criticism of existing shows, it is not the best of times for TV's networks. Add to this the periodic economic boycotts by groups like the Moral Majority, and perhaps the only safe conclusion is that it is very hard to please all of the people all of the time. Nevertheless, you can be assured that this is exactly what the networks will continue to try to accomplish. In any event, the road ahead does not look smooth for commercial television's network decision makers.

The Ratings War

At the heart of the relationships between producers and networks, and at the center of network fortunes, is the ratings system. All networks subscribe to the A. C. Nielsen Company's service. Until 1987 Nielsen chose some 1,700 homes at random to represent all viewers and installed an Audimeter, which automatically recorded which channel the set was tuned to while it was on.

The controversial "people meter," instituted in the fall of 1987, is a sort of deluxe Audimeter that requires viewers to "punch in" when they sit down to watch. Thus, specific information is provided regarding exactly who is watching. The idea is simple, but all three networks expressed misgivings about the new device. ABC researchers, stating that viewers would tire of pushing buttons, canceled their contract with Nielsen. NBC issued a statement indicating that it believed younger people would drop the button-pushing habit first, thus distorting the ratings. CBS also canceled its contract with Nielsen but said it wanted to continue to work with the company to "rectify the problems."

Advertisers were far more enthusiastic about the device, saying it would supply them with more accurate information. Essentially the problem was network concern that the people meter would mean lower ratings and thus lower advertising revenues.

As the networks feared, the fall 1987 TV ratings were significantly different as a result of the use of people meters. According to *Business Week,*

> People meters seem to help shows that appeal to younger urban viewers, especially men. That's good news for ABC, the No. 3 network, which has targeted a youthful, hip audience with programs such as "Moonlighting" and "Perfect Strangers." . . . CBS, however, loses points on nearly 80 percent of its prime-time shows, including some of its more popular offerings such as "Murder, She Wrote" and "Falcon Crest."

Eventually all the networks learned to accept the people meter. Today Nielsen is experimenting with a "passive people meter" that uses "Smart Sensing," a radarlike tracking system. No buttons need to be pushed by viewers. The system can tell precisely who is watching and even whether a specific commercial is seen. The accuracy of the passive people meter when integrated with existing Nielsen databases on the product-purchasing characteristics of sample households could revolutionize the way advertisers assess the effectiveness of their messages.

Generally, a Nielsen family or household is so designated for a 4-year period. Household members are sworn to secrecy and are not paid. Nielsen does pick up half the TV repair bills during this period, however. The findings are described in the Nielsen Television Index (NTI).

The NTI provides the fastest possible way for networks and advertisers to know how many households will be reached by a given program. Often "overnight" information is available about TV programs that aired the night before. People meters are wired via telephone lines directly to Nielsen headquarters in Florida. Normally the meter is "called" automatically by a computer twice a day to yield tallies of viewer habits.

The company also surveys a *matched sample* of some 2,400 additional homes. Members of these households keep a diary that reveals their viewing habits as well as their demographic characteristics: age, sex, ethnic origin, and other data. Nielsen combines this information with that obtained from the meters for its final NTI reports.

These reports are then used by national advertisers to determine their *CPM,* or cost per thousand (the "M" comes from the Roman numeral designation for 1,000). CPM is a vital statistic for advertisers because it allows them to determine how much money they paid to reach each 1,000 viewers during a particular show. Obviously, the lower the CPM, the greater the bargain for the advertiser. CPM figures are utilized by radio stations and networks, magazines and newspapers, as well as TV networks and stations in order to help them sell advertising.

A second service provided by Nielsen is the Nielsen Station Index (NSI), oriented to the local television market. Nielsen divides the country into 220 designated market areas (DMAs). There is a separate NSI for each DMA. Information from viewers in these markets is gathered exclusively via the diary method. More than 90,000 diaries are mailed out annually.

The NSI tells advertisers which TV stations in each local market viewers report they are watching. Thus the NSI report is essential to both local and national advertisers. All of these surveys are very expensive, and about 80% of the costs are borne by the stations themselves. Charges are based on the size of the market. It is not unusual for a station in a major market to pay more than $50,000 a year for the service; stations in small markets may pay as little as $10,000 annually.

Nielsen's main competitor in the TV ratings business is Arbitron, which also uses the diary method, surveying more than 200 TV markets each year. Like Nielsen, Arbitron issues regular reports, usually four times a year in major markets.

All the networks subscribe to both services, as do most local stations. They often choose the one that reports the best ratings to ballyhoo in their sales literature. Although Arbitron is recognized as the leader in radio ratings, it has continually lagged behind Nielsen in TV.

In recent years, Arbitron has begun using meters in some of the major markets in an attempt to topple Nielsen from first place. Ironically, there is a war even between those who provide the ratings for the ratings war.

Rating the Ratings: Problems and Paradoxes

A glance at prime-time ratings tells the story of the ongoing battle for TV viewers (see 8.3). In addition, Nielsen and Arbitron provide viewer information categorized by age, sex, and countless other subdivisions. The temptation for most of us is to believe what is written there. Yet at the back of each ratings book, they remind us in small type: *"Remember, ratings are only estimates."* That crucial little reminder is often overlooked by advertisers and stations alike. A number of things can influence ratings and affect their usefulness.

First, both Arbitron and Nielsen suggest that any figures they issue can vary by plus or minus 5% due to "sampling errors." Because it is not practical for ratings services to survey every TV user in the country, they must choose a *sample* to represent all viewers. Nielsen claims that its sample can deliver estimates that do not vary more than plus or minus 5% from the actual number of people watching. Some critics argue that the Nielsen sample is not truly random and thus ratings can be distorted to a greater degree than Nielsen is willing to admit.

Diaries can give supplemental information that meters cannot, but do they? There is a phenomenon known as viewer fatigue. Viewers might be diligent about filling in their diaries for the first few days during the week, but they inevitably lose interest as the week goes on. This problem became so acute that some years ago both services began starting their survey week on Wednesday or Thursday so that viewer information during the crucial weekend period would be more accurate.

Certainly there must be some viewers who, knowing they will be counted as representing thousands of households, cannot resist the temptation to "play God" by reporting that they watched programs *they think* the rest of the country should be watching, rather than what they actually watched.

Diary participation is another problem. Only about 54% of all diaries mailed are returned in usable order. Do the viewing habits of those who do not return their diaries or those who fill them out improperly differ from those who do? Both ratings services contend that they do not, but no one knows for sure.

Another phenomenon that influences ratings is the sweep period. These typically occur four times each year, when the ratings taken will determine what the advertising rates will be for that "book." It means that local news shows will be running more sensational stories and that TV networks will introduce their blockbuster films, mini-series, and other specials with high ratings potential. Viewers without VCRs often face tough decisions, because two or three "must-see" programs may run at the same time. Of course, this also means that during nonsweep weeks there may be little of interest on any channel for many viewers.

Given all of these considerations, it's safe to say that ratings should be taken with at least a few large grains of salt. After all, they are only estimates. Advertising agencies, stations, and networks, however, all tend to treat them as gospel. Until these attitudes change, or until passive people meters or some other, more accurate and economically feasible way of gathering ratings appears, we are all stuck with them pretty much the way they are.

Public TV

Shielded from the "tyranny" of the ratings, Mediamerica's public television system seems the ideal place for quality television to flourish. Indeed, PBS has been responsible for some of TV's finest moments.

It all began in the 1950s when there was much excitement about a possible educational TV network, one that would provide traditional classes and create a "university of the air." But educators found that they could not simply tape lectures, broadcast them, and interest an audience, even when they offered college credit. The programs were not visually appealing. Content criteria were borrowed from print, and often too much information was crammed into too short a time.

Although the TV-university idea of the 1950s did not work, public television still ex-

ists in the form of noncommercial stations funded by government, corporate, and viewer contributions. In 1970 the alliance known as the Public Broadcasting Service (PBS) was formed.

At first glance it would seem that noncommercial stations have a big advantage over their competitors: They offer programs uninterrupted by hypes for denture adhesives or kitty litter. Yet in every major market, noncommercial viewers constitute less than 5% of the total audience. Why?

Until recently, it was safe to say that public TV stations did not succeed with the mass audience because their programming did not meet audience expectations created by the slicker commercial stations. In fact, some public TV programmers deliberately avoided appearing slick. Smooth acting, professional editing, expert lighting, and perfect timing were and still are the hallmark of commercial prime-time programming.

Many noncommercial outlets lagged behind and presented "talking heads" (two or three people sitting on stage just talking to one another). Our experiences with commercial TV have shown us that visual form can be much more important than story content.

Today, however, PBS' visual standards have improved, and many programs rival those of the commercial networks in terms of visual quality. The success of "60 Minutes" proved that the mass audience could be drawn to documentary material if it was packaged in a form that met its expectations. Paradoxically, the "gritty" quality of the new brand of commercial TV's reality shows such as "America's Most Wanted" and "Cops" seemed integral to their success.

Historically on PBS, English imports like "Upstairs, Downstairs," "Civilisation," and "Brideshead Revisited" have garnered strong ratings. More recently, "The Civil War" delivered a large segment of the mass audience. "Sesame Street" (see 8.4) is a collage of bright colors, clever editing, and professional production techniques. As such, its form became a model for commercial children's programs.

Of course, such productions are more expensive than talking heads. Thus public TV stations must be funded adequately if they are to compete for the mass audience. But Congress is getting tired of underwriting a television network that serves so few citizens. If this vicious circle continues, there will be no public television in America, and a great opportunity will have been lost.

Not everyone would agree that public TV has failed. Some contend that noncommercial stations exist to offer an alternative to commercial fare. It's true that as long as *anyone* is watching, they have succeeded to some extent. But again, television is a *mass* medium, and the *mass* audience is what it's there for. In all fairness, some public stations have taken steps in recent years to increase their audience, utilizing extensive promotion practices and offering syndicated programming with a decidedly commercial flair. Nevertheless, there are those who argue that public stations are still not doing enough.

On the other hand, PBS supporters contend that in a television environment where the audience is increasingly fragmented and demographically defined, PBS, like the cable channels A&E (Arts and Entertainment) and Discovery, targets and delivers an upscale audience that knows and appreciates precisely the programming it finds there.

UHF and LPTV

Of the more than 1,100 commercial TV stations on the air, about 50% are UHF, channels 14–83. UHF also accounts for almost two thirds of the 350 noncommercial stations. When the FCC ended the freeze on new licenses in 1952, it added 70 new UHF channels to the 12 existing VHF channels, 2–13. (It was subsequently reduced to 55.) But there were already millions of TV sets in America not

8.4

Big Bird is one of the stars of *Sesame Street*, PBS' highly acclaimed learning experience for children.

equipped to receive the new channels. It wasn't until 1964 that manufacturers were required to add UHF. By the late 1970s some commercial UHF stations were earning a profit, particularly those in smaller cities where they were the only outlet for local TV advertising.

Most UHF stations in major markets have had an uphill battle. Many commercial UHF stations are independent because they entered the market too late to be affiliated with one of the big three networks, though some have now affiliated with Fox. With no affiliation, they

Minorities in the Broadcast Media: A Score Card

Because the television industry holds such a special place in our society, with its tremendous influence on the way we perceive reality, concern has been growing about the role that women and minority groups will have in shaping its future. Of course, the place where these groups can have the most influence is within the structure of the industry itself. Hence many stations and other employers, with an occasional nudge from the FCC or the federal government, have been making extra efforts to hire women and minority group members. Here are the results to date and some predictions for the future.

Women began more aggressive campaigns seeking media employment in the 1970s. Particularly irked by the hiring of women exclusively as secretaries and receptionists, they demanded that networks and stations recruit women for management positions.

Until the mid-1980s, the FCC examined the employment practices of virtually every station at license-renewal time, and its "rule by raised eyebrows" method was somewhat successful. In the Reagan era, minority hiring guidelines were relaxed. At present, women make up about one third of the work force at the network headquarters and at network-owned and -operated stations.

Currently, women control less than 2% of broadcast properties; American Women in Radio and Television (AWRT) offers seminars for women who want to get involved in station ownership.

In the area of sales, however, things are booming. It is not unusual for a major-market radio station to have more women account executives than men. The reason is quite simple. Stations are finding that men, who make the majority of media-buying decisions, are more likely to buy from a woman than they are from another man.

Women with technical expertise can virtually write their own ticket, according to one source, because there are so few of them. Thus the prospects in engineering and production will be particularly bright for women in the years ahead.

African Americans have been particularly prominent in the

---

must pay for all the programs they air, which limits them to first-run syndication, syndicated shows that ran in network prime time years ago, old movies, and locally produced efforts hardly up to network standards. Some TV sets in service are still without UHF, and all noncable households need a special antenna to receive the higher channels. Given these drawbacks, most viewers stay with the VHF channels.

The UHF band does have one distinct advantage: It has a lot more room for growth. UHF is routinely available in markets where there is high cable penetration because, until recently, the FCC insisted that cable franchises carry all local signals, regardless of the ratings. Viewing habits have certainly diversified as more channels have become available. The pattern is similar to that of radio in the 1950s. Rather than relying on a few mass-audience stations, viewers in those markets tend to seek out programming most closely in tune with their own particular tastes and interests.

The advent of cable and the refinement of broadcast transmission techniques have induced the FCC to authorize licenses for a large number of new UHF stations. Several minority groups have been active applicants for these

programming side of television in recent years. In the 1960s Bill Cosby costarred in "I Spy" and thus became the first African American continuing character in a network prime-time series. Since then, of course, numerous programs featuring African American characters have aired, many of them situation comedies: "The Jeffersons," "Good Times," "Sanford and Son," "The Cosby Show," "Fresh Prince of Bel Air," and "Martin" to name just a few. From a strictly statistical point of view, African Americans are currently overrepresented in prime-time TV. But the crucial question may be, *How* are they represented?

While some people argue that African American characters are still stereotyped, many shows in recent years have featured African Americans in nonstereotypical ways. The Huxtable household on "The Cosby Show" was headed by a doctor and a lawyer, and the kids were mostly college-bound. "A Different World" was set on a college campus. One of the most successful lawyers on "L.A. Law" was an African American Harvard graduate, and positive African American role models can be found on numerous other shows.

Latinos are making their presence increasingly felt in broadcasting. Organized professional groups such as the California Chicano News Media Association have been instrumental in placing a growing number of Latinos in broadcasting positions. Nevertheless, their absence from prime time continues to be a problem.

"Sesame Street" is one of a number of television programs that have begun to introduce Latino culture into the mainstream. Chances are that a greater awareness of Chicano and other Latino cultures will spur a growth in the number of industry positions open for Latino job seekers.

Advertisers are just now beginning to realize the tremendous potential in Spanish-language stations operating in such diverse communities as El Paso, New York, and San Francisco. Employment opportunities at such stations are obviously geared toward Latinos; the important challenge lies in bringing more Latinos into the traditionally "Anglo" electronic media and in giving those already employed the opportunity for upward mobility.

---

new licenses (see 8.5), but large corporations and other traditional applicants are competing for them as well.

The new low-power television stations (LPTV) are also making their mark. Like the additional UHF stations, LPTV was made possible by new technological breakthroughs, and as with UHF, black and other minority applicants are currently in the forefront.

When it first authorized the new service in 1982, the FCC estimated as many as 4,000 new stations could be licensed. By 1984 more than 37,000 applications were pending, and the FCC adopted a lottery system to determine

who would be granted licenses. In 1986 alone, some 60 new LPTV stations went on the air, and by 1993 there were about 1,200 stations.

The impact of LPTV is not clear, and the extent to which LPTV can help increase diversity in programming and program services remains to be seen. One major problem is that cable carriers are not bound to include LPTV stations, so viewers in some markets will not have access to them via cable. Nevertheless, the LPTV possibilities remain enticing. In Chapter 17 you'll find more information about how the new broadcast technologies may affect our viewing habits.

Eric Sevareid once pointed out: "Until a few years ago every American assumed he possessed an equal and God-given expertise on three things: politics, religion, and the weather. Now a fourth has been added: television." Television, like the weather, is something everybody talks about but few people do anything about.

TV viewers can often be heard wondering aloud how so many "poor-quality" programs get on the air. It's equally hard to understand how a station pledged to operate in the *public* "interest, convenience, and necessity" can devote so much air time to commercials touting the *private* enterprises of thousands of sponsors. For that matter, a sizable minority of TV's potential audience finds nothing in the medium that interests it, so it watches little or none at all.

But what can the public do about such matters? And isn't the FCC supposed to act as a watchdog, making sure TV stations are programming in the public "interest, convenience, and necessity"?

Some of the most salient criticism of network television practices has come from Nicholas Johnson, an FCC commissioner during Lyndon Johnson's administration. His book *How to Talk Back to Your Television Set* (1970), which deals with the whole issue of who controls television, will never *really* be dated, though broadcast licensing procedures have changed drastically since that time (see 8.6). Although deregulation has had an impact, the licensing process remains theoretically similar to the one established in 1934.

As with radio, TV channels have practically become the property of the licensees. Only on the rarest of occasions does the FCC refuse to renew a license, and then only for flagrant violation of broadcast law. More often, warnings will be issued, or some other less formal method will be used for resolving any outstanding problems.

Johnson's book points out that there is really no deep, dark conspiracy between the broadcast industry and the agency that is supposed to regulate it. It's much more subtle than that. Over the years, friendships develop; lawyers meet lawyers and go out to dinner. It's just a lot more "pleasant" if licenses are granted as a matter of course, and a lot more practical as well.

The deregulation of TV in 1984 took the FCC another step away from controlling broadcasters. License-renewal periods were extended, and most of the cumbersome paperwork previously required was eliminated. In the current political climate, the FCC is not actively involved as a public advocate.

Johnson concludes that if the public wants change, it is going to have to invest its own time and energy, do the necessary research, and submit findings to the FCC, the press, and anyone else who will listen. He suggests that though the FCC responds to pressure from the broadcast industry, it also responds to pressure "from anybody." Ralph Nader has shown just how much impact citizens' groups can have. Citizen lobbies made significant inroads into corporate America in the 1970s. Many groups have used the courts in their quest, and class-action suits have appeared with greater frequency. Perhaps it is a fantasy to envision citizens banding together to sue local stations for presenting inferior programs, but after all, the local station is still legally pledged to operate in your "interest, convenience, and necessity." If you feel that it's breaking that pledge or could be doing a lot better, there are ways to bring about change.

Letters to the local station are not thrown away but are carefully filed. You will get a response, particularly if you mail a carbon copy to the FCC, which also keeps all letters it re-

8.6

He has been called everything from the "hostile hippie" to the "citizens' least frightened friend in Washington." He is Nicholas Johnson, author of *How to Talk Back to Your Television Set,* one-time FCC commissioner, and still a force to be reckoned with in broadcasting. So critical of the corporate interests controlling broadcasting was Johnson that the industry magazine *Broadcasting* predicted there would be "dancing in the streets" when his term ended. When he left office in 1973, no unusual dancing was seen to take place, but some reported a huge sigh of relief from broadcasters all over the country.

aired each hour? Is enough time devoted to public-service announcements? What about the balance between news, entertainment, and other types of programs? A quick check of the TV schedule will tell you how many hours a week are devoted to various program types.

Many women's groups brought about change by taking apart the content of the shows themselves. Are minorities fairly represented? Remember that even if a show is piped in by the network, *your local station* is responsible. The FCC does not license networks; it licenses local stations.

The urgency of consumer action seems particularly acute now that the deregulation of TV is in place. The guidelines that forced stations to offer a certain percentage of nonentertainment programming have been eliminated.

Many organizations have been formed by citizens determined to improve television offerings. All provide literature and suggestions about what you can do to improve TV programming.

All of this may sound like a lot of work and bother, and perhaps it is. Still, one letter can sometimes make all the difference. Take heart from the story of John Banzhaf, a lawyer who got tired of seeing all of those cigarette commercials on TV in the 1960s. He reasoned that if stations are required to give various political partisans "equal time," why weren't antismoking forces given air time, too?

He challenged all stations indirectly but narrowed his focus to one. He authenticated his claim by monitoring New York's WCBS-TV and citing specific commercials. That one letter, carefully documented, opened the door for a new FCC ruling: Stations had a responsibility to air the other side of the smoking question. Millions and millions of dollars' worth of broadcast time was offered to antismoking groups, who produced a series of clever ads. Eventually, cigarette commercials were banned from radio and TV. And it all started with one letter.

ceives. This material is reviewed when the station's license comes up for renewal. Be as specific as you can about your complaint; write one letter for each practice or program you find objectionable. Sponsors are particularly sensitive to letters of this type.

Your letters take on increased significance when you have collected data to back your value judgments. Is your local station airing too much advertising? Get out a stopwatch: Exactly how many minutes of commercials are

1   Do you feel that the incessant competition among TV networks helps or hurts the quality of television programs currently offered? Why/why not?

2   Critics argue that in trying to "offend no one," the networks tend to offer TV programs that appeal to the "lowest common denominator." Do you agree? Can you think of programs that defy the lowest-common-denominator label? Explain.

3   Are you a zapper? Know any zippers? Interview five friends about their use (or nonuse) of the remote control while watching television. Some questions to consider: How often do they change the channel? Why? When viewing with others, who controls the remote control? Do women seem to make different uses of the remote than men do?

4   Many TV critics contend that the quality of TV programs should be improved. But network programming executives are quick to point out that the ratings offer solid proof that the public would rather watch "The Simpsons" than Shakespeare. Make a list of all the ways you can think of that the ratings, as they are currently conducted, affect network-program decision making. Discuss.

5   Do you have cable TV in your area? How much does it cost a month? What does cable provide that broadcast TV cannot?

What public-access offerings are available? Many cable outlets offer you the chance to produce, direct, and star in your own TV show. Investigate. Write up a brief proposal for a show you'd like to produce. (Look out "Wayne's World"!)

6   Compare and contrast a random hour of public TV with an hour of commercial TV. What could commercial programmers learn from public programmers and vice versa?

7   You have just been awarded an LPTV license for your area. What types of programs do you intend to put on the air? Why?

8   After reading 8.5, do you think that commercial-television employers and programmers are doing enough to encourage minority participation in the broadcast media? If not, can you think of three specific suggestions that might help?

9   List three advantages and three disadvantages that might be associated with the use of passive people meters. Do the advantages seem to outweigh the disadvantages?

10 Passive people meters are the latest thing in ratings technology. What's next? How might ratings be measured (if at all) in the year 2000? In the year 3000?

Readings and References

Pioneers

Erik Barnouw
A History of Broadcasting in the United States.
3 vols. Vol. 3, *The Image Empire: From 1950.*
New York: Oxford University Press, 1970.

This is the third volume of one of the most often quoted historical treatments of the rise of the electronic media. *The Image Empire* deals with television as a societal force. The book has ample material on the early TV hardware and software pioneers.

Tube of Plenty: The Evolution of American Television. 2d rev. ed. New York: Oxford University Press, 1990.

This is an updated and abridged version of Barnouw's treatment of TV in his historical trilogy. Included are sections on prime time and the rise of the major network corporations and advertising. An all-new chapter ("Progeny") has been added to this edition. Includes a chronology and bibliographic notes.

The Growth of Television

Laurence Bergreen
Look Now, Pay Later: The Rise of Network Broadcasting. Garden City, N.Y.: Doubleday, 1980.

A highly readable, inside view of the rise of network broadcasting in the United States. The final section, "Signs of Obsolescence," critically examines the prospective role the networks will play in shaping broadcasting's future. For an update, read Ken Auletta's *Three Blind Mice* (listed here under "The Networks").

William Boddy
Fifties Television: The Industry and its Critics. Champaign: University of Illinois Press, 1990.

Good history of the development of television during the pivotal 1950s. The focus is on the scheduling, production, and sponsoring of prime-time programs.

Fay C. Schreibman
"Searching for Television's History." Chapter 2 of Joseph R. Dominick and James E. Fletcher, eds., *Broadcasting Research Methods* (pp. 16–45). Boston: Allyn & Bacon, 1985.

This chapter highlights historical research methods and lists organizations, archives, and reference materials for exploring the growth of television.

Programs and Producers; The Networks

Ken Auletta
Three Blind Mice: How the TV Networks Lost Their Way. New York: Random House, 1992.

In 656 pages, Auletta paints a detailed and fascinating picture of life at the big three (ABC, CBS, NBC). The focus is on the top decision makers who run the networks, and all the big names are covered: who they are, what they do, where they came from, and where they are likely to go. Auletta is hardly charmed by what he sees at the networks; this book is no love letter.

Alex Ben Block
Outfoxed. New York: St. Martin's, 1990.

Billed as "the inside story of America's fourth TV network," this engaging (and sometimes gossipy) history traces one of the most significant arrivals on the network scene: Fox TV. It's all here, from Joan Rivers to Jason Priestly.

Muriel G. Cantor
The Hollywood TV Producer. New Brunswick, N.J.: Transaction Books, 1988.

Though dated now, this book remains a pioneering study of the people who create prime-time television. The author interviewed 80 producers in preparing the book. In this revision of the classic study (originally published in 1971), Cantor provides an all-new introduction and update.

Marc Eliot
Televisions: One Season in American Television. New York: St. Martin's, 1983.

Where were you in '82? Marc Eliot was busy watching television (and watching the people that put it all together). This book is a unique, anecdotal, in-depth look at a single television season, 1981–82. Eliot examines the programs as well as the producers.

Todd Gitlin
Inside Prime Time. New York: Pantheon, 1983.

In this widely read book, Gitlin (a sociologist at UC Berkeley) probes the process of creating prime-time television. Based on 200 interviews with a wide range of television personnel. Includes a long section on "Hill Street Blues," the only program Gitlin seems to have any affection for; the author does not seem to be a TV *fan,* by any means.

Richard Levinson
William Link
Stay Tuned: An Inside Look at the Making of Prime-Time Television. New York: St. Martin's, 1981.

Both Levinson and Link have written and produced a number of successful television programs. This interesting book gives us a glimpse behind the scenes, into the creative process, as well as the controversy that sometimes surrounds it. Recommended.

Richard D. Lindheim
Richard A. Blum
Inside Television Producing. Boston: Focal Press, 1991.

An excellent overview of the complexities of producing; very practical and up to date. The authors develop case studies of "Coach" and "Law and Order"; the complete pilot scripts for both shows are included. Recommended.

Bruce M. Owen
Steven S. Wildmon
Video Economics. Cambridge, Mass.: Harvard University Press, 1992.

Frankly, not the most exciting book I've read. But this text ranks among the most contemporary, comprehensive, and accessible introductions to the business and economic realities of today's television industry. Covers both theory and practice in terms of emerging network, technological, and marketing trends. Ample tables and diagrams help sort everything out.

Robert J. Thompson
Adventures on Prime Time: The Television Programs of Stephen J. Cannell. New York: Praeger, 1990.

This book covers more than just the career of Cannell, one of the medium's most fascinating creators. Through Cannell's story, we get a picture of the complex nature of television "authorship" and the nature of formula/genre.

The Ratings War; Rating the Ratings: Problems and Paradoxes

Susan Tyler Eastman
Sydney W. Head
Lewis Klein
Broadcast/Cable Programming: Strategies and Practices. Belmont, Calif.: Wadsworth, 1989.

Excellent introduction to the theory and practice of television programming. Covers all the essential bases: programming strategies, the networks, cable, personnel, and more. Especially good on ratings and audience research. Includes selected bibliographies for each chapter; useful glossary.

James G. Webster
Lawrence W. Lichty
Ratings Analysis: Theory and Practice. Hillsdale, N.J.: Lawrence Erlbaum, 1991.

A more advanced treatment of the ratings. The authors cover the uses of ratings in academic research, programming, and advertising. Ratings are examined as both research technique and business practice.

Arbitron and Nielsen can be helpful in supplying students and others with support materials regarding their respective ratings services. Arbitron publishes a monthly newsletter, *Beyond the Ratings* (address inquiries to Arbitron, 1350 Avenue of the Americas, New York, NY 10019; if you live in a major market, contact your local Arbitron branch office). Nielsen publishes a periodical booklet called *The*

Nielsen Report and a useful annual *Report on Television* (address inquiries to Nielsen Media Research, Nielsen Plaza, Northbrook, IL 60062).

Public TV

Carnegie Commission on Educational Television. *Public Television.* New York: Harper & Row, 1967.

The Carnegie Commission spent 18 months reviewing the status of public television before issuing this impressive report. Its conclusion ("a well-financed, well-directed educational television system . . . must be brought into being if the American public is to be served") is as convincing now as it was in 1967.

Carnegie Commission on the Future of Public Broadcasting. *A Public Trust.* New York: Bantam Books, 1979.

This follow-up to the seminal 1967 report contains a number of provocative suggestions for addressing some of public TV's perennial problems. However, Congress has never seriously acted on any of these recommendations.

UHF and LPTV

For more on the evolution of cable and other new television technologies, see the readings and references listed for Chapter 17.

Issues and Answers: Who's in Charge Here?

Nicholas Johnson
How to Talk Back to Your Television Set. New York: Bantam Books, 1970.

This might be the book people will look back on in 30 or 40 years and say: "This is where it all began. People actually started taking charge of their own media." A must. In many ways, still as relevant as when it was written. Also

worth looking at is Johnson's *Test Pattern for Living* (New York: Bantam Books, 1972).

Denis McQuail
Media Performance: Mass Communication and the Public Interest. Newbury Park, Calif.: Sage, 1992.

A comprehensive look at media assessment and evaluation. Among the questions tackled by McQuail: Do the media have covert messages or intentions? How is the quality of media regulated? What roles do governments and businesses play in determining media content?

Kathryn C. Montgomery
Target: Prime Time — Advocacy Groups and the Struggle over Entertainment Television. New York: Oxford University Press, 1989.

An interesting history of how various groups — African Americans, women, gays, and others — have attempted to take charge of television and influence programming in a positive direction. The book includes useful lessons for anyone committed to "talking back" to television. Highly recommended.

C. C. Wilson
Felix Gutiérrez
Minorities in the Media. Newbury Park, Calif.: Sage, 1985.

Though limited to a select range of minority groups, this book makes an important contribution to the literature. As always, current trends and issues must be tracked in the trade press (*Broadcasting, Variety,* and so forth). A number of groups have established various media advocacy and professional associations (such as American Women in Radio and Television, and the National Black Media Coalition), which are well worth investigating. The nation's oldest newsletter covering women in the media is the excellent *Media Report to Women,* carried by many libraries.

9

Patterns and Programs:
The Content of Television

**The problem with television is that
people must sit and keep their eyes
glued on a screen; the average
American family hasn't time for it.
Therefore, the showmen are convinced
that for this reason, if no other,
television will never be a serious
competitor of broadcasting.**

New York Times, March 19, 1939

Remember high school? It wasn't so long ago. All the kids had new cars, and lots of them chatted with each other on their car phones. During the summer everybody hung out at the beach club. In the fall everyone was decked out in the latest fashions. Sure there were problems, but nothing that couldn't be wrapped up in an hour. Two hours, tops.

If that doesn't sound exactly like your high school experience, don't worry. In the TV world of Brandon and Brenda such occurrences seemed to happen on a daily (weekly?) basis. Welcome to the mediated world of "Beverly Hills, 90210." So what if some of these people are pushing 30 in real life? They're in college now! Exceptions are Dylan, who keeps trying to spend his money, and bad-girl Brenda, who has conveniently departed the scene.

It's easy to assemble a list of differences between the typical "real" high school experience and that found on Fox's hit show. But to do so is to miss the point. For "Beverly Hills, 90210," like much of TV's mediated reality, represents an idealized and very fictional version of life in Mediamerica.

TV's Mediated Reality

To understand the relationships between real life and TV's special brand of mediated reality, we can again use the *cone effect* (see Chapter 1

The cast of "Beverly Hills, 90210" (left to right): Ian Ziering, Jennie Garth, Tori Spelling, Brian Green, Gabrielle Carteris, Jason Priestley, Shannen Doherty, and Luke Perry.

and 9.1). We know that TV situations are based on real-life experiences. There really is a Beverly Hills, and "90210" has dealt with a number of very real teen social issues including alcoholism, drug abuse, and teen pregnancy. The fact is that all TV programming differs considerably from real life. Yet it all begins with somebody's real-life experience.

TV's constructed mediated reality (CMR) presents a world that is funnier, sexier, bolder, more violent, and more intense than our own. This is because those who construct the genres, or categories, of TV programming realize that the successful CMR must contain certain qualities in order to attract and hold that audience and become a part of their perceived mediated reality (PMR). These qualities also involve the gratification of basic real-life needs (see 9.2).

Our response to what we see on television can be subtle or very dramatic. Shannen Doherty, who plays Brenda Walsh, told *TV Guide* that "there are thousands of Brenda imitators cutting their hair just like mine. . . . I'm stressed out." She has discovered that playing the role has its own responsibilities.

In fact, it's surprising how often viewers take their PMR and apply it to their own real-life situations. In one episode, Brenda was supposed to be worried about losing 5 pounds as the bikini season approached. Doherty told the executive producer: "I'm the thinnest girl on this show. If girls hear Brenda say she can't go to the beach unless she loses weight, they're going to become bulimic." The line was eventually cut.

Television has become a vast resource, the ultimate educational device, not because it teaches traditional curricula but because it supplies *roles*. Countless characters parade through our lives each day via TV: priests and politicians, doctors and lawyers, private detectives and public enemies, sex objects and sex offenders. Each character supplies us with bits of information about what his or her role is like. We have personal contact with a few people every day, but television gives us contact with a cast of thousands. These roles may have a direct impact on how we perceive ourselves and our own roles in our personal day-to-day environment (see 9.6).

Of course, our lives are made up of many social experiences. Our parents and friends all have an influence on the attitudes we develop and the decisions we make. But the hundreds of people we have "known" from TV also have an effect. We carry around their images in our heads, and we can recall them in an instant.

Are you skeptical? Okay, try this. Close your eyes and make your mind a complete blank. Then think of Bill Cosby as Dr. Cliff Huxtable. Try it before reading on.

What did you see? Yes, it was Cosby in his most famous role. No doubt he was wearing one of those outrageous multicolored sweaters. You probably pictured him in the living room of the Huxtable home (set?) or perhaps in bed with his lovely wife. His face is more familiar to you than many people you have met in real life. Who conjures up the clearest picture — Cosby or, say, your third-grade teacher?

For many viewers, conceding that television has any impact is difficult. At times it seems like such a shallow medium; the stories are so simple. But television is the most powerful and the most influential of all mass media; ignoring it won't make it go away. So no matter what your opinion of TV may be, try to keep an open mind as we explore the genres of TV programming.

The Genres of Prime Time

I once passed by a Chicago ice cream shop with this sign posted in the window: "31 Flavors — Instant Gratification!!!" The mediated reality of television is the ice cream shop of the imagination. It offers many things to gratify us.

Back in the 1960s, broadcast researcher Stuart Hyde, who teaches at San Francisco State University, came up with a list of various gratifications that watching TV provided in that era. The list presented in 9.2 differs somewhat from his original, but it can be argued that some of the basic gratifications that were offered by the westerns and variety shows of the 1960s are still applicable to "Roseanne" and "The Simpsons" today. TV fulfills these needs by presenting various types, or genres, of programming. Each program is aimed at a slightly different set of needs.

This is a different way of looking at the influence of media. Traditional media research centers on how media change attitudes and beliefs; the "uses and gratification" approach looks instead at how television and other media meet our social and individual needs.

The concept is not of a passive audience soaking up information and reacting to medi-

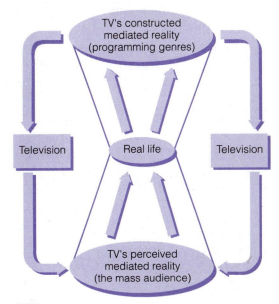

9.1

Here we see the cone effect applied specifically to television. Scriptwriters, newswriters, and others in the industry use real-life experiences and fashion a constructed mediated reality from them. This CMR may take the form of a situation comedy, game show, newscast, or any of TV's other program genres. The final version is distributed through the TV set to the audience, where it enters their perceived mediated reality. This PMR is then taken back and incorporated into the real lives of viewers.

ated reality but instead of an active audience "deliberately using the media to achieve specific goals." The studies that have been produced thus far are based on a "common set of assumptions" about TV and other media:

- Media use is goal directed. We use mass media to satisfy specific needs. These needs develop out of our social environment.

- Receivers (viewers) select the types of media and media content to fulfill their

31 Possible Gratifications from Watching Television*

Vicarious

1 The need for vicarious, but controlled, emotional experience

2 The desire to live vicariously in a world of significance, intensity, and larger-than-life people

3 The desire to experience, in a guilt-free arena, the extreme emotions of love and hate

4 The need to confront, in a controlled situation, the horrible and the terrible

5 The desire to see villains in action

6 The desire to imagine oneself a hero or heroine

7 The need to be purged of unpleasant emotions

8 The need to experience the beautiful and the ugly

9 The desire to experience vicarious financial reward

10 The desire to engage in vicarious gambling or risk taking

11 The desire to vicariously explore dangerous territories and experience totally new situations.

Escapist

12 The need to be distracted from the realities of life

13 The desire to believe in the miraculous

14 The desire to return to "the good old days"

15 The desire to be amused

16 The desire to believe in romantic love

17 The desire to experience "the happy ending"

18 The need to find outlets for the sex drive in a guilt-free context

Social

19 The need to have shared experiences with others

20 The need to share in the suffering of others

21 The need to feel "informed"

22 The need to see authority figures exalted

23 The need to see authority figures deflated

24 The need or desire to feel superior to a social deviant

25 The desire to see others make mistakes

Spiritual and Moral

26 The need to believe that spiritual or moral values are more important than material goods

27 The need to identify with a deity or a divine plan

28 The desire to see evil punished and virtue restored

29 The need to explore taboo subjects with impunity

30 The need for spiritual cleansing

31 The need to see order imposed on the world

*Based on course outline, "History and Analysis of the Public Arts," by Stuart W. Hyde.

---

needs. We are able to "bend" the media to our needs more readily than they can overpower us.

- There are other sources of need satisfaction that must compete with TV and other media, e.g., family, friends, work, leisure.

This research, along with the list of 31 gratifications, helps us understand more completely the complex relationships between the mass audience and their favorite television programs. In this section we'll take a look at these program genres: sitcom, variety, western, doctor and lawyer shows, action-adventure, and drama. Surprisingly these six, along with the current wave of "reality" shows, account for the vast majority of all successful prime-time programming.

It seems likely that the popularity of these various genres reflects the times, because audience needs and gratifications may differ somewhat from one decade to the next. Thus we can talk about traditional American values evident in the westerns of the 1950s, or the need for an escape into the past evident in certain popular sitcoms of the 1970s like "Laverne and Shirley" and "Happy Days." The family-oriented sitcoms of the 1980s certainly reflected the Reagan era while the current crop of TV's gritty reality shows reflects Mediamerica's preoccupation with crime, gossip, and scandal. Our brief tour of the evolution of prime-time programming probably will give you a lot to think about. If you look carefully, you may even spot a few trends of your own!

Sitcom

Situation comedy has been part of television from the beginning. "I Love Lucy" (1951–61) was one of the first and certainly wins the longevity award. It probably has been recycled more than any other program on TV. Lucille Ball was the first of many "dingbat wives" who became stock characters in sitcoms. The husband and father, played by Desi Arnaz, wasn't too bright, but he patiently tried to keep the "situation" from getting out of hand. Of course, it is precisely when the situation gets out of hand that it begins to be funny.

Unlike the durable "I Love Lucy," most sitcoms don't last long; the average life span is a season or less. Most are based on situations that seem funny at first, but the writers soon run out of ideas, and a new show is always waiting in the wings. In the 1950s, a show was guaranteed a berth for 39 weeks. Now a show may be canceled after only 6 weeks on the air. NBC began something called the "second season" in the mid-1970s to promote new shows replacing the fall failures. With the TV season now less than 25 episodes long, many predict that the "season" concept will soon disappear. Fox's plans for 1992 included a commitment to "year round programming." It may not be long until shows will just come and go at will,

being replaced as ratings fall. In many ways, it's already happening.

Cable TV, with its huge capacity for programming, is recycling a number of classic sitcoms from the past, everything from Jack Benny and Burns and Allen to "Leave it to Beaver" and "The Brady Bunch." A number of independent TV stations air these reruns as well, giving viewers a unique opportunity to study the evolution of the genre.

During the 1970s, TV viewers showed a marked preference for sitcoms; they occupied more prime time then than did any other genre. Many were the product of one of the most prolific sitcom producers ever, Norman Lear. Lear first hit prime-time pay dirt with "All in the Family" in 1971. He rapidly launched a string of sitcoms based on the success of Archie Bunker and company, including "Good Times," "Maude," and "The Jeffersons." Most were readily identifiable by the Lear formula: "realistic" dialogue and a tendency toward racial and ethnic controversy. Plots often revolved around sex and drugs.

Lear deserves more credit than any other single person for introducing previously taboo subjects to TV shows. He forced television to grow up, contending that the audience was ready for something a little different. By 1977 nine different Lear productions were on the air, leading more than one critic to conclude that his "fresh new approach" was no longer fresh.

Nevertheless, his shows revolutionized the genre. Sitcoms had been easy-to-swallow little stories reinforcing traditional American values (for example, a benevolent father is the head of the household). Lear's shows explored suicide, unemployment, racism, and women's liberation. Not everyone was enthusiastic, of course; many feel such matters are better examined in a more sober context, such as a documentary. But Lear's commercial success assured him a place on TV.

Another stable of 1970s sitcoms was built by the producers of the highly rated "Mary

Bill Cosby and Phylicia Rashad were dressed for success as doctor and lawyer in NBC's "Cosby Show." (1984–92).

Tyler Moore Show" (1970–77). Some, like "The Bob Newhart Show" (1972–78), featured all-new characters; others, like "Rhoda" and "Phyllis," were spinoffs from "Mary Tyler Moore."

The spinoff is an interesting phenomenon for many reasons. In the industry, such shows are known as safe properties, because they have a built-in audience from the "mother show." One example of a successful spinoff is "A Different World," slotted into the highly coveted position immediately following its "mother," "The Cosby Show."

Spinoffs and their highly rated mother shows are often where innovative approaches to the genre are attempted. In the 1970s, one such trend involved scripts with multiple situations. Several subplots would be woven in while the main plot was working itself out. This technique lent diversity, provided new joke material, and seemed to involve the audience a bit more. Sitcom producers of the 1970s were also bent on convincing the audience that their characters had depth, which involved more complex scripts that allowed a character who had been stereotypically "funny" to experience a serious situation.

During the seasons that "The Mary Tyler Moore Show" headed CBS' Saturday-night lineup, the characters developed significantly. Mary grew from a nervous doormat to a capable working woman. Mr. Grant developed from a no-nonsense boss to an often troubled and sensitive person. In fact, in various episodes the character created by Ed Asner went through a divorce (there was never a reconciliation) and became a borderline alcoholic. Hardly "Father Knows Best"! The character was so strong, it was spun off into the hour-long drama series "Lou Grant," which many critics hailed as one of the best shows of the decade.

The success of hit series like "Happy Days" (1974–84) and spinoff "Laverne and Shirley" (1976–83) was due in part to a nostalgia craze. Both were set in the 1950s and originally aimed at the audience that had been in high school during that time. (People in the 25–49 age group are the most desirable audience because they buy most of the products advertised on TV.) These shows won that audience and much more. Young people turned their stereos off long enough to watch their favorite characters, particularly the Fonz.

"Happy Days," "Laverne and Shirley," and "Mork and Mindy" formed a triumphant trilogy of sitcoms for Garry Marshall, who headed one of TV's most successful production companies. Marshall admits that most of his programs stressed the belly laugh rather than social awareness.

The most successful sitcoms of the early 1980s seemed to reflect this belly-laugh philosophy. "The Dukes of Hazzard" was continually rated among the top 10, along with

"Three's Company" and "Mork and Mindy." Only "M*A*S*H" (1972–83) seemed to be able to draw top ratings while making serious social comment, perhaps because it combined that comment with a lot of visual comedy.

During its 11-season run, "M*A*S*H" became a national pastime. When the crew of the 4077th at last packed up and returned to the States, the 2½-hour final segment became the highest-rated single episode in the history of the medium, surpassing previous champion "Dallas." Widely syndicated, the exploits of Hawkeye and the gang can still be seen up to a half-dozen times each day in many major markets.

Many critics said that "M*A*S*H" added new depth to the sitcom genre, proving once and for all that there is a place on commercial network television for intelligent and meaningful humor that appeals to a diverse audience.

Other 80s sitcoms seemed to signal a return to a more traditional family orientation. Known collectively as "warmedies," "The Cosby Show" (see 9.3), "Who's the Boss?" "Growing Pains," and "Family Ties" were all based on family situations. "Ties" became the catalyst for the whirlwind success of Michael J. Fox, one of the few television personalities whose sitcom stardom has translated into big-screen box office appeal.

"Kate and Allie" offered up the unconventional story of two middle-aged divorced women and their children sharing a house against a backdrop of "real" events and characters. Drama was also mixed with comedy in the offbeat "Frank's Place," the brainchild of Hugh Wilson, a sitcom innovator whose previous hit was "WKRP in Cincinnati" (1978–82). Tim Reid, who had played WKRP's Venus Flytrap so convincingly, was equally adept in his new role as a Boston college professor suddenly in charge of a Cajun restaurant in New Orleans.

"Frank's Place" was one of four "dark comedies" in prime time during the 1987–88 sea-son. ABC's "Hooperman" was another. The so-called dark comedies utilized no laugh track and often seemed to be more drama than sit-com, tackling such topics as death, drugs, and divorce. Two of the dark comedies were the work of writer/director/producer Jay Tarses: "The Slap Maxwell Story" starred Dabney Coleman as a self-centered newspaper sports-writer, while "The Days and Nights of Molly Dodd" was based on the rather confused life of a middle-aged single woman with psychological problems and a collection of odd relatives. For all of their innovations, the success of more enduring and traditional sitcoms like "Cheers" during this period proved that dark comedy had a very limited audience.

The 1990s brought some fresh half-hour attempts to combine comedy and drama including "The Wonder Years," "Doogie Howser, M.D.," and "Brooklyn Bridge." Yet none enjoyed the success of the "in your face" humor found in shows like "Roseanne" and "Married . . . With Children." "Roseanne" is still near the top of the ratings each week, while "Married" has developed a big cult following and is also doing very well in syndication. These shows are often regarded as being more "realistic" than their competition, because they portray a decidedly blue-collar environment.

What's next for the American sitcom? It's anybody's guess. If you can come up with the definitive answer to that question, fame and fortune can be yours.

Variety

Variety shows offered something for everybody. Often they were centered on the personality of a single star or a troupe of familiar faces. Ed Sullivan was the acknowledged king of the variety format; his Sunday-evening show (1948–71) was top rated for more than 20 years. Sullivan prided himself on being a good judge of talent and entertainment trends. It was he who boosted Elvis Presley to prominence on TV (although Elvis had appeared on

In 1964 Ed Sullivan introduced the most popular rock 'n' roll group of all time to an enthusiastic TV audience.

a few TV shows previously). Later came the Beatles (see 9.4) and dozens of other rock groups. But that was only a small part of the story. No matter what your entertainment tastes, you could find something each week on the Sullivan show: stand-up comics, opera stars, elephant acts, talking dogs, jugglers, cartoonists, you name it.

Sullivan himself was an enigma. Before working in TV, he had been an entertainment columnist for a New York newspaper. He had absolutely no skill as a performer and seldom got involved with his talented guests. Dozens of comics loved to do imitations of him, often while he watched. It was his very lack of talent that seemed to help him become such a success. He spent little time in front of the camera,

simply introducing the acts and getting out of the way.

Musical hosts dominated the variety format for a time. Unlike Sullivan, they participated directly with guests in comedy skits and musical duets. Among the more popular of these shows were those hosted by Perry Como, Dinah Shore, Tennessee Ernie Ford, and Andy Williams.

Comedy-based variety accounted for a number of hit shows. Early hosts of successful comedy-variety programs were such colorful personalities as Jackie Gleason, Milton Berle, Red Skelton, Jack Benny, and George Gobel.

The 1960s brought "The Smothers Brothers Comedy Hour" and "Rowan and Martin's Laugh-In." The Smothers Brothers began with the usual variety approach but rapidly became recognized program innovators. Tom and Dick Smothers, guitarist/songwriter Mason Williams, and resident comic Pat Paulsen became heroes to those who believed TV shouldn't shy away from controversy. They had a habit of inviting guests who were politically outspoken.

Often the brothers' material was allowed because their skits were satirical and thus the audience was "not taking them seriously," but when folk singer Joan Baez made some remarks against the war in Vietnam, CBS censors snipped them out. The problem was that TV is a *mass* medium. The network and some sponsors thought a part of the mass audience might become alienated. The Baez incident was one of several that accelerated the conflict between the Smothers Brothers and the network. After extensive negotiations and a lot of publicity, the show was abruptly canceled in 1969, despite good ratings. All was forgiven in 1988, when a reunion special aired on CBS, but ratings were marginal.

"Rowan and Martin's Laugh-In" (1968–73) got away with things the Smothers Brothers could not. The secret of their success was the special format of the show. Quick and lively skits were punctuated with hundreds of pieces of videotape. There were one-liners, recurring situations, and bad jokes. "Laugh-In" was the first program to use electronic editing devices extensively to piece together a collection of "out-takes." Dick and Dan would march out on stage at the beginning and say hello. An hour later, they'd come back to say goodbye. In between, anything could happen. John Wayne and Richard Nixon did cameos, series regulars got cream pies and cold showers. Many, including Goldie Hawn and Lily Tomlin, went on to successful solo careers.

"Laugh-In" was the first show to point out that TV audiences could handle a lot more entertainment "information" than other shows were offering. Because it relied so heavily on editing and visual devices, "Laugh-In" was uniquely TV. The mass audience gave thundering approval, and the show (originally scheduled as a 13-week summer replacement) became, for a time, TV's most popular program. The critics loved it too, and "Laugh-In" won a flock of Emmys.

Variety shows of the 1970s borrowed heavily from the "Laugh-In" format. Everything had to be sped up; the more elements the better. These shows depended heavily on technicians and those behind the camera to "create" a new, more visually exciting television. Costuming and set decoration became key factors, as the audience expected to be visually entertained while listening to a song or laughing at a comedy sketch. "Carol Burnett," "Sonny and Cher," "Donny and Marie," and others flourished, in part, because their producers realized that visual appeal, rapid pacing, and diverse guest lists were a necessity.

The British import "Monty Python" took the "Laugh-In" formula one step further (see 9.5). It was a nonstop barrage of satirical sketches interspersed with animation in the tradition of the Beatles' film *Yellow Submarine*. BBC censorship standards were considerably more relaxed than those of their American counterparts; nudity and irreverence abounded. The same relaxed standards applied when the show was aired over public TV in America, as there were no irate sponsors to object. Besides, as in "Laugh-In," everything happened so quickly that it was hard to know exactly what was being said.

"Monty Python" became an underground hit. But when one of the networks bought the rights to the shows and aired them in competition with late-night rock shows, regular "Python" viewers set up a howl. Whole sketches and scenes were missing. The performers themselves finally sued to stop commercial airing unless shows were aired uncut. "Monty Python" quickly disappeared from commercial TV but remained a success on PBS.

Meanwhile NBC's "Saturday Night Live," which premiered in 1975, was breaking ground of its own (see 9.5). It had no regular emcee but a weekly guest host whose role was often overshadowed by the antics of the Not Ready for Prime Time Players. The comic skits offered satire with a bite, but the late-night hour kept network censorship to a minimum. Where else could TV viewers watch a sketch about a brand of jam called Painful Rectal Itch or see a live fish chopped to bits in a blender?

The extraordinary success of the show led to stardom for a number of its talented regulars, including Dan Aykroyd, Gilda Radner, Jane Curtin, Bill Murray, Chevy Chase, and John Belushi. But as these stars left the show one by one, they seemed to take a lot of the original energy with them. By the fall of 1980, producer and guiding force Lorne Michaels had left, as had the rest of the original cast. In their place was an entirely new cast of characters.

Slow to win followers, the new "Saturday Night Live" nevertheless gradually built its own audience, helped along considerably by a young "unknown" comic named Eddie Murphy. Belushi's brother Jim joined the cast in 1983. By the time Murphy departed in 1984, the show was a hit all over again. Michaels rejoined the show in 1985. Today "SNL" continues to entertain late-night viewers while

Two of television's most memorable comedy ensembles: (top) The fun-loving group that was "Monty Python's Flying Circus" and (bottom) the original cast members of NBC's "Saturday Night Live." The creators and stars of "Monty Python's Flying Circus" (left to right): John Cleese, cartoonist Terry Gilliam, Terry Jones, Graham Chapman, Michael Palin, and Eric Idle. The original SNL cast featured (left to right) John Belushi, Jane Curtin, Garrett Morris, Laraine Newman, Dan Aykroyd, Gilda Radner, and Chevy Chase (not pictured).

providing a launching pad for the careers of many regulars like Dennis Miller and Dana Carvey.

The 1970s also brought a flood of variety-type shows that appealed to a youthful late-night audience. "The Midnight Special," "Don

Kirschner's Rock Concert," and "In Concert" all featured rock music. Many were built around major rock personalities, but occasionally a little humor would be thrown in for diversity. Though rock generally was still not popular enough for TV's prime-time audience, the Friday and Saturday late-night spots seemed ripe, and ratings were good.

Today the variety format has all but disappeared. Perhaps the idea of "something for everyone" worked more effectively in TV's early years. Those who grew up with vaudeville and radio variety have aged and died. In addition, as programmers became more sophisticated in constructing TV's mediated reality, they were able to focus more directly on the various sub-audiences that make up the mass audience. Reruns of variety shows did not fare well in the ratings and thus did not provide lucrative syndication profits. Cable was yet another culprit in variety's downfall. As the network's share of the total audience has diminished (see Chapter 8), succeeding with a "something for everyone" format has become increasingly difficult.

Westerns

Another genre that enjoyed its biggest success during television's early years was the western. Westerns are uniquely American and once made up a large share of the programs that America exported to other countries. As a result, the myths about those gun-toting American pioneers get plenty of reinforcement. (Perhaps they should—Americans own more handguns per capita than do residents of any other country.) At its best, the western, like all TV genres, was entertaining, informative, amusing, and enlightening. At its worst, it was trite, boring, and downright offensive.

"Gunsmoke" (1955–75), the longest-running TV western ever, was a slow-moving, comfortable show with a cast of characters from every age group and social background. Matt (James Arness) was tall, quiet, and rugged. His sidekicks, Chester and Festus, offered comic relief. Kindly old Doc played the grouch, while attractive Miss Kitty supplied an offbeat romantic angle. Kitty was the stereotypic belle of the old West. She was a bit naughty (after all, she did run a saloon) but had a heart of gold (see Huber Ellingsworth's guest essay in Chapter 6). When "Gunsmoke" finally bit the dust after 20 years, there wasn't a dry eye in the house.

"Have Gun, Will Travel" (1957–63) and my favorite, "Maverick" (1957–62) (see 9.6), merit special consideration because their scripts were often literate. Both took the genre beyond the good guys–bad guys clichés and allowed characters to develop real personalities.

The most popular western of the 1960s was "Bonanza" (1959–73). The NBC show was originally conceived as a showcase for the new color TV sets conveniently being manufactured by parent company RCA. It was one of the first all-color shows to air on network TV and probably was responsible more than any other show for the rapid increase in the sale of color sets during this period. Ben Cartwright (Lorne Greene) and his boys dominated the ratings for years (they were finally knocked out of the number one spot by "Laugh-In"), and the show was a true believer's potpourri of traditional western values with an emphasis on home and family.

Cartwright's three sons provided identification enough for everyone. There was Adam (Pernell Roberts), the quiet, articulate man in black; Hoss (Dan Blocker), the comic relief, with a heart as big as all outdoors and a stomach to match; and the rebellious Little Joe (Michael Landon), darling of the teenage viewers who saw him as one of their own. Joe often refused to do Pa's bidding and struck out on his own. I doubt if there was any "baby" of a family who didn't readily identify as well. Landon parlayed his success in "Bonanza" into two more long-running NBC hit series, "Little House on the Prairie" and "Highway to Heaven."

Ben provided a hero image for older viewers, and more than one plot revolved around his straight shooting. He also provided a firm but gentle, understanding father figure. The Ponderosa was their kingdom. Owning property, of course, is a vital part of the American dream. Plots often involved others' attempts to infringe on the Cartwright domain.

Despite its stereotype trappings, the Western format is so flexible that it can meet virtually all 31 of the needs listed in 9.2. Perhaps this explains the enormous success of the western format during television's early years.

With the 1970s, however, came increasing viewer sophistication. As a result, the popularity of the western diminished. Attempts to resuscitate the Western in the early 1980s met with little success. Despite the occasional network attempt to revive the genre ("The Young Riders"), the sun seems to have set on the TV western.

Doctors and Lawyers

The doctor format enjoyed great popularity during the first two decades of TV. "Ben Casey," "Dr. Kildare," and "Marcus Welby, M.D." (1969–76) satisfied viewers who had "the need to share in the suffering of others" and "the desire to believe in the miraculous." The success of these shows probably owes something to the high status we have given the medical profession; the genre has repaid its debt by giving the profession something extra: romantic glamour. Though these men and women were only human, we saw them perform heroically week after week under tremendous pressure, and their patients always seemed to recover.

A more realistic view of the medical scene came in 1982 with the premiere of "St. Elsewhere." "St. Elsewhere" was to hospital drama what "Hill Street Blues" was to police drama. It showed doctors as human, fallible, emotional, and sometimes cold and uncaring as well. For

Who Is the Tall Dark Stranger There?

*Who is the tall dark
stranger there?
Maverick is his name
Riding the trail to who
knows where
Luck is his companion
Gambling is his game . . .*

Those lyrics heralded the beginning of each episode of "Maverick." ABC's popular "western with a sense of humor" premiered in the fall of 1957. James Garner would star as Bret Maverick for just three seasons, but before he was through, he had left quite an impression on at least one young viewer. That viewer was Edd Whetmore.

I was thinking about all of this one day as I compiled a list of my own lifelong interests:

• **Gambling:** I have always been preoccupied with cards and the track. I keep coming up with plans to break the bank. (So far the bank is still intact.) It started when I was 14 — I'd sneak into the race track (no one under 21 was admitted without a parent) and find kindly old men to place bets for me.

• **Travel:** At 16 I dropped out of high school and drove my old Pontiac thousands of miles, crisscrossing the country like a madman, looking for . . . anything — action, adventure, whatever. There was something glamorous about being

on the road, traveling from town to town.

• **Work:** I had always hated it. Not a day went by when I wasn't up to some scheme, legal or slightly illegal, to beat it. Growing up in Oregon I looked around at everyone doing an 8-hour shift at the sawmill and thought, My God — this isn't for me. A job may be fine temporarily, but I couldn't do it for a living.

My parents were disturbed, to say the least. How could such an antisocial set of values have evolved? Then I turned on the television set. There was a rerun of an episode from the old "Maverick" series. It sent me back. I could vividly remember my brother and me keeping time on Sunday afternoons by "how many hours it is till 'Maverick.'" Now that's devotion!

Bret Maverick was the anti-hero of the Old West. A hero was virtuous, but Bret was expedient. A hero was strong, stable, and hardworking; Bret abhorred work. He always took the coward's way out; whenever trouble developed, he left town. A home was something he never needed; he just wandered from place to place, meeting beautiful women and playing poker. He always had fine clothes and plenty of money; his was the life of ac-

Suddenly it struck me. My entire life had developed around "Maverick"! All of those

inexplicable impulses — it was as if I had been playing out the Maverick role. The lessons I learned from Bret Maverick, like so many of the lessons we all learn from television, remain lifelong and indelible.

When I finally met James Garner last year at the Emmy awards, I shook his hand. He smiled and then he was gone. I never got to tell him how much "Maverick" meant to me, but perhaps that was for the best. I'm sure he's heard it all before. Though a 1994 *Maverick* Hollywood film featured Mel Gibson in the starring role, it is Garner who remains Bret Maverick in this writer's mind. I can still see him smiling as he lays down a winning poker hand, tipping his hat to a pretty lady, or high-tailing it out of town because things are a little too messy. He's played a lot of roles over the years, but James Garner will forever remain the "tall dark stranger" to me.

several seasons, "China Beach" used the Vietnam War as a medical backdrop. Nevertheless, television's mediated reality of the medical world remains more fiction than fact.

Television doctors are usually larger than life. Many real-life patients have been disappointed because their doctors could not provide the instant cures or hours of personal attention of a Marcus Welby. This "Marcus Welby syndrome" carries over to many facets of real life. We develop expectations about the roles of others from watching TV and are disappointed when they prove erroneous. We expect police officers to solve cases within the hour and lawyers to see justice done whether the client can afford it or not.

The best-known lawyer of television was Perry Mason, played by Raymond Burr. Though it was shot in black and white, "Perry Mason" (1957–66) enjoyed success in syndication during the 1970s and 1980s and has become a television staple. The plot was the same each week: Someone unjustly accused would come to Mason for help. Mason, along with secretary Della Street and detective Paul Drake, would eventually unravel the mystery. Usually Mason would break down the real culprit on the witness stand while his client was being tried.

In the final moments, Mason would meet the client and staff for coffee or a drink and explain how he had figured it out. That portion of the format, known as the *denouement,* was so successful that a number of other shows soon adopted it. Burr reprised his role as Mason in several successful made-for-TV movies.

All of these shows cashed in on our desire to experience a happy ending. Of course, the illusion of the happy ending—common to all media, except for news-oriented publications and programs—can be a dangerous one. If we expect each episode of our lives to end happily, and if we believe that everything will always turn out for the best, we may often become frustrated and discouraged.

Contemporary legal practices were explored in "L.A. Law," (1986–94). The brainchild of Steven Bochco ("Hill Street Blues," see 9.7), "L.A. Law" lived up to its advance billing as one of the finest dramatic series ever to reach the small screen. Utilizing the ensemble casting that had worked so well on "Hill Street," "Law" offered a no-holds-barred look inside a successful law firm and confronted difficult and complex legal issues with extraordinary humor and pathos. By the time it went off the air, Bochco had crafted "NYPD Blue," yet another critically and commercially successful drama.

Action-Adventure

The action-adventure program is typically about a police officer or a private eye, but science fiction and other varieties also exist. What they all have in common is *pacing.* The audience is constantly tossed between conversation and car chase, conversation and fist-fight, conversation and murder.

Since the beginning, action-adventure shows have come in for criticism, particularly about their use of violence. There are a couple of schools of thought here: One says that violence on television encourages violence in real life. Another contends that the vicarious experience of violence substitutes for the real thing. If the latter is correct, it would seem the more violence on TV the better! Generally, network executives have tried to cut down on the violence over the years, but the most successful action-adventure series such as "Starsky and Hutch" and "The A Team," were often the most violent as well. Action-adventure series play to the audience's need to share in the suffering of others, to confront the horrible and terrible in a controlled situation, and to see villains in action.

One obvious arena where audiences can find gratification is the world of cops and robbers. Some successful action-adventure shows were "Dragnet" (1952–59) and "Highway

Patrol" in the 1950s, "The FBI," "Naked City," and "Dragnet" (1967–70) in the 1960s, "Kojak" and "Hawaii Five-0" in the 1970s, and "Simon and Simon" and "Magnum P.I." in the 1980s. All featured plots in which stars tracked down criminals and brought them to justice with great finesse. Police dramas of the 1970s emphasized the personality of the star. Scripts for "Colombo," "McCloud," "Kojak," and "Baretta" spent as much time developing the hero's character as they did getting the crooks.

Believable character development was also a key factor in the success of "21 Jump Street," one of the Fox network's first highly rated series. Premiering in 1986, "21 Jump Street" traced the lives of three young undercover police officers as they infiltrated high schools and street gangs. Ratings indicated that the show appealed primarily to teens and viewers aged 18–24, an audience that generally watches MTV and little else.

The work of private detectives, too, lends itself to action-adventure gratifications. "77 Sunset Strip" (1958–64) was one of the most successful. In that program, the office contained a secretary and a group of "characters" of various ages and social statuses for maximum audience identification. "77 Sunset Strip" starred good-looking, clean-cut Roger Smith and Efrem Zimbalist, Jr., plus an added attraction: Edd "Kookie" Byrnes. Kookie became something of a cult hero, for he appealed directly to the teen audience and helped make "77 Sunset Strip" a smash. Later detective series like "Mannix," "Switch," "The Rockford Files," "Charlie's Angels," and "Barnaby Jones" featured heroes, heroines, and villains of various ages and ethnic backgrounds. There was something for everybody.

TV critic Horace Newcomb notes that new types of action-adventure characters emerged in the 1970s. They were usually part establishment and part antiestablishment. The kids of the "Mod Squad" were first; then came "Baretta," "McCloud," "Spenser: For Hire," and others. Though unorthodox, all worked within the system.

Many of the action-adventure series seemed intent on reassuring us that even the fattest ("Cannon," "Jake and the Fatman"), clumsiest ("Colombo"), and most severely disabled (*Ironside* and *Longstreet*) among us can be heroes. We are *all* potential stars despite our physical and mental shortcomings.

But the most talked-about, most heavily watched action-adventure series was a one-of-a-kind phenomenon. The original "Star Trek" was on NBC for only three seasons (1966–69), but it still enjoys tremendous ratings in reruns. Its creator, the late Gene Roddenberry, described it as a kind of "Wagon Train" of the stars. Each week, the Starship "Enterprise" would venture into the universe and right some cosmic wrong. Its 5-year mission was to "seek out new life and boldly go where no man has gone before."

Contrary to popular belief, "Star Trek" was not canceled because of some evil Klingon conspiracy. Rather, it was a victim of the ratings system. Ratings measure the *number* of bodies watching TV, but they don't account for the emotional depth of the audience or the loyalty they might have to a given show (see Chapter 8). "Star Trek's" viewers were relatively small in number at the time, but they were intensely devoted. When the show was canceled after the second season, they set up an unprecedented howl, enough to keep it on for an extra year.

In the long run, "Star Trek's" problem was that it was a bit ahead of its time. The integrated crew included blacks, Asians, Russians, and even Vulcans. Women were given roles as geologists and psychiatrists. Plots revolved around war, politics, and racism. This would not be unusual for a sitcom of the 1970s, but for an action-adventure show of the 1960s it was unheard of. "Star Trek" got away with it for a while because it was set in the future. Wars were between planets with strange names, and the names of the "races" were equally unfamiliar. In a few years, mass-audience tastes caught up with "Star Trek," but by then the show was in syndication.

Long-suffering "Star Trek" fans were finally rewarded with a series of successful films starring the original cast in the 1980s and a new prime-time version, "Star Trek: The Next Generation" with an all-new cast in 1987.

"Star Trek" was not the only science-fiction program to find its way to prime time (others included "Land of the Giants," "Lost in Space," and "Space 1999"), but it was the only one to offer consistently believable scripts that seemed to center on people instead of events. None of the original "Star Trek" actors were particularly famous or talented, but the chemistry between them created dialogues that seemed genuine. The plots had plenty of violence and sex, but the believability of the characters was the key. It created the intense audience involvement that still brings fans out to "Star Trek" conventions and keeps them watching reruns. As a result, "Star Trek" lives. KTVU, a Fox affiliate in California, has been running the show off and on for years; according to sales manager Jim Diamond, "People just don't ever seem to get tired of the thing."

Soaps and Scenarios: Drama in Prime Time

In the early years of television, it was easy to identify prime-time drama — it consisted of theatrical works taken intact from the stage to TV. As television programming became more sophisticated and the genres more clearly defined, the distinction between, say, action-adventure and drama became blurred.

Early dramatic efforts were generally anthologies, with stories taken directly from theater or literature. "Kraft Television Theater" (1947–58) was one of the most durable and is remembered fondly by TV's "golden age" enthusiasts. This is also the case with "Playhouse 90" (1956–60), which offered a completely original 90-minute TV drama each week. Most of these shows were done live, which contributed to their theaterlike quality.

The big-budget live shows did not endure as long as a number of other highly regarded dramatic series, many of them of the half-hour variety. "Alfred Hitchcock Presents" (1955–65) was one amusing example, and the program still does quite well in syndication, as does the original "Twilight Zone" (1959–64).

The most successful dramatic series of the 1970s was "The Waltons" (1972–81). The Waltons were a Depression family with very little money, but they had a lot of beautiful land and each other. The Depression actually became "the good old days," as John-Boy recalled the hardships and obstacles that led to a weekly renewal of faith in land and family.

"The Waltons" took place in real time, with children growing up and getting married much as you would expect in real life. Critics had a field day lambasting the "cornball" attitudes toward social problems, but the mass audience loved it. Again, a broad range of ages was represented. Grandparents were in their 70s; the youngest children attended elementary school. "The Waltons" seemed to be one of those shows that transcended simplistic scripts and plots to come alive for the mass audience.

"Lou Grant," set at a daily newspaper, first aired in 1977 and immediately pleased the critics who had panned "The Waltons" as too unrealistic. Indeed, the show was advertised as dealing with "stories right out of today's headlines," and plots involved themes such as nuclear power, drug use, and freedom of the press.

Realistic drama was also a key element in the success of "Hill Street Blues" (see 9.7). "Blues" broke new ground by combining traditional dramatic elements with innovative camera work and scripting. Of particular interest were the developing and ever-changing relationships between regular characters.

In the 1980s, Lorimar Productions (see Chapter 8), the company that first found

"Hill Street Blues": A Different Kind of Drama

In one episode of "Mork and Mindy," Mork (Robin Williams) was deeply troubled by a rather perplexing subplot, when he suddenly stopped in the middle of the action, looked into the camera and deadpanned "Oh, wow, this is more confusing than an episode of 'Hill Street Blues.'" Confusing or not, "HSB" was the object of the attention of millions of television viewers each week during its prime-time run (1981–86).

The program did not immediately zoom to the top of the ratings. In fact, when it premiered it was at the bottom. However, its huge success at Emmy time signaled an upturn, and during the 1981–82 season, "HSB" garnered more than comfortable ratings.

Trying to understand the program is reminiscent of the story of the six blind men and the elephant. If you'll recall, one blind man held the elephant's tail and described it, another the trunk, a third described the elephant's leg, and so on. All had different perceptions of what an elephant was, and it may be that different viewers have different perceptions of "Hill Street Blues."

"Hill Street" did not fit easily into any one of the six genres of prime time. The program actually combined elements of comedy, police-detective, action-adventure, and traditional drama. In addition, its film technique created a documentary feel. The opening of the show, for example, had a definite documentary look, and credits appearing throughout the first few minutes gave it a cinematic quality.

To make matters even more confusing, the show was built on a soap-opera structure similar to that of "Dallas" and the daytime serials. Recently I directed a group of students doing in-depth research into why people are so intensely drawn to soap operas. One of our most interesting findings was what we call the "hump factor." The greater number of subplots and characters, the more difficult it is for viewers to "get over the hump" and become regular fans of a particular soap. "HSB," with its large cast of characters, experienced this problem.

Once the hump was mounted, viewers found themselves getting involved with "real people" and "real emotions." "HSB's" action-adventure elements may have reminded viewers of "Magnum, P.I." and even the ancient "Dragnet." As with "M*A*S*H," a relatively small amount of bloodshed was shown, but what was shown took on meaning because of the involvement with the characters who experienced it.

The popularity of "HSB" said something significant about the increased sophistication of television writers and producers *and* the ability of viewers to understand what they're up to. It also provided a measure of satisfaction for those of us who (despite the shrill cries of "boob tube" critics) have contended that the possibilities for the still-developing television art form are both exciting and limitless.

With his signature high-fashion clothes and Rolex watch, "Miami Vice's" Don Johnson was once dubbed the "sexiest man on TV" by *People* magazine.

success with "The Waltons," followed up with two new prime-time dramatic series that were to have far-reaching consequences for the dramatic genre. "Dallas" and its spinoff, "Knots Landing," became enormously popular. "Dynasty" and "Dallas" vied for the top spot in the ratings through the early part of the decade. "Dynasty" produced a spinoff of its own in 1985 with the premiere of "Dynasty II: The Colbys" (later, simply "The Colbys"), but it was canceled in 1987 and many of the characters returned to the mother show. The content of these shows might be called soap opera, though their form is big-budget, prime-time drama.

Form also played a large role in the success of "Miami Vice" (see 9.8). By any estimation, the plots of the show were flimsy at best; the real story was the visual splendor of the locations and the sartorial glamour of Crockett and Tubbs. The "Vice look" became standard fare for many prime-time shows, including "Vice" producer Michael Mann's action-adventure drama, "Crime Story," set in the 1960s.

The 1985–86 TV season brought a short-lived renaissance of sorts for prime-time drama with the return of anthology series like "The Twilight Zone" and "Alfred Hitchcock Presents." Movie mogul Steven Spielberg contributed "Amazing Stories" in an attempt to spread his movie magic to the small screen. But none of these anthology dramas were as successful as the prime-time soaps.

Two highly regarded dramatic series made their debuts in 1987. "Thirtysomething" (9.9) depicted the struggles of the yuppie generation; "A Year in the Life" traced the paths of a Seattle family. Both shows stressed realistic dialogue and a kind of documentary visual style that ranked them with the best dramatic efforts in the history of the medium.

More recently the fate of the one-hour drama has been in some doubt (see Chapter 8). High production costs and dwindling network ratings have often led to the cancellation of finely crafted dramatic series. Remember "Twin Peaks" or "China Beach"? How about "Homefront," "Civil Wars," and "South Central"? In contrast, quality one-hour dramas such as "Northern Exposure" and "NYPD Blue" have become hits. Each season the networks continue to air at least a few examples of the genre. Will the one-hour drama survive in today's cluttered video environment? You'll have to stay tuned to find out.

Daytime TV and the Common Cold

When prime-time soap operas were flourishing, they sparked an interest in daytime programming among many students. Some were even willing to come forward and confess that they had been daytime-TV fans all along. I was thinking about this during a week when I spent my days (and nights) at home with a temperature of 101 degrees and the usual sinus miseries. During that week I must have seen 100 commercials suggesting remedies for my ailment. I hadn't realized how dependent TV is on the common cold. If it is ever cured, TV is in real trouble!

Colds always seem to come at the wrong time, but this one came at the right time for me. It gave me a chance to make some notes on daytime TV:

- Game shows are everything you are not when you're sick. Game-show contestants are happy, excited, and competitive. It reminds me of my mother's favorite tongue-in-cheek cliché: "It's not whether you win or lose that counts . . . but the thrill of wiping out a friend." Game-show hosts insist that contestants "know" each other a bit before they do battle. Only then can we find out if "The Price Is Right."

- "Studs" and "The Love Connection" are not really about winning or losing. It's how you play the game and who "scores" that really counts.

- Soap operas are by far the most intricate programs offered on television today. The way the writers carefully weave and reweave characters and situations together is positively incestuous.

- There is a lot more steamy sex on the soaps now than there used to be. Men routinely run around without their shirts on. Women jump in and out of the shower with only a towel wrapped strategically around them. These people have definitely never learned how to "just say no."

- Program options change drastically when the kids get home from school. A lot of cartoons and western reruns are shown

9.9

ABC's hit series "thirtysomething" featured the trials and tribulations of advertising agency partners Elliot (Tim Busfield, left) and Michael (Ken Olin).

after 3:00 P.M. There are also various after-school specials aimed at this audience. Meanwhile, parents are urged to explore the real social issues (like the lesbian striptease controversy) by the likes of Oprah, Phil, and Geraldo.

- By the time the news comes on, I'm ready for something different, but the news is made up of the same elements as soaps, games, and reruns: suspense, murder, intrigue, money, and violence.

All three major networks derive more total advertising revenues from daytime shows than from prime time even though each ad costs less in the daytime. Some 14 hours of TV are considered non–prime time. These include the daytime hours (7:00 A.M. to 6:00 P.M.) and an increasingly longer late-night period (11:00 P.M. to 2:00 A.M.). Networks supply packaged entertainment to take care of the special audiences that watch during these hours.

In the early years, TV networks supplied no daytime programs. The first major network morning effort was aimed at an audience hungry for information. NBC's "Today" show and later ABC's "Good Morning America" featured extensive interviews, film footage of various public figures, and other diversions. The content was often oriented to entertainment and soft news. These early-morning formats have been very successful. "Good Morning America" finally caught "Today" for the first time in the morning ratings in 1979. It continues to vie with "Today" for the title of Mediamerica's most watched morning information show.

Daytime Soap Operas

Though dozens of different daytime formats have been tried, daytime network TV is still pretty much soap operas and game shows. The soaps were introduced when daytime TV began, deriving their name from the soap manufacturers that were often sponsors. The soap-opera format was brought intact from radio, and its basic premises have changed little over the years. Protagonists get into conflicts usually involving close friends or relatives and must make decisions to resolve those conflicts. Some soaps, such as "The Guiding Light" and "As the World Turns," boast 30 or more years on daytime TV and a loyal audience.

Unlike prime-time shows, soaps are often shot only a week or two before they are aired. The five-show-a-week schedule takes its toll on cast and crew. The budget seldom allows for retakes, and sometimes missed cues and blown lines must be aired. It really keeps the cast on its toes. One advantage to the schedule is that the soap script may incorporate recent news events, whereas prime-time shows, shot as much as 6 months in advance, cannot.

The soap opera depends so much on human interaction that we may use the term to describe our own conflicts. ("Gee, my father isn't speaking to my mother, my sister is getting divorced, and I'm flunking out of school. My life is really a soap opera!") In reality, few lives are as troubled and confused as those on the soaps. As with much of TV, our real lives may be dull but safe by comparison.

Soap-opera characters are carefully created for the mass audience. They are usually young (25 to 35), well dressed, and financially comfortable. Leading men are doctors, lawyers, and successful business executives. Leading women are attractive and well manicured. Indoor sets are actually small, but look unusually large on camera and boast lush carpeting, plush drapes, and built-in wet bars. Soap-opera characters tend to do a lot of eating, drinking, and arguing.

Critics contend that all soaps are nauseatingly similar, but actually each is aimed at a special segment of the audience. Although 70% of that audience is female, men and younger viewers increasingly are getting involved with the soaps.

Soap operas have always been popular with college students. On almost any campus you can find students gathered around TV sets during the lunch hour. The marriage of Luke and Laura on ABC's "General Hospital" in 1981 was a major campus event. If you don't schedule your classes around your favorite soaps, you probably know some students who do.

Other soaps that have won favor with younger viewers are "The Young and the Restless" (number one in the ratings and a personal favorite; I've been watching it for 15 years!) on CBS, "Days of Our Lives" on NBC, and ABC's highly rated "All My Children." In 1983 Agnes Nixon, the creator of "All My Children," introduced a new half-hour soap, "Loving." Beginning as a made-for-TV movie, "Loving" was unique in that it featured plot lines which unfolded on college and high school campuses.

Many other soaps soon followed suit, in an attempt to entice younger viewers. Younger characters are often given fatter parts in the summertime when a younger audience is more likely to be watching.

Regular viewers can name all the characters in a given soap and describe their history in detail. The casual observer gets lost in the plot, which has more twists and turns than a mountain highway.

Soap operas are a fascinating study of audience-character relationships. No other media audience is so involved with its programs and so devoted to its characters. When soap characters have an on-camera birthday, they can expect a lot of cards from fans. When they are sick, thousands of viewers send get-well greetings. If a popular character dies, viewers protest. And, unlike the prime-time audience, soap watchers tend to have a good handle on what they receive from their programs. The desire to believe in romantic love, the desire to see evil punished and virtue rewarded, and the desire to see others make mistakes are most often cited by viewers themselves.

Soap characters are usually good or evil, positive or negative, with well-defined personalities. However, it is not unusual for a character to gradually change from good to evil, then back to good again.

Today's daytime soap operas explore social issues ranging from racism to AIDS and are faster paced and considerably more erotic than their predecessors. They remain one of television's most enduring and popular programming genres.

Game Shows

Originally introduced to compete with the soaps, game shows now outnumber them. They are actually cheaper to produce, despite the cash they give away. Salaries for the actors, actresses, scriptwriters, and set designers of a soap opera add up, but the game show requires only a couple of contestants, a limited production crew, a cheap set with a lot of sequins, and a moderator with a lot of teeth. The contestants do the rest.

One game-show producer, interviewed by a network TV crew, was very explicit when asked what he thought was at the bottom of his success: "Greed . . . it's American as apple pie." There is no doubt that the desire to experience financial reward, however vicariously, is at the root of the game format's success. Often we can't help playing along and trying to outguess the contestants.

Each semester I bring a TV set into the classroom and treat my students to a game show. In the beginning things are rather quiet, but as the show progresses, more students begin to participate. At the end everyone is yelling directly at the contestants and criticizing the moderator. The mood is infectious. Even in the college classroom, students who insist they "hate" TV *have* to get involved.

It is precisely this ability to involve the audience that spells high ratings for game shows. By playing along, we can engage in risk taking in a safe and controlled way:

Do you want to keep or trade away your jogging outfit, a year's supply of frozen TV dinners, 200 pet hamsters (with cages), and four thousand eight hundred twenty-six dollars in cash? Or do you want what's behind door number two?!

The first game shows were a comparatively tranquil lot. "Who Do You Trust?" "What's My Line?" and the original "You Bet Your Life" were all good-natured get-togethers in which contestants were given time to get acquainted with the emcee. Playing the game was only incidental. This changed in 1955 with the introduction of "The $64,000 Question." It was the first show to offer really big prize money, and the emphasis shifted to the game itself and the huge sums that went to winners. Contestants were put in an "isolation booth" where they were unable to hear audience hints. Emcee Hal March added to the suspense by constantly reminding the audience: "This question could mean sixty-four thooouuusand dollars!" Contestants seemed to ponder, look perplexed, sway from side to side, and then suddenly pull the answers out of nowhere. The suspense was unbearable — almost unbelievable.

Before long, we knew it really *was* unbelievable! Participants had been coached ahead of time. In those days, sponsors produced programs, then "rented" space from the networks for airing. As it turned out, executives of Revlon (which had sponsored the show and several offshoots) had decided which contestants could "win" and which were to "lose." A congressional investigation followed.

In 1960 the networks began to take more direct control of program production and the last big-money shows were taken off the air. Those that remained, like "The Price Is Right" and "Concentration," gave away very little cash. Instead, prizes were furnished by sponsors in return for an on-air plug.

In 1966 "The Hollywood Squares" premiered, with nine Hollywood personalities trying to bluff contestants with right or wrong answers to questions based on material from sources like "Dear Abby" and the *National Enquirer.* Again, prizes were furnished by sponsors, but the real show was the stars, who ad-libbed and joked until there wasn't really much time left to play the game.

During the late 1970s, some big-money game shows began to reappear, including "Treasure Hunt" and "Name That Tune." Ironically, an updated version of the old Revlon favorite, "The $128,000 Question," was among them. But the new big-money contests were compulsively honest, with answers stored in a computer miles away and sealed envelopes certified by private agencies. Network officials sat in on every taping, and if anything looked remotely fishy, they pulled the plug.

A game-show-junkie friend of mine who lives in Los Angeles attends several tapings daily. One time he got his big chance to become a contestant on "The Hollywood Squares." After being interviewed several times, he was finally brought to the studio on taping day. The show treats all contestants to lunch at the NBC commissary. There he stood in line with Vincent Price (a "Squares" regular). He asked Price what time it was, and before the star noticed my friend's yellow warning badge, he answered the question. That was all it took; a network supervisor told my friend he could not compete on the show: He and Price might have discussed a possible answer! Disappointed, he pleaded with producers to give him another chance. They told him they'd call. That was in 1975, and he's still waiting.

Increasingly in the 1970s, game shows seemed bent on milking every last drop of anxiety out of their frantic contestants. "Treasure Hunt" and "Let's Make a Deal" would play the poor contestants' emotions until they were exhausted. One minute they would win, the next they would lose. The emcee would tell them to sit down, then call them up on stage to "give them another chance." Audiences loved it.

Today "Wheel of Fortune" is TV's most successful syndicated program. Aired on over 200 stations, it can be seen in 98% of Mediamerica's households and regularly beats "The Oprah Winfrey Show" and "Star Trek: The Next Generation" in the syndicated ratings race. "Jeopardy" is often a close second. The key to game-show success remains emotion — the capacity for audiences to identify with contestants. As long as that process continues, there will always be a place on the dial for America's game shows.

Talk Shows

Talk shows often appear in the morning, late afternoon, or late evening, but seldom in prime time. Like many of their game-show competitors, "The Arsenio Hall Show," "Donahue," "The Oprah Winfrey Show," and "Geraldo" are syndicated, or sold to stations on an individual basis. That's why they appear at different times across the country.

However, the granddaddy of them all is a network effort, NBC's "Tonight Show." With its hosts Steve Allen, Jack Paar, Johnny Carson (along with countless guest hosts), and Jay Leno, "The Tonight Show" has ruled late-night TV ratings since 1954.

During the 1980s, Carson had hosted the show for so long that most people simply referred to it as "Carson" — "Did you see Carson last night?" Johnny Carson had become NBC's number one money-maker. As the late-night audience grew over the years, so did the price sponsors paid to push their dog food or aspirin. "The Tonight Show's" overhead is comparatively low; the sets are inexpensive, and the one production crew is not large. Bob Hope, Madonna, and the kazooist from Southeast Asia are all paid the same union minimum (about $750).

Carson's rise to success on "The Tonight Show" probably was due to his own affable personality. Raised in the Midwest, he seemed folksy yet smooth. He seldom dominated the show but kept things going if the guests let down. Many were Hollywood actors and actresses who needed little prompting. And success is often a matter of chemistry: Carson's onstage rapport with announcer Ed McMahon and overdressed bandleader Doc Severinsen was legendary.

What do audiences want from a talk show? "The Tonight Show" may offer four or five guests on a given night, some well known, some lesser known, and some not known at all. A common lineup is a vocalist, a comedian, a well-known personality, and a pop "intellectual" guest — perhaps a sociologist explaining some current social or sexual trend. Audiences like this mixed bag because it has something for everybody. The pace is not nearly so frantic as in the prime-time variety shows of old. Viewers can nod off if they like. For years in most markets, "The Tonight Show" was aired from 11:30 P.M. to 1:00 A.M. and lost half its viewers by sign-off time. When NBC signed Carson to a new contract in 1980, part of the agreement was that the show would be reduced to 60 minutes. Today the show airs at 11:35 in most markets; the extra 5 minutes were carved out for more affiliate commercials and promotional spots.

Despite his success on NBC's "Late Night with David Letterman," Dave was denied a shot at Johnny Carson's throne. Ironically, his victory in head-to-head competition with Jay Leno has given the gap-toothed comedian the last laugh.

Over the years, both ABC and CBS have tried to imitate "The Tonight Show's" success. Joey Bishop (1967–69) and Merv Griffin (1969–72) each lasted less than 3 years opposite Carson, although Griffin continued for a time with a successful syndicated show. Dick Cavett (1969–72) gave Carson his biggest challenge. Critics loved Cavett, calling the Yale alumnus the "thinking man's Carson." He tried to upgrade the genre by offering the audience in-depth interviews with reclusive legends like Marlon Brando and Katharine Hepburn. Cavett also used something called the "theme" show. He'd bring on, say, five singers from the 1930s, or six psychologists to discuss human sexuality. For all his innovations, Cavett's show didn't last. Apparently the mass audience prefers something a little more casual that late at night.

Late-night talk has been a graveyard for the careers of many who went up against "The Tonight Show." "Wheel's" Pat Sajak was unable to find an audience at CBS. Rick Dees failed at ABC. "Saturday Night Live's" popular Dennis Miller failed in syndication. Carson's legacy seems safe, but "The Tonight Show" no longer rules as it once did. While Jay Leno's ratings have been good, David Letterman has now emerged as the ratings king of a late-night environment where competition has never been more intense.

Sorely missed on the late night airwaves is "The Arsenio Hall Show." Its ebullient host had a winning personality, and his offbeat guests were generally "younger and hipper" than those on "The Tonight Show." Arsenio carved out a formidable niche in late-night, and his unique, urban-oriented perspective seems all but irreplaceable, despite the proliferation of new talk shows.

While the host's personality is a central ingredient in any talk show, the real key to the talk-format success may be "talk" itself. We all like to know something about the personal lives of those larger-than-life show-business people. Are they just plain folks in reality? How closely do they resemble their mediated images?

Late night's most popular talk show seems to stress the oddest aspects of guest behavior, but perhaps that's part of the reason for its success. When "Late Night with David Letterman" appeared in 1982, critics were perplexed. James Wolcott wrote in *New York* magazine that "Letterman loves polishing his giant doorknob and planting it on his desk, but then these pesky guests come on and spoil all his fun." Nevertheless, the surreal humor practiced by Letterman and his crew has found a home with the late-night audience (as well as with early-to-bed VCR owners).

Letterman's 1993 move to CBS created quite a stir. Despite the title change (It's now "The Late Show") and the earlier time slot,

Letterman's appeal remains essentially the same. More than ever, viewers seem hooked.

Why do they watch? Is it the inherent appeal of the giant doorknob? The thrill of seeing a grown man in a nice suit covered with potato chips and lowered into a giant vat of onion dip? Who knows?

They do know that by the end of the show they will see Letterman skewer guests with questions that Carson would simply have never asked. Letterman defended his interview technique while being interviewed himself in *Newsweek*: "If the person seems defenseless you have no business getting in there and hurting their feelings. But if the person seems to be an incorrigible show-business buffoon then I think they're a fair target." There have been many targets. Joan Collins, Cher, and Shirley MacLaine have never returned. The key to being a successful Letterman guest is never to take yourself too seriously.

Much has been written about Letterman's unique sense of humor. Even the staff refers to it as "strange." It has certainly never appeared on network television before. His goal is simply to do something different. Letterman explains: "It's great if you can get people to actually talk about something they have seen on television. In the first years of television that's all people did talk about because there never had been television before. But now, heavens, we've just seen it all." Well, maybe not quite everything. In 1995 Letterman celebrated his 13th year on late-night network television. Despite Dave's longevity record, you get the feeling that he still has a few surprises up his sleeve.

Children's Shows

Of all television genres, children's programs are of most concern to researchers, because children are thought to be most vulnerable to concepts they find on TV. If TV is as powerful as some say, what kinds of ideas are we putting into the heads of tomorrow's adults?

In the beginning, there were "Captain Video," "Kukla, Fran and Ollie," and "Howdy Doody." These were evening shows ("Howdy Doody" was usually aired at around 5:30 P.M.). When the networks introduced daytime programs, they included "Romper Room," "Captain Kangaroo," and other low-key entertainment designed to amuse and occupy the toddlers. The commercial success of such programs in the 1950s prompted a barrage of children's shows on Saturday mornings.

Many of these slots were filled with cartoons. Though cartoons have changed over the years (there are now fewer animals and more people), the basic formula remains the same. A central character or set of characters is placed in conflict with another character or set of characters. Action results from the conflict. In the end, all is resolved when *our* character wins.

The classic example is the "Roadrunner" series, which still appears on TV and in movie theaters. The roadrunner does nothing but emit a pleasant little "beep beep" and run up and down desert paths at 100 miles per hour. He is simple, good, and innocent. Villain Wile E. Coyote plots and schemes to catch him, but his elaborate traps always seem to backfire, leaving Wile E. the worse for wear. One study identified "Bugs Bunny–Roadrunner" as the most "violent" program in all of television.

Occasionally the cartoon format appears in prime time, and audience researchers find that Mom and Dad are looking over their kids' shoulders. "The Flintstones," "The Jetsons," and "Top Cat" all made it in the 1960s. The 1970s saw a dozen "Peanuts" specials in prime time and even one featuring the characters from "Doonesbury."

More recently, the success of "The Simpsons" brought a flock of prime-time animated shows. However, "The Simpsons" is obviously aimed at the adult audience, and to consider it a children's show might make its devotees "have a cow."

The only prime-time children's show to span three decades was Walt Disney's (1954–81). (The program had four different names, but they were all essentially the same show.) The Disney show offered cartoons, action-adventure, and other programs appropriate for children. Parents trusted Disney to deliver what was good for their kids; in a sea of sex and violence, it was an island of wholesomeness. The Disney magic was resurrected once again in 1987 with the Sunday night "Disney Movie" on ABC. Today the Disney Channel is one of cable TV's success stories.

By far the most innovative new children's program in the 1980s was "Pee-wee's Playhouse" (see 9.11). Until it was canceled, it was seen by an estimated 9 million viewers each Saturday. Despite Paul "Pee-wee" Reubens' much publicized brush with the Florida police, the show will go down in history as a unique children's program. *Newsweek*'s Harry Waters called Pee-wee

9.11

Paul Reubens as Pee-wee Herman, host of "Pee-wee's Playhouse."

an archetypal man-child. Pee-wee somehow blends bits and pieces of Soupy Sales, Pinky Lee, Jerry Lewis, Uncle Floyd, Snoopy and E.T. into an altogether original persona that is, in a word, weird . . . a David Letterman for five-year-olds and a freaked-out Howdy Doody for their parents.

The set is a kind of hallucinogenic ecosystem in which, thanks to some wonderful special effects, everything inanimate is alive. An overstuffed armchair hugs and tickles its occupants. A talking window announces who's coming up the walk. When Pee-wee peers into a mouse hole, he discovers a family of tiny dinosaurs playing tennis.

If all of this sounds very strange, it was. Yet there's no denying that Pee-wee struck a responsive chord in his audience, one third of whom *were over 18.*

Children and TV Advertising

Critics have long been wary of commercials aired during children's shows, asserting that children may be more susceptible to advertisers' messages and should be protected from the gimmicks used to sell products to adults. The products themselves are often deplored. Some claim that war toys encourage kids to poke one another's eyes out and that "sugar-coated" cereals are more sugar than cereal.

Parents are equally uneasy about commercials and children's programs in general. That uneasiness stems from their instinctive knowledge of the power of television. They see their children hypnotized by the colorful images careening across the screen and wonder what will come of it. This was particularly true of parents who experienced the medium for the first time as adults. Today's younger parents

HEY, KID, GUESS WHAT! I NEVER EVEN **WENT** TO SCHOOL! AND YET HERE I SIT WITH MY OWN TV SHOW!

EARLY SATURDAY MORNING WHILE **YOU'RE** STILL ASLEEP

ZIEGLER

Reprinted by permission: Tribune Company Syndicate, Inc.
Drawing by Ziegler; © 1981 The New Yorker Magazine, Inc.

grew up with TV and may not fear it as much. "After all," they say, "we watched TV constantly, and we turned out all right." What they may not realize is how much of what they are now is a product of that small screen.

Sports

Competing with kids for rights to the family set on weekend mornings is the sports fan. Much has been written about the impact of sports on TV and vice versa. When sports coverage began, it seemed like a natural. After all, TV could "put you there" in a way radio never could. Live sports coverage was a big part of the 1950s. Dominating all was the broadcast of major heavyweight boxing matches and baseball's World Series. The technical capabilities of TV improved to make diversified sports coverage a reality in the 1960s. An experimental broadcast of the 1940 World Series had involved one camera located on the sidelines. By the 1960s a dozen cameras were being deployed, and by the 1980s a roving "mini-cam" had been added, along with cameras in helicopters, hot-air balloons, and locker rooms. Exhaustive coverage was designed to give the audience the best seat in the house.

This tremendous sense of participation, of being involved with everyone else in experiencing a spectacle, explains a lot about the popularity of baseball and other sports on TV. ABC figured this out in the late 1960s and began quietly buying up rights to air the Olympics. By the 1970s, ABC had pulled off a ratings coup, putting the games on night after night in prime time and beating the competition.

Though the Olympics had been aired before, ABC showed them with a clearer understanding of TV form. The TV audience never had to wait for any event. Olympic schedules were altered so that one event would take place here, another one 5 minutes later somewhere else. Cameras were set up at every location, and viewers were treated to colorful nonstop action supplemented with "personality profiles." Interviews with Olympic stars were taped in advance but aired just before the crucial moment of "the thrill of victory" or "the agony of defeat."

The 1984 summer Olympics was a dazzling technological feast for the senses. ABC described it as "the biggest show in the history of TV," and a *Broadcasting* editorial called it "the perfect match of television and spectacular event." The network edited 1,100 hours of coverage into 180 on-air hours. Events were held at 30 locations hundreds of miles apart, but for 80 million prime-time viewers it was front row center every night.

Ratings were also outstanding for ABC's coverage of the 1988 winter Olympics. During the week of February 24 of that year, all six nights of prime-time Olympic coverage were among the top 20 rated shows. CBS pulled out all the stops for the 1992 winter games from France, canceling its entire prime-time schedule (except for "60 Minutes") in favor of the Olympic drama that unfolded on the ice and snow. Records were shattered when ratings skyrocketed even higher for the 1994 games in Lillehammer, Norway. *Entertainment Weekly* proclaimed that for CBS there was "no biz like snow biz."

Recent ratings have also been good for ESPN. The upstart cable network built a large following of sports fans with its tightly edited, yet comprehensive sports coverage. ESPN began airing NFL games in 1987. In the 1990s, the network's comprehensive major-league baseball coverage established it as a major, some say *the* major, force in television sports.

Baseball may always be the national pastime, but the real story of TV sports is football. The Super Bowl seems to break its own rating records year after year. Each year more than half the men and women in Mediamerica tune

in to the spectacle. The Super Bowl has become a hit in Mediaworld as well and now can be seen live, around the globe.

It's hard to imagine, but football was once a second-class professional sport. In the 1950s, far more attention was focused on college games. The average National Football League (NFL) player was earning about $6,000 a year. TV changed all of that. In the days before cable, it was economically impractical to televise baseball every day; no *one* game ever meant enough, and besides, baseball was so long and drawn out. Football was different; it had plenty of action, with balls thrown and kicked and guys running into each other. Football was so, well . . . so *visual!* What's more, when the clock ran out, that was it. No overtime (prior to the 1983 NFL season) meant no unscheduled pre-emption of other network programs. When TV networks approached NFL owners, they found them eager to talk. This was in sharp contrast to baseball teams, which were enjoying record attendance and didn't want to rock the boat. The television-football marriage was born.

Football provides many of the same gratifications as do other TV genres. It fulfills the desire to believe in the "miraculous" ("That catch was a miracle, Al"). It fulfills the desire to imagine oneself a hero ("Mildred, did you see that? That was just like the touchdown I scored at Tech back in '67—remember?"). It fulfills the need to experience the ugly and the desire to share in the suffering of others ("Look at that field—it must be frozen solid. Why, it's 17 below zero out there, and with the wind chill factor . . .").

According to communications researcher Michael Real, football represents a microcosm of American social values. For example, it is a game of territory; the winner is the one who gains the most. Football is competitive, played by the clock, and full of "deadlines" and penalties, much like real life. Of course, football also supplies heroes with whom we can identify. The Super Bowl in particular is a communal festival. Many Super Bowl watchers interviewed admitted that they seldom watched other football games but felt that they *had* to watch this one because "everybody is doing it, and everyone will be talking about it tomorrow."

While TV has expanded the audience for sports, it has also altered the games themselves. Sports purists decry such manipulative actions, saying that TV has forever altered the true spirit of sport. They point to football referees working directly with TV crews, calling time out for commercials, and the dreaded instant-replay rule. But these critics miss the point: Football is no longer a game played on the gridiron for thousands of fans; it is a game played on television for millions. Football *is* television for many viewers, as are tennis, golf, bowling, basketball, and even baseball.

I was thinking about all of this at a recent baseball game. It was Los Angeles at Cincinnati, and we had choice seats just over home plate. I noticed that the guy next to me had a portable television set and a radio. Both were tuned to the game we were watching. After a few beers I got up the courage to ask him, "Why all the paraphernalia?" He looked up from the TV, turned up the radio, and gazed at the field through his binoculars. "Whaddya mean?" he said impatiently. "Why, without this stuff I wouldn't have any idea what was going on."

We need to have real life filtered through mass media channels before we really feel that we have experienced "the total event." Particularly in sports, the media actually determine the nature of the experience. Some claim that media coverage has become more important than the event itself.

Sports, like the other TV genres, gives us everything we always wanted in real life and could never have, everything we always wanted in real life but were afraid to have, everything we used to have in real life but lost. In doing this, television programming has actually become real life, influencing much of what we do and say.

Reality Programming

According to media analyst Joe Saltzman, reality programming is easy to define: "It's cheap programming that's very popular with the mass audience. . . . If you can come up with a formula in Hollywood to create a cheaper product and get people to watch, it's gold." With reality shows typically budgeted at 25–50% less than half-hour sitcoms and 33–75% less than hour dramas it's easy to see why they have become so popular. In fact, reality programming is the 90s' hottest TV trend, yet it's been around since the beginning of the medium.

"This Is Your Life" (1952–61) and "You Asked for It" (1950–59) were two of TV's earliest and most popular shows. "Life" host Ralph Edwards surprised a celebrity or some other person of note at the opening of each show by announcing that they were to be the week's subject. Then old friends and acquaintances were brought on stage one by one. "You Asked for It's" formula was simple. Viewers would send in suggestions on a postcard, and the show's cameras would go inside the vault at Fort Knox or wherever they needed to go in order to get the whole story.

The appearance of news magazine shows "60 Minutes" (1968) and "20/20" (1978) proved that TV viewers can be entertained by fact as well as fiction. Then NBC added a twist. Its "Real People" was the surprise hit of 1980 and spawned a number of imitators, including "Those Amazing Animals," "That's Incredible," and "Speak Up, America." These shows were part of a movement dubbed "the new populism" in TV programming. The idea was to point out to the viewer that real people are just as fascinating as those fictional characters they have been watching on TV. However, the same basic gratifications were involved. "Real People" featured sex (the stripper who has "done her thing" nonstop for 13 days), violence (daredevil stunt people driving motorcycles over recreational vehicles and breaking their necks), and all the other ingredients that make up the appeal of fictional programs. TV critics scoffed at most of these shows, but they were very popular for several years.

The most recent chapter in the reality-programming saga began with the appearance of "America's Funniest Home Videos" in 1989. Camcorder technology lent a new twist to an old truth: People love to see themselves on television. "America's Funniest People" soon followed. Both shows continue to do well in the ratings.

Currently, about half of all reality programming involves law enforcement. "Top Cops" producer and ex-narcotics officer Sonny Grosso sums it up this way: "Most cops make less than $40,000 a year to do what most people wouldn't do for a half million. . . . But people get this vicarious thrill from watching." Indeed they do. That's why we have "America's Most Wanted," "Cops," "FBI: The Untold Stories" and many more. Other successful reality shows providing vicarious thrills and appealing to similar gratifications include "Rescue 911," and "Unsolved Mysteries."

If nothing else can be said for reality programming, at least it affords us an opportunity to examine the differences between our own everyday experiences and those that form the basis for TV's mediated reality. You probably have your own ideas about why certain aspects of real life provide the grist for so much reality programming. Increased awareness of the process should be an important part of your education, one that will help you become a more sophisticated and informed consumer of mass communication in the years to come.

Television News: The Tossed Salad

Despite all the new reality shows, when it comes to reality on television, most of us still think of the news. Television news began as a simple rip-and-read operation. TV newscasters delivered the script taken directly from the AP and UPI radio wires. A considerable amount of TV news still reaches us this way. Local newscasts are often a tossed salad culled from radio wire copy, newspapers, and other sources. Still slides are used along with film, and more recently Betacam and camcorder footage.

Former CBS anchor Walter Cronkite has observed that the concept of an anchorperson unifying these separate parts may become a thing of the past:

> If we can illustrate all stories there is no further need of a news broadcaster to read half the items to the public. Disembodied voices can narrate the film, reporters on the scene will be seen when the situation demands, and there will be no need for a news master of ceremonies in the studio.

Indeed, the whole idea of an anchorperson may be left over from commentators of the radio era. Yet today's anchors seem far less opinionated and pioneering than their radio counterparts. Of more importance is their visual appeal to the audience (see 9.12). According to author Irving Fang, the five most important qualities for the TV anchorperson are:

- Speaking clearly
- Imparting the sense of the news
- Convincing viewers you know what you are talking about
- Keeping the newscast running smoothly
- Maintaining contact with the audience

Nowhere on the list do we find skills involving more traditional journalistic practices or ethics. The question of the journalistic integrity of popular news anchors provided grist for the highly successful 1987 film *Broadcast News*. William Hurt played the part of the classic "know nothing" anchorman who was all flash and no substance. Nevertheless, by the

Not Just Another Pretty Face: The Christine Craft Case

Christine Craft was relatively happy in her job as anchor of the evening newscast on KEYT-TV in Santa Barbara, California. A media consulting firm liked what it saw and, without her knowledge, sent a tape of one of her newscasts to Kansas City's KMBC-TV, a station in search of a new female anchor. KMBC contacted Craft and in January 1981 hired her away at almost double her KEYT salary.

While Craft was being interviewed for the Kansas City job, she told them she resented the treatment she had gotten while working for CBS Sports. In 1978 management had in-sisted that she bleach her hair blonde and change her makeup technique. Despite the changes, she was eventually fired, and she didn't want a repeat performance. But that is exactly what she got.

From the day she arrived at KMBC, she was told what to wear, when to wear it, and what kind of makeup to apply. Craft didn't like it but went along. Despite a rise in the program's ratings, she was fired 7 months after she began. The station manager told her that a consulting firm had found that she was "too old, too unattractive, and not deferential enough to men." Craft sued Metromedia, owner of the station, charging sex discrimination. "No one cares what John Chancellor and Roger Mudd look like," she told *People* magazine. "If we can have uncles on television, why can't we have aunts?"

During the trial it became clear that it was the consultant's findings regarding her looks that had cost her the job. A member of the firm had been taped in a conversation with viewers where he declared, "Let's spend 30 seconds destroying Chris Craft. Is she a mutt?" In addition, the consultants reported that she did not appeal to men and "the women viewers dislike you the most. They resent the fact that you don't hide your intelligence."

With that kind of evidence, it didn't take the jury long to decide. On August 8, 1983, they awarded her $500,000 in

---

end of the film, the Hurt character had risen to become the evening news anchor at a major network.

Perhaps the ultimate extension of form over substance came when ERA, a San Francisco research firm, was hired by Los Angeles' KNXT-TV to find out why its news ratings were slipping. News consultants, or "news doctors" as they are known in the industry, have become commonplace. Their job is to identify factors that may increase news shows' ratings. In this study, the galvanic skin response (GSR) of viewers chosen at random was measured while they were shown film clips of the station's anchorpeople. GSR works like a lie-detector test: When viewers get excited, they begin to sweat slightly, and the GSR device picks up the subtle difference. Newscasters who produced sufficient GSR responses were kept; those who didn't were fired.

George Putnam, a rival newscaster and longtime Los Angeles TV personality noted for his own ability to elicit emotional audience response, objected to the practice. "This ERA thing is frightening. I'm sure if they showed Adolf Hitler up there on the screen the needle would jump right out of the glass. But that's no reason to let Adolf anchor the five o'clock news!" Nevertheless, those who anchor newscasts realize that their jobs are as much cosmetic as substantive (see 9.12 and 9.13).

Friendly Teamness . . . Teeming Friendliness

ABC-owned stations in San Francisco and New York pioneered the "Eyewitness News" format in the early 1970s. These shows have also been called "friendly teamness" and

damages and urged the judge to find the station guilty of sex discrimination. The jury foreman said, "We hope we have helped women in broadcasting."

The decision sent shock waves through the industry and raised some questions about TV news practices. Should anchors be hired for their journalistic skills and experience, or is the way they look of prime importance? TV executives say that they must be free to hire and fire anchors and other news personalities at will as they struggle to compete for ratings. ABC News vice-president David Burke was quoted as saying, "Women in this business face pressures that men do not, but those pressures often stem from the public." In-

deed, a 1981 survey of 1,200 anchors found that almost half the men but only 3% of the women anchors were over 40.

The 38-year-old Craft returned briefly to her Santa Barbara job but quit shortly after the 1983 judgment was awarded to write and speak on the lecture circuit. Currently, Craft carries on the fight for changes in TV news practices but admits that it is an uphill battle. Shortly after the verdict she confided, "This is a victory for civil rights, but I have no illusions that it will make a huge difference in TV news."

The August 8 verdict, however, was thrown out by U.S. District Judge Joseph F. Stevens in October 1983. A retrial was scheduled, and on

January 13, 1984, the new jury awarded Craft $325,000 — $225,000 for actual damages and $100,000 in punitive damages. Craft's lawyer argued that punitive damages should be awarded for their "deterrent effect," to discourage other stations from similar practices. That award was also overturned on appeal. The debate over the appropriate weighing of form and content, of viewer appeal and solid journalistic practice, continues. Meanwhile, Craft has joined the news staff of a radio station in Sacramento, California, and is attending law school there.

"happy news." They differ from other local newscasts in a number of ways, but most notably in the way members of the news team relate to one another. Gone is the old stiff-collared, serious approach. Friendly team members are relaxed and at ease with their news.

Between stories there is light chitchat about the day's events and whatever else comes to mind. News stories emphasize human interest. A group of Boy Scouts is going on a hike in Tarzana; a new flower seller has set up shop on Fourth Street.

Journalists still debate the ethics of "friendly news," but no one questions its success. ABC hit the ratings jackpot in both San Francisco and New York. The network promptly supplied the format outline to local affiliates, and soon Eyewitness News teams began springing up in most of the country's ma-

jor markets. Other newscasts were forced to follow suit in hopes of winning back viewers.

In part, this urge to imitate is a product of the new competitiveness among local newscasts. In recent years, local newscasts in large markets have become very profitable, despite high production costs.

In addition, at many stations the local news is directly followed by prime-time offerings. If a large audience is tuned in for the local news, more will stay tuned when it's over. So "teeming friendliness" is desirable because it means a larger audience than does the more traditional approach. Why?

ABC called in Marshall McLuhan to explain the phenomenon. McLuhan contended that friendly newscasters *share* the news with the audience rather than reporting it in a more objective way. The happy chat between newscasters lets the audience in on what's happening. "The press," he said, "is concerned with what *has* happened. TV news is more successful when it concerns itself with what *is* happening."

Eyewitness News is really "I" witness news. It's a warmer, friendlier, more relaxed coverage of events that allows the viewer to participate. The news team has direct dialogue with the audience. The old newscaster says, "That's the way it is"; the friendly news team says, "This is the way *we are*." The reporting of the event *becomes* the event, overshadowing the original story.

The same can be true of news at the national level. Network anchors are stars or celebrities in their own right. When Ted Koppel interviews an official from Kuwait, he is actually the story because he's far better known than the interviewee. ABC's "Nightline" has become the most talked about program of its kind.

In 1988 CBS introduced "48 Hours" with news anchor Dan Rather. Each week several CBS news correspondents and crews immerse themselves in some newsworthy topic, filming as many different aspects as possible in a 48-hour period. Early shows featured everything from two typical days in a major community hospital to two days inside the pressure-packed Final Four college basketball tournament. More recently the show has focused on urgent social and political controversies.

TV News in the 1990s

TV's emphasis on friendly news points up the changing nature of local TV news. Once upon a time, local news was something you had to put on to keep the FCC off your back. Most stations tried to keep it to a minimum, and budgets were meager. More recently, the audience for local TV news seems to have multiplied exponentially. Now local TV newscasts vie for ratings points just like game shows and prime-time movies do.

The cost of producing a top-quality newscast is tremendous. There are salaries, sets, and expensive electronic equipment. The use of helicopters and satellite delivery has be-

Anchors Catherine Crier, Lou Waters, Susan Rook, and Ralph Wenge on the Atlanta newsroom set of the Cable News Network.

come routine. Yet local newscasts in most metropolitan markets make a good profit. This turn of events came about as a result of an increasing public hunger for news and information of every kind. Why the sudden hunger? Perhaps in an increasingly complex and troubling world, we all feel helpless. Somehow, being "informed" gives us the feeling that we are more in control. Or it may be that we are experiencing a kind of isolation from our fellow human beings, and following the news helps us feel more interconnected with one another. In any event, our increased need for news brought about the success of all-news radio in the 1960s and increasing local TV news coverage in the 1970s. As early as 1970, one Los Angeles TV station was presenting 2½ hours of local news coverage each evening.

The logical extension of this trend came in 1980 when Ted Turner, the controversial cable TV tycoon, inaugurated his Cable News Network (CNN) (see 9.14). Fed to about 3.7 million cable subscribers across the country, CNN was the first 24-hour-a-day, 7-day-a-week TV news service. In its first 2 years of operation, CNN increased its potential audience immensely, and by 1982 it could be received in more than 15 million homes. By 1993 CNN reached over 60 million households in America alone. The news network's coverage of the Gulf War catapulted it to prominence around the world (see Chapter 8). There seems to be no end to the public's insatiable quest for news. As long as this remains true, CNN, the networks, and the local stations will continue to provide it.

Issues and Answers: Beyond Programs and Patterns

We've come a long way from those early newscasts to CNN, from "The Beverly Hillbillies" to "Beverly Hills, 90210." Or have we? Television programming trends appear and disappear at the speed of light, only to reappear before our very eyes. Reality programming was there at the beginning, yet at the moment it is TV's hottest trend. The West was won every prime-time night in the 1950s, but we haven't seen much of the West lately.

It's tempting to survey the chaotic world of TV programming and come away concluding that there is no way to predict what will happen next. Or that no matter what happens next, it has happened before, and will happen again.

Then again you may still feel that "it's only television, so what does it matter anyway?" You're not alone. Even TV professionals can succumb to this. Working under intense deadline pressure they can often be heard reminding one another, "Hey, it's just television, it's not brain surgery."

Television may not be brain surgery, but it does have an effect on our brains, and on the rest of us too for that matter. TV's critics are fond of saying that TV fare is turning our brains to vegetative mush, yet our programming choices are greater than ever before, running the gamut from Academy Award–winning films and hard-hitting documentaries to bikini contests and tractor-pulls.

Television may not be the most intimate medium (radio) or the most prestigious (film), but it is the most pervasive and as such it deserves our attention. Television was only a few years old in 1956 when researcher Leo Bogart eloquently stated the case for the increased understanding of the medium in *The Age of Television:*

> In its brief history television has become the American people's most important source of ideas, apart from interpersonal contact. It has changed the position of other mass media, and profoundly affected the way in which we spend time with our families, and outside the home. It has influenced our outlook on the world and our political decisions, and it has an even greater potential for doing this.

In this chapter, you have been given a number of "tools" to help you understand what television is and how it affects us all. You now know more about the relationships between television programming and real-life experience. You have developed a better understanding of the gratifications that motivate the mass audience. As a member of that audience, you will spend the rest of your life watching. Perhaps you have decided to join the ranks of those who are professionally involved in the medium. If you do, you will be directly involved in determining the future of television and of the culture that it continually reinvents.

Whatever your role, you will be profoundly affected by the small screen with the large potential. Realizing that potential was the key to Robert Lewis Shayon's *The Eighth Art* (1962). Shayon's words are as relevant today as they were 30 years ago: "Let us by all means continue to find out all we can about what television 'is.' But there remains a larger task: to determine what it *should* be and take steps to bring it nearer to the heart's desire."

In the end, it is your heart's desire that will shape the future of Mediamerica and Mediaworld. More than any other medium, television supplies important clues about who we are, where we've been, and where we are headed. Resist the temptation to ignore it or trivialize its effects. TV is here to stay. The viewing choices we make each day and our collective effort to understand them are of critical importance. There's a lot to be done, and it's time we all rolled up our sleeves and got to work.

Queries and Concepts

1 High schools have served as the settings for a number of popular, prime-time television programs. Can you think of any reasons for this? What sorts of gratifications might such school-based programs provide? Using the cone effect model, ex-

amine any TV program in which a school or the educational process plays a central role.

2 What is your favorite television program currently on the air? How about when you were 10 years old? Can you think of ways these programs might have affected the person you are?

3 If you could trade places with any television character for a day, who would it be and why? What does this tell you about that character? About yourself? About television?

4 Check this week's TV schedule and make a list of all prime-time TV series. Then break them down in terms of genre, using the criteria found in this chapter. Does any particular genre seem to dominate? Do the same thing, using a TV schedule or *TV Guide* from 15 years ago (check your library for old copies, or consult the Brooks and Marsh directory, listed in "Readings and References"). Compare and contrast your findings.

5 Using the 31 gratifications listed in 9.2, pick a television show and watch it carefully, keeping the list in front of you at all times. Can you find specific plot instances that match some gratifications? Have a friend do the same, and then compare notes.

6 Make a list of current heroines and heroes in prime-time TV. What do these images suggest about our society?

7 Turn on the TV set at 9:00 A.M. and leave it on all day no matter what. Make notes about what you find. Discuss.

8 Pick a Saturday morning, turn on the TV set, and enter the world of children's programming. Take notes on anything that strikes you; be sure to examine both the programs and the advertisements. If it's possible, watch with your little brothers, sisters, or neighborhood kids. Ask them about the programs, the ads, the characters, and so on. Their answers might startle you.

9 What is the total amount of weekend TV time devoted to sports programs? To men's sports? Women's? Would you rather watch a favorite sport on TV, view it in person, or directly participate in it?

10 You are a local television reviewer. Sit down and watch a network series that you have never seen before. Write a review based on your knowledge of prime-time programming patterns.

11 Check your local TV newscast for any evidence of the "friendly team" approach. You might want to look at all the TV newscasts in your market and decide which has the "friendliest" team.

12 Reread the "Issues and Answers: Beyond Programs and Patterns" section of this chapter. Do you agree or disagree with the position taken? In five pages or less, sketch your vision of television 30 years from today. What is your *heart's desire*?

Readings and References

TV's Mediated Reality

John Fiske
Television Culture. London: Methuen, 1987.

Fiske has a unique aptitude for penetrating TV's mediated reality. The content of this book ranges widely: the TV industry, TV content, and social-cultural effects are all considered. Recommended.

Jerzy Kosinski
Being There. New York: Bantam, 1970.

Captivating novel about Chance the gardener, an improbable product of television's influence: "By changing the channel he could change himself." Made into a movie that is also worth investigating.

Robert Kubey
Mihaly Csikszentmihalyi
Television and the Quality of Life: How Viewing Shapes Everyday Experience. Hillsdale, N.J.: Lawrence Erlbaum, 1990.

One of the most original books on the impact of television to be published in a long time. The authors have engaged a unique research technique (the Experience Sampling Method) to gauge television's contributions to the emotional and psychological quality of everyday life. While I think the research method creates its own set of problems (which are not adequately addressed), I have no reservations about recommending this book as a substantial contribution to our understanding of television. Essential reading.

James T. Lull
Inside Family Viewing. New York: Routledge, 1991.

This collection of Lull's research studies offers an *ethnographic* approach to understanding television. The focus is on the complex ways in which audiences interact with television in natural settings. A unique contribution.

David Marc
Demographic Vistas: Television in American Culture. Philadelphia: University of Pennsylvania Press, 1984.

A much-discussed book. Marc takes a sensitive and meticulous look at our relationship to TV's mediated reality. Recommended.

David Morley
Family Television: Cultural Power and Domestic Leisure. London: Comedia, 1986.

A pioneering study of how people make use of television in their everyday lives. Morley inter-viewed families in their homes about the ways in which they watch, interpret, and are influenced by television.

The Genres of Prime Time

Ien Ang
Watching "Dallas": Soap Opera and the Melodramatic Imagination. New York: Methuen, 1985.

Ang is one of the freshest and most insightful television analysts to come along in quite a while. Here, she explores the complex relationship between the soap opera and its audience.

Tim Brooks
Earle Marsh
The Complete Directory to Prime Time Network TV Shows: 1946–Present. 4th ed. New York: Ballantine Books, 1988.

This is the ultimate book for any TV fan. It includes a listing for every network prime-time show that has ever been on the air. Some entries are brief, but the more important shows receive more extensive treatments. Also included are charts of top shows and season-by-season listings of prime-time schedules. Good for research or just to put on top of the TV set at home.

John Fiske
John Hartley
Reading Television. London: Methuen, 1978.

This unique book lays the groundwork for new ways of understanding how we perceive the content of television and incorporate it into our lives. Chapters on the functions, modes, codes, and signs of television. A lot to think about here. Recommended.

Stuart M. Kaminsky
Jeffrey H. Mahan
American Television Genres. Chicago: Nelson-Hall, 1985.

The authors examine genres from critical, historical, psychological, and sociological perspectives. Simple and straightforward, the book is a useful introduction to the unique qualities of genre and formula in television.

E. Ann Kaplan
Regarding Television: Critical Approaches — An Anthology. Frederick, Md.: University Publications of America, 1983.

An outstanding series of essays that cover a lot of territory: television criticism, news, sports programming, soap operas, commercials, made-for-TV movies, and more. Margaret Morse's essay on TV sports is particularly effective. A selected bibliography is also included, though (unlike the essays themselves) this has become somewhat dated.

Horace Newcomb
TV: The Most Popular Art. Garden City, N.Y.: Doubleday, 1974.

Includes sections on the sitcom, action-adventure, western, and other genres. Newcomb is a pioneer, among the first scholars to write about the genres of television with anything less than abhorrence. Instead, he offers insight into *why* these programs are popular. In doing so, he creates a catalog of American myths and values. This is one of the most important books ever written on the content of commercial television.

Television: The Critical View. 4th ed. New York: Oxford University Press, 1987.

A follow-up to *TV: The Most Popular Art,* Newcomb offers a collection of essays on the genres of TV, plus a piece on the meanings behind the myths. Includes sections on seeing television, thinking about television, and defining television.

Karl Rosengren
Lawrence Wenner
Philip Palmgreen, eds.
Media Gratifications Research: Current Perspectives. Beverly Hills, Calif.: Sage, 1985.

The idea of an *active* audience seeking gratifications from television is rooted in a research tradition known as "uses and gratifications." This collection of essays examines recent developments in that research area. For a good overview, I also recommend essays by Austin Babrow ("Theory and Method in Research on Audience Motives," *Journal of Broadcasting & Electronic Media,* vol. 32, no. 4, 1988, pp. 471–487) and David L. Swanson ("Gratification Seeking, Media Exposure and Audience Interpretations: Some Directions for Research," *Journal of Broadcasting & Electronic Media,* vol. 31, no. 3, 1987, pp. 237–254).

Daytime TV and the Common Cold

Mary Cassata, ed.
"Day Time Television." Special issue of the *Journal of American Culture,* vol. 6, no. 3, 1983.

Daytime Soap Operas

Muriel Cantor
Suzanne Pingree
The Soap Opera. Beverly Hills, Calif.: Sage, 1983.

An academic look at the soap-opera genre. Includes chapters on radio soaps, content, and the soap audience. For a glimpse of how *fans* relate to soaps, pick up a copy of a fan magazine at your local newsstand or supermarket; *Soap Opera Digest* and *Soap Opera Weekly* are both revealing.

Suzanne Frentz, ed.
Staying Tuned: Contemporary Soap Opera Criticism. Bowling Green, Ohio: Popular Press, 1992.

Covers some of the same ground as Cantor and Pingree's *The Soap Opera,* though this collection is much more current. Essays explore the effects of viewing, whether women view soaps differently than men do, the treatment of sexual activity on the soaps, dominant themes in daytime dramas, and more.

Alfred P. Kielwasser
Michelle A. Wolf
"The Appeal of Soap Opera: An Analysis of Process and Quality in Dramatic Serial Gratifications." *Journal of Popular Culture*, vol. 23, no. 2, 1989, pp. 111–124.

These researchers argue that the appeal of a soap opera is much like the appeal of a friendship that evolves over time; the more you think you invest in it, the more you seem to get out of it. For a related study, see Edward Jay Whetmore and Alfred P. Kielwasser, "The Soap Opera Audience Speaks: A Preliminary Report" (*Journal of American Culture,* vol. 6, no. 3, 1983, pp. 110–116).

Edward Jay Whetmore
"It's NOT a Waste of Time." *Soap Opera Digest,* May 3, 1988, pp. 84–86.

Children's Shows; Children and TV Advertising

Robert M. Liebert
Joyce Sprafkin
The Early Window: Effects of Television on Children and Youth. 3d ed. New York: Pergamon Press, 1988.

This book is an excellent source for a quick overview of the massive research literature in this complicated—and often controversial—area. Highly useful reference section.

H. F. Walters
"Pee Wee's Playhouse." *Newsweek,* May 18, 1987, pp. 83–84.

Michelle A. Wolf
Deanna Morris
Alfred P. Kielwasser
Factfile #19: Resources on Children and Television. Los Angeles: American Film Institute, 1989.

This slim volume is a step-by-step guide to the literature on children and television. Includes an overview of print and audiovisual resources, media organizations, and indexes. Hundreds of annotated references. This Fact-file is part of a series published by the American Film Institute; write for details: AFI, Education Services, 2021 North Western Avenue, Los Angeles, CA 90027.

George Woolery
Children's Television: The First Thirty-Five Years, 1946–1981. Metuchen, N.J.: Scarecrow Press, 1985.

This book is essentially the kid's TV equivalent of the Brooks and Marsh directory listed earlier. Fills an important gap, as many children's programs are not aired in prime time.

Thousands of books and articles have been written on the subject of children and television, and interest is hardly waning. For current articles, check *Reader's Guide to Periodical Literature.* For current research studies, look in *Communication Abstracts,* an index that can be found in the reference sections of most libraries.

Sports

Michael Real
"Super Bowl: Mythic Spectacle." *Journal of Communications,* Winter 1975, pp. 31–43.

Lawrence Wenner, ed.
Media, Sports and Society. Newbury Park, Calif.: Sage, 1989.

An academic look at mediated sports realities. Essays touch on a number of important and provocative areas.

Television News: The Tossed Salad

Shanto Iyengar
Donald R. Kinder
News That Matters: Television and American Opinion. Chicago: University of Chicago Press, 1987.

A technical, empirical look at the effects of television news on viewers. On the basis of a number of experimental studies, the authors provide some compelling evidence for the pronounced effect that TV has on setting the "public agenda," what issues we come to think of as important and worthy of our attention. Consequences associated with presidential power and the electoral process are discussed.

Kathleen Hall Jamieson
Karlyn Kohrs Campbell
The Interplay of Influence: Mass Media & Their Publics in News, Advertising, Politics. 2d ed. Belmont, Calif.: Wadsworth, 1988.

Well-written introduction to some of the social consequences associated with television news. The study of rhetoric provides the context. Special attention is given to political reporting. Recommended.

Ivor Yorke
The Technique of Television News. 2d ed. Stoneham, Mass.: Focal Press, 1987.

A very practical, skills-based introduction to television news. The author covers all the basics: reporting, interviewing, writing, graphics, studio design, personnel.

Issues and Answers: Beyond Programs and Patterns

Leo Bogart
The Age of Television. New York: Ungar, 1972. (Originally published in 1956.)

Robert Lewis Shayon
The Eighth Art. New York: Holt, 1962.

Both of these books rank among the first — indeed, the classic — calls to take television seriously. That call is more urgent than ever. See also the readings and references listed for the "Issues and Answers" section of Chapter 8 and the discussion of media advocacy groups in Chapter 13.

10

The Big Picture:
Film as Popular Art

**People tell me that the movies should
be like real life. I disagree. It is real life
that should be more like the movies.**

Walter Winchell

How long has it been since you saw a *great* movie? See if you can make sense out of this little seven-part scenario:

1 "E.T., phone home."

2 "You do know how to whistle, don't you? You just put your lips together and blow."

3 "If that plane leaves the ground and you're not with him, you'll regret it. Maybe not today, maybe not tomorrow, but soon—and for the rest of your life."

4 "In 10 or 15 years none of this will be important to you."

5 "I'm mad as hell, and I'm not going to take this anymore!"

6 "What are you rebelling against?"
   "What have you got?"

7 "Frankly, my dear, I don't give a damn."

If any of these lines have a familiar ring to them, then perhaps you won't need to phone home to get the answers to this little quiz. If there are some you don't recognize, please read on.

Each example is a snippet of famous dialogue from a classic American film—just seven of the thousands and thousands of films that have been produced in Mediamerica over the past century. From *The Life of an American Fireman* to *Backdraft*, from *Birth of a Nation* to *Born on the Fourth of July,* these "moving

Scarlett (Vivien Leigh) visits Rhett (Clark Gable) in his prison cell shortly after the end of the war. These love scenes represent our very definition of romance in America.

pictures" have entertained, excited, and sometimes even illuminated us all. How do they do it?

Life Is Like a Movie

Film provides us with a giant mirror — a reflection of the values, the half-truths, and the ideals of our culture. This does not happen by accident, at least most of the time. Writers, directors, producers, and others know how to rifle our personal emotional treasures and translate them to film where we buy them back at the box office. The more closely a film approximates our own myths and values, the more likely we are to see it and recommend it to others.

For example, fear is a universal emotion. We have all been afraid at one time or another, afraid we were going to die some horrible, lingering, and unjust death. The master of suspense, Alfred Hitchcock, successfully played to these fears and became one of the largest legends in filmdom in the process.

More recently, *Fatal Attraction* and *The Hand That Rocks the Cradle* struck raw nerves as they successfully tapped in to some of our greatest fears, unleashing a media blitz and causing us to reexamine our feelings about some timely and controversial concerns.

Of course there are other ways to reach an audience. *Gone With the Wind* played on our romantic emotions (see 10.1). Rhett Butler was a rogue who had a way with women. Scarlett O'Hara was a beautiful, spoiled belle of the Old South whose affair with Ashley Wilkes was never to be. We wanted to jump into the screen and plead: "Oh Scarlett, can't you see it is Rhett who really loves you?" But we couldn't, she didn't, and at the end of the movie when she asks Rhett, "Where shall I go, what shall I do?" he replies, "Frankly, my dear, I don't give a damn." Scarlett's life was never the same, despite the sequel.

These are universal emotions — fear, love, anger, disappointment — but few of us have experienced such total ruin, complete love, paralyzing fear, and savage violence. The big screen inflates universal emotions until they are larger than life. When we come upon a situation in real life that is intense, we say, "This is just like a movie." Our very way of perceiving vivid experience is shaped by what we have seen on film.

In F. Scott Fitzgerald's final novel, *The Last Tycoon,* an admirer marvels at the power a movie producer, Stahr (based on real-life producer Irving Thalberg), has had over her life: "Some of my more romantic ideas actually stemmed from pictures. . . . It's more than possible that some of the pictures which Stahr himself conceived had shaped me into what I was."

Indeed, the power of the filmmaker to shape our notions about intense experience and provide a series of fictional encounters through which we filter real life, is unrivaled in

all of mass communication. Somehow, the mediated reality we see "up there" takes on an inexplicable significance.

At first glance it's easy to distinguish between real life and "reel life." If I asked you what the difference was, you probably would respond rather indignantly that you could "certainly tell the difference between fact and fiction." However, it's not always that simple.

We have seen how all mass media play a large part in formulating our attitudes, beliefs, and ideals, because we all incorporate perceived mediated reality into our real lives. For example, most of us have never experienced a major crime firsthand, so we formulate our ideas about it from what we see in films or on television. If we actually do witness a crime, we can't help but compare it with what we have seen on the screen. We might even react to a given situation by imitating behaviors of those we have seen in the movies or on TV!

Our notions about romantic love are almost completely derived from mass media. All of us are waiting for that great scene when we will take that special person in our arms for the first kiss. It will be a long, smooth, beautiful kiss. Everything will be perfect. The skyrockets will explode, and we will go off and live "happily ever after," just like in the movies.

The Magic Lantern

Like all mass media, film has two component parts, *form* and *content*. The form of film involves cast, costume, and location, as well as the mechanical phenomena that make it go. The content is the story, plot line, and cast of characters that deliver the message to us. As with most mass media, when we experience moving pictures, we seldom think of the form but concentrate on content in order to derive the message.

Moving pictures do not actually move, but they seem to, thanks to a physiological process called persistence of vision (see 10.2). When a series of still pictures is flashed before your eyes faster than you can perceive each one individually, your mind runs them together, creating the illusion of motion—like those cartoon books that instruct you to thumb through rapidly and "watch the characters come to life."

This phenomenon was discovered almost 2,000 years ago by the astronomer Ptolemy, but it eventually would be Thomas Edison who put it to work. His incandescent bulb was so strong it could project pictures on a wall, making them visible to a large audience (see 10.3). This is how "moving" pictures differed

1895 Auguste and Louis Lumière perfect a projection system and exhibit films to a paying public. The movie theater is born.

1915 D. W. Griffith's *Birth of a Nation* becomes the most successful American film.

1800

1900

1925

1820s In England, Peter Mark Roget and John Paris conduct experiments and publish findings involving persistence of vision.

1839 In France, Louis Daguerre develops a workable system of still photography.

1882 Dr. E. J. Marey, a French physiologist, develops a photographic "gun" that takes 12 pictures a second.

1888 Thomas Edison and assistant William Dickson develop the first workable motion picture camera.

1900 Edison, Biograph, and Vitagraph are competing companies in the new film industry.

1903 Edwin S. Porter releases *The Great Train Robbery.*

1905–1910 Era of the nickelodeons.

1906 British inventors Edward R. Turner and G. Albert Smith devise Kinemacolor, the first practical natural-color film process.

1909 The Motion Picture Patents Company (MPPC) if formed.

1922 Technicolor is introduced.

1927 *The Jazz Singer* is the first "talkie."

1929 *On with the Show* is the first all-talking color film.

1930 As the decade dawns, almost all new films are talkies.

1933 Fred Astaire and Ginger Rogers team up for *Flying Down to Rio* and become film's most successful couple.

1939 *Gone With the Wind* is the film of the year, sweeping the Oscar awards.

1941 *Citizen Kane,* perhaps the greatest American film of the sound era, is released.

1946 Film's biggest box office year; 90 million Americans are going to the movies every week.

10.2 The History of Film in America

1975

Robert Altman's *Nashville* breaks new ground in entertainment films with the vignette approach.

1992

"Home movies" are a hit. Over 100 million video-cassettes are rented in the first week of the year, a new record.

1950

1975

1950s The film audience is younger than ever. Many adults give up films, opting to watch television instead.

1960 Alfred Hitchcock's *Psycho* is released.

1968 The MPAA's new rating system is introduced.

1969 *Easy Rider* typifies youth-oriented films with a message.

1970s Disaster films *Towering Inferno, Earthquake,* and others are successful.

1972 X-rated *Deep Throat* pioneers pornography for the mass audience.

1975 *Jaws* spreads terror in theaters, takes big bite of box office.

1977 *Star Wars* breaks theater attendance records, surpasses *Jaws*.

1978 *Grease* is the word.

1980 *Star Trek: The Motion Picture* costs $40 million but disappoints at the box office. There will be more. Meanwhile, *The Empire Strikes Back* draws huge audiences.

1982 *E.T.* is released, becomes all-time box office champ.

1983 *Terms of Endearment* successfully reaches the female audience.

1986 *Platoon* is the year's low-budget success story.

1987 22 million Americans go to the movies each week.

1988 *The Last Emperor* wins nine Oscars, including best picture and best director.

1989 *Batman* reigns at the box office but is shut out of the Oscar race.

1990 *Ghost* and *Pretty Woman* are unexpected hits. *Dances with Wolves* dances its way to Oscar glory.

1994 Steven Spielberg's year! *Jurassic Park* becomes the all-time box-office champ, while *Schindler's List* is anointed by Oscars.

Thomas Edison demonstrates an early version of the motion picture projector.

from other media utilizing persistence of vision. Many such machines were already popular in the late 19th century. Kinetoscopes and vitascopes were one-person peep shows usually found in a penny arcade. You put in a penny and turned a crank. When turned at the proper speed, the pictures appeared to move.

In the late 1880s, one of Edison's assistants, William Dickson, developed a camera and a projecting device using the new bulb. His first effort at filmmaking was not exactly an aesthetic masterpiece; it lasted 15 seconds and recorded a man sneezing. Yet many films with equally dull content—random scenes at a downtown location; the sun rising in a cornfield—played to large audiences around the turn of the century. The admission price was usually 5 cents, thus the theaters were dubbed *nickelodeons.*

As is often the case with a new medium, the inventive form carries it for a while; refinement of content comes later. Ask some older people about the early years of television. They'll tell you that when they saw their first set, they just stared and stared. There was only one station, and it didn't matter what it showed—they'd watch commercials, a test pattern, anything.

The first motion pictures designed for an audience were made by two French brothers, Auguste and Louis Lumière. These early shorts were being shown to audiences in Paris as early as 1895. Another Frenchman, Georges Méliès, provided major creative contributions to early films.

After the turn of the century, filmmakers were suddenly everywhere. Many who have written about this era have romanticized it, overlooking the seamier side of things. In *Two Reels and a Crank,* Albert E. Smith (who helped found Vitagraph, one of the early motion picture companies) recalls the period a little more realistically. According to him, there was tremendous competition among early filmmakers to cash in on this new revenue source. Smith himself admits to "pirating" pictures of major boxing matches by sneaking in a huge camera under his overcoat. He faked footage of major battles of the Spanish-American War and passed them off to an unsuspecting public as the real thing. At the same time, he relates fascinating stories of legitimate photographic missions. He claims to have filmed the charge up San Juan Hill with Teddy Roosevelt, the first American president introduced to the people via a nonprint mass medium, the film newsreel. Smith was filming a speech by President McKinley when suddenly a shot rang out. The president had been mortally wounded, and it was all on film.

Often the most vicious film battles never made it to the screen—they were fought in the courtroom by competing companies vying for patent rights to cameras and projector components. They "borrowed" one another's inventions shamelessly. For years Edison maintained he should receive *all* the revenues from motion pictures, claiming his inventions and patents had made them possible. By the time he organized a court fight, the situation was out of hand. Too many improvements had come along. In the end a collective was formed, and agreements were reached among the major patent holders. They formed the Motion Picture Patents Company (MPPC) and pooled the use of all patents, providing benefits to the inventors. All movie companies were required to pay a flat fee each time they shot a film. Edison held the largest number of patents, and eventually his share of pool funds reflected it.

Some filmmakers were unhappy with this arrangement, particularly those at smaller companies that operated on slim budgets and preferred to pay no fees at all. Their solution was to leave the East and go so far away that the MPPC would have a hard time tracking them down. Because all films had to be shot outdoors (indoor lighting for film had not yet been perfected), they decided to locate where the sun shone year round. Most ended up in a farm area just north of Los Angeles, called Hollywood. Here was the ideal location for film-making, a quiet, sunny area close to a major West Coast town. But it wasn't quiet for long.

Hollywood became a fairy-tale land. Even today, for all its tackiness and vulgarity, Hollywood inspires adjectives like beautiful, thrilling, amazing, and spectacular. You can still walk down Hollywood Boulevard and read the names of the stars on the sidewalks or buy a "map to the homes of the stars." Films, movie companies, and stars may come and go, but the myth of Hollywood endures. It's still "the dream factory."

The Quiet Years

The birth date of significant content in film is generally regarded as 1903. An American, Edwin S. Porter, had experimented with moving pictures that told a story in his *Life of an American Fireman* the year before, but it was quite by accident. Now he set out specifically to construct a "story" film — one that would go beyond capturing a random event and convey a complete plot. Porter believed that by using stage actors, a script, and joining disparate pieces of film together he could convey a storyline to the audience.

It hardly seems revolutionary now, but it had never been done before. Many were skeptical about such a venture, but Porter filmed *The Great Train Robbery* and made plans to show it around the country. It was a western, and the plot was pretty flimsy. In the final scene a robber shoots a gun directly at the audience for no apparent reason. Yet it was a tremendous commercial success, paving the way for more complex subject matter. Apparently there was an audience for films that told a story. Was there ever!

Twelve years later, film took its greatest leap forward. A former Porter actor, D. W. Griffith, had shot a number of short films that were enormously popular. Many were based on American history — pioneering, the West, American Indians, and the like. When Griffith decided to make a large-scale film, one subject came immediately to mind. The Civil War was the perfect historical backdrop, because it was the most turbulent time in American history — a time when conflicting ideologies were at a peak and unprecedented violence swept the land. But Griffith could not capture such a monumental event while confined to the existing form of film. He expanded it to fit, using a large screen to reproduce marvelously photographed outdoor battle scenes. He also employed moving shots, extreme close-ups, and a host of other film innovations (see 10.4). *Birth of a Nation* was issued complete with a score to be performed by a full orchestra. It became a huge box office success and was the most popular film ever until 1939, when another Civil War epic, *Gone With the Wind,* replaced it at the top of the list.

So advanced was *Birth of a Nation* that almost all film critics agree it was the most influential silent film ever made. For a number of reasons it is difficult for students viewing the film today to assess its impact properly. The film's heroes are members of the Ku Klux Klan. (This reflects Griffith's own racial prejudices and his southern background.) Though the content is socially archaic, the achievement of form remains as brilliant today as it was all of those years ago.

10.4

Director D. W. Griffith at work.

Griffith continued making epic films. His next effort, *Intolerance*, was on an even grander scale. One of the most expensive silent films ever made, it contained four interwoven stories, and the film skipped from one to the next. That is a common technique in today's cinema but one that confused the 1916 audience. Griffith was ahead of his time, and he couldn't take the audience with him. In 1948 he died alone and almost forgotten. It was only after his death that his genius was truly recognized.

While moviegoers of the quiet years flocked to see short comedy films with stars like Charlie Chaplin and the Keystone Kops, epic films flourished, too. Audiences gradually became used to full-length feature films such as *Cleopatra, Ben-Hur,* and *The Ten Commandments.* These names may be familiar to you because remakes were done in the sound era.

The tendency to redo existing material did not start when sound came to film. Just as today, many successful films in the quiet years were based on books and stories popular at the time. Griffith's *Birth of a Nation* was taken from the novel *The Klansman.* As the practice became more commonplace, many discovered that stories lifted directly from print were simply not the same on the screen. We know now that they couldn't be. Whenever we transfer content from one medium to another, it must change to accommodate the new form. But in the quiet years there was little radio and no television, and audiences were not used to the process of adaptation. According to novelist Elinor Glyn, the transferral process was often painful:

> All authors, living or dead, famous or obscure, shared the same fate. Their stories were re-written and completely altered either by the stenographers and continuity girls of the scenario department, or by the Assistant Director and his lady-love, or by the leading lady, or by anyone else who happened to pass through the studio; and even when at last after infinite struggle a scene was shot which bore some resemblance to the original story it was certain to be left out in the cutting-room or pared away to such an extent that all meaning which it might once have had was lost.

The Star Is Born

Critics and authors had yet to learn what the public knew instinctively: Story content was only part of the film phenomenon. The audience was less concerned with *what* and more concerned with *who.* The star system was being born.

Early silent-film stars came from all walks of life. Some, like Charlie Chaplin, had enormous talent; others had only tremendous visual appeal. Most popular of all were those who projected a romantic, sexual image. Douglas Fairbanks and Rudolph Valentino were cast as romantic rogues, while Mary Pickford (10.5) and Lillian Gish (10.6) projected virginal innocence and breathtaking beauty. Soon, titles of films appeared at the bottom of the marquee — at the top was the name of the

Mary Pickford (1893–1979) reigned supreme as "America's sweetheart" for an entire generation. Her active career spanned 23 years, 125 short features (as the one- and two-reel early silent pictures were called) as well as 52 full-length motion pictures. Cecil B. DeMille, one of her many directors, once wrote about the "America's sweetheart" label that "thousands of such phrases are born daily in Hollywood. . . . About once in a generation such a phrase lives, because it is more than a phrase: it is a fact."

film's best-known performer. People began to ask each other: "Have you seen the new Valentino film?" *Story* had been replaced by *star*.

Cults grew around the great stars, and the public hungered for details of their private lives. Fan clubs abounded. The studios were more than happy to cooperate, sensing that a cluster of stars under contract meant financial success. They did not foresee the days when stars would make exorbitant salary demands and become free agents, moving from one studio to the next. Every major film studio in

Lillian Gish (1896–) was one of famed director D. W. Griffith's "discoveries" shortly after he joined two other noted directors, Thomas W. Ince and Mack Sennett, to form Triangle Film Corporation. In *The Stars,* film critic Richard Schickel noted that Griffith kept moving his cameras closer and closer to the faces of the actors and actresses, thus his need for "unlined youthful faces for his close-ups . . . and unwrinkled minds which he could command absolutely." Apparently, Gish filled the bill; she was one of his most successful actresses and starred in a number of films including *Broken Blossoms* (1919), *Way Down East* (1920), and *Orphans of the Storm* (1921). She was presented with the American Film Institute's Lifetime Achievement Award in 1984. In 1987, at the age of 91, she starred with Bette Davis in *The Whales of August.*

America was built on the star system, yet it was that same system that eventually led to a decline in big-studio control of the industry.

The Sound and the Fury

In the late 1920s, my father played the organ for the silent pictures in one of Los Angeles' major movie houses. He made $60 a week, which was more money than he had ever seen in his life. He drove a brand-new Jowett and, needless to say, this put him at the top of the social heap at Manual Arts High School.

But suddenly tragedy struck. A theater down the street began showing *The Jazz Singer,* and overnight, as he recalls it, the lines in front of his theater dwindled while people waited for hours to see (and hear) the talkies. The theater owner assured him it was "just a fad." The quality of silent pictures produced during the late 1920s was superb, whereas the talkies were crude and simplistic by comparison. Surely the audience would soon come to its senses! When it didn't, my father found himself out of a job and playing in bars for $2 a night. He was understandably bitter; he had to sell the Jowett, and for years refused to go into a theater to see a talkie.

Technological change in mass communication can often come so quickly that even those closest to the media are unable to fathom it. The same producers who had been successful with silent pictures were bewildered by talkies. Studios that got into sound early flourished; others perished. Stars who had commanded six-figure salaries were suddenly unwanted because their voice did not match the voice audiences had "created" for them in their collective imagination. Twenty years later history repeated itself with a twist when radio stars could not make the transition to a medium where their visual image did not match audience expectations.

Critics were quick to condemn the talkies. Paul Rotha, in *The Film Till Now* (1930), wrote:

> It may be concluded that a film in which the speech and sound effects are perfectly synchronized and coincide with their visual images on the screen is absolutely contrary to the aim of the cinema. It is a degenerate and misguided attempt to destroy the real use of the film and cannot be accepted as coming within the true boundaries of the cinema. Not only

are dialogue films wasting the time of intelligent directors, but they are harmful and detrimental to the culture of the public. The sole aim of their producers is financial gain, and for this reason they are to be resented.

Come to think of it, "financial gain" is still a pretty big motivator for producers! For better or worse, the public wasn't listening to the critics; it was listening to the soundtracks of the new movies. By 1930 virtually all films appearing for general public release were talkies. The change was sudden, complete, and irrevocable.

Talkie producers found that material suitable for silent films did not always work with sound. So they looked to the stage for new stories and fresh faces whose voices were a proven success. This led to a crop of stars with Broadway and other theatrical experience, including Fredric March, James Cagney, Spencer Tracy, and Fred Astaire. A precious few, like Greta Garbo and Marie Dressler, survived the transition from silent to talkie because they had stage experience and their voices were much as silent film fans had imagined.

1930s: Guns 'n' Music

The one element that seemed to thread through all the successful films of this era was escape from reality. Few films were about real life, because life during the Depression wasn't very entertaining. Films offered an escape from a world of poverty and worry to one of singing, dancing, laughter, fair play, and justice for all.

The emphasis on sound led to the birth of the movie musical. After all, now that pictures could talk, why not have them sing? And sing they did; major studios began producing a series of musical extravaganzas. MGM's *That's Entertainment* (Parts 1 and 2), released in the early 1970s (and still available on video), is the most complete film record of this wonderful genre.

No single couple dominated entertainment films of the 1930s more than Fred Astaire and Ginger Rogers. They first appeared together in 1933 in *Flying Down to Rio*. Then came a string of box office smashes, including *The Gay Divorcee, Follow the Fleet,* and the most famous, *Top Hat.* Plots were secondary in the Astaire-Rogers films; emphasis was on the dance numbers sprinkled throughout. Though the formula was the same from film to film, audiences of the period never seemed to tire of it. Most critics agree that the last "great" Astaire-Rogers film was *Carefree* in 1938. There, for the first time, Fred kissed Ginger on screen, and for some reason that seemed to break the spell. The two films that followed weren't quite able to recapture the magic.

Like the Fred-and-Ginger movies, the 1930s films of the Marx Brothers draw large audiences at revival houses and on TV even today. The zany brothers were never concerned with plot. In fact, Groucho would often leave the story altogether to address asides directly to the audience: "I told you this story would never get beyond the second reel," he'd say impishly and dive back into the action. Marx films had a number of obligatory musical production numbers, but the brothers seemed to enjoy doing them. Sound suited the Marx approach perfectly, for the brothers delivered an avalanche of dialogue filled with double and triple connotations.

Visually, the Marx films were unrivaled. There were sinks hidden beneath coats, horns and harps under the table, smashed hats and cream pies. The secret of the Marx Brothers' success was their ability to poke fun at authority figures. Kings and queens, dime-store employers, underworld bosses, society matrons, and military commanders were all treated with the same joyous irreverence (see 10.7).

The 1930s also saw a curious public preoccupation with crime. Actors such as James Cagney and Edward G. Robinson were filmed fighting and killing one another in an endless parade of St. Valentine's Day Massacres. Perhaps this is one time when mass communica-

10.7

A scene from *A Night at the Opera,* one of the Marx Brothers' zaniest films. Their form-over-content approach to films is one reason their popularity has not diminished in 60 years.
From the MGM release A Night at the Opera © 1935 Metro-Goldwyn-Mayer Corporation. Copyright renewed 1962 by Metro-Goldwyn-Mayer Inc.

tion simply reflected a public longing for justice. While hundreds of successful pictures like *Little Caesar* and *Public Enemy* ended with gangsters getting their just deserts, real public enemies Al Capone and Machine Gun Kelly seemed to be, literally, getting away with murder. Nevertheless, these films were often criticized for showing criminals in a sympathetic light and encouraging hero-worship. Some things never change!

Gone With the Wind

Gone With the Wind was the most successful film of the 1930s, and it has captivated generation after generation since. It has endured because it has everything: the swaggering Rhett, the ruthless Scarlett, the goody-goody Melanie, and the lovable, stereotyped black mammy. And of course it also has the Civil War: the Yankees, the carpetbaggers, and the burning of Atlanta.

Adapted from the best-selling book of the time, the film was produced by David O. Selznick, who spared no expense on lavish sets and period costumes. It was directed by Victor Fleming, whose *Wizard of Oz,* produced the same year, was also a classic.

Gone With the Wind milked every cinematic cliché and success formula that had emerged in the first 40 years of the medium. It stands as a classic, for in it we can see pieces of every one of its successful predecessors. One American Film Institute membership survey named it the greatest film of all time.

1940s: The Movies Grow Up

The 1940s were a period of abrupt and rapid change for many Americans. Along with increasing prosperity came a devastating war. Likewise, the era was a period of abrupt change in American movies and in films all over the world.

Citizen Kane and the American Dream

Released in 1941, *Citizen Kane* is considered by many to be the most important American film made in the sound era. Like *Birth of a Nation,* it advanced the state of the art by developing entirely new ways of delivering a cinematic message.

In many ways the story of the making of *Citizen Kane* is the story of one man, Orson Welles. He starred, directed, supervised casting, and co-authored the script. He was only 26 when he made *Citizen Kane,* yet when he died at 70 in 1985 it was for this film he was best remembered.

Welles had become a national celebrity in 1938 with his *War of the Worlds* broadcast (see Chapter 6). He received several offers to do films, but according to film critic Pauline Kael,

he held out until he could get *complete* artistic freedom and an ample budget. RKO finally gave him that opportunity in 1940, and he moved to Hollywood, bringing his "Mercury Theater on the Air" cast with him. The young sensation looked over the facilities at RKO and exclaimed: "This is the biggest choo-choo train a kid ever had."

It took Welles less than 6 months to film *Citizen Kane,* and he did it for less than $1 million. The plot was a fictionalized version of the life of William Randolph Hearst, the newspaper tycoon, whose reputation for sensationalism and subterfuge was well known to the public at the time (see Chapter 3). It's not a flattering portrait; Hearst banned any mention of it in his papers and offered to pay RKO all production costs if the prints and negatives were destroyed. The studio released the film anyway, hoping it would become a moneymaker. It didn't, at least not right away. Although reviews of the innovative film were glowing, public response was lukewarm. It took many years for RKO to recoup its initial investment.

For all of its artistic virtues, *Citizen Kane* was not exclusively a "personal statement" in the later tradition of Fellini, Bergman, or even Oliver Stone. Rather, it was designed to entertain the mass audience. It tells a relatively simple story. In the best tradition of the entertainment film, the tycoon rises to the top and is transformed from a brash, idealistic playboy to a bitter, defeated old man. Sounds like grist for any one of hundreds of films. What made *Citizen Kane* so special?

Plot The film does not tell the complete story but offers up instead some crucial glimpses into the life of Charles Foster Kane. It begins with Kane's death and works backward. A reporter from a news weekly interviews those closest to Kane and pieces the story together. The opening few minutes of *Citizen Kane* are done as a newsreel, "News on the March" (an imitation of the "March of Time" movie newsreels of the 1940s). This gave the audience the necessary background, and it was so like an actual newsreel that many thought it was real (shades of "War of the Worlds"!).

Sound Welles' experience in radio had taught him how sound could be utilized for maximum audience impact. Remember, talkies were only beginning their second decade, and the use of sound was still considered an aesthetic handicap to true film art. Welles turned this around by making sound work for him. He used all the tricks of radio production, including echo, recorded sound effects, and music, to help tell the story.

Technique Because Welles had never directed a feature film or even appeared in one, every decision about the storytelling function of film was rethought. Cameramen would scream, "It's never been done," but that didn't stop the boy wonder. For example, in one scene Kane's ex-wife sits alone in a large, dark restaurant. Outside the rain is falling; the exterior of the building is bleak and foreboding. The scene begins with a full shot of the neon sign on the roof, which says, "Susan Alexander Kane appearing twice nightly." Then the camera goes *through the skylight* on the roof and zooms in to where Mrs. Kane is talking with the reporter. Welles combined animation and live footage to give the audience the zoom impression, and the scene became the model for all the films that followed. This is but one example of the dozens of completely new cinematic techniques that *Citizen Kane* contributed to the art of film, among them new lighting effects and innovative use of mirrors, shadows, and extreme close-ups (see 10.8).

In one scene, Kane and his wife are at Xanadu, their mansion in Florida (Hearst's mansion was in California's San Simeon), having a dispute. The emotional distance between them is symbolically represented by the physical dimension of the huge room; they are so far apart they practically have to shout to be understood

10.8

Citizen Kane star and director Orson Welles in a scene depicting a festive staff meeting. Note how the ice sculptures in the foreground frame this shot. Innovative visual effects helped make *Kane* one of the most influential American films ever to reach the screen.

by one another. The camera lens distorts the distance, emphasizing it even more. An echo effect makes their voices seem to rebound against the castle walls.

No discussion of *Citizen Kane*, no matter how brief, would be complete without mentioning "Rosebud." "Rosebud" was the thread that wove the *Kane* tapestry together. A reporter sets out to find why Kane murmured the word just before his death. At the end of the film, the reporter concludes that he'll never find out what Rosebud was. The audience does find out, however, in the last shot of the film. The use of such a hook was not entirely new, but never had it been so skillfully employed, and never had the screen told such a powerful story with such believable irony.

Eventually, *Citizen Kane* was successful in bridging the gap between "popular" entertainment and the personal "artistic" statement. Over 50 years later, it remains the most discussed and analyzed American film of the sound era.

Play It, Sam

It started out to be just another spy story and ended up one of the best-loved movies of all time. *Casablanca*, made in 1942, featured Humphrey Bogart as the proprietor of Rick's Café Americain in occupied Casablanca, Morocco. He claims he cares not for politics and disdainfully informs the Germans that "the problems of the world are not my department. I'm a saloon-keeper." In the end, however, he does "the right thing" and is welcomed into the fight against the Germans by the man who is married to the only woman he ever loved.

Numerous lines from the Oscar-winning screenplay (by Julius J. and Philip G. Epstein and Howard Koch) have become famous, including "I'm not good at being noble, but it doesn't take much to see that the problems of three little people don't amount to a hill of beans in this crazy world," and Rick's warning to his beloved Ilsa (played by Ingrid Bergman) to get on a departing plane with her husband or she would regret it "maybe not today, maybe not tomorrow, but

soon—and for the rest of your life."

Most famous of all, however, is the moment in the film when Sam, the bar's pianist (played by Dooley Wilson), is asked to "Play it, Sam. Play 'As Time Goes By.'" Woody Allen's film notwithstanding, no one in *Casablanca* ever actually said "Play it *again,* Sam."

Bogart was a star before *Casablanca,* but the success of the film made him one of Hollywood's most famous leading men for the rest of his life. Since his death in 1957, his legend—and the audience's fascination with *Casablanca*— seem to increase with each passing year. It would appear that the sentimentalists are right: There will never be another Bogart, or another *Casablanca.*

Humphrey Bogart and the Detective Movie

The single most popular genre of the 1940s was the detective story. These films were designed to entertain the mass audience by offer- ing an escape from everyday life into a world of danger, suspense, and intrigue. One of the first great detective films appeared the same year as *Kane. The Maltese Falcon* was John Huston's directing debut; he cast in the lead an experienced but little-known actor who had mainly played supporting roles in second-rate pictures. His name was Humphrey Bogart.

Bogart became *the* leading man of the 1940s (see 10.9). His successes, *The Maltese Falcon, Casablanca, Key Largo, The Big Sleep,* and *The Treasure of Sierra Madre,* to name but a few, are as well known today as they were when they first thrilled audiences of their day. Bogart performed equally well as a laconic detective in *The Big Sleep* and as an exuberant mercenary in *The African Queen.* The key to his success seemed to be his image as a loner.

An unlikely hero and an unlikely leading man, Bogart was always tough, streetwise, and looking out for number one. Yet inevitably, plots would lead him to a confrontation that pitted those self-serving values against the public good. His decision was usually to opt for good in spite of himself.

Bogart wasn't handsome in the Clark Gable or Rudolph Valentino mold. He became the screen's leading man because he projected a visual image that was unique; there was only one Bogie. He was tough and tender, selfish and giving, irreverent and sympathetic. As with all successful stars, any picture he appeared in seemed to become *his* picture.

Perhaps the ultimate detective film was Howard Hawks' *The Big Sleep*. Bogart starred opposite a very young Lauren Bacall. (They later married.) The great novelist William Faulkner wrote the screenplay from the Raymond Chandler novel. The result was a film that defied understanding. There were so many bodies scattered about and so many evil characters that the audience never did understand "whodunit," but it didn't matter! The real story was Bogart, rescuing damsels in distress and trading sizzling one-liners with Bacall (among them, the famous "You do know how to whistle, don't you?"). Dozens of films and television programs in the detective genre (remember "Moonlighting"?) can be traced directly to Bogart's detectives Sam Spade and Philip Marlowe.

The Best of Times, The Worst of Times

The 1940s saw the full flowering of financial success for American films. In 1946 over 90 million Americans went to the movies every week. The industry would never have that large an audience again. By 1993 that figure had dropped to about 20 million a week.

The decline of the movie business in the late 1940s had many causes. New tax regulations made films less desirable as investments. Some antimonopoly rulings meant the studios were forced to relinquish their theater holdings, hence they could no longer exert such complete control. The House Un-American Activities Committee was investigating the industry, and the blacklisting of some top film stars and writers did not help the industry's image. But what really hurt was television. Within a few years, TV would replace movies as America's favorite entertainment pastime. Like radio, the movie industry would have to undergo tremendous change to adjust to its new role as a secondary source of entertainment.

1950s: A New Film Audience

The 1950s film audience demanded that a movie deliver an evening's entertainment significantly different from what was available on television. Thus, controversial subject matter that was inappropriate for TV became the staple of the big screen.

Increasingly, the movie theater became the hangout of young people. Adults stayed home and watched TV while kids went to the movies to get away from Mom and Dad, engage in a little heavy petting, and nibble a box of popcorn. The new youth audience put pressure on filmmakers to produce movies young people could identify with. It remains so today.

A younger Marlon Brando delivered a memorable performance in 1954's *The Wild One*.

One such film was *The Wild One* (1954), featuring Marlon Brando as a mumbling motorcycle leader whose gang terrorizes a small town, pillages the local shops, and leaves folks devastated in a senseless rampage of violence. Yet Brando emerges as an antiestablishment hero of sorts, sought after by the local "good girl." (It was she who asked what he was rebelling against — his famous response, "What have you got?") The plot was borrowed from grade-B westerns (horses became motorcycles), yet somehow it worked. The picture was a huge commercial success and launched his career.

Another hero in the antiauthority mold was James Dean. His most noted film, *Rebel without a Cause,* told the story of the new kid in school who is roughed up by some juvenile-delinquent types. Dean must take his stand, of course, and this involves a "chickie-run," a contest where he and a rival head their cars for the edge of a cliff and jump out at the last moment. The first one to jump is a "chicken," perhaps the most scathing epithet among youth of that day. More telling than any other scene in the film is the confrontation between Dean and his father (played by Jim Backus). When his son asks if he should go ahead with the chickie-run, Dad says simply: "In 10 or 15 years, none of this will be important to you."

Like rock music, *Rebel without a Cause* seemed to strike a responsive chord with a bored teen audience. James Dean was someone that teenagers could look up to, a younger Humphrey Bogart, whose main concern was his most cherished possession, an automobile. So strong was audience identification with Dean that he became something of a cult hero after his tragic death in 1955 at age 24 in a car accident. Though he starred in only three pictures (*East of Eden* and *Giant* were the other two), he was, with the possible exception of Elvis, the era's greatest young idol. The appeal of stars like "90210's" Dylan (Luke Perry) can be traced directly back to James Dean.

The 1950s also spawned a new kind of horror movie — the science-fiction film. True sci-fi buffs may recoil when they hear the term applied to movies like *The Fly, The Thing,* and *The Blob,* all box office smashes in which some technological disaster transformed men and women into robots, insects, or the like.

Often the culprit was a visitor from outer space, bent on conquering and destroying the earth. Usually a scientist was in charge of the good guys. Often his teenage son/daughter/student would play a role in the victory, thus allowing the young audience to identify. These films were usually made by small, independent studios like American International Pictures. But their success caused many major studios to rethink their policies. Most ventured into the B-film business while continuing to issue "major" releases.

Many of the greatest cinema westerns were made during the 1950s. *High Noon* and *Shane* both drew positive attention from film critics. More than any other entertainment form, the western is totally American. The story of the American cowboy is a vital component of the American dream. Like the detective story, the western also offers the vicarious violence Americans seem so fond of.

The need for vicarious physical experience of a different kind may help explain the success of those largely forgettable, but very popular films starring the sex queens of the 1950s: Marilyn Monroe and Jayne Mansfield. Plot served as the vehicle for the sex goddess to parade her charms before the camera. Like violence, sex became a vital ingredient in the success of many features. Here was something they couldn't do on television! There had been sex in the cinema long before the 1950s, but it was usually served as an appetizer, not as the main course.

1960s: The Young and the Restless

Movies in the 1960s continued the accent on youth and reflected the anxieties of a generation born into the atomic age. The period was one of tremendous social upheaval, and some of it ended up on film.

Stanley Kubrick's *Dr. Strangelove* came not long after the Cuban missile crisis of 1962 and brought home the real possibility of nuclear holocaust to a nervous public. Fear of the bomb had been an American preoccupation since 1945. During the late 1950s and early 1960s, many Americans had spent time and money building bomb shelters in their basements. *Dr. Strangelove* played on this panic for laughs, but the humor was very black indeed. The military elite were portrayed as mindless puppets reveling in the ultimate destruction. Kubrick uses the film to mock the military-industrial complex, and we laugh until we cry. *Dr. Strangelove* still attracts large audiences whenever it is shown in theaters, despite frequent appearances on television. Perhaps its popularity during the latter part of the 1960s was bolstered by opposition to the Vietnam War. Young moviegoers, suspicious of the military and its motives, approved of Kubrick's message.

Another dark vision came with *Psycho*, perhaps Alfred Hitchcock's greatest horror film. There have been hundreds of horror films, some good and most bad, but film critics and the moviegoing public agreed *Psycho* was a masterpiece.

Janet Leigh plays a character who steals money from her greedy, insensitive boss and flees to the Bates Motel. Yet by the time a half hour goes by, she has decided to return the money and face the music. She steps into the shower and lets the water run down her body as if to cleanse it of this terrible sin she has committed. Then an unknown person pulls the shower curtain back and stabs her repeatedly. The audience has no idea why; it all seems so senseless. Suddenly we are transferred from one story to another that is far more brutal and terrifying.

The stabbing itself is a cinematic miracle. We never actually *see* the knife enter the body, but through hundreds of quick shots, we watch the knife gleam, see the flesh gyrate, and gasp as blood mixes with the swirling water. It is probably the most violent and chilling piece of film ever shown on the screen, yet the murder happens entirely in the viewer's imagination. (I remember seeing the film shortly after it came out—I couldn't take a shower for a month afterward.)

Hitchcock was called the "master of suspense" because he was the most successful in creating that suspense in the minds of his audience. The famous director was an artist but said he was "merely an entertainer." Perhaps exact definitions of the fine line between art and entertainment will always be blurred, but

Dennis Hopper (left) and Peter Fonda rode off in search of America and made film history in *Easy Rider*.

Hitchcock knew his audience, and the result was a string of commercial triumphs. There has never been another Hitchcock.

In a less scary vein, three films starring the Beatles rang up profits during the 1960s. *A Hard Day's Night, Help!* and *Yellow Submarine* were all resounding commercial successes. Though the popularity of the group was an obvious asset, film critics eventually were forced to admit that the genius of the Beatles infected all of their media efforts. On film they performed very much like the Marx Brothers. There was little plot; rather, the screen was a vehicle for chaos, music, and madness.

As with the Marx Brothers, so much happens in a Beatles movie that you find something new each time you watch. There are puns galore, along with the music and the message. All three films went much further than simply setting film to music. They explored how each medium could reinforce and expand the other. The significance of that contribution became more apparent in the 80s when filmmakers like John Hughes (*The Breakfast Club, Pretty in Pink*) discovered that combining rock and film can lead to box office profits.

In 1969 the commercial success of *Easy Rider* set off a wave of youth-oriented "protest" pictures. Dennis Hopper, who directed and starred in the film, may have been the first American director since Orson Welles to have so much freedom with his product. *Easy Rider* was privately financed (for a bargain basement $370,000) after being turned down by the major studios, who felt that the plot was an open endorsement of drugs and might alienate the audience.

Easy Rider connected with young moviegoers because it articulated, in the most graphic and basic way, the concerns of the 1960s. Two long-haired trippers, Captain America and Billy (Peter Fonda and Hopper), set off on their motorcycles to chase down some drugs and the American Dream. Along the way they visit a commune, a couple of prostitutes, and a southern lawyer (Jack Nicholson), who gets them out of the local jail. Nicholson is the first to die a violent death at the hands of the rednecks. Captain America and Billy die at the end of the film as well. *Easy Rider* seemed to vindicate a large subculture of antiestablishment young people who used marijuana and opposed the war in Vietnam.

Audiences left the theater stunned by the violent ending. The film provided a warning to society and a plea for understanding. Like the Beatles films it also provided music, lots of it. The use of songs like "Born to Be Wild" solidified youth identification and made *Easy Rider* one of the most socially significant films of the decade. Rock remains a central component in many recent provocative features (*The Commitments, Grand Canyon*).

1970s: Snatching Victory from the Jaws of Disaster

The key to big box office in the 1970s was disaster. A string of hits beginning with *The Poseidon Adventure* (about the shipwreck of a luxury liner) proved that the mass audience was hungry for well-known stars and giant catastrophes. *The Towering Inferno* was the story of a huge office-building fire. *Earthquake* told of the inevitable destruction that finally came to Los Angeles. It also featured Sensurround, a sound technique that practically shook the audience out of their seats.

But a bigger box office success than all of these was a disaster film of a different color. Steven Spielberg's *Jaws*, about a shark that devours tourists at an East Coast beach resort, played to millions and became one of the most talked-about movies ever. Millions screamed in terror as the skilled camera crew convinced them the giant shark was about to come out of the screen and eat them alive.

Critics argued that moviegoers were becoming jaded, that they demanded increasing doses of stimulus and titillation. This raises a more significant issue: Are there moral implications to the relationship between audience and filmmaker? Can the audience that gasps when a shark gobbles up a victim be somehow psychologically damaged in real life? Can manufactured anxiety become destructive?

Nashville and *Network*

Many have argued that the movies of the 1970s were devoid of aesthetic merit and notable only for their commercial success. Two films about mass media defy this analysis: Robert Altman's *Nashville* and Paddy Chayefsky's *Network* (directed by Sidney Lumet). Altman has directed a number of first-rate films, including *M*A*S*H, McCabe and Mrs. Miller,* and *California Split,* but *Nashville* remains his masterpiece.

Nashville defied film convention. In an almost documentary fashion it traces the paths of dozens of characters as they attempt to crawl to the top of the country-music scene in Nashville. There is the established C&W star, the teenybopper just in from California, the bevy of C&W starlets eager to make their way into the music business. There is also the politician who sends advance men to convince a country group that this is a good time to support his candidacy, the promotion man's wife who sleeps with the young lead singer, and the singer himself, who lives and loves one day at a time and sings his "special" song to every woman who will listen.

There's also the music — more than a dozen country tunes sung by superstars and would-be superstars. All the songs in the film were written by the actual performers, few of whom had any real professional musical experience. However, this didn't keep Keith Carradine from winning the Academy Award for best song for "I'm Easy."

Oddly enough, that's the only Oscar the film won, though it was lauded by reviewers. It wasn't a commercial failure, but it did fail to match its critical success with comparable box office receipts. This has been the case with most of Altman's movies, including his 1992 satire on Hollywood, *The Player.*

The form of *Nashville* is both its strongest virtue and its greatest handicap. The dozens of subplots are interwoven in a series of vignettes, so the audience never has a chance to get to know the characters as well as it might in other films. Yet Altman turns this into a strength, because *Nashville* is not the story of one star but of the star system. It doesn't matter what kind of stardom you're after (film, country music, political); *Nashville* tells a universal saga of media power and prestige with its glorious, but arbitrary and sometimes capricious, rewards.

Critics still mention *Nashville* in conjunction with a new technique here, a new approach there, a whole new kind of film somewhere else. In a decade when the movie industry seemed interested only in box office numbers, *Nashville* stood out like a beacon.

More commercially successful was *Network* (see 10.10). The 1976 film captured four Oscars, including those for best actor and best actress. The story involves the behind-the-scenes activities at UBC, a mythical fourth TV

"I'm mad as hell, and I'm not going to take this anymore!" screams Peter Finch in his final role as Howard Beale, the "mad man of the airwaves." Finch posthumously won the 1976 Oscar for best actor for his work in *Network*.

network. When a wild-eyed anchorman goes off the deep end on camera, ratings skyrocket. He's left on the air despite his strange ravings because it is UBC's first hit show.

Unlike *Nashville,* this story is told in a very traditional way, but it is an important story. Chayefsky's animosity toward the influence of TV struck a responsive chord in the filmgoing audience. Both the audience in the theater and the depicted TV audience seem to respond unanimously when the anchorman urges them to begin shouting (for no special reason), "I'm mad as hell, and I'm not going to take this anymore!" *Network* proved that, though the protests of the 1960s had subsided, a bubbling undercurrent of frustration remained.

1980s: Galactic Allegories and Psychological Dramas

In the 1980s, successful films were hard to categorize. George Lucas's trilogy, *Star Wars, The Empire Strikes Back*, and *Return of the Jedi*, told straightforward stories involving danger and heroism (see 10.11). The audience's need for these simple storylines, plus the spectacular impact of the space epics' special effects, spelled unprecedented box office success.

E.T. The Extraterrestrial, the most popular film of 1982 and the all-time box office champ, centered on the impact of a visitor from outer space on an average American family. Compared to Lucas' space epics, this Steven Spielberg film featured more heartwarming drama and fewer special effects. Other Spielberg success stories were *Raiders of the Lost Ark* and its Indiana Jones sequels.

Escapism wasn't the only route to success, however. *Ordinary People* (1980), directed by Robert Redford and starring Mary Tyler Moore, was a taut psychological drama set in suburban America where a young man (Timothy Hutton) tries to come to grips with himself, often with disturbing consequences. *The Big Chill* (1983), a film that won both popular acceptance and critical praise for writer/director Lawrence Kasden, centered on the reunion of a group of college friends from the 1960s at the funeral of one of their old gang who had committed suicide. Each had found different ways of coping with the "real world," but in one way or another felt that their college years in that turbulent time represented the finest part of their lives.

A similar theme was explored with great impact in *St. Elmo's Fire* (1986) and in John Hughes' *Breakfast Club* (1985), in which a diverse group of high school students learn about life and each other during a Saturday detention period.

The prolific Hughes also made his mark with two other exceptional entertainment films documenting teen life in America in the 80s. *Sixteen Candles* and *Pretty in Pink* both starred Molly Ringwald and were characterized by their extensive use of rock music and quick-cut editing techniques. One never has time to get visually bored while watching these films. The realistic teen dialogue helped make the characters ring true with the young movie audience. Hughes went on to score with 1991's most successful film, *Home Alone*.

The 1980s were also a time when films tackled the social, political, and personal issues that had roots in the women's movement of the 1970s. *Lianna* explored with sensitivity the problems encountered in a lesbian relationship. *Terms of Endearment* spotlighted the evolution of a mother-daughter relationship. *9 to 5* offered frustrated working women a chance for revenge. More recent films such as *Thelma and Louise* and *Fried Green Tomatoes* have mined this territory successfully.

The divisive war in Vietnam was the setting for Sylvester ("Rocky") Stallone's early Rambo pictures. Many critics found them a simplistic and self-indulgent expression of the "American might makes right" mentality. A more critically acclaimed view of Vietnam was Oliver Stone's *Platoon*. The hard-hitting war epic set off a wave of films about Vietnam and also provided the backdrop for Stone's *Born on the Fourth of July*.

At the same time, there was a tendency for the Academy of Motion Picture Arts and Sciences to award its highest honor to the sweeping epic pictures that seemed to rekindle the spirit of the Hollywood of old. Oscars for best picture went to *Amadeus* (1985), *Out of Africa* (1986), and *The Last Emperor* (1987). Bernardo Bertolucci's *Last Emperor* traced the life of Chinese Emperor Pu Yi from the time he assumed the throne in 1908 to his death as a long-forgotten private citizen in Red China in 1967. It won Oscars in all nine of its nominated categories, making it the Academy's most honored film since *West Side Story* won 10 Oscars in 1962.

At the end of the decade, *Rain Man*, *Driving Miss Daisy*, and *Dead Poet's Society* found commercial and critical success. *Rain Man*, about a disoriented mental patient and his con-artist brother, might have been just another TV movie, but director Barry Levinson teamed Dustin Hoffman and Tom Cruise and produced a poignant and highly regarded film.

The small, character-driven *Driving Miss Daisy* won the 1989 Oscar for best picture. *Dead Poet's Society* showcased the talents of several talented little-known young actors alongside those of Robin Williams.

Film in the 1990s

Though no single unifying theme has emerged in the 1990s, there have been some success stories. *Dances with Wolves* turned Kevin Costner into one of the highest paid movie stars in Hollywood and won a flock of Oscars as well. Oliver Stone's *J.F.K.* was vilified by many critics, yet it broke new cinematic ground and sparked unprecedented interest in the assassination 30 years after the fact.

In 1994 it all finally came together for Steven Spielberg. *Jurassic Park* surpassed *E.T.* to become the all-time box-office champ, while *Schindler's List* won massive critical acclaim and brought Spielberg the Oscars that many felt he should have won long ago. Finally, *The Lion King* roared through the summer as, once again, Disney discovered animated gold at the box office.

The Critics, Promotion, and Success

Throughout this chapter I have continually referred to "the critics" as if they were a group of men and women who perceive film on an altogether different plane from the mass audience. Although this portrayal is somewhat simplistic, there may be some truth in it. Film critics do not generally reflect the mass audience's taste, and therefore they do not have the power to make or break a film the way a record reviewer for *Rolling Stone* could once make or break an album.

George Lucas: "From Modesto to Magic"

As a child, George Lucas seemed less like a budding film executive and more like an impossible dreamer. The producer and creator of the *Star Wars* trilogy spent most of his childhood lost in comic books or in front of the television set. Perhaps that is why he is so much in touch with today's generation of children.

Lucas graduated from high school in Modesto, California (later the setting for his *American Graffiti*), attended a community college for two years, and eventually wound up in film school at the University of Southern California where he met Francis Coppola. Coppola went on to direct *The Godfather* and helped Lucas find financial backing for *THX 1138* (1970), a film about a futuristic world that served as a kind of prototype for *Star Wars*.

The two collaborated on *American Graffiti* (1973), a film reflecting Lucas' own boyhood. *Graffiti*, made for a scant $780,000, returned some $145 million in box office revenues worldwide. That success led to the making of *Star Wars* (1977). Its $10 million budget seemed high at the time, yet it earned more than $500 million in world box office revenues, making it far and away the most profitable film up to that time. (*E.T.* surpassed it in 1982, with $637.6 million.)

The third *Star Wars* film, *Return of the Jedi,* was but one more chapter in what Lucas hopes will eventually be a nine-film series. In fact, at the beginning of *Jedi,* it is identified as episode VI. The three existing films form a middle trilogy for what may well be the most ambitious mythical undertaking in the history of entertainment. Walt Disney himself could not have created a fairy tale on any grander scale.

How much of Lucas can be found in the *Star Wars* sagas? In an interview with *Time* magazine, Lucas says: "A lot of the stuff in there is very personal. There's more of me in *Star Wars* than I care to admit." After all, Luke Skywalker didn't get to be called Luke by accident. Lucas admits that the character played by Mark Hamill is, in many ways, his alter ego.

Lucas currently presides over a 3,000-acre filmmaker's paradise in northern California called Skywalker Ranch. The ranch has become a magnet for moviemakers and would-be moviemakers from all over the world. His Lucasfilm company, located near the ranch, oversees the millions of details associated with a project the size of the *Star Wars* trilogy. Once *Jedi* was launched in mid-1983, Lucas announced he was taking a two-year sabbatical, and rumors circulated about a possible retirement.

Lucas resumed his moviemaking career with the release of *Howard the Duck* in 1986, proving that even he was capable of laying an egg. However, the failure of *Howard* has not slowed him down. In

For example, there are hundreds of commercially successful films that have received nothing but poor reviews from all major film critics. Of the top all-time money-makers—films like *E.T, Star Wars, Return of the Jedi, Batman,* and *Terminator 2*—not one has had the critical acclaim of *Citizen Kane* or *Nashville.*

Movies have been around longer than radio or television and have developed a certain artistic integrity in the minds of the cultural elite. Like the novel, the film medium has a swarm of reviewers who make a living judging each new effort and pronouncing its place among all other works. The TV shows that attract the most attention from critics are those known to the mass audience: "L.A. Law," "Roseanne," and "Cheers," for example. But the films most critics like to talk about, "artistic" films like *Rules of the Game, Jules and Jim,* and *8½,* may be virtually unknown to the mass audience.

1988 he produced two films, the fantasy-adventure *Willow* and *Tucker,* directed by Coppola. Today his "Industrial Light and Magic" company is the film world's leading source of special effects.

In an interview with *Rolling Stone* Lucas was asked why he hasn't resumed work on the long-awaited sequel or prequel to the *Star Wars* trilogy:

> I can make more *Star Wars* and make zillions of dollars, but I don't need to do that, and I really don't have the interest right now. There *is* a story there I would like to tell. It's just that it isn't beating in my head hard enough to say "I have to get this out of here." I'm more interested in other things.

Yet Lucas proudly shows interviewers the large binder that contains notes on the entire nine-part *Star Wars* saga. One gets the feeling that it won't be too long before he's back into production with another seg-

ment. At least that's what the millions of *Star Wars* fans throughout the world are waiting and hoping for. Meanwhile the Lucas magic continues via Industrial Light and the *Star Wars* saga finds new fans thanks to video. For Lucas it's been a long road from Modesto to "a galaxy far away."

A clear difference exists between the elite interpretation of film as art and the mass-audience perception of film as entertainment. Many film critics like to think of themselves as celluloid gourmets, telling the public what tastes good and what's in good taste. In all fairness, the best film critics can lead interested viewers to films of lasting value. And praise from them can mean a lot more to directors and actors than tons of fan mail. There is much to be said for artistic films and their audiences.

Yet despite this, the public seems to develop its own tastes, largely ignoring the critics.

For this reason, movie studios do not go overboard trying to woo the critics. Instead, they try to appeal directly to the moviegoing public through publicity and promotion. But even these tools do not always do the job.

For example, *The Great Gatsby* was released in 1974 amid one of the loudest ballyhoos of the decade. A lot of people were rereading the Fitzgerald novel. The studio

Understanding the Movies: High Concept in Hollywood

If you read the preface of this book, you may remember that I mentioned I currently divide my time between teaching, writing textbooks, and pursuing a career as a screenwriter in Hollywood. It is in the latter capacity that I discovered the term *high concept.*

To understand what high concept means to you as a moviegoer, you need only think back to those films you have seen that contain an immediately recognizable storyline. In Hollywood this storyline is called the "log-line," a term derived from those little blurbs you see in *TV Guide.* The current wisdom is that stories which contain an immediately

recognizable premise are those most likely to draw the largest audience. This is crucial because the movie business is, after all, a *business.*

When you team Arnold Schwarzenegger and Danny DeVito as *Twins,* you have a high-concept movie. When you ask what happens when Peter Pan grows up, you have *Hook.* When you have a typical suburban family that discovers an alien in their back yard and helps him return home, you have *E.T. The Extraterrestrial.* All of these films are successful examples of the high-concept theory.

On the other end of the spectrum are the so-called soft stories like *Terms of Endearment, Driving Miss Daisy, Dead Poet's Society,* and *Grand Canyon,* which derive their audi-

ence appeal primarily from the unique aspects of the *characters.* In Hollywood-ese these films are "character driven" whereas the high-concept films are "story-driven." While most everyone in the industry longs to be associated with "quality" films like *Terms,* the bulk of what sells to the major studios today is high concept.

As a writer, this reality influences the choices I make as I ponder what my latest "spec" screenplay will be about. (Spec means on speculation — a script that I own and intend to have my agent sell, as opposed to an assignment done for one of the studios.) Needless to say, I am not the only screenwriter in Hollywood thus influenced.

Most moviegoers automatically associate "quality" with

spared no expense, hiring Robert Redford to play Gatsby and casting Mia Farrow as Daisy. *Time* magazine put it on the cover, and everyone was set for a box office bonanza. Within a few weeks, most theaters showing the film were empty. The word was out: *Gatsby* was a bomb, and no amount of publicity could save it. Six months later it was on television. Similar scenarios have been repeated since. Remember *Heaven's Gate, Ishtar,* or *Hudson Hawk?*

Most movie producers agree that the feature film, more than any other medium, has one elusive requirement for commercial success: *word of mouth.* The audience sees a film and tells friends. They in turn see the film and pass the word along. Pretty soon there are long lines waiting to see film A, while film B, which may have cost the same to produce, opened at the theater next door, and enjoyed an equal

amount of advance promotion and critical acclaim, is shunned.

At the heart of the process is the intricate relationship between studio, critic, and audience. Critics want movies that advance the state of the art or make strong social statements or both. The public is usually content with less and tends to gravitate toward simple and predictable stories. The studios would like to produce winners that are loved by the mass audience and critics alike, but the primary concern remains filling theater seats. This has become increasingly difficult for them to do.

Nineteen ninety-one was the first year since 1976 that less than a billion tickets were sold domestically. Annual domestic box office grosses, which had been above the $5 billion mark, dropped to $4.85 billion that year. In the end it is the highly selective and slowly di-

character-driven films like *Awakenings* or *Fried Green Tomatoes,* and they are often right. Yet another favorite Hollywood axiom is that "it's all in the execution." Thus a high-concept film like *Batman* can be very well executed while a character-driven film like *Family Business* can be poorly executed. (You don't remember *Family Business?* That's my point.)

It's tempting to criticize Hollywood's preoccupation with high-concept ideas in its eternal quest for the next summer blockbuster. Many screenwriters I know lament the fact that they can't sell their character-driven scripts. "All they want is high concept" is a familiar lament around town. Yet the fact remains that high-concept ideas are much easier to understand and can be "pitched" or verbally described with ease. Thus the studio executive can make a quick decision.

The real dilemma is that a good script is not simply words on a page. It must *evoke* the movie, help the reader see the film in his or her mind as the script is read. That's what sells the script and convinces top talent to come aboard. With a hot director and a star or two contractually committed ("attached" in Hollywood-ese) to the project it stands a much better chance of winding up on the screen. It is considerably easier for the writer to accomplish this formidable task when starting with a high-concept idea.

As a moviegoer you know which films you have enjoyed over the years. If you make a list of your all-time top 10 and classify them according to whether the basic idea can be described successfully in a line or two, you'll be able to arrive at your own high-concept quota. You might find the results surprising. If your preference is for high-concept films, you are not alone. What's more, as long as people flock to the theaters to see these films, you can bet we writers will keep cranking them out.

Oh, by the way, if you have a great high-concept idea for a movie, send it along. Who knows? Maybe we can write the next summer blockbuster together!

---

minishing feature-film audiences, paying an average of $5 per ticket, that will determine the winners and losers.

Majors and "Indies": The Movie Business

Moviegoers are a fickle lot. What worked in yesterday's blockbuster may not work tomorrow. Paradoxically, the very nature of corporate endeavor involves assessing various risk factors and coming up with a formula for success (see 10.12). When no formula can be found, heads roll, and fortunes are jeopardized.

This is precisely the dilemma of Buena Vista, Columbia, Fox, MGM, Paramount, Tri-Star, Universal, and Warner Brothers, the eight major motion-picture production studios. Of the 400 or so English-language feature films released annually, about half are produced by these studios. In the movie-crazy 1940s, the majors released 40 or 50 features each year. Today each produces 15 to 25 titles annually.

Generally the majors have attempted to stay with established or "bankable" stars and tried-and-true success formulas. Into this creative vacuum has come the independent filmmaker, or "indie." *Time* magazine explains it this way:

> The major studios left an opening for such films by sticking too long with expensive formulas calling for car chases, special effects and predictable stars. While these features have perennial appeal for teens, the baby

Spike Lee has come a long way from the low-budget *She's Gotta Have It* to the epic *Malcolm X.*

kets such as videocassette distributors and cable channels. These new markets offer an alternative to the tedious task of financing via traditional theater distribution channels.

The Academy of Motion Picture Arts and Sciences has long recognized the quality of independent films. In 1986, for example, four of the five nominees for the best-film Oscar were produced outside the major studios and on comparatively minuscule budgets. The most successful film that year was *Platoon,* despite its paltry budget of $6 million.

Among the most intriguing independent success stories was that of Robert Townsend and his *Hollywood Shuffle* (1987). In this film an out-of-work black actor (played by Townsend) finds himself on an unending merry-go-round of auditions for stereotypical black roles. Townsend financed his film using a savings account of only $20,000 and another $40,000 he charged on his credit cards. He had only a month to sign a distribution deal before the bills came due. He found one, promptly paid off his credit cards and the cast, and finished making the film. Final cost: about $1 million, a drop in the bucket by Hollywood standards.

Another independent black filmmaker who hit pay dirt was Spike Lee. *She's Gotta Have It* (1986) was made for a mere $200,000 but eventually earned $7 million. The film also appeared on cable, and Lee's next film, *School Daze,* was produced by Columbia. His controversial 1992 release, *Malcolm X,* was produced in association with Warner Brothers and came in considerably over budget at about $35 million.

In the 1980s, there was much talk of "the rise of the indies." David Puttnam, a former head of Columbia Pictures, noted in *Newsweek* that "the underground has become the 'overground.' They're already a major creative reality." But Puttnam's prediction that the indies would flourish in the 90s proved wrong. The deep pockets of most majors continue to give them the edge in the very competitive feature business.

boom generation is developing a taste for movies about relationships and eccentric characters, films that often take less money but more ingenuity to make.

While the major studios continue to invest $20 million or more per picture, the indies can produce films for far less, sometimes a few million dollars. What's more, the final product is often *better* than what the major studio turns out. Director John Sayles (*Eight Men Out, City of Hope*) says, "You have a sense that you are closer to the ground when you're watching an independent movie."

According to Amir Malin, president of independent Cinecom, "The major studios have to make a tremendous profit to meet their overhead, so they go for the home run. We go for singles." Independent filmmakers are also finding it easier to finance their projects thanks to advance money from *ancillary mar-*

In addition, the major studios exert control over the flow of domestic production by dominating the *distribution* process. To achieve any kind of commercial success, independent films must sign a distribution contract with one of the majors to get their films into theaters. Today it is common practice for the majors to book as many as 2,000 theaters for a single film. This "wide release" strategy leaves very few theaters available for films without a studio distribution contract. This is one reason why former independent directors like Lee now labor for the major studios.

In a word, the problem is money. Today the *average* feature film costs between $20 million and $25 million to make. *Terminator 2* came in at a record $95 million. Carolco, which financed the Schwarzenegger action hit, and Orion (*Dances with Wolves*) were regarded as the two largest and most successful independent studios — the so-called mini-majors. Carolco teetered on the verge of bankruptcy in 1992 until it was taken over by Japanese and Italian interests. Orion did go bankrupt that year, falling victim to the recession.

There remain a few bright spots. Most of the survivors have kept production costs down. Miramax has succeeded through clever marketing and the careful nurturing of films like *sex, lies and videotape* and Madonna's *Truth or Dare*. New Line Cinema has survived, thanks largely to its Teenage Mutant Ninja Turtle franchise.

Meanwhile, the majors have encountered their own financial problems. As a result, many have been acquired by foreign interests. Sony now owns Columbia and TriStar while Matsushita controls Universal. Many in Hollywood have warned that Japanese control of the American feature-film industry could lead to problems. Jeff Katzenberg, head of Disney's Buena Vista, released a controversial memo that said in part:

A clash between Hollywood and Japanese sensibilities is inevitable because filmmaking at its essence is about the conveyance of emotion and the Japanese culturally err on the side of withholding emotion. . . . The Japanese are getting into a business that is to some extent outside of their cultural context.

Be that as it may, the Japanese remain major players in the feature-film industry, and the lure of foreign investment dollars may prove too strong for all but the most successful majors to resist. Of course there are also larger implications. According to *Variety*, "Given the cost efficient record of the Japanese and their growing dominance of the world economy, it isn't only Hollywood that's worried about how to position itself vis-a-vis the Japanese."

"Home" Movies: The Hollywood Video Boom

It was only a few years ago that seeing a recently released motion picture meant going to a theater. Today you can rent a videocassette and watch it in the privacy of your home. About 6 million Americans do it every day.

When VCRs were first marketed in the 1970s, the film industry lined up solidly with TV program producers to denounce the new technology as a threat to their economic survival. There must have been some very red faces when, a few short years later, videocassette sales represented bigger profits to moviemakers than box office receipts!

According to *Business Week*, the video industry is now experiencing a "shakeout period." One industry executive says flatly, "The videocassette market is showing the classic signs of becoming a mature industry. . . . The novelty has worn off."

To keep the profits coming, Paramount Pictures has taken the lead in reducing the retail price of many of its video releases in the hope that consumers will buy rather than rent. Paramount pioneered this strategy when it released *Top Gun* on video in 1986 for just $26.95, compared to the industry average of

$75. The lower price was made possible, in part, by a deal Paramount made with Pepsi. Each *Top Gun* videocassette began with a 30-second Pepsi commercial. More recently, Fox's *Home Alone* sold for less than $15.

Still, the rental market remains strong. More than 100 million videos were rented in the first week of 1992, shattering all previous records. Of course, not all videos are movies. An unending array of instructional and "how-to" videos, led by the phenomenal success of the Jane Fonda workout tapes, are also available. Nevertheless, it is the feature motion picture that continues to support the burgeoning videocassette industry.

At the retail level, video rentals were initially dominated by so-called mom-and-pop stores with names like Video Spot and The Video Store. But major retailers such as 7-Eleven and K mart have invested heavily in video and now rent popular movies for as little as 49 cents. The result has been a shakeout at the retail level, and many of the estimated 25,000 original retail outlets now find themselves out of business.

For the consumer, the options have never been better. A company called Blockbuster Video has pioneered a new kind of supermarket video store that carries some 7,000–12,000 titles, compared to the 500–2,000 available at most outlets.

The video boom has also been blamed for the latest technological technique in film, the computer "colorizing" of black and white movies, initiated by media mogul Ted Turner. Woody Allen calls it "criminal mutilation"; the Directors Guild of America has referred to it as "artistic desecration." Writing in the *New York Times,* Richard Mooney contends that "it will inevitably drive the original versions out of circulation."

But Charles Krauthammer argues in *Time* that "colorizing leaves the original black and white prints unmolested. Only a tape of the film is colorized. Nothing is (irrevocably) altered. Colorization is not like painting a mustache on the Mona Lisa, it is like painting a mustache on cheap prints of the Mona Lisa." He goes on to say that "the critics' real fear is that colorization will win the market [and] so corrupt tastes that people will lose their appreciation of the beauty of the black and white original."

Given the history of the film industry, one cannot help thinking of the initial reaction to the talkies. It seems that each new technology brings with it a torrent of criticism from film purists. Inevitably, colorized versions of great old film classics such as *Casablanca* and *It's a Wonderful Life* will introduce these films to new generations of movie fans. As with all new technologies, we will have to wait to see how the public accepts these new versions of old favorites. But the smart money says that a decade from now we will all look back and wonder what all the fuss was about.

Issues and Answers: Self-Regulation

Looking back at ups and downs of the film industry over the past 40 years, we can identify some patterns. For example, the trend toward explicit sexuality in films in the 1950s culminated with a series of movies that seemed to capitalize on an increasingly permissive society in the 1960s. A Swedish import, *I Am Curious (Yellow)* (1967), showed sexual intercourse on the screen. Parents seemed reluctant to send their children to see anything but Walt Disney films for fear the kids would be exposed to language they considered unsuitable.

Seeing a threat to their pocketbooks and drawing from a long history of self-censorship, the members of the Motion Picture Association of America (MPAA), a trade organization, instituted a new rating system in 1968. It was designed to give audiences an idea of what kind of picture they were going to see. After some modifications, five now-familiar categories have emerged:

- G: For all ages; no nudity or sex and only a minimal amount of violence.

- PG: Parental guidance suggested. Some portions may not be suitable for young children. Some mild profanity may be present, and violence is permitted as long as it is not "excessive." A glimpse of a nude body is permitted, but anything more makes it:

- PG 13: Parents are strongly cautioned to give special guidance to children under 13. Some material may be inappropriate for young children.

- R: Restricted, those under 17 must be accompanied by a parent or guardian. This is an adult film in every sense of the word and may contain very rough violence, explicit nudity, or lovemaking.

- NC-17: No one under 17 is admitted, with or without a parent or guardian. This rating, formerly known as X, is generally reserved for films that are openly pornographic, though some serious films by noted filmmakers have received it.

The ratings do not represent censorship per se. But studios know that certain ratings draw specific audiences. Teens will rarely turn out to see a G picture. On the other hand, given the large youth audience, major studios hesitate to make films that will exclude anyone under 17. Though the absurdity of evaluating a film according to the number of seconds a bare buttock appears on the screen is self-evident, the ratings seem to have accomplished what they set out to do.

Of course it also must be noted that not everyone is happy about the current system. Los Angeles archdiocese Cardinal Roger Mahoney sent shock waves through the industry in 1992 when he proposed a reinstitution of the restrictive production codes and standards that preceded the current rating system. According to Mahoney, "In an age of rape, date-rape, sexual harassment, child molestation, sex addiction, serial killings, AIDS and vene-

real disease epidemics, Hollywood simply must stop glorifying evil."

The ratings have the same problem as all attempts to identify what makes a media presentation "objectionable." Guidelines must be flexible enough to incorporate shifting community standards, but which community? Frontal nudity on the screen may be acceptable in Manhattan but unheard of in Minneapolis.

The most obvious flaw in the code is its approach to violence. Though hundreds of sexually explicit films received the old X rating, it wasn't until 1974 that a martial-arts film, *The Street Fighter,* received it for showing objectionable violence.

The implication seems to be that our society will tolerate arbitrary violence but objects to arbitrary sex. In fact, it remains unclear to moviegoers what aspects of a film might prompt a particular rating. While drug use, profanity, violence, or nudity may affect a rating, it is fair to say that not all of these things may be equally objectionable, given the context of a particular film.

Millions of words have been written attempting to define obscenity. But it's an elusive term; today's obscenity is tomorrow's art. No attempt will be made to define obscenity here, but it's worth taking a moment to think about the rating code itself and what it may hold in store for other mass media.

During the 1970s, television networks began to show more explicit material (usually films), preceding it with a "warning" that parental discretion was advised. Some cable TV companies showed uncut X-rated movies during late hours. The time slot of a network show sent a message to the audience. The "family hour" experiment that began in the mid-1970s was designed to reassure parents that their children would be safe watching shows during the early evening.

The "success" of the MPAA rating scheme may eventually lead to a similar code for radio and television programs. The large audiences watching controversial TV shows in prime time as well as the offerings of various outlets like HBO and Showtime mean there is a public that is ready for "adult" TV fare. But their desires often conflict with those determined to protect children by keeping sex and violence off the air. A self-imposed TV rating system could go a long way toward resolving this conflict.

Queries and Concepts

1 Choose three top films now showing in your local theaters. Can you make a list of myths and values associated with each of them?

2 Make arrangements to see a silent film (your library or video rental store are likely sources). Keep a journal of observations regarding the differences between silents and talkies. Which seem to move faster? Which use the visual aspect of film more effectively?

3 Do any young film stars of today enjoy the same idol worship as James Dean? If not, why not? If so, who are they and *why* are they?

4 Do you think that editing "R" and "NC-17" films for television broadcasts harms or somehow undermines the artistic integrity of these films? Do you support the showing of such films, unedited, on commercial television stations? Explain.

5 In one concise page, describe the standards you believe are prevalent in your community with respect to obscenity.

Can you think of any films or publications that seem to violate these standards?

6 Are any of your notions of romantic love derived from movies you have seen? Can you recall any time in your life when you expected things to happen "just like in the movies"? Did they? Explain.

7 Clip a recent movie review from a newspaper or magazine, and then "review the reviewer." Does the reviewer offer an elite interpretation? Is she or he sensitive to mass-audience perceptions? What, in your opinion, are the major strengths and weaknesses of the review? As an alternative project, locate an old film review, published 30 or more years ago. Does the review still hold up? Did the reviewer make any predictions about the film that did or did not pan out? Does the review seem hopelessly bound to its time, or does the writer say anything universal and timeless?

8 Take another look at the Walter Winchell quote that opens this chapter. Do you agree or disagree with the statement?

Readings and References

Richard B. Armstrong
Mary Willems Armstrong
The Movie List Book: A Reference Guide to Film Themes, Settings, and Series. Jefferson, N.C.: McFarland, 1990.

What films have featured one or more zombies? Have any movies been made about people with "unusual" occupations? These and

other categories are included in this book, which provides a list of films, stars, and release dates for each.

Life Is Like a Movie

F. Scott Fitzgerald's *The Last Tycoon* (New York: Charles Scribner's, 1941) is still one of the best sources on the lingering emotional impact of film. Some social and critical approaches to film may be found in Lewis Jacobs, ed., *The Movies as Medium* (New York: Farrar, Straus, & Giroux, 1970), Garth Jowet and James M. Linton, *Movies as Mass Communication* (Newbury Park, Calif.: Sage, 1980), Arthur Knight, *The Liveliest Art* (New York: New American Library, 1979), and James Monaco, *How to Read a Film* (New York: Oxford University Press, 1977).

The Magic Lantern

Albert Smith
Two Reels and a Crank. Garden City, N.Y.: Doubleday, 1952.

A particularly rewarding first-person account of the early years of film from a nickelodeon to the silent screen, told with relish and conviction.

The Quiet Years

Raymond Lee
The Films of Mary Pickford. Cranbury, N.J.: A. S. Barnes, 1970.

I bought this book at a used-book store for $1 . . . here's hoping you have that kind of luck. A short introduction is followed by hundreds of incredible stills from Pickford's most famous films.

Edward Wagenknecht
The Movie in the Age of Innocence. Norman: University of Oklahoma Press, 1962.

Silent-screen star Lillian Gish calls this "the best book on films I've ever read." It turns out she is a personal friend of the author, but her enthusiasm is warranted. The book concentrates on the silent film, particularly its heroines.

The Star Is Born

Richard Dyer
Heavenly Bodies: Film Stars and Society. New York: St. Martin's Press, 1986.

Dyer, a film critic and media scholar, has written a number of seminal essays about "stars" and the relationship between film and society,

between "reel life" and "real life." Recommended reading.

Roger Ebert
A Kiss Is Still a Kiss. Fairway, Kans.: Andrews, McMeel and Praker, 1985.

Most of you are already familiar with this author; he's the "larger" of the famous "Siskel & Ebert" film critic team. Though I find him vastly irritating, Ebert is a thoughtful, insightful, Pulitzer Prize–winning critic. This is his take on some of the industry's stars, from Marilyn Monroe to Jerry Lewis.

Richard Schickel
Allen Hurlburt
The Stars. New York: Dial Press, 1962.

Schickel has served as a film critic for *Life* and *Time,* so this is more than a fan's-eye view of some "classic" stars. Their lives and influences are examined in the context of their audiences. Good reading, lavish pictures.

The Sound and the Fury

Thomas W. Bohn
Richard Stromgren
Light and Shadows: A History of Motion Pictures. 3d ed. Mountain View, Calif.: Mayfield, 1987.

A historical account of the rise of cinema. See particularly Chapters 3–6 on the rise and influence of the silent film. Chapter 7 deals exclusively with the furious impact of sound.

Paul Rotha
Richard Griffith
The Film Till Now. New York: Springs Books, 1967.

This book was originally written in 1930 and is obviously dated. Yet it was the first monumental history of film ever written, compiled before the intellectual establishment was taking film seriously. Rotha notes in an updated introduction that he would like to take back some of his earlier opinions, particularly those on sound films. (He had thought they were a passing fad.)

Citizen Kane and the American Dream

Pauline Kael
The Citizen Kane Book. New York: Bantam Books, 1973.

This includes the original review by Kael as well as the full shooting script and over 100 hard-to-find stills from the film. Once you have seen *Citizen Kane,* you probably will want to pick up this book.

1930s Through 1990s

Tino Balio, ed.
Hollywood in the Age of Television. Boston: Unwin Hyman, 1990.

The film and television industries have been linked for decades, though most books continue to treat them as if they were separate entities. This anthology looks at the connection between film and television. Part I deals with the rise of commercial television and its impact on film; Part II covers trends in the 1970s and after.

William Bayer
The Great Movies. New York: Grosset & Dunlap, 1973.

An excellent examination of "great films" of the sound era, easy and fun to read. Bayer is a film critic with a gift for getting to the point. The book is filled with more than 300 photographs and a text that provides convincing rationale for the author's choice of the 60 "greatest" films ever made.

Richard Griffith
Arthur Mayer
The Movies. New York: Simon & Schuster, 1970.

A decade-by-decade fan's-eye view that covers films into the 1960s. One of the largest (9″ × 11″) and most enthusiastic histories around.

Mark Thomas McGee
The Rock and Roll Movie Encyclopedia of the 1950s. Jefferson, N.C.: McFarland, 1990.

This unique reference book capsulizes the plots of 35 films. In addition, the author provides quotes from reviews and information about the music, cast, and credits. Useful reference lists and bibliography.

William J. Palmer
The Films of the Seventies: A Social History. Metuchen, N.J.: Scarecrow Press, 1987.

This book focuses on "quality" films from a decade that many regard as something of a wasteland (at least as far as films are concerned). Especially interesting is a section on *Go Tell the Spartans,* a forgotten Vietnam War film that preceded such popular films as *Apocalypse Now, Born on the Fourth of July, The Deer Hunter,* and *Platoon.*

Two general historical accounts of the movies provide fine background material for those seeking information on specific films through the early 70s. Gerald Mast's *A Short History of the Movies,* 3d ed. (Indianapolis: Bobbs-Merrill, 1981) is just that, but it covers virtually every important film ever made during the period from an international perspective and includes sections on the rise of the film industry. John L. Fell's *History of Films* (New York: Holt, Rhinehart & Winston, 1979) covers similar turf in somewhat less detail but emphasizes the medium's more daring and avant-garde directors such as Fellini, Antonioni, Godard, and Bergman.

The Critics, Promotion, and Success

Peter Hay
Movie Anecdotes. New York: Oxford University Press, 1990.

In addition to the critics, gossip columnists spend their lives writing about the movies and the people who make them. This collection is described as "period pieces that evolved from real-life and reel-life happenings reported by the gossip columnists." Can you believe what you read? Of course not! But you might have fun sorting through the fact and fiction that is so much a part of film lore.

Cobbett Steinberg, ed.
Reel Facts: The Movie Book of Records. New York: Vintage Books, 1982.

Just about everything you always wanted to know about movie facts and figures. A massive "book of lists" for the movie buff. Included are sections covering the Academy Awards and all other major awards, the marketplace (most popular films on TV, annual box office receipts), the studios, stars, and festivals. Plus a section of the codes and regulatory functions of the industry.

For a discussion of popular versus critically acclaimed films, see David Shaw, "The Film Critics — Power of Pen Has Sharp Limits," *Los Angeles Times,* July 6, 1976, p. 1.

Majors and "Indies": The Movie Business

Alexandra Brouwer
Thomas Lee Wright
Working in Hollywood. New York: Avon Books, 1990.

Among the best introductions to the film industry. This comprehensive book covers all facets of Hollywood through interviews with the pros who are working in the industry. Recommended.

S. Koepp
"Lights! Camera! Cut the Budget!" *Time,* Mar. 30, 1987, p. 57.

Roy Paul Madsen
Working Cinema: Learning from the Masters. Belmont, Calif.: Wadsworth, 1990.

Each chapter in this book is co-authored with an expert in the field. The text is incredibly well illustrated.

Jason E. Squire
The Movie Business Book. New York: Fireside Books, 1988.

This collection of amusing and informative interviews with film personalities and professionals provides a behind-the-scenes peek. Not to be missed: the Mel Brooks chapter on the business of movies and the Russ Myer chapter on low-budget films.

Peter Steven, ed.
Jump Cut: Hollywood, Politics and Counter-Cinema. New York: Praeger, 1985.

A collection of essays from *Jump Cut,* a film magazine that publishes unique and often controversial articles. In addition to an examination of Hollywood (the "dominant cinema"), many of the authors explore independent productions (the "counter-cinema"). Included are essays on independent filmmaking, women's counter-cinema, gay and lesbian cinema, and radical third-world cinema.

Issues and Answers: Self-Regulation

See the readings and references listed for Chapter 13. Many books about freedom of expression, obscenity, and pornography include some discussion of film. See the references listed at the end of Chapters 2 and 4.

Bohn and Stromgren's *Light and Shadows: A History of Motion Pictures,* 3d ed. (Mountain View, Calif.: Mayfield, 1987), gives equal time to sex, violence, and ethnicity and their roles in the MPAA ratings. For an interesting account of the lengths that must be taken to bring R-rated films to G-rated television, read Eric Mankin's "Bleep, Bleep: Censoring Movies for TV," *Electronic Media,* April 18, 1988, p. 40. For current issues, check such periodicals as *Film Quarterly, Journal of Popular Film & Television, Jump Cut, Screen,* and *Variety.* The *Film Periodicals Index* is an excellent guide to articles in the legion of film magazines and journals, and that old standby *The Reader's Guide to Periodical Literature* will help out as well. Both are library reference-room staples.

Beyond the Media: The Phenomena of Mass Communication

So far we have concentrated on the evolution and current practices of the media themselves — what they are, where they have been, and how they work today. This final section explores some media-related phenomena, topics chosen to help you make sense of your own participation in Mediamerica and Mediaworld.

Chapter 11 provides a look at advertising. From the classified ads in your local "home shopper" to the multi-million-dollar TV ad extravaganzas premiering each year at Super Bowl time, advertisers compete with one another in a relentless battle for our hearts, minds, and pocketbooks.

Public relations practitioners (Chapter 12) have come to play an increasingly significant role in supplying the information-hungry media. No longer mere publicists, today's PR counselors work to build strong relationships between organizations and their publics. Without them, the media system as we know it would cease to function. What's more, advertising and PR now account for over half of all media-related employment opportunities.

As our mass communication systems become increasingly pervasive, there is a renewed sense of urgency for all of us to examine the ethical and moral considerations involved. Recently, defining and encouraging "responsible communication" has become a leading topic in mass communication courses. Chapter 13 examines these and related issues, providing a current context for the ethical-behavior codes that have emerged over thousands of years of human history.

Another consequence of our growing reliance on mass media has been the advent of the serious study of popular culture. Though a relatively new academic discipline, popular

three

culture is attracting the attention of a lot of students and professors as well. I hope that Chapter 14 will lead you to additional thought about its meaning in your everyday lives.

We have all witnessed the extraordinary political and social upheaval that has transformed our world these last few years. The breakup of the Soviet Union, a reunited Germany, and the new European alliance have forged a new world order. Any true understanding of the media must be global in nature. Chapter 15 offers a look at some of Mediaworld's leading mass communication systems.

Traditional and empirical kinds of media research are being conducted daily to answer the kinds of questions that have been raised in *Mediamerica, Mediaworld*. One danger involves the myriad ways that exist to conduct and report research. Often we can be easily influenced by articles that attempt to simplify findings. Chapter 16 offers some sample studies and is designed as an introductory consumer's guide to the measurable consequences of the form and content of mass communication.

Our final chapter explores some of the new communication technologies. In the past, we have tended to think of technological breakthroughs as isolated scientific curiosities. But communication patterns are changing so rapidly in Mediamerica and Mediaworld that the form and content of the information we receive today may be radically different tomorrow.

If it seems to you that these final chapters cover a lot of territory, you're right. In fact, thousands of books have been written about these topics. I urge you to use the Readings and References section at the end of those chapters that spark your interest to discover more about these phenomena of mass communication.

Hearts and Minds: Advertising Yesterday and Today

News, by its very definition, is bad; if one hears good news—it must be advertising or PR.

Marshall McLuhan

"It's *good* for your skin." "It makes you feel *good* all over." "It's so *good* and *good* for you!" Any way you slice it, dice it, chop it, or cut it, most of the thousands of bits of good news we see and hear each day come to us via advertising. Advertising, from the Latin *advertere,* meaning "to turn the mind toward," is not a mass medium, but it does rely on the media to convey its message. Often that message contains a promise that we'll look, feel, smell, and be better if only we'll buy the product or use the service.

These messages come from everywhere: Standard Oil, Ralston Purina, Marlboro, Nike, Alpo, Duncan Hines, and even the good folks at Goodyear Tire and Rubber. In our informa-tion environment, these businesses are but a few of those that compete for our attention on a daily basis. Behind each effort is a full-time staff of advertising professionals whose job it is to turn hearts and minds toward the product or service, and ultimately to influence *you*, the information consumer.

The Information Environment

Media visionary Marshall McLuhan reminded us that our world continues to change rapidly. In the last few decades we have, in a sense, gone from an industrial society to an information society. We have witnessed "the creation of the worldwide information environment" that McLuhan dubbed a "worldpool of information." In fact, "information itself has become by far our largest business and commodity."

In some ways, the functions of advertising differ little from those of the mass media themselves. As in print, radio, and television, a message is created from real life, and a mediated reality is constructed and designed to reach a mass audience. But the advertising message must do more than keep the audience's attention. It must influence attitudes, beliefs, and behaviors. No matter how clever a message campaign may be, if it fails to influence, it fails. What's more, the advertiser may have only 30 seconds of air time or a few column inches of space to make it happen.

The Advertising Business Develops

Mass advertising developed along with mass media. Early ad forms were handbills and printed signs. Actually, newspapers came into being as vehicles for advertising. By the early 1800s there were thousands of such publications. George Washington used newspapers to sell real estate, and Ben Franklin wrote some of Mediamerica's first promotional handbills. Most transactions were made at the local level, but as marketing techniques became more sophisticated and long-distance travel more common, many businesses wanted to expand to new markets.

To fill this need, the advertising *agency* was born. Volney Palmer organized the first one in the United States in 1841 (see 11.1). Early agencies represented publishers, not products, going directly to potential advertisers to offer space for sale. Agencies were awarded a small

fee by the publishers, usually based on the total amount of revenues they generated.

Soon the advertising business became unwieldy. Advertisers were constantly in doubt as to which publications would be most effective and what their ads should say. Circulation figures were suspect, and there was no way of knowing for certain the real "cost per thousand" of readers reached. Into this vacuum stepped the N. W. Ayer & Son Agency. In 1875 it began offering ad counseling directly to the people with the product, advising them how to get more for their advertising dollars. The idea was a great success, and this basic structure remains intact today.

Advertising agencies represent clients, dream up copy for their ads, recommend media outlets, and receive a portion of the total advertising dollars spent (usually 15%). One additional twist makes the relationship between agency and client interesting. Most media outlets offer a 15% *agency discount* on all ad rates, a practice that grew from their desire to sell as much advertising time and space as possible. In theory at least, agencies live on the discount and clients receive agency services for free.

Early Excesses

Advertising practices during the first half of the 20th century were often more expedient than ethical. Print media and radio stations received consumer complaints by the thousands, accusing advertisers of making exaggerated claims for their products.

In 1911 advertisers started a crusade to clean up the industry. This was in large part a reaction against the shady campaigns of the purveyors of patent medicines. A number of organizations tried to adopt codes of ethics to encourage truth in advertising and discourage questionable practices. They reasoned that the public might come to distrust all advertising if something wasn't done.

The 1929 Code of Ethics of the National Association of Broadcasters laid down guidelines for the regulation of commercials, placing the responsibility for commercial content on the broadcast licensee. Broadcasters were urged to prohibit advertising making "false, deceptive, or grossly exaggerated claims." Obscene material was to be banned. The client's business product should be mentioned "sufficiently to ensure him an adequate return on his investment, but never to the extent that it loses listeners to the station." That's a magic formula most stations would still like to have today!

The problem comes in defining the terms used in the 1929 code or in any of the other advertising codes that followed. At what point do we reach "excessive" advertising claims? When does zealous representation of the product end and outright "exaggeration" begin? Advertising remains advocacy for a product. Most consumers know by now that advertising agencies exist to portray the sponsor's product in the most favorable light. A product's weaknesses are going to be ignored while the competition's will be exploited.

"Take tea and see." Lyons' Tea sponsored this appearance of the two Nippys. Early advertising practices often involved such stunts.

Truth in Advertising

In an effort to keep advertisers and advertising honest, dozens of government and private agencies have become involved. At one time or another the Federal Trade Commission, the FCC, the U.S. Postal Service, the Food and Drug Administration, the Securities and Exchange Commission, and the Public Health Service have all acted as consumer watchdogs. Consumer advocate Ralph Nader's Center for the Study of Responsive Law is one of the best known of the independent, nongovernmental forces in the consumer arena. The 1970s brought a tremendous surge in the consumer-advocacy movement. With it has come an increasingly critical focus on advertising practices.

In addition, the courts have generally become more favorable toward the consumer in cases where consumer interest and advertising practices conflict. Severe judgments have been delivered against companies by judges and juries sympathetic to the consumer perspective. In short, more than ever, advertisers are *liable* for what they advertise.

In *The Advertising Answerbook*, author Hal Betancourt lists five general rules of thumb for the advertiser and the agency that want to stay out of hot water:

1   Refrain from advertising a product that is unsafe or potentially hazardous.

1837 Settlers are lured to Illinois by publications subsidized by land speculators.

1929 The first Code of Ethics issued by the National Association of Broadcasters provides guidelines for the regulation of broadcast commercials.

1800

1800 Early printers like Benjamin Franklin produce promotional sheets to supplement their income.

1828 Andrew Jackson's election to the presidency is attributed, in part, to his ability to manipulate the press.

1841 Volney Palmer organizes the first ad agency in America.

1875 N. W. Ayer & Son Agency begins offering ad counseling directly to advertisers.

1896 McKinley-Bryan presidential race marks the beginning of modern political campaign methods.

1900

1911 Advertising professionals, led by industry trade paper *Printer's Ink*, begin a crusade to "clean up the industry" that spells the beginning of the end for patent-medicine vendors and other shady advertisers.

1922 The first radio ad, for a real-estate development company, is aired in New York.

11.1 The History of Advertising in America

1973

Subliminal Seduction by Wilson Bryan Key alerts the public to the use of alleged hidden messages in advertising.

1950

1954 For the first time, TV ad revenues top $500 million and exceed those of radio.

1957 Vance Packard's controversial book *The Hidden Persuaders* documents excesses in the advertising industry.

1979 Psychographics is the latest ad-industry methodology.

1980 Ronald Reagan's election signals the deregulation of advertising thanks in part to a less aggressive Federal Trade Commission.

1984 "Great Communicator" Reagan is reelected by one of the widest margins in history.

1988 George Bush's successful presidential campaign is characterized by numerous "negative" 30-second TV spots.

1989 Research indicates that for the first time, over half of all students enrolled in U.S. journalism and communications programs hope to find jobs in advertising and PR. Despite this, the number of news-oriented majors remains constant.

1991 The recession is blamed for large advertising cutbacks.

1993 With advertising revenues down, there are dire predictions of "the end of advertising." Insiders contend that reports of advertising's demise are greatly exaggerated.

1995 Advertising revenues surge, led by big increases in syndicated television and cable. Magazine and newspaper income are also on the upswing.

2 Refrain from false claims that lead a customer to expect a better product than he or she will actually get.

3 Refrain from creating false impressions — by the use of the word "free," or testimonials, or reduced special prices that are phony — in order to motivate sales.

4 Refrain from unfairly hurting competition through comparative advertising that disparages a competitor's products.

5 Refrain from making claims for a product without substantiation or some reasonable basis for making such claims.

Betancourt concludes with a simple statement: "Fooling the customer these days is a risky and expensive proposition." He is only one of a growing number of advertising professionals who believe that we have gone from a society that once said "caveat emptor" (let the buyer beware) to one that now says "caveat venditor" (let the seller beware).

It is also fair to say, however, that the government's willingness to take a hard line against advertising diminished significantly in the 1980s, given the Reagan administration's laissez-faire "marketplace" philosophy.

A leading industry publication, *Printer's Ink,* is responsible for the Printer's Ink Model Statute, a strongly worded model for legislation against false and deceptive advertising practices, which has been passed in one version or another in most states. The statute spells out specific guidelines for advertisers and identifies practices that are "deceptive or misleading." It covers radio and television as well as print practices and is responsible, in part, for a growing movement toward truth in advertising.

Radio Advertising

There has always been a difference between public perceptions of print and broadcast advertising. From the beginning, people seemed

Consumer advocate Ralph Nader has often been an outspoken critic of corporate advertising practices.

to take print advertising for granted. Few objected in the 1800s when most newspapers developed a heavy dependence on advertising. For example, the benefits of newspaper classified advertising to everyone involved are easy to recognize. But the public seemed to feel that broadcast ads were an intrusion into their own private space. Many still do.

Only 5 years after the first radio ad ran in 1922, radio advertising was commonplace. Into the chaos of advertiser claims and counterclaims stepped the federal government, and in 1927 the first act regulating radio broadcasting was passed. The provisions of the act made it obvious that the American system of broadcasting was to be "commercial." What might have happened had the government taken a different tack? In Britain and many other European nations, all broadcasting was put under control of the national government in the 1920s (see Chapter 15). No advertising was allowed, and listeners paid for their entertainment via a special tax on home receivers.

The commercial nature of American radio continued to be challenged. As recently as 1929, the National Association of Broadcasters, an industry organization, was trying to discourage advertising during what we now call television prime time. Its Code of Ethics stated that there was a "decided difference between what may be broadcast before and after 6:00 P.M." They reasoned that before 6:00 P.M., radio is part of the listener's business day. But after that time, radio should be used for "recreation and relaxation." The 1929 code limited advertising between 6:00 and 11:00 P.M. to a dignified "good-will type" identification of sponsors.

Such idealism soon gave way to a more pragmatic approach. It was precisely during the evening hours that most people were listening. Broadcasters quickly learned they could charge more for advertising time when the audience was larger.

By 1930 the CBS and dual NBC radio networks were going strong, boasting more than 100 affiliates among them. Programs the networks supplied were not their own creations, but those of sponsors and their advertising agencies. Thus during the 1920s and 1930s many successful programs bore the names of products: *Lux Radio Theatre,* *The Eveready Hour,* and *The Purina Chow Checkerboard Boys.* Often the name of the product was woven into the theme song of the show. Radio stars unabashedly endorsed everything from soap to cigarettes.

Today advertisers pay about $8.5 billion each year to tout their products on radio stations and networks (see 11.2). In contrast to the early sponsored shows, virtually all radio advertising is now done on a "spot" basis, with advertisers running their brief commercials during various times of the day. In radio the most sought-after periods are the crucial drive-time slots: 6 to 9 in the morning and 3 to 6 in the afternoon. During these periods the radio audience swells as commuters tune in.

11.2

The high cost of advertising on television is the theme of this ad, designed to reach advertisers and agencies. Radio has had an uphill battle to hold on to its share of revenues since TV, the "ultimate advertising medium," was introduced in the late 1940s.

Television: The Ultimate Advertising Medium

Though radio remains a vital force in advertising, it is generally acknowledged that after World War II, television became the dominant American entertainment medium. It was only natural that it should become the principal advertising medium as well. By 1993 advertisers were spending over $20 billion annually to purchase broadcast TV time. Another $2 billion was spent to reach cable viewers.

In the beginning, television was a new challenge for advertisers—they could now picture the product as well as describe it. A lesson first learned in radio was doubly applicable to television: In a marketplace flooded with similar products, the form of the ad was at least as important as the content. Cigarette commercials in the mid-1950s, for example, showed scene after scene of lush springtime countryside. A playful couple cavorted flirtatiously while smoking. Clearly the message was that smoking (for whatever unknown reason) is like a springtime experience, embodying all the joys of youth, love, and an ant-free picnic.

In 1952 the sale of radio time still accounted for more than 60% of every broadcast advertising dollar, but 2 years later television surpassed radio with sales that exceeded $500 million. By 1956 the total spent buying network radio time had dropped to $44 million, about a third of what it had been at the beginning of the decade. Today TV accounts for over 70% of all broadcast advertising revenues.

As in radio, most network television programs were *sponsored*—conceived, created, and paid for by sponsors and their agencies. In 1959 the public was outraged at having been deceived by those rigged quiz shows (see Chapter 9) and blamed the networks. With some justification, all three maintained that they were only conduits, selling time to others who created the shows.

The networks quickly realized that they would have to more carefully control the content of programs they aired. Increasingly, new shows were conceived and produced by the networks themselves. This led to the rise of spot advertising. The spot advertiser does not buy any one show but hundreds of 10-, 30-, or 60-second spots to be run at specified times.

Save Me a Spot

Spot advertising is the backbone of broadcast advertising. Here's how it works:

1   The ad agency meets with the client and determines media strategies most appropriate for the product.

2   A time buyer employed by the agency meets with a station representative, who may handle dozens of radio and TV sta-tions. Together they try to determine which "buys" will be most effective for the client.

3   The station rep designs a package of buys, specifying stations and air times.

Sometimes a client will intervene by putting other constraints on the time buyer. Often the station rep will try to stick time buyers with the less than desirable times they are under pressure to sell. Eventually the client's spot, conceived and produced by the agency, appears on the station at the time and date specified.

What I've just described is a simplified version of what happens at the national or regional level. At the local level, advertisers may deal directly with the station salespeople. In very small markets, those salespeople may also be on-the-air personalities or perform some other function at the station.

Advertising: Making a Living

More than half a million people are employed in advertising in America today. Some of them are station reps and time buyers. Some deal exclusively in print: layout, design, illustrations, and graphics. Others work for newspapers, magazines, or other media outlets. Some are involved with broadcast copywriting and production.

A typical advertising agency is run by a board of directors that chooses a president, who deals with department heads, each with a specialized staff. These typically include the following:

Market Research

This is the agency's statistical arm, which informs clients of the most lucrative geographic and demographic targets for their products. Often market research involves field interviews with potential buyers.

Media Selection

This is done by print-space buyers and broadcast-time buyers as well as those who handle outdoor, yellow pages, direct mail, and specialty buys. All do their best to place the client's message where it is likely to get maximum response for minimal expense.

Creative Activity

Creativity is what most of us think of when we imagine an advertising agency. It involves the people who write the words and create the visuals of the ads we see and hear each day. Photographers, graphics experts, copywriters, and others are often employed by the agency on a full-time basis. Much of this work is also farmed out to production companies or freelancers.

Account Management

These are the executives who deal directly with the client and are constantly on the lookout for new clients to bring into the agency fold. Account executives, like radio and TV salespeople, are generally among the highest-paid staffers. Without them, there would be no need for other staff members, because there would be no clients.

Many college graduates fortunate enough to land an entry-level advertising position start as salespeople at local media outlets. If you go to an agency, you might start in the media department, planning and buying time and space. Many of these positions were traditionally filled by men. However, an increasing number of entry-level opportunities for women are found in account management.

Women will find that initiative is rewarded more rapidly in advertising than anywhere else in media — not because ad agencies are pro-feminist but because they are pro-achievement. Advertising is an upwardly mobile business. Once you get over the demeaning lower hurdles, you'll be able to rise as far as your brains and talent will take you. And even at the lowest levels, advertising positions tend to pay substantially more than comparable media jobs. A beginning copywriter at an agency can expect to earn 20% more than someone doing similar work at a radio or TV station. This holds true for employees in production, art, and other areas as well.

You'll have a much better chance of success if you're competitive, aggressive, hardworking, and mix well with all kinds of people. The world of advertising is one of *compromise*. Ad people are hardheaded realists: Their business is to help clients sell. *What* they're selling makes little difference.

Advertising can be used effectively in "selling" many things that are not products in the traditional sense (see 11.3). It was the public-service antismoking spots on TV that helped lead to a ban on cigarette commercials in the medium. Many top advertising agencies regularly contribute their time and energies to charities (cause-related marketing) and environmental groups (green marketing).

Form and Content: How Advertising Works

The effectiveness of advertising is attributable to the considerable media skills of people in the industry. The most clever copywriters, best artists, and most talented graphic designers labor over the national advertising campaigns that bombard us. This collaboration led Marshall McLuhan to observe: "The ad is the meeting place for all the arts, skills, and all the media of the American environment."

The television-commercial scriptwriter has only 30 seconds to tell the story. Television advertising dispenses with plot line and brings us action, music, and visuals (see 11.4 and 11.5). The scene may shift several dozen times in those 30 seconds. First a close-up of a hand holding a drink — suddenly a plane flies overhead — a flight attendant pours a cup of cof-

ADVERTISING SELLS A LOT MORE THAN CARS, COOKIES AND COMPUTERS.

Just name the good cause and chances are awfully good that advertising has given it a helping hand.

Corporations, advertising agencies, and communications media — through the Advertising Council — have been donating their time, talent and money for 30 years.

Because advertising works for cars and cookies and computers.

And it works just as hard for education and health and peace.

Ad agencies remind readers that they sell education, health, and peace as well as products — and themselves.

You Say You Want a Revolution?

Like so many trends in popular culture, a recent fad in TV advertising first came to public attention thanks to the Beatles — some 17 years after the group broke up! In 1987 the Nike shoe company launched a $7 million advertising campaign with a series of controversial, fast-paced, black-and-white spots prominently featuring the group's 1968 hit "Revolution." Nike's agency reportedly paid a huge undisclosed amount to current copyright owner Michael Jackson for the rights to use the song, marking the first time that an original Beatles recording had been used for advertising purposes.

Beatles fans were not pleased. Chris Morris, a rock critic for the *L.A. Reader,* noted: "When 'Revolution' came out in 1968 I was getting teargassed on the streets of Madison. That song is part of the sound track of my political life. It bugs the hell out of me that it has been turned into a shoe ad."

The Beatles agreed. The three surviving members and Yoko Ono sued Nike, contending that the "persona and good will" of the group were being used without permission.

But the success of the spot has spawned a number of such uses, and now the airwaves are full of them. Marvin Gaye's "I Heard It Through the Grapevine" became a pitch for California raisins; the Four Tops' "I Can't Help Myself" suddenly referred to the urge to consume a cake made with Duncan Hines's mix. Ritchie Valens's "La Bamba," which was a big hit in the 1950s, and came to our attention in the movie of the same name, also became the soundtrack for a Pop Secret microwave popcorn spot.

Some artists have steadfastly refused to authorize such uses, among them Bruce Springsteen, John Mellencamp, and R.E.M. Some go even further than that. Chrissie Hynde of the Pretenders attacks such practices directly on the LP *Get Close* by asking, "How much did you get for your soul?"

While music historian Jon Wiener contends that "Revolution" "had a meaning that Nike is destroying" and Lennon and McCartney obviously did not have shoes in mind when they wrote the song, this type of tie-

in seems to work well for advertisers as baby boomers become big consumers. The process continues unabated. Craig Hazen, music director for the Young & Rubicam agency, used hits from the 1960s in a successful series of spots for Mercury cars. He says, "Right now it is a very pronounced trend in advertising."

Where will it all end? Ironically, Bob Seger's "Like a Rock," a powerful anthem on the foibles of male machismo, now describes the masculine virtues of a certain pick-up truck. Seger must be laughing all the way to the bank.

No doubt you can think of a few special songs that you simply cannot imagine as the soundtrack for a TV commercial. ("Here's Guns 'n' Roses for Winchester Rifles!" — "Nirvana says Old Spice smells like teen spirit!") We all associate hit songs with our own "soundtrack for life," and the use of them for commercial purposes may be disorienting at best. Perhaps an audience backlash will come when we finally heave a collective sigh and say "Enough already!" Now *that* would be a revolution.

---

fee — a child laughs in glee while being served a hot dog as the clouds roll by outside the window.

Form is the important thing; content is secondary. The ad for a shirt company shows a field of daisies — no shirt and no people. The voice-over tells us: "This shirt makes you *feel like a daisy.*" It's like Picasso's painting *Man in Chair.* There is no man, no chair, only a collection of skewed lines that, according to McLuhan, represent what it *feels like* to sit in a chair.

Commercials:
The Best Thing on TV

In his book Commercials: The Best Thing on TV, *Jonathan Price extols the virtues of the TV commercial. Though we are conditioned to think of these 10-, 30-, and 60-second messages as mere interruptions, Price maintains that they involve the audience far more than the programs themselves do.*

More fun than a gorilla with a suitcase, more explosive than a camera that blows up, more entertaining than the programs they interrupt, more informative than most network news, commercials are often the best thing on TV. And the best commercials outpace the television programs they sponsor in at least a dozen ways.

Commercials are dangerous to make: The ad men who go out on location often risk their lives for even less than an Oscar; they do death-defying stunts for the sake of five seconds of film to advertise a car — or peanut butter.

• They're violent to products: Unlike regular programs, commercials don't hurt people; they torture products.

• They're almost obscene: also unlike regular programs, commercials hint and flash but never deliver; the suggestions are enough to arouse, but these clean scenes never come to climax.

• They're emotional: In thirty seconds, not thirty minutes, a commercial can make your eyes moisten, your adrenaline accelerate, and your heart thump.

• They're coldly calculated: Since a commercial is designed as part of a marketing strategy, its objectives are studiously worked out beforehand; compared to program writers, the creators of commercials are far more conscious of the impact they are making.

• They're carefully written: Since every second costs more than two thousand dollars, crack writers sand every idea and plan every camera angle for maximum effect, making the authors of 60 Minutes look like tourists casually writing home.

• They're overdirected: Shooting one hundred feet of film for every one they use, commercial directors caress every detail until it glows; particularly on food, hair, and cars, the results are bravura.

• They're star-studded: There are more Oscar winners playing the breaks than the shows, and commercials sometimes turn unknowns into superstars in a few months.

• They're extravagantly produced: Since more money goes into the production of some thirty-second spots than into half-hour shows, commercials often have flashier locations, bigger casts, stranger sets, snappier graphics, and funnier ideas.

• They're highly edited: Our culture is learning faster perception per second thanks

Print media, particularly magazines, are replete with examples. A full-page ad for vodka pictures a lone fingerprint (see 11.6). In another ad, a "machine wash" tag somehow symbolizes Nike apparel (see 11.7). A Marlboro billboard plants a colossal cowboy in an urban landscape (see 11.8). In each case, visual space is given over to a scene that has a minimal "logical" connection with the product. The theory is that by surrounding the product with an unusual environment, the ad can entice the consumer to try it.

But the consumer is also busy learning other things. Ads tell us a great deal about our society, and they help influence and change that society. Although the first business of ads is to sell products, their influence doesn't stop there. In fact, that's where it begins. As McLuhan points out, "Advertising itself is an information commodity far greater than any-to editing techniques that show us a hundred bottles of beer on a wall in twenty-seven seconds or sixty-five pictures of McDonald's breakfasts in sixty seconds; we follow them, and when we return to the slower editing of regular programming—not to mention the scenes of real life—we may find the pace unaccountably dull.

• They're regulated and censored: Commercials have to submit to many more censors and many more taboos than regular programming; since freedom of expression does not apply to advertisers, the commercials must do a fine tap dance down the line of conventions, a discipline that keeps commercials politically agile and diplomatically astute.

• They're even rated PG: When parents cannot ban products, they band together to prevent advertisers from mentioning the rotten stuff to kids; as a result, ads to children are now much more honest than the programs—and kids still like candy.

Culturally, commercials have trained our eye to accept fast cuts, dense and highly paced imagery, very brief scenes, connections that are implied but not spelled out—in brief, a new style of visual entertainment.

Historically, we see commercials more often than the shows (the same spot may be run six to sixty times a season), and we recall them in more detail, often with more fondness. People feel great nostalgia for the White Knight, the Green Giant, Speedy Alka-Seltzer, Tony the Tiger, Snap, Crackle, and Pop—these are the elves of our country's imagination.

Financially, commercials represent the pinnacle of our popular culture's artistic expression. More money per second goes into their making, more cash flows from their impact, more business thinking goes into each word than in any movie, opera, stage play, painting, or videotape. If commercials are artful, then the art is objective; capitalist, not rebellious; part of a social activity rather than a personal search for expression; more like a Roman road than a lyric poem. Their beauty is economic.

Yes, some are dumb. Some guy leaning out of the screen to yell at us because we supposedly tried to make him change beers just makes us hate Schlitz. People going gaga when they walk into a bank, just because the bank accepts savings accounts, make me gag. But then I don't love Lucy much. And I'm glad Gilligan has to stay on his island.

Commercials are not all superb. But the best are lively, very American mini-dramas, tiny films, high-speed epics. Taken as a whole, commercials offer a rough catalogue of our consumer economy and a wild tour of our unconscious fantasies.

From The Best Thing on TV by Jonathan Price. Copyright © 1978 by Jonathan Price. Used by permission of Viking Penguin, a division of Penguin Books USA, Inc.

thing it advertises." In their rush to sell a product, advertisers sometimes don't even recognize the more important effects of their collective art—selling life styles and social values to generation after generation of Americans.

Advertising is the first to reflect and encourage social trends. According to McLuhan, advertising "responds instantly to any social change, making ads in themselves invaluable means of knowing where it's at." For example, America's interest in ecology during the 1970s showed up often in advertising: Ads featuring the "natural" environment sold everything from cigarettes to silverware. The women's movement had barely gotten started when television ads began picturing women as mechanics and bank presidents. Ads are first to reflect social trends because they *have* to be one step ahead. Competition in advertising is

ARCO Marine, Inc. Salutes the Children's Hospital of Orange County Clinic

ARCO Marine, Inc.

300 Oceangate
Long Beach, CA 90802-4341

11.6

Large corporate sponsors such as ARCO often use their ad space to promote the interests of worthy non-profit organizations.

For more information on Nike Apparel call 1-800-645-7898.

11.7

The tag is the thing in this Nike apparel ad. What does it say to you?

far more fierce than in programming. Thus, advertising is often more arresting than the program it interrupts (see 11.5).

Advertising also teaches us how to behave through little socialization lessons. They show us how and when to love one another. A wife makes her husband happy by straining his coffee through a special filter. A husband amazes his wife with the latest innovation in diapers. In many ways, advertising provides a context and a meaning for all sorts of everyday experiences. In contemporary society, virtually all our everyday experiences are somehow influenced by advertising.

Case in Point: The Great Pet-Food War

I want tuna,
I want liver,
I want chicken,
Please deliver.

The cat that sang this refrain for Meow Mix was supposed to persuade us that our cats would never be happy until we delivered the product to them. This is one of the dozens of pet-food commercials in recent years that have "humanized" pets and featured a number of "stupid pet tricks." But when you stop and think about it, pets aren't human at all. Or are they?

Behind these commercials are thousands of hours of research designed to exploit our feelings about pets and to sell us one particular brand of pet food over another. Most veterinarians agree that pets are colorblind and that even the taste of a particular food matters very little. Yet most of us are convinced about the virtues of the pet food we buy. Why?

Pet-food commercials afford the perfect example of the victory of form over content in advertising. In Europe most animals get along on table scraps, but in Mediamerica our pets *must* have pet food.

This phenomenon is a fairly recent one. According to an article in the *New Yorker,* until about 1960 there were only a few pet foods on the market. But by 1965, Americans were spending $700 million on their pets, and a scant 15 years later that figure had jumped to over $3.2 *billion.* Today it has surpassed $5 billion. Virtually all of this growth can be attributed to advertising. Our pets may be no healthier or happier, yet we believe they *must* have these products.

The advertising agencies have us neatly divided into three camps: the "premium" buyer, who purchases only the best — brands advertised as "100% meat and meat by-products"; the "practical" or "functional" consumer, who buys whatever is cheapest — the cereal products; and in the middle, the buyer of the "moist meal" pet foods packaged in convenient foil pouches but supposedly tasting like they "just came out of the can."

One of the most celebrated coups in the industry was the triumph of the Alpo dog-food campaign of the middle 1960s, which insisted "Your dog *needs* meat." The goal was simple: to convince owners that their dogs *had* to have the premium-priced Alpo brand. In 1970 the

11.8

Urban cowboy? The western image has long been associated with Marlboro cigarettes. Ironically, Marlboros were originally designed to appeal to women.

Federal Trade Commission intervened. Its tests indicated that pets really don't *need* meat at all. In fact, all pet foods — canned, moist, and cereal — had long been meeting government regulations requiring certain minimum nutritional content.

The new Alpo cry was: "Your dog *loves* meat!" Ralston Purina asserted that its Chuck Wagon was "meaty, juicy, chunky." Nevertheless, Chuck Wagon did not contain one speck of meat.

What motivates us to spend all this money on our pets? The first response is obvious: We love them. We want them to have a "balanced diet," one that's good for them. We have feelings about our pets that have been successfully exploited by sponsors and their agencies. Besides, who can resist a close-up of a kitten or puppy (see 11.9) or the antics of Morris, the "finicky" cat? Pets are so . . . well . . . visual!

11.9

Form or content? Purina contends that it puts more "wow" in its cat food. What is wow?

That's why pet-food commercials work so well on television. Despite healthy budgets for radio and print, TV remains first in the pet-food ad business.

Television advertising has been the biggest single contributor to the rapid economic growth of many key industries like pet foods, which sell their products to a large number of consumers. Through heavy use of TV, today's unfamiliar brand name becomes tomorrow's institution.

Of course, the pet-food war is but one example of thousands of advertiser wars being waged for our consumer dollars. As early as

The Siren's Song: A Theory of Subliminal Seduction

Luigi Manca and Allesandra Maclean Manca taught and studied mass media and sociology, respectively, in New Orleans, where they were involved in research related to subliminal images. Here they suggest some reasons that such images are used and why we "need" the amazing things advertisers promise us.

In the mid-1950s Vance Packard exposed the extensive use of hidden, or subliminal, messages by advertisers selling products. In the 1970s Wilson Bryan Key began to find all kinds of sex and death images embedded in magazine ads and radio and TV commercials. Inspired by their books, an alert student in a Loyola University mass persuasion course discovered the words "you love" delicately, but unmistakably, traced in the shadow by Ted Kennedy's nose on the cover of the November 5, 1979, issue of *Time*.

Apparently we are being bombarded with a variety of subliminal stimuli. But, with the possible exception of Professor Key and his students, those of us who are supposed to study and teach mass media practices really do not know very much about what is going on. What's more, we do not know what sort of social impact or significance the use of subliminal communication may have.

Among all the media enterprises, the advertising industry is the most directly involved in systematically using subliminal stimuli to manipulate consumer behavior. As Packard pointed out, at first advertisers were concerned primarily with informing the public about the quality and the availability of their products. Eventually, however, marketing research demonstrated that most consumers were not persuaded to buy by cool, logical arguments but rather by hidden, seemingly irrational motivations.

Advertising, therefore, could no longer be based on a cool mode of communication but had to rely on emotional and aesthetic appeals. The manipulation of consumers through subliminal stimuli was a logical consequence.

Since subliminal communication has become a part of our daily lives and, therefore,

our culture, the role it plays in our society should certainly be examined. It may be that subliminal communication is part of what we may call the emotional-aesthetic dimension of our mass culture and that it is being used in certain media in the creation of a feeling of mass intimacy and spirituality.

Since it is no longer a matter of cool, logical transmission of information in order to persuade reasonable people, the concept of truth in advertising has acquired a novel dimension. Are the popular images used to appeal to emotional and aesthetic values true or false?

When Catherine Deneuve greets TV viewers with a throaty meow from atop a luxury sedan, is the meow true or false? In a sense, the ad is certainly false, since at a subconscious level it is promising the male consumer a sexy European blonde and the female consumer her glamour and sex

What particular market might this ad be aimed at?

appeal as part of the package. And we know that Catherine Deneuve definitely does not come with the car. Or does she?

As Ernest Dichter pointed out, consumers tend to act toward a product as if it had a soul or a personality of its own. The function of advertising is therefore to suggest or even create this soul in the minds of the consumers. In the case of the luxury sedan, the soul is the sexy European blonde. It follows that in a consumer so- ciety, commodities are no longer marketed for what they really are but for the fantasies and ideals they represent to the buyer.

For example, Marlboro and Virginia Slims are both

Continued on next page

Have you ever seen a grown man cry?

In *Subliminal Seduction,* Wilson Key suggests that liquor ads often use distorted and grotesque faces hidden among glass and ice cubes to play on the death wish of alcoholics. The face circled in this Crown Royal ad seems to verify this. Can you find any other hidden images here?

manufactured by Philip Morris and probably contain essentially the same tobacco. But the soul of Marlboro is the rugged cowboy roughing it in the untamed West, while that of Virginia Slims is a sleek, svelte woman with a chic touch of liberation.

On the surface, most of us simply dismiss such ads as so much Madison Avenue fluff. However, their impact on our behavior is very real. The same people who laugh at the ads when they see them in a magazine would not even consider buying the cigarette whose soul was of the opposite gender.

At a subconscious level, the preoccupation with the soul of the products we consume seems to have given an almost spiritual dimension to what used to be (and in reality still is) a basically materialistic society. We are promised the experience of a nearly transcendental joy as we caress the upholstery of our shiny new cars or take the Nestea plunge. We should feel a deep, forbidden thrill when we finally get to squeeze the Charmin or rub our armpits with Tickle. We'll see the light with 7-Up . . . and we know, of course, that Coke adds life.

This is obviously a pseudospirituality. Viewing the crime, fear, organized violence, poverty, racism, and genocide that are also part of our daily lives, it seems likely that we actually have a great spiritual void. Perhaps our ability to perceive the suffering of other human beings as something touching us has been numbed by the siren's song.

1957 in *The Hidden Persuaders,* Vance Packard pointed out that advertisers exploit our fears, hopes, dreams, and anxieties. We must become more aware of this process if we are to make sensible choices about how we spend our money.

Packard maintains that advertisers with their "depth manipulation," or probing of our wants and needs, often make us do things that are irrational and illogical:

> The most serious offense many of the depth manipulators commit, it seems to me, is that they try to invade the privacy of our minds. It is this right to privacy in our minds — privacy to be either rational or irrational — that I believe we must strive to protect.

Another controversy along these lines has centered on the debate about so-called *subliminal* advertising, or the use of hidden images in magazine and TV ads (see the guest essay "The Siren's Song"). *Subliminal Seduction,* a 1973 book by Wilson Bryan Key exposing this alleged practice, stirred quite a response from the industry and the public as well, though virtually everyone in the industry denies that such practices exist.

In the late 1970s, *psychographics* became the latest advertising rage. It was no coincidence that this method became popular just as computers were winning widespread acceptance in the advertising industry. Psychographics involves the data-based identification of mass-population segments into such categories as the *belongers* (38%), who are happy with mainstream values and are reluctant to change brands, and the *achievers* (20%), who tend to be more upscale and more independent in their product decision-making. Interestingly, only 5% of the population were identified as *experientials,* or those who are willing to try new things and "experience life fully."

Thanks to computer technology, all manner of obscure group attributes could be identified. For example, researchers contend that experientials attend fewer high school and college sporting events than do certain other types but are just as likely to attend a professional sporting event. Go figure.

The biggest news for advertisers in the 1980s came from Washington. During the Carter years, the Federal Trade Commission (FTC) had played an increasingly larger role in policing advertising practices by encouraging truth in packaging and truth in lending legislation. The Reagan administration insisted on a downsized and less aggressive FTC as part of its deregulation-minded "marketplace" philosophy. Consumer activists protested, but these policies continued during the Bush years.

Decreases in the government watchdog functions over advertisers have led to increasing concerns regarding the long-term impact of advertising. These involve some very central questions about the impact of advertising in our society. In their guest essay, Ronald K. L. Collins and Michael Jacobson ask one such question: Are we consumers or citizens?

Advertising Today

As with other media industries, the early 1990s have been the worst in recent history for advertising. Not surprising, since 80% of all newspaper revenues and over half of all magazine revenues come directly from advertising. Add to that a couple of recent annual double-digit slides in TV and radio revenues and it's not a pretty picture.

In *Newsweek,* ad man Robert Samuelson recounts the various theories used to explain all of this. Among them: the recession, the emergence of alternative marketing strategies such as coupons and consumer prizes and promotions, and large cutbacks by traditional big advertisers like tobacco and liquor companies. But Samuelson contends that the real problem is "the bust after the boom." The advertising-media complex overexpanded and now it's paying the price. The past decade's boom was driven by abnormally high consumer spending. As that has abated, so has advertising."

Are We Consumers or Citizens? A Call for Reclaiming Our Traditional Noncommercial Values

Ronald K. L. Collins, visiting associate professor of law at Catholic University, and Michael F. Jacobson, executive director of the Center for Science in the Public Interest, are on the board of directors of the Center for the Study of Commercialism in Washington, D.C.

Commercialism Is Wrecking America

Our cultural resources are dwindling. The very ideal of *citizen* has become synonymous with *consumer*.

The omnipresent signs of commercialism's stamp are so numerous that we are in danger of becoming oblivious to the obvious. Ads are tucked in books, displayed on giant screens at sport events, projected from subway monitors, pumped into doctors' reception rooms, posted in public restrooms, inscribed on clothes, embedded in arcade games, zapped through fax machines, and emblazoned (thanks to food dyes) on hot dogs.

One hundred and thirty billion dollars is dumped annually into advertising. That's more money than the gross national product of our oil-rich ally, Saudi Arabia.

There is the long-standing American ideal of simple and honest living, of moderation in the marketplace. Frugality used to be a key word in America's civic vocabulary. Yet ever since World War II we have allowed businesspeople to exalt one value—consumption—to the near exclusion of all others. This treads on our moral and civic tradition like a bulldozer in a flower garden. In this one-value universe, the ideal of consumption too often obliterates other important social and environmental values, such as the following:

- **Psychological well-being:** Our system of advertising purposefully promotes envy, creates anxiety, and fosters insecurity. The tragic end product of this is kids killing kids for $100 name-brand sneakers.

- **Communal values:** The soul of a community cannot thrive in a relentlessly

Nevertheless, he cautions those who predict "the end of advertising." "Ad budgets are being trimmed, not terminated. American life won't become noticeably less commercial, even if some enterprises that subsist on advertising don't survive the slump. . . . Somehow advertising triumphs over its limitations. It helps create and preserve markets."

Samuelson contends that some good things may even emerge from the current crisis. "People in the press have been reminded that the normal laws of economics apply to them too. This may build character."

The jury is still out on the character issue, but it is oddly comforting to know that endearing characters like the Eveready bunny and the Pillsbury doughboy will somehow endure. Advertiser efforts to win our hearts and minds are so much a part of the fabric of Mediamerica and Mediaworld that it is impossible to imagine what our lives would be like without them, even if there are times when we would like to try.

Issues and Answers: TV and the Selling of the President

Of all the controversies that swirl around advertising and television, none stirs more public passion than media involvement in the presidential election process. Back in 1960, when TV's role in politics first became glaringly apparent, *Life* magazine quoted one campaign

commercial environment. Civic-mindedness is an alien concept to a people mesmerized by consumer goods. This is the "me only" world, the world where politicians feed the great political beast with disingenuous promises of "no new taxes." In this world, public institutions that depend on government are forced to turn to business dollars to survive. The resulting cost, of course, is the commercialization of schools, art museums, and nonprofit organizations.

- **Egalitarian values:** The materialism promoted by Madison Avenue is bound to accentuate class differences. This is because differences between the commercial haves and have-nots become the measures of one's rank in society. Championing excessive consumption exacerbates social disparities and class conflicts, especially along racial lines.

- **The value of thought:** Much advertising substitutes imagery, sloganeering, and a brand-name mentality for rational, fact-based decision making. A fantasized "truth" appeals to our impulsive side. That kind of advertising accustoms us to be more accepting of irrational sales schemes and encourages mindless and wasteful shopping binges.

- **The value of political discourse:** When the distorted "logic" of advertising becomes the currency of political, social, economic, and other forms of once-serious discussion, democratic government suffers. The difference between commercial advertising and political campaigning is blurred. This development, says broadcast journalist Bill Moyers, "is wrecking the polity of America, destroying our ability as a cooperative society to face reality and solve our problems."

Unchecked commercialism has the potential to destroy America. We need not, however, allow this potential to be realized. We can stem the tide, individually and collectively, by reconsidering our priorities and then acting.

Excerpted with permission from The Christian Science Monitor *(Sept. 19, 1990).*

---

strategist as saying, "I can elect any person to office if he has $60,000, an IQ of at least 120, and can keep his mouth shut."

Highly publicized TV debates between candidates in 1960, 1976, and 1980 appear to have affected the outcomes. In 1960 Richard Nixon (the early favorite) probably would not have lost to John Kennedy were it not for his poor showing on TV (see 11.10). Similarly, the 1976 debates probably clinched Jimmy Carter's narrow victory over Gerald Ford, and the 1980 debates helped Reagan upset Carter. Political observers agreed that Reagan looked and sounded a lot better than Mondale in 1984.

The 1992 Democratic primaries served as another reminder of the power of the debate format. With six major candidates, none of whom were well known before the process began, voters had little choice but to watch a series of TV debates to find out who the candidates were as well as where they stood on the issues.

What effect does television have on the candidates themselves? It certainly dictates priorities that are different from those of an earlier day. The physical appearance of the candidate is increasingly important. Does he or she look fit, well rested, secure? Losing candidates Adlai Stevenson (1952, 1956), Hubert Humphrey (1968), Walter Mondale (1984), and Michael Dukakis (1988) all looked "bad" on TV.

Nixon overcame his own negative TV image in his reelection campaign of 1972 with ads that featured longer shots of him being "presidential" — flying off to China, for

The first televised presidential debates stirred controversy about TV's role in politics and helped establish the charismatic Kennedy image in the minds of the electorate.

example. Close-ups were avoided. Bumperstickers never mentioned Nixon by name but simply read: "Reelect the President."

Kennedy and Carter seemed more at home with TV, perhaps because both were youthful, informal, and physically active outdoor types. Dwight Eisenhower, Lyndon Johnson, and George Bush seemed to project a paternal, fatherly image on the small screen. Every recent president has learned how to use the medium to his advantage, by "staging" events so as to receive maximum favorable coverage. This practice has added to the considerable power of incumbency.

Yes, television has diminished the significance of issues. It can be argued that, since the 1960 presidential debates, we have elected people, not platforms, a major departure from earlier years. Franklin Roosevelt's radio charisma cannot be denied, but he was swept to power by a single issue — the Great Depres-

sion. Jimmy Carter's spectacular rise to power was a testament to the new image orientation. No one really knew *what* he was going to do when he took office; his entire campaign had been geared toward developing a relationship of trust with the electorate. "Trust me," he said as he looked directly into the camera. "I'll never lie to you." For a while it worked.

Some would contend that the election of Ronald Reagan in 1980 represented the ultimate television victory. After all, what other country has elected an actor as president? It can be argued that Americans were tired of Carter and that Reagan simply offered an alternative. Yet throughout the campaign that alternative was really only a vague (but visually attractive) media "vision" of a "shining city on a hill." His reelection campaign in 1984 offered more of the same and led to one of the biggest victory margins in history.

These lessons were not lost on Bush in 1988, thanks to his "thousand points of light" campaign. A new twist was added with the largely negative campaign against Dukakis, including one controversial TV spot that blamed the Massachusetts governor for allowing black convicted killer Willie Horton to enter a furlough program so that he could "kill again." In 1992 Democrats successfully cited the spot as proof that Bush had "divided the nation along racial lines."

My father, a longtime politician in southern California, used to say, "The worst thing a candidate can do is get bogged down in the issues." The tendency to focus on personality instead of position has alarmed countless media critics. Politicians, newscasters, and others have stood in line to denounce it. They assert that the important thing is *what the candidates stand for,* not the candidates themselves. Almost everyone seems to agree that television has been detrimental to American politics and has clouded the issues and confused the electorate.

On the other hand, media researchers Thomas E. Patterson and Robert E. McClure say that the power of TV has been overrated and that (1) "viewers of the nightly network newscasts learn almost nothing of importance about a presidential election," and that (2) "people are not taken in by advertising hyperbole and imagery. . . . Exposure to televised ads has *no effect on voters' images of the candidates* [italics mine]." I respectfully disagree on both counts. Nor do I feel that TV has clouded the minds of the electorate.

We need a president we feel we *know* and can *trust*. Print afforded us no opportunity to get a "feel" for the person. We could study the issues, read the speeches, yes — but how would we "know" the candidate as we might a neighbor or casual acquaintance? Television provides an audiovisual record of the candidate under all sorts of circumstances. Bill Clinton's 1992 campaign exemplified this process. Accusations involving his marital infidelity and Vietnam era draft record had to be faced head-on. Voters developed a real sense of how he would react in crisis conditions. Such knowledge can help us choose someone of integrity, or at the very least someone with honorable intentions.

Of course, TV cannot guarantee honest candidates, but we rejected Richard Nixon in 1960 and we might have again had he not so successfully *avoided* any informal coverage. (He wouldn't let TV reporters near him unless he had a suit on. For all we know, he wore a suit while walking on the beach.) Once he was president, it was the intimate nature of the medium that helped bring him down. Even his well-rehearsed Watergate denials wouldn't work. He would sit there surrounded by flags and piles of transcripts and swear he was innocent. Yet the sweat on his brow and the look in his eyes seemed to confirm his guilt.

Some may argue that skillful media manipulators like "the great communicator" Ronald Reagan can utilize television to their advantage in a way that Nixon never could. Yet despite his acting ability, most conclude that Reagan believed in what he was saying. Despite being tagged "Slick Willie," Bill Clinton was finally able to convince voters they could trust him to lead the nation.

Issues come and go, but we elect *people* to the presidency. In this fast-moving information environment, today's burning issue is tomorrow's historical footnote. It's far more important to develop a sense of what kind of person we are electing to the nation's highest office. Whatever else it might do, television affords us that opportunity in a way no other medium can.

Queries and Concepts

1   Design a print ad for your favorite product. Then follow up by writing copy for a 30-second television or radio ad. Which more effectively sells the product? Why?

2   Write the copy for a 30-second radio ad for each of the following products or services: (a) your favorite beverage, (b) the course for which you are using this textbook, and (c) you.

3   Take an inventory of all the products in your medicine cabinet or on your refrigerator shelves right now (or make an inventory of a friend's things if you're feeling nosy!). Are there any brand names there? Any generic items? Why did you (or someone else) purchase these products?

4   Find three examples of magazine advertisements you think are in bad taste. How could they be changed so that they still sell the product without using the tactics you consider offensive?

5 Using an audiocassette or videocassette recorder, tape five radio or TV commercials. Is there anything in any of them that might violate the truth-in-advertising guidelines given in this chapter?

6 Think of the television commercial you hate more than any other. Write four paragraphs on what you find so objectionable about it. No fair using vague, general words like "stupid" or "dumb" — be *specific*. Have you ever used the product? Do the same activity, writing about a commercial you think is better than any other.

7 Who feeds the pet in your house? Interview some pet owners about their pets' eating habits. What brand(s) of pet food do they usually buy and why?

8 Visit your library and look through magazines or newspapers published *at least* 30 years ago. Photocopy any interesting ads you come across. How do these ads compare to ads today? What are the most significant differences? Similarities? If a product is one of the old ads is still being sold today, compare the older ad with a more recent one. What do you find?

9 Do you think that political spots help or harm the electoral process? Are there any political advertising practices that you find objectionable? Explain. Can you recall any time that a political spot helped you make a vote choice?

10 As a candidate for mayor in your city, you haven't been doing very well. The polls place you 14 points behind your opponent. But wait! You've just received a videotape showing your opponent (a married woman) in a compromising position with an unmarried, younger man (not her husband). Your campaign manager wants to run the tape as part of a new television ad campaign. Do you approve?

Readings and References

The Information Environment

Steven M. L. Aronson
Hype. New York: William Morrow, 1983.

How are superstars born? Reborn? How does one get into exclusive New York restaurants without a reservation? These intriguing questions are answered in this flip and devastating treatise on information manipulation. Fun to read.

Christopher Lasch
The Culture of Narcissism. New York: Warner Books, 1979.

A brilliant — and deeply disturbing — examination of "American life in an age of diminishing expectations." Lasch is concerned with our society's turn toward self-involvement, a turn encouraged by advertising and consumer culture. Advertising, argues Lasch, "manufactures a product of its own: the consumer, perpetually unsatisfied, restless, anxious and bored."

Marshall McLuhan
Culture Is Our Business. New York: Ballantine Books, 1972.

This is McLuhan on advertising and its social and cultural consequences. He juxtaposes full-page ads from magazines with a series of probes, exploring the way advertising creates cultural norms and predicts social trends. Fascinating stuff, but take it in small doses. The book is now out of print but is available in most libraries and many used-book stores.

The Advertising Business Develops

Charles Goodrum
Helen Dalrymple
Advertising in America: The First 200 Years.
New York: Harry N. Abrams, 1990.

Comprehensive and current. Some of the chapters are: "Cereals, Soap and Sex," "Guilt, Shame and Blame," "A Century of Cigarettes," "The Automobile," "Gender Change," "Lingerie, Hosiery, and Underwear—Selling the Package for the Form Divine," and "Causes—Advertising in the Service of the Community."

A nice five-page mini-history of advertising is found in Agee, Ault, and Emery's *Introduction to Mass Communications,* 7th ed. (New York: Dodd, Mead, 1982). Advertising history is also woven throughout Emery and Emery's *The Press and America,* 6th ed. (Englewood Cliffs, N.J.: Prentice-Hall, 1988).

Truth in Advertising

Hal Betancourt
The Advertising Answerbook: A Guide for Business and Professional People. Englewood Cliffs, N.J.: Prentice-Hall, 1982.

Agencies, budgets, copywriting, artwork—you name it, it's here. A professional, hands-on approach to the advertising business. Highly recommended.

Michael Gartner
Advertising and the First Amendment. Winchester, Mass.: Priority Press, 1988.

Is advertising a worthy form of speech, protected by the U.S. Constitution? Gartner thinks so. A lawyer and newspaper editor/owner, the author considers the regulation of commercials to be a form of censorship. Major court rulings are discussed.

Jef Richards
Deceptive Advertising: Behavioral Study of a Legal Concept. Hillsdale, N.J.: Lawrence Erlbaum, 1990.

This unique text examines deceptiveness as both a legal and a psychological concept. The author proposes a theory of how deceptiveness affects us.

Radio Advertising; Television: The Ultimate Advertising Medium

Michael J. Arlen
Thirty Seconds. New York: Penguin, 1980.

An often-hilarious, step-by-step account of the making of one 30-second TV commercial, an AT&T "reach out and touch someone" spot. Arlen's sense of humor about the extraordinary lengths involved in manufacturing such a spot is obvious when, for example, he interviews the man whose job it is to "soften" the colors to give them just the right luster. Arlen ranks among the most respected television critics of the century.

Huntley Baldwin
How to Create Effective TV Commercials. Lincolnwood, Ill.: NTC Business Books, 1989.

Chapters on strategy, how to come up with ideas, visual storytelling, storyboards, preproduction and production, and much more. A fine how-to text on the creation of TV commercials by someone who knows the business inside out.

Jim Hall
Mighty Minutes: An Illustrated History of Television's Best Commercials. New York: Harmony Books, 1984.

You might not agree with the author's selection of television's "best" commercials, but this book might spark a few powerful memories just the same.

Elizabeth Heighton
Don R. Cunningham
Advertising in the Broadcast and Cable Media.
2d ed. Belmont, Calif.: Wadsworth, 1984.

A solid treatment of real-world advertising practices in the broadcast media. Well illustrated and easy enough for beginning students to read. There are chapters on audience research and spot sales, and an entire section is devoted to social responsibility. Recommended.

Advertising: Making a Living

Alan Fletcher
Thomas A. Bowers
Fundamentals of Advertising Research. 4th ed. Belmont, Calif.: Wadsworth, 1991.

Market research has become *the* fuel that drives the advertising industry. This comprehensive introduction covers all the research basics. Includes sections on strategic planning, sampling, questionnaire design. Must reading.

A. Jerome Jeweler
Creative Strategy in Advertising. 4th ed. Belmont, Calif.: Wadsworth, 1992.

The first text I know of that deals extensively with the problems of the advertising copywriter. Offers a practical, step-by-step approach to solving various advertising and layout problems. For an additional, highly practical introduction to writing commercials, I recommend Milan D. Meeske and R. C. Norris's workbook, *Copywriting for the Electronic Media: A Practical Guide* (Belmont, Calif.: Wadsworth, 1987).

Form and Content: How Advertising Works

Arthur Asa Berger
Media Analysis Techniques. Rev. ed. Newbury Park, Calif.: Sage, 1991.

A brief and simple (in some cases, *too* simple) handbook of various methods that can be used to study media content (semiotics, psychoanalytic theory, sociology, Marxist criticism).

Berger offers a case study in the analysis of advertising; how ads work (and work us over). Enjoyable reading.

Alice E. Courtney
Thomas W. Whipple
Sex Stereotyping in Advertising. Lexington, Mass.: Lexington Books, 1983.

Advertising and sexism have often gone hand-in-hand (with some notable exceptions). Why is the "voice of authority" in TV commercials always a *man's* voice? Why do some ads depict women as helpless, vain, caretakers? Read this book for further details.

Sammy R. Danna, ed.
Advertising and Popular Culture: Studies in Variety and Versatility. Bowling Green, Ohio: The Popular Press, 1992.

Fifteen essays that explore advertising in our culture. The book is divided into five sections: comment and criticism in advertising, subliminal perception in advertising, unusual advertising types and uses, specialized advertising forms and applications, and gender and advertising. Covers a lot of territory. Illustrated.

John Phillip Jones
What's in a Name? Lexington, Mass.: Lexington Books, 1986.

About advertising and the concept of brand names. Includes sections on factors that shape a brand during its growth and maturity, advertising campaigns and pressures, and how to develop better advertising.

Wilson Bryan Key
Subliminal Seduction. Englewood Cliffs, N.J.: Prentice-Hall, 1973.

Media Sexploitation. Englewood Cliffs, N.J.: Prentice-Hall, 1976.

These two books present Key's controversial theories about *subliminal* advertising. Both are easy enough to read and include ample illustrations. Readers are encouraged to spot the male genitals in ice cubes and discern other "embeds," such as the word "SEX" written all over Ritz crackers. You can take or leave these notions as you please, but beware: You may never be able to look at a Ritz cracker in the same way again!

Carol Moog
Are They Selling Her Lips?
New York: William Morrow, 1990.

Dr. Moog's even-handed examination is a kind of updated *Hidden Persuaders* (see below). Interesting reading.

Vance Packard
The Hidden Persuaders
New York: D. McKay Co., 1957.

Packard was one of the first to call public attention to the "depth manipulation" strategies that were little known outside the advertising industry. This classic work sold well and paved the way for a plethora of popular books examining the advertising process. Several more came from Packard as well.

Thomas Whiteside
"Onward and Upward with the Arts (Pet Food)." *New Yorker,* Nov. 1, 1976, pp. 51–98.

Judith Williamson
Decoding Advertising: Ideology and Meaning in Advertising. London: Marion Boyers, 1978.

Few books have so challenged my understanding of the consequences of advertising as this one. The text is both an overview and an in-depth treatment of the way advertising works its own seductive "magic." Williamson focuses on print ads, but her arguments and insights can easily be extended to other media. Over 100 ads are dissected in this occasionally haphazard but thoroughly rewarding book.

Carl P. Wrighter
I Can Sell You Anything. New York: Ballantine Books, 1972.

Though often humorous in tone, this book addresses the rather serious ways in which advertisers coax us into parting with our money.

Writing from his vantage as an advertising executive, Wrighter (a pseudonym, by the way) delves into the uses of deceptive language, evasive guarantees, tricky visual demonstrations, and more. Illuminating reading.

Advertising Today

Robert J. Samuelson
"The End of Advertising?"
Newsweek, Aug. 19, 1991, p. 40.

For up-to-date discussions of current trends and research, check out copies of these indispensable trade magazines and research journals: *Advertising Age, Ad Week, Broadcasting, Journal of Advertising, Journal of Marketing Research,* and *Public Opinion Quarterly.* Useful reference resources include *Standard Directory of Advertisers* and the *Advertising Age Yearbook.*

Issues and Answers: TV and the Selling of the President

Donna Woolfolk Cross
Mediaspeak: How Television Makes Up Your Mind. New York: Mentor, 1983.

A readable, enjoyable (and inexpensive!) critique of television. See especially Chapter 6, "It Sells Soap, Doesn't It?" and Chapter 7, "Hail to the Chief."

Edwin Diamond
Stephen Bates
The Spot: The Rise of Political Advertising on Television. Rev. ed. Cambridge, Mass.: MIT Press, 1988.

Perhaps the most complete and studious history of American political advertising. Illustrated. Highly recommended.

Leo Jeffres
Mass Media Processes and Effects. Prospect Heights, Ill.: Waveland Press, 1986.

A concise catalog of thousands of studies on mass media effects. Section 7 covers "Political Effects of the Media."

Joe McGinnis
The Selling of the President, 1968. New York: Trident Press, 1969.

An inside look at Richard Nixon's successful campaign for the presidency in 1968. McGinnis focuses on the media-related aspects of the campaign. A classic.

For an interesting account of the relationship between press and presidential candidates, read Timothy Crouse's *Boys on the Bus* (Westminster, Md.: Random House; paperback from Ballantine Books, 1976).

Dan D. Nimmo
James E. Combs
Mediated Political Realities. 2d ed. New York: Longman, 1990.

A thoughtful analysis of the relationship between politics and the media. Chapters on the mediated world of election campaigns, TV news as fantasy-land, political celebrity in popular magazines, and more.

Thomas E. Patterson
Robert D. McClure
The Unseeing Eye: The Myth of Television Power in National Politics. New York: Putnam, 1976.

The authors argue that the influence of TV has been far overrated by media analysts. One problem: Much data for the empirical conclusions is taken from the 1972 Nixon-McGovern race, an atypical election in a number of ways. Fascinating reading.

Thomas E. Patterson
The Mass Media Election: How Americans Choose Their President. New York: Praeger, 1980.

A series of important studies on the involvement of mass media in the electoral process. Dry and difficult reading in some places for the beginning student, but the book is considered a pioneering effort, a virtual classic.

Philip Schlesinger
Politics, Media, Identity. New York: Routledge, Chapman and Hall, 1990.

An advanced book for those interested in the complex intersections of political sociology and media studies. Topics covered include consorship, information management, power and control, images of enemies, and more.

Tony Schwartz
Media: The Second God. New York: Anchor, 1983.

Schwartz has worked on a number of advertising campaigns, including political races (he created the infamous "Daisy Ad," perhaps the best-known political spot of all time). In this book, he offers a number of intriguing insights into that process. See especially sections on "The John Jay Campaign," "Political Communication," and "How Commercials Work."

Contemporary Public Relations: Promotion, Perception, Persuasion

In the high tech public relations business, a very thin line runs between tactical brilliance and tactless buffoonery.

Craig J. Settles

It made sense for Polaroid's Mag-Media division to enter into a cooperative marketing deal with FoundationWare software. Both companies agreed that computer users who bought their new products in tandem could reduce the number of mistakes that destroy valuable computer data. But how to get the word out?

Simple. Hire PR practitioner Craig J. Settles. Settles' Successful Marketing Strategies firm, located in Berkeley, California, was famous for its innovative PR ideas, and this time was no exception. Settles came up with a surefire idea. Because users without the new system would be "shooting themselves in the foot" by destroying their own data, why not a three-step "tease and deliver" campaign aimed at the largest computer trade magazines? The campaign was approved by phone and timed to coincide with a major trade show.

Settles mailed envelopes sporting a bullet decal (but no return address) to 50 reporters, analysts, and editors at several leading trade magazines including *Byte, InfoWorld, Computer Software*, and *PC Computing*. Inside was a note that read: "Who's been shooting [name of publication] readers?" Taped to the note was a spent bullet shell.

A second mailing was planned for a few days later to explain that it was the readers who were shooting themselves in the foot and that Settles' two clients had teamed up to save the day. Complete information on the new systems would be supplied later as the third and final step of the campaign.

Meanwhile, at *Byte* the editors were disturbed. Some crackpot was sending threatening letters. What's more, the crackpot had a gun. The Berkeley postmark confirmed their worst suspicions since the town was famous for its campus radicals. The security staff was called in. By the time the second package arrived, they swung into action. Their conclusion was that the second envelope contained a bomb detonator. The mail-room was shut down and a bomb squad called in to examine the package. When x-rays finally determined the true nature of the mailing, Settles got an irate phone call from the security chief, who "read him the riot act."

Quickly concluding that "our firm and the reputation of our client were on the brink of a public relations disaster," Settles called everyone on the mailing list. Many were quite upset. *Computer Software* had sent its bullets to the FBI, *InfoWorld* settled for the local police, while *PC Computing* had opted for a "crises specialist" to handle the matter.

Settles quickly arranged to meet each editor in person at the trade show and apologize. (Sometimes you just have to byte the bullet!) He noted in recounting the story for the *Public Relations Journal* that there were valuable lessons to be learned from the experience — notably that the offended parties more quickly forgive the person who "stands up, apologizes for the offenses, and swears never to do anything like it again." He also noted that "journalists have long memories. Burn few bridges if you plan to stay in the public relations business."

In addition, it is always desirable to have the client approve such a mailing only *after* seeing it. Sometimes a phone approval just isn't good enough. When employing a promotion in which "art imitates life" in a potentially discomforting way, materials should carry some kind of tip-off that it's part of a promotional campaign. In this instance, if the first mailing had read "Who's been shooting [name of publication] readers *in the foot?*" it would have been less threatening. Three little words can sometimes make a great deal of difference!

Settles concludes that "success in public relations comes from the ability to incorporate the lessons learned from past mistakes into bold future steps. If you are unwilling to pick yourself up from a disaster (or near-disaster) and try again to stretch the boundaries of creativity, you risk denying your company or client the greatness they expected when they hired you."

Embodied in this story are many of the functions, risks, and rewards of the public relations business. In many ways, PR specialists put themselves and their reputations on the line with each new campaign they create and every new client they sign. Far from being the nondescript corporate types that many envision, today's PR counselors are as creative and innovative as any who labor in the media.

What Is PR?

PR practitioner Margaret Norman, writing in *Reader's Digest,* explains the business this way:

> When I accepted a position in Public Relations, a friend remarked that the job would be a breeze for me with my advertising/promotion background. I explained that the areas are quite different, and I illustrated my point with this example. "If the circus is coming to town and you paint a sign saying *Circus coming to fairground Saturday,* that's advertising. If you put the sign on the back of an elephant and walk him through town, that's promotion. And if the elephant walks through the mayor's flower bed, that's publicity."

> "And," he chimed in, "if you can get the mayor to laugh about it, that's public relations."

This story illustrates many of the numerous facets of mass communication's fastest-growing profession, public relations. In fact, the field has so many aspects that there is no general agreement regarding the most appropriate name for it. Some practitioners think the term *PR* carries a negative connotation. They prefer to think of themselves as *information specialists,* which indeed they are.

Although one specific definition cannot cover every function, the British Institute of Public Opinion defines PR as "the deliberate, planned, and sustained effort to establish and maintain mutual understanding between an organization and its publics." The PR practitioner is the intermediary between the interest represented and all of the involved publics.

Because PR has its origins in press agentry, many conclude that is all there is to it. According to Frances Friedman of the GCI Group, "We will always be publicists, because there is no substitute for a well-executed media placement." But this is only the beginning.

In *This IS P.R.,* authors Doug Newsom and Alan Scott contend that "there is a hazy line between the old press agentry and today's promotion. Although promotion incorporates special events that could be called press agentry, it goes beyond that into opinion making, for promotion attempts to garner support and endorsement for a person, product, institution or idea. . . . Examples of promotion are various fund-raising drives conducted by churches, charities, health groups and conservation interests."

Many top corporations coordinate all information-related functions through a *corporate communications* department. Corporate communications functions might include advertising, employee publications, community relations, government affairs, and even a consumer hotline.

Public affairs is another term for PR that is used in many corporations as well as educational institutions. In other companies you'll find the term *marketing communications* used to describe product publicity and promotion. The idea of obtaining editorial rather than advertising space to promote a product gets us

Gulf Oil Company generates organizational good will by sponsoring National Geographic specials on public television.

back to one of the central functions of PR as opposed to that of advertising.

In *Public Relations: Strategies and Tactics,* authors Dennis Wilcox, Phillip H. Ault, and Warren K. Agee point out a number of significant differences between advertising and PR:

- Advertising deals with the selling of goods and services; public relations generates public understanding and fosters good will for an organization.

- Advertising works almost exclusively through mass media outlets; publicity relies on a number of communication tools — brochures, slide presentations, special events, speeches, news releases, feature stories, and the like.

- Advertising is addressed to external audiences — primarily consumers of goods and services; public relations presents its message to specialized external audiences (stockholders, vendors, community leaders, environmental groups, and so on) and internal publics (employees).

- Advertising is readily identified as a specialized communication function; public relations is broader in scope — dealing with policies and performance of the entire organization, from the morale of the employees to the way telephone operators respond to calls.

- Advertising is used as a communication tool in public relations, and public relations activity often supports advertising campaigns. Advertising's function is to sell goods and services; the public relations function is to create an environment in which the organization can thrive. This calls for dealing with economic, social, and political factors that can affect the organization.

If you ask the average person what a PR person does, the first thing that will come to mind might be those publicists who work in personal and entertainment functions. Often referred to as "spin doctors," these publicists represent only a small percentage of PR practitioners. Public relations specialists are employed primarily in the corporate sector, but a large number also work for trade associations, labor unions, professional and cultural societies, and various social and religious organizations. There are PR practitioners in education, politics, and the military as well. Sometimes a PR job involves answering the phone and giving information. More often it requires skills in journalism, broadcasting, advertising, international relations, and other fields.

The PR agent acts as a liaison between client and public. Whereas advertising agencies generally try to reach the public directly through paid messages in the mass media, PR practitioners usually deal with editors and reporters, who then disseminate information to the public via the media. Effective PR counselors facilitate the flow of information by providing reporters with facts and figures and other background materials. Seasoned journalists know how to "use" PR people and their materials to avoid doing costly and time-consuming research.

In one survey, reported in *Public Relations: Strategies and Tactics,* a group of public relations directors stated the qualifications they consider most important for a PR agent, in descending order:

- Ability to write
- Verbal skills
- Professionalism
- Maturity
- Poise
- Appearance

The PR directors also indicated that other desirable traits include the ability to see things from another person's point of view, skill at expressing a viewpoint with clarity and succinctness, and a willingness to perform behind the scenes. Would-be PR practitioners are less likely to succeed, according to the survey, if they need excessive independence, have an inflated opinion of their own writing ability, or tend to resist compromise. Employment in a PR capacity calls for a certain flexibility. It always has.

Press-Agentry Pioneers: P. T. Barnum & Co.

PR is as old as media. As long as there have been public information channels, there have been people who would use them to influence public opinion (see 12.1). Dennis Wilcox and colleagues quote Peter Osgood, president of Carl Byoir & Associates:

> The art has many roots. For example, the practice of dispatching teams to

prepare the way for a traveling dignitary was not invented by Harry Truman or Richard Nixon. Their political ancestors in Babylonia, Greece, and Rome were quite adept at it. St. John the Baptist himself did superb advance work for Jesus of Nazareth.

Authors Newsom and Scott maintain that one of the earliest recorded "staged" PR events occurred in the 11th century when Lady Godiva rode nude through the streets of Coventry, England, to persuade her husband to lower taxes. Her tactics may have been considered outrageous, but they got the job done. Taxes were lowered.

The acknowledged king of American PR pioneers was Phineas Taylor Barnum, who was responsible for the success of midget Tom Thumb and Jenny Lind, the "Swedish Nightingale," as well as the "Feejee Mermaid" and Jumbo, the world's largest elephant. Barnum was adept at creating and sustaining legends. And of course he ran a circus that bore his name. So effective was Barnum's PR that his name remains a part of Americana a century after his death.

When Barnum died in 1891, *The Times* of London had nothing but good things to say. "His death removes an almost classic figure, and his name is a proverb already, and a proverb it will continue to be until mankind has ceased to find pleasure in the comedy of the showman and his patrons — the comedy of the harmless deceiver and the willingly deceived."

The term *public relations* did not come into being until the 20th century. Before that, PR was known as press agentry. The press agents were masters at planting stories in newspapers. This kind of publicity was much more valuable than paid-for advertising, and it was free. Many such campaigns were waged during the late 19th century, but most notable, according to historian Marshall Fishwick, was the rise of Buffalo Bill.

Fishwick notes that a half-dozen writers helped shape Buffalo Bill into the greatest American folk hero of all. "No one should underestimate their endeavors. More spectacular men had to be outdistanced. Mountains had to be made out of molehills." Almost all the folk heroes of this era were virtually created through press agentry, among them Wyatt Earp, Calamity Jane, and Wild Bill Hickok. Some stories began with fact, but most were primarily fiction.

PR's entry into the political fray can be traced to Andrew Jackson's election to the presidency in 1828. Jackson employed Amos Kendall, a former newspaper editor, as part of his "kitchen cabinet" to direct the publicity efforts from the White House, making him, in effect, the first presidential press secretary.

The 1896 McKinley-Bryan presidential race marked the beginning of modern political campaigning methods. Posters, pamphlets, and publicity, much of it concocted by party press agents, were deployed. The information tools have changed a bit as the candidates have moved to the electronic stage, but tactics remain essentially the same today.

The patent-medicine scandals and other questionable business practices that came to the public's attention around the turn of the century also furthered the PR industry. The first decade of the new century was the era of journalism's muckrakers (see Chapter 3). Many of the muckrakers' favorite targets were wealthy businessmen such as John D. Rockefeller. Public pressure on government and government agencies became so great that a number of business-reform bills were passed, restricting corporate activities.

Business leaders like Rockefeller gradually became convinced that they could no longer ignore public opinion. Thus the "press agent" also began to function as publicity counsel for management. The most prominent PR practitioner and very first public relations counsel was Ivy Ledbetter Lee. A Princeton graduate and former business reporter for the *New York World*, Lee got his start in 1906 when he was hired by the coal industry to present management's side during a bitter strike. He gradually

1891 P. T. Barnum, the king of the PR pioneers, dies in London, receives good press.

1931 Alfred P. Sloane, president of General Motors, is prominent among the new breed of executives who show great faith in public relations.

1800   1900

1828 Andrew Jackson's election to the presidency is attributed, in part, to his ability to manipulate the press.

1837 Settlers are lured to Illinois by publications subsidized by land speculators.

1896 The McKinley-Bryan presidential race marks the beginning of modern political campaign methods.

1906 PR pioneer Ivy Ledbetter Lee signs his first client, the coal industry. They want him to give management's side during a bitter strike.

1914 John D. Rockefeller, Sr., is promoted to the public as a great humanitarian by Ivy Ledbetter Lee.

1917 "The Creel Committee," a group of journalists and press agents, cajoles magazines and newspapers to donate space to the war effort.

1923 Edward L. Bernays' classic book about PR practices, *Crystallizing Public Opinion,* is published.

1941 Radio news personality Elmer Davis heads the Office of War Information, to promote the U.S. war effort.

12.1 The History of Public Relations in America

1981

Megatrends correctly predicts the increasingly important role of the PR specialist in an information-oriented society.

1960

1960s Public relations comes of age in journalism and communications departments nationwide.

1968 The top 50 PR firms have a collective fee income of $59 million.

1988 The top 50 PR firms report a collective fee income of $875 million.

1989 Research indicates that over half of all students enrolled in U.S. journalism and communications programs hope to find jobs in advertising and PR.

1990s Leading PR practitioners call for a "redefinition" of the industry, stressing the global and multifaceted functions of the modern PR professional.

1993 Clinton's election places environmental issues and health-care practices at the top of the PR agenda.

1995 Increasing trend toward sale of PR agencies to advertising firms puts new pressure on practitioners to contribute to parent company bottom line, raises ethical issues.

PR for peace. In Minnesota, Honeywell Computers cosponsored and funded "Prospects for Peacemaking," a series of public discussions on national security and arms control.

persuaded them to give up their "public be damned" attitude.

Lee contended that the public could no longer be ignored. Neither would it continue to be fooled. In his "Declaration of Principles," Lee articulated his concerns: "In brief, our plan is, frankly and openly, in behalf of business concerns and public institutions, to supply the press and the public of the United States prompt and accurate information."

In another famous case in 1914, John D. Rockefeller hired Lee to help resolve a strike at the family's Colorado plant. Lee arranged what are now called photo opportunities that featured Rockefeller eating in the dining hall with workers and having a beer with them after work. This approach worked well, and soon the public began to perceive Rockefeller as genuinely concerned about the workers and their families.

So successful was Lee in these efforts that he was put on permanent retainer as the family's publicist. It was he who helped craft the image of John D. Rockefeller, Sr., as a great humanitarian and philanthropist.

During World War I, the U.S. government relied on the Creel Committee, a group of journalists and press agents assembled by for-mer newspaper reporter George Creel, to help it convince the American public of the urgency of the Allied cause. The committee helped induce newspapers and magazines to donate advertising space encouraging the sale of Liberty Bonds.

The emerging role of the public relations counsel was documented by Edward L. Bernays in his 1923 book, *Crystallizing Public Opinion*. That same year Bernays taught the first course in public relations ever offered in higher education, at New York University. Meanwhile, he was devising many successful campaigns for his famous clients. The roster included Procter & Gamble, Lucky Strike cigarettes, *Good Housekeeping* magazine, and even President Calvin Coolidge. Through all these endeavors, Bernays became known as the father of modern public relations.

Other PR pioneers were at work during the period between the wars. Benjamin Sonnenberg's efforts for Texaco are especially notable. Rex Harlow was probably the first full-time PR educator. He also founded the American Council on Public Relations, which eventually became the Public Relations Society of America (PRSA), the industry's largest and best-known trade organization.

During World War II the Office of War Information, headed by journalist and radio commentator Elmer Davis, was instrumental in promoting the sale of war bonds and convincing the public of the necessity for the wartime rationing of food, clothing, and gasoline.

After the war the booming economy contributed to the increasing prominence of public relations. More and more companies began opening PR departments, and independent PR agencies sprang up everywhere.

Public Relations in the Global Village

Today more than 650,000 people in the country work in some PR capacity. The burgeoning job opportunities in the field have led to dramatic enrollment increases in college and university journalism and communications programs that emphasize public relations. Today about half of all communication and journalism students are preparing for a career in advertising and/or public relations.

Virtually every media position open to the entry-level employee has a counterpart in PR. PR is by far the fastest-growing arm of mass communication and, as such, supplies an increasingly large number of beginning jobs for those desiring a career in media. Administration, finance, research, and even legal departments flourish at most medium-size and large agencies. Small agencies offer the beginner the opportunity to gain experience in many areas of media, experience that might take years to acquire in other fields.

One reason for the PR boom is the increasing value — and the increasing cost — of access to major media channels themselves. Sponsors may pay $1 million for one commercial during the Super Bowl. Many advertisers turn to PR counselors, who often help snare valuable media space free of charge.

Each of the 200 largest corporations in America employs a public relations staff of at least 100. Large PR firms may have as many as 500 employees. Reporters who leave journalism for PR can expect an immediate salary increase of 25% or so. The chances are very good that when they return to the newsroom to see old friends 10 years later, they will be earning double the salary of colleagues who stayed.

In large corporations, the PR staff has monumental responsibilities. Stockholders want maximum return on their investment, employees want higher wages, and some consumers will always be convinced that all corporations are run by white-collar criminals. The PR department is expected to make everyone happy. It attempts to do so by using the primary tool of the trade: information. Stockholders' meetings are held, and quarterly reports are issued that speak in glowing terms of profits. Employee newsletters help create a sense of community and harmony. News re-

leases tell of acts of benevolence performed by corporation executives.

As America shifts from the industrial age to the information age, the role of public relations experts becomes increasingly important. In 1982 John Naisbitt's best-selling book, *Megatrends*, offered a number of predictions involving the profession. Among them:

- Public relations firms will emphasize information-gathering and computer data searches for clients. Information will be a commodity with sales value.

- Specialization in public relations will increase. These fields will include employee relations, government affairs, investor and financial relations, high-technology product publicity, and international public relations.

- Public relations activities and job opportunities will shift from so-called sunset industries such as steel, automobiles, textiles, and heavy industrial manufacturing to sunrise industries such as electronics, robotics, biology, and alternative energy sources.

- Increased specialization of the mass media, including magazines, broadcast narrowcasting, and cable networks, will require more sophisticated and knowledgeable public relations experts.

In fact, virtually all of these predictions have already come to pass. In reviewing the 80s decade for the *Public Relations Journal*, Frances Friedman notes that "it's fine to talk about the future. But for public relations the future is here already. By strategy or by necessity our profession has changed dramatically over the past ten years."

Friedman says that most "publicists" now prefer to be referred to as counselors, but the public perception of the profession as simply a way to obtain "free advertising" lingers. She stresses the need for PR to be *redefined* to clients as well as the public. In addition, top people must be hired who can "truly be accepted

Public Relations— Beyond Theory

Beverly Beck Ellman is co-principal and director of public relations for DME Communications in San Diego, California.

What They Didn't Tell Me in School

None of my professors at Loyola Marymount University in Los Angeles or California State University, Northridge, told me that part of my job as a publicist would be to have my hair cut off on live television by a famous Beverly Hills coiffeur, to sit next to the Easter Bunny on a helicopter, to have my picture taken with Senator Pete Wilson at an exclusive party in La Jolla, to cajole an unhappy and balking celebrity artist into appearing on a live television talk show two minutes before air time, to stage an injury accident scene in the middle of rush hour traffic, to make incognito phone calls to a client on talk radio when the talk show host expressed concern about the lack of audience response, or to pace nervously in a television studio waiting for my client, who had arrived promptly, but at the wrong TV studio.

My college experience also didn't prepare me for the satisfaction I would feel in putting together projects to help the homeless, the elderly, and troubled teenagers, or the joy I would experience from getting coverage for clients.

Public relations people are the unsung heroes, the behind-the-scenes professionals the public rarely sees, although once I did leap to the foreground and actually grab the microphone away from a television talk show host to introduce my client, who had failed to introduce himself. That's my job—to ensure that the public recognizes the positive contributions and qualifications of my client.

Getting Started

I've worked in the field of public relations for 11 years. In college I studied everything in communications from journalism, radio, and television to popular culture and interpersonal, group, and organizational communications. I wanted to know a little about a lot of disciplines in the media. I felt that this would give me a better chance at landing a job, any job, as a writer. I always believed that I would become a "new journalist" in the Tom Wolfe genre.

When I graduated from California State University, Northridge, in 1980, I immediately relocated to San Diego. In Los Angeles I had choices, connections, and job offers. San Diego was the West Coast paradise. Everybody south of Long Beach seemed to be a writer. My first job was as the public relations director for the Campfire Council. What I learned there was how much I had to learn. I really had no concept of media relations, creating newsletters, brochures, working with celebrities, or staging special events. What I could do was write a good press release.

I quickly discovered that public relations was hard work. One doesn't just disseminate a press release and have the media arrive with minicams. It's actually a bit more complicated.

A Word to the Wise

Know your media. When you send out a press release, make sure it is newsworthy and that the facts are correct.

Most press releases received by reporters, editors, and producers each day get trashed or lost. I recently called a well-known San Diego newspaper editor to check on a release. She responded that she hadn't opened her mail in two weeks and would probably just toss everything on her desk and start over. What this means is that even if you write a good release, it might not get read by the right person, or read at all.

Knowing your media helps resolve this predicament. Every press release sent must be followed with persistent phone calls, beginning the week after the press release is mailed. If possible, meet the reporter face-to-face. Most newspeople *do* respond well to a publicist worth his or her salt, contrary to what you may have heard or read. Sometimes reporters and editors recognize that the information in a press release does not always constitute "real" news, but they still need it to fill gaps and add color to what might otherwise be a rather bleak 6:00 P.M. news report.

As a public relations professional, I often find myself selling stories—really pitching my clients. I don't push when a reporter is busy or on deadline. On these occasions, I simply ask when I can call back. I learn each person's schedule. Everyone has a different deadline. If I'm careful, skillful, and prepared, I can reach the people I need to talk to, even news anchors.

I asked Michael Grant, columnist at the *San Diego Union*, what he thought of PR people. He said, "Take them away for one week and you'll see all the journalists running after them." Most journalists won't admit how much they depend on public relations people for ideas and information.

Leonard Novarro, feature editor of the *Tribune* in San Diego, commented, "Most PR people call me and say, 'I've got this client. Can you write a story about him?'" Novarro explained that he cannot assign a story without substance. He

needs a news element, a reason for writing a story beyond merely giving a PR person's client free space.

If a newsperson seems uninterested in your ideas, have other suggestions available. Work with them. Get to know who does what and try to work directly with the decision makers. I enjoy talking to people, and I usually meet personally with all the reporters, editors, producers, and talent. We need to trust one another.

Public relations professionals must be diligent and responsible. Recently, I acquired a major account. When I told the producer of a popular San Diego television talk show about my good fortune, she seemed particularly pleased. The producer then confided that, previously, she would not

Continued on next page

have this client on her show because the client's last agency failed to give her people adequate advance information and to prepare the client correctly for live television. She added that the PR agency had even sent the client to the studio on the wrong day.

PR Is Hard Work

My husband and I own and operate DME Communications, a full-service public relations and advertising agency in San Diego. Our clientele runs the gamut from medical and legal to automotive and high-tech. We've worked hard establishing the agency. We both be-

lieve in working on a task until it is completed according to our high standards, regardless of how long it takes. We may work 12 to 14 hours a day. Often we work weekends. We take our work home, digest it with dinner, discuss it after the kids are asleep, and wake with it in the morning. My six-year-old son, Matthew, already plans on joining the firm as a writer; my nine-year-old daughter, Elizabeth, wants to be our graphic designer, if she doesn't become a ballerina instead.

We admit that this life is not for everyone. Clients need us for special events, which usu-

ally occur during holidays, or for special reassurance, which may come at any hour of the day or night. The competition for new accounts is arduous and often unfair. Connections are everything. Once we get a client, we must perform; it's a client's market. It's a strange, exhilarating, exhausting world. We're never bored. The stress level is outrageous. Fortunately, one of our clients is an internationally acclaimed stress management psychologist. We have his home phone number.

---

by members of top management as valuable counselors, rather than functionaries or publicists." She argues convincingly that "to reposition ourselves in the minds of our clients and prospects we need to address the makeup of our own staffs, how we can reshape and build on traditional roles and assignments, how we charge for our services and how we handle the media."

PR in the 90s

Like all media-related industries, PR has suffered as a result of the downturn in the economy. Corporations desperate to reduce operating expenses have been tempted to reduce their PR budgets by switching agencies or laying off key information personnel. Yet such moves can often be "penny wise and pound foolish" according to Robert L. Dilenschneider, president and CEO of Hill and

Knowlton. He argues that as long as PR practitioners supply businesses with the things they "must have" to compete successfully in the 90s, agencies and clients will continue to prosper together. According to Dilenschneider, the five key areas where PR can function most effectively for business clients are:

- *Monitoring:* Businesses today want to see around the corners. They want to know the new issues they will be facing from all the different directions that can have an impact on them. We will, therefore, be spending much more time analyzing information on a continual basis, and using this information to launch first-strike programs.

- *Knowledge:* Public relations once worked because of a well-turned phrase or the well-placed pal. Today it is as knowledge-driven as any professional service business. We are becoming masters of sampling and surveying, of focused research and intricate problem solving. Soon, I am sure, we will pioneer the use of artificial intelligence in solving problems.

- *Specialization:* Once public relations was the second career for retired newspaper people. But look at the lawyers, accountants, scientists, and senior government officials who are now selecting public relations as their second career. Managers no longer want advice that isn't backed by seasoned operating experience.

- *Global reach:* Businesses today expect the same high standards of performance in Barcelona as they do in Buffalo; in Singapore as in Santa Clara. Businesses will continue to globalize, and smart managers recognize the worldwide risks and opportunities. Management expects us to be strong both globally and locally.

- *Innovation:* Business wants much more than a logistical support program. It expects innovative strategies, bold ideas, superior execution and sophisticated understanding of mores and customs that distinguish businesses, governments, and cultures around the world.

Dilenschneider remains decidedly upbeat about the role of PR in the current decade. "The 90's will be all about performance. It will be a great time to be in this business because we can deliver the results."

Management and Policy Functions: The New PR?

In 1992 the *Public Relations Journal* polled their readership and found that 86% agreed that "today's public relations practitioners are more involved in providing strategic counsel to top management than they were five years ago." The results were part of an overall trend to-

ward an increased respectability for and appreciation of the profession, especially at the highest management levels.

Part of this trend can be attributed to increased management awareness of the vital functions of mass communication in Mediamerica and Mediaworld. More than ever before, PR practitioners are being acknowledged as media professionals whose expertise and knowledge can be put to work at every level of management activity.

The image of the PR practitioner as someone to be called in when things go wrong has increasingly been supplanted with one that is more consultant oriented—someone whose counsel is valued throughout various steps of the management decision-making process.

Corporate culture is a term used to describe a belief system that defines an organization's or company's mission and values. Today's PR practitioner is often involved in creating employee education programs and coordinating internal and external communication that describes and sometimes defines management style. At the same time, PR experts are involved in developing effective employee interaction. In short, it is up to the practitioner to effectively communicate what an organization stands for and to do it proficiently inside the organization as well as to the organization's various publics.

When corporate culture shifts or changes, the practitioner knows it's time to get to work. In the *Public Relations Journal*, Robert Kinkead and Dena Winokur maintain that

regardless of what stimulates change, the corporate communicator is generally charged with implementing it and making it work. As strategist, facilitator, observer and two-way communicator, the practitioner spreads the news about cultural change and collects feedback from stakeholders both within and outside the corporate structure.

This can be especially challenging when management seeks significant change in traditional employee-relations methods. When GM started its Saturn division the goal was to create "an entirely new car company" and a new corporate culture to go along with it. To compete effectively with the quality image of Japanese autos, Saturn had to find new methods of dealing with employees, and that involved every aspect of the communication process.

According to Bill Quigly, GM's executive in charge of corporate communications:

> GM public relations is certainly involved in the culture change process. Our employee information function is a strong tool, not merely for distributing corporate messages, but helping to generate feedback, allowing for a more precise monitoring of changes.

The creation of a more participatory culture is vital in the success scenario of Saturn and has been designed to provide one way for Saturn to differentiate itself in the competitive auto market. At the heart of this process are PR practitioners who labor to make sure that the word gets out. Robert B. Tripolsky, Saturn's manager of product information, says that "people who work here are team members. We don't describe anyone as our employee."

The Saturn experiment is being watched closely in the auto industry. In the annals of PR it's also being viewed as a test of keen management awareness of the vital role that corporate communications plays. Saturn's policies are at the cutting edge of the changes in corporate culture designed to increase productivity and product pride. If those policies succeed, acknowledgment of the role of PR practitioners as management and policy experts will succeed along with it.

In any event, those in the profession sense a growing awareness of their value in providing strategic counsel to top management. If it's not "the new PR," then it certainly qualifies as a new level of PR achievement and undoubtedly blazes the trail for the next generation of practitioners.

Issues and Answers: Ethics, Journalists, and PR

It is ironic that the industry in charge of maintaining a good public image for its clients seems unable to do the same for itself. The public at large may not even distinguish between advertising and PR, but when it does, PR is often perceived as a shady practice. Part of this public mistrust is probably the result of a lack of information about what PR people actually do. Part of it also centers on the uneasy relationship between PR practitioners and journalists.

Journalists complain that PR practitioners attempt to "color" the news or grab free advertising for their clients. Reporters also resent the fact that many of their own give up reporting for higher-paying PR positions.

PR practitioners have their own complaints against journalists. They often claim that their clients are victims of sensational-type reporting of news and that quotes and other information from releases are taken out of context.

Frances Friedman cautions practitioners that "it is essential for us to draw distinctions between honest respected media and sensational 'news as entertainment' media—and use the latter only when we're sure it's to our client's benefit."

The Public Relations Society of America has been active in promoting PR as a positive and integral part of the mass communication system. In 1954 it adopted a Code of Professional Standards (revised, 1988), and at times it has acted to penalize and expel members for violating that code.

In its Declaration of Principles, PRSA acknowledges PR counselors' role as communicators:

> In serving the interests of our clients and employers we dedicate ourselves to the goals of better communication, understanding and cooperation among the diverse groups and institutions of society. . . . We pledge

to conduct ourselves professionally with truth, accuracy, fairness and responsibility to the public.

Modern PR practices have come a long way toward living up to these standards in recent years. The task of informing the public about the true nature and functions of the industry and familiarizing them with the positive aspects of public relations presents a challenge to all of the current and future members of the profession.

Queries and Concepts

1   Sketch out your idea for a three-step "tease and deliver" campaign to promote the first CD being released by a relatively unknown musical group. Your campaign is aimed at the largest music and radio industry trade publications. (Try to anticipate and avoid the pitfalls encountered by Craig Settles' PR firm, examined at the beginning of this chapter.)

2   In stating that "John the Baptist . . . did superb advance work for Jesus of Nazareth," Peter Osgood points out that PR efforts have always been a part of history, even before the term *public relations* was coined; the story of Lady Godiva makes the same point. Can you think of any other historical events (prior to the 1800s) that involved public relations in some capacity?

3   Look through all the mail you receive in one week. Can you find any examples of public relations at work? Which efforts are more effective than others? Why?

4   What sorts of PR materials are being used on your campus right now? Go on a "treasure hunt," finding as many of these PR examples as you can. Don't forget to include materials produced by your own

college or university. Bring these examples to class and evaluate them.

5   PR professionals continue to play a big part during wartime, just as they did during World War I (the Creel Committee) and World War II (Office of War Information). What's your opinion on the use of public relations during times of war?

6   Most of the PR professionals quoted in this chapter seem pretty optimistic about the positive, expanding role PR will play in the 90s. But is that "just more PR"? That is, are these professionals actually doing PR work for PR itself? Or do you agree with their assessment? Explain.

7   Do some additional reading and come up with a list of four more significant events that could be added to the time line (12.1) on page 316. Make two additions to the past and two additions for this year.

8   You are a public relations agent for a baseball player who has held out for a $15-million contract and has been booted off the team. In a fit of rage, he has beaten up the owner and his manager. The press is calling for a statement, and you can't find your client anywhere. What do you do?

Press-Agentry Pioneers: P. T. Barnum & Co.

Scott M. Cutlip
Allen H. Center
Effective Public Relations. 6th ed. Englewood-Cliffs, N.J.: Prentice-Hall, 1985.

First written in 1952, this text has become a standard in the field. The authors are heavily committed to the positive aspects of PR, and the book reflects that perspective. It is comprehensive and includes historical information on the pioneers of PR.

R. E. Hiebert
Courtier to the Crowd: The Life Story of Ivy Lee. Ames: Iowa State University Press, 1966.

Lee is considered one of the two founders of modern PR (along with Edward L. Bernays). This is a good, thorough history, written by a media educator and scholar.

Many advertising histories (see Chapter 11) include accounts of the PR pioneers and the evolution of public relations in the United States.

Public Relations in the Global Village; PR in the 90s

Robert Dilenschneider
"A Make-or-Break Decade." *Public Relations Journal,* Jan. 1990, p. 29.

Frances Friedman
"Redefining Ourselves to Clients." *Public Relations Journal,* Jan. 1990, p. 31.

Danny Moss, ed.
Public Relations in Practice. London: Routledge, 1990.

Fourteen case studies examine successful PR campaigns, the strategies behind them, and the gains that each achieved. These campaigns all took place in Great Britain, but many of the lessons are universal.

John Naisbitt
Megatrends: Ten New Directions Transforming Our Lives. New York: Warner Books, 1982.

Doug Newsom
Alan Scott
This Is PR: The Realities of Public Relations. Belmont, Calif.: Wadsworth, 1989.

This up-to-date text has become one of the standards in the field. Includes chapters on PR activities, research, and the PR audience.

Frank Walsh
Public Relations Writer in a Computer Age. Englewood Cliffs, N.J.: Prentice-Hall, 1986.

A concise and well-illustrated introduction. The focus here is on the craft of *writing,* but the author also covers speeches, meetings, audio-visual material, crisis and emergency communications, and public relations law. Publicity case studies are included, and the PRSA Code of Professional Standards for the Practice of Public Relations is appended. No index, unfortunately.

Dennis Wilcox
Philip H. Ault
Warren K. Agee
Public Relations: Strategies and Tactics. 2d ed. New York: Harper & Row, 1989.

An excellent overview to the field. Includes sections on role, process, strategy application, and tactics. This latest edition includes an increased emphasis on PR ethics. I am indebted to the authors of this text for much of the background information that appears in this section.

Important periodicals to investigate include *Communication World, Public Relations Journal,* and *Public Relations Review.*

Management and Policy Functions: The New PR?

Robert W. Kinkead
Dena Winokur
"Navigating the Seas of Cultural Change."
Public Relations Journal, Nov. 1991, pp. 14–34.

"Practitioners Report Growing Role and Respect." *Public Relations Journal,* Aug. 1992, p. 13.

Issues and Answers: Ethics, Journalism, and PR

Ben H. Bagdikian
The Effete Conspiracy and Other Crimes of the Press. New York: Harper & Row, 1972.

Ben Bagdikian is a journalism educator and a highly respected critic of the press who has written a number of important books and articles. This book includes his observations about the problematic relationship between journalism and public relations. Recommended reading.

Daniel J. Boorstin
The Image: A Guide to Pseudo-Events in America. New York: Atheneum, 1961.

Written decades ago, this book has become something of a classic. In it, Boorstin critically examines the creation of "pseudo-events," events that are staged precisely because they will be reported as "news." In many ways, psuedo-events are still very much a part of modern public relations practices. Boorstin continues to comment on the media; you might have heard him on National Public Radio.

Joyce Nelson
Sultans of Sleaze: Public Relations and the Media. Toronto: Between the Lines, 1989.

This scathing indictment actually began as a documentary series on Canada's CBC Radio in 1981 and 1982. Nelson is convinced that the PR industry is engaged in a "circus of deception" that "constitutes a clear and present danger to our collective future." You might not agree with the hard-line approach that Nelson takes, but you'll be given a lot to think about just the same.

Doug Newsom
Bob Carrell
Public Relations Writing: Form & Style. Belmont, Calif.: Wadsworth, 1990.

A basic introduction. More than 80 examples of effective writing are provided, and new developments in technology are discussed. A chapter new to this edition takes a look at the ethical and legal responsibilities of the PR writer.

The Public Relations Society of America (PRSA) can provide you with further information about the association and its code of ethics. Write to the PRSA (33 Irving Place, New York, NY 10003-2376). For more on media ethics, see Chapter 13 and the readings and references listed there.

Morality and the Media: Ethics in Mass Communication

Since you cannot survive the effects of media if you huddle or hide, you must rush out and kick them in the guts — give them what for — right in the midriff. And they respond very well to this treatment.

Marshall McLuhan

On the night of March 4, 1983, photographer Ronald Simmons and sound technician Gary Harris were on duty at WHMA-TV in Anniston, Alabama. The phone rang. On the other end of the line, a distraught voice announced: "If you want to see somebody set himself on fire, be at the square in Jacksonville in 10 minutes." Simmons and Harris notified the police and drove to the scene.

When they arrived, the news crew found no police officers in sight. However, the caller — Cecil Andrews, an unemployed roofer — was already there, dousing himself with gasoline. Harris and Simmons set up their equipment, turned the television camera on the scene, and began to record Andrews's efforts to set himself on fire. Harris eventually attempted to stop this ghastly suicide attempt, but not before Cecil Andrews had been on fire for perhaps 30 seconds and already suffered severe burns. Images of the man in flames were shown later that evening on local stations and network newscasts.

This incident in Alabama created a wave of controversy across the nation. As good journalists, should the two reporters have covered the story objectively, watching the scene from a distance? Or, as good citizens, should they have intervened immediately and perhaps saved the man from burning himself? Did the presence of a news crew encourage the suicide attempt? Is such an event actually "news" in the first place? Should this and other gruesome scenes be shown on television at all? These and many other questions were asked following the events of that troubled night on the square in Jacksonville.

In response to widespread criticism, the news director at WHMA defended his staff. Philip Cox, who had dispatched Harris and Simmons to the scene, argued that his crew had done only what was professionally expected of them. In his own defense, Simmons, the camera operator, declared: "My job is to record events as they happen." Harris, who was 18 years old at the time, concurred. He said simply: "My conscience is clear."

The story of WHMA and the man who set himself on fire is now legendary. But the ethical questions raised by those long-ago events are as current as ever. Journalists still struggle with defining their role in society. Station managers are still criticized for what they do and do not broadcast. And the rest of us are still left with the daunting task of figuring out who is right and who is wrong.

Defining Media Ethics

As the influence of mass communication continues to expand, touching on almost every facet of society, it is vital that we strive to understand not only what we *can* do but also what we *should* do with the media in our lives. We need to explore what the mass media *ought* to be doing for us—and to us. The study of media ethics involves questioning the moral dimensions—the "shoulds" and "oughts"—of mass communication.

"Ethics" is one of those complex terms—like "love" and "beauty"—that have many meanings and evade precise definition. Gener-

ally speaking, the study of ethics involves the struggle to determine what is right or *good* and, consequently, what is *evil* or somehow wrong. In short, "doing ethics" involves figuring out how to "do the right thing."

In working through ethical dilemmas, we are often led into an examination of *responsibility*. The ethical individual attempts to understand his or her responsibilities to self and others and is able to rationally evaluate the possible consequences of actions—both responsible and irresponsible—from a range of personal and social perspectives. In his book *Ethics in Human Communication*, Richard Johannesen defines ethics by emphasizing the concept of responsibility:

> Responsibility includes the elements of fulfilling duties and obligations, of being accountable to other individuals and groups, and of being accountable as evaluated by agreed upon standards. . . . That is, the responsible communicator would carefully analyze claims, soundly assess probable consequences, and conscientiously weigh relevant values. In a sense, a responsible communicator is *response able*. She or he exercises the ability to respond (is responsive) to the needs and communication of others in sensitive, thoughtful, fitting ways.

In many ways, we can think of mass media ethics as the continuing attempt to encourage greater "response ability" on the part of both media creators and consumers (see 13.1).

Ethical Theories and Moral Reasoning

Various philosophical principles, or ethical tests, have been developed to help us determine the moral superiority of one action over another and, in the process, become more "response able." Developing theories of ethics has occupied the efforts of philosophers for some time, and a few central theories have risen to prominence. Among the major schools of thought are *utilitarian, Kantian, social justice, natural law,* and *Aristotelian* ethics.

Utilitarian Ethics: It All Adds Up

Utilitarian ethics — or utilitarianism — is largely derived from the work of two philosophers, Jeremy Bentham (1748–1832) and John Stuart Mill (1806–1873). The foundation of the utilitarian perspective is the "greatest happiness principle." According to this principle, the right thing to do is that action which results in the greatest good for the greatest number of people. When an action has the potential to create happiness for some and unhappiness for others, the right — or ethical — thing to do is whatever creates the *greatest sum amount* of happiness. In this way, utilitarianism is largely concerned with consequences, or the results of our decisions and actions. How such results are achieved is secondary to their effect. The ends justify the means.

Kantian Ethics:
The Principle of the Matter

Kantian ethics — or Kantianism — derives its name from the seminal advocate of this philosophy, Immanuel Kant (1724–1804). Kant claimed that looking only at the consequences of actions is not sufficient for determining whether those actions are ethical. Kant argued that we must look at the *principles* that underlie our actions. We need to examine our *motives.* If a morally sound principle guides our actions, then our actions — regardless of their outcome — are also morally sound. A watered-down Kantian ethic is being applied, in fact, whenever we dismiss the transgressions of another individual by saying something like, "Yeah, but at least he *meant* well." From a

Kantian perspective, the means are used to justify the ends.

One of Kant's fundamental principles is known as the *categorical imperative.* This principle holds that a person should be guided by standards that she or he would apply categorically, as a "universal law." Thus, for example, if you are thinking of cheating on the final exam in your Introduction to Mass Media course, the decision to cheat would be ethical *only* if you felt that cheating was *always* the right thing to do and that *everyone* ought to do it. In other words, everyone ought to be bound to the same ethical principles; double standards are generally unethical.

Social Justice Ethics:
Playing Fair

Social justice ethics — sometimes referred to as egalitarianism — is a derivative of Kantianism. Though social justice theory has varied proponents, 20th-century philosopher John Rawls is perhaps the most widely recognized. Where utilitarians seem most concerned with the welfare of the majority, Rawls argues for a greater sensitivity to the welfare of the minority and, indeed, the well-being of the individual. From a Rawlsian perspective, we might say that the means and the ends must justify each other.

Rawls proposes that a "veil of ignorance" be adopted when making ethical judgments. When deciding what is right or wrong, persons should assume that they are utterly ignorant of their own economic, social, and political status. Behind the "veil of ignorance," each person is equal to every other person. Thus, decisions are made according to what is fair — and therefore just — for each individual, not simply for the majority. In fact, egalitarian ethics rejects the "majority rules" concept. On an island inhabited by nine cannibals and one vegetarian, for instance, the noncannibal does not deserve to be eaten, even if the majority of

1873 Anthony Comstock founds the New York Society for the Suppression of Vice.

1938 The "War of the Worlds" broadcast panics listeners and sensitizes the nation to the power of radio; investigations probe the ethics of mediated deception.

1800   1900

1833 With the motto "It shines for ALL," the *New York Sun* begins publication; all are not pleased with the paper's redefinition of news—crimes, scandals, disasters, and gossip become the mainstay of the highly successful "penny press."

1898 Newspaper publisher William Randolph Hearst is accused of starting the Spanish-American War.

1923 The American Society of Newspaper Editors adopts the Canons of Journalism, the first national code of mass media ethics in the United States.

1929 The first code of ethics issued by the National Association of Broadcasters (NAB), the *Radio Code,* provides guidelines for news, entertainment, and advertising.

1934 Henry Forman's book *Our Movie Made Children* indicts popular films as the latest menace to the moral development of American youth.

1947 The Hutchins Commission issues its seminal report, *A Free and Responsible Press*, outlining requirements for journalistic responsibility.

13.1 The History of Ethics and Mass Communication in America

1952 The NAB adds the Television Code to its Radio Code. Both codes of "good practices" would be suspended in 1983.

1967 One of the few activists ever to grace the FCC, commissioner Nicholas Johnson publishes *How to Talk Back to Your Television Set.*

1950

1960

1954 Frederic Wertham's *Seduction of the Innocent* is published and also appears as "Blueprints for Delinquency" in *Reader's Digest;* Wertham's warnings precipitate "The Great Comic Book Scare."

1954 The Public Relations Society of America adopts a code of Professional Standards.

1955 *Rebel Without a Cause* strikes a responsive chord with a new, youthful film audience; James Dean becomes the antihero for teens, parents become worried.

1959 The payola scandals rock the recording industry as unethical liaisons between the radio and music businesses are uncovered.

1959 The quiz-show scandals sweep over the television industry; game-show rigging strains the faith of television viewers.

1965 "I Spy" premieres on NBC; Bill Cosby is the first African American cast in a continuing role on a prime-time TV series.

1965 Despite changing times, the American Newspaper Advertising Code continues to forbid the mention of bust measurements and prohibits the use of such words as "lust," "lesbian," "naked," and "homosexual."

1968 The Motion Picture Association of America (MPAA) enacts a system of self-regulation; the movie ratings are born as the old Hays Office production codes die.

1970

Concerns over the influence of rock music take a new turn, as "drug-related" lyrics are debated; some radio stations ban Peter, Paul and Mary's "Puff the Magic Dragon," fearing that the folk song might really be about marijuana.

1977

Troubled teen Ronald Zamora robs and murders a grandmother; lawyers argue unsuccessfully that watching too much violence on television is to blame.

1960   1970

1968 The press and the police clash violently during Chicago's Democratic National Convention. Police–press relationships continue to be a source of numerous ethical dilemmas.

1969 In a confrontation between censors and comedians, CBS cancels "The Smothers Brothers Comedy Hour"; the political satire practiced by the brothers is too controversial, by the network's standards.

1970 The Congressional Commission on Obscenity and Pornography releases the results of a 3-year study; the Commission concludes that pornography is harmless, but President Nixon concludes that the report should be rejected.

1971 In just 13 days, the Supreme Court argues the Pentagon Papers case, upholding the right of the New York Times to publish the papers; ethical questions regarding press leaks and national security loom large.

1971 "All in the Family" premieres; the situation comedy breaks a number of television taboos, dealing with sexism, racism, rape, homosexuality, politics. Creator Norman Lear would later found People for the American Way.

1972 Bob Woodward and Carl Bernstein's Washington Post articles expose the Watergate scandal and fuel debate over the ethics of investigative journalism.

1973 In his best-seller Subliminal Seduction, Wilson Key argues that hidden images and messages adversely influence the media audience. The debate over subliminal communication continues to the present day.

1974 NBC broadcasts the TV-movie Born Innocent; a 9-year-old California girl is raped by juvenile assailants who claim they were copying a scene depicted in the movie.

13.1 (continued)

1987

R. Budd Dwyer, Pennsylvania state treasurer, calls a news conference and shoots himself in front of the television cameras.

1991

Tight control over media coverage of the Persian Gulf War makes for controversy; media coverage of antiwar demonstrations also becomes the focus of intense debate.

1980

1980 William Friedkin releases his feature film *Cruising;* activists mount a major, nationwide protest over the film's extremely negative stereotyping of gays.

1981 KMBC-TV news anchor Christine Craft is fired because she hasn't got the right "looks" for the job.

1981 Janet Cooke wins — and then loses — a Pulitzer Prize; her *Washington Post* series on heroin addiction falsely portrays a composite character as a real person.

1983 Widespread criticism follows WHMA-TV's coverage of a suicide attempt by Cecil Andrews, who set himself on fire in front of a television news crew.

1983 The United States invades the island nation of Grenada; members of the press are not invited to the war.

1985 *An Early Frost* is the first made-for-television movie to deal with AIDS.

1986 The controversial final report of the U.S. Attorney General's Commission on Pornography is released; the report bolsters a renewed call for stringent moral standards and stepped-up legal regulation of pornography.

1987–1988 The ethics of America's "electronic churches" are questioned as leading televangelists fall from grace.

1990

1990 Several major record labels strike up an agreement with the Parents' Music Resource Center (PMRC) and enact a voluntary labeling system; "warning stickers" are affixed to potentially offensive music.

1991 National Public Radio reports the contents of a leaked FBI file; Clarence Thomas and Anita Hill square off on Capitol Hill as the nation looks on.

1992 The National Endowment for the Arts adopts new standards to curtail funding of "objectionable" projects.

1995 Debate continues over media coverage of O. J. Simpson fiasco, free press versus fair trial issues abound. How much is too much?

the residents were to hold an election and decide (by a 9 to 1 vote!) that eating their vegetarian brother would be the best thing to do.

Natural Law Ethics: In the Beginning . . .

Natural law ethics attempts to explore the very nature of human goodness and probes the thorny question of why we desire to be good in the first place. In answering this question, natural law theories tend to adopt a *theological* perspective and assume that a creator god has made human beings with certain tendencies or potentials. This sort of ethical reasoning is reflected in the Declaration of Independence, for example, where this famous assumption is made: "We hold these truths to be self-evident, that all men . . . are endowed by their creator with certain unalienable rights, that among these are life, liberty and the pursuit of happiness."

According to natural law ethics, good actions work toward the realization of our innate potentials, while evil actions work against our natural tendencies. From this perspective, certain actions are intrinsically good (for example, telling the truth) and others are intrinsically evil (for example, lying). Because evil must be avoided at all costs, the ends *never* justify the means whenever those means involve some evil action. Evil must never be used to produce good. Both the ends and the means used to achieve those ends must be free from evil.

Aristotelian Ethics: A Compromising Position

A central tenet of Aristotle's (384–322 B.C.) ethics is the "golden mean." According to Aristotle, virtuous or ethical conduct involves avoiding *extremes*. The goal of ethical analysis is to identify extreme positions and then locate some middle or moderate ground between those extremes. It is this middle ground that we call the golden mean.

As is the case with Kantianism, the ends do not automatically justify the means in an Aristotelian system of ethics. Indeed, in this system it is often necessary to compromise and to moderate both the ends and the means in order to arrive at the middle ground. For example, pornographic movies are viewed by some people as harmful or evil. For others, these films are a useful means of entertainment, a form of free expression and free trade. How can we balance the interests of these opposing groups? Limiting the manner in which such films can be shown, sold, and advertised represents a golden mean between the extremes of banning the films altogether and doing nothing to regulate where, when, and to whom they are shown.

For some reasonable people, however, there might be no middle ground. First Amendment absolutists — persons who believe that freedom of speech and press must *never* be abridged — could make a sound ethical argument for the unencumbered distribution of pornography. For such persons, accepting any middle ground of even limited regulation would seriously compromise their absolutist ethic.

It is also important to note that the concept of the golden mean does not work very well unless the extreme positions are identified through a process that is both rational and reasonable. It would hardly be ethical for a murderer to decide that, given the extreme options of either killing a person or letting him live, breaking the victim's legs would be a "moderate" course of action. In this case, the extremes of life and death are not reasonable options, particularly from the victim's point of view!

What's a Reporter to Do? The Case of the Mayor's Diary

In order to gain a fuller appreciation of these differing ethical theories, we can apply them to a hypothetical dilemma. Let's assume that you are a reporter for an all-news radio station in your city. A trusted source has informed you that the mayor received a number of illegal campaign contributions during the last election. Though the mayor's record has been exemplary since being elected, violating election laws is a serious offense and you think that such information ought to be made public. However, your source informs you that the only hard evidence of the wrongdoing is contained in the mayor's private diary. Your source was able to have the diary stolen, photocopied, and then returned to the mayor's bedroom. All of this happened while the mayor was on vacation and her house was being painted. The mayor is apparently unaware that her private diary has been photocopied. In such a situation, what's a reporter to do?

This situation raises a number of serious ethical (and legal) problems. First, you are faced with two competing vices. On the one hand, theft is generally considered the wrong thing to do. On the other hand, political corruption is also a serious ethical violation. In accepting the purloined documents, you will become complicit in the theft. By ignoring those same documents, you might be allowing political corruption to go unchecked. Additionally, your radio station might have certain policies regarding the use of anonymous sources or illegally obtained information, and you will have to consider those codes of professional ethics as well (see 13.3 on p. 342). For the sake of expediency, however, we can reduce this dilemma to a basic question: Should you accept the stolen documents and report the information they contain?

From a utilitarian perspective, you could justify the decision to accept the photocopies and expose the mayor's misdeeds. After all, the mayor is only one individual. The citizens of your town deserve an honest government. Within a utilitarian framework, the needs of the many outweigh the needs of the few, or of the one. Thus, exposure of political corruption would lead to the greatest good for the greatest number. The ends (better and more honest government) justify the means (theft of a private diary).

Kantian ethics does not offer an easy justification for reporting information from the mayor's diary. If you decide that using stolen documents is ethical, the categorical imperative requires you to be guided by the principle that such theft is *always* the right thing to do. Indeed, if you accept the photocopied diary, you should do so only if you believe that stealing secret papers ought to be a routine journalistic practice, perhaps supported by a "get the news at any cost" principle.

The categorical imperative resembles the old golden-rule adage: Do unto others as you would have them do unto you. That is, if you accept the mayor's diary, you ought to have no ethical quarrel with someone who might decide to steal *your* private papers, if such papers could reveal important information about some misconduct. For instance, another reporter at a rival radio station might decide to steal your notes, hoping to find out who stole the mayor's diary in the first place. In short, Kant's categorical imperative suggests that alternative ways to achieve the results should be considered in the case of the mayor's diary. The ends (exposure of corruption) might not justify the means (theft) in the long run.

Social justice theory requires that you move behind the "veil of ignorance" when deciding whether to accept and publish details from the mayor's diary. Behind the veil you cannot know if you are an "average citizen," a broadcast journalist, or even the mayor. How would you feel if you *were* the mayor? There are no clear or easy answers to such a question, of course. Obviously the mayor is bound to feel badly — and even violated — if her diary is made public. But perhaps the mayor would also feel relieved. "At last this terrible secret has been revealed," the mayor might reason. "A great burden has been lifted from my conscience." Well . . . maybe not. But the mayor has chosen to be a public official, after all, and she is fully aware of the fact that public officials are exposed to a unique level of media surveillance. In any case, social justice ethics suggests that the reporter seek out the mayor's perspective before the details of the diary are published. To be fair, the mayor must at least be confronted with the material prior to your report. Her story deserves to be told from her point of view.

Natural law ethics offers a number of interpretations for the case of the mayor's diary, and we can deal with only the most simple one here. Generally, theft is regarded as an evil deed. Because good ends never justify evil means, the theft of the diary must be rejected at the outset. The evil of stealing the mayor's diary does not justify the good of reducing government corruption. Of course, the mayor clearly committed an act of evil as well, but "two wrongs don't make a right." As an ethical reporter, you should never accept stolen information, regardless of its value.

Finally, we can consider the case of the mayor's diary from an Aristotelian point of view. Recall that Aristotle was concerned with the virtue of the golden mean, a middle ground between extreme vices. In this case, you are confronted with at least two extremes: You can accept and expose the documents, or you can do nothing. Neither of these seems to be a fundamentally ethical course of action. Is there some middle path you might take? Perhaps you could look for other sources that would provide the same information that the diary contains. In this way, you could seek out evidence of the mayor's misdeeds, yet you avoid accepting stolen material from your source.

So, what have you decided? Oh, by the way, the mayor's diary also contained some pretty steamy descriptions of her romantic life. Reporting those salacious details could easily boost the sagging ratings at your station. You could also make many thousands of dollars by selling this "extra" information to a tabloid newspaper. And *now* what's a reporter to do?

No Easy Answers

As you can see, there are seldom easy answers to ethical questions. The important thing, however, is that we ask such questions in the first place. By engaging in a process of moral reasoning — rather than acting blindly — we are more likely to consider the consequences of our decisions and develop sound reasons for our actions. The point of moral reasoning, after all, is not that everyone agrees as to what is right or wrong but that we can at least understand each other's motives, actions, and principles. An editorial in *The Quill*, a publication of the Society of Professional Journalists, put the matter this way:

> Ethical judgments are like that. No matter who makes them, they are seldom easy, and they are almost certain to strike some of us as perfectly proper while others regard them as wrong-headed, stupid, unfair, and — possibly — as evidence of intellectual and/or moral decay.

> All of which is a wonderful thing. Differing definitions of ethical behavior help keep our minds awake and our spirits inflamed. If everyone agreed on all ethical principles, life might be more orderly, but it surely would be more boring.

The ethical dilemmas associated with mass comunication involve all of us. In confronting these dilemmas, we are dealing with problems that impact, rather directly, the quality of our lives. The chaotic and confusing realm of mass media ethics is anything but boring.

To help bring some order to this chaos, ethicist Louis Day has developed a model for moral reasoning. In his book *Ethics in Media Communications,* Day presents the "SAD formula" (see 13.2). Despite its unfortunate acronym, this model provides a useful map of the moral reasoning process. In this model, the

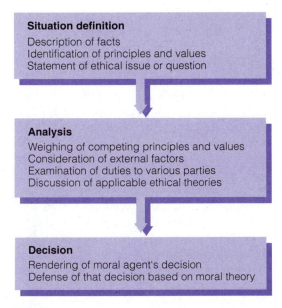

Situation definition
Description of facts
Identification of principles and values
Statement of ethical issue or question

Analysis
Weighing of competing principles and values
Consideration of external factors
Examination of duties to various parties
Discussion of applicable ethical theories

Decision
Rendering of moral agent's decision
Defense of that decision based on moral theory

13.2

The *SAD formula* is a model of the ideal moral reasoning process.
From Louis A. Day, Ethics in Media Communications: Cases and Controversies. *(Belmont, CA: Wadsworth, 1991), p. 60. ©1991 by Wadsworth, Inc.*

seemingly infinite number of variables that must be considered when making ethical decisions are organized into three general stages: *Situation definition, Analysis,* and *Decision.*

First, the *situation* must be clearly defined. The facts must be ascertained, and the essential ethical question needs to be posed. The conflicting values and interests that have created this ethical quandary must be identified.

Second, we need to engage in an *analysis* of the situation. In this important step we must use all of the information gathered in the first stage and then evaluate the ethical alternatives. This evaluation should be both rigorous and imaginative. Essentially, this stage involves considering the various pros and cons involved in the ethical dilemma we are working on; various ethical theories should be tested on the problem at hand. We must explore what

external factors—such as various laws or codes of ethics—might impact our decision. We might look for any precedents for our case. We should also consider how others will react to our decision and how each of the parties involved will be affected by the course of action we might take. As a newspaper reporter, for example, you would need to consider not only the effects of your decision on your readers but also on your company.

Finally, stage three brings us to a *decision.* At this point, we explain our judgment and defend our decision. This defense can be based on an appeal to any of the theories of ethics discussed earlier.

Of course, ethical problems are typically complicated affairs. In the real world, we might find that a "snap judgment" is required or that certain facts are simply unavailable. Nonetheless, we must be as careful in our moral reasoning as we can, and our decision-making process should be open to inspection. Using the SAD formula can help us achieve both of these goals.

Media Self-Regulation: Codes and Censors

While morality and law are closely related, many of the concerns of mass media ethics do not directly involve legal matters. For example, there is no law against advertising condoms on television. Nevertheless, many stations—in fact, most stations—will not carry such advertisements, fearing that this content would offend the moral sensibilities of the audience. Thus, the decision to exclude condom advertising is an ethical one. Restricting condom advertising is an act of *self-regulation* exercised by many media industries. Self-regulation can take one of two forms: codes of ethics or industry censorship.

Codes of Ethics

Many mass media professions maintain some form of ethical *code*. These codes govern the behavior of print journalists, public relations professionals, advertising executives, news anchors, and other media professionals whose work has the potential for significant social impact. Of course, compliance with the specifics of such codes is voluntary, though many codes have been enacted to avoid the threat of government regulation.

The first national code of ethics adopted by a mass media industry in the United States was created by the American Society of Newspaper Editors. The ASNE Canons of Journalism were adopted in 1923 and, in part, they declared:

> The right of a newspaper to attract and hold readers is restricted by nothing but considerations of public welfare. The use a newspaper makes of the share of public attention it gains serves to determine its sense of responsibility, which it shares with every member of its staff. A journalist who uses his power for any selfish or otherwise unworthy purpose is faithless to a high trust.

The ideals of responsible newspaper journalism expressed in the Canons continue to be espoused in the ASNE's current code of ethics, the Statement of Principles adopted in 1975. The original ASNE code encouraged later media industries to adopt similar ethical guidelines.

One of the most famous (and infamous) movie industry codes originated in the 1920s. The Motion Picture Production Code came to be known by various names, usually in reference to the current head of the Motion Picture Producers and Distributors of America: the Johnson Office, the Hays Office, and the Breen Office. William H. Hays—a former postmaster general—is the best known of these administrators. He developed a rather restrictive code, which film producers were bound to follow. Unless a film received code approval, it could not be screened in U.S. theaters.

The code developed through the Hays Office was, for the most part, concerned with sexuality. The 1927 version of the code absolutely prohibited the depiction of such things as "any licentious or suggestive nudity—in fact or silhouette," "miscegenation—sex relationships between the white and black races," "sex hygiene and venereal diseases," "scenes of actual childbirth—in fact or silhouette," and "any inference of sex perversion." Scripts were reviewed by Hays Office censors, and code prohibitions were enforced with an exacting—and often exasperating—attention to detail. In an effort to censor all depictions of homosexuality, for example, the Hays Office issued a 1933 memo banning the use of the word "pansy" in any film; even a male character using such phrases as "My dear boy" was frowned on and blue-penciled by Hays Office censors as "homosexual dialogue."

By the late 1960s, the Production Code had lost much of its force. The emphasis shifted from reviewing scripts and banning films at the box office to rating completed films so that the public could anticipate any questionable content. This classification system—the Motion Picture Association of America's rating system—remains in effect today (see Chapter 10).

Critics of the old Hays Office code point out that its strict censorship did not protect "public morality" but actually stunted the growth of film as an art form and a medium of free expression. However, the echoes of the 1920s Hays Office can still be clearly heard in the 1990s. A renewed interest in morality and "family values" at all levels of society, especially in government-funded projects, has sparked calls for stricter control over media content. Interestingly, the new list of "offensive" material looks remarkably similar to the old list of Hays Office taboos.

In addition to guidelines for film content, codes of ethics have also been developed for the broadcast media. With the rise of commercial radio in the United States came the formation of the National Association of Broadcasters (NAB), a professional industry organization established in 1923. The NAB enacted a code of ethics in 1929 that covered the full spectrum of radio content—policies related to advertising and entertainment were spelled out. Of course, it was not coincidental that this code arrived two short years after Congress enacted the Radio Act of 1927. The NAB Code was not simply a statement of lofty ideals but also a direct attempt to ward off further government interference in the lucrative business of broadcasting. As with most codes of ethics, the Radio Code was part idealism and part public relations.

In 1952 the NAB adopted its Television Code, a detailed document that addressed many of the same issues covered in the Radio Code. However, it was not until 1961 that the NAB established a Code Authority, a commission assigned with the responsibility of ensuring that member stations were following the rules of the codes. Over the years, the radio and television codes underwent numerous revisions until, in 1982, a federal court ruled that certain code provisions dealing with the length and number of commercials were a violation of antitrust law. Eventually, the NAB agreed to suspend the codes entirely. Today, no industry codes of ethics govern radio or television stations on a national level. However, many local stations operate under guidelines similar to those found in the old NAB codes.

A number of other ethics codes address specific segments of the mass media industries. For example, the Radio-Television News Directors Association (RTNDA) has enacted a national code for broadcast journalists (see 13.3). Other important codes are those espoused by the Society of Professional Journalists and the Associated Press Managing Editors. There are also the Advertising Code of American Business and the Code of Professional Standards of the Public Relations Society of America.

Do codes of ethics actually help media professionals become more responsible? That's a tough question. Critics point out that because these codes are essentially voluntary, there is no mechanism by which various media organizations—let alone the general public—can ensure that code guidelines are being followed. Additionally, the language of most codes is vague. Because codes avoid specific regulations, they are open to wide interpretation. For example, the RTNDA Code of Broadcast News Ethics states that it is improper to identify people by race unless it is "relevant." Of course, different broadcast journalists will hold differing definitions of such "relevance."

Likewise, the Advertising Code of American Business includes the following provisions:

- *Truth.* Advertising shall tell the truth, and reveal significant facts, the concealment of which would mislead the public. . . .

- *Taste and decency.* Advertising shall be free of statements, illustrations or implications which are offensive to good taste and public decency. . . .

- *Unprovable claims.* Advertising shall avoid the use of exaggerated or unprovable claims.

- *Testimonials.* Advertising containing testimonials shall be limited to those of competent witnesses who are reflecting a real and honest choice.

This code has been endorsed by many organizations. But obviously, not everyone would agree on what constitutes such things as "good taste," "public decency," or "a real and honest choice." And what, for that matter, constitutes an "exaggerated" claim? For instance, is it exaggeration to suggest that the right toothpaste

Radio-Television News Directors Association Code of Broadcast News Ethics

The responsibility of radio and television journalists is to gather and report information of importance and interest to the public accurately, honestly, and impartially.

The members of the Radio-Television News Directors Association accept these standards and will:

1 Strive to present the source or nature of broadcast news material in a way that is balanced, accurate, and fair.

    a They will evaluate information solely on its merits as news, rejecting sensationalism or misleading emphasis in any form.

    b They will guard against using audio or video material in a way that deceives the audience.

    c They will not mislead the public by presenting as spontaneous news any material which is staged or rehearsed.

    d They will identify people by race, creed, nationality, or prior status only when it is relevant.

    e They will clearly label opinion and commentary.

    f They will promptly acknowledge and correct errors.

2 Strive to conduct themselves in a manner that protects them from conflicts of interest, real or perceived. They will decline gifts or favors which would influence or appear to influence their judgments.

3 Respect the dignity, privacy, and well-being of people with whom they deal.

4 Recognize the need to protect confidential sources. They will promise confidentiality only with the intention of keeping that promise.

5 Respect everyone's right to a fair trial.

6 Broadcast the private transmissions of other broadcasters only with permission.

7 Actively encourage observance of this Code by all journalists, whether members of the Radio-Television News Directors Association or not.

Source: Radio-Television News Directors Association/RTNDA, 1717 K Street, NW — Suite 615, Washington, DC 20006/(202) 659-6510.

---

or jeans will improve your sex life? Or are such claims merely part of the hype and promotion that advertising is all about? The slick and surreal quality of many contemporary advertisements — especially those for sexuality-enhancing fashions — makes ethical analysis even more challenging (see 13.4).

Standards and Practices: The Censors

In addition to codes of ethics, radio and television networks are under the guidance of Standards and Practices personnel, more commonly known as "the censors." While the people who work in various Standards and Practices departments play a vital role in determining what gets on the air, they have traditionally kept a low profile. In *Feedback* Herb Kaplan, a former NBC censor, recalls:

> In 1968–9, I was a Senior Editor in the Broadcast Standards Department at NBC. Whenever someone in the company asked where I worked, I responded "Standards" and they asked, "What's that?" I learned to reply, "The censors." Relatively few of the thousands of employees of NBC, outside of the Sales or Programming departments and the top executives, knew of the existence of the NBC Codes or what it was that the Broadcast Standards Department actually did. Even then, mentioning the censors revealed that they did not know what it was we were "censoring" or how we went

about it — what standards we followed.

The ethical implications of Kaplan's observation are startling. While most of us remain unaware of who the censors are and what it is that they do, they nonetheless determine — to a significant extent — what millions of Americans are allowed to see and hear over radio and television.

Sometimes, the work of the censors takes on a higher profile, usually when a writer or an actor feels that his or her work has been hurt by the Standards and Practices people. Such was the case in the 1960s, when CBS censors clashed with the Smothers Brothers over comedy skits about such sensitive issues as the Vietnam War. In that struggle, CBS seemed to be the victor. "The Smothers Brothers Comedy Hour" was canceled despite good ratings (see Chapter 9). Nevertheless, Tom and Dick Smothers publicly expressed their outrage at CBS and, in the process, exposed the seemingly arbitrary and sometimes hypocritical nature of the censorship process.

In their efforts to protect the sensitivities of the mass audience, a difficult if not impossible task, the censors have often made decisions that seem ridiculous in retrospect. For example, when Lucille Ball became pregnant in the 1950s, she was not allowed to use that word to describe her condition on the highly rated situation comedy "I Love Lucy." Instead, she and husband Ricky had to announce the news that Lucy was "in the family way." Television viewers at that time would have no direct evidence of just how Lucy got that way either, as she and Ricky never slept in the same bed. That too was a television "no-no."

Today, of course, the censors have loosened up a bit. Still, some of the "logic" behind the censors' actions is still hard to fathom. For example, ABC felt that the network could get away with showing two gay men in the same bed, lighting up a cigarette to suggest that they had just had sex, on "thirtysomething." How-

13.4

What's for sale here: The product or the model? The bargain (a consumer value) or the body (a social value)? In contemporary advertising it's sometimes hard to figure out exactly what is being sold. Do these ads conform to the Advertising Code of American Business?

ever, the men could never be shown kissing or otherwise actually expressing any outward affection for each other.

As noted earlier, most network television stations still refuse to carry condom advertisements. This too has been deemed hypocritical by some critics. Because most network television programs are loaded with implied sex, the critics point out, the networks have a moral obligation to allow advertising for a product that could save lives and prevent unwanted pregnancies. Such advertising is still almost unknown on any of the major networks, however. To their credit, though, a number of television programs continue to include references to safe sex and condoms as part of their storylines. The Fox network and MTV also feature ads for condoms; some of the MTV spots are aimed at a target audience as young as 14 years old.

Standards and Practices personnel often claim that their job is not to censor but to achieve balance in order to maintain an "offend no one" policy. In fact, many censors describe their work in utilitarian and Aristotelian

13.5

This Tom Tomorrow cartoon seems to agree with the critics' contention that American mass media favor blandness over controversy, asking the "easy questions" while hiding behind the smoke-screen policy of "exposition, not advocacy." Do you agree with Biff? © 1991 Tom Tomorrow; reprinted by permission.

terms. For example, Alan Wurtzel, ABC's vice-president for Broadcast Standards, does not like the "censor" label at all. "If anything," he maintains, "I would say that we *add* complexity. . . . If you have a program that advocates a single point of view, it's simplistic. . . . We have a policy that says, basically, 'exposition not advocacy.' We want balanced views on our network."

Television critic Donna Woolfolk Cross strongly disagrees with Alan Wurtzel's position. Cross maintains that the networks' concept of "balance" is actually an attempt to eliminate anything that challenges the social status quo. Often, Cross maintains, the censors do little more than protect the vested interests of advertisers. She argues:

> To provide the best possible environment for their product messages, both networks and sponsors try to steer clear of "controversial" topics. Controversy is avoided for two reasons: Viewers who do not agree with the message might boycott the sponsor's product; and viewers who are deeply moved or politically aroused are less likely to be receptive to deodorant soap commercials.

The result of network censorship, according to critics like Cross, is not balance but blandness (see 13.5).

Enduring Issues and Persistent Questions

In the volatile world of mass communication, change is the keynote. Seemingly new and different ethical problems arise almost daily, involving both the producers and the consumers of mass media. However, underlying most of the specific cases are a smaller number of *enduring* ethical issues or themes. These themes include: (1) press responsibility, (2) privacy, (3) morally offensive or questionable content (such as violence, pornography, and stereotyping), (4) children and mass communication, (5) the uses of persuasive mass communication, such as propaganda and advertising, and (6) economic interests and business practices.

Of course, there are other general concerns, but these basic themes encompass most of the central ethical controversies involving the mass media. In the remainder of this chapter, we will take a closer look at a few of these controversies. Let the readings and references at the end of the chapter guide you to further examination of these and other persistent questions in media ethics.

Press Responsibility

The Bill of Rights guarantees a free press in the United States. But with freedom comes responsibility. Just as free speech does not include the freedom to falsely yell "Fire!" in a crowded theater, freedom of the press does not grant journalists the privilege of lying, endangering the general public, or maliciously ruining the lives of individual citizens. In fact, there are legal restrictions against doing most of these things. The press is free, but only to a point.

The *legal* constraints on the press concern only those things that a journalist can or cannot do if she or he wishes to stay out of jail or avoid paying hefty fines. The *ethical* constraints cover a wider terrain and involve those things that a journalist should and should not do if she or he wishes to be a responsible member of the press.

Of course, one of the primary responsibilities for a journalist is to tell the truth. But what, exactly, constitutes the "truth"? Is it ethical, for instance, when a journalist makes up an "anonymous" quote? Or writes a story from an eyewitness perspective, having never really been on the scene? And what about inventing situations altogether? Is it ethical to create a composite character in order to convey some sense of the "truth"? Apparently, *Washington Post* reporter Janet Cooke thought so. Her 1980 *Post* series on heroin addiction began with the story of "Jimmy":

> Jimmy is 8 years old and a third-generation heroin addict, a precocious little boy with sandy hair, velvety brown eyes and needle marks freckling the baby-smooth skin of his thin brown

arms. . . . There is an almost cherubic expression on his small round face as he talks about life — clothes, money, the Baltimore Orioles and heroin. He has been an addict since the age of 5.

Cooke won a Pulitzer Prize for the series. Yet, in the attention lavished on her following the receipt of the award, Cooke's story began to unravel. Soon, she admitted that she had actually invented the character of "Jimmy," having based her composite on interviews with social workers. The prize was rescinded, and Cooke resigned her position at the *Post*. Critics were quick to condemn the Janet Cooke affair as a sharp blow to the integrity of honest and objective reporting.

Absolute objectivity is an impossible ideal for journalists, and some form of bias creeps into most news stories. In fact, a number of media advocacy groups devote considerable attention to exposing what they see as *systematic* distortion in the news. According to these organizations, Americans are often getting only one side of a story. In many cases, however, we might not be getting the story at all (see 13.6).

Accuracy In Media (AIM), a politically conservative media watchdog organization, claims that most journalists give a liberal slant to the news they report. The result, according to AIM members, is a virtual blackout of conservative viewpoints. Other groups, such as People for the American Way, take the opposite position and lobby against conservative control over the media, arguing that right-wing influences are choking free expression. Groups such as People for the American Way claim that AIM and similar organizations actually want to restrict rather than expand the range of views and the diversity of information available to the public.

Related to the question of bias is another, more basic question: Are the media doing a good job of keeping the public informed about

Project Censored: All the News That Didn't Fit

What the American people don't know can kill them.

Fred W. Friendly

Critics often point out that the *New York Times* slogan "all the news that's fit to print" ought to read "all the news that fits." Not every newsworthy event receives coverage in the nation's newpapers and newscasts. Some stories do not "fit," and they are largely overlooked or underreported. Ethical questions are raised by the possibility that there is a *pattern of exclusion*, that certain types of stories are routinely ignored, presumably to serve the vested political or economic interests of those who manage our national news industries.

Did you know that George Bush appointed Nazi sympathizers to key campaign slots during his 1988 run for the presidency or that he purchased real estate with deeds containing "whites only" provisions? You probably haven't heard about these things. These news items are listed by Project Censored as among the most underreported stories of 1988. These and other subjects were covered in the alternative press, but went largely ignored by the mainstream media.

Project Censored annually examines news stories that, despite their significance, have received minimal press coverage. Every year since 1976, Project Censored has published a report on the year's most ignored — or "censored" — news stories. The selection committee has hosted a distinguished roster of experts, including Ben Bagdikian, of U.C. Berkeley's Graduate School of Journalism, former FCC commissioner Nicholas Johnson, and televison journalist Bill Moyers.

Among the stories included on past "censored" lists are:

- "The Abuse of America's Incarcerated Children"
- "Project Galileo: The Risk of Nuclear Disaster in Space"
- "Radioactive Waste and the Danger of Food Irradiation"
- "Acid Rain — One of America's Biggest Killers"

What news stories do you think deserve wider attention? Project Censored encourages nominations from the public. Nominated stories "should have received minimal coverage, be on issues affecting a large number of people, have reliable sources, be of national or international scope, and be timely." Send a copy of any overlooked news story to Dr. Carl Jensen, Director, Project Censored, Sonoma State University, Rohnert Park, CA 94928.

---

important issues? Critics maintain that contemporary journalism is shallow and sensational. In lieu of facts and in-depth reporting, these critics contend, the mass media offer us sound bites and titillation.

Among the more controversial journalism trends in the past few years is "tabloid television" or, more simply, "trash TV." News and talk shows in this genre, which program creators prefer to call "guts TV," focus on the sorts of sensational news items typically found in such supermarket tabloids as the *National Enquirer* and the *Weekly World News*.

Controversial talk show host Geraldo Rivera is credited with creating the trash TV format, and he became the object of intense criticism in the wake of his highly publicized documentaries on devil worship and drug abuse. He has continued to be no less controversial as the host of two daily television programs, "Geraldo!" and "Now It Can Be Told."

The formats of the various tabloid television shows are varied, but the subjects covered generally fall into a few categories. Sex, crime, the occult, and celebrities are the most common subjects. Many times these categories are combined: "Devil-worshipping prostitutes who have had sex with the ghost of Elvis . . . That's the focus on this edition of 'Geraldo!'"

The success of "Geraldo!" has had an impact on all talk shows and their hosts. Oprah Winfrey, Sally Jesse Raphael, Joan Rivers, Maury Povich, and Phil Donahue now host tabloid-like programs. When Phil Donahue invited Jimmy Carter's mother, Lillian, onto his talk show, she replied: "Phil, I don't wear an IUD, I'm not a homosexual, and I don't smoke pot—just what am I going to talk about?"

According to its detractors, tabloid television represents the lowest form of broadcast journalism. Much of the criticism, however, is not directed at the topics found on tabloid TV—their *content*—but at the sensational manner in which those topics are addressed—the *form*. After all, many of the subjects covered on these shows—sexuality, drugs, rape, abortion, racism—are undeniably important. But, the critics ask, when these subjects are discussed in a "freak-show" environment, can the audience actually become better informed? For the critics, such a *consequence* seems unlikely.

Defenders of guts TV point out that these shows are, in fact, giving the public what the public wants. In defending his documentary "Satan's Underground," Geraldo Rivera had this to say to his detractors:

> You know something, people said that the devil worship show was pornography. I will bet my life savings that you could have put two hours of pornography opposite the devil worship show, you could have two hours of pure fornication and people still would've watched my program. Because it's a real issue that, unlike my critics, the real people were very concerned about, and it was done in a professional and responsible and in-

teresting way. Television doesn't have to be boring to be righteous.

Perhaps the fundamental question is not whether people are getting what they *want* from the nation's major news sources but whether or not the public is getting what it *needs*. Many Americans, for example, appear to be fundamentally ignorant of the American political system. When asked, quite a few citizens are unable to name the U.S. senators who represent their state. Too many Americans are unable to identify each of the rights guaranteed by the First Amendment, let alone those covered by the first 10 amendments to the U.S. Constitution.

Citizens are not only lacking in political knowledge but appear to be rather uninformed about such basic issues as nuclear power, ecology, and public health. Information about these subjects could, quite literally, save lives. Yet, in "giving the public what it wants," TV producers often give these subjects second billing to celebrity gossip and sensational crime stories. Television viewers might very well be more interested in devil worship than the status of the ozone layer. But the question remains: Whose fault is that?

The Press and Privacy

Often, the public's right to know is pitted against an individual's right to privacy. In this battle the press is accused of invading the private lives of public persons, incessantly harassing them in order to get that one extra tidbit of information. Public figures like Michael Jackson and Princess Diana frequently complain of being hounded by members of the press. Rob Lowe's sexually oriented home videos were shown on television stations all over the country, much to the actor's chagrin. More recently, Tonya Harding's explicit private videotapes found their way on to the nations' TV sets and into video stores. Elizabeth Taylor's most recent wedding was invaded by an army of journalists, including one determined photographer who parachuted onto the scene. Michael Jackson and Lisa Marie Presley were married for weeks before anyone found out. Their publicists explained that the object was to keep the ceremony from becoming "a public spectacle."

The ethical issues surrounding press treatment of public figures are complicated by the fact that professional celebrities achieve their fame through media interest in the first place. The stars of the entertainment industry need press coverage as much as they rant against it. Astute superstars like Madonna have, in fact, made a virtual art form out of manipulating press interest in their private affairs. In her film, *Truth or Dare,* and book, *Sex,* Madonna seemed to be taking the upper hand, placing her private life in the glare of the media spotlight and revealing her personal "secrets" before the press could have a chance to do so.

Of course, it can be argued that the public does not really have a *right* to know the details of Madonna's sex life, or what she thinks of her brothers, or how she looks without make-up. Sure, we might *want* to know such things, but we don't really *need* that information. On the other hand, do we have a real need and, in fact, a right to know about the "private life" of our state's attorney general? The local police chief? Or a nominee to the Supreme Court of the United States?

The debate over the press and privacy heated up dramatically in October 1991, as the saga of Anita Hill and Clarence Thomas unfolded on television screens and newspaper pages across the nation. Just prior to the U.S. Senate vote that would have elevated Clarence Thomas to the Supreme Court, a confidential FBI report was leaked to the press. National Public Radio first announced the shocking news that a credible source had accused Judge Thomas of sexual harassment while he was the director of the Equal Employment Opportunity Commission. The Senate, panicked by the leak, scheduled special hearings to further

investigate the allegations. The source, law professor Anita Hill, flew to Washington, D.C., and the unprecedented hearings began.

For three remarkable days, Americans were able to watch nonstop television coverage of the Senate hearings — coverage that included the most intimate details of the lives of Anita Hill and Clarence Thomas. The subject of sexual harassment was instantly moved to the top of the national agenda. The topic was discussed on virtually every news and talk show, featured prominently in every newspaper and magazine, and debated in classrooms as well as barrooms.

The ethical questions raised in the midst of these debates were many, and they continue to be asked. Republican leaders — including President Bush — began an immediate hunt for the source of the news leak, claiming that not only journalistic ethics had been violated but also Senate rules had been breached. Two conservative political action groups offered a $5,000 reward to anyone who could identify the person who had leaked the report to National Public Radio. For her part, Nina Totenberg, the NPR reporter who first received the story, argued that she was simply doing her job and had performed a valuable service by bringing to the public's attention an important issue that the Senate planned to ignore. She was not about to compromise the confidentiality of her source. The *Washington Times* entered the foray by naming Senator Paul Simon as the source of the leak, a claim Simon refuted as irresponsible journalism.

Journalism historians added context to the scandal, pointing out that news leaks frequently perform a valuable function in our democracy. The leaking of the Pentagon Papers provided Americans with a more accurate picture of the Vietnam War. The leaks associated with Watergate and the Iran-Contra scandal helped expose serious political corruption.

However, the highly personal nature of the Hill-Thomas hearings set this incident apart from the others. Certainly, it matters a great deal if a potential Supreme Court justice is guilty of sexual harassment or perjury. But how much does it matter if he watches pornographic movies? Or if he boasts about his sexual prowess? Where should the line be drawn between what is relevant information and what is truly a private affair? To some observers, the testimony given before the Senate Judiciary Committee offered up details seemingly provided for entertainment rather than enlightenment. President Bush condemned the nationally televised hearings for becoming "more like a burlesque show than a civics class."

A few critics argued that the press did not go nearly far enough into the personal lives of these "instant celebrities," particularly in the case of Clarence Thomas. Judge Thomas indignantly refused to answer many questions about his private life and his personal beliefs, claiming that such matters were irrelevant for determining his fitness to serve as a justice of the Supreme Court. Those questions remain unanswered.

In an effort to remain "objective," the press might have been too cautious, failing to fulfill its investigative role as an advocate for the public. In *The Mass Media: Opposing Viewpoints,* Jack Newfield makes an interesting point about some of the pitfalls of this sort of Aristotelian objectivity:

> The point is not to equate objectivity with truth. It was objective to quote Joe McCarthy during the 1950s; it was the truth to report that most of what he had to say was unfounded slander. . . . The goal for all journalists should be to come as close to complex truth as humanly possible. But the truth does not always reside exactly in the middle. Truth is not the square root of two balanced quotes. I don't believe I should be "objective" about racism, or the tax loopholes for the rich. . . . Certain facts are not morally neutral.

13.7

Press coverage of the Hill-Thomas controversy often came in the form of "he said/she said" quotes.

In the search for the "truth" during the Hill-Thomas controversy, the news media often did little more than pit quote against quote (see 13.7). Was this *responsible* journalism?

Whether or not the press acted responsibly in covering the Hill-Thomas controversy, one thing is certain. In the wake of the Senate hearings, some Americans probably felt that they knew more about the private lives of Anita Hill and Clarence Thomas than they knew about members of their own families. Ironically—though not unexpectedly—Clarence Thomas was sworn in as the 106th justice of the Supreme Court on October 23, 1991, in a ceremony that was *not* announced to the press.

Even as the tide of press coverage receded, scriptwriters began to work the Hill-Thomas controversy into a number of television programs. Only weeks after they concluded, the hearings were the subject of such situation comedies as "Designing Women" and "Murphy Brown," spear-heading a new trend that television crtitics dubbed "situation commentary."

Of course, politicians, celebrities, and other national figures are not the only persons affected by "invasions of privacy." There are many other urgent issues involving privacy and the press that touch on the lives of average citizens. When, if ever, should the names of rape victims or AIDS patients be published? When are the details of a person's physical or psychological health newsworthy? For what reasons and by what means should a person's sexual orientation be revealed? What ethical guidelines ought to cover the use of secret videotaping or audiotaping? As is the case with so many ethical issues involving the media, there is no shortage of questions, only a shortage of answers.

Perhaps the very concept of "privacy" needs to be reevaluated. Our mothers might have warned us against it, but in the age of mass communication — through books, radio, and television — we "talk to strangers" every day. And they talk to us. Marshall McLuhan and Quentin Fiore, writing some 25 years ago, observed that the processes of modern mass communication have forever blurred the distinction between "private" and "public" knowledge. "In an electronic information environment," they wrote, ". . . too many people know too much about each other. . . . We have become irrevocably involved with, and responsible for, each other." Is this new level of "mediated involvement" a negative or a positive development? McLuhan and Fiore had no concrete answer to offer. Do you?

Questionable Content: Sex, Violence, and Stereotypes

The combination of sex and mass communication has always been an explosive one. On February 13, 1886, the latest issue of *Electrical World* carried a small news item on "The Dangers of Wired Love." The wires involved were telegraph wires and the love was sparked between two telegraphers, a married railroad employee and a young woman who worked in her father's store. This unique relationship blossomed, thanks to modern technology, and caused quite a scandal. Eventually, the young woman had to go so far as to have her own father arrested when, upon hearing of the "wired love affair," he became so enraged that he threatened to physically harm her. Commenting on this story, communication historian Carolyn Marvin points to "its sensational distrust of new media, its fears of women using technology, and other typical themes, such as the fear that new media would destroy the family group." These fears are with us still.

From an audience perspective, many issues in media ethics center on content that is perceived as somehow questionable or even dangerous, usually because it deals with sex, violence, or stereotyping. These dilemmas are not limited to the news media but most frequently involve fiction and fantasy, media content primarily intended for entertainment purposes. Comic books, romance novels, blockbuster movies, popular music, and situation comedies have all been the objects of intense ethical scrutiny.

Do violent movies and television programs contribute to real-life violence? A number of anecdotal stories suggest as much, but social scientists have no definitive answers to this question. The same is true for questions surrounding the impact of pornography. Heated debates rage on, but there is little scientific evidence to reliably prove that pornography has any harmful effects on those who enjoy it. And those who enjoy pornography, of course, often claim it has certain undeniable benefits.

Because we are uncertain about the effects of sex or violence in the media, however, we are hardly absolved from probing the ethical issues involved in either creating or consuming such content. In fact, the lack of definitive media research only underscores the need for media ethics. Since we are often uncertain about the precise effects the mass media may have on our lives, we ought to at least explore and explain what effects we hope they might or should have. In the face of incomplete or contradictory *facts,* we can still work at developing reasonable and rational *opinions.*

We can take strong ethical stands on many issues without having to prove, for example, that violence on television causes real-life harm or that pornographic magazines encourage rape. After all, ethical questions are frequently concerned with intangible beliefs and values that are not easily examined through the methods of science. Yet it is still imperative that we keep in mind the distinction between what we *know* the media do and what we *believe* the media should or ought to do as responsible forces for social good.

Too often, arguments over questionable media content draw on dubious "research" claims to bolster one side or another in the debate. It is one thing to claim that pornographic magazines and X-rated videotapes are morally offensive, an argument that can be reasonably supported on ethical grounds. It is quite another thing to argue, as did the report of the 1986 Meese Commission on Pornography, that there is a causal link between violent pornography and violence toward women. There is simply insufficient research to either prove or disprove such a claim. Misrepresenting the results of mass media research seriously undermines the process of moral reasoning that is fundamental to the search for mass media ethics.

In addition to moral clashes over sex and violence, the use of stereotyping remains one of the most hotly and consistently contested issues in mass media ethics. Stereotypes of ethnic and national minorities (for example, African Americans, Arabs, and Native Americans), the elderly, the disabled, women, sexual minorities (gays, lesbians, and bisexuals), and even certain professions and religions, have been variously debated.

There is ample evidence that we rely on stereotypes to help us make sense of a fantastically compex world. The media, which are also in the business of sense-making, frequently use stereotypes as easily recognizable and readily understood dramatic conventions. The problem, of course, is that stereotyping in the media can lead to prejudice in the real world, frequently with dire consequences. At the very least, some stereotypes — presented over and over again in films, television programs, novels, and popular songs — do little to reduce real-life bigotry and ignorance.

Certainly, mediated images of African Americans have, until very recently, been restricted to a few, very unflattering stereotypes. Native Americans, Asians, and Hispanics are routinely ignored or negatively stereotyped. Women have fared little better, though the women's movement has made a number of notable gains in achieving more diverse representation. The physically disabled and the elderly have also raised their voices against media images that portray them as helpless and pathetic victims of circumstance. Gays and lesbians are frequently excluded from the media altogether — a form of defamation by omission — and must fight for simple inclusion as well as fairer and broader representation. In each of these cases, we can see a history of degrading media stereotypes that has largely gone unchecked and unbalanced, a situation that can hardly be defended in light of the unjust treatment these groups continue to experience in real life.

Media ethicist Louis Day points out that it is particularly "when we make inaccurate judgments about others on the basis of these mental images that ethical questions arise to confront our prejudices." He sees the fundamental dilemma in these terms:

> Ethical issues arise when the employment of media stereotypes becomes so pronounced as to dull the audience's critical faculties in making value judgments concerning individual members of society. In a pluralistic culture such as ours, media practitioners have an obligation to consider the fundamen-

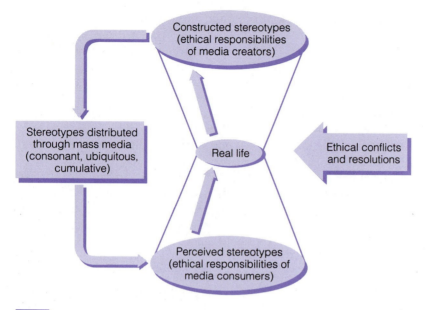

Constructed stereotypes
(ethical responsibilities
of media creators)

Stereotypes distributed
through mass media
(consonant, ubiquitous,
cumulative)

Real life

Ethical conflicts
and resolutions

Perceived stereotypes
(ethical responsibilities of
media consumers)

13.8

Here, the cone effect is used to represent stereotyping. Note that different sorts of ethical issues arise at various stages of the mass communication process, but all ethical conflicts must ultimately be resolved where the effects of stereotypes are felt — in real life.

tal fairness of a system that has traditionally projected stereotypical images of certain segments of society.

Once again, we can refer to the cone effect model to help us begin to sort out some of the ethical issues associated with stereotyping (see Chapter 1 and 13.8). In this version of the model, we can see that stereotypes are drawn from real life; there is usually a kernel of truth in even the most exaggerated portrayals. Media professionals — such as producers, actors, scriptwriters, and network censors — need to examine what sorts of stereotypes they are creating. What aspects of real life do they choose to exaggerate? What processes of selection are involved, and who is making these decisions? Who is consulted in this process? Are representatives from groups that might be offended or hurt by a stereotype asked for their input? These and other questions ought to be asked by responsible distributors of mediated reality.

A number of unique ethical problems arise when stereotypes pass through a mass medium, particularly when the same sorts of images are distributed again and again. This process — known as *cumulation* — means that the strength of some stereotypes builds up over time, through repeated use. For example, a single stereotype of a slovenly Russian woman or a murderous lesbian might not seem to pose a serious problem. But, when such an image appears in many films and television programs and has been used frequently in the past, significant ethical questions must be answered by those who would choose to use such stereotypes again. Indeed, the problem becomes especially acute when these similar — or *consonant* — images are delivered through many different media sources. Moreover, these various sources have the capacity to deliver irresponsible stereotypes to a vast audience, because the mass media are indeed *ubiquitous* — they are everywhere. In short, the ethical consequences associated with stereotypical content are made more acute by the unique form of the mass media.

The ethical dilemmas associated with stereotyping do not end when an image passes through a mass medium. In many ways, the problems have just begun. Consumers of media content apply stereotypes—in different ways—to their own, real-life experiences. This is unavoidable. What can be avoided, however, is the thoughtless use of stereotypes to fuel real-life bigotry and prejudice.

As consumers of mediated reality, we must be willing to check stereotypes against experiences in the real world. We need to be ever-mindful of the fact that mediated reality is *not* real life but a careful distortion—an exaggerated, "blown-up," and larger-than-life version of reality. Media consumers need to be especially vigilant when their own experiences in regard to a particular group of people have been relatively limited.

For example, many Americans have had very limited contact with Iraqi citizens; most of what we know about Iraqis is derived through the mass media. In such instances, there is always a greater danger of indiscriminately incorporating these mediated realities directly into our real lives. The result is that we behave as if we know what Iraqi citizens are like when, in fact, we can know for certain only what the media say Iraqis are like.

It is, ultimately, in our real lives that ethical conflicts must be resolved. It is the responsibility of both media creators and media consumers to continuously monitor stereotypes as they endlessly flow through the mass communication process.

The Media Menace: Children, Youth, and Mass Communication

On the evening of September 25, 1991, the majority of American teenagers viewing television had *SEX* on their minds. More specifically, 53% of teens viewing TV that night had

"Doogie Howser, M.D." ad from *TV Guide*.

tuned in to the season premiere of "Doogie Howser, M.D.," to see 18-year-old whiz kid "Doogie" lose his virginity. Advertisements for the episode announced: "Tonight, Doogie and Wanda say goodbye . . . to each other *and* to virginity." Needless to say, the show raised a few eyebrows. The ethical questions surrounding mediated sex become especially urgent and passionate whenever children are involved.

In "television years," Doogie Howser is something of a late bloomer. Over a decade ago, 16-year-old James Hunter, a character played by actor Lance Kerwin, lost his virginity on a controversial series aptly titled "James at 16." Currently, many of the young characters who inhabit "Beverly Hills, 90210" are sexually active. Sexuality, condoms, abortion, AIDS—each of these subjects has come up on "90210," the most-watched television program among young viewers during the series' second season. Such a program is a far cry from "The Brady Bunch," one of many televison shows that—not so long ago—featured a cast of children who never did anything more daring than develop a crush on the "groovy" boy or girl next door.

Concerns about children's media habits seem perennial, transferring from one medium to another as each new technology emerges. In the *Republic*, Plato asked: "Then shall we simply allow our children to listen to any story anyone happens to make up, and so receive into their minds ideas often the very opposite of those we shall think they ought to have when they are grown up?" Centuries later, the question continues to be asked.

Gabriel Tarde, a noted 19th-century French criminologist, blamed newspapers for the rise in juvenile delinquency in his country. In 1898 he wrote: "It is the trashy and malicious press, scandal mongering, riddled with court cases, that awaits the student when he leaves school. The little newspaper, supplementing the little drink, alcoholizes the heart." Thirty years after Tarde made this complaint, film would replace the newspaper as the greatest menace of all time.

Film was among the first of the "new" media to appeal to a unique mass audience of children. By 1929, an estimated 28 million American youth were going to the movies on a weekly basis. In the 1930s, not unexpectedly, worried parents and policy-makers turned their attention to this popular medium. "What do children learn," they asked, "while sitting for hours in darkened movie theaters?" In his book *Our Movie Made Children*, published in 1934, Henry Forman thought he had some answers.

Forman interviewed a number of "juvenile delinquents" in an effort to see if the popular movies of the day had contributed to these young lives of crime. His conclusion: "The road to delinquency, in a few words, is heavily dotted with movie addicts."

Forman's conclusion is tainted by the fact that his research stood upon the shakiest of scientific grounds. He seemed to look only for evidence that would support his conclusion, and his sample was hardly representative of American youth in general. Nonetheless, his studies give us some insight into the popular ethical concerns of his era, concerns that are *still* quite evident today. Forman reports this observation, made by one of the delinquent girls he interviewed:

> The most responsible thing for getting me in trouble is these love pictures. When I saw a love picture at night, and I had to go home alone, I would try and flirt with some man on the corner. If it was the right kind of a bad man he would take me to a dance or wild party; at these parties I would meet other men that would be crazy for fast life.

Another response, from a 14-year-old girl, is typical of the sorts of "facts" that Forman uncovered: "After I see a romantic love scene . . . I feel as though I couldn't have just one fellow to love me, but I would like about five."

Two decades after Henry Forman published his research, American parents were alerted to yet another media menace in what has come to be known as the "Great Comic Book Scare." The scare was largely the doing of one man, psychiatrist Frederic Wertham, and his widely read book, *Seduction of the Innocent*, published in 1954. Among a host of consequences, Wertham believed that homosexuality, crime, and suicide were the result of too much comic book reading. In particular, he argued that the graphic violence depicted in popular "crime story" comic books of the day desensitized children to real-life violence. Heavy comic book readers, claimed Wertham, were more likely to harm others and themselves. Wertham's data suggested that these youth had lost the ability to distinguish mediated reality from real life.

As with many of the claims made about the influence of movies, Wertham's notions about the effects of comic books do not stand up under serious scientific scrutiny. Nonetheless, he captured the public's imagination and obviously struck a resonant chord with many parents who were baffled by their children's preoccupation with comic books. Under pressure from the U.S. Senate, the comic book industry responded with a stringent code of ethics designed to appease parental fears about comic book immorality. Portions of this code are included here in 13.9.

The Comics Code remains in effect today. Two revisions were added in 1971, restricting depictions of drug use and goverment corruption. Only books that meet the Code's standards can display the Comics Code seal on their covers.

Considered one of the most restrictive media codes in existence, the Comics Code has always been controversial. Critics contend that the code has stifled the growth of the comic form. Code defenders claim that these guidelines protect impressionable young minds and guard over the welfare of an easily manipulated readership.

Concerns over the impact of mass media on the moral development of children continue unabated to the present day. Currently, popular music seems to have taken center stage in this arena. Many of the same concerns connected with movies and comic books are now being raised in connection with pop music. In the 1950s, parents frowned on the gyrating hips of Elvis Presley. In the 1990s, they might be taken aback by the spectacle of an all-female rock group singing about masturbation, which The Divinyls did — with great success — in their hit song:

> I don't want anybody else.
> When I think about you,
> I touch myself.
> I touch myself.

According to a *Rolling Stone* magazine poll, 48% of the once-radical 60s generation now believe that rock music is a "bad influence" on American youth. Much of the current criticism is directed at rap music. The March 19, 1990, edition of *Newsweek* featured a cover story on this "rap rage," declaring: "Yo! Street rhyme has gone big time. But are these sounds out of bounds?" The subject even entered the 1992 presidential elections, when Democratic candidate Bill Clinton attacked the "pro-violence" and "racist" lyrics of rap singer Sister Souljah.

Songs about sexuality — as well as violence, drugs, and the occult — continue to provoke passionate and widespread condemnation from various segments of society. Some of these attacks appear rather extreme, if not ridiculous. Claims about "back-masked" or subliminal messages in rock music remain unsubstantiated. Yet, however unfounded these fears might be, angry citizens routinely burn rock records that they believe contain harmful, hidden messages — messages usually associated with devil worship and the occult (see 13.10).

A somewhat more rational response to the questionable content of rock songs has come from the Parents' Music Resource Center. The PMRC has proposed a labeling code, not unlike the current movie ratings system. A number of record companies now put labels on albums, cassettes, and CDs that contain music deemed "offensive" by the PMRC — music that parents might not want to find in the hands of their children (see Chapter 7).

Of course, many critics — children and teenagers among them — are unhappy with the Aristotelian (or golden mean) approach of the PMRC. Leon Miletich, a former disc jockey, sees little value in labeling music:

> It becomes obvious that if you really want to shield kids from sex and violence — from life itself — *everything* better have a warning label on it. And if music is going to be blamed for anti-social behavior, you'd better ban the Bible too. On August 22, 1986, an 18-year-old Miami high-school student named Alejandro Martinez stabbed his grandmother to death. He told police she interrupted him while he was reading the Bible and he thought she was the devil. For the well-being of the world's grand-

Code of the Comics Magazine Association of America

Code for Editorial Matter

Institutions. In general, recognizable national, social, political, cultural, ethnic and racial groups, religious institutions, and law enforcement authorities will be portrayed in a positive light. These include the government on the national, state, and municipal levels, including all of its numerous departments, agencies, and services; law enforcement agencies such as the state and municipal police, and other actual law enforcement agencies such as the FBI, the Secret Service, the CIA, etc.; the military, both United States and foreign; known religious organizations; ethnic advancement agencies; foreign leaders and representatives of other governments and national groups; and social groups identifiable by lifestyle, such as homosexuals, the economically disadvantaged, the economically privileged, the homeless, senior citizens, minors, etc.

Socially responsible attitudes will be favorably depicted and reinforced. Socially inappropriate, irresponsible, or illegal behavior will be shown to be specific actions of a specific individual or group of individuals, and not meant to reflect the routine activity of any general group of real persons.

If, for dramatic purposes, it is necessary to portray such a group of individuals in a negative manner, the name of the group and its individual members will be fictitious, and its activities will not be clearly identifiable with the routine activities of any real group.

Stereotyped images and activities will not be used to degrade specific national, ethnic, cultural, or socioeconomic groups.

Language. The language in a comic book will be appropriate for a mass audience that includes children. Good grammar and spelling will be encouraged. Publishers will exercise good taste and a responsible attitude as to the use of language in their comics. Obscene and profane words, symbols, and gestures are prohibited.

References to physical handicaps, illnesses, ethnic backgrounds, sexual preferences, religious beliefs, and race, when presented in a derogatory manner for dramatic purposes, will be shown to be unacceptable.

Violence. Violent actions or scenes are acceptable within the context of a comic book story when dramatically appropriate. Violent behavior will not be shown as acceptable. If it is presented in a realistic manner, care should be taken to present the natural repercussions of such actions. Publishers should avoid excessive levels of violence, excessively graphic depictions of violence, and excessive bloodshed or gore. Publishers will not present detailed information instructing readers how to engage in imitable violent actions.

Characterizations. Character portrayals will be carefully crafted and show sensitivity to national, ethnic, religious, sexual, political, and socio-economic orientations. If it is dramatically appropriate for one character to demean another because of his or her sex, ethnicity, religion, sexual preference, political orientation, socio-economic status, or disabilities, the demeaning words or actions will be clearly shown to be wrong or ignorant in the course of the story. Stories depicting characters subject to physical, mental, or emotional problems or with economic disadvantages should never assign ultimate responsibility for these conditions to the character themselves. Heroes should be role models and should reflect the prevailing social attitudes.

Substance Abuse. Healthy, wholesome lifestyles will be presented as desirable. However, the use and abuse of controlled substances, legal and illicit, are facts of modern existence, and may be portrayed when dramatically appropriate.

The consumption of alcohol, narcotics, pharmaceuticals, and tobacco will not be depicted in a glamourous way. When the line between the normal, responsible consumptions of legal substances and the abuse of these substances is crossed, the distinction will be made clear and the adverse consequences of such abuse will be noted.

Substance abuse is defined as the use of illicit drugs and the self-destructive use of such products as tobacco (including chewing tobacco), alcohol, prescription drugs, over-the-counter drugs, etc.

Use of dangerous substances both legal and illegal should be shown with restraint as necessary to the context of the story. However, storylines should not be detailed to the point of serving as instruction manuals for substance abuse. In each story, the abuser will be shown to pay the physical, mental, and/or social penalty for his or her abuse.

Crime. While crimes and criminals may be portrayed for dramatic purposes, crimes will never be presented in such a way as to inspire readers with a desire to imitate them nor will criminals be portrayed in such a manner as to inspire readers to emulate them. Stories will not present unique imitable techniques or methods of committing crimes.

Attire and Sexuality. Costumes in a comic book will be considered to be acceptable if they fall within the scope of contemporary styles and fashions.

Scenes and dialogue involving adult relationships will be presented with good taste, sensitivity, and in a manner which will be considered acceptable by a mass audience. Primary human sexual characteristics will never be shown. Graphic sexual activity will never be depicted.

---

mothers, better prohibit sales of that book to minors.

In the ongoing debate over children and the mass media, there are endless anecdotes that can be called up to "prove" almost any point, a fact that Miletich's satirical tone betrays. In 1973, for instance, a group of youngsters in Florida poured lighter fluid on sleeping homeless people, set them on fire, and laughed as their victims screamed; the children had apparently copied the hideous crime from a TV movie that aired 3 weeks earlier. In an even more famous case, another Miami

Administrative Procedure. I. All comics which member publishers wish to bear the Comics Code Seal will be submitted to the Code administrator for review prior to publication. The administrator will review them according to the guidance he has received from the permanent committee and will either approve them to bear the seal, or return them to the publisher with his comments. The responsible editor from the publisher will either revise the comic in accordance with those comments, or discuss with the administrator the concerns raised with him and reach agreement on how the comic can properly bear the Code Seal either without being revised or with a mutually-agreeable set of alternative revisions. In the event no agreement can be reached between the editor and the administrator, the matter will be referred to the permanent committee, which will act promptly to determine if, or under what conditions, the comic in question can bear the Code Seal. Decisions of the permanent committee will be binding on the publishers, who agree not to place the Code Seal on any comic on which it is not authorized.

II. The members of the Comics Magazine Association of America include publishers who elect to publish comics that are not intended to bear the Code Seal, and that therefore need not go through the approval process described above. Among the comics in this category may be titles intended for adult readers. Member publishers hereby affirm that we will distribute these publications only through those distribution channels in which it is possible to notify retailers and distributors of their content, and thus help the publications reach their intended audiences. The member publishers agree to refrain from distributing these publications through those distribution channels that, like the traditional newsstand, are serviced by individuals who are unaware of the content of specific publications before placing them on display.

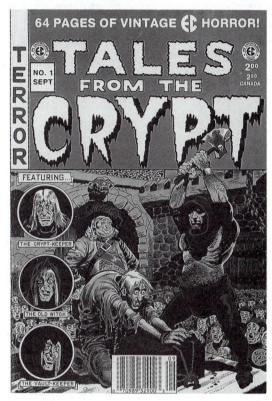

Though one of my favorites, this comic book does not carry the Comics Code seal of approval. Any ideas why?

III. Recognizing that no document can address all the complex issues and concerns that face our changing society, the member publishers have established a permanent committee composed of the senior editor of each member's staff. This committee will meet regularly to review those issues and concerns as they affect our publications, and to meet with and guide the administrator of the Comics Code, and will replace the previous written guidelines of the Comics Code.

Code for Advertising Matter

1   Liquor and tobacco advertising is not acceptable.

2   Advertisement of sex or sex instruction books is unacceptable.

3   The sale of picture postcards, "pin-ups," "art studies," or any other reproduction of nude or semi-nude figures is prohibited.

4   Advertising for the sale of knives, concealable weapons, or realistic gun facsimilies is prohibited. . . .

teen — Ronald Zamora — stabbed a grandmother in 1977 and blamed it all on "television intoxication." Television, Zamora's lawyer argued, had "narcoticized" his client.

In many of these cases — from Tarde's condemnation of the newspaper that "alcoholizes" the young heart to Zamora's indictment of television, the menace that "narcoticizes" — responsibility for some unwanted effect is shifted fully to the media. However, honest and rigorous ethical analysis requires that we also consider the responsibility of other agents — parents, school systems, religious leaders, politicians, and of course, the children themselves.

BLOOM COUNTY

by Berke Breathed

13.10

"Bloom County" by Berke Breathed. © 1982, Washington Post Writers Group. Reprinted with permission.

Issues and Answers: Talking Back, Taking Sides

Ethical analysis ultimately leads to the question of *personal* responsibility. Whether you think that television corrupts or enhances young lives or that pop music is a force for good or for evil, you should be willing to examine the reasoning behind your beliefs with an open and questioning mind. Once you have probed your own beliefs and evaluated the positions of others, you should then be willing to take upon yourself the personal responsibility of acting on your convictions.

Though moral convictions are often deeply personal, you'll find that many other people share in your vision of what's right and wrong with the media. Various *media advocacy groups* devote considerable energy to monitoring ethical issues in mass communication.

One well-known advocacy group, Action for Children's Television (ACT), lobbied for decades to promote better programming for young television viewers. Claiming that her group had achieved all it had set out to, founder Peggy Charren disbanded ACT in 1992. The National Black Media Coalition and the National Asian American Telecommunications Association continue to work for more responsible media images of ethnic minorities. Other national organizations, such as the Parent-Teacher Association, monitor violence in the media.

Some groups, like the New Mexico-based Society for the Eradication of Television, believe that the mass media are essentially unredeemable and advocate a "just say no" approach. Anti-television activism has been popularized in a number of books. Among the more widely read are Jerry Mander's *Four Arguments for the Elimination of Television* and Marie Winn's *The Plug-In Drug*.

A number of advocacy groups not only must confront the media but also are often at odds with other organizations working toward very different goals. For instance, the efforts of the Gay and Lesbian Alliance Against Defamation (GLAAD) are pitted directly against those of the ultra-conservative American Family Association. Likewise, Planned Parenthood's efforts to have pro-choice themes represented on television often come up against the National Right to Life Committee's desire to battle, in the words of NRLC president John Willke, "spineless politicians, misled judges, radical feminists, and especially the arrogant members of the national media who have relentlessly promoted the horrible nightmare of abortion in America." As noted previously, People for the American Way and Accuracy In Media have also been longtime combatants, especially over the complicated issue of censorship (see 13.11).

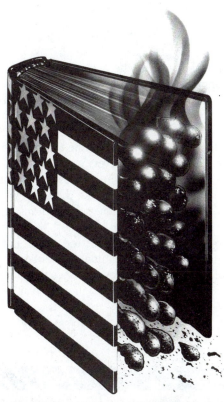

CENSORSHIP IN A FREE SOCIETY: IT'S A BAD MATCH

Censorship is the greatest tragedy in American literature. It constricts the mind, teaches fear and leaves only ignorance and ashes. A political movement today wants to eliminate all forms of expression that don't conform to their narrow views. So all over the country, books are being banned, burned and censored. Teachers, students, librarians and book and magazine publishers are being harassed. The attacks of these self-appointed censors are endorsed by our silence. The freedom to read is one of our most precious rights. Do something to protect it. Call People For the American Way's special **artsave** hotline to report an incident of censorship or to lend your support in the battle for free expression.
Call
artsave
A project of People For the American Way
1-800-743-6768

PEOPLE FOR THE AMERICAN WAY
Defending Constitutional Liberties

13.11

Founded by TV producer Norman Lear, People for the American Way is one of many media advocacy groups that put theory into practice in the ongoing struggles over mass media ethics.

Most cities host a number of different media advocacy groups. Often, national organizations will have local chapters around the country. These organizations represent an excellent opportunity for you to use your knowledge of the mass media in working for social change. Media advocacy groups are one means for acting on your personal media ethics.

For those of you who intend to become media professionals, of course, there will be opportunities to work for change from the "inside." But whether or not you work in the mass media industry, you will continue to be a consumer of the media for the rest of your life. Inasmuch as the influence of the mass media cannot be ignored, neither can we ignore our moral responsibilities. As citizens of Mediamerica — and inhabitants of a Mediaworld — it is imperative that we all strive to become more "response able."

We might find it difficult. There are many more issues than there are answers. But the task of exploring mass media ethics is vital. The stakes are high.

As he accepted the Nobel Peace Prize in 1986, Elie Wiesel admonished his audience to take a stand on the moral issues that confront us: "Take sides. Neutrality helps the oppressor, never the victim. Silence encourages the tormentor, never the tormented."

Whatever your personal ethical convictions might be, it is important that you act on them and make them known. It is important that you *take sides* and *talk back* to the media, accepting Marshall McLuhan's challenge to "kick them in the guts." The alternative is a surely formidable silence. For ultimately it is only our own silence that allows the mass media to be used in unethical, and even harmful, ways.

Queries and Concepts

1 Using the SAD formula, analyze a current issue involving mass media ethics. Your situation should involve an event that took place this year. Share your decision with others. Do they tend to agree or disagree with your assessment?

2 Conduct an informal survey of five people, asking them to define the term *ethics*. Compare and contrast the answers you get. Can you develop one definition of ethics with which each of your five respondents agrees?

3 Create a media ethics case, using "The Case of the Mayor's Diary" as your model. Your case can involve any controversy you choose. Be imaginative, but ground your case in realistic concerns. Don't forget to explain how your controversy might be resolved using each of the five theories of ethics outlined in this chapter.

4 In general, do you think that codes of ethics encourage media responsibility or do they hinder free expression?

5 You've just been hired to work in the Standards and Practices Department at NBC. Your first task is to devise a list of five items that you think constitute inappropriate content for your network's prime-time programming schedule. In other words, what would you censor? Defend your selections. If you decide that nothing should be censored, defend that position.

6 Reread the provisions of the Advertising Code of American Business included in this chapter. Can you think of specific advertisements that seem to violate any of these provisions? Explain.

7 Using the cone effect model as a guide, analyze an experience you have had that

involved stereotyping in the media. Be precise, and limit your analysis to a specific example found in one mass medium (for example, you might examine the depiction of women in a particular comic strip, or a gay character in a film, and so on).

8 Look over the provisions of the Comics Code. With which, if any, do you agree? Disagree?

9 Who is in the best position to determine what music is acceptable for adolescents: parents, the courts, communication researchers, advocacy groups (like the PMRC), Congress, the music industry, or teens themselves?

10 Write a letter to a newspaper or a radio or TV station in your community, offering a compliment or complaint about something you found either ethical or unethical. Be specific. For example, rather than complain that "there's too much violence on this TV station!", indicate a specific incident that you found objectionable. Are you satisfied with the response you receive?

11 Prepare a brief report on an existing media advocacy group that interests you (and if you are not a member, consider joining). As an alternative, describe a media advocacy group that *could* be organized to address issues that concern you. Provide a concrete plan for starting such a group in your college or city (and, if you're motivated, do it!).

Readings and References

Donald F. Ungurait
Thomas W. Bohn
Ray Eldon Hiebert, eds.
Media Now. New York: Longman, 1985.

This anthology contains a number of contributions on "Ethics and Responsibility of the Mass Media." Howard Polskin's article, "Reporters' Dilemma: Save a Life or Get the Story," examines the case of WHMA-TV and the man who set himself on fire.

Defining Media Ethics

Karen Joy Greenberg
Conversations on Communication Ethics. Norwood, N.J.: Ablex, 1991.

A range of viewpoints are presented in these "conversations," which are primarily concerned with the formal study of ethics from a communication perspective. The role of ethics is examined in institutional, mass-mediated, and intercultural contexts. A history of communication ethics is included.

Richard L. Johannesen
Ethics in Human Communication. 2d ed. Prospect Heights, Ill.: Waveland Press, 1983.

Though not exclusively concerned with media ethics, this book offers a broad introduction to ethics at all levels of communication. Many basic issues are covered; specific subjects include sexist language, advertising, formal codes of ethics, and truth. Useful bibliography.

Ethical Theories and Moral Reasoning

Clifford Christians
Kimberly B. Rotzoll
Mark Fackler
Media Ethics: Cases and Moral Reasoning. 3d ed. New York: Longman, 1991.

A thoughtful collection of cases, covering a wide range of urgent and provocative issues. The authors offer a concise introduction to major ethical theories, then provide dozens of cases for putting theory into practice.

Louis A. Day
Ethics in Media Communications: Cases and Controversies. Belmont, Calif.: Wadsworth, 1991.

Should Santa Claus be used as a PR tool? When should a newspaper publish the names of people with AIDS? Should nudity be shown on television? These and many more questions are explored in this excellent introductory text, which includes chapters on the foundations and principles of ethics, plenty of relevant and interesting cases, and a number of codes of ethics. Good bibliography. Recommended.

"Sports, Ethics and Ideas." *The Quill*, Jan. 1987, p. 2.

Media Self-Regulation: Codes and Censors

Donna Woolfolk Cross
Mediaspeak. New York: Mentor/New American Library, 1983.

A provocative, engaging examination of television and some of the ethical abuses associated with the medium. Cross challenges the censors.

L. J. Davis
"Looser, Yes, But Still the Deans of Discipline." *Channels*, July/Aug. 1987, pp. 10–11.

A look at the work of the network censors. Davis includes a listing of some "television taboos."

Conrad C. Fink
Media Ethics: In the Newsroom and Beyond. New York: McGraw-Hill, 1988.

This introduction to the ethics of mass communication focuses on journalism and issues confronting the press.

Herb Kaplan
"I Didn't Think of It That Way: On Teaching Ethics in Broadcasting Curricula." *Feedback*, vol. 31, no. 4, Fall 1990, pp. 14–18.

William L. Rivers
Cleve Mathews
Ethics for the Media. Englewood Cliffs, N.J.: Prentice-Hall, 1983.

Not one of the best books on media ethics, this text is still useful for its inclusion of a number of professional codes of ethics.

Enduring Issues and Persistent Questions

Neal Bernards
Thomas Modl, eds.
The Mass Media: Opposing Viewpoints. St. Paul, Minn.: Greenhaven Press, 1988.

This handy little book covers a lot of territory. Excerpts present the differing positions of dozens of authors through a point-counterpoint approach. The issues debated include: press responsibility, bias, press freedom, advertising, the impact of the mass media, and more.

Kath Davies
Julienne Dickey
Teresa Stratford, eds.
Out of Focus: Writings on Women and the Media. London: The Women's Press, 1987.

Dozens of (very) brief articles that cover a lot of ground: age, race, class, disability, sexuality, violence, romance, health, work. The final section deals with practical options: how to organize, complain, and work for better media. For some interesting perspectives on issues surrounding men and the media, see Steve Craig, ed., *Men, Masculinity, and the Media* (Newbury Park, Calif.: Sage, 1992).

Everette E. Dennis
John C. Merrill
Media Debates: Issues in Mass Communication. New York: Longman, 1991.

The authors examine 18 enduring issues in mass media ethics. Major arguments are briefly presented in a pro and con debate format. Each debate set includes research and bibliographic resources, chosen with the beginning student in mind.

Henry Forman
Our Movie Made Children. New York: Macmillan, 1934.

"Geraldo Rivera: Bloodied, but Unbowed." *Broadcasting*, Dec. 19, 1988, pp. 43–45.

Tom Goldstein
The News at Any Cost: How Journalists Compromise Their Ethics to Shape the News. New York: Simon & Schuster, 1985.

A controversial, close-up examination of the techniques and attitudes of working reporters. Includes chapters on such topics as "lost credibility," when journalists *become* the story, and reporters who use deceit to get the story. Much to think about.

Craig McLaughlin
"Project Censored." *The San Francisco Bay Guardian*, May 24, 1989, pp. 15–18.

Philip Patterson
Lee Wilkins
Media Ethics: Issues and Cases. Dubuque, Iowa: Wm. C. Brown, 1991.

E. Barrett Prettyman, Jr.
Lisa A. Hook
"The Control of Media-Related Imitative Violence." *Federal Communications Law Journal*, vol. 38, no. 3, Jan. 1987.

A quick review of a number of important lawsuits brought against various media organizations, including the case of Ronald Zamora.

Stephen A. Smith, ed.
Free Speech Yearbook. Vol. 26. Carbondale: Southern Illinois University Press, 1987.

In particular, see these essays: "Why Superheroes Never Bleed: The Effects of Self-Censorship on the Comic Book Industry," by J. P. Williams (pp. 60–69); "Media Intrusion and Evolving Legal Standards of Privacy," by Mary Hart (pp. 117–124); "How and Why Social Science Research Can Inform the Pornography Debate," by R. Brian Attig (pp. 125–134).

Michelle Wolf
Alfred P. Kielwasser, eds.
Gay People, Sex and the Media. New York: Haworth Press, 1991.

This unique anthology examines issues surrounding mediated representations of sexuality and sexual identity. Topics covered include AIDS, adolescent sexual socialization, pop music, stereotyping, free speech, and more. Extensive bibliography.

The *Journal of Mass Media Ethics* is an outstanding source for scholarly, topical, and substantive essays; for a sample issue, write to Lawrence Erlbaum Associates, 365 Broadway, Hillsdale, NJ 07642. Current topics in media ethics (especially journalism) are routinely covered by the *Columbia Journalism Review*, *The Quill*, and the *Washington Journalism Review*.

Issues and Answers: Talking Back, Taking Sides

Kathryn C. Montgomery
Target: Prime Time—Advocacy Groups and the Struggle Over Entertainment Television. New York: Oxford University Press, 1989.

A readable, highly recommended history of advocacy groups—their origins, strategies, and impact. For information about existing advocacy groups, you might check the *Encyclopedia of Associations* in your library reference room.

George Orwell
1984. New York: Signet/New American Library, 1983.

Perhaps the most powerful case study in media ethics ever written. Orwell's classic book examines the ultimate consequences that can eventuate when silence is the only response to media and government abuses. This "1984 commemorative edition" includes a preface by Walter Cronkite.

Joseph Turow
"Pressure Groups and Television Entertainment: A Framework for Analysis." In W. D. Rowland, Jr., and B. Watkins, eds., *Interpreting Television,* pp. 142–162. Beverly Hills, Calif.: Sage, 1984.

Popular Culture and Mass Communication

Popular culture is a constant classroom in which education can take place virtually 18 hours a day. The trick is to make passing the time of our lives, of entertainment, into an educational exercise.

Ray B. Browne

opular culture is "the stuff of everyday life." Thus there was popular culture in ancient Greece, during the Renaissance, and so on. Most of it was local and regional in nature. However, with the coming of mass communication technology, more and more of contemporary popular culture has become national and global in nature. Popular culture, or *mass culture,* is best defined as those everyday things that we all share through mass media and industrial technology. By definition, that which is mass produced (and successful) is "popular," thus becoming part of the popular arts and popular culture.

Some examples of popular culture at work involve the icons and artifacts of our society:

McDonald's golden arches, the Kodak camera, the Coke bottle, and the T-shirt. In addition there are many globally successful films and television programs. These things are produced for and utilized by ordinary people all over the world.

Popular culture is so pervasive that it is almost invisible. Marshall McLuhan (see 14.1) contended that all environments are invisible, and he used the fairy tale of the emperor's new clothes to illustrate that we see only what we are conditioned to see. All the well-conditioned subjects saw the emperor's new clothes; it took the unconditioned child to exclaim, "But he has nothing on at all!" One instructor likes to begin his mass media course each semester by

Who Was Marshall McLuhan?

Herbert Marshall McLuhan (1911–1980) was the director of the University of Toronto's Center for Culture and Technology. Although he received his Ph.D. in English, he concentrated on developing a group of theories about the impact of electronic media.

McLuhan was the most controversial figure in mass communication and popular culture. Shunning traditional research methods, he liked to tell his critics: "I don't pretend to understand all my stuff—after all, I'm very difficult!"

Empirical researchers seem most upset by his complete lack of proof to back countless assertions. McLuhan offered a theory, gave one or two brief examples, and then went on to the next theory. He seldom cited serious academic research or offered footnotes. To those who criticized this technique, McLuhan responded, "I don't explain, I explore."

His argument that it is how (form), not what (content), a medium communicates that matters seems to defy common sense. He maintained that watching television actually requires more involvement than reading a book and that it is the amateur, not the professional, who can best solve complex technical problems in everything from physics to marketing.

In person, he delivered lectures in an offhand and matter-of-fact way, as if everyone could see the obvious logic of his argument. (If you saw Woody Allen's film *Annie Hall,* then you caught a glimpse of McLuhan in action.) His books are hard to read, because he jumps from one thought to another with very little connection. When criticized for his writing style, he simply maintained that it used what he called "interface," or the placing side by side of two things that seem unrelated until you look more closely.

Though he was accused of favoring electronic media over print, McLuhan spent most of his time reading and said he watched very little television. He was called everything from the "electronic guru" to "that nutty professor from Canada." When he died in 1980, we lost the most original media observer in recent memory. A synopsis of "The Gospel According to McLuhan":

History: 600 Years of Linear Thought

Since Gutenberg, people have been trained to believe that all "real" truth and knowledge are in books and printed material. This belief has perpetuated the fallacy of linear thought. We live our lives the way we read, knowing it is the "correct way."

We discuss one topic at a time, take things and teach things in "logical" sequence: You have to walk before you run, you have to crawl before you walk! McLuhan says walking may come first, or running may come first. "There is absolutely no inevitability as long as there is a willingness to contemplate what is happening."

What: The Medium Is the Message/Massage

The medium is the *message* because our technological and social progress has always been affected more by the nature of what we communicate *with* than by individual messages contained in the communication.

The medium is the *massage* because it prods us thousands of times each day. We are virtual prisoners of an infinite array of unrelenting media form and content. These media have a profound effect on the way we think and behave toward one another.

The Media and Technologies: Human Extensions

The media, like other technological innovations, have been designed by us to extend the functions of the body and brain. The radio is an extension of the ear, just as the wheel is an extension of the foot, and the computer an extension of the central nervous system. Radio and television have catapulted music to a mass emotional experience unprecedented in the history of art.

Where: The Global Village

Early people clustered in small villages for convenience and self-protection. Enter industrial progress and the population explosion. Tribes grew bigger and bigger, jobs became more specialized, and a change in identity developed. Rivalries became more acute. People were now grouped in cities, towns, and nations. Print encouraged factions to develop, because it failed to perceive the whole. Now air travel and the electronic media are shrinking the world back to tribal size, and tribalization is encouraged by the demise of print. Hence we are becoming once again a village, but this time a global village. Such upheavals do not come easily. According to Alfred North Whitehead, "The major advances in civilization are processes that all but wreck the societies in which they occur."

How: Collide-o-Scope

The electronic media tend to break down the social and ethnic barriers between people by familiarizing everyone with everyone. Information is instantaneous. The poor see the rich, blacks see whites, and with increased awareness comes increasing unrest. The electronic media are both the enemy of ignorance and factors in social havoc. Then they *amplify* that

Photo © by Harry Benson, 1976.

havoc through instant news coverage. They bring together divergent ideas, views, and ethics in a collide-o-scope of change.

When: Instantaneous Communication and Information

The electronic media make possible instant communication worldwide. Technology provides instant access to all but a few forms of private communication. Their privacy violated and their most cherished patterns threatened, generations raised without these electronic media are bombarded with them in later stages of life

when they are less able to accept rapid change. This fact (plus the H-bomb, a technological extension of the club!) has created a unique fissure between the postwar generation and its elders.

Who: We Are "Them"!

It becomes increasingly absurd to talk about protecting "us" from "them." The global village is running out of elbow room. Pollution, radiation, global warming, and other related problems are of concern to all of us. We are "them." We are the children of the global village. We are the tribal members of humanity.

writing on the blackboard, "The fish will be the last creature on earth to discover water." Mass communication and popular culture are so much a part of our everyday life that we have to step back from participating in order to see them. Think of this chapter as your invitation to do just that.

Another way to define popular culture is by what it *isn't*. It isn't *elite* culture. Our elite culture, which comes primarily from the Western or European tradition, is anything deemed worthy of study and included in the traditional curricula of colleges and universities: art, history, medicine, law, philosophy, and science.

Popular-culture enthusiasts find that confining academic study to these pursuits alone denies the rich diversity of America's many cultural sources and ignores the present in favor of the past. According to Ray B. Browne and Arthur G. Neal:

> The center of the culture they [traditional academicians] wish to promote consists of white, male, Eurocentric, middle class values. In their view, racial and ethnic minorities are, and will continue to be, seriously disadvantaged unless they internalize this core culture of ideas, concepts and factual information.

By way of contrast, popular culture is not what we study but what we *live*. Popular culture represents a common denominator, something that cuts across most economic, social, and educational barriers.

In America, Rembrandt represents elite culture, but Leroy Nieman's sports paintings are popular culture. Chamber music is elite, but rap is popular. The study of law may be considered elite, but "L.A. Law" is popular culture.

At the center of the difference between elite and popular culture is our cultural definition of what constitutes "art." The Balinese, for example, have no word for *art*; they say that they simply do everything as well as they can. For

Television's "L.A. Law" represents our collective vision of the legal profession. Such occurrences are common in the context of Mediamerica's popular culture.

the Balinese there is little difference between popular and elite culture.

Writer/editor Tad Friend argues that mass culture is an art form all its own and that the so-called entertainment media supply us with far more than mere entertainment. Writing in *The New Republic* he points out that

> to be genuinely entertaining you have to appeal to the audience's common humanity — yes — to include rather than exclude, to interest by a considered appeal to intelligence. . . . Art, all art, should disclose not secrets to the few but treasures to the many.

Some advocates of elite culture argue that the masses would be better off if they became "cultured." But the masses are already steeped in culture — mass culture. Although it is fair to say that today's elite culture may very well color the popular culture of tomorrow, much of the mass culture of today will be the elite culture of the future.

Shakespeare, whose plays are now considered the epitome of elite culture, supplied sex and violence to the masses of his day. Charles Dickens is now considered a "classic" writer, and his works are often read and analyzed in traditional English literature classes. Yet he was the most "popular" writer of his time. Who knows? Someday "Star Trek" may become elite culture; it can be argued that "Star Trek" provides much the same sort of material to the masses today that Shakespeare and Dickens did in their era, and for many of the same "commercial" reasons.

Mass culture is largely uncharted as far as academic study is concerned. We have been studying the elite for so long that we have ignored the culture we all have in common. But this is changing, and popular culture is becoming, at last, an object of serious study at some universities.

Bowling Green State University in Ohio, which boasts the nation's leading department of popular culture, has close to 1,000 students discovering the social significance of such things as Volkswagens, comic books, science fiction, sports, film theory, women in literature, and more. According to department head Ray B. Browne: "Popular culture is a very important segment of our society. The contemporary scene is holding us up to ourselves to see; it can tell us who we are, what we are, and why."

Of course, popular culture is an even newer academic discipline than communication. As a result, there is a great deal of debate about exactly what it is and whether it's an academic discipline at all. In this respect, it's developing like such disciplines as psychology, sociology, journalism, and business administration, all of which had to earn their way into acceptance during the first half of the 20th century.

In academe, the study of popular culture draws on many disciplines, including American studies, sociology, psychology, anthropology, and communication. But it is with communication that it seems most at home, for mass culture has become the consequence of mass communication: Print, radio, film, and television are today's channels of popular culture.

The Link Between Mass Media and Popular Culture

Before Gutenberg, the artist survived through subsidies from the wealthy classes. This is how we derived the term *patron of the arts*. Novelists, poets, and painters would dedicate and/or deliver their work to those who could afford to support them.

With the rise of mass literacy came a new kind of patron and a change in the relationship between patron and artist. Artists were at the beck and call of not one patron but thousands. The newly literate consumer had tastes that were noticeably different from those of the wealthy elite. If the artist were to profit, these tastes had to be satisfied — hence the arrival of the "commercial," or popular, artist and the popular arts.

Print was the first medium to offer a palette for the commercial artist; eventually film, radio, and television followed. These newer mass media have been almost exclusively given over to the popular arts. Electronic media are in the business of attracting an audience; this means catering to public tastes. The popular artist, now as always, calculates the wants and needs of the mass audience, creates a work in response to those needs, then delivers it to millions of patrons through mass media channels. What's more, it is done very quickly. The 15th-century writer may have taken years to complete a book. The modern mystery novelist may take only a few weeks. Some TV scripts are written in even less time. Popular art is art in a hurry.

Researchers have long debated whether the mass media create popular culture or simply act as a mirror reflecting popular tastes and values. Actually, TV and all mass media probably *refract* reality. The mediated reality we see on the TV screen, for example, is similar to real life, yet distorted. It is America as filtered through the eyes and minds of producers, directors, and scriptwriters. It "imitates" life while creating a separate reality for the mass audience. Those who disdain popular culture believe this distortion may be harmful.

Yet it can be argued that the often simplistic world of mass media may offer consumers a buffer between themselves and the complexities of modern life. Further study could reveal that one function of mass media in our time has been to ease the transition from the relatively simple life styles of a few decades ago to the accelerated and stress-filled life styles of today and tomorrow. If TV is partly responsible for what author Alvin Toffler dubbed "future shock," it may also provide a temporary cure. To know for sure, we must put popular culture under the microscope of serious academic investigation.

Accomplishing this can be a formidable task. According to Ray B. Browne,

> the sticking point will be in getting interested people in all levels of education to accept popular culture as a worthwhile and effective tool in teaching instead of as a distracting and weakening diversion. . . . The popular culture around us is well known. . . . Therefore we should use it as an educational device in promoting literacy and love of education and learning.

Some research examining popular culture in this context has been done (see Chapter 16),

and much remains to be done. But everyone agrees that an important link exists between mass media and popular culture. If the mass media do not actually create popular art and popular culture, they certainly help make it conspicuous and available. People who favor elite art may believe (with some justification) that they are drowning in a sea of popular culture, promoted and perpetuated by the mass media. In any event, popular culture is so much a part of our mass communication system that distinctions between mass media and popular culture have become increasingly blurred.

Icons and Artifacts

Of the numerous ways to examine the impact of popular culture, one of the most useful and interesting involves examining icons and artifacts. Icons are special symbols that tend to be idolized in a particular culture. Artifacts are products of a culture that receive less attention.

To understand the importance of icons, we need to try to imagine a world without words. For the cave-dwelling family, communication was a system of grunts and gestures. Cave dwellers drew pictures of animals and of themselves, leaving them for future generations. Early tribal civilizations lived in a world of symbols, just as we do today. But their symbols were *visual*, more direct than the written word.

In a sense, words take us away from all that is direct and create a complex and confusing system of communication. Inside all of us, there is a cave dweller yearning to be free. So we develop a devotion to *things,* visual two- or three-dimensional objects.

Religion and politics have always made use of icons: the crucifix, the St. Christopher medal, the Union Jack, the swastika. Icons have become an especially visible part of our lives since our "retribalization" by television. TV has reintroduced us to thinking in pictures. So, like the cave dwellers, we are beginning to rely more on visual and three-dimensional objects for communication and as symbols of worth.

Among the more treasured icons is the automobile. Our cars have always been more than just a way to get from one place to another. They reflect and communicate our values, hopes, and dreams. Are you the practical, no-nonsense driver of a Honda? Or perhaps the proud owner of a sporty gas-guzzling Corvette? Whatever the case, you have developed a personal and emotional commitment to the car of your choice.

"Diamonds are a girl's best friend," while "clothes make the man." Even a book can be an icon, appreciated more for form than for content. Have you ever been to a house full of tasteful leather-bound books that have never been opened? The television is an icon of paramount importance. Likewise, the stereo can be a status symbol. Portable CD players have become a very personal expression of this phenomenon.

But one does not need to be wealthy to have a hoard of personal icons. In *Icons of America,* pop-cultural analyst Marshall Fishwick points out:

> Even the poorest among us has his private icon bank. We make deposits there regularly, and withdraw more than we know. Just as we tuck away special treasures (notes, emblems, photos, medals) in the corners of drawers, so do we tuck away iconic images in the corners of our mind. We draw interest from our deposits. Icons have a way of funding us, sustaining whatever sense and form our lives assume. When we can no longer draw from an icon bank, we quickly go bankrupt.

Michael Jackson's internationally recognized image, used here to sell Pepsi Cola, was one of popular culture's most enduring until the superstar was accused of child molesting.

So it would seem that our icons are essential to our emotional well-being. They are with us now more than ever, encouraged by mass advertising.

A thousand years from now, archaeologists will measure the worth of our culture from the objects we have left behind. As with the cultures of old, the objects most likely to remain are icons. Cultural artifacts disappear because they are thrown away. We may keep the special wine bottle and throw away the cork. We keep our books but throw away our magazines. An icon is forever.

But what about our artifacts? Andy Warhol's painting of a Campbell's tomato soup can and Claes Oldenburg's pop depiction of a hamburger serve to remind us that it is the everyday things in our consumer society that make up our lives. It is as if the artists are saying, "For better or worse, this is *your* art; these are the objects you have chosen." So even our artifacts can be icons if they have a special symbolic meaning for us. The Coke bottle (did you see *The Gods Must Be Crazy*?) is perhaps

God and the Super Bowl

Marshall Fishwick, professor of humanities at Virginia Polytechnic Institute in Blacksburg, is one of the best-known scholars in the field of popular culture. He is a past president of the Popular Culture Association and has written more than a dozen books on American history and popular culture.

An Episcopal bishop recently commented that he was tiring of the NFL — it was too High Church. He gave this version of the Lord's Prayer:

> *Our football, which art on*
> *television*
> *Hallowed be thy game.*
> *Thy fullback run, thy pass*
> *be flung*
> *In Miami as it is in Dallas.*
> *Give us this day our four*
> *quarters*

> *And forgive our trips to the*
> *bathroom*
> *As we forgive our fumblers.*
> *And lead us not into*
> *conversation,*
> *But deliver us from off-*
> *sides;*
> *For this is the power and*
> *the popular culture*
> *Forever and ever. Amen.*

The Super Bowl provides the basis not only for recreation but for religion as well. This application of the word *religion* offends because our way of regarding religion as an institution prevents us from seeing the "sacred" or sacrosanct in everyday life. We *want* religion locked into a pietistic Sunday morning service, and we mold our language accordingly. Look at the faces of people listening to Easter sermons on the church's Super Sunday (Easter), and compare them

with faces watching football's Super Sunday. Where is there more involvement?

Several years ago in Colorado (where the Denver Broncos roam), a fan attempted suicide by shooting himself in the head on the day after the Broncos fumbled seven times against the Chicago Bears.

"I have been a Broncos fan since they got organized," he wrote in his suicide note. "I can't stand their fumbling anymore."

He fumbled, too — the bullet did not reach a vital spot. Otherwise it would have been a classic example of blood sacrifice demanded by a merciless God.

Traditional rituals were attuned to the seasons; throughout central North America, say anthropologists, they took the form of war games between

the best-known American icon; its shape — and its meaning (things go better with Coke!) — are recognized in every corner of the globe.

The Events of Popular Culture

Each year on a Sunday in January, 100 million Americans sit down in front of their television sets and spend a few hours watching a small army of uniformed men carry a pigskin ball up and down a hundred yards of real or artificial grass. The event is the Super Bowl, and the teams are the winners of the National and American Conferences of the National Football League. To decide which team is "the best," a one-game playoff is held.

The Super Bowl, the World Series, and other mass-communicated sporting events are a vital part of our culture, reflecting its priorities and values. As with all popular culture, careful study yields clues about the sociological and psychological games we play in everyday life (see the guest essay by Marshall Fishwick).

tribes. How has this come down to our times? As battles between rival teams, with incantations, cheerleaders, and fans (short for *fanatics*) to urge armed (at least padded) warriors forward.

This "friendly game" is a minutely observed and monitored battle between aggressive male teams, who use cunning, deceit, and violence to attain their ends. Does this sound like a corporation or bureaucracy? Is the Bowl merely a mirror image of life out there?

And what about up there? Teams both play and pray to win. Former head coach George Allen of the Washington Redskins insisted on locker room prayers. The Miami Dolphins have a public pregame prayer. "How touching a scene," reports Colman McCarthy of the *Washington Post*. "Giant men, bruised and

asweat, kneeling to acknowledge that however almighty their win may have been, there is still another Almighty, the Divine Coach." In such a scene the true meaning of popular culture can be found—if only we know how to find it.

Super Sunday dawns. Ten times ten thousand go to the Bowl itself. Millions more witness the events on television screens, "against the beautiful skyline." The destiny-laden pregame coin flip (the coin, incidentally, is worth $4,000) sets the scene. Players come onto the field, amidst acclamations louder than any heard outside ancient Jerusalem's walls. They run, collide, bruise, bash. Now for the halftime festivities. Ten lines of young people march forth, precise as pistons in a well-tuned engine . . . females in yellow or orange, males in blue, white teeth shining as

they sing, "It's a Good Time to Know Your Neighbor." Four priest warriors dance on the drumhead/godhead. Now the hundred thousand worshipers are on their feet, tears in their eyes, singing:

> *America, America,*
> *God shed his grace on*
> *thee. . . .*
> *Amen.*

The Cult in Popular Culture

Webster's New World Dictionary defines *cult* as "devoted attachment to, or extravagant admiration for, a person, principle, etc., especially when regarded as a fad." In most cases, mass media play an important role in bringing about popular cults.

Cults may form around political candidates or other opinion leaders who strike a responsive chord among a segment of the population.

When thousands of long-haired, brightly clad hippies descended on San Francisco in the summer of 1967, they had a number of political and social beliefs in common, many dealing with questions of religion. That movement, fanned by mass media coverage, can be justifiably labeled a cult.

It is not surprising that cults, like most other aspects of popular culture, often involve mass media in some way. Certainly the ritualistic tribal gatherings at rock concerts to hear the Grateful Dead, Michael Jackson, U2, Madonna, or even the New Kids on the Block are cultlike. In the eyes of the devoted, these figures can do no wrong. Thus the New Kids survived their "lip-sync" scandal. In the presence of their favorite artists, followers find a symbolic or mythic truth.

A tremendous cult sprang up around *Star Wars, The Empire Strikes Back,* and *Return of the Jedi.* Some devotees claimed to have seen the movies hundreds of times. Box office figures indicated that a large number of people saw them more than once. Similar responses have been cited in connection with a wide range of films, including *Woodstock, This Is Spinal Tap, Blue Velvet,* and especially *The Rocky Horror Picture Show.* Likewise, some television programs, such as "The Brady Bunch" and the original "Twilight Zone," can best be described as "cult classics."

One of the most widespread cults to center on a television program is that of the Trekkies, fanatic devotees of the "Star Trek" series. Trekkies come in all ages, though most are 15–35 years old. Each year thousands of them gather at conventions ("cons") held in various major cities. Here they view "Star Trek" episodes they have seen countless times before. Exhibitors are there selling everything from plastic Spock ears to metal phaser guns.

Trekkies do not sit passively and observe. Many dress up in the costumes of their favorite heroes and heroines: Captain Kirk, Mr. Spock, Klingons, robots, even tribbles, the round, faceless, furry creatures featured in an early episode. Similar devotion can now be observed in connection with "Star Trek: The Next Generation."

Participants swap stories about their favorite episodes and trade trivia questions. Several years ago I participated in an academic panel at a Los Angeles con. There were half a dozen of us who had taught seminars on "Star Trek" or used it as a jumping-off point for analyses of TV's influence in society. I thought I was quite an expert, having read every available book and even talked with the late Gene Roddenberry, the series' creator and producer. I quickly

discovered I was among the most poorly informed at the con! These people had spent hours every day for years learning every detail. At a moment's notice they could tell you who starred in a given episode, what it was about, and even describe the last scene before the first commercial! More recently, the life of the Star Trek phenomenon has been prolonged by the success of a series of films documenting the continuing adventures of the crew of the *Enterprise* and "Star Trek: The Next Generation." To the delight of trekkies, the wide-screen versions and the new series drop obscure references to their favorite old TV episodes.

Examining Popular Culture

One of the reasons for including popular culture in a book about mass media is to interest you in the global consequences of mass communication. I have found that my students are willing to spend more time investigating history and current issues if they can link them up to the real world around them.

For too long we have ignored popular culture in favor of a more traditional elite approach. Mass media and popular culture are important because you *live* them every day. You wake up to popular culture in the morning and fall asleep with it each night.

You should also wake up to things around you. What you find in textbooks (including this one) may not be much help. You need to examine your own life style, icons, artifacts, television-viewing habits, favorite singers, and favorite foods in order to understand yourself and your relationships with others.

Because you *live* popular culture, you may not think it is important. Nothing could be further from the truth. This may indeed be something you need to do on your own, but it is critical. When Socrates said, "The unexamined life is not worth living," he could hardly have envisioned our vast electronic environment full of instant gratification and information. If he were here today, he might add, "The unexamined environment is not worth living *in*."

In a society clamoring for a "back to basics" approach to education, we should never forget what Ray B. Browne has so eloquently pointed out: "Popular culture has never left the basics — it *is* the basics, the fundamentals, the everyday and indeed it should be so used. . . . Properly presented the entertainment of life is an unending source of knowledge and training."

Queries and Concepts

1 Make a list of your five favorite books or films. Which would be considered popular culture and which elite? Why? Do any of these books or films have qualities of both elite and popular culture? Explain.

2 Develop a time line that covers the past 500 years of world history, divided up into five 100-year-long segments. For each century, list one example of popular culture and one example of elite culture from that period. (If anything elite later becomes popular or vice versa, you can list the same item twice on the time line.)

3 Investigate your backpack and dresser drawers to find your own icons. Why are you saving them? Write a paragraph about two or three of these icons, explaining their significance. (If you can't justify saving them, throw them away!)

4 The Super Bowl is not the only event of popular culture that takes on spiritual overtones. Can you think of others?

5 Can you think of several popular cults not mentioned in this chapter? Are you a member of any organization, formal or informal, that could be considered a cult?

6 Visit a newsstand or bookstore and look for magazines that have cultlike qualities, such as those written for professional-wrestling fans, thrashers (skateboard enthusiasts), soap-opera viewers, and the like. Buy an issue that particularly interests you, and prepare a brief report on what the magazine reveals about this popular-culture phenomenon.

7 Which group is in the best position to investigate and evaluate popular culture: (a) those in elite culture who have "risen above it"; (b) those who experience it firsthand all the time; or (c) Martians coming to Earth for the first time? Choose one and explain why.

8 Reread the last section of this chapter. Do you agree or disagree with Ray Browne's position? Is the study of popular culture one of "the basics"? Explain your position.

9 Does the history department at your college offer any courses that deal with popular culture? Write a brief proposal for an *advanced* course in popular culture that could be taught in the history department. Be specific. Define the subject area and list the books, videos, or other instructional materials that would be used in teaching the course.

10 Pick one of McLuhan's arguments, summarized in 14.1 (pp. 366–367). Defend or refute the argument, using examples of contemporary media or popular culture to make your point.

Ray B. Browne
Arthur G. Neal
"The Many Tongues of Literacy." *Journal of Popular Culture,* Summer 1991, pp. 157–186.

John Fiske
Understanding Popular Culture. Boston: Unwin Hyman, 1989.

A good introduction to a field of study that is now coming into its own. Chapters include: "The Jeaning of America," "Commodities and Culture," "Productive Pleasures," "Offensive Bodies and Carnival Pleasures," "Popular Texts," "Popular Discrimination," and "Politics." Fiske gives special attention to the relationship between popular culture and capitalism.

Tad Friend
"The Case for Middlebrow." *The New Republic,* Mar. 2, 1992, pp. 24–27.

Herbert J. Gans
Popular Culture and High Culture: An Analysis of the Evaluation of Taste. New York: Basic Books, 1977.

In this classic little book, Gans examines the distinctions between popular and elite culture. His notion of "taste publics" is still useful, though his categories must now be reconciled with the emergence of new and seemingly more diverse "publics" as the mass media — and the mass audience — become more specialized.

Marshall McLuhan
The Mechanical Bride: Folklore of Industrial Man. Boston: Beacon Press, 1967.

A complicated adventure through the landscape of popular culture. It's easy to get lost along the way, but the journey is worth taking! McLuhan examines magazine ads, newspaper pages, western movies, comics, and more. Many intriguing illustrations. The book is out of print, so look for it in your library.

The emperor's new clothes analogy is from Marshall McLuhan and Quentin Fiore's *The Medium Is the Massage: An Inventory of Effects* (Westminster, Md.: Random House, 1967). The tale of the fish that has not discovered water is included in another book by McLuhan and Fiore, *War and Peace in the Global Village* (New York: Bantam, 1968).

A "must-read" for all pop-culture analysts is the *Journal of Popular Culture.* A subscription to *JPC* includes membership in the Popular Culture Association. For details, write to Popular Culture Center, Bowling Green State University, Bowling Green, OH 43403.

Popular Culture and Mass Communication

Arthur Asa Berger
Popular Culture Genres: Theories and Texts. Newbury Park, Calif.: Sage, 1992.

The aim of this book (the second volume in Sage's new "Foundations of Popular Culture" series) is to empower the reader to decipher popular culture through the study of various media genres, formulas, and formats. Plenty of examples ("texts") are provided to demonstrate how different sorts of analysis ("theories") can be used. A case study of the classical mystery genre is included. Among the texts examined: *The Maltese Falcon, Frankenstein,* and *War of the Worlds.*

Ray B. Browne
"Popular Culture: Medicine for Illiteracy and Associated Educational Ills. *Journal of Popular Culture,* Winter 1988, pp. 1–15.

Sean Cubitt
Timeshift: On Video Culture. London: Routledge, 1991.

Much of pop culture is really video (or television) culture, and this book explores that culture with both wit and wisdom. The book is described as "a collection of approaches to a protean area of cultural practice, each of them less an essay than . . . a raid." Chapters range from "How Music Became Visible Again" to "My Father Will Heal You With Love." Intrigued? Read on.

Icons and Artifacts

Ray B. Browne
Marshall W. Fishwick
Kevin O. Browne, eds.
Dominant Symbols in Popular Culture. Bowling Green, Ohio: Popular Press, 1990.

A comprehensive collection of essays that examine popular-culture symbols from a range of unique perspectives. Among the symbols explored in this "icon bank" are: the movie theater, cars, fast food, and pink flamingos.

Marshall Fishwick
Ray B. Browne
Icons of America. Bowling Green, Ohio: Popular Press, 1978.

This highly regarded text includes articles on the most talked-about modern icons. A highly recommended anthology.

Tom Tumbusch
Illustrated Radio Premium Catalog and Price Guide, Including Comic Character, Pulp Hero, Cereal, TV, and Other Premiums. Dayton, Ohio: Tomart Publications, 1989.

What really counts is *not* how a cereal tastes but what prize is in the box! These prizes, and other "premiums," now rank among the most amusing, interesting, and collectible artifacts in our culture. This is a catalog of premiums popular from the early 30s to the middle 50s. Nothing analytical here, but worth looking at for its 2,000 illustrations of every imaginable ring, badge, decoder, and other "amazing gadgets." Fun.

The Events of Popular Culture

Ray B. Browne, ed.
Rituals and Ceremonies in Popular Culture. Bowling Green, Ohio: Popular Press, 1981.

The events of popular culture surround us, but do we really know what's happening? That question seems to shape most of the essays in this collection. Many sorts of pop rituals are discussed.

Michael Real
"Super Bowl: Mythic Spectacle." *Journal of Communication,* Winter 1975, pp. 31–43.

The Cult in Popular Culture

Roberta Pearson
William Uricchio, eds.
The Many Lives of the Batman: Critical Approaches to a Superhero and His Media. New York: Routledge, 1991.

The Batman cult is but one of many cults in popular culture, though it is one of my personal favorites (next to "Star Trek," of course). Essays in this fascinating book focus on a variety of topics, from the nature of Batman's following to the economics of cult heroes. All relevant media are covered: film, television, comic books.

Susan Sackett
Letters to Star Trek. New York: Ballantine Books, 1977.

The author traces the early history of the "Trekkie" saga (the preferred term now, of course, is "Trekker"). One of the better books about the original television series is Stephen E. Whitfield and Gene Roddenberry's *The Making of Star Trek* (New York: Ballantine Books, 1973).

There are numerous books written by, for, and about virtually every popular cult in the United States, from *The Rocky Horror Picture*

Show to "The Brady Bunch." Check your local bookstore for recent examples. Other good sources are the numerous "fanzines," magazines devoted to various pop-cult phenomena—professional wrestling, heavy metal, thrashers, teen sex idols, UFO sightings . . . whatever the subject, there's probably a magazine for the fan or fanatic. These books and magazines can offer fascinating insights into the inner workings of popular cults.

Examining Popular Culture

Ray B. Browne, ed.
Forbidden Fruits: Taboos and Tabooism in Culture. Bowling Green, Ohio: Popular Press, 1984.

Popular culture often challenges the values of the dominant, elite culture. However, even in popular culture, some things are "taboo." Essays in this book examine a variety of taboos and the logic (or illogic) behind them. A number of important cultural taboos are left out of this collection, but the book is still an excellent place to start exploring the subject.

Barry Brummett
Rhetorical Dimensions of Popular Culture. Tuscaloosa: University of Alabama Press, 1991.

The author argues that traditional ways of studying elite culture do not always work when we are examining popular culture. To that end, he presents his own theory for deciphering the rhetoric, or meaning, of various pop-culture manifestations.

Iain Chambers
Popular Culture: The Metropolitan Experience. London: Methuen, 1986.

Chambers is a master at interpreting popular culture, examining the stuff of everyday life and offering a number of surprising insights. This book covers both historical and contemporary themes and gives ample attention to popular music. Excellent reference list.

M. Thomas Inge, ed.
Handbook of American Popular Culture. 3 vols. 2d ed. Westport, Conn.: Greenwood Press, 1989.

A pop encyclopedia, these three volumes offer a good place to start investigating almost every conceivable aspect of pop culture: TV, radio, the occult, graffiti, cartoons, and more. Each of the 55 chapters is written by an expert in the field, and each includes a history of the subject and recommended resources (books, articles, journals).

15

Mediaworld: Mass Communication in the Global Village

I'm inside and I'm outside at the same time

And everything is real . . .

when the world crashes into my living room

Television made me what I am

Television Man

I'm watching everything. . . .

David Byrne/The Talking Heads

Like many Americans, I found myself glued to the television set during December of 1989. The images were startling, to say the least. Thousands of German citizens danced in front of the Berlin Wall. Many of the revelers climbed up and on top of the wall, popping champagne bottles, waving flags and banners, and smiling into the hundreds of television cameras gathered to record this historic event. The granite and steel barrier that had separated East and West Germany was coming down—chipped into souvenir-sized bits, the latest commodities in the pop-culture marketplace (see 15.1).

These images entered my home nightly through sophisticated, international media systems. The events that flashed across my television set traveled along satellite networks that span the globe and link us together in a vast, media membrane. Marshall McLuhan pointed out that these new media links have reshaped the world "in the image of a global village." Just as ancient villagers shared in the day-to-day routines of their neighbors, so we share in the day-to-day triumphs and tragedies that unfold across the globe—thanks to mass communication.

15.1

An East German border guard peers through one of the many holes chipped out of the Berlin Wall. Overnight, the world was drastically changed and, thanks to international media, global villagers everywhere watched these events unfold.

country participating in the Olympics, and I watched that happen as well. The Soviet Union had ceased to exist a few months earlier, and the red "hammer and sickle" flags that usually dominate these international games were gone. So much had changed, so quickly. But Gutenberg would have been proud, I thought, as those modern-day German heroes accepted their Olympic medals in Albertville, France, while I watched it all from my living room in the United States, taking notes for a chapter in a textbook that would, in turn, be read around the world.

The Gutenberg press made mass communication possible. Those first, few pages that the German printer produced in 1456 were much more than reproductions of the Bible. These were the first invitations to a *truly* new world order. Today, I can still read the very words that Gutenberg printed. I can watch the Berlin Wall crumble all over again. I can look in on the Olympic games in France or Spain, or witness the latest upheaval in Russia or Iraq. You can, too. In the age of mass communication, the world has become our back yard. The globe is, indeed, our village.

The Berlin Wall is now gone. But it still exists, too. It exists in photographs, on videotapes, and in chips of stone scattered across the planet. And it exists in my memory, as well. For in some sense, I was "there" when the wall came down. I saw it happen, right along with millions of other global villagers.

As I watched the Berlin Wall come down, I couldn't help but recall a quite different event that took place, also in Germany, almost 600 years earlier. As Johannes Gutenberg slid the first ornate pages off his printing press, he pushed forward a chain of events that would lead, unbroken, to those worldwide broadcasts from Berlin in the winter of 1989.

In the winter of 1992, a new *unified* Germany went on to win more medals than any

International Media Systems

This book has been concerned primarily with the development of mass communication systems within the United States. But every country has developed its own methods for using mass media technology. Pop music, television programs, magazines, and other media flow into and out of the United States every day. The only way to fully understand modern media systems is to place them in an *international* context.

In many ways, media systems are similar throughout the world. Television in the United States looks pretty much like television in Russia. An American magazine and a Japanese magazine look like magazines, even though we read them in different directions. But, of course, *looks* can be deceiving. While they share similar forms, the world's media systems are organized differently from country to country, according to different social, economic, and political customs. Likewise, the content of the mass media varies widely from one nation to the next.

Most countries have not opted for a commercial media system to the extent that the United States has. In fact, many countries severely restrict the kinds of advertising allowed. Some allow no advertising on radio or TV at all.

To give you an idea of how other nations control their mass media, we'll first review four basic theories that have guided the development of mass media systems all over the globe. Then we'll take a look at specific media systems in the United Kingdom, Canada, Mexico, the Netherlands, Japan, and Brazil. We will also review some of the unique issues confronting the nations that comprise the European Community. This "tourist's guide" is but a sampling of the variety and richness of our mediaworld, but hopefully it will stimulate your interest in further exploring some of the lesser-known corners of the global village.

Mass Media and National Governments: Four Theories

In 1956 Fred Siebert, Theodore Peterson, and Wilbur Schramm codified competing notions about international media systems in their classic book, *Four Theories of the Press*. As the book's title suggests, the authors collapsed all of the world's media systems into four general categories that describe each system's organization within various political and ideological contexts. Most simply, these theories describe the sorts of relationships that exist between governments and media in different nations. The four theories they examined were: authoritarian, Communist (or "Soviet"), libertarian, and social responsibility.

Of course, collapsing the world's media systems into these four categories is both restrictive and misleading. Certainly, there are more subtleties than can be accounted for, and many countries have experimented with various combinations of these four theories. Still, most mass media systems can be described as adhering *predominantly* to one of the four theories outlined below.

Authoritarian Theory

What most characterizes mass media systems in authoritarian countries is how fully these media are under the control of the ruling government — a government that is typically dominated by one individual, such as a monarch or dictator. The only press freedoms are those that the nation's ruler will allow, and not surprisingly, there is usually very little freedom in authoritarian systems. Government control of the media can take a variety of forms, including censorship, licensing of media professionals and services, and even threats of imprisonment or physical harm if regulations aren't followed.

Though the government exerts almost absolute control over them, newspapers, broadcast stations, and other media are often privately owned in authoritarian systems. The owners and operators of these media must answer to the national leader, however, so the press routinely serves to bolster the image of the existing government and its policies.

Authoritarian theory has guided the development of many mass media systems throughout the world. The earliest printing press operations were often under the control of a monarch. In 1529, for example, Henry VIII issued a list of books that printers were not allowed to publish. In 1534 the infamous king established the first government licensing system, which required printers to obtain royal permission before they could practice their profession. In spite of these measures, a small "black marketplace" of ideas developed, and a few printers were able to circulate forbidden writings. Much the same situation exists in authoritarian countries today.

Certainly, authoritarian theory runs contrary to the free-press philosophies of the United States and other democratic nations. However, in even the most enlightened countries, strains of authoritarian theory can be found. Book banning, for instance, has been popular in many countries, including the United States (see Chapter 2). While it is easy to identify media abuses in obviously repressive countries, we are sometimes less mindful of authoritarian notions when they are advanced closer to home.

Communist Theory

Communist media theory draws heavily from the philosophy of Karl Marx, especially as practiced in what was once the Soviet Union. In fact, Communist theory is also known as the "Soviet theory" or "Marxist theory" of the press. Essentially, the mass media in Communist systems are owned and operated by the government and, as such, serve to advance the goals of socialism. The mass media might carry advertising as one means of supporting their continued operation, but the goal is never profitability.

In the People's Republic of China, for example, media executives are Communist Party officials. Thus, the mass media are not controlled *by* the government (as in authoritarian systems) but are literally *part of* the government. Ultimately, the media—along with other agencies of the government—aspire to the promotion of Communist ideology. In theory, this system exists to spread the "truth," or at least the truths as revealed in Marxist philosophy. In practice, however, the "facts" are often brushed aside in order to present this "truth," a situation that was vividly demonstrated during the 1989 Tiananmen Square massacre in China.

In the summer of 1989, troops of the People's Liberation Army marched on peaceful demonstrators gathered in Beijing's Tiananmen Square, killing perhaps as many as 5,000 people. Though Western journalists recorded this bloodshed, the Chinese press—as a part of the government—denied that the massacre had taken place at all. Chinese officials declared that news reports carried on television stations outside of China were using technological trickery to make it look as if the army had attacked Chinese citizens. According to the official Chinese media, not one person died in Tiananmen that day. Even now, most of China's 1 billion citizens have received only this official version. This event in the history of international journalism reads like a page from George Orwell's *1984*: "The Party could thrust its hand into the past and say of this or that event, *it never happened*. . . . And if all others accepted the lie which the Party imposed—if all records told the same tale—then the lie passed into history and became truth."

Despite the travesty of Tiananmen, it has become increasingly difficult for Communist nations to exert overt and absolute control over the flow of news and other information in the global village. New technologies—such as fax and photocopy machines, personal computers, and desktop publishing systems—can be mobilized locally and internationally without the cooperation of large government agencies.

During the 1991 coup that attempted to topple Soviet leader Mikhail Gorbachev, Communist hard-liners and the Communist press reported that Gorbachev had taken ill and could no longer carry out his duties as president of the Soviet Union. However, nonofficial news sources, both inside and outside the USSR, told a much different story. Most likely, Gorbachev had been deposed and was being held against his will. The news spread: This was a coup, not a cold. This information traveled throughout the world, instantly. In Moscow small printing presses, photocopiers, and fax machines worked day and night to report developments and call for protests. Through such media channels, Russian leader Boris Yeltsin was able to gather support and crush the attempted coup.

Boris Yeltsin's efforts were boosted by the moral support he received throughout the world, a support communicated to him through makeshift networks of telephone lines, fax machines, and shortwave radios. Artyom Borovik, a Russian journalist who was with Yeltsin during the coup attempt, puts it this way: "The media were our tanks and armored vehicles. When I was talking on the air to Dan Rather, I felt that Rather—and his 15 million viewers—were in the Russian White House (the parliament building) with us. It was a very strange feeling. It made us bigger and stronger."

Today, only the remnants of Communist theory guide media systems in the newly formed Commonwealth of Independent States. Even the once-mighty newspaper *Pravda*, based in Moscow, has undergone a revolutionary transformation (see 15.2). However, communism is not dead. Communist theory still dominates the structure of media systems in Cuba, China, and other Communist and Marxist-oriented nations. In one form or another, Marxist philosophies will continue to guide media developments in both Communist and non-Communist countries.

Libertarian Theory

Of the four press theories, libertarianism is the one most closely associated with the development of the mass media system in the United States. A libertarian philosophy is clearly reflected in the U.S. Constitution, particularly in the Bill of Rights. The foundations of libertarian thought can be found in the writings of British philosophers John Locke and John Stuart Mill, British poet John Milton, and American revolutionary Thomas Jefferson. John Milton's book *Areopagitica,* published in 1644, is considered to be the classic libertarian plea for freedom of the press.

Essentially, libertarian theory advocates the widest possible freedoms for the mass media and rejects any unnecessary government control, particularly censorship. In fact, the media often serve as government watchdogs in libertarian societies. The basic idea behind libertarianism is that the public will be best served by having access to the widest array of information and entertainment. According to this theory, "truth" will always win out in the end, through the competition that takes place in a sort of "free marketplace of ideas." In practice, however, such systems do not enjoy absolute freedom of the press. Certain restrictions—for example, those governing obscenity, libel, and access to the public airwaves—can be found in most libertarian media systems.

Generally, the media are privately owned in libertarian systems. These media are operated as commercial businesses, designed to turn a profit. While each citizen may have the right to use and own such media, that right is actually limited to those who have the means to participate. For example, every adult American has the right to watch MTV or CNN, but only those who can afford cable television or a backyard satellite dish may actually do so.

Some critics have argued that the need to turn a profit greatly determines the content of the mass media in libertarian systems. Thus, the "free marketplace of ideas" may be dominated by messages that promote the interests of a wealthy, elite class of businesspersons. Just as Marxism shapes media content in Communist systems, capitalism structures the output of the media in capitalist nations.

Social Responsibility Theory

In many ways, social responsibility theory attempts to address some of the pitfalls of libertarianism noted above. Many of the mass

Pravda: The Truth in Transformation

Until recently the mass media in Russia and other nations that were once part of the Union of Soviet Socialist Republics were government-owned and operated agencies of the Communist Party. The social policies of Soviet President Mikhail Gorbachev — *glasnost* ("openness") and *perestroika* ("restructuring") — led to a number of press reforms. However, the greatest changes in Russian media arrived after the aborted August 1991 coup that attempted to depose Gorbachev.

For the duration of the 3-day coup, the coup plotters took control of all Soviet media, including one of the nation's most prestigious and popular papers, *Pravda* (the Russian word means "truth"). The 70-year-old newspaper dutifully printed the statements and decrees issued by the Communist leaders who were attempting to overthrow Gorbachev. Editors claim that they had no choice but to do so. Nonetheless, Russian President Boris Yeltsin shut the paper down after the coup failed.

When it next appeared in print, *Pravda* no longer car-

As never before in history, international news services captured the sights and sounds of this century's most dramatic political upheaval. These emotionally charged images — such as the removal of this statue of KGB founder Felix Dzerzhinsky — came to symbolize the collapse of Soviet communism.

ried the customary picture of Vladimir Lenin and the front-page banner declaring allegiance to the Central Committee of the Communist Party. Under Soviet control, *Pravda's* daily circulation topped 10 million (compare that to the circulation of your city's daily paper!). The paper's success within the new Commonwealth of Independent States is less certain.

Currently, *Pravda* operates as an independent newspaper.

Without Communist Party financing, the cost of a single issue has risen more than 50%. A plea made on *Pravda's* front page reflects the enormous changes experienced by many media outlets in the former Soviet Union: "*Pravda* is left practically without any financial support whatsoever. In this critical situation for the newspaper we appeal to our readers: The publication of *Pravda* will depend largely on you yourselves."

---

media systems in the modern world have come under the control of a few, large corporations. The loudest voices are not necessarily the worthiest voices — they are often simply the wealthiest voices. Control and ownership of radio, television, and print media are generally restricted to the "media elite," those who can afford to buy into the system. Libertarian theory does not adequately account for such a situation.

Social responsibility theory recognizes that freedom of the press entails certain responsibilities. That is, those who own and operate the mass media enjoy a special privilege and should honor that privilege by striving to be responsible to society. This responsibility involves a commitment to truthfulness, accuracy, the public welfare, diversity of opinion, and so on. In the United States, the 1947 report of the Hutchins Commission on Freedom of the Press — *A Free and Responsible Press* — has become a classic manifesto for social responsibility theory, even though the report never specifically used the phrase "social responsibility" (see Chapter 4).

According to the theory of social responsibility, the mass media should be allowed to operate with relative freedom and independence, but the government should be ready to step in and curtail any media abuses. Government regulation must ensure media responsibility when self-regulation fails to do so. Ideally, this government supervision should take the form of gentle reminders to the media. Official, stringent regulations are generally avoided, though they are often posed as threats. In response to such threats, many media operations have devised various forms of self-regulation, including codes of ethics. Social responsibility theory underpins most codes of media ethics, such as those examined in Chapter 13.

Of all the media theories, social responsibility is the most recent and is still evolving. Many countries — such as the United Kingdom, the United States, and Canada — appear to be experimenting with combinations of libertarian and social justice theories. Calls for deregulation of the media usually rely on libertarian concepts, whereas pleas for responsible regulation draw from the theory of social responsibility. As national boundaries shift and the relationship among mass media and national governments continues to undergo rapid change in many of the world's nations, we can expect increasing experimentation with existing theories and, perhaps, the development of entirely new mass media systems.

Mediaworld: A Tourist's Guide

The United Kingdom: Media in the Motherland

Our impression of the United Kingdom is largely formed by the popular culture that it exports to us. We think of Big Ben, Charles and Di, "Monty Python's Flying Circus," the Beatles, "The Young Ones," and "Doctor Who." At the same time, people in the United Kingdom think of the Statue of Liberty, "Dallas," Elvis Presley, the Wild West, and Abe Lincoln. Obviously, both impressions are incomplete.

Mass-produced newspapers were available in England as early as 1622. Today the British are voracious readers and support dozens of daily newspapers, ranging from sensational tabloids that print prictures of partially nude women every day to the detailed coverage of the day's events found in the London *Times*.

The British were interested enough in radio to support Italian inventor Marconi's efforts to make the "wireless" a practical communication system. When radio grew to become a consumer-oriented medium in the early 1920s, the British were ready. The British Broadcasting Company (BBC) was formed in 1922 and became a public corporation in 1927. The BBC is independent, financed by a license fee collected from each citizen who owns a television set, as well as government grants. The BBC uses these revenues to build and maintain radio and television stations and to pay for the programming it broadcasts.

Today the BBC has five radio channels, which can be heard throughout the country. Radio 1 and Radio 2 carry popular music. The first, a rough equivalent of the Top 40 format in the United States, plays songs that are selling in the music stores. Radio 2 is more like our album-oriented rock (AOR) stations, playing selected album cuts as well as the hits. These two channels are by far the most popular, and together they account for about four of every five radio listeners. Like their counterparts in the United States, these radio services also offer news, weather, and traffic reports.

Radio 3 airs classical music, drama, and other more elite cultural fare, including discussion programs about philosophical and sociological questions. Radio 4 offers many programs similar to our news and news-talk formats. Especially popular have been the news-magazine shows such as "The World in Focus" and "PM Reports." Public radio stations in the United States and elsewhere carry the popular BBC "World Report." Introduced in 1990, Radio 5 features sports, education, and youth-oriented programming.

The BBC introduced the world's first television service in 1936. Just as in the United States, the development of TV took a back seat to World War II. Regular BBC-TV programming was suspended in 1939 and resumed in 1946. Today the BBC produces many of the programs it airs; others come from independent producers both at home and abroad. BBC-TV programming is world-famous, and its productions are shown in over 100 nations.

In 1954 the government established the Independent Television Authority (ITA), which later became the Independent Broadcasting Authority (IBA) when commercial radio was introduced. Today the Independent Television Commission (ITC) and the Radio Authority are the governing bodies charged with regulating non-BBC stations. Unlike the BBC, these stations are commercial; each is allowed to carry a specified number of commercials each hour. Every independent radio and television station is responsible for its own success or failure and must answer to the appropriate governing body for the quality of its programming.

Independent stations have been quite successful in competition with the BBC, though they do not dominate the airwaves the way the commercial stations in the United States overpower PBS. In fact, it wasn't until 1982 that viewers all over the United Kingdom could receive a second commercial television channel. Four channels are now available to all viewers:

two run by the BBC (BBC 1 and BBC 2) and two independent commercial outlets. In 1990 Parliament authorized a fifth national TV network that is scheduled to premiere in 1994.

The ratings for BBC and independent stations traditionally run neck and neck, and although the British do not place the tremendous emphasis on ratings that we do, a healthy awareness of what most viewers are watching exists. Generally most observers agree that independent competition has been good for the BBC.

On the legal front, a number of serious disputes over press freedom have involved the United Kingdom's Official Secrets Act of 1911. The Act has been used to suppress news that reflects poorly on the ruling government — in short, the Act sanctions political censorship in the United Kingdom.

Despite press restrictions, the British media system has been praised by many in the United States as superior to ours. Perhaps our admiration for the British system comes from the feeling that people there enjoy the best of both worlds by having access to commercial and noncommercial outlets in more or less equal measure. Most everyone agrees that American media outlets can still learn a thing or two from those in the "Motherland."

The Canadian Compromise

Like the United Kingdom, Canada has long had a tradition of quality mass communication. The first Canadian newspapers were printed in 1751. Many of the newspapers have taken their lead from developments in the United Kingdom. At the same time, many magazines and some newspapers have patterned their approach after successful counterparts in the United States. Among the more prominent of the Canadian periodicals are the *Globe & Mail* and *Maclean's* magazine.

Since Newfoundland was chosen as the reception point for Marconi's first transatlantic wireless experiments, Canada has been a leader in establishing radio communication.

Broadcasting is regulated by the Canadian Radio-Television and Telecommunications Commission, an agency of the government somewhat analogous to the FCC. It consists of 5 full-time members and 10 part-time members, whose votes are always taken on crucial issues such as license revocation.

The Canadian Broadcasting Act of 1968 clearly established that the airwaves belong to the public and that licensees "have the responsibility for programs they broadcast, but the right to freedom of expression and the right of persons to receive programs . . . is unquestioned."

The Canadian Broadcasting Corporation (CBC) offers a broadcasting service similar to the United Kingdom's BBC. The CBC offers many news, public affairs, and documentary shows as well as entertainment fare. Unlike its British counterpart, however, the CBC does accept commercials. There is also a CTV television network, the counterpart of the United Kingdom's IBA. These stations are privately owned and are operated for profit.

Of special concern over the years has been competition from nearby media outlets in the United States. Some major U.S. magazines produce a Canadian edition. Most of Canada's population lives near the U.S. border, so competition between U.S. and Canadian broadcast stations has always been lively. The Canadian government restricts Canadian advertising on U.S. stations by limiting the tax deductions Canadian businesses can take on such expenditures. For many years Canadian radio stations were prohibited from playing too many songs by U.S. artists.

Though Canada still receives a relatively large influx of American television programs, a number of U.S. shows are shot on location in Canada. It's simply cheaper. Canada has also produced the world's first mini-series for high-definition television (HDTV), "Chasing Rainbows."

The unique characteristics of the Canadian population create another problem. In order to serve all the people, much of what appears in the print and broadcast media must be duplicated for the French-speaking segment of the population. Most feel that both segments get adequate service, but the issue has heated up as a result of a separatist movement among French-speaking Canadians (particularly in the province of Quebec).

Another concern involves cross-media ownership and monopoly. One report indicated that over half of all daily newspaper circulation is controlled by two large corporations. Just as in the United States, this calls up the question of news manipulation and control and could mean that Canadians are not getting as much diversity in their news as some think they should.

In many ways, the Canadian media system is a compromise between the systems of the United Kingdom and the United States. Canadian broadcast media, especially, seem to be able to maintain the fine tradition of the BBC while bending to some of the economic realities that govern broadcasting in the United States.

The Mexican Challenge: Serving All the People

Since the first newspaper was founded in 1722, Mexico has had a rich tradition of print media. Despite this, the country's literacy rate has consistently lagged behind that of its northern neighbor. Today, however, more Mexican citizens can read than ever before (see 15.3).

The Mexican broadcast system is dominated by the government. Three agencies are involved with radio and television at various levels: the Ministry of Transport and Communications, the Ministry of Internal Affairs, and the Ministry of Education. These agencies oversee the government-operated stations. In addition, all privately owned stations must give up 12.5% of their air time to the government.

Four television channels are loosely affiliated in a federation known as *Televisa*. Each channel is programmed to reach different

15.3

Periodicals have been available in Mexico since 1722. *La Jornada* is a contemporary offering.

segments of the population during various time periods. Mexico is a relatively young country, demographically speaking. Well over 60% of the population is under age 30, and broadcasters must provide adequate programs for this significant audience. Mexican television viewers can find most anything they would find in the United States, including game shows, soap operas, talk shows, and "Plaza Sesamo," a Mexican version of "Sesame Street." In U.S. cities with large Spanish-speaking populations, a number of these shows are broadcast daily.

Mexican television also includes some American, Japanese, and British programs. According to one estimate, 45% of Mexico's TV programming is imported. Programs such as "Hill Street Blues," "Dynasty," and "Falcon Crest" have been very popular in Mexico.

There has been some concern in recent years, however, that certain programs from the United States and elsewhere might be too violent or otherwise unacceptable by Mexican standards. Another concern has been radio stations situated on the U.S.-Mexico border. These stations are licensed by the Mexican government but aim virtually all of their programming and advertising at the more affluent audience to the north.

The Netherlands: Democracy Leads the Way

It has been said that nowhere in the world are people more dependent on print than in the Netherlands. Over 98% of the population is literate, and the Dutch have a large appetite for print, especially books and newspapers. They take their politics seriously, so the newspapers generally take a stand on most issues of the day. Despite their political orientation, however, the Dutch have achieved worldwide recognition for their objectivity.

The interest in politics carries over to the broadcast system, which is a unique experiment in democratic telecommunications. Major social, political, and religious groups can band together to form a *broadcast group* and petition the government for air time. About 70% of all broadcast programming is created by these groups, with the rest used for educational and entertainment purposes. According to the Media Act of 1988, a group must have at least 150,000 dues-paying members to gain regular air time. However, time is also reserved for groups with 60,000 members to help them achieve the 150,000 target required for full participation in this system. Other blocks of time are also reserved specifically for cultural and educational institutions, churches, and political parties. The Netherlands Broadcasting Foundation coordinates all of these services.

Although broadcasting is under the jurisdiction of a government ministry responsible for welfare, health, and culture, no government agency has the right to edit or censor programs aired by participating groups, despite their occasional inflammatory nature. However, some restrictions are placed on the use of obscenities and similarly "objectionable" programming. This open system of broadcasting typifies the rather enlightened social policies of the country.

The first radio station in the Netherlands was on the air in 1919, a year before America's first station (KDKA) went into operation. Until the 1960s, however, no advertising was allowed on Dutch broadcast stations. This absolute prohibition of commercials vexed some commercial interests, and in 1964 one company took the situation in hand by starting a pirate station on an abandoned oil rig 5 miles offshore. After some debate, the police were authorized to close down the station at the end of the year.

Meanwhile, the debate over allowing commercials continued. In *Broadcasting in the Netherlands*, Kees Van der Haak attributes the fall of one ruling coalition government, in part, to the heat of that debate. Finally an on-air Advertising Foundation was created in 1965 and commercials were allowed. They were kept to a minimum, however, with a maximum of 95 minutes a week on television. The figure has since advanced to around 2½ hours a week, still very low by U.S. standards. (An average of four hours of commercials appear each week in the U.S. in prime time alone.) Beginning in 1968 the three radio channels were allowed to carry 26 minutes of advertising each day among them.

In addition to broadcast programming, cable television has experienced great success in the Netherlands. The country is one of the most highly cabled in Europe, with cable penetration now exceeding 70%.

Unlike other programming forms, radio and TV news is produced by an independent group without political or religious affiliations. News shows carry out the print tradition of in-depth reporting and objectivity. Many consider the media system of the Netherlands the best in Europe, if not the world. At the very least, it presents a unique system that the rest of the world should watch with interest.

Made in Japan: Technology and More

Japan's mass communication system is technologically the most highly developed in the world, even though it got off to a relatively late start. The first Japanese newspaper did not appear on a regular basis until 1864, and as late as World War II the Japanese media were considered quaint and rather sluggish by Western standards. Today, however, hundreds of daily newspapers — including a number of national dailies — are printed in Japan. Perhaps the most prestigious of these newspapers is *Asahi Shimbun* ("Rising Sun Newspaper"), which boasts an enormous editorial staff of 3,000 editors and reporters. These journalists undergo tough training and examinations and, once hired, tend to remain with *Asahi* for the duration of their professional lives.

The Japanese are also voracious consumers of magazines. According to one report, the small island-nation produces 2,600 different magazines and that number is growing! Magazines that top Japanese circulation lists include *Shukan Pureiboi* ("Weekly Playboy," a version of the American *Playboy*), *Ie No Hikari* ("Light of the House," a family-oriented monthly), and *Riidaazu Daijesto* (a Japanese version of *Reader's Digest*).

Since the war, the Japanese have developed media technology to the fullest, especially in broadcasting. One need only think of the quality of the electronic products available from such Japanese firms as Sony, Panasonic, and Mitsubishi to get some idea of just how far the country has come in a short time. The vast majority of all video recorders for sale in the United States are made in Japan, and virtually all of the various models were designed there.

Tokyo Broadcasting System

15.4

In Japan about 70 million TV sets are tuned into a variety of noncommercial and commercial program services, including NHK, Nippon Television Network Corporation, and the Tokyo Broadcasting System.

Currently the Japanese are the world leader in fiber-optics applications (see Chapter 17) and have developed some cable and closed-circuit TV systems that put any in the West to shame.

Nippon Hoso Kyokai (NHK), the government broadcast service, has been compared favorably with the BBC. The system is financed by license fees similar to those in the United Kingdom and the Netherlands. The NHK operates two TV channels, one for educational programming and the other for informational and entertainment programming. Thus, the service is able to offer traditional Japanese theater and cultural programs as well as numerous reruns of popular programs from other countries, notably the United States. One NHK program that is seen regularly in the United States is the newscast "Japan Today," which airs daily on many PBS television stations. The NHK also operates three radio networks, with stations tailored to local and regional interests.

Since 1950 the NHK has had to compete with numerous commercial broadcasters, such as the Nippon Television Network Corporation, the largest commercial network in Japan, and the Tokyo Broadcasting System (see 15.4). The result has been an abundance of programs for Japanese citizens. Commercial

television experienced a tremendous boom during the 1958–71 period, mirroring the fantastic growth of the Japanese economy. During this same period, Japan's gross national product went from an annual $25 billion to over $200 billion. More than 100 different broadcast companies are now operating an astounding total of some 6,000 radio and television stations. Japan's success in developing broadcasting has amazed the world.

American visitors to Japan observe that they are right at home with Japanese television stations, which broadcast 24 hours every day in the major cities and offer a number of American programs dubbed in Japanese. A number of Japanese films and television programs have achieved popularity in the United States, as well. Japanese characters as diverse as Godzilla, Ultraman, and Speed Racer have become a part of American culture.

Though government regulations prohibit multiple ownership of local stations, four large stations in Tokyo are major powers in the industry. Cable penetration is relatively low, but developing rapidly. Many VCRs are equipped with a special scanning device that sets the timer to record when the device is waved across bar codes that appear in Japanese TV guides.

With its tremendous edge in electronic hardware, Japan is looking toward the future with optimism. Satellite broadcasting is already a reality, and plans are under way to reach the last few Japanese homes without TV reception utilizing direct broadcast satellite (DBS) technology.

Brazil: Turned On and Tuned In

In 1964 Brazilian President Joao Goulart was booted out of office by the military, which ruled the country for the next two decades. Under military control, mass media systems developed as the country modernized. The military established the Ministry of Communications, the National Department of Telecommunications, the Brazilian Telecommunications Enterprise, and the National Communication Council. These government organizations pushed forward the military's goal of using the mass media to modernize the country. The government expected Brazil's media to support the military's rule and to foster a national identity. As such, the emphasis was placed on domestic media production. Foreign media were eyed with suspicion, and stringent censorship was the norm.

In the 1970s, a new spirit of cultural and intellectual freedom emerged in Brazil, but the emphasis on domestic production remained. Today, Brazil is the home of the most-watched commercial television network in the world, *Rede Globo*. Some 60 to 80 million people tune in each night to view the network's programs, most of which are original offerings. Over 75% of Brazilian households have a television set, and there are more sets in Brazil than in all other Latin American countries combined. Brazil is truly a television nation, "turned on and tuned in."

Telenovelas, or soap operas, are the most popular television programs in Brazil. These shows air six nights a week but, unlike prime-time soaps in the United States, the *telenovelas* have a built-in ending. Much like a very long mini-series, a single *telenovela* lasts about 6 or 7 months and is then replaced by another story.

Cultural anthropologist Conrad Kottak has studied the *telenovela* phenomenon in Brazil. He reports that audience devotion to these programs is so intense that even the arrival of Secretary of State Henry Kissinger once went virtually unnoticed during the broadcast of one *novela's* pivotal episode:

> Kissinger's plane arrived early [at Brasília Airport]. Finding no welcomers, the secretary and his entourage walked into the terminal and discovered the greeting party watching the final chapter of an especially popular *novela*. The murderer, whose

identity people all over the nation had been speculating about for weeks, was about to be revealed.

When such popular episodes are broadcast, they come close to being watched by 100% of Brazilian TV viewers — that's a perfect rating, a fantastic 100 share! As Conrad Kottak notes: "No program in the United States achieves such a share [of the audience] — not *The Cosby Show*, the Super Bowl, a presidential debate, a World Series game, *Roots*, *The Day After*, or the last episode of *M*A*S*H*."

The European Community

Though made up of numerous sovereign nations, Europe is becoming increasingly unified through political, economic, and cultural agreements that have established a common "European Community." This new union has created new possibilities as well as problems for mass media systems — especially telecommunications — in Europe. Jean Cluzel, vice-president of the Senate Committee of France, commented in an issue of *Media Bulletin*:

> One of the major tasks which the parliaments and governments of the European Community will have to undertake is that of creating a "European audiovisual space." Indeed, Europe will become a single, homogeneous, powerful economic and cultural entity only if it can gradually establish a common human outlook, the main channel for which will be audiovisual communication. When that happens, the efforts which are now being made to construct a single Europe . . . will take on their full significance.

Of course, member nations are not in full agreement on how to go about constructing this "common human outlook," and there have been numerous conflicts over issues of media regulation and cultural identity.

Euro-Pop: New Unity in the Old World

Roger Tredre is a journalist with The Independent, *where this essay first appeared in 1992. According to Tredre, cultural unity seems to have outpaced political unity in Europe. While politicians argued over the Maastrict Treaty that will formally unify the 12 nations of the European Community, a common pop culture has already emerged.*

Never mind the politicians feeling their way toward European unity post-Maastrict. For many young Europeans, unity is already a *fait accompli*. The worlds of fashion, music and clubbing are overlapping as never before in Europe. British fashion companies are revising their marketing campaigns to promote a specific European identity. Their model is Emporio Armani, the Italian company with stores in London and Glasgow which last year published an in-store magazine with a strong Euro-flavor.

Research conducted among teenagers in Glasgow by Pepe, the British jeans company, suggests that young people are more open than older generations to the idea of cultural interchange. Chris

European nations contribute to global pop culture through a variety of media. Italy's *Mondo Uomo* magazine is a leading fashion trendsetter, an international arbiter of "Euro-style."

Stephenson, advertising manager, said: "Their horizons are expanding. Teenagers in Glasgow want to recreate the cafe culture of Paris or the paninari style of Milan."

Ironically, a prime medium for the evolution of Euro-style is MTV, the American music video TV channel that was launched in Europe in 1987. Although Anglo-American rock videos still dominate air time, some of the channel's biggest audiences are reported for "120 Minutes," a two-hour survey of new acts, and "The Pulse," a fashion show with a strong European slant. A readers' poll in *Melody Maker,* the popular music publication, listed "120 Minutes" as one of the most influential shows in television.

Of particular concern is "transfrontier television," television programming that is delivered from one nation to many other nations in the European Community. Member nations are seeking a balance between opening up a free and common telecommunications marketplace and preserving national and regional cultures and standards (definitions of "obscenity," for example, vary from country to country). Meanwhile, as in the United States,

While MTV is recognized as the single most powerful youth marketing medium in the United States, the European version of MTV has achieved substantial distribution across Europe: 31.5 million households at the end of 1991, compared with 14 million a year earlier.

Bill Roedy, managing director, said: "18-year-olds in Stockholm have realized that they have more in common with 18-year-olds in Paris than they do with their own parents."

According to a survey of attitudes among the European Community for *Reader's Digest* 1991 Eurodata report, young people under 24 are more confident about the European Community than any other age group: 66 percent of 18- to 24-year-olds are confident, compared to 61 percent of 35- to 49-year-olds.

Simon Silvester, planning director of Burkitt Weinreich Bryant Clients & Company, a British advertising agency that is researching youth attitudes across Europe, said: "You get the feeling that there is a real sense of integration among the young."

But he added that Britain was still lagging behind continental countries. "Young people here (in England) still tend to look to the U.S. before Europe."

Euro-skeptics claim the trend represents a disturbing drift toward a drab cultural homogeneity, but for Euro-enthusiasts, the free-flowing interplay of cultures is a positive sign.

In the world of fashion design, old snobberies are being pushed aside. Every nation can make its mark where once only the French, Italian and British were deemed worthy of note. Among the countries producing designers who are making a Europe-wide impact are Germany (Jil Sander), Austria (Helmut Lang), Spain (Sybilla), Belgium (Dries Van Noten), and Sweden (Marcel Marongiu).

Marysia Woroniecka, a fashion marketing executive, said: "The snob attitudes that dominated European fashion for years are no longer relevant. It doesn't matter where designers come from any more; if they're talented, they can make it."

Disk jockeys who work in clubs across Europe say the broadening of horizons dates to the birth of house dance music in the late '80s. Jeremy Healy, 29, from London, who has worked in France, Italy, Spain and Belgium, said: "It started in Ibiza in 1988, the 'summer of love.' Now we're traveling all over the continent."

Individual countries are making different contributions to the boom in house dance music. The Belgians have added the harsh techno-sounds of the clubs of Antwerp and Ghent. The Italians have contributed a sense of melody and piano breaks, exported from the studios and clubs of Bologna and Rimini.

Michael Leahy, an Irish-born rock critic working in Belgium, cites the success of Black Box (Italy) and 2 Unlimited (Belgium) on the British dance charts, and Urban Dance Squad, a Dutch band with a continent-wide following. "Dance music is striking the same responses in Dresden and Bristol. There is a genuine European style emerging. Linguistically, I should have more in common with Americans. But I feel most at home with other Europeans."

While politicians debate the future, it seems that the young are simply getting on with it.

From: Roger Tredre/The Independent, "New Unity in the Old World—Young Euros Trash Continental Drift to Meld Music, Fashion," San Francisco Examiner, Jan. 19, 1992, pp. D-1, D-7.

European advertisers and broadcasters are demanding little or no government regulation of programming and advertisements, while many citizens' advocacy groups are seeking more stringent safeguards and guidelines to ensure that programming truly serves the interests of the pan-European audience. While specific solutions to these problems are still being sought and debated, many observers agree that the general trend is toward deregulation.

Though politicians seem preoccupied with the complexities of transfrontier television, popular music is perhaps the strongest cultural force now washing over the European Community. For centuries, Europe has had a worldwide impact on musical developments. Today, pop-music groups from European nations regularly top the charts and dominate the dance clubs in the United States and elsewhere. "Euro-pop" has become an especially prominent feature on the playlists of college and alternative radio stations. In Europe, observers have noted the appearance of the "Euro-teen," European youth who share a new, common identity as the first generation of citizens to come of age in the European Community. That identity is being maintained through popular music (see the guest essay by Roger Tredre on pages 392–393).

The Global Village: Consequences of International Mass Communication

In their books *The Medium Is the Massage: An Inventory of Effects* and *War and Peace in the Global Village*, Marshall McLuhan and Quentin Fiore examine the impact of mass media on global life. In *The Medium Is the Massage*, McLuhan first argued that modern mass communication "recreates the world in the image of a global village" as it

> pours upon us instantly and continuously the concerns of all other men. It has reconstituted dialogue on a global scale. Its message is Total Change, ending psychic, social, economic, and political parochialism. The old civic, state and national groupings have become unworkable. . . .
>
> Our new environment compels commitment and participation. We have

become irrevocably involved with, and responsible for, each other. . . .

> Ours is a brand-new world of allatonceness. "Time" has ceased, "space" has vanished. We now live in a *global* village . . . a simultaneous happening. . . . We have begun again to structure the primordial feeling, the tribal emotions.

In many ways, *The Medium Is the Massage* is a book bound to its time—the 1960s. McLuhan wrote the book with a cryptic, "hip" prose characteristic of that era. But his insights—and his questions—are as relevant today as they were a few decades ago. Though he made his observations when the first telecommunications satellites could do little more than send blips and beeps back to Earth, McLuhan perceived many of the profound consequences of living in a world linked by rapid, instantaneous, mass communication (15.5).

In particular, McLuhan understood that international mass communication impacts the most basic units of society, which he divided into "you," "your family," "your neighborhood," "your education," "your job," "your government," and "the others." Today, we can take a look at McLuhan's categories in light of recent developments in the structure of worldwide mass media systems.

You

Who are *you*, as a tribal member of the global village? What struck McLuhan most about our notions of "you" were the ways in which mass communication has eroded privacy in the name of "the community's need to know." He wrote: "The older, traditional ideas of private, isolated thoughts and actions—the patterns of mechanistic technologies—are very seriously threatened by new methods of instantaneous electric information retrieval, by the electrically computerized dossier bank—that one big gossip column." In short, he notes, "We have become so involved with each other."

In the global village, "you" are always involved with "them." Isolationism is impossible. Events in Russia, Germany, Japan, and Iraq are as real as the events in your own city. Are you a Californian? Are you an American? Are you a North American? Are you an Earthling? In the age of international mass communication, you may be all of these, and more. The whole world is watching (15.6).

And who do "they" think "you" are? What do the citizens of England or Malaysia or Japan think of Americans? In the global village, we paradoxically know more *and* less about each other. The prime-time soap opera "Dallas" was once wildly popular around the world. In the month of May 1987, the program was seen by over a million Malaysians alone! What lessons about "American life" might programs like "Dallas" be teaching our neighbors in the global village?

In *The Medium Is the Massage*, McLuhan answers the question "And who are you?" with a quote from Lewis Carroll's *Alice in Wonderland*. Says Alice: "I—I hardly know, sir, just present—at least I know who I was when I got up this morning, but I think I must have changed several times since then." Have you ever felt like Alice? Living in the global village, it is hard not to be confused.

Your Family

"The family circle has widened," according to McLuhan. "The worldpool of information fathered by electric media—movies, *Telstar*, flight—far surpasses any possible influence mom and dad can now bring to bear." Teenagers in Japan rebel against authority by dressing like Elvis Presley. American youth immerse themselves in the latest pop music from European bands. Movies, films, books, magazines, CDs, and more crisscross the planet, often passing among the younger members of the global village. To what "family" do these villagers belong?

In 1989, MTV projected that within 5 years 30% of the company's revenues would be de-

15.5

"Ours is a brand-new world of allatonceness. . . . We now live in a *global* village . . . a simultaneous happening."

rived from international ventures. Speaking before the New York Television Academy, MTV Networks president and CEO Tom Freston observed:

> Common sense dictates, and sophisticated research confirms, that a 23-year-old in Amsterdam has more in common with a 23-year-old in New York or Paris or Sydney than he does with his own parents. . . . Rock music really transcends international boundaries, cultures and ideologies.

Certainly, not everyone is pleased with such a "transcendence." Various critics around the world have decried what they see as the erosion of the "traditional family," an erosion typically attributed to the impact of modern forms of mass communication. The family has traditionally been a microcosm of a nation's beliefs and values, and world leaders as well as heads

The Whole World Is Watching!

Television programs crisscross the globe every day, creating a common set of experiences— a common popular culture— shared among the inhabitants of the global village. To commemorate *TV Guide*'s 2,000th issue, published July 27, 1991, the magazine's editors polled well-known persons, reporting their current favorite and all-time favorite TV shows. Here's what some of our Mediaworld's leaders have been tuning into . . .

Elizabeth II
Queen, England
All-time favorite: "I Love Lucy"
Current favorite: "Dallas"

George Bush
President, United States
All-time favorite: "The Ed Sullivan Show"
Current favorites: "Murder She Wrote," "Hallmark Hall of Fame."

Jerry Falwell
Fundamentalist religious leader, worldwide ministry
All-time favorite: "Little House on the Prairie"
Current favorite: "Matlock"

Margaret Thatcher
Former British Prime Minister
All-time favorite: "Yes, Prime Minister"
Current favorite: "CNN"

Saddam Hussein
Dictator, Iraq
All-time favorite: "Charlie's Angels"
Current favorite: "Little House on the Prairie"

From: TV Guide Commemorative Edition, *July 27, 1991, pp. 5, 6, 11.*

---

of households are alarmed at the intrusion of "outside influences" carried across borders— national and local— by the mass media.

Your Neighborhood

McLuhan argued that the concept of the "neighborhood" was virtually obliterated by modern mass communication. "You can't *go* home again," he declared. The world has come *to* you; wherever you are, you are in the midst of the vast, global village. It is quite possible that you know more about events in Russia than you know about what is happening in the house next door.

Global villagers also spend much of their time in mythical places, mediated realities. We live on Sesame Street, somewhere in Mister Rogers' Neighborhood, near a Little House on the Prairie. "Time has ceased, space has vanished." In the global village, where is *your* neighborhood?

Your Education

Today's child is immersed in the concerns of the world— famine, oil spills, war, nuclear disasters, peace treaties, and coups. Traditional educational programs were designed to introduce the child to the world. In the global village, education must equip the child with the skills needed to understand the world in which she or he is *already* deeply immersed.

For the "television child," however, the classroom is often seen as lagging far behind the living room, where the TV set incessantly brings the world home in a chaotic flow of sound and image. This curriculum— delivered through the processes of international mass communication— may very well be teaching us more about life in the global village than we appreciate.

Your Job

Competition in the marketplace of the global village is fierce! The wealth (or the poverty) of nations is demonstrated daily on newscasts. We see the bread lines in Russia and the newest technologies in Japan. The media foster a sense of urgent competition: Will you lose your job to a "foreigner"?

The global village is a global marketplace. Work "here" affects work "there." Kentucky Fried Chicken is sold in the People's Republic of China, and you can buy Chicken McNuggets in Moscow (see 15.7). What common identity, if any, is shared by a McDonald's employee in New York and one in Moscow? What are some of the possible cultural consequences involved in the exportation of images like "The Colonel" and "Ronald McDonald"?

Many jobs in the global village depend on the international connections forged by mass communication—newspapers, faxes, video-conferences, and specialized newsletters flow in massive quantities among workers in every part of the world. Mass media industries are increasingly transformed into giant, complex, global conglomerates. The business of the global village is mass communication.

15.7

McDonald's in Moscow. The Soviet Union has gone, but Chicken McNuggets remain.

Your Government

As international media systems continue to connect disparate parts of the planet, we must consider the political consequences of these developments. Just as you, your family, and your neighborhood have been reconfigured through the processes of international mass communication, world governments are also taking on strange new shapes. According to McLuhan, "A new form of 'politics' is emerging and in ways we haven't yet noticed. The living room has become a voting booth. Participation via television in Freedom Marches, in war, revolution, pollution, and other events is changing *everything*."

Government officials in developing countries have argued that they are suffering under the *media imperialism* of nations like the United States. The global communications order is not very democratic. The richest and most powerful nations create, export, and control most of the world's media. Concerns over this situation heated up significantly in the United Nations in the early 1980s, as many nations called for a "new world information and communication order." The United States has resisted these efforts (see "Issues and Answers").

Some critics have argued that American films, television programs, pop music, and comic books may actually threaten the national identity of some countries, subverting the historical values and interests of a nation's citizens. In the global village, political leaders might have less influence than large media industries.

Certainly, international mass communication has affected the way we view our political leaders. The "public" has been replaced by the "mass audience," and the mass audience is now a global phenomenon. When, during a 1992 visit to Japan, President George Bush vomited at a formal dinner, images of the "event" were immediately sent around the world. Just a few decades earlier, few people in the United States—let alone other countries—knew that President Franklin D. Roosevelt was paralyzed, a victim of polio and confined to a wheelchair.

Of course, as McLuhan is careful to point out, the mass audience is routinely deprived of substantive political power. Though the mass audience has the potential to be a "creative, participating force," it is instead "merely given packages of passive entertainment. Politics offers yesterday's solutions to today's questions."

Other critics of the global village make a similar point. Renowned propaganda expert Jacques Ellul argues that the "global village" is a myth:

In the real village, information transmitted from one individual to other inhabitants was relevant to their lives (even if the information was a joke, gossip, or slander). Such information caused a change (for example, in the relationship between families), and it almost always led to action. On the contrary, the information I receive today through the media is usually not related to my life. I cannot change my behavior because of this information. What can I do against the advance of the desert in the Sahel, against worldwide hunger, against the Pol Pot regime, against the condition of the Cambodians in the camps in Thailand, against the invasion of Afghanistan or Lebanon? Information may be instantaneous, and bring about a new mode of thinking, but it has not changed our world into a global village. At most, it has caused the disappearance of real villagers!

In a similar vein, columnist Stephanie Salter argues that television in particular fosters a misleading sense of participation and political awareness. Her observations about TV's role following the 1991 Soviet coup echo a common complaint:

> Thanks to TV we were eyewitnesses to just about everything that occurred in the USSR except Boris Yeltsin sitting at home in his undershorts. Yet we finished up the week with more questions than ever. . . . In other words, we *saw* everything but know almost *nothing*.

"Just because we witness something," Salter reminds us, "doesn't mean we know what the hell happened."

The Others

In the global village, "the others" are hard to ignore. If the world has become our neighborhood, then the world's inhabitants have become our neighbors. However, it is important to keep in mind that much of what we know about these "neighbors" comes through the mass media. As always, we must be careful to distinguish mediated reality from real life. Certainly, for instance, it would be a mistake to form an impression of the "typical" citizen of Iraq, Israel, or Kuwait based only on the images broadcast over our television sets during the 1991 Gulf War. Unfortunately, however, stereotypes are confused with real persons, a situation that has not helped foster global harmony.

Try this experiment: Close your eyes and form a vivid, clear image of Iraq's Saddam Hussein. Imagine you are in the same room with Hussein, standing very near him. Then, form another, vivid image of Tom Cruise. He's standing on your other side. As you imagine these men, which one smells better? Yes, it's an odd question. But it's surprising how many people report a malodorous Hussein. The point here is that you probably haven't met either of these people, but you do have opinions and feelings about them just the same. These feelings and thoughts are largely based on images transmitted through the mass media.

On a more general level, our images of other nationalities are greatly affected by the mass media. During World War II, for example, the mass media were used to paint an ugly picture of the Japanese (see 15.8). After the war, international media helped foster a new spirit of cooperation between Japan and the United States. In the 1990s, however, that relationship was again strained, as American news reports began to depict the Japanese as money-hungry tycoons, bent on buying up businesses operated by "lazy" Americans. These images contributed not only to international tensions but also to increased racial attacks in the United States. According to journalist Steven C. Chin:

> Asian Americans are particularly vulnerable to racial attacks because many Americans associate all Asians with Ja-

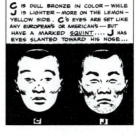

15.8

During World War II, the U.S. government used various forms of mass media to create ugly and threatening stereotypes of the Japanese. The psychological consequences of such wartime communication can be felt long after the physical conflict has ended.

pan, regardless of their national origin, and resent Japan's economic success. . . . The problem is compounded by a tendency to view all Asians as foreigners, even when they are native-born U.S. citizens.

A 1992 report from the U.S. Commission on Civil Rights pointed to the role of media portrayals in perpetuating anti-Asian sentiments and hate crimes. The report encourages the media to "provide balanced, in-depth and sensitive coverage of Asian Americans." Of course, such a recommendation would apply equally well to mediated depictions of native Japanese and other ethnic and cultural groups.

Keeping in mind the differences between mediated reality and real life will help curb the *ethnocentrism* that plagues the global village. Ethnocentrism involves the belief that the norms, values, and customs of one's own society or national group are somehow right or good for everyone else. Evaluating one society or culture according to the values of another is typically ethnocentric. Of course, mass communication can either foster or hinder ethnocentrism. Our ability to peacefully coexist in the global village depends, now more than ever, on our willingness to use the mass media to encourage global awareness rather than global ignorance.

Issues and Answers: A New World Communication Order

The idea of global awareness—of living in a *truly* global village—suggests that there is honest, open interaction among all of the "villagers." As you know, this is not the case. Most international media activities are centered in a few, "First World" nations—the wealthy, capitalist societies of Europe, Japan, and North America. The so-called "Third World," which is made up of the poorer, developing nations

in Africa, Asia, and Latin America, has been virtually excluded from the existing international media system or "world communication order."

For decades, international news has primarily been gathered and distributed by just five major wire services: Associated Press (AP, the United States), United Press International (UPI, the United States), Reuters (Britain),

Agence France-Presse (AFP, France), and Tele-grafnoie Agenstvo Sovetskavo Soiuza (TASS, the former Soviet Union). This dominance by the "Big Five" has resulted in a disproportionate coverage of First World news and a corresponding lack of interest in (and general ignorance about) events in the developing nations of the planet. In the existing communication order, news tends to flow from the First World to the Third World; the reverse flow is rare. According to a number of critics, international news about less-developed nations is typically negative and lacks coverage of positive events taking place in these countries. In short, it's all "bad news" for the Third World.

When we think of developing nations, we often think of countries that lack the economic clout of Japan, Germany, or the United States. But developing nations are not simply impoverished in a monetary sense. In the global village, there is an ever-widening gap between the "information-rich" and the "information-poor." Telecommunications satellites, so much a part of daily life in the United States, are too costly for most developing nations. Though these satellites circle a planet we all share, such technology is owned and operated by a mere handful of global villagers.

According to a United Nations report, no more than 20 radios are available for every 1,000 persons living in less-developed countries. In the United States, by comparison, there are 2,000 radios for every 1,000 Americans. The number of television sets available to Third World citizens is, as you might guess, even lower. Even so common a medium as the daily newspaper is relatively rare in a number of less-developed countries, which do not enjoy access to a wide range of periodicals. Yet, in the age of mass communication, access to information is vital. The information-poor are "starving."

Some of us might be tempted to look with envy at the information-poor of the world. Perhaps they are better off without "I Love Lucy" and Michael Jackson. Maybe. But international media communicate more than entertainment

(important as that is). These media also carry news about birth control, farming, and AIDS. And what are we, the information-rich, losing out on? After all, we seem to have it all. Maybe. We must keep in mind that we might be getting a rather narrow view of the world. Surely, there are things that less-developed nations could teach us — in the areas of politics and literature, to name two. Does this information reach us, in the existing communication order?

These and other questions have been at the heart of an ongoing controversy surrounding the development of a New World Information and Communication Order, more commonly referred to as "NWICO." Much of this debate has taken place through UNESCO, the United Nations Educational, Scientific and Cultural Organization. In the late 1970s, UNESCO convened a special commission to study the problem of world communication priorities. The MacBride Commission (named after the chair, Sean MacBride of Ireland) issued its seminal report in 1980: *Many Voices, One World*. This detailed and often technical document explored many of the problems that have plagued global harmony under the "old" information and communication order. Critics maintained that the report called for undue press controls and would inhibit the freedom of expression. Supporters argued that the report simply called for social responsibility on a global scale. This debate continues today.

The United States government has generally taken a stand against the development of a new world communication order. So have many other First World nations. In fact, both the United Kingdom and the United States withdrew entirely from UNESCO in 1984, declaring that the organization had become a propaganda machine for those with an anti-Western axe to grind.

However, the inequities of the global communication order will not go away if we ignore them. Ninety percent of all global news still originates in four countries. Ninety percent of all international shortwave radio frequencies are still controlled by Western nations. Eighty percent of the world's books continue to be produced in the industrialized nations. Something is wrong in the global village.

Perhaps as we enter a new era of global cooperation, one free of cold war anxiety, we may yet find ways to improve international mass communication. The global village *can* become a much nicer place to live. These improvements might come from another generation of media watchers, who envision new solutions to these complex problems.

1 Spend a week taking notes while you watch television, keeping your eyes open for stereotyping that might contribute to ethnocentrism. What do you find? As an alternate activity, watch five of the top-rated TV programs in one week. This time, take notes on what these shows might teach people in other countries about life in America. If you want, use five popular magazines instead of television programs.

2 Why does popular music seem to occupy such a special place in the global village, transcending national borders and uniting an audience of youthful listeners? Is pop music a unique "international language"?

3 Of the various media systems reviewed in this chapter, does any seem better than the others? Explain.

4 Go to your library or newsstand and look over some magazines from different countries. How do their form and content compare with that of magazines in the United States? What sorts of advertisements do these foreign magazines contain? Bring copies of interesting ads or articles to share with the class.

5 Prepare a five-page report on the media system of a country *not* described in this chapter. Include details about all types of media, and explain which of the four media theories best describes the system in the country you selected.

6 Congratulations! You have just been appointed as an ambassador to the United Nations. You can select the country you would like to represent. Your first task is to prepare a written summary of your position on the idea of a "New World Communication Order." What do you say?

International Media Systems; Mass Media and National Governments

Thomas W. Cooper
Clifford G. Christians
Frances Forde Plude
Robert A. White
Communication Ethics and Global Change. New York: Longman, 1989.

A unique examination of "ethical theory in a global setting," this book details media ethics in a variety of countries, including Poland, Spain, the Netherlands, Nigeria, Korea, Japan, China, and Australia. Includes selected national and international codes of ethics. Recommended.

Sydney W. Head
World Broadcasting Systems: A Comparative Analysis. Belmont, Calif.: Wadsworth, 1985.

Though world events change more rapidly than textbooks can be written, this standard is still a good source for students. Head offers up interesting content in an easy-to-digest form. The consequence: Recommended reading.

Neil Hickey
"TV's Biggest Coup: Covering the Week That Shook the World." *TV Guide,* Sept. 21, 1991, pp. 20–22, 34.

Chin-Chuan Lee, ed.
Voices of China: The Interplay of Politics and Journalism. New York: Guilford Press, 1990.

This anthology reviews Chinese journalism after the Tiananmen massacre in 1989. Journalists, educators, and politicians from both the United States and China examine press practices in China as well as U.S. media coverage of China. The media implications of China's 1997 acquisition of Hong Kong are also discussed.

John Martin
Anju Chaudhary
Comparative Mass Media Systems. 2d ed. New York: Longman, 1990.

This introductory textbook is comprehensive, current, and readable. Covers some of the same ground as Head's book (above), but with a more diverse focus.

Fred S. Siebert
Theodore Peterson
Wilbur Schramm
Four Theories of the Press. Urbana: University of Illinois Press, 1963.

This book, originally published in 1956, is a classic. Of course, it is now rather dated, and a number of scholars have seriously challenged the usefulness of the authors' four-part scheme. Still, the book remains standard reading for students of international media.

Mediaworld: A Tourist's Guide

Jean Cluzel
"Europe's Audiovisual Future." *Media Bulletin,* Mar. 1989, p. 3.

Conrad Phillip Kottak
Prime-Time Society: An Anthropological Analysis of Television and Culture. Belmont, Calif.: Wadsworth, 1990.

Kottak spent 4 years studying television in Brazil, and he reports his observations in this fascinating and well-written book. He illuminates the role of television in the global village through a comparison of Brazilian and American television usage.

James Lull, ed.
World Families Watch Television. Newbury Park, Calif.: Sage, 1988.

The editor provides a unique collection of descriptive accounts of television viewing in Great Britain, Venezuela, West Germany, India, People's Republic of China, and the United States. Students will be relieved that Lull and his contributors offer readable, firsthand accounts. You won't have to wade through a mist of indigestible pie charts and redundant bar graphs to get the message.

Jeremy Marre
Hannah Charlton
Beats of the Heart: Popular Music of the World. New York: Pantheon, 1985.

An overview of music in more than a dozen different cultures, including South Africa, China, Puerto Rico, and Japan. The book is well illustrated and includes a discography (a reference list of recordings).

Michele Mattelart
Armand Mattelart
The Carnival of Images: Brazilian Television Fiction. New York: Bergin & Garvey, 1990.

A critical and comprehensive examination of the *telenovela* phenomenon. The authors pay particular attention to the impact of the *novelas* on worldwide television, and they consider the relationship between these serials and the social and cultural climate of Brazil.

Ithiel de Sola Pool
Eli M. Noam
Technologies Without Boundaries. Cambridge, Mass.: Harvard University Press, 1990.

This book "on telecommunications in a global age" examines the global flow of messages, regulation of international communication, satellites, and communications for less-developed nations. Though he died before this book could be published, Pool remains a highly respected expert on the subject.

Roger Rollins, ed.
The Americanization of the Global Village: Essays in Comparative Popular Culture. Bowling Green, Ohio: Popular Press, 1990.

This series of essays examines the production and consumption of popular culture on a worldwide scale. Cases compare and contrast mass culture in two different countries or regions of the world and evaluate the impact of pop culture on national identities.

Philip T. Rosen, ed.
International Handbook of Broadcasting Systems. Westport, Conn.: Greenwood Press, 1988.

The editor has included a wide range of useful information in this reference book, which covers history, regulation, technology, economics, and programming.

Cynthia Schneider
Brian Wallis, eds.
Global Television. New York: Wedge Press, 1988.

A provocative collection of unique essays. Among the topics you'll find here: "Dallas," international television flow, New World Information and Communication Order, video and the counterculture, Michael Jackson, media representation of AIDS. Recommended.

Anyone interested in international journalism should consult *World Press Review.* This monthly journal provides English-language versions of press reports appearing in newspapers and magazines all over the world. An added bonus: *WPR* also features editorial cartoons. Another magazine worth investigating is *The Democratic Journalist,* a colorful monthly published by the International Organization of Journalists (IOJ).

The Global Village: Consequences of International Mass Communication

Jacques Ellul
"Preconceived Ideas About Mediated Communication." In E. M. Rogers and F. Balle, eds., *The Media Revolution in America and in Western Europe,* pp. 95–107. Norwood, N.J.: Ablex, 1985.

John Martin
Ray Eldon Hiebert, eds.
Current Issues in International Communication. New York: Longman, 1990.

This book covers current issues and enduring themes, placing them in a thoughtful and accessible context. Subjects covered include: the New World Information and Communication Order, international media flow, comparative systems for controlling the media, consequences of global communication.

Marshall McLuhan
Quentin Fiore
The Medium Is the Massage: An Inventory of Effects. New York: Bantam Books, 1967.

War and Peace in the Global Village. New York: Bantam Books, 1968.

Both of these innovative books probe the restructuring of the world through mass communication. Though a bit difficult to follow at times, many of the insights offered in these classic and creatively designed books are as fresh today as they were decades ago. Recommended for any McLuhan fan.

Marshall McLuhan
Bruce R. Powers
The Global Village: Transformations in World Life and Media in the 21st Century. New York: Oxford University Press, 1989.

Published 9 years after McLuhan's death, this book is a good (re)introduction to the major concepts developed in McLuhan's earlier books. Current media technologies, including computers and satellites, are considered.

Stephanie Salter
"TV Went to U.S.S.R., But What Did We Learn?" *San Francisco Examiner,* Aug. 29, 1991, p. A-15.

Herbert Schiller
Mass Communication and American Empire. Boston: Beacon Press, 1969.

Communications and Cultural Dominance. White Plains, N.Y.: E. M. Sharpe, 1976.

Schiller ranks among the most widely cited critics of what he argues is U.S. "media imperialism." He bases his challenging observations in Marxist theory. Recommended reading.

Jack G. Shaheen
The TV Arab. Bowling Green, Ohio: Popular Press, 1984.

The author's detailed analysis of Arab stereotyping offers useful insights that apply to a host of problems associated with ethnocentrism in the global village.

Jeremy Tunstall
The Media Are American. New York: Columbia University Press, 1977.

The author examines the history of U.S. influence in the international media marketplace. Considered a pioneering book on the subject.

Issues and Answers: A New World Communication Order

Enrique Gonzalez-Manet
The Hidden War of Information. Norwood, N.J.: Ablex, 1988.

This book addresses the difficult subject of communications inequity and isolation in the Third World, particularly Latin America. Proposals for the new world communication order are examined, and the United States' decision to withdraw from UNESCO is discussed.

International Commission for the Study of Communications Problems
Many Voices, One World. London: Kogan Page, 1980.

Also known as the MacBride Report, this detailed, technical UNESCO report sparked immediate controversy. That controversy continues to this day in debates over NWICO—the New World Information and Communication Order.

16

Mass Communication Research: A Beginner's Guide

Social scientists insist that any important conclusions about the effects of media be supported by solid evidence. . . . Most are quite wary of any simple answers or unverified conclusions concerning causal relations between media content and undesirable conduct.

Melvin DeFleur

It is surely no wonder that a bewildered public should regard with cynicism a research tradition which supplies, instead of answers, a plethora of relevant, but inconclusive, and, at times, seemingly contradictory findings.

Joseph Klapper

By now the pattern has become all too familiar. A violent film depicting gang activity opens, and real life imitates art as violence breaks out in the theaters. Civic leaders deplore the situation. Filmmakers are dubbed "irresponsible" even as they point out that the film carries an *antigang* message. Meanwhile, another "slasher" film is condemned by feminist groups for its depiction of violence against women.

A controversial new rap group releases an album that some feel is "obscene." Some record stores refuse to carry it. Others insist on doing so, citing the group's freedom of speech. Civic leaders deplore the situation. Record companies are dubbed "irresponsible."

A daytime soap opera incurs the wrath of community leaders when it is found to be "too steamy" for an audience that includes an increasing number of young people.

These are but a few of the familiar media-related controversies that we read and hear about each day. In a world where mass communication has become a relentless presence in our lives, it is increasingly important for each of us to understand something about the connection between the form and content of the media and its consequence or influence on the mass audience. For answers to these very complex and troublesome questions, we look to mass communication researchers.

When compared with medicine, which is thousands of years old, or even with modern psychology, which is a product of this century, the formal study of mass communication is in its infancy. We have only begun to research the effects of mass media, the dynamic force that is reshaping our lives.

Patterns in Mass Communication Research

The direction of research in mass media is largely determined by the people who hold the purse strings. Much of the funding for large-scale studies comes from some level of government. These studies are often about violence or involve the interests of minority groups. They are prompted by the concern of the people (as expressed through their government) that certain media programs or practices may be harmful to society.

A second group of studies is done by students who write theses and dissertations in graduate schools. Usually these are directed by senior-level faculty members, who either steer students to favorite research topics or let them make their own decisions. Studies are also funded by universities or private sources such as the media themselves or their professional organizations.

All of these efforts contribute *something* to the accumulated knowledge that we have about issues in mass communication. But because research in mass media is so new, we have very few hard and fast conclusions. Not enough studies have been done in most areas to give us conclusive results.

Another problem involves the *situational perspective* that we have on our media consumption. In brief, not all media consumption affects everyone in the same way. Violence on TV may stimulate certain types of young people to behave violently in real life; for others it may have the opposite effect. All studies that involve large numbers of subjects inherently assume that those subjects are somehow similar. But in the real world we are all very different.

We need more research in mass media because the media themselves are constantly changing. They are not stable, like a chemical formula; instead, they are flexible and volatile in both form and content. I spent 3 years working on a dissertation involving sex-role socialization on four popular TV shows. All of them were off the air within a year of its completion. This can be very frustrating. But it also indicates that we need more research in the field to help us keep current and cope with change.

The study of mass media is so new that there is still some debate about whether it should be housed with arts, humanities, or social sciences. The creation of effective mass communication via print, radio, television, or film is an art. It involves the efforts of one or more artists. Each medium can point to its best and proudly proclaim it a unique art form. But mass communication is also a branch of human learning and belongs with the rest of the humanities, like English and foreign languages. Each medium has a "literature" all its own: In radio, it's sound; in film and television, pictures.

As far as research is concerned, mass communication is usually regarded as a social science. To understand its effects we borrow procedures from psychology and sociology. In fact, many of the most important communication researchers are psychologists and sociologists. These pioneers have developed methods for examining attitudes, beliefs, and behaviors. All admit that the methods of the social scientist are not as exact or as pure as those of the physical scientist; human behavior is simply not as predictable as a chemical solution or a physics experiment. But it *is* predictable to some degree. Social scientists adopt many of the statistical procedures used in the physical sciences in order to make more definite predictions about human behavior.

Procedures and Problems of Communication Research

We all have opinions about the influence of mass media, just as we have opinions about everything. These opinions are often based on information we have gathered and ideas we have been taught by our parents, teachers, and television sets. Occasionally we engage in debate with others. We match our opinions against theirs and offer facts to back them. But if that's all we do, what we end up with is what we started with: *opinions*.

Of course, it is possible to gather opinions in a systematic way. We might go to everyone in the country and ask what he or she thinks about TV and violence. We might find that 76.2% think there is a relationship between TV viewing and violence. But this does not mean there is a relationship, only that more than three quarters of the people *think there is*.

In recent years, all social sciences have placed more and more emphasis on empirical research, which relies not on soliciting opinions but on observing behaviors. The researcher gathers data systematically and makes conclusions based on the data. Several steps are involved in designing an empirical study, and each has its own pitfalls.

The first step is to identify an idea that is to be tested. The field is wide open, with an unlimited number of hypotheses — some far too general to be tested and some so small or obvious that they are not worth testing. The beginning research student often makes the mistake of asking too large a question. It might be impractical, for instance, to test whether TV violence causes violence in real life, but we could design a nice study documenting the TV viewing habits among inmates of a juvenile detention school versus those of students in a public school. By obtaining this information, we might contribute a small bit of data to help resolve the larger question.

A common way to test a hypothesis is to go at it backward by gathering data in an attempt to disprove a *null hypothesis*. The null hypothesis claims that no relationship exists between the elements in question. In this case our null hypothesis would be: There is no difference between the viewing habits and program preferences of the two groups being studied.

Then we must make a decision about research design. How can we gather data to test our null hypothesis? Are we going to ask these kids to report how many hours a day they watch TV? That's one simple way, but does it tell us what we want to know? And how do we know that their answers will be accurate?

Some subjects may report fewer hours than they actually watch, because there seems to be a social stigma attached to spending too much time with the "boob tube." In addition, TV watching is something we do on an irregular basis (some days we watch 5 hours, other days none), so the chances are great that some error will be made. Stationing someone by the TV set in both the private and detention homes to see how many hours each kid watches it would help, but it would be difficult and time-consuming. Moreover, if we do manage to observe the subjects, are they going to watch what they normally would, knowing that we are watching them? These are just some of the problems of research design.

Once we have data, we have the job of analyzing and interpreting it. The first question: Did we get enough data? Perhaps our N (number in the sample) was only 20. Does this really represent the institution and the school? The community? All children in Mediamerica? Children of the world? We must be careful when inferring that others behave like our test group.

The greatest pitfall in empirical research involves the problem of establishing *causal inferences*. It is all too easy to leap to conclusions. We may *infer*, for example, that because Lee Harvey Oswald was once a Marine, and because he allegedly shot John F. Kennedy, all ex-Marines are somewhat prone to violence, and therefore military training tends to make trainees more violent. But what about the ex-marine who now heads a committee for strict gun-control legislation? That example seems to "prove" that military experience leads to a realization of how destructive guns can be. Who is right?

To test a theory, the researcher attempts to establish *causality*, that is, the relationship of one phenomenon to another. Richard J. Hill, editor of *Sociometry* and a leading authority on statistical research, used to tell a story that illustrates the problem of establishing causality: Many years ago, researchers discovered that the water level of the Potomac River dropped in direct proportion to the number of peanuts consumed in Washington, D.C. The more peanuts consumed, the less water there was in the river. The obvious conclusion? People eating all of those salted peanuts got thirsty and drank up the water!

This makes sense, of a sort, but it doesn't have anything to do with reality. In the spring, ice melts and the river rises. In the summer, water evaporates and the level goes down. Meanwhile, baseball season goes into full swing (Washington had a team in those days), and the number of peanuts consumed rises, thanks to peanut-hungry fans. Baseball and melting ice were *intervening variables* that accounted for the peanut consumption and water levels.

We must be careful not to establish causality simply because the statistics (data) *seem* to support a certain theory. It is one thing to say that real-life crime rates and the number of crimes committed on TV have both risen in the past 10 years. It is quite another to establish a *causal relationship*, to say that one "causes" the other.

Causal ordering is another problem. It seemed to make sense that the peanut consumption caused the lower water levels, but the statistics offered equal support for the theory that lower water levels caused a higher consumption of peanuts. Of course, both hypotheses are nonsense, but causal ordering can be critical. If more real-life crimes encourage TV writers to think more about crime and put it into their scripts, that's one thing. If the true causal ordering is the reverse, we have an entirely different problem.

Finally, there is always a great temptation to yield to our own opinions and biases in such cases or to design studies so that results will verify gut-level feelings. Yet it is the difference between gut-level feelings and empirical research that gives credibility to a point of view.

To avoid all of these pitfalls we must choose the right statistical method to test our theories. A battery of tests is available to help us decide whether any significant difference exists between groups. There will always be differences between any two groups; we want to know whether any of them are *statistically significant* differences that relate to our hypothesis. Choosing the appropriate statistical test helps us make that decision. All such tests have limitations. Some can be used only for certain kinds of data, others only when N is large.

A Sampler of Research Studies

The balance of this chapter contains three research articles that were published in three leading communication journals. These journals are designed primarily for graduate students, researchers, and college professors. Yet some of their articles can be useful to the undergraduate student.

Each article deals with an important area of mass communication research. Obviously it would not be possible to present or summarize all the relevant articles in each area or to try to represent all the areas that are being investigated. However, you may want to use these articles as a jumping-off point to learn more about research and about the questions being studied by mass communication researchers across the country.

To help guide you through each article, a list of "Tips and Touts" is given for each study as well as annotated material. These should be useful in helping you understand the unique aspects of each example. From blunt "slasher" films to the subtle nuances of soap operas and rock 'n' roll, research projects like these are carried out each day in an attempt to "make sense" of the often confusing and contradictory consequences of mass communication.

Are "Slasher" Horror Films Sexually Violent? A Content Analysis

James B. Weaver, III

This article originally appeared in the Summer 1991 issue of the *Journal of Broadcasting and Electronic Media*. © 1991.

One of the principal tools of communication researchers is a technique known as content analysis, *using a careful, objective collection of data that can be counted in some way. This study involves a content analysis of selected scenes from the 10 most successful "slasher" films in recent years and attempts to answer questions concerning the filmmaker's decisions to choose male or female victims and the ways in which the victims are portrayed.*

James B. Weaver, III
(Ph.D., Indiana University, 1987) is associate professor of mass communication and director of the Behavioral Research Laboratory at Auburn University. His research interests include the use and effects of mass media messages.

Tips and Touts

1   As with many studies, this one begins by reviewing various earlier studies in the area. The central dilemma appears to be that some research concludes that such films contain scenes involving violence that is "primarily directed against women" while other research contends that men and women are equally victimized.

2   In the method section, the author describes how he arrived at the list of 10 films and how each was identified as a member of the slasher genre.

3   *Intercoder reliability*, as described in the coding section of this study, is often a key issue. Researchers seek some way of guaranteeing that there is some general agreement regarding the content of each scene among those who view it — in other words, that we all tend to "see" it the same way.

4   Try not to be put off by the long strings of numbers, such as those found in the appearances section. While it's not feasible for us to go into the numbers in detail here, you'll still get the essence of the findings if you read the entire study carefully.

5   The discussion section, usually found at the end of each study, reviews the findings and helps the reader make sense of them. This study seems to conclude that while men and women are equally victimized, scenes involving female victims tend to run longer, in an attempt to appeal to male and female audience members alike. Do you agree or disagree?

6   This study deals with gender issues *and* the research was carried out by a man. Is that significant? Might men and women ask different sorts of research questions and even come to different conclusions based on the same data? Increasingly, questions like these are being asked about the role of the researcher in the research process. The researcher's gender, sexual orientation, ethnicity, and socioeconomic status can all have a tremendous impact.

Horror films have traditionally experienced considerable audience acceptance (cf. Bunnell, 1984) and this genre of motion pictures has enjoyed a burgeoning popularity, especially in the last decade (Waller, 1987). Much of this growth has resulted from a particularly strong fascination among teenage and young adult viewers for the horror subgenre commonly referred to as "slasher" films (Farber, 1987; Waller, 1987). The appeal to young viewers of slasher films — which typically accentuate, if not celebrate, the graphic, gory victimization of young adults — has fostered considerable critical and empirical dialogue (cf. Grant, 1984; Tamborini, 1991). One prominent point of contention to emerge from this discourse concerns explication and interpretation of the content characteristics of these movies (cf. Weaver, 1991).

In this debate, most analysts acknowledge that slasher film plots typically follow a rather rudimentary formula. Wolf's (1989) summary of this plot formula is representative:

> Take a certain number of attractive high school or college age men and women and put them into a dark or shadowy place, then intrude into that erotic setting the presence of a maniac with a knife, an axe or a cleaver. Let the camera caress every shadow for as long as possible, while the young people caress each other until the killer kills — brutally, ingeniously, swiftly, spilling as much blood as possible. (p. 89)

Divergent opinions have been advanced, however, over whether male or female characters suffer the brunt of this fictionalized violence.

One position argues that slasher films provide a "spectacle of pure killing" in which men and women are victimized equally (Maslin, 1982; Polan, 1984). Maslin (1982), for example, observes

As you now know, mass media content is usually formulaic — various genres are utilized to cater to specific audience needs, desires, and expectations.

that "murdering pretty young women excites him [the killer] most, but he's really not particular. He'll gladly butcher anyone who gets in his way" (p. b-1). Consistent with this idea, Dickstein (1984) suggests that the equitable victimization of male and female characters is essential for the aesthetic and dramatic development of most slasher films.

Alternatively, it is argued that the violence of slasher films "is overwhelmingly directed at women" (Donnerstein, Linz, & Penrod, 1987, p. 113). Logas (1981), for example, asserts that slasher films are "filled with scene after scene of terrified, half-dressed women, screaming with pain and horror as they are raped, stabbed, chopped at, and strangled" (p. 21). In a similar vein, Linz, Donnerstein, and Penrod (1988) contend that the slasher subgenre consists primarily of "sexually violent films" that feature "scenes of explicit violence primarily directed toward women, often occurring during or juxtaposed to mildly erotic scenes" (p. 759).

Are men and women inequitably victimized in slasher film violence? Do sexually-aggressive assaults of women punctuate such productions? Under what circumstances are assaults typically depicted? This investigation was designed to address these questions. Specifically, 10 slasher films were systematically sampled from the population of commercially successful horror movies. The content of these films was then analyzed to determine (a) the extent to which aggressive, sexual, and sexually aggressive actions are depicted; (b) the number, gender, and dramatic role (i.e., protagonist vs. antagonist) of the characters portrayed in each action; (c) the consequences of each action, including the demographic attributes of all victimized characters; and (d) the extent to which nudity is portrayed.

Here the research questions are posed. Developing precise, thoughtful, and manageable research questions is one of the most important tasks in the research process.

Method

Sample Selection The sampling of films involved two stages. First, the titles of all horror films included in *Variety*'s annual compilation of movies ("All-Time Film," 1987)[1] were identified by a panel of 12 judges. This task, which was facilitated by several annotated film reference sources (Frank, 1982; Nash & Ross, 1985–1987; Willis, 1972–1984), yielded a list of 66 films.

In the second stage, the judges reviewed in-depth synopses of each film (Nash & Ross, 1985–1987) to isolate those that fell into the "slasher" subgenre. These synopses often contained very vivid descriptions of the films, including comments such as "an above-average slasher film" and "another one of those 'you've seen one, you've seen then all' slasher films." After reading the synopses, the judges indicated which of the 66 movies they considered "slasher" films. Eighteen titles were identified by the majority of the judges as fitting the "slasher" subgenre. However, in order to minimize redundancy because of the serialization of several titles (e.g., *Friday the 13th, Part 2* through *Part 6*), only the first release of a same-titled series was retained. This yielded a final sample of 10 films that, in descending order based on rental income, included: *Halloween, Friday the 13th, Texas Chainsaw Massacre, Nightmare on Elm Street, Prom Night, Happy Birthday to Me, Maniac, Nightmare, The House on Sorority Row,* and *Drive-In Massacre.* The average box office income was $8.8 million, with *Halloween* ($18.5 million) recording the highest and *Drive-In Massacre* ($4.1 million) the lowest rental performance.

Coding of Content Characteristics The unit of analysis for this investigation was "the scene," which was defined as an uninterrupted sequence of behaviors occurring within a given physical context. Transitions from one physical context to another (e.g., walking from outdoor to indoors), rather than movement within a single physical context (e.g., walking around outdoors), were operationalized as the beginning and ending parameters of a scene. Each scene was coded for (a) duration (in seconds); (b) the number, gender, and dramatic role (i.e., protagonist vs. antagonist) of all characters; (c) the general type of action depicted; (d) the specific nature of each action; (e) the resolution, if any, of each action; and (f) the involvement of nudity.

Each scene was assigned to one of four general type of action categories (aggression, sexual, sexual aggression, or other) based on its predominant theme. Each scene was further categorized into one of several, more descriptive specific actions. Acts of aggression, for example, were coded as involving either verbal abuse, an attempted attack, or an attack on a person or persons. Sexual actions were classified as depictions of voyeurism/exhibitionism, sexual caressing/foreplay, or sexual intercourse. Scenes of sexual-aggression were defined as intercourse via either verbal or physical coercion, rape, or sadomasochism. Other scenes were further categorized as involving personal care, socializing, or other.

It must be recognized that, as a result of dramatic license, the specific theme of some scenes rapidly evolves by shifting from one type of action to another. Many critics have noted (cf. Waller, 1987) that this phenomenon is particularly evident in the "slasher" films, especially when sexual context is juxtaposed with violence (e.g., a young couple engaging in precoital behaviors is attacked and brutally murdered by a crazed killer). To accommodate this stylistic feature, the consequence or resolution of each scene involving a victimization of a character was

Here the author explains his "coding" and "operationalization." Coding refers to the actual process of labeling and counting specific aspects of the film and placing them in appropriate categories. Operationalization means defining variables (in this case, features of slasher films) in terms of how they are measured. For example, you probably can think of a number of definitions for "nude scene." But an operational definition might be "when a character appears for 10 seconds or more with no clothes on."

recorded. The number, gender, dramatic role of each victim, and whether the action was terminated by their escape, being wounded, or by their death was also coded.

Finally, the extent to which nudity was employed in the sampled films was examined. The number, gender, and dramatic role of each character depicted as either completely or partially nude was recorded.

Content Coders Three undergraduates were recruited as coders. Following extensive training, they viewed and coded one of the 10 films (Friday the 13th) in order to test intercoder reliability. This test, which involved the coding of 55 scenes or about 13.5% of the total scenes in the sample, produced a reliability coefficient of 94.5 using Holsti's (1969) method. To permit efficient use of the data generated by this reliability test, the responses of one coder were randomly selected for inclusion in the final data set. Each coder was then randomly assigned to view three of the remaining nine films over a 5-day period. Working independently, the coders watched videotapes of the films in a supervised setting.

Results

A total of 406 scenes was coded across the 10 films. The average scene length was 153.3 seconds. Overall, 24.1% of the scenes depicted acts of aggression, 6.2% showed sexual actions, 0.5% depicted acts of sexual-aggression, and 69.2% involved other actions. Because of the extremely low frequency of scenes portraying sexual aggression (i.e., two scenes of sadomasochism), these data were collapsed into the sexual actions category for subsequent analyses.

To determine if the number and length of scenes differed significantly across the three types of action, one factor analyses of variance were computed. These tests revealed a significant effect for the number of scenes, $F(2, 27) = 27.3, p < .001, \hat{\omega}^2 = .64$, but not for the average duration of scenes, $F < 1$. Subsequent tests revealed that the number of scenes involving portrayals of aggressive ($M = 9.8$) or sexual actions ($M = 2.7$) was significantly ($p < .05$ by Scheffé's test) smaller than those depicting other actions ($M = 28.1$). Comparison of the average number of scenes of aggression and sexual acts approached significance ($p < .10$).

Examination of the specific nature of the actions showed that scenes of aggression ($n = 98$) typically involved an attack on at least one individual (67.4%). Scenes depicting an attempted attack (26.5%) or verbal abuse (6.1%) were less frequent. The data also show that the majority of scenes categorized as sexual ac-

Intercoder reliability is a measure of the extent to which these students (the coders) counted up the same sorts of things in the film clips they saw. For example, two people might not agree that a particular scene in a film represents an "act of sexual-aggression." To increase reliability, the researcher must provide coders with very specific, detailed, operational definitions for each category being used.

Analysis of variance is one sort of statistical technique used to determine if the results are "significant," that is, if they are not due to random chance. Statistical symbols and jargon might seem unusual, but they are not really complex. In fact, they often refer to fairly simple procedures that any good stats book can help you sort out.

tions ($n = 27$) presented sexual caressing or foreplay (51.9%). Scenes portraying either sexual intercourse (22.2%) or voyeurism/exhibitionism (18.5%) were less frequent. Finally, the most frequently categorized types of other actions ($n = 281$) were socializing (34.9%) and personal care (6.4%).

Consideration of the resolution of each scene revealed a distinct pattern. The most prevalent outcome of aggressive actions was death, with 62.2% of such scenes involving the victimization of at least one character. In contrast, the injury of a character was a less common (22.4%) outcome. Just over one-third (37.0%) of the scenes involving sexual actions ($n = 27$) concluded with the death of one or more characters. The death of one male protagonist was depicted in a scene involving other actions.

Portrayals involving partial or full nudity ($n = 10$) represented a small proportion (2.5%) of the total scenes. All depictions of full nudity presented female characters exclusively.

Appearances and Deaths of Protagonists   Approximately 13% of the 406 scenes presented in the sample of films involved the death of protagonists. Further, the data show that while protagonists typically appeared in pairs ($M = 1.99$), they were most often killed in solitude ($M = 1.3$).

In order to test for potential inequities in the overall appearance of protagonists, the data for the number of persons, number of scenes, and average duration of scenes were summarized within each film for male and female characters. Analyses conducted on these measures (t tests, $df = 18$) revealed no significant differences in the overall appearance of male and female characters in slasher films.

To allow examination of the data on depictions of the death of protagonists, the number of victims, number of scenes, and average duration of death scenes were summarized within each film as a function of character gender (male, female) and type of action (aggressive, sexual).[2] The data were then subjected to 2 × 2 analyses of variance that revealed significant ($p < .0001$) type of action main effects for both the number of victims, $F(1, 36) = 18.4$, $\hat{\omega}^2 = .51$, and number of death scenes, $F(1, 36) = 21.2$, $\hat{\omega}^2 = .32$. A gender main effect for the duration of death scenes measure, $F(1, 36) = 5.5$, $p < .05$, $\hat{\omega}^2 = .10$, also emerged. The character gender by type of action interaction approached significance, $F(1, 36) = 2.92$, $p < .10$, $\hat{\omega}^2 = .03$, for the number of scenes measure. All other effects yielded nonsignificant variation.

Examination of the means associated with these effects revealed that a larger number of victims ($M = 2.7$) and death scenes ($M = 2.4$) resulted from aggressive actions than sexual actions (victims, $M = .65$; scenes, $M = .65$). The means also show that the average length of death scenes for female characters ($M = 217.2$) was longer than scenes involving males ($M = 107.7$).

Subsequent tests on the interaction means revealed that scenes portraying the death of female characters as a result of aggressive actions ($M = 3.0$) were significantly ($p < .05$ by Scheffé's test) more frequent than scenes depicting the death of characters of either gender as the resolution of sexual actions (females, $M = 0.6$; males, $M = 0.7$). The frequency of scenes involving the death of male characters following aggressive actions ($M = 1.8$) was intermediate to these extremes.

Appearances and Deaths of Antagonists In contrast to the findings for protagonists, the data show that antagonists were typically depicted as acting alone ($M = 1.13$). The apparent death of an antagonist (males $= 7$; females $= 3$) was a common characteristic presented in 8 of the 10 films sampled. Further, examination of the portrayal of antagonists as a function of character gender revealed no significant differences (t test, $df = 18$).

Discussion

The ultimate attraction of horror movies, it has been suggested, rests on the fact that they offer viewers "a safe, routinized way of playing with *death* [emphasis added]" (Dickstein, 1984, p. 69; also see Zillmann, Weaver, Mundorf, & Aust, 1986). Consistent with this idea, the data at hand document that the depiction of graphic, gory violence typically resulting in the death of one or more characters is a common component of contemporary horror films. Indeed, the findings illustrate that the "slasher" label assigned to this subgenre of horror films is well justified.

More important, the results revealed that there was no significant difference in the number of male and female characters suffering violent victimization, that the circumstances of these deaths (aggressive vs. sexual) did not differ as a function of gender, and that no scenes involving nonconsenting sexual aggression (i.e., rape) were observed. These findings, taken together, challenge the assertion that slasher movies present violence that "is overwhelmingly directed at women" (Donnerstein, Linz, & Penrod, 1987, p. 113; Logas, 1981). Instead, the findings appear most consistent with the observation that the intermingling of sex and violence may best be characterized as conveying the message that "boys and girls who play around get murdered by the maniac while the virginal [or at least abstentious] heroine survives — evidently because she refuses what the films picture as a kind of moral decadence" (Polan, 1984, p. 202).

Here we see that death scenes for women are longer than those for men. What does this suggest to you?

How else might the attraction of horror films be explained? Do any of the 31 gratifications listed in Chapter 9 offer possible explanations?

This finding is interesting because the mass media are so often accused of being "immoral" when, in fact, they often seem to reinforce traditional values. A similar finding is reported in the soap-opera study included in this chapter.

One aspect of the data at hand, however, indicates that the victimization of men and women in fictionalized slasher film violence is not entirely equitable. Specifically, the findings disclose that scenes portraying the death of female characters were significantly longer than those involving male characters. One possible explanation is that male characters are often shown attempting to defend themselves when attacked and, because of this stand and fight reaction, are dispatched in short order. Female characters, on the other hand, often exhibit a flight reaction and, because of their initial elusiveness, delay the ultimate confrontation with their attacker.

Interestingly, such a proposition is quite consistent with expectations concerning the enjoyment of horror films projected by the gender-role socialization model of affect (Zillmann et al., 1986). Research based on this model has shown, for instance, that men enjoy scenes from slasher films most in the company of distressed women, while women report the greatest enjoyment in the company of men who display mastery in response to such gory depictions (Zillmann et al., 1986). Given that those who produce horror films appear, at least intuitively, to recognize these considerations (Dickstein, 1984; Farber, 1987; Maslin, 1982), it should be expected that slasher film characters would be treated in a manner that could maximize enjoyment for both female and male viewers. The fact that the death of male characters is presented in a quick, straightforward manner should minimize the anxiety experienced by the male viewer and provide him with an opportunity for the maximum display of mastery. Similarly, the extended length of scenes depicting the victimization of female characters should, it would seem, provide the female viewer a particularly advantageous opportunity to display anxiety and/or distress and to seek and receive comfort from her companion. Clearly, exploration of these considerations should be encouraged in future research.

How do these observations stack up against your own experiences when viewing horror films? Can you think of any alternative explanations?

Taken together, the data at hand provide considerable clarification of the content attributes of the most widely viewed of contemporary slasher films. It should be recognized, however, that there are other films within this subgenre which have not enjoyed extensive commercial success and were excluded from this analysis. Consequently, further research examining other samples of slasher films, and especially those distributed primarily via nontraditional outlets such as videotape rental, should be encouraged. Also, additional research utilizing alternative coding schemes could prove informative. One particularly interesting approach, for example, would be to use the character rather than the scene or behaviors as the unit of analysis. The resulting data would provide a detailed sketch of how

Here the author notes any limitations of his study and offers suggestions for future research projects.

life and death are portrayed in this type of film. Finally, the findings illustrate that any attempt to build our theoretical and empirical understanding of the appeal and impact of contemporary horror films should be grounded upon careful quantification and description of the content characteristics of such productions.

Notes

1   This roster includes all films earning at least $4 million via distributor rentals in the US-Canadian market. As noted by the *Variety* editors, although data based on world-wide rentals might provide greater generalizability, reliable information of this type is not available. Similarly, extensive data concerning income from videotape distribution were not available when this study was conducted.

2   The death of a single male protagonist that was originally coded as the resolution of an "other" type of action was collapsed into the aggressive category for these analyses.

References

All-time film rental champs [of the US-Canada market]. (1987, January 14). *Variety*, pp. 30, 66, 68, 70, 72, 74, 76, 78, 80, 82, 101, 103.

Bunnell, C. (1984). The gothic: A literary genre's transition to film. In B. K. Grant (Ed.), *Planks of reason: Essays on the horror film* (pp. 79–100). Metuchen, NJ: Scarecrow Press.

Dickstein, M. (1984). The aesthetics of fright. In B. K. Grant (Ed.), *Planks of reason: Essays on the horror film* (pp. 65–78). Metuchen, NJ: Scarecrow Press.

Donnerstein, E., Linz, D., & Penrod, S. (1987). *The question of pornography: Research findings and policy implications.* New York: Free Press.

Farber, J. (1987, July). Blood, sweat, and fears: Why are horror movies such a slashing success? *Seventeen*, pp. 108–109, 140–141, 149.

Frank, A. (1982). *The horror film handbook.* Totowa, NJ: Barnes & Noble Books.

Grant, B. K. (1984). *Planks of reason: Essays on the horror film.* Metuchen, NJ: Scarecrow Press.

Holsti, O. R. (1969). *Content analysis for the social sciences and humanities.* Reading, MA: Addison-Wesley.

Linz, D. G., Donnerstein, E., & Penrod, S. (1988). Effects of long-term exposure to violent and sexually degrading depictions of women. *Journal of Personality and Social Psychology, 55,* 758–768.

Logas, M. B. (1981, June). Chicago critics team up against film violence. *Ms.,* p. 21.

Maslin, J. (1982, November 21). Bloodbaths debase movies and audiences. *New York Times,* pp. B-1, B-13.

Nash, J. R., & Ross, S. R. (1985–1987). *The motion picture guide* (Vols. 1–9 and 1986 Annual). Chicago: Cinebooks.

Polan, D. B. (1984). Eros and syphilization: The contemporary horror film. In B. K. Grant (Ed.), *Planks of reason: Essays on the horror film* (pp. 201–211). Metuchen, NJ: Scarecrow Press.

Tamborini, R. (1991). Responding to horror: Determinants of exposure and appeal. In J. Bryant & D. Zillmann (Eds.), *Responding to the screen: Reception and reaction processes* (pp. 305–328). Hillsdale, NJ: Erlbaum.

Waller, G. A. (Ed.). (1987). *American horrors: Essays on the modern American horror film.* Champaign: University of Illinois Press.

Weaver, J. (1991). The impact of exposure to horror film violence on perceptions of women: Is it the violence or an artifact? In B. Austin (Ed.), *Current research in film* (Vol. 5, pp. 1–18). Norwood, NJ: Ablex.

Willis, D. C. (1972–1984). *Horror and science fiction films: A checklist* (Vols. 1–3). Metuchen, NJ: Scarecrow Press.

Wolf, L. (1989). *Horror: A connoisseur's guide to literature and film.* New York: Facts on File.

Zillmann, D., Weaver, J. B., Mundorf, N., & Aust, C. F. (1986). Effects of an opposite-gender companion's affect to horror on distress, delight, and attraction. *Journal of Personality and Social Psychology, 51,* 586–594.

The Emotional Use of Popular Music by Adolescents

Alan Wells and Ernest A. Hakanen

This article originally appeared in the Spring 1991 issue of *Journalism Quarterly*. © 1991.

Popular music obviously speaks to the high school audience in some very strong and emotional ways. This study attempts to document that process via the results of a questionnaire administered to over 1,500 high school students. The grouping of respondents into various "clusters" using a computer technique helps identify how various subgroups of the high school population respond to the music and how they "use" it in their everyday lives.

Alan Wells is visiting professor of mass communication at the National University of Singapore and professor of communication in the Department of Radio, Television, and Film at Temple University.

Ernest Hakanen is assistant professor of broadcast and electronics communication at Marquette University.

Tips and Touts

1 The authors open with a plea for more serious academic inquiry into popular music. It's interesting to note that while rock 'n' roll has been a social force among young people since the 1950s, it wasn't until the 1980s that much of the research began to appear. Note how the authors carefully build on that research and use it to lead the reader to his or her own findings.

2 In the results section, the authors find that men tend to cite TV as their most used medium while women tend to favor radio listening. Does this finding match your own experience?

3 Table 1 lists a wide array of emotions that respondents cite in conjunction with their feelings about the music. How do they compare to your own responses? Table 2 breaks them down according to gender. Can you think of any reason why men's and women's reactions to various songs may be different?

4 Levels of proof are indicated in various sections of the study where you see $P = .0001$, $P < .05$, and so on. These claims are made to show that the trends reported by the authors are not merely the results of chance occurrence.

5 According to this study, women are much more likely than men to use music for "mood management," although both men and women find music useful in that regard. Can you think of possible explanations for this gender difference?

6 In Table 4, the authors begin to break findings down according to respondent membership in one of four "musical taste" groups. While such divisions may seem arbitrary in some ways, they do help us organize the large number of respondents and explore the differences among them. The authors leave the door open for later studies to build on these definitions and use them to find out more about the relationships between popular music and the young audience.

7   This study uses the *survey method,* where a questionnaire is given to gather data. Other approaches could also have been taken. *Content analysis* could be used to examine the content of various songs, to see what sorts of emotions are dealt with in them. *Ethnographic* or *field research* could explore how music is used by adolescents in natural settings (such as in their homes or schools or at dance clubs). An *experiment* could be conducted to test the effect of different songs on various groups of adolescents. Finally, *critical* or *cultural analysis* could be used to explore the deeper meanings in music, such as the ideological messages they might contain. Note that each method produces unique results.

Popular music holds a central position in contemporary mass media. It is the main content of radio, and music videos have made it a growing component of television viewing. Music also appears to be an increasingly important part of feature film production. With records, tapes and compact discs, along with live concerts and performances, popular music is a ubiquitous medium in its own right.

However, serious study of popular music is relatively new to mass media research. During the 1980s some book length treatments emerged[1] and scholarly journal articles have added to existing knowledge. The frequency of programmatic statements in the literature, however, indicates the still emergent status of popular music research. Lewis[2] noted the dearth of "uses and gratifications" studies and Curtis[3] claims that technology and the audience are the least studied aspects of popular music. Chaffee[4] has summarized existing research in his appeal to legitimize music study. More recently, Denski[5] has set out a comprehensive program for music research.

This study attempts to fill some existing gaps in the knowledge about consumption and uses of popular music by adolescents. The research is in what Denski calls the "micro levels of analysis": we investigate the uses and experience of music and their relationship to age, social class, gender, academic success

This section is known as the literature review. Here the authors review what has already been done in this area and explain how their study will offer a unique contribution. That is, they need to prove that they are not just covering old territory or working on research questions that others have already exhausted.

and race. We then focus on the emotional and mood management[6] uses of music.

Review of Literature

In a study using electronic pagers by Larson and Kubey,[7] respondents reported that they were listening intently to music for 1.4% of the total self-report time. However, as a reported secondary media activity, music was reported 6.4% of the time. This suggests that music is more frequently used as background.[8] When listening to music, adolescents reported greater emotional involvement, higher motivation, greater excitement and more openness than for other media.[9] The study concluded that the adolescents demonstrated that music is much more successful in engaging youth than television. The authors explain why such findings are important: it speaks to adolescent concerns, from heterosexual relationships to autonomy and individualization. Rock in particular may be embraced by the young, because its very sounds and words mirror the intensity and turbulence of adolescent experience. The music reflects the extreme emotional experiences adolescents encounter from moment to moment as part of their daily realities. Thus it is no wonder that this medium has much power to engage the young.[10]

Can you think of other reasons that music seems to be particularly important to youth?

Christianson and Lindlof[11] have summarized what is known from the scarce studies of the effects of music on children. It may "... have a significant emotional and effective impact ... there is evidence that two of the prime determinants of children's musical preferences are the mood and sentiment of the music. .... Most rock music is by its very nature an excitatory stimulus and can arouse the listener."[12] The same effect can be expected in young adults.

Gantz et al.[13] studied the gratification of popular music claimed by a sample of secondary and college students. The listeners were found to use music primarily to relieve boredom, ease tensions, manipulate their moods and fight loneliness. Music preference or use was not examined by the researchers.

Precise use of terms is important in research. However, sometimes the jargon can confuse rather than clarify. In stating that rock music is an "excitatory stimulus" the authors simply mean that youth tend to experience intense emotions (excitement) when listening to rock. What terms might adolescents themselves use to describe this phenomenon?

Rosenbaum and Prinsky[14] asked a junior and senior high school sample to choose their three favorite songs and select one of seven reasons for liking them. In order of preference, the reasons the songs were chosen were: "It helps me to relax and stop thinking about things" (30% male, 34% female); "Helps get me in the right mood" (25% male, 29% female), "It's good to dance to" (16% male, 35% female), "Words express how I feel" (17% male, 24% female), "It creates a good atmosphere when I'm with others" (16% male, 13% female); "It helps pass the time" (13% male, 10% female); and "I want to listen to the words" (11% male, 7% female).[15] Dance or emotional impact are highly represented. Except for dance, differences between the genders were small.

Melton and Galician[16] consciously employed a uses and gratifications model. They found that "Respondents felt that both radio and music videos provided need satisfaction in passing time, relieving tension, relaxation, mood shifting, and forgetting about problems."[17] Gender was dropped in their regression analysis of popular music consumption: it may have less significance in music use than would be expected from gender role hypotheses. Hochschild[18] analyzed some of the complexities of a single emotion, love, and the differing ways that males and females deal with it. To have their full impact, an audience would have to perform three social acts to absorb them: the music would have to be attended to, codified and managed. The artist, too, presumably must construct the emotion in the same way to be convincing. Hochschild[19] has also persuasively argued that the genders manage their emotions in different ways. One can therefore hypothesize gender differences in the emotional use of music.

Love, in its many varieties, is widely acknowledged to be the most common component of western popular music. Denisoff and Bridges[20] have cited the numerous studies on the love component of American popular music and the differing uses of music by males and females. Similarly, Frith[21] discusses at length the meaning of pop music to British teens. He describes the features of female youth culture[22] that produces the "dream lover" phenomenon while males gravitate to "macho" music. While he notes that rock has been a force in liberating sexuality,[23] there is neither sexual equality among performing artists nor a unisex homogenization of musical tastes. Of course, the expression of a range of emotions in popular music is complex. The music itself may imply emotions, and the artist's interpretations of lyrics can convey other than their surface meaning. The analysis herein suspends such considerations and deals only with the emotional content of music as perceived by the listener.

Using a list of emotions from the Dictionary of Emotional Meaning,[24] Wells[25] asked college students to identify the emotions that they most associated with their favorite songs. He found that "Contrary to the pernicious 'nonemotional' stereotype of males, they do in fact exhibit strong emotional use of music. Overall, there is a striking congruence of the frequency of male and female selections of emotions." Gender differences did

As you recall from Chapter 7, "love" is perhaps the most common theme in popular music. Do you think men and women interpret this theme differently? In what ways might pop music be "sexually liberating"?

not appear to be great. Women chose songs that express hope, happiness, passion and grief slightly more than men. Men were more likely to choose excitement, delight, anger and hate. While popular music exposes the listener to a broad range of emotional feelings, the most frequently chosen were happiness, excitement, love, hope, confidence, delight and passion.[26]

Many studies attest to the intense effects of music. In Wells'[27] study most respondents expressed an emotional, personal impact that is probably far more important to them than, for example, watching a television soap opera or reading a textbook. Both males and females commonly associated songs with current or past loves. Songs can also evoke other memories, sometimes sentimental or tragic ones. Music seems to be a major link of biography and nostalgia.

This point was also made in Chapter 7. Pop music has a unique ability for "marking" significant events in our lives.

Wells[28] examined mood management and music. He found a high percentage of both males and females claim to use music to change a mood. The most common for both genders was combating depression or being upset. Music, they claimed, could lift their spirits. Others claimed that music was used to calm them down or to relax. Few respondents claimed both uses of music.

All of the studies cited imply some link between music use and emotional management. Mood management theory[29] eloquently addresses the psychological choices of music for the regulation and management of emotional states. Zillman expands on dissonance theory and its selective exposure theory[30] as his theory "deals with all conceivable moods rather than with a single, specific affective state, such as dissonance."[31] He[32] explains:

> The theory is based on the hedonistic premise that (a) individuals strive to rid themselves of bad moods or, at least, seek to diminish the intensity of such moods, and (2) individuals strive to perpetuate good moods and seek to maintain the intensity of these moods.

> The theory then posits that, to the extent possible, individuals arrange internal and external stimulus conditions so as to minimize bad moods and maximize good moods.

Again, the point here is rather simple: We do what feels good. We avoid pain.

The research herein examines mood management as respondents are asked to identify moods that they associate with their favorite music and how they use music to enhance particular moods. "Mood management theory does not stipulate that individuals need be cognizant of the reasons for their choices. Recognition of the causal circumstances is not ruled out, however."[33]

Method

A questionnaire was administered to respondents from all of the sections of English education (every student must take English) at a Northeastern small city high school.[34] In addition to demographic information, respondents were asked to rate each of the following emotions on a progressive scale (0 through 9) as to how they felt when they listen to their favorite type of music: Love, Hope, Fear, Pride, Grief, Anger, Sadness, Passion, Delight, Happiness, Excitement and Confidence. Respondents were also asked to rate each of the five completions to the following using the same progressive (0 to 9) scale: I use music to . . . (1) lift my spirits, (2) calm me down, (3) mellow me out, (4) get me pumped up, and (5) strengthen my moods.

How might the fact that the study took place in a "small city" be significant?

The respondents were also asked to choose their spare time media preference from a list provided and to rate their liking, on a progressive scale of 0 (most dislike) through 9 (most like), of each of the following: Rock, Classical, Reggae, Easy Listening, Heavy Metal, Jazz, R & B/Soul, Country, Pop and New Wave.

Because the research questions address an examination of music and emotions and preference differences across gender and grade level, appropriate tests which imply difference were applied. Since we proposed to investigate taste clusters and since respondents could prefer more than one type of music or feel more than one type of emotion, a quick cluster (SPSS) method was applied to define interest groups and emotion groups. Cluster analysis computes the similarity or distances between all pairs or objects that are computed. Based on these, similar objects are grouped using preselected criteria. Because of the great size of the data base, a quick cluster program, in which the number of clusters must be specified, was used. These music preference groups and emotion groups were then analyzed as to their gender and grade level make-up.

Here the sort of questionnaire used is described so that the reader can evaluate its valid-ity, if it indeed measures what the authors claim it does. Also, this allows other re-searchers to replicate (re-peat) this study to see if they get the same results. Such replication helps us estimate the reliability of a study.

Results

Males ($n = 732$) rated TV as their most used medium (42.6%) followed by recorded music (32.8%) and radio (14.8%). Females ($n = 800$) rated radio listening highest (38.5%) followed by TV (25.5%) and records (25.1%). Listening to music, either on the radio or records, is clearly the predominant media use by females and is also strong for males. Both genders rated movies, books, magazines and newspapers very low as a premier media activity. Television use decreased with grade in school (40.4% in 9th to 26.9% in 12th), while recorded music as a first choice rose steadily from 22.6% in 9th grade to 33.1% among 12th grade.

Interesting. Why might males watch more TV than females? Conversely, why might fe-males be more inclined to lis-ten to the radio?

Table 1: Association of Emotions with Favorite Music

	"Does Not Reflect"	"Intermediate"	"Reflects a Great Deal"
Rating	(0–3)	(3–6)	(7–9)
Emotion			
Love	10.8	20.0	69.2
Hope	16.4	30.6	53.0
Fear	40.2	34.4	25.4
Pride	17.7	32.7	49.6
Grief	41.2	36.3	22.5
Anger	35.3	30.0	34.6
Sadness	29.3	33.0	37.7
Passion	21.1	29.8	48.9
Delight	16.7	32.5	50.8
Happiness	7.4	21.5	71.3
Excitement	6.2	17.6	76.1
Confidence	15.2	27.4	57.4

In Table 1, we see that "love" is the emotion that respondents most often said "reflects a great deal" upon how they feel when listening to pop music. In Table 2, we see that females were somewhat more likely (with a mean, or average, score of 7.67) than males (with a mean score of 6.05) to give this answer.

Table 2: Emotion Ratings by Gender

Emotion	Females		Males		T Value
	Mean	SD	Mean	SD	
Love	7.67	2.14	6.05	3.03	12.12*
Hope	6.23	2.76	5.60	3.02	4.27*
Fear	4.17	3.22	3.46	3.00	4.45*
Pride	5.56	2.99	6.00	2.97	−2.87*
Grief	3.82	3.09	3.51	2.96	1.95
Anger	4.26	3.35	4.75	3.31	−2.88*
Sadness	5.59	3.10	3.84	3.09	11.00*
Passion	6.06	2.96	5.10	3.24	6.00*
Delight	6.15	2.74	5.41	3.03	4.99*
Happiness	7.37	2.26	6.72	2.60	5.20*
Excitement	7.48	2.25	7.26	2.40	1.87
Confidence	5.94	2.89	6.37	2.92	−2.91*

*$p < .005$ d.f. range from 1515–1525

Most respondents were able to identify strong links between music and emotions. As Table 1 shows, excitement, happiness and love are the emotions most frequently associated with music.

Emotion ratings varied significantly by gender. As shown in Table 2, women tend to associate emotions with music more than do men. The only emotions rated higher by men than by women were confidence, anger and pride. Gender differences were significant ($P < .005$) for all emotions except grief and excitement, the two emotions with the most extreme ratings.

Analysis of Variance was employed to test the difference between emotion ratings and selected social variables. The Tukey procedure was also used to examine where the significant differences occurred. Because many of the respondents did not know thier class or father's occupation, father's education was used as an indicator of social class. None of the emotions were significantly related ($P < .05$) to social class or to race and ethnicity.

Grade in school was related to four emotions. ANOVA for love ($F = 261$, $P = .05$) was attributable (Tukey $P < .05$) to 12th graders rating it higher than 9th graders. Despite the image of music appealing to young teens, apparently love strikes later. The same also holds for grief ($F = 3.06$, $P = .03$). Sadness ($F = 7.09$, $P = .0001$) is experienced by 11th graders and 12th graders significantly more than 9th graders. Passion follows a slightly different pattern ($F = 4.8$ 1, $P = .002$) with 10th and 12th rating it significantly higher than 9th graders. For love, grief, sadness and passion, there appears to be a maturation effect, with 9th graders associating these emotions with music less than upper classpersons. Success in school (self evaluation grade) of the respondents was not significantly related to emotions ratings.

A cluster analysis (SPSS quick cluster routine) was used to identify homogeneous groups of cases based on selected attributes. The attributes in this case were the twelve emotion variables. After examining different numbers of clusters, a set of five clusters (see Table 3) was used based upon its comparative non-ambiguity and clarity.

Table 3: Emotion Clusters and Cluster Centers

Cluster	1	2	3	4	5
		Highly			
Name	Unemotional	Emotional	Romantic	Angry	Self-Assured
Emotion					
Love	2.36	7.98	7.40	5.91	6.48
Hope	1.16	7.06	5.48	4.29	5.89
Fear	1.61	5.62	3.82	3.13	1.80
Pride	2.13	6.67	3.33	3.20	6.41
Grief	1.52	5.58	2.48	3.38	1.60
Anger	2.20	6.20	2.07	6.79	2.32
Sadness	1.89	6.67	3.92	5.83	2.47
Passion	1.43	7.23	6.52	3.29	4.61
Delight	1.88	6.84	3.57	2.20	6.52
Happiness	3.36	7.68	6.11	4.52	7.90
Excitement	4.21	7.85	5.05	6.62	8.09
Confidence	1.62	6.61	4.58	4.96	7.15
N	116	716	84	117	464

In this table, we see how various groups of students relate to music. Among the "angry" students, for example, music is often associated with "excitement," whereas among the "romantics," music use is most often associated with "love."

By far the largest group of respondents fell into the "highly emotional" cluster. Love, excitement, happiness and passion are strongly associated with their favorite music, but so are other emotions. In contrast, the "unemotional" group rate every emotion lower than any other group. They clearly do not associate emotions with music. The second most populous group, the "self-assured," associate music with the positive emotions of happiness, confidence and so on. They reject the negative emotions of fear, anger and sadness. The "romantic's" primary emotions are love, passion, hope and excitement. The "angry" cluster also associates excitement with music, but its distinguishing emotions are anger, love and sadness.

A cluster analysis was used to identify homogeneous groups of cases based on the 10 music choices. After examining different numbers of clusters, a set of four clusters was used based upon its comparative nonambiguity and clarity.

The four clusters represent four distinct musical taste cultures (see Table 4). Cluster I was labeled "mainstreamers." They like the main types of commercial music aimed at youth through radio, record promotion, MTV and concerts. "Mainstreamers" give relatively high positive ratings to rock, pop and new wave and are relatively tolerant to easy listening. Another large group, cluster IV, seems to specialize in rock and heavy metal. These "heavy rockers" are the most hostile group in their ratings of R&B/Soul, new wave, reggae, classical, country and jazz. Cluster II, by contrast, gives low ratings to all types of music. While they like reggae more than the other groups, no music genre gets a positive rating, and the only music that they dislike more than the other groups is heavy metal. They are, therefore, labeled "indifferent." The last group represented by cluster III are named "music lovers." They rate rock higher than any other group, enjoy heavy metal pop and easy listening, and even give a positive rating to classical, country and jazz, strongly disliked by the mainstreamers and heavy rockers.

Table 5 shows the relationship of music taste and emotional identification. The "unemotionals," as would be expected, fall disproportionately into the indifferent music cluster. "Highly emotionals" and "romantics" are both slightly overrepresented in their choice as "music lovers," and underrepresented as "indifferents." The emotionally "angry" are "indifferent" or favor heavy rock music. They are under represented as "mainstreamers." "Self-assured" are evenly distributed among the music taste choices.

Thus far, adolescent associations of music with emotions have been examined. Now, we turn to an examination of music and its use in emotional management. Respondents were asked

Table 4: Music Preference Cluster Centers
(Means of cluster method 0–9 scale)

Music Labels	I Mainstream	II Indifferent	III Music Lovers	IV Heavy Rockers
Rock	7.61	3.72	8.02	7.82
Pop	7.19	3.23	6.40	4.00
R&B/Soul	4.40	2.38	3.43	1.88
New Wave	5.25	4.45	3.73	2.37
Heavy Metal	2.81	1.01	6.31	7.55
Easy List.	4.97	1.78	6.59	2.09
Reggae	3.47	4.47	3.65	1.84
Classical	1.58	3.84	5.86	1.01
Country	1.14	0.97	5.19	0.62
Jazz	1.93	3.01	5.28	1.38
N	662	112	101	630

In these tables, various "music taste cultures" are identified. For example, "heavy rockers" don't seem to listen to much classical music, whereas "music lovers" seem to listen to a much wider range of music. Which category do you fall into?

Table 5: Musical Taste by Emotional Cluster

Music Cluster Count Col. Pct. Tot. Pct. Emotion	Main-streamers	Indifferents	Music Lovers	Heavy Rockers	Row Total
Unemotionals	35	20	2	58	115
	5.5	18.3	2.1	9.4	7.9
	2.4	1.4	.1	4.0	
Highly Emotional	345	35	53	266	699
	53.8	32.1	54.6	43.2	47.8
	23.6	2.4	3.6	18.2	
Romantics	36	3	7	37	83
	5.6	2.8	7.2	6.0	5.7
	2.5	.2	.5	2.5	
Angry	35	15	4	63	117
	5.5	13.8	4.1	10.2	8.0
	2.4	1.0	.3	4.3	
Self-Assured	190	36	31	192	449
	29.6	33.0	32.0	31.2	30.7
	13.0	2.5	2.1	13.1	
Col. Totals	641	109	97	616	
	43.8	7.5	6.6	42.1	

Chi square = 58.21 d.f. = 12 P < .000

Table 6: Percentage of Distribution of Emotional Uses

	Lift Spirits	Calm Down	Mellow Out	Pumped Up	Strengthen Mood
Rating Don't Use Music					
0	8.9	18.1	19.6	7.2	6.8
1	1.5	2.2	2.4	1.3	1.2
2	2.8	4.1	4.5	.9	1.5
3	1.8	3.5	5.4	2.6	1.5
4	2.2	3.9	4.4	1.8	2.7
5	6.3	9.9	9.7	5.5	6.2
6	5.1	5.4	6.4	4.3	5.5
7	8.4	9.1	8.4	6.7	9.6
8	13.4	8.8	7.6	11.2	12.6
9	49.6	35.0	31.6	58.5	52.3
Use a Great Deal					
N	1531	1531	1529	1532	1530

Table 6 shows that over half the respondents use music to get "pumped up," whereas less than 10% do not use music for this purpose. What other interesting results can you find in this table?

to rate five (progressive scale, 0–9) of the uses for music derived from open-ended questions in Wells'[35] studies. The distribution of ratings is shown in Table 6. Most respondents claim high levels of emotional management through music use (see Table 7). Getting "pumped up" is the most frequent use. This energizing is followed in popularity by "mood strengthening" and also "lifting spirits." All three may be seen as mood enhancing using music as a stimulant. Less frequent, but clearly established, is the use of music as a tranquilizer. Thus about a third of the respondents use music a great deal to "calm down" and "mellow out."

Women use music for mood management significantly more than men. T-tests reveal differences ($P < .002$) for all uses except "get me pumped up." This is the most popular choice for males and it is the only use that they rate higher than do female respondents.

The only significant relationship between social class and music use was an association with "strengthen my mood" ($F = 2.03$, d.f. $= 7$, $P = .048$) due to differences (Tukey $P < .05$) between high school and master's degree paternal education.

Race/ethnicity was related to some emotional uses. "Lifts my spirits" ($F = 4.84$, $P < .0005$) was claimed more by black respondents than whites (Tukey $P < .05$). "Getting pumped up" ($F = 4.84$, $P = .0005$) was significantly lower for Asians than for whites, blacks and others.

Grade is related to the use of music to "lift my spirits" ($F = 6.88$, $P = .0001$), with 9th graders significantly less likely to

Table 7: Emotional Management by Gender

| | Females | | Males | | |
Emotion	Mean	SD	Mean	SD	T Value
Lift my spirits	7.53	2.48	6.34	3.23	8.13*
Calm me down	6.24	3.28	5.05	3.49	6.86*
Mellow me out	5.72	3.43	4.97	3.45	4.24*
Get me pumped up	7.34	2.73	7.35	2.71	−0.07
Strengthen my mood	7.43	2.54	7.01	2.78	3.05*

*P < .005
d.f. range from 1525 to 1530

do so than 11th and 12th graders. The same pattern is true of "mellow me out" ($F = 6.01$, $P = .0005$). The other uses of music are not significantly related to music.

Conclusion

Listening to popular music is a major media use by adolescents, and it increases with age. The respondents clearly associated particular emotions with music they liked. The choice of music was closely related to emotional uses. Emotional use was related to some social variables (gender, grade in school) but not to others (social class, academic success).

Does this strike you as a particularly significant conclusion? Why or why not? What sorts of other studies might be conducted to elaborate upon the research reported here?

A cluster analysis was used to identify five emotional types: "unemotional," "highly emotional," "romantics," "angry" and "self assured." Four taste clusters were identified: "mainstreamers," "heavy rockers," "indifferents" and "music lovers." The relationship between emotional clusters and musical taste was investigated.

Most respondents claimed to use music for emotional management, either mood enhancing (energizing, strengthening or lifting) or tranquilizing. Women engage in this management significantly more than men. There were also some differences in specific emotional uses by social class, race/ethnicity and grade in school. Overall, it is clear that for many adolescents who like popular music, it is a powerful tool for expressing and managing emotions.

References

1   Simon Frith, *Sound Effects: Youth, Leisure and the Politics of Rock 'n' Roll* (New York: Pantheon, 1981) and James Lull, ed., *Popular Music and Communication.* (Beverly Hills, Calif.: Sage, 1987).

2   G.H. Lewis, "The Meaning's in the Music and the Music's in Me: Popular Music as Symbolic Communication." *Theory, Culture and Society, 1*(3), (1983),

pp. 133–141; "Towards a Uses and Gratifications Approach: An Examination of Commitment and Involvement in Popular Music," *Popular Music and Society, 8*(1), (1981), pp. 10–18.

3   J. Curtis, *Rock Eras: Interpretation of Music and Society, 1954–1984* (Bowling Green, OH: Bowling Green University Press, 1987).

4   Steven Chaffee, "Popular Music and Communication Research: An Editorial Epilogue." *Communication Research* 12:413–424, (1985).

5   Denski, "One Step Up and Two Steps Back: A Heuristic Model for Popular Music and Communication Research." *Popular Music and Society, 13*(1), pp. 9–21, (1989).

6   D. Zillman, "Mood Management: Using Entertainment to Full Advantage," In L. Donohew, H. Sypher, and T. Higgins, (Eds.), *Communication, Social Cognition and Affect* (Hillsdale, N.J.: Erlbaum, 1988); and D. Zillman, "Mood Management Through Communication Choices," *American Behavioral Scientist,* (31), pp. 327–340.

7   Richard Larson and Robert Kubey, "Television and Music: Contrasting Media in Adolescent Life," *Youth and Society,* pp. 13–33, (Spring, 1983).

8   Ibid., p. 19.

9   Ibid., p. 25.

10   Ibid., p. 26.

11   P.G. Christianson and T.R. Lindlof, "The Role of the Audio Media in the Lives of Children," *Popular Music and Society 9*(3), (1983), pp. 25–40.

12   Ibid., p. 36.

13   Walter Gantz, H.M. Gartenburg, M.L. Pearson, L. Martin, S.O. Schiller, "Gratifications and Expectations Associated with Pop Music Among Adolescents," *Popular Music and Society,* 6:81–89, (1978).

14   J. Rosenbaum and L. Prinsky, "Sex, Violence and Rock 'n' Roll: Youth's Perceptions of Popular Music," *Popular Music and Society, 11*(2), pp. 78–91, (1978).

15   Ibid., p. 26.

16   G.W. Melton and M. Galician, "A Sociological Approach to the Pop Music Phenomenon: Radio and Music Video Utilization for Expectation, Motivation, and Satisfaction," *Popular Music and Society, 11*(3), (1987), pp. 35–36.

17   Ibid., p. 41.

18   Arlie R. Hothschild, *The Managed Heart: Commercialization of Human Feeling* (Berkeley, Calif.: University of California Press, 1983).

19   Ibid.

20   Serge R. Denisoff and J. Bridges, "Popular Music: Who are the Recording Artists?" *Journal of Communication* 32: 132–142, (Winter, 1982).

21   Simon Frith, *Sound Effects: Youth, Leisure and the Politics of Rock 'n' Roll* (New York: Pantheon, 1981).

22   Ibid., pp. 225–234.

23   Ibid., pp. 235–248.

24   J.R. Davitz, *The Language of Emotion* (New York: Academic Press, 1969), p. 11.

25   Alan Wells, "Gender, Emotions and Popular Music." Unpublished paper presented at the Midwest Sociological Society annual meeting. St. Louis (1985).

26 Ibid., p. 8.

27 Alan Wells, "Popular Music and Emotions: Emotional Uses and Management." *Journal of Popular Culture,* forthcoming (1988).

28 Ibid.

29 D. Zillman, "Mood Management: Using Entertainment to Full Advantage," In Donohew, H. Sypher and T. Higgins, (Eds.), *Communication, Social Cognition And Affect* (Hillsdale, N.J.: Erlbaum, 1988). D. Zillman, "Mood Management Through Communication Choices," *American Behavior Scientist,* (31), pp. 327–340.

30 Festinger, *A Theory of Cognitive Dissonance* (Stanford, Calif.: Stanford University Press, 1957).

31 D. Zillman, "Mood Management Through Communication Choices," *American Behavior Scientist,* (31), p. 328.

32 Ibid.

33 Op cit., p. 329.

34 The availability sample consisted of 1,547 respondents (52% female and 48% male) from ages 11 to 19. Many (77.5%) intend to continue their education beyond high school. Using father's occupation as an indicator and A. Edwards "Comparative Occupations in the U.S., 1870 to 1940" (Washington, D.C.: Government Printing Office, 1943) as a classification scheme, about one-third (34.5%) are from upper middle to upper class backgrounds. About half (47.2%) fall into middle class classifications. Almost one-tenth (9.5%) were from working and lower class backgrounds. The remaining respondents (8.8%) did not answer or have households in which the providers were not in the work force, unemployed, or deceased.

35 Wells, A. (1985). "Gender, emotions and popular music." Unpublished paper presented at the Midwest Sociological Society annual meeting. St. Louis.

The Treatment and Resolution of Moral Violations on Soap Operas

John C. Sutherland and Shelley J. Siniawsky

Soap operas have been increasingly analyzed in research journals. It is important to note that this research used content analysis technique but that the source is a secondary one. Rather than analyze a year's worth of episodes of "All My Children" and "General Hospital," the authors have chosen to accept the condensation in Soap Opera Digest *as their source. Nevertheless, the findings refute one of the most often voiced objections to daytime drama: that soap operas condone or encourage immoral behavior.*

John C. Sutherland, at the time this was written, was an assistant professor at the College of Journalism and Communications, University of Florida.

Shelley J. Siniawsky was a graduate student at the same school.

Tips and Touts

1   Note how the authors present several points of view about the moral point of view of soap operas before discussing their own findings. This is often done in research studies to help present a "balanced" perspective.

2   Note the list of 14 moral "stands" that the authors chose to represent "established" moral codes. Do you agree with all of these? How about your community at large?

3   Note in Table 4 that over 60% of all the moral issues were not resolved or were resolved in an unclear manner. This means that the study's conclusions are actually based on the minority of issues that were resolved.

4   In the final paragraph of the study, the authors make an excellent point that relates to all content analysis. Simply counting how often things occur in the media (*x* number of murders, for example) does not tell us nearly so much as when further analysis can be applied to help us understand *why* such things appear with great frequency. This article offers perspectives on why things occur as they do in soap operas.

5   The numbers within parentheses in this study refer to other related studies, which are listed by number in the References section at the end. Those interested in a particular point may track down the original study for more information.

A frequent criticism of soap operas is that they present and condone immorality. According to Herzog (12), soap operas function as a "school of life," where moral truths are taught by example and advice. Similarly, soap operas fit into Chesebro's (4) mimetic form of communication, as a reflection of ordinary life. Over repeated exposures, some critics maintain, viewers come to believe that the behavior and moral stands to which they are exposed are socially accepted. According to Katzman (13), soap operas "suggest how people should act in certain situations. . . . They can legitimize behavior and remove taboos. . . ." As morals are treated more liberally and violators of moral standards are unpunished, so this argument goes, viewers learn more liberal and perhaps new moral standards.

Other critics take a middle ground. Modleski (14, p. 15) maintains that soap operas only introduce those issues that can be forgiven in the long run, but that soap operas may ultimately have a liberalizing effect. Comstock (5) suggests that while television program content cannot transgress established morals and beliefs, programming does flirt with nonconformity.

Finally, some critics believe that soap operas are only "propaganda for the status quo" (1, p. 43) and that soap opera content has not changed since the days of radio (8). If soap operas have such a strong effect on moral standards, these critics might ask, why have these standards changed so little over time?

The opinion of the public on the effects of soap operas on morality is mixed as well. Over half the respondents in a 1970 Canadian survey (3) believed television contributed to a breakdown of morals. In a 1971 Harris poll only 26 percent of those interviewed believed soap operas are "meant for me" (6, p. 40). Polls conducted for NBC by the Roper Organization and for ABC by the National Survey Research Group found that few viewers scorn television violence and sex (9). The Roper poll concluded, "There is little dissatisfaction with the treatment of sex, less dissatisfaction with violence, and even less sentiment for taking these programs off the air because of sex, profanity or violence." Sixty-four percent of the respondents to the ABC poll believed that "primary responsibility to determine what is acceptable belongs to the individual viewer."

Research of soap opera and other programming content has attempted to clarify the issues. Goldsen (10) and Katzman (13) analyzed soap operas to determine their moral content. These studies found plots revolving around murder, child abuse, poisonings, infidelity, illegitimacy, and incest. Durdeen-Smith's analysis of CBS and ABC soap operas found emphasis placed on moral and emotional crises rather than on characters (7, p. 19).

As with most studies, different points of view about the question are discussed and summarized. Those interested in the studies cited can look them up and read them in full.

The question of "moral points of view" is raised often in media research. Perhaps you have one particular favorite program. Can you see any implications here for the characters on that show?

Ryan's (16) analysis of one episode of "Kung Fu" found the major character to have a highly developed moral system; villains had less developed moral systems. Examining violent content in films, Martin (cited in 17, p. 153) argued that the effect of violence is mediated by the reason for it; violence for the sake of decency should be less "harmful" to viewers. A similar conclusion was reached in a 1976 Canadian Senate content analysis of programming (19), which maintained that strong conclusions could not be reached about television content without studying how the audience perceived that content.

Previous research on soap operas has focused on the moral content of the programs and the number of instances in which moral dilemmas arise. However, merely tabulating the instances in which moral questions arise does not reveal how these questions were resolved. It may be that moral dilemmas are treated and resolved in a manner that is consistent with a moral code.

We selected two popular soap operas for analysis — "All My Children" and "General Hospital," both highly rated, one-hour shows on ABC. While the results of this study clearly cannot be generalized to all soap operas, our objectives here were best met by examining popular, trend-setting soap operas which are frequently criticized. Each report of these two soap operas in issues of *Soap Opera Digest* from January 8–December 23, 1980, was analyzed. Since each issue of *Soap Opera Digest* covers about two weeks of programming or ten episodes, this study analyzed roughly 440 episodes (220 episodes per series).

While there are limitations inherent in the use of such a secondary source, only two present serious difficulties (11). First, because *Soap Opera Digest* runs several weeks behind regularly scheduled broadcasts, and the number of episodes reported in each *Digest* varies, it was impossible to determine accurately exactly when events occurred. However, this was not considered relevant to our study. The second limitation is more serious. Written capsule descriptions cannot provide all the information presented in a television broadcast. Hence subtle messages conveyed by music, facial expressions, and voice inflections could not be taken into account. Given soap operas' use of repetition and their heavy reliance on dialog, however, this limitation was not considered a debilitating one. The benefit in using *Soap Opera Digest* was that it permitted analysis of a full year of programming, which we considered necessary to allow story lines to reach resolutions. The time and costs of analyzing one year of broadcasts would have been prohibitive.

Moral standards are difficult to define because they differ among individuals and they are continuously evolving. We reviewed soap opera criticism and discovered 14 moral standards frequently claimed by critics to be violated on soap operas.

Here the authors must deal with the fact that using Soap Opera Digest *is not exactly the same as watching the shows themselves. They maintain that the differences are not significant enough, however, when compared with the benefit of being able to monitor the shows for such a lengthy period. Such methodological shortcuts are common in research. Can you think of any problems this kind of shortcut might pose?*

1 Premarital/extramarital sex is wrong (8, 10, 13, 14, 15).

2 Bigamy is extramarital sex and wrong (10, 13).

3 Children should be born in wedlock (8, 10, 13, 15).

4 Abortion is wrong (8, 14, 15).

5 Incest is wrong (18).

6 Rape is wrong (15).

7 Divorce must be carefully considered and not rushed into (10, 14, 15).

8 Parents should not neglect their children (10).

9 Children should obey their parents (15).

10 Alcohol abuse/addiction is wrong (8, 14).

11 Drug abuse/addiction is wrong (13, 15).

12 Deception of others is wrong (5).

13 Blackmail is wrong (13, 14).

14 Murder is wrong (13).

Each instance of a moral violation was coded according to the action taken. Instances in which the character intended to violate a moral [standard] but took no action were coded as "intended" — for example, if a character purchased a gun to commit murder but did not attempt the murder. Instances in which a character attempted an action that violated a moral standard but was unsuccessful were coded as "attempted" — for example, if a character fired a weapon at a victim with the intent to kill, but missed; or if a male attacked a female with the intent to rape, but was stopped by another character's intervention. Instances were coded as "actual" if a character carried out an action that violated a moral standard.

Treatment, or what happens to the character who violates a moral [standard], was coded into three categories. Treatment was considered "condoned" if a character's immoral action was supported either socially or economically in the story line. For example, if one who violated a moral standard was agreed with or offered aid, this was considered a "condoned" treatment. When Palmer and Myra allowed Daisy to remain in Pine Valley without revealing her true identity to Nina on "All My Children," they "condoned" her deceit. Treatment was "not condoned" when immoral action was opposed, as, for example, when the transgressing character was "warned" by another, was "suspected," or suffered social or economic penalties. This category was also indicated by emotional reactions, such as guilt, shock, or worry. Complications, such as a "close call" or an argument, also indicated treatment that was "not condoned." Finally, "not indicated" covered a situation in which the violation was mentioned but no reaction was described. For example, a reporter told Anne the details of Paul's affair with Ellen on "All My Children," but according to the description Anne did not exhibit emotion or use the information in any way.

Every story involving a moral dilemma was examined for the moral lesson in its conclusion. This concluding lesson was the resolution. If the resolution was punishment, the resolution was coded as "consistent"; if the resolution was reward, it was coded as "inconsistent." For example, on "All My Children," Claudette Montgomery killed Eddie Dorrance. Although she was not accused of murder for six months, others began to suspect her. When Claudette was chased by the police, she drove her car into a river. She died in the hospital after confessing. Since Claudette was punished for her actions, this resolution was coded as being "consistent" with the moral injunction "do not kill." If a character violated a moral injunction but was rewarded, the resolution was coded as "inconsistent" with the moral code. In some instances the resolution was coded as "not clear." On "General Hospital," for instance, Mitch and Susan had an affair. There was no clear reward or punishment; the affair ended because of extraneous circumstances. Finally, story lines not resolved by the end of the *Soap Opera Digest* year were coded as "not resolved."

There were 68 instances of moral issues coded, 36 on "All My Children" and 32 on "General Hospital." As shown in Table 1, deceit was the most frequently raised moral issue, followed by murder and premarital and extramarital sex. No other moral issue arose more than five times. Neither incest, illegitimacy, nor bigamy was addressed. As a result, all moral issues except deceit, murder, and sex were collapsed into an "all other" category for analysis.

It is common practice to give examples of situations and how they affected the collection of the data. Obviously some subjectivity on the part of the researchers is called for here, in terms of how they categorized what they saw. Such subjectivity may influence a study's findings.

Table 1: Moral Issues Addressed by
All My Children and General Hospital

Moral Issues	n	%	Moral Issues	n	%
Deceit	20	29.4	Drinking	1	1.5
Murder	16	23.5	Child obedience	1	1.5
Premarital/			Parents must not neglect		
extramarital sex	11	16.2	their children	1	1.5
Blackmail	5	7.4	Incest	0	0.0
Drugs	4	5.9	Illegitimacy	0	0.0
Other	4	5.9	Bigamy	0	0.0
Divorce	2	2.9			
Rape	2	2.9	Total	68	100.1
Abortion	1	1.5			

Table 2 shows that the majority (72.1 percent) of the moral issues involved actual violations: someone told a lie; someone murdered someone; or someone had premarital or extramarital sex. The remaining instances involved intent to violate a moral injunction (19.1 percent) or attempted violations (8.8 percent). The majority of situations involving murder led to intended or attempted violations; most of the instances involving other moral issues resulted in actual violations.

There were 489 treatments of moral issues, 298 on "All My Children" and 191 on "General Hospital," an average of 7.19 treatments per moral. As shown in Table 3, the majority of moral violations (64 percent) were not condoned, more than the combined number of treatments condoning the violation and treatments where the stand taken was not indicated. The percentage of treatments condoned on "General Hospital" was greater than on "All My Children," as was the percentage of situations in

In other words, when examining the "moral issues" they had identified, the plot resolutions usually involved some rejection of the notion that it was okay to lie or cheat.

Table 2: Moral Issues by Type of Violation on
All My Children and General Hospital

| | | | Type of Violation | | | |
| | Intended | | Attempted | | Actual | |
Moral Issues	n	% of total	n	% of total	n	% of total
Deceit	1	5.0	0	0.0	19	95.0
Murder	9	56.3	2	12.5	5	31.2
Sex	2	18.2	0	0.0	9	81.8
All others	1	4.8	4	19.0	16	76.2
All moral issues	13	19.1	6	8.8	49	72.1

$\chi^2 = 19.691$, $df = 6$, $p < .05$ Blalock's (2) correction for continuity was used for small expected values.

Table 3: Treatment of Moral Issues on
All My Children and General Hospital

| | All My Children | | General Hospital | | Total | |
	n	%	n	%	n	%
Condoned	41	13.7	31	16.2	72	14.7
Not condoned	203	68.1	110	57.6	313	64.0
Not indicated	54	18.1	50	26.1	104	21.3
Total	298	99.9	191	99.9	489	100.0

which the stand was not indicated. However, for both soap operas, more than half the treatments did not condone the moral violation.

Of the 68 instances of moral issues raised, 44.1 percent were not resolved during the time frame of this study (see Table 4). Of the remaining 38, 56.1 percent were resolved in a manner consistent with moral standards, 18.4 percent were resolved inconsistently with moral standards, and 29 percent were resolved in an ambiguous way. The majority of the latter violations involved deceit and the "all other" category, which included the more controversial issues. No difference in resolution was found between soap operas. Nor were there differences in the type of resolutions among the different moral violations. Regardless of type, moral violations tended to be resolved consistently with moral standards.

While there was no significant difference between male and female characters in terms of the percentage of violations committed, there was such a difference for the types of morals they violated. As shown in Table 5, male characters were more often involved with murder, while female characters were more often involved with deceit.

Table 4: Resolution of Moral Issues on
All My Children and General Hospital

	n	% of Total	% of Total Resolved
Resolved consistent with moral standards	20	29.4	52.6
Resolved inconsistent with moral standards	7	10.3	18.4
Resolution not clear	11	16.2	29.0
Not resolved	30	44.1	—
Total	68	100.0	100.0

Table 5: Sex of Characters (Perpetrators) Involved in Moral Issues
on All My Children and General Hospital

Moral Issue	Male n	Female n	Total n
Deceit	7	14	21
Murder	14	2	16
Sex	6	8	14
All others	14	7	21
Total	41	31	72

$\chi^2 = 12.81$, $df = 3$, $p < .05$.

While it is true that moral issues are frequently discussed on these soap operas, the most frequently raised moral issues — murder, deceit, and sex — have always been the mainstay of dramatic conflict. More controversial moral topics, such as incest, illegitimacy, bigamy, abortion, and drugs, were rarely raised.

This is interesting in light of the fact that we usually assume these issues are soap opera staples.

The soap operas analyzed also tend to punish those who violate moral standards, either socially or economically; they support the status quo. Although almost half the violations were not resolved during our one-year time period, those that were resolved tended to be resolved consistently with "traditional" moral standards. Many of the resolutions were left open to viewers' interpretations; traditional attitude theory would suggest that the audience is most likely to perceive such situations in a manner consistent with their existing beliefs and morals, which should further support the status quo. Many of these instances tended to involve the more controversial moral issues.

There are instances, although they constituted a minority, when soap operas do allow a person who violates a moral to "get away with it." Some characters do "get away with" murder, deceit, and/or premarital or extramarital sex.

In sum, the issue of soap operas' presentation of moral issues is not as clear-cut as many would have the public believe. Research that simply counts the number of instances in which moral issues are raised without taking into account the treatment and resolution of these issues adds little to an understanding of the interaction of soap opera content and societal morals.

References

1   Barnouw, E. "Television as a Medium." *Performance*. July/August 1972.

2   Blalock, H. M., Jr. *Social Statistics* (2d ed.). New York: McGraw-Hill, 1972.

3   Canadian Government, Special Senate Committee on Mass Media. *Mass Media,* Volume 3: *Good, Bad, or Simply Inevitable*. Ottawa, Ontario: Queen's Printer for Canada, 1970.

4   Chesebro, J. "Communication, Values, and Popular TV Series — A Four-Year Assessment." In G. Gumpert and R. Cathcart (Eds.), *Inter-Media: Interpersonal Communication in a Media World*. New York: Oxford University Press, 1979.

5   Comstock, G. *Television in America*. Beverly Hills, Calif.: Sage, 1980.

6   "Do We Like What We Watch?" *Life* 71(11), September 10, 1971.

7   Durdeen-Smith, J. "Daytime TV — Soft-Soaping the American Woman." *Village Voice,* February 8, 1973.

8   Edmondson, M., and D. Rounds. *From Mary Noble to Mary Hartman: The Complete Soap Opera Book*. New York: Stein and Day, 1976.

9   "Few Scorn TV Sex, Violence," *Tampa Tribune*, June 20, 1981.

10 Goldsen, R. K. *The Show and Tell Machine: How Television Works and Works You Over*. New York: Dial Press, 1977.

11 Gordon, Ruth. *Soap Opera Digest.* Telephone interview, April 17, 1980.

12 Herzog, H. "Daytime Serials." In P. Lazarsfeld and F. Stanton (Eds.), *Radio Research 1942–1943.* New York: Essential Books, 1944.

13 Katzman, N. "Television Soap Operas: What's Been Going on Anyway?" *Public Opinion Quarterly* 36(2), 1972, pp. 200–212.

14 Modleski, T. "The Search for Tomorrow in Today's Soap Operas." *Film Quarterly* 33, Fall 1979.

15 Ramsdell, M. L. "The Trauma of TV's Troubled Soap Families." *The Family Coordinator,* July 1973.

16 Ryan, K. "TV as a Moral Educator." In D. Cater and R. Adler (Eds.), *Television as a Social Force: New Approaches to TV Criticism.* New York: Praeger, 1976.

17 Skornia, H. J. *Television and Society.* New York: McGraw-Hill, 1965.

18 Soares, M. *The Soap Opera Book.* New York: Harmony Books, 1978.

19 Williams, T. M., M. L. Zabrack, and L. A. Joy. "A Content Analysis of Entertainment TV Programs." *Report of the Royal Commission on Violence in the Communication Industry,* Volume 3. Ottawa, Ontario: J. C. Thatcher, Queen's Printer for Canada, 1976.

Issues and Answers: Mass Communication Research and You

You've now had the opportunity to read three of the hundreds of mass communication research studies that are published each year. Such research is important because it represents the only way that we can go beyond speculation and our own aesthetic responses and make definitive statements about the effects of mass communication.

A number of complex issues involving mass communication face us today. Some examples: We need to know more about how TV affects children and how newspapers influence our political decisions. We need to know how women pictured in magazine ads affect our perception of women and our interpersonal relationships in general. We may speculate all we like about such things, but until we have definitive research along the lines of the examples presented here, we can't be sure what to do about it all. To put it as plainly as possible, we need more legitimate mass communication research, and we need it to be as concise as possible.

To accomplish this, we'll eventually need a lot of help from students like yourselves. Those of you considering teaching careers should think seriously about the possibility of contributing to efforts such as those presented here. Each completed study adds something to our total knowledge and takes us one step closer to a true, comprehensive understanding of the mass communication process.

Queries and Concepts

1 Look through some recent issues of newspapers or magazines, scanning for an article about a media-related controversy. Does this article mention any research studies? If so, attempt to track down a copy of the original study. Does the news article fairly reflect the content of the original research report?

2 You are a newspaper reporter, and your assignment is to report the results of one of the research studies reprinted in this chapter. Remember: You are writing for the "general public," and you are limited to four paragraphs.

3 What are some of the advantages of government funding for large-scale research studies? The disadvantages? What about private funding by media organizations, such as a television network? Do you think the funding sources can have any impact on how the results of a study are treated?

4 Make a list of 10 statements that include causal inferences. How many of these could be tested empirically?

5 Other than those mentioned in the text, can you think of at least three important media-related questions that might be addressed by research projects such as those reported here?

6 No single research effort can answer every relevant question about the consequences of mass communication; research results often raise new questions. What questions do you think remain unanswered by the research projects reported in this chapter? Select a question that interests you, and describe a study you would do to answer it.

7 Do the studies reported here successfully avoid the research pitfalls described in the text? Why or why not?

8 If very aggressive boys watch a lot of violent cartoons on television, would it be

safe to conclude that such heavy television viewing causes increased aggression in young boys? Why or why not?

9 Identify at least three areas where you think media research would be valuable to you, in your own day-to-day life.

Readings and References

Patterns in Mass

James Anderson
Timothy P. Meyer
Mediated Communication: A Social Action Perspective. Newbury Park, Calif.: Sage, 1988.

This advanced text can amount to tough reading for beginning students. Yet this is one of the most inventive and enlightening books on mass communication theory and research to be published in some time. Difficult but recommended reading.

Charles R. Berger
Steven H. Chaffe, eds.
Handbook of Communication Science. Newbury Park, Calif.: Sage, 1987.

The focus here is not on mass communication, though media research is covered as part of the broader field of "communication science." Many of these state-of-the-art essays were written by top names in the field. In a heavy (literally and figuratively) 946 pages, this book covers history, methods, theory . . . everything you wanted to know, and more.

Shearon A. Lowery
Melvin L. DeFleur
Milestones in Mass Communication Research: Media Effects. 2d ed. New York: Longman, 1988.

In this historical overview, the authors examine a number of major mass communication research efforts, successful and otherwise. The surgeon general's report on TV violence, research on the "War of the Worlds" radio broadcast, and "The Great Comic Book Scare" are among the milestones examined.

Lee Thayer
On Communication: Essays in Understanding. Norwood, N.J.: Ablex, 1987.

For decades, Thayer has ranked among the most eloquent and insightful observers of communication research and theory. This book offers a mix of some of his essays. Go right to the most intriguing contribution: "The Idea of Communication: Looking for a Place to Stand."

Procedures and Problems of Communication Research

James A. Anderson
Communication Research: Issues and Methods. New York: McGraw-Hill, 1989.

This is a well-written, comprehensive introduction to communication research. The book is unique in that it provides both the "how" and the "why" of research. In a way few writers have, Anderson dissects the methods of science to get at the assumptions and presuppositions that guide research. Recommended.

Hubert M. Blalock, Jr.
Causal Inferences in Nonexperimental Research. Chapel Hill: University of North Carolina Press, 1964.

The opening chapter offers a simple introduction to causal thinking and theory, along with problems in the field and the causal model. Blalock is a widely recognized authority on empirical research in the social sciences.

Melvin L. DeFleur
Sandra Ball-Rokeach
Theories of Mass Communication. 4th ed. New York: Longman, 1982.

Research without theory isn't very useful. This easy-to-follow treatment of theory has been widely cited. The overview is designed to advance the authors' own theory of media dependence.

Joseph R. Dominick
James E. Fletcher, eds.
Broadcasting Research Methods. Boston: Allyn and Bacon, 1985.

Though the quality of individual chapters varies, most are useful, concise introductions to basic research methods: content analysis, physiological research, uses and gratifications, sex-role socialization, children and television, ethnographic research, and more.

Lawrence R. Frey
Carl H. Botan
Paul G. Friedman
Gary L. Kreps
Investigating Communication: An Introduction to Research Methods. Englewood Cliffs, N.J.: Prentice-Hill, 1991.

A broad-based, practical book that covers experimental design, survey research, textual analysis, ethnography, stats. Good chapter on "Asking Questions," and a much-needed section on "Reading Scholarly Journal Articles."

H. J. Hsia
Mass Communication Research Methods: A Step-By-Step Approach. Hillsdale, N.J.: Lawrence Erlbaum, 1988.

This text is primarily concerned with the study of media effects, using empirical research. Among the better chapters are those on survey research, experiments, and research article preparation (which also discusses converting research reports into popular articles). Fairly comprehensive, with over 600 pages of material.

Thomas R. Lindlof, ed.
Natural Audiences: Qualitative Research of Media Uses and Effects. Norwood, N.J.: Ablex, 1987.

The first collection of media ethnographies ever published in the United States, the research reported here attempts to describe and explain the consequences of mass communication as they unfold in natural settings. If you don't care much for statistical formulas, lab experiments, and general "number crunching," this book is for you.

Rebecca Rubin
Alan M. Rubin
Linda Piele
Communication Research. Belmont, Calif.: Wadsworth, 1990.

This book is *the* place to start for students new to communication research and resources. A highly recommended "beginner's guide."

Keith R. Stamm
John E. Bowes
The Mass Communication Process: A Behavioral and Social Perspective. Dubuque, Iowa: Kendall/Hunt, 1990.

In 10 readable chapters, the authors cover everything from historical developments to the role of research in today's "information societies." Advertising, entertainment, political communication, and other topics are examined, in addition to the methods of content analysis, surveys, and experiments. Many interesting and practical anecdotes are included, as is a 17-page glossary of key terms.

Frederick Williams
Ronald E. Rice
Everett M. Rogers
Research Methods and the New Media. New York: Free Press, 1988.

Covers most of the basics, while focusing on new media such as computers and emerging telecommunications networks. The emphasis here is on the industrial, or business, side of things (such as measuring the factors that influence adoption of new media).

Roger D. Wimmer
Joseph R. Dominick
Mass Media Research: An Introduction. Belmont, Calif.: Wadsworth, 1991.

A clear introduction to the research process and to various approaches to mass media research. Recommended for students wanting to know more about research methods and their practical applications to mass media problems. For a more conceptual approach, check out James Anderson's *Communication Research: Issues and Methods,* listed above.

A Sampler of Research Studies

Jeffrey Katzer
Kenneth H. Cook
Wayne Crouch
Evaluating Information: A Guide for Users of Social Science Research. 2d ed. Reading, Mass.: Addison-Wesley, 1982.

This brief, enjoyable book takes you on a guided tour of research studies. Though you might never actually conduct research yourself, you will read (and read about) research studies for the rest of your life. The authors offer the "consumer's point of view," explaining

how to interpret and critically evaluate a research study. Essential and highly recommended reading.

Academic journals are the place to look for the latest research in mass communication. Listed here are some of the more prominent journals, as well as a few personal favorites. Most libraries subscribe to some or all of these: *Communication, Critical Studies in Mass Communication, Journal of Broadcasting and Electronic Media, Journal of Communication, Journal of Popular Culture, Journalism Quarterly, Media, Culture & Society, Public Opinion Quarterly, Screen.*

Useful collections of research are also published annually, in volumes in these book series: *Communication Yearbook* (Newbury Park, Calif.: Sage), *Mass Communication Review Yearbook* (Newbury Park, Calif.: Sage), and *Studies in Communication* (Norwood, N.J.: Ablex).

Issues and Answers: Mass Communication Research and You

John Downing
Ali Mohammadi
Annabelle Sreberny-Mohammadi, eds.
Questioning the Media: A Critical Introduction. Newbury Park, Calif.: Sage, 1990.

An eclectic array of short, comprehensible essays on the media. Each chapter will lead you further into an exploration of important issues in mass communication theory and research. Recommended.

Fred Inglis
Media Theory: An Introduction. Cambridge, Mass.: Blackwell, 1990.

The title is a bit misleading; this "introduction" will certainly challenge your thinking about the media. Throughout, Inglis is concerned with forging vital connections between abstract concepts and our daily lives, connections between "research and you."

Michael R. Real
Super Media: A Cultural Studies Approach.
Newbury Park, Calif.: Sage, 1989.

Real also engages the formidable task of integrating communication research with our media experiences in everyday life. The book reflects an expanding emphasis on synthesizing research methods from the humanities and the social sciences. Includes case studies of politics, the Olympics, Bill Cosby.

17

New Technologies and the Future of Mass Communication

The major advances in civilization are processes that all but wreck the societies in which they occur. . . . It is the business of the future to be dangerous.

Alfred North Whitehead

I f you take a moment to flip back to the beginning of Chapter 1, you might recall that we began our journey through Mediamerica and Mediaworld in 1962 with the blastoff of *Telstar,* the first communications satellite. Over 30 years and 400 pages later we're still trying to get a handle on what McLuhan called "the new electronic interdependence" that "recreates the world in the image of a global village."

We have seen that today's Mediaworld is a very different place than it was a generation ago when Telstar began relaying electronic signals around the globe (see 17.1). Once upon a time we were taught that "east is east and west is west and never the twain shall meet." But thanks to the new communication technolo-

gies, the distinctions between east and west, north and south, have become increasingly blurred. Now we turn our attention to the electronic future of Mediaworld. What's in store for us?

For thousands of years, many Eastern cultures have been guided by the "tenets of Zen." Among them are two that seem to apply quite readily as we consider our collective future:

- The realities of life are most truly seen in everyday things and actions.

- Everything exists in relation to other things.

The impact of the new technologies is best observed in the events that take place every

1975

Sony introduces Betamax,

the first home video

recording system.

1960

1960	
1962	*Telstar* is the world's first communications satellite.

1970

1970	
1970	Ted Turner buys Atlanta's WTBS.
1975	HBO becomes the nation's first satellite TV network.
1975	Western Union launches its own domestic communications satellite.
1977	Steven Jobs and Steve Wozniak launch Apple Computer; they envision systems that will "offer freedom to workers and executives who are prisoners of time."

1980

1980	
1980s	The decade of the cellular phone.
1981	MTV is the first music video network. Youth culture will never be the same.
1981	IBM markets its first personal computer.
1983	Direct-broadcast satellite transmissions begin on an experimental basis.

17.1 A Short History of the New Technologies

1985

The Home Shopping Network becomes the first national electronic home shopping service.

1991

Congress allocates $3 billion to begin construction of a national fiber-optic "data highway."

1990

1984 In a 5–4 decision, the U.S. Supreme Court rules that home video taping is legal.

1984 HBO begins scrambling its signal. Other channels soon follow in an attempt to thwart the signal pirates.

1985 VH-1 goes on line as a sister service of MTV.

1987 Cable is deregulated, subscriber fees soar.

1988 Half of Mediamerica's households are wired for cable.

1991 Premium cable services experience their first subscriber losses after 15 consecutive years of growth.

1992 The FCC votes to allow broadcast networks to own cable outlets, but on a very limited basis.

1992 Candidate Bill Clinton appears on MTV in an attempt to woo young voters.

1992 Cable reregulation legislation is passed, despite presidential veto.

1993 The FCC attempts to balance priorities as it deals with HDTV standards.

1994 More than 25 million people worldwide use the Internet computer network. America boasts 33 million homes equipped with personal computers.

1995 After several 1994 congressional setbacks, the Clinton administration pushes hard for increased funding for the nation's information superhighway. Technical problems involve data compression, storage, and interactive capabilities.

day. When we watch MTV or ESPN, we are experiencing the new technologies in action. Perhaps sometime today you have worked on a personal computer, placed a long-distance phone call via a fiber-optic system, or listened to the latest CD from R.E.M. It's hard to believe that these simple everyday activities were unheard of even a decade ago.

Mass communication texts and the teachers who use them have long talked of the "communications revolution." It has been widely projected as a time when new technological devices would change the way we communicate with one another. Those changes in turn were expected to radically alter our daily lives.

Although some feel the communications revolution has been decidedly slower to arrive than expected, it now appears that the next decade will transform our daily communication patterns in ways that even the most radical visionaries failed to anticipate.

Television by satellite. Camcorders that turn your living room into a TV studio. Record "albums" that never scratch or wear out. Word-processing equipment that corrects spelling and grammatical errors. The communications revolution is here at last!

In *The Coming Information Age*, Wilson P. Dizard explains how this came to be:

> The so-called communications revolution is, in reality, a succession of three overlapping technological stages that have taken place during the past one hundred and fifty years. The first of these was the Wire Age (1844–1900), the second was the Wireless Age (1900–1970), and the third is the one we are now entering—the Integrated Grid Age, in which wire and wireless technology are brought together in powerful combinations which will form the structure of the future global information utility.
>
> The technological advances that occurred between the beginning of the

Wire Age and the present are awesome. The early Western Union telegraph machines that opened the Wire Age could relay about forty words a minute. Western Union's first domestic communications satellite, the successor to the old telegraph line, was placed in orbit in 1975 with a capability of transmitting eight million words a *second*.

One of the reasons the communications revolution has been so late in arriving involves economic reality. No technological breakthrough can have much impact until it is recognized by a significant number of people. Consumers must be able to afford to buy a new device or hook up to a new service before it can become part of their lives. The innovations made possible by microcircuitry, fiber optics, and satellites are already at work in millions of living rooms across the nation. Virtually all of us are touched by the new technologies. Our task now is to discover the ways we can use them to take us where we want to go. The ultimate consequences of the communications revolution are strictly up to us.

Throughout this book we have explored some of the ways the introduction of technological devices, from the printing press to television, has altered the outlook of the population of what Buckminster Fuller called our "Spaceship Earth." What follows is a brief overview of the new technologies and some of the things we might expect to happen as they become increasingly integrated into our culture.

Linkups: The Foundation of the Communications Revolution

To understand what is happening with the new technologies requires far more information than is possible to include in this brief overview. However, any understanding begins with an awareness of the basic elements at work. Because "everything exists in relation to other things," we need to focus on those elements and understand how they work together to produce change. You're already more familiar with them than you might think.

A historical case in point is Ted Turner (see Chapters 6 and 9) and his Atlanta-based superstation, WTBS. Turner bought the failing UHF station for $2.5 million in 1970, against the advice of just about everyone he knew in the industry. His idea was relatively simple: Why not link up the station's output of old movies, syndicated reruns, and sports programs with some of the thousands of cable systems across the country? Once this was accomplished, his audience would be truly national and the rates he could charge advertisers would be multiplied.

Using Home Box Office (HBO) as his model, Turner rented the facilities of a communications satellite to beam WTBS to local cable companies, who then distributed it as part of their basic cable service. Cable operators got another reason to urge viewers to sign up, and Turner got his national audience. By 1993 Turner's "superstation" could be received by 60 million cable subscribers, and annual profits were estimated to be in the $75 million range. Turner used some of that money to start CNN and TNT, and to purchase MGM/United Artists, thus ensuring his superstation a catalog of movies for the future.

Turner's success was a stunning accomplishment. Most high-tech endeavors take years to turn a profit, and many never do. Sponsors are reluctant to try a new medium, and competition in all areas of the new technologies is intense. Turner overcame these odds. WTBS became the prototype for media to come.

At the heart of this success story is the marriage of two technologies, *cable television* and *satellite communication*. These two elements have now been joined by *computers* and dozens of new *home video and telephone* products to produce the communications revolution.

The Wired Nation: Cable TV

Former FCC member Nicholas Johnson (see Chapter 8) once said that "the difference between ordinary television and cable is the difference between a garden hose and Niagara Falls." This analogy is not as far-fetched as it may seem. Broadcast TV has a limited channel capacity, and in some markets viewers receive only a handful of stations. State-of-the-art cable systems now deliver up to 150 channels of programming.

In the strictest sense of the word, cable cannot be considered a new technology since it is hardly new. In fact, cable has been around almost as long as TV itself. But the marriage of cable to satellite and computer technologies makes it an integral part of the "new technologies."

Currently most cable companies offer a multiplicity of special-program channels as part of their basic service. TBS, Cable News Network (CNN), Entertainment and Sports Programming Network (ESPN), Music Television (MTV) (see 17.2), and the USA Cable Network are but a few of these. *Network* is an appropriate term for all of these services because structurally they do exactly what ABC, CBS, NBC, and Fox do since they can be received simultaneously across the country.

In addition, there are the so-called *premium* channels such as HBO, Showtime, Cinemax, the Movie Channel, and the Disney Channel. Subscribers to these services pay an extra fee each month.

All of these "new networks" come via satellite and owe their existence to that technology. In 1975 HBO became the first satellite cable network. By 1993 it had over 17 million

I Want My MTV!

August 1, 1981. 12:01 A.M. In a makeshift set designed to look like a family rumpus room, curly-haired New York radio personality Mark Goodman became the world's first "veejay" when he introduced a video aptly titled "Video Killed the Radio Star." The song's message became prophetic. Music Television (MTV) was born. Rock 'n' roll, radio, television, and youth culture would never be the same.

MTV finished that first year by celebrating the fact that it could be received in over 2 million homes. Today it is beamed to over 60 million homes in Mediamerica. Add to that another 100 million households in Europe, Asia, South America, Russia, and just about everywhere else on the planet and you have the living proof of MTV's international programming philosophy: "Think globally, act locally."

MTV's "founding father," Bob Pittman, notes that MTV has had a profound impact on every aspect of world culture: "In music, fashion, politics, art, advertising and movies. . . it popularized a whole new kind of music and made visual appeal a prerequisite for musical artists."

Ironically, 1981 was a bad year for the record industry. Sales were down and budgets were being slashed. Record companies had experimented with rock videos but had little proof that they generated additional sales. Pittman and his cohorts raced to get the new service on the air in time to convince the companies to keep making videos. Only about 250 were available when MTV was launched (30 were by Rod Stewart!). Pittman realized that if record companies cut back on video production, MTV would die before it found an audience.

The key to MTV's success was the perception of TV's mediated reality in an entirely new way. Pittman explained it to the *Los Angeles Times*:

> We realized that almost all TV was narrative in form . . . the structure of beginning, middle and end. The appeal of music, however, has nothing to do with that structure. Music is about emotion and attitude—it makes you feel. *It moves you. With the creation of MTV we changed the form of TV to fit the music as opposed to trying to fit the music into a narrative structure.*

Attitude is a key factor in MTV's success. MTV's founders vowed that "no rule would be left unbroken." What emerged was an irreverent yet relevant programming service aimed squarely at the 12–34 audience. From the beginning, Pittman understood that audience would eventually grow out of MTV. (A second service, VH-1, was created to give them an alternative.) Pittman turned traditional TV programming on its ear vowing that "we would stay ahead of our audience—not follow the TV programming tradition of mirroring the audience."

To accomplish this he staffed MTV with a very specific type of employee. "I was looking for a unique blend—smarts and ignorance. We put together a group of smart, aggressive people, yet none of them had ever done the jobs they were hired to do," he explains. "Everyone was ignorant of the traditions and conventions of the job, freeing us all to do it a new way." Do it they did.

In the beginning no one knew what would work. The biggest concern was whether storytelling-type concept videos or concert-footage–type videos would predominate. In the end that proved to be a false dichotomy. "Videos that worked were videos in which the visuals created the same emotion and attitudes that the music did. . . . It was compatibility that mattered, not techniques," Pittman explains.

In 1982 cable operators were reluctant to add the controversial new service to their basic lineup. MTV countered with a now-famous campaign that exhorted teens everywhere to call their local cable company and tell them in no uncertain terms "I want my MTV!" It worked.

In 1983 MTV weathered criticism that it did not feature enough black artists. Eventually, Michael Jackson proved to be the breakthrough black act MTV was looking for. His 14-minute "Thriller" was the "first video of any major popularity with an extensive nonmusic, dramatic wrap-around, and the first to be made by a major feature-film director," explains writer Chris Willman. It set new standards for the genre and turned the album into one of the most successful releases of all time (see Chapter 7). Today "Yo, MTV Raps" is one of the most successful segments on music television.

In 1985 sister station VH-1 went on the air. Billed as the "adult" version of MTV it too enjoyed tremendous success. Meanwhile, Dire Straits released "Money for Nothing," and guest vocalist Sting sang the famous refrain, "I want my MTV." It was supposed to be satirical, of course, yet it was voted the best video of the year by MTV's viewers. Go figure.

By 1986 many of the original MTV veejays were phased out and Downtown Julie Brown

joined the lineup. A year later her "Club MTV" premiered, and "Remote Control" became TV's most unusual game show. After all, where else can viewers get a chance to answer questions in such categories as "Dead or Canadian?" or "Brady Physics"?

In 1990 "MTV Unplugged" became the hottest artist showcase on TV and vacuous Pauley Shore joined the MTV staff. In 1992 the music channel scored a coup with the presentation of "Choose or Lose: A Conversation with Bill Clinton." Who would have imagined that MTV would become a must appearance for a presidential candidate seeking the youth vote? Clinton has vowed to return to MTV as president.

Through it all, MTV has not escaped criticism. In a speech on the Senate floor, Senator Robert Byrd (D.–W. Va.) claimed that "most rock musicians and actors in music videos emerge as sneering antisocial, unkempt, undisciplined and arrogant punks, male and female alike."

Respected rock critic Dave Marsh, while lauding shows like "Yo, MTV Raps" nevertheless feels that MTV's programming "reflects a male supremacy that is uncomfortable to watch." Professor Stuart Ewen says that "MTV represents a sea of change in media, in which a form of advertisement

is perceived as entertainment." Indeed, it has forever changed the way records are promoted. According to Steve Leeds of Polygram Records, "MTV is the biggest radio station on the planet and it's very difficult to have a hit record without support from [MTV]."

Madonna's controversial "Justify My Love" video was banned from the music channel but became a hit anyway—thanks in part to a full airing on ABC's "Nightline." Despite this, Madonna owes her success to MTV, as do such acts as Duran Duran, Stray Cats, Culture Club, Paula Abdul, Janet Jackson, and even the infamous Milli Vanilli.

Through it all, MTV executives have remained unruffled. Tom Freston admits, "Yes, there are some things we wish we hadn't done." But he also adds that "MTV is a very good window on the world for young people."

That window has expanded considerably with the end of the cold war and the proliferation of worldwide satellite distribution systems. Now "Beavis and Butthead" can be seen around the world! Despite the trend toward less music videos and more special programming, the channel's fans still want their MTV. Now there will be more MTV fans than ever before.

subscribers, making it cable's most popular premium channel.

Why do consumers sign up for cable service? How does it alter their viewing habits? One *Consumer Reports* readership survey found:

- 61% of cable subscribers said that they wanted more movies.

- 49% said that they wanted to receive out-of-town channels.

- 44% said that cable improved picture quality.

- 41% opted for more news.

- 38% said that they wanted more sports. (These figures add up to more than 100 percent because respondents could check multiple choices.)

Not surprisingly, 44% said that they were attending fewer movies, and 26% admitted that they had cut back on their "reading for pleasure" time. Yet a surprising 41% said that their leisure activities had not changed significantly since hooking up to cable.

One definite impact has been felt by the broadcast networks. Little by little, the new cable networks and Fox have nibbled away at the big piece of the pie long enjoyed by the so-called big three. Since 1975 the portion of viewers who tune in to the big three during prime time has dropped from over 90% to around 60%, and that number continues to shrink each year.

The situation is complex, but the basic appeal of cable is simple. ABC can't offer movies without commercials 24 hours a day. NBC can't run 24 hours of music videos. CBS can't offer nonstop sports. They must cater to a large general audience. The smaller networks with lower costs zero in on various demographic groups and offer them exactly what they want. This process (sometimes called *narrowcasting*) involves target programming for specific audiences and has long been a factor in most mass

media marketing strategies. Narrowcasting is good news for advertisers who wish to reach these types of special audiences.

By 1988 more than half of all the nation's homes were subscribing to a cable service. Today 11,000 different cable systems serve about 60 million households. We are rapidly becoming a "wired nation" tuned in to what has been called the "television of abundance."

Of course, *more* is not necessarily *better*. (Remember Bruce Springsteen's "57 Channels and Nothin' On"?) There is no shortage of ideas for new services and new communication possibilities; whether these will result in an aesthetically improved product remains to be seen. Marketplace constraints also have an effect. Just how much television do we really want? How much can we afford?

Premium and Pay-Per-View

Cable operators have found that consumers are willing to pay extra for certain types of programs. In the 1980s, viewers were excited about seeing first-run movies uncut, live music concerts, and similar events. Ironically, other new technologies such as home video have now cut deeply into that market. In 1991 most premium channels experienced their first subscriber shrinkage after 15 years of steady growth. One woman summed it up while being interviewed in the *Los Angeles Times*: "I know that I can go to the video store and rent a movie for $1.90. . . . It just seems to me that paying $20.00 extra a month for cable is no longer worth it."

In addition, many front-line cable "events" are now available only on pay-per-view (PPV). While this service remains in its infancy, cable operators are discovering that some people are willing to pay $4 or $5 for a movie that is not yet available via a premium channel. Request Television, Viewer's Choice, and several smaller services that cater to hotels are the main players in this field. Yet despite the fact that Request and Viewer's Choice each boasts a potential audience of more than 8 million viewers, neither has turned a profit yet.

Nevertheless, many remain upbeat on the future of PPV. According to Jessica Reif, cable analyst for Oppenheimer and Co., "By the time the 21st Century rolls around, the typical cable system will be transmitting as many as 300 channels, and more than one third of these will probably consist of PPV movies."

Cable and Information Services

According to *Variety*, there are many cable operators and programmers "who believe the cable industry is entering an extraordinary era of new services and growth." Management at one pay-per-view service, recently advised its stockholders, "Not since the advent of the satellite have there been so many momentous technological developments."

Many believe that cable's future will involve expanding existing operations while providing new information services to consumers. To accomplish this, leading multiple system operators (MSOs) are experimenting with *digital video compression*, *multiplexing*, *smart TV*, and *interactive* technologies.

Pioneered by AT&T, digital video compression "compresses the vast amount of data contained in a TV signal so several programs can be sent at once on one cable channel." According to AT&T, this could boost the channel capacity of today's cable systems by up to 13 times and save cable companies from a costly rewiring of their systems, many of which can now carry only 35 channels. Compression technology evolved as part of AT&T's research on high-definition television (HDTV).

With the imminent availability of additional channels, programmers are already envisioning what might be on them. There is already a comedy channel, a science fiction channel, a weather channel, and of course a lot of shopping channels.

The Home Shopping Network (HSN) became the first truly national home shopping service in 1985. Its rise to prominence was spectacular, but not without problems. *Channels* noted that "criticism mounted over HSN's selection of merchandise. Batches of defective fur coats and personal computers were returned, and best-selling — some say 'schlocky' — items such as cubic zirconium jewelry . . . and electronic flea collars came to represent all that was wrong with HSN and the home shopping craze."

Despite these problems, HSN and rivals such as QVC continue to be dominant forces in home shopping, accounting for billions of dollars in annual revenues. That's a lot of electronic flea collars! In 1994 MTV began offering products, ranging from clothing to compact discs, in special "shopping segments." Since cable operators share directly in home shopping revenues, you can bet they will continue to find a place for these channels.

According to Dick Green of CableLabs, an industry research consortium, "The movement in cable is toward more diversification, similar to what happened in the print industry. . . . More special services are being created in which you have a revenue stream coming from the subscriber and the advertiser. The narrower the interest, the more costly the subscription fee. It's the same process that magazines went through" (see Chapter 5).

One potential use for the new channels is multiplexing. This technology provides a single program service on several different channels. For example, Time-Warner's experimental 150-channel system in New York now offers HBO, HBO2, and HBO3. All run the same programming, but at different starting times. While one HBO channel airs a comedy, another runs a drama, the third an action picture. Thus, viewers can access three different movies for the price of a single channel. According to Betsy Brice of HBO, "With multiplexing we're giving them a package of channels. . . . The benefit to subscribers is more choice at any time."

Smart TV technology is not necessarily tied to cable, but the marriage of the two seems inevitable. Smart TV provides on-screen menu-oriented computer technology, similar to, but far more sophisticated than that currently found in some newer VCRs. Michael Faber, president of InSight, a leading smart TV company, contends that the system "makes the television set truly intelligent, in that it's able selectively to tell the viewer what's on."

According to *Broadcasting*, current prototypes will allow the viewer "to see program titles on screen as they "graze" channels, search for programs by theme or category, call up or record a program by title and provide a kind of electronic TV guide by calling up a seven-day program listing organized by channel and time."

Most imaginative of all potential cable innovations are the interactive technologies, an amalgam of computers and television that gives viewers a high degree of control over what they see. Bob Pittman, president and CEO of Time-Warner Enterprises, says that interactive is a logical marriage of computers and TV. "The computer industry is trying to make their computers full motion video and the TV people are trying to make their TV smart. We're both coming to the same location."

Pittman, who had a hand in the creation of MTV (see 17.2), Nickelodeon, and VH-1, sees a definite generation factor in interactive TV. "The generation weaned on personal computers and video games does not view inactivity as a way to assist the use of conventional TV, but as an element they seek out and desire."

Pittman describes a kind of future home shopping system where "viewers can ask their TV to seek out specific merchandise, have it go through every digitalized catalogue and find numerous options. Viewers will be able to narrow their search through a series of menus and look at moving images." He contends that "interactive TV will be as pervasive as narrowcast specialized networks are today."

ACTV created a buzz in the industry in 1991 when it announced its "interactive broadcasting" system that would allow cable viewers with specially equipped boxes to participate directly in programming. Football fans, for example, could zoom in on the quarterback or change their viewing angle at will. There was even an interactive blackjack game that allowed viewers to hit or stand. ACTV President Leonard Schaier claimed that "in five or ten years people will wonder how they ever watched television without interactivity."

More recently, *Broadcasting* reported that ACTV has been frustrated because "cable channel operators want to wait for channel compression to become reality before helping develop programming." The current system requires multiple channels, and most cable operators simply don't have the space.

Despite some setbacks, TeleCommunications Inc. President John Malone recently told a gathering of cable executives that while continuing to provide its more traditional video services, "cable can enhance its position as the most cost-effective highway to the home for every imaginable communications service." National Cable Television Association President James Mooney agreed: "The biggest telecommunication story of the decade may turn out to be . . . cable technology and architecture [becoming] the most efficient means of delivering the next generation of communication services."

Cable at the Crossroads: Reregulation

During the 1960s and 1970s, cable systems began springing up all over the country. This period of phenomenal growth was monitored very closely by various government agencies. Local governments were given the power to award cable franchises while the FCC passed a series of complex regulations designed to keep subscriber costs down and encourage cable companies to operate in the public interest.

As we have seen, the Reagan years were characterized by the sweeping deregulation of all media businesses. In January 1987 it was cable's turn. The results were predictable. In the next 5 years the average cable bill climbed 60%. In some metropolitan areas like Los Angeles, subscriber bills doubled.

In recent years, the 50-million-member Consumer Federation of America has led the congressional battle to reregulate the industry. It contends that Congress could save consumers up to $6 billion per year in cable fees, if Congress would only act. Meanwhile, the explosion of new technologies and a weakened economy have turned the battle into a slugfest among TV networks, broadcasters, the Hollywood studios, cable operators, and other high-tech segments of the industry. Numerous bills and amendments have been offered. Among the major issues being debated:

Price Guidelines Should the FCC once again set guidelines and prices that cable operators can charge for "basic" services such as local broadcasting and government channels?

Retransmission Consent Should local stations be allowed to *charge* cable operators for the privilege of carrying their signal? Until now, cable has always gotten such broadcasts free.

Compulsory License From 1976 to 1985 cable operators were forced to carry all local broadcast signals as part of their basic service. In addition, the distant superstations were purchased at mandatory below-market costs. Should marketplace forces be allowed to determine these costs? Should cable operators choose which stations they want to carry?

Network Cross Ownership Should TV broadcast networks be allowed to own cable systems and vice versa? Some already have financial interests in certain cable program services. Financially strapped networks are looking toward ownership of lucrative cable companies as a way to boost their sagging financial fortunes. In 1992 the FCC voted to allow such ownership, but on a very limited basis.

Mandatory Program Access If true competition is to develop between cable and competing technologies such as "wireless cable" or direct-broadcast satellite (DBS), shouldn't the newer technologies have access to such popular cable networks as ESPN and MTV? Cable operators contend that they have provided the funds which built these networks and that they cannot afford to "give them away" now.

Most of these issues were addressed in a 1992 bill that was passed, despite a Bush veto. In 1994 the FCC also managed to push through a small mandatory cable rate decrease. While cable began as a way for those with poor TV reception to receive a clear picture, it has blossomed into an entirely new industry, as revolutionary as printing or television itself. Congress and the Clinton administration continue to attempt to provide some sort of balance between the many opposing market forces involved. It remains to be seen if they can also keep in mind the interests of Mediamerica's 65 million cable households.

Fiber Optics

An engineering breakthrough pioneered by Western Electric is bound to have great impact on cable, and many other communication services as well. Fiber optics has made it theoretically possible to carry 100,000 phone calls or transmit the entire broadcast spectrum through a cable the size of a human hair.

Traditional wires use radio signals for transmission; fiber optics employs light waves. Today our personal and industrial computers talk to one another utilizing modem technology. Information moves at the speed of sound.

A few thousand words might take several minutes to travel across the country. With fiber optics, data would travel at the speed of light and arrive within a second or so.

In 1991 the federal government authorized the expenditure of some $3 billion as the first step in the construction of what has been dubbed a national "data highway." Proponents contend that the "fiber-optic spinal chord," a new information infrastructure, will do for the nation's economy and life style "what the interstate highway system did for America in the 1950s."

Industry observers are keeping a close eye on Japan, which expects to be fully fiber-optic by 2015. According to Fred Weingarten, executive director of the Computer Research Association, "Without that infrastructure, in the 21st century we're going to be a third class nation."

In the new communication environment of fiber optics, it may soon be possible to use one wire to receive phone, TV, and all other electronic communication. According to *Newsweek*, on-ramps to the data highway will eventually find their way to everyone's front door:

> Students could search through the Library of Congress, farmers could read detailed geographical maps from satellite photos for crop data and ultimately, as the computer network is made available at home, couch potatoes could become their own TV programmers, ordering up, say, every love scene from every movie made in 1975, or the last five minutes of every Super Bowl since Game I.

In fact, fiber optics is already in use in some international phone services. Remember when USA-Sprint began promoting its FON card? FON enables subscribers to utilize a fiber-optic network while making long-distance phone calls. Fiber optics brings exciting possibilities because it represents an almost unlimited channel capacity. Information from a virtually unlimited number of sources may soon be available, all at the speed of light.

Satellite Communication

As we have seen, when *Telstar,* the first communications satellite, was launched in 1962, a new concept was launched with it. Five years earlier the Soviet Union had shaken the world by launching *Sputnik I.* America soon followed with *Explorer I.* These early efforts were aimed at increasing our knowledge of space. As it turned out, the most intriguing role of satellites would not be in exploring space but in transforming life on earth through the infusion of new communication channels. *Telstar* was the first satellite designed exclusively for such purposes.

The theory behind satellite communication is fairly simple. Satellites actually act as radio relay stations, receiving electronic messages from the ground that are transmitted through "uplinks" at earth stations and retransmitting them to "downlinks" at other earth stations.

Satellites can relay such information with relative ease because they are placed in a synchronous orbit 22,300 miles above the earth. Since satellites revolve around the earth at the same speed the earth rotates on its axis, they are constantly in the same position in relation to earth stations. This gives them the ability to beam signals all over the planet with equal ease (though rarely with equal signal strength), something that no ground-to-ground device could possibly do (until the advent of fiber optics) at such a comparatively low cost.

Put most simply, satellites like *Telstar* have made instantaneous global communication possible. By the mid-1980s, there were 20 such satellites owned by the United States in the air. Television traffic was most heavy on *G.E. Satcom 1, Hughes Galaxy 1,* and *G.E. Satcom 3.* Meanwhile, the Japanese and European

Pirates in Space

It all began in 1976, just after HBO became the first satellite network. Taylor Howard, a Stanford University electronics professor, put together some surplus military parts and came up with a 30-foot "antenna" that allowed him to receive satellite signals free of charge. The first home earth station was in operation.

Howard wrote to HBO and offered to pay the company for reception of its service, but his letter went unanswered. Nobody was really concerned with the first space pirate — but that changed in a hurry. Before long the loss of potential revenues became a major issue for all satellite-program distributors.

For years, satellite programmers threatened to scramble their signals to thwart home dish receivers. When they made good on their promise, only dish owners who were willing to pay a monthly fee and purchase a $395 decoder could receive a scrambled channel.

Howard's original earth station cost about $30,000 to assemble, but prices dropped over the years as more companies got into the business. By 1986 some mini-dishes were available for as little as $800. Sales were brisk until that year, when scrambling began in earnest. Since then they have fallen dramatically, and many small mom-and-pop dish companies have been forced out of business.

Today the scrambling system and the proliferation of DBS ventures have all but eliminated the space pirate controversy. What *Channels* magazine once called the "do-it-yourself TV reception movement" is largely a historical footnote. Nevertheless, it remains a lesson in the economics of telecommunications. If the space pirates had been successful in their efforts to "free the airwaves," we might have a very different system than the one in place today.

---

communities built and launched "birds" of their own.

In 1975, when Home Box Office began using *Satcom I* to transmit its movies, it became the first satellite network and altered forever the shape of the television landscape. No longer was television earthbound, tied to phone lines or the other ground devices used by broadcast networks.

The average consumer is probably not aware of the technology that makes HBO or any of the other services possible. But that will change with the proliferation of personal satellite receiving dishes. Some 3 million American homes have an earth station, enabling them to receive many of the satellite signals.

Most who send those signals were not particularly pleased with "signal pirates" — dish owners who did not pay any fee to receive them (see 17.3). The legality of dish ownership and the ownership of the signals themselves were the issues. Earth-station owners contended they were simply receiving information that should be free to all, just as radio and TV earthbound signals are free to all. Those paying large fees to utilize satellite distribution felt they were being cheated by not receiving revenues from the pirates.

In 1984 HBO announced it would begin scrambling its signals to thwart signal pirates. Most of the major satellite networks have now followed suit. Dish owners who wish to receive these signals must purchase or lease special unscrambling equipment and pay a monthly fee as well. Generally, premium programming is sold in packages that contain a dozen or so channels with fees in the $25 per month range.

In addition, there remain approximately 70 "in the clear" or unscrambled channels including the Fox network, Home Shopping

Network, Court TV, SportsChannel, and Much-Music, the Canadian MTV-type music video channel.

DBS: Direct-Broadcast Satellites

A variation on the home dish is the direct-broadcast satellite (DBS). The first experimental DBS transmissions began in 1983. Unlike HBO or Showtime, DBS signals are intended to go directly to the consumer, without benefit of a cable "middleman" (see 17.3). These services beam channels to consumers who have specially equipped dishes installed on their roofs. The dish combined with a descrambler unit allows consumers to receive satellite transmissions beamed directly to them, thanks to a technological development providing transmission of a signal up to 40 times stronger than signals used for other transmissions. As a result, the dish is comparatively small (about the size of an umbrella) and considerably easier and less expensive to operate than a traditional dish. Of course, DBS enthusiasts can receive only what is beamed to them, and they are charged a monthly fee.

Nevertheless, the future of DBS is intriguing from an economic point of view. It is the first technology that lets consumers bypass traditional TV stations, networks, and cable systems altogether. The immediate future for DBS may be in areas where cable is not available. By some estimates, up to 30% of all U.S. homes are unable to be wired economically; these have become prime markets for DBS programming.

A number of DBS services have come and gone during the first decade of the new technology. After years of unsuccessful attempts to get DBS off the ground, Comsat pulled the plug in 1984. The United Satellite Communications venture, launched in 1983, was well financed but attracted fewer than 10,000 subscribers and filed for bankruptcy in 1985. One investor reportedly lost $70 million. Sky Cable offered 100 channels of programming and was backed by some of the biggest names in the entertainment business, but failed nonetheless in 1991 (see also 17.4).

The most recent entry in the DBS market is Hughes Communications' DirecTv. Hughes gathered programming service contracts in 1993 in preparation for a 1994 launch and offered consumers an 18-inch dish for only $700, approximately one third the going rate for larger, more cumbersome earth stations. Initially, Hughes offered a 20-channel package on five transponders but has room for many services thanks to advanced digital compression technology. It is hoped that the new technology, affording DBS consumers more channels than ever before, will be the solution to the financial blues that have plagued the fledgling industry.

A successful DBS prototype can currently be found in Japan where 4 million households subscribe to DBS. That number will reach 10 million in 1995, much to the chagrin of Japan's cable industry. The American cable industry has opposed DBS, but proponents contend that the new service represents a great opportunity for cable programmers to reach millions of unserved households. Cable reregulation decisions will directly affect the DBS industry, particularly those involving mandatory access to programming. When compared to cable, current DBS operators pay four or five times the per-subscriber fee for access to the popular cable networks they send to the backyard dish market.

Commercial Satellite Applications

In *The Communications Revolution,* Frederick Williams lists a number of commercial applications that will be possible with the construction of "communication platforms" — giant satellites that can be put into orbit from our

Pioneer Television's New Frontier!

Most direct-to-home satellite services by-pass local participation. But one group in the satellite space-race believes that free TV delivered with the help of local television stations has a bright future. United States Satellite Broadcasting Company, Inc.

We're adding space-age technology to local service ... making free, advertiser-supported news, sports and first-run entertainment available to every American home via satellite with local station participation!*

Pioneer the future! Join us!
Call Bob Fransen at (813) 576-4444 or (612) 642-4467 today.

United States Satellite Broadcasting Company, Inc.
3415 University Avenue St. Paul, Minnesota 55114
*Pending F.C.C. approval.

17.4

The now-defunct U.S. Satellite Broadcasting Company tried a slightly different approach to the satellite game. Rather than have its signals transmitted by cable, it offered them to local stations that could set up their own dish and beam programming to viewers via their broadcast transmitter. The ad implied that stations could do this at no cost to themselves because the signal also carried commercials that "paid" for the service. Seemed like a good idea at the time.

Videoconferencing offers the opportunity for economical face-to-face business meetings, no matter where participants are located.

already operational space shuttle. Among them:

- A worldwide communications network linking all individuals on earth by means of wristwatch-size communication units
- Improved broadcasting of radio and television directly from satellite to rooftop dishes on houses or apartment buildings
- Communications networks for business and government, significantly reducing costs of teleconferences, electronic mail, and sharing of computer data
- The teaming up of large computer and data systems for computer-assisted management or design
- Linkage of small hand-held computer terminals, like pocket calculators, with sources of information such as banking records, the stock market, transportation scheduling, a library of games, or useful computer programs

- Movement toward electronic mail systems where electronic movement replaces paper movement
- A nationwide educational communications network, one capable of supplying instructional materials from a central library of supporting computer-assisted instructional systems now too costly for schools, even systems that can link into the home

Among the most innovative business uses currently available is *videoconferencing*. By using satellite signals, corporations with branches spread out across the nation or around the world can hold "meetings" without having to pay costly plane fares and hotel bills. Executives simply gather where there is an uplink and downlink and communicate via giant TV screens. Hundreds of such networks are already in operation; there were only three as recently as 1982. Susan Irwin of Irwin Communications, a consulting firm that assists corporations in setting up their own video networks, says: "Business TV is certainly one of the fastest-growing applications of satellites."

Though business meetings and conferences are the most immediately applicable use of this new technology, some envision college classrooms and universities without walls using satellite transmissions.

As strange as it may seem, there is already talk about the limitations of satellite technology. The single most important element in that technology is the *transponder*. Each transponder is capable of relaying one color television channel or handling 1,000 phone calls. Most current satellites pack a payload of 24 transponders; those launched during the 1990s carry 40 or more.

But the industry must now compete with fiber-optic networks. When Sprint switched from satellite transmission to fiber optics, it left plenty of satellite space available for rent. One high-growth area that has helped offset this trend is the use of satellites for news gathering (SNG). The economics are such that TV stations in major markets can now afford to rent satellite space to beam reporters' stories live and direct to their news rooms.

In summary, satellite technology combined with cable is the most immediately applicable and financially practical marriage among the new technologies. Such a marriage combines wireless and wired technologies and forms the basis for what Dizard calls the "integrated grid age."

HDTV: The Couch Potato's Dream

If you have ever been to Europe, you may have noticed that TV sets there seem to have a sharper and clearer picture. It wasn't your imagination. Many European systems employ a higher resolution, or definition, than do their U.S. counterparts. The result is better picture quality.

The current American system, established in the 1940s, uses 525 scanning lines across the screen. Some European systems use more. The more lines used, the clearer and sharper the picture. Enter HDTV.

This new type of television transmission system will use 1,125 or 1,250 digital lines. The result is every couch potato's dream: movie-film clarity and compact-disc-quality audio, all in the comfort of your living room. Forty- and 50-inch screens will become commonplace. HDTV requires no new scientific breakthroughs; the technology has long been in place. In fact, several technologies are already in place, and that's part of the problem. For years the FCC has debated which HDTV system would become the new national standard. In 1992 it put broadcasters on notice that a decision was imminent.

According to current FCC plans, all TV stations will be required to switch to HDTV by 1998. This means that all domestic stations will need to buy new cameras and equipment; costs are estimated at $10 billion for broadcasters and ultimately $100 billion for Mediamerica's consumers. Of course, the FCC will make sure that any new system will be compatible with current receivers and VCRs, much as it did when we made the move from black and white to color in the 1960s. As with color, it is highly unlikely that anyone is going to want a 525-line set once they've seen HDTV.

Broadcasters are concerned about having to shell out anywhere from $5 million to $15 million apiece to make the transition, but there is an upside: Because HDTV employs digital technology (and thanks to current advances in digital compression) broadcasters could theoretically send out considerably more than a single TV signal. According to *Broadcasting*, "HDTV could allow broadcasters to compete directly with telephone and cable companies, offering voice and data services from their broadcast towers and opening up entire new streams of revenue." It will be up to the FCC to decide if they will be allowed to do so.

Portable computers that could be used at home and at the office had a large impact on the personal computer marketplace in the latter part of the 1980s.

In the meantime, the industry is gearing up for the change. Peter Fannon of the Advanced Television Test Center warned broadcasters at a recent convention that "from our perspective, it is clear that the future of HDTV is close at hand." Long a topic of discussion, the dawn of HDTV is here at last. Our entire perception of television is about to be altered forever.

The Computer Revolution?

In 1996 IBM will celebrate the 15th anniversary of the introduction of its first personal computer. Today the personal computer industry has annual revenues in the $30 billion range, and 33% of Mediamerica's households are equipped with one or more PCs (see 17.5).

According to Stanford University Professor Robert Textor, the personal computer is symbolic of "what will be seen by historians as nothing less than the third great revolution in mankind's culture-building career—as pro-

found in its implications for the human condition as the agricultural and industrial revolutions." With computers becoming commonplace in offices and schools across the country, it won't be long before using a computer will be second nature to a new generation of consumers.

But there are those who maintain that talk of the computer revolution may be premature, especially where PCs are concerned. According to Anthony Oettinger, professor of Information Resource Policy at Harvard, "To talk about the PC being revolutionary is a bit of salesmanship on the part of computer companies." He believes that personal computers have not really lived up to their revolutionary promises because "they are still too difficult for the average person to use and the average price tag . . . is financially out of reach for most consumers."

Despite the many possible applications of PCs, he contends that "people still prefer to write letters with a pen, balance a checkbook with a calculator and play games with a deck of cards. . . . Most people cannot find even one task that provides a good enough justification to buy a PC."

Humorist Erma Bombeck agrees. She bought one five years ago and laments that "it has no sense of humor whatsoever." According to *USA Today*, she's abandoned it and returned to her IBM typewriter. She's hedging her bet, though. "I want to be sure it's not a flash in the pan. . . . I was going to make it into a planter. But if it's going to be around for a while, OK, maybe I'll learn it."

Nevertheless there are a lot of satisfied PC users. Actor Sam Behrens ("Knots Landing") uses his to write and study scripts and says, "You can do without it, but once you've had it, you cannot imagine life without it." Portland Trail Blazer Buck Williams uses his to follow stock investments. "The computer makes these numbers all talk to me. . . . I love it. At the rate the computer era is going, if you're not involved in the technology you're going to be out in the cold."

Desktop publishing is a recent computer innovation that supplies one good reason for those who write for a living to buy a PC. According to *Byte* magazine, "Desktop publishing is a deceptively simple description for an extremely complex group of hardware and software tools . . . which provide a method for producing professional-looking documents without the need for outside typesetters or graphic artists. You can now write text, edit text, draw illustrations, incorporate photographs, design page layouts, and print a finished document with a relatively inexpensive computer and laser printer."

Many contend that the next generation of personal computing will come in the form of the so-called pen computers that are designed to be held in one hand and written on by the other. These PCs can be trained to recognize the handwriting of the user and translate it directly to a file. Tim Bajarin of Creative Strategies International believes that by 1995 over 40% of all portable PCs will be pen based: "This is the first PC technology that could get a computer in the hands of everybody."

When Steven Jobs and Steve Wozniak formed Apple Computer back in 1977, they envisioned systems that would "offer freedom to workers and executives who were prisoners of time." PCs have saturated the workplace, but results have been mixed. Pacific Bell bought 40,000 PCs for its 60,000 employees, but director of office systems Dennis Kavenaugh reports that while some users are productive "others would actually be more productive if PCs were yanked out of their office."

He explains that putting a powerful computer on everyone's desk is "like giving everyone a powerful race car and hoping they will win the race. But giving everyone a powerful race car is not enough because it can't drive itself." Operating the average PC remains too difficult. "The PC is not a mature technology

Writers can also become artists, graphic designers, and publishers, thanks to desktop publishing.

and its relative immaturity places a great burden on the user."

Byte technical editor Stanley J. Wszola reminds users that although the new technology offers new freedom, "There is a price to be paid for this freedom. With total control comes total responsibility." In fact, the issue of social responsibility in our new computer age has long been a topic of debate among computer enthusiasts.

PC Magazine publisher David Bunnell is concerned with the long-term social effects of the so-called computer revolution. Ironically, many PC pioneers who built and marketed the first machines were 1960s-style advocates of social change. Bunnell, a former college chapter president of the radical Students for a Democratic Society, notes that "while personal computer technology has the potential to make society more equal, it's having the opposite effect since upper-middle-class people can afford them and lower-class people cannot."

In addition, the ways that computers are used to monitor the activities of their users have evoked anxiety about "Big Brother." According to writer John Eckhouse, "Over 7 million Americans now have their work paced, controlled, and monitored by computers." Langdon Winner, a professor of political science at the Rensselaer Institute, says that a computer is "more restrictive and powerful in the way it controls people than the old-fashioned assembly line." This can lead to what some have called "techno-stress." Irritated eyes, back problems, and other physical symptoms have also been associated with the extensive use of computers.

Byte's Jane Morril Tazelaar envisions an office of tomorrow equipped with furniture that is "ergonomically designed for the health and safety of its workers. Paper is nearly non-existent. You receive all mail electronically. . . . In meetings you take notes on pen-based computing pads and feed them directly in to your computer. . . . Presentations are multi-media based: Pulling them together is simply a matter of "mousing" around and combining various objects. All linkage between them is automatic. . . . You can talk to your computer in a normal voice with continuous speech. It understands the natural language it hears and then either speaks in human tones or displays its responses on a large screen in nonfatiguing colors." If this all sounds a little far-fetched, she insists that "everything I've mentioned so far is available today, although in a more primitive form."

Perhaps the safest conclusion is that while PCs in the office and at home have come a long way, they still have a long way to go. Although the personal computer may not have had the liberating impact some predicted, the combination of computer technology with satellite, cable, video, and telephone technologies into state-of-the-art multimedia systems does promise innovations that would have seemed astonishing just a few short years ago.

IBM's ThinkPad is one of the new generation of pen-based computers.

Video Technology: The Consumer Takes Control

In 1975 Sony introduced Betamax, the first videocassette recorder (VCR) intended for home use (see 17.6). VCRs can now be found in over two thirds of all TV households. Shows can be taped and played back at a later, more convenient time. One show can be taped while another is being watched because a VCR is actually a small "recording" TV set without the picture tube.

Originally, VCRs were sold in two non-compatible formats, Beta and VHS. Beta purists argued that picture quality was better with their format; VHS fans boasted that their system allowed more hours per tape. VHS won the battle, and Beta went the way of the eight-track tape and vinyl record (see 17.7).

What can be accomplished with a state-of-the-art "smart" VCR is truly amazing. Most VCRs now offer viewers such options as freeze

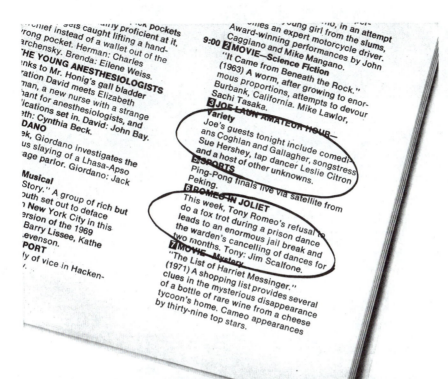

17.6

Sony introduced home video recording with the Betamax unit in 1975. The two-shows-at-once and time-shift functions are still major marketing features for all of today's VCR manufacturers.

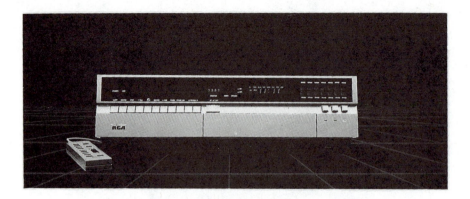

17.7

The RCA Selectavision was one of the first high-tech video recorders to hit the market. Today's VCRs weigh less than half of those in use a decade ago.

frame and slow motion. Most important from a consumer point of view is the scan feature, which allows viewers to "zap" commercials and other unwanted programming segments at will. On-screen programming and stereo sound are now commonplace.

Camcorders have also become popular in recent years, offering consumers the chance to make their own "funniest home videos." Many state-of-the-art camcorders offer all the trappings of a good VCR including stereo sound and flexible editing capabilities (see 17.8).

17.8

Hitachi was one of several companies to enter the rapidly expanding camcorder marketplace. Appearing just as the sales of home video units began to level off, camcorders were the key to growing video markets in the latter 1980s.

In 1988 the Super-VHS (SVHS) system appeared. This high-quality VHS is not totally compatible with current VHS units; tapes recorded on SVHS cannot be played back on a regular VHS machine. SVHS units currently go for about $1,000 or more and have not exactly been snapped up by consumers.

Nevertheless, the popularity of home video recording machines has increased significantly as prices have dropped. Currently, VCRs can

17.9

Magnavox obviously did not want to be left out of the home video revolution. This ad stressed a complete home video system including a television, a video game unit, a home video recording system that records off the air (as well as allowing the consumer to make home video movies with the addition of a camera), and "Discovision," a video disc system. This was one of the first attempts to integrate components into a single system and served as a forerunner of the new multimedia systems now appearing on the market.

be found for as little as $150 or as much as $1,600, depending on the options chosen. The most economical machines are those manufactured in Korea.

The legality of home taping was in question for some time. Originally the courts had held that such taping, even for private home use, may be in violation of copyright law. The case was finally settled in 1984 when the Supreme Court ruled 5-4 that home taping was legal. Video manufacturers and VCR owners breathed a sigh of relief. Meanwhile, those who own the rights to movies and television programs continued to pressure Congress to enact a special tax on machines and tapes to make sure they would receive appropriate copyright payments.

Compact and Laser Discs

Competing with VCRs for the home video market are *video disc players*. Unlike VCRs, these units cannot record; they play only prerecorded programs. Featuring high-quality sound and pictures, they surpass all VCRs in these crucial categories. Thus the consumer is told that no home system is complete without one (see 17.9). The public has clearly shown a preference for VCRs, however, with their ability to record, play back, and erase. Though video discs were marketed as a great breakthrough in home viewing, sales have lagged as variations on basic VCR formats have proliferated.

Much more successful are the audio compact discs. What were once known as "record stores" have now become CD stores with large blocks of space given over to the shiny discs. Consumers are paying $15.98 each for new releases of these high-quality, virtually indestructible "albums" (some older titles sell for less). Just why they cost so much remains a mystery.

A *Los Angeles Times* probe into the cost factors yielded some interesting statistics. The average manufacturing costs are about $2.35 per disc. Add to that the artist royalty ($1.85), songwriting royalty ($.60), and marketing costs ($1.20) and you come up with $6.00. In 1993 the old "long box" packaging was all but eliminated, saving manufacturers another half dollar per unit.

So how come they retail for $15.98? Music retailers claim the fault lies squarely with the record companies. Arnie Bernstein, executive vice-president of the Musicland chain, says, "When CDs first came out, retailers were led to believe that as costs dropped, prices would come down. . . . The companies asked us to hang in there until it happened. We're still waiting."

Rich Kudolla of Columbia Records says, "We believe that consumers are paying a fair price for an exceptionally durable product that is extremely entertaining. CDs are infinitely better than albums or tapes, so why shouldn't they cost more?" Everyone agrees that the high cost of CDs is hurting the music industry that generates some $8 billion in revenues each year. CDs account for about half of that amount, and record company executives say there is little chance that costs will come down. Meanwhile, consumers are buying less music than ever and the used-CD market is booming.

Video disc manufacturers are watching these trends closely. Current video disc programming is primarily movies; thousands of titles are available. Yet VCRs may have cornered that market. So video makers are now planning more interactive software: cooking demonstrations, exercise programs, and the like. Such programs utilize video disc capabilities much more effectively, but the public will have to be educated in how to use them. Meanwhile, CD technology has become a crucial component in the new multimedia systems. Of all the home video technologies, laser discs appear to have the brightest long-term future and the most intriguing possibilities, despite their current marketing and cost problems.

Dialing the Future: New Telephone Technologies

Marketing and cost dilemmas also play a crucial role in the vast array of new telephone technologies that are arriving at a heady rate. Most prominent is cellular telephone technology, which is already changing the way we communicate and do business with one another.

The 1980s was clearly the decade of the coming of age of the portable, or cellular, phone system. Cordless phones are now commonplace, and personal portable phones utilizing cellular technology can now be seen daily on the nation's freeways. In 1980 a car phone cost about $5,000, clearly out of reach for all but the most upscale business users. Today a complete system may sell for as little as $300.

No longer confined to cars, the portable phone is actually a miniature radio transmitter that communicates with different hexagonal-shaped cells (hence the cellular name) dispersed throughout the phone company's service area. These relays retransmit the signal to land-based telephone lines and complete the call.

When the recession hit, many predicted that cellular phones were little more than

Today's cellular phones are virtually "free" to consumers willing to commit to using the airwaves of super-competitive cellular systems.

"yuppie toys" and cellular stocks plummeted. Nevertheless, the number of users doubled from 1989 to 1991, and annual cellular revenues have climbed to over $6 billion. Currently, about 10% of Mediamerica's phone users have portable capability. Industry estimates indicate that figure could rise to over 30% by the end of the century.

Industry analysts say that the key to cellular's continued growth lies in the flexibility of systems to deliver various services to the consumer. According to *Business Week*:

> Subscribers are no longer satisfied with a cellular phone that simply allows them to make and receive calls while tooling around town. These days they want calls to reach them wherever they are—in their home, at the office, or in a distant city. And wherever they move, they want to be able to use all the features that they pay for, including conference calling and voice mail.

The cellular telephone may be the first step toward Frederick Williams's prediction of "a worldwide communications network linking all individuals on earth by means of wristwatch-size communication units." In 1992 Bell Atlantic introduced a small hand-held "personal communicator" (Beam me up Scotty!) that "can do triple duty as a cordless phone in the home, a wireless adjunct to the office phone system and a conventional cellular phone on the road."

Meanwhile, at a recent international conference of radio officials, excitement was generated by proposals to open up a new band of radio frequencies that *U.S. News & World Report* says "would connect calls by satellite from one hand-held phone to another anywhere on the earth's surface."

Motorola seems to have taken the lead in this technology by

> developing a $3.2 billion system called Iridium that promises to connect any two mobile phones in the world when commercial service begins in 1997. Signals from a hand-held phone would be beamed to one of 77 satellites circling the globe. . . . Despite high initial costs of $3,000 for an Iridium handset and $3 a minute to call, business travellers who go to parts of the world where phone service is poor or unavailable are likely to find the service attractive.

While cellular technology remains the most obvious innovation in phone technology, there are a number of other services on the horizon that could help shape our phone future. We are already growing accustomed to answering machines, automatic dialing, and call waiting. Office voice-mail systems now route calls automatically and allow users to direct their calls to the most appropriate departments and leave messages in individual "mailboxes." New "smart phone" services include:

- Phones that trace or block calls
- Phones with special rings to identify callers before you pick up
- Pagers that flash messages on tiny screens
- Intelligent 800 numbers that offer interactive capability

How will consumers react to all of this? It's hard to say. Fewer than 10% of the phone customers who pay for three-way calling and speed dialing actually use them. The problem: confusion over how to program the phone to take advantage of these services.

In addition, there are concerns regarding the intrusive nature of what some feel is a relentless telephone technology. Not everyone thinks that being reachable at all times is a good idea. In an interview in *Money* magazine, sociology professor Rosanna Hertz contends that "there is no longer a separation between work and family life." Professor Donald Norman concurs: "The telephone has badly distorted our lives. We all need downtime for our minds and bodies."

Just how much telephone technology we need, and what it may ultimately mean to our society, remains to be seen. Market forces will play a crucial role. College professors will study the effects. What was once a simple two-way communication device has blossomed into an incredibly complex and comprehensive system that Alexander Graham Bell would hardly recognize.

Wire to Wire: The Marriage of Cable and Phone Technologies

Once upon a time there were two distinct and separate home services: cable TV and the telephone. Safely surrounded by a wall of government regulation, these two giants seemed to have little in common. But today technological change is poised to force a shotgun marriage of the two, and each is scrambling for its "fair share" of the consumer information pie. According to telecommunications expert Arthur D. Little, "The cable industry and the telephone industry are headed toward each other like two steaming locomotives."

As we have seen, the introduction of fiber optics will create a vast data highway into the home. At issue is who will build and ultimately control access to that highway with its estimated $1 trillion in revenues by the year 2000. According to media analyst Fritz Ringling, "The winner would wind up calling the shots and the loser could end up with an electronic white elephant."

Initially, it appears that the phone companies hold the edge. According to *Time* magazine, phone industry assets are currently in the $200 billion range while cable assets are around $50 billion. What's more, *Time* reports that the regulatory mood in Washington has shifted significantly:

> Traditionally, the telephone company was the utility that the public loves to hate. Cable now appears to hold that distinction, thanks to growing public resentment over the rapid rise in cable rates.

Phone companies began laying fiber-optic lines about 10 years ago, but cable operators are catching up quickly. Phone companies are pressuring the government to deregulate the industry. U.S. Telephone President John Sodolski explains: "If it's going to be a race between us, then we want to run with both legs like cable, not with one leg tied down."

When Democratic Congressman Rick Boucher introduced a bill to allow phone companies to own cable systems, he explained, "The only way you can stop unregulated monopoly of cable from gouging subscribers is to introduce competition."

However the economics play out, the marriage of cable and telephone technologies will ultimately lead to home information systems that will provide services in a few short years that boggle the imagination. Among them:

- Television programs and movies on demand. Viewers will simply call them up on one of their 300 channels, with charges appearing on a monthly bill.

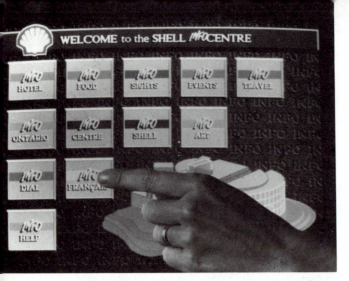

Interactive multimedia systems offer users a dazzling array of choices.

- TV remote-control devices that can do everything from ordering a pizza to picking which TV news stories are to be covered in depth.
- Home shopping and electronic yellow pages.
- Full banking services.
- Video picture phones.
- Access to electronic classrooms where viewers can ask questions, take tests, and earn a degree without ever leaving the home.

Many of these services are already in operation in an experimental system in Cerritos, California, being offered by General Telephone. According to the *Los Angeles Times*, "High-tech, hybrid telecommunication systems that combine traditional telephone and cable TV services could become commonplace under a plan by the FCC to allow local telephone companies to provide cable television to their customers."

The centerpiece of the phone company's plans for our electronic future is the Integrated Services Digital Network. ISDN allows the phone company to become the pipeline for every conceivable communication service including faxes, newspapers, videoconferencing,

and home shopping services, as well as radio and TV.

Special ISDN fiber-optic networks are being constructed that promise to integrate all existing communication networks into a complete range of telecommunication services — voice, data, image, and video — in a single network, cheaper, faster, and with greater accuracy.

As the FCC and Congress sort through the competing demands of cable and phone companies, consumers await a vast new array of services that will soon find their way into Mediamerica's homes.

Multimedia Systems

The marriage of phone and cable technologies is only one part of the trend toward converging home electronics systems. For years, manufacturers have been encouraging consumers to link their home electronic components together (see 17.9). Enter multimedia. Current multimedia systems are essentially a melding of the PC, CD, and TV. This technological "alphabet soup" makes it possible for TV viewers to control and create their own interactive video experiences. Several multimedia systems are already on the market, and more are on the way. According to *Business Week*:

> The interactive part is the key. Instead of just watching *Sesame Street* . . . kids can participate in it. Ernie and Bert appear on the TV, invite you into their apartment, and guide you through activities. Using a hand-held remote control with a tiny joystick, you can examine items in their living room. Select a book and it will open so that you and Ernie can read together. Pick the Muppet's TV and they'll guide you through an interactive arithmetic lesson.

For adults, there are programs like "ABC Sports Golf: Palm Springs Open," which allows you to choose your club, determine the trajectory, and play simulations of various real-life courses. Hit a poor shot and "a snide British commentator weighs in with caustic remarks" like, "I think dehydration is setting in, Jim."

Other programs offer a self-guided tour through the Smithsonian Institution or encyclopedias with moving pictures and sound. In addition, you'll be able to store still pictures on a CD and "take standard video from a VCR, edit it, add sound, graphics and text and then send it back to the VCR for viewing."

All of this is accomplished "by harnessing computer chips to blend digitalized text, still photos, graphics, CD-quality voice and sound, and eventually full-motion video. Information is stored on special CDs called CD-ROMS [read-only memory]."

Is multimedia a mere linkage of present systems? The next great wave of personal computing? (See the guest essay by Peter Scisco.) Or perhaps an electronic gateway to a future that affords us a set of entirely new problem-solving capabilities? Only time will tell. Meanwhile, the enthusiasm for multimedia systems with their infinite possibilities continues to grow.

Virtual Reality

You're in a primordial world. The smell of the dense underbrush permeates the air. The swish-swish of your feet can be heard as you hack your way through the primitive jungle. Suddenly a SCREAM from above. A 100-foot-long 'dactyl is headed your way, and it looks like it means business. Startled, you look up, pull out your weapon, and blast it out of the sky. Direct hit! Its body thunders to the ground with the force of an earthquake.

Welcome to virtual reality (VR for short). "Dactyl Nightmare" is but one experience featured on "Virtuality," the prototype VR arcade game of tomorrow that's already in place in selected shopping malls on the West Coast. VR technology has finally left the research lab and made its way to the consumer. And it's only the beginning.

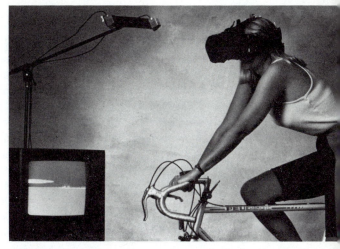
Virtual reality cyclists can race around the world without ever leaving their living rooms.

Writer Brenda Laurel contends that "VR techniques and technologies will be standard features of many entertainment, business and communications environments." VR delivers what computer scientists call telepresence — "a medium or technology that can give a person the sense of physically being in a different place or time, either real or imagined."

So what? It can be argued that any good movie or computer game can create the sense of being in another world, thanks to our ever-so-willing suspension of disbelief. But telepresence is much more — it means you take your body with you into that world. Computers accomplish this electronic sleight of hand by head-tracking, which allows them to adjust what you see and hear according to where you are looking. If you move toward a window, you can hear what's going on "outside." The proper computer-ese term is "viewpoint-dependent imaging."

You slip on a helmet, or perhaps a body suit, and suddenly find yourself in a computer-generated world of light, color, sound, and even smell. VR techniques have been largely developed at NASA and at several small independent research labs in California.

Multimedia—The Next Generation?

Peter Scisco's succinct commentary on the social and political impact of the computer revolution is a welcome voice amid the sea of technical articles that generally appear in computer magazines. You might say that he is one of the most "user friendly" computer writers in America today. This article first appeared in the June 1991 issue of Compute *magazine.*

If you're among the many computer users who've been bombarded by the latest technological buzzword, *multimedia*, your understanding of that term may revolve around a vague and tenuous idea of television pictures, stereo music, and a PC. But multimedia isn't a new phenomenon spon-sored by advanced technology. It has its roots in various intellectual movements—from art to philosophy—that span the last 20 years.

As an art form, multimedia gathers disparate images into a single, focused vision—not as a sluice channels water, but as a laser channels light. It's particularly fitted to this post-modern world of visual impressions, fragmented narratives, information overload, and accelerated living.

Multimedia isn't just a collection of computers and programs coupled with camcorders and CD players. Computer hardware and software makers have seized on multimedia as a means of packaging products for consumers. (And that's not a criticism; it's a fact. Turn on MTV if you want to see the standards under which software—in this case, music—is packaged for your consumption.)

The most vocal proponents of multimedia insist that the hardware and software born from this latest technological wave will integrate computing into suites of mutually enhancing applications with an unlimited capability for creating new ways of teaching, working, and playing.

But using that word *multimedia* to define a class of computer activities and applications underscores a compelling, if rarely stated, axiom about the PC: It's not the amount and availability of information that defines the usefulness of computer technology; rather, it's the presentation of and access to information that makes the PC such a powerful medium.

Most folks don't think of the personal computer as a me-

Telepresence comes in two forms: virtual environments, the computer-generated kind represented in "Dactyl Nightmare," and remote presence, the ability to experience a real location that is remote in space and time. Here is where NASA has pioneered with space simulators that get future astronauts used to the real thing before they blast off.

You probably don't need a lot of prompting to imagine the possibilities of this technology, particularly as it might link up to your own computer and video hardware. VR is already useful in helping engineers design everything from cars to custom furniture. Feature-film set designers now have a VR program that allows them to walk through computer-generated sets, view them from every angle, and make creative decisions before costly construction begins.

If you're tempted to write VR off as mere arcade entertainment, remember that today's powerful PCs began in the late 1970s as simple conduits for video games (remember Pong and Pac Man?). Many experts are predicting that VR technology will be readily available for home use by the end of the century. Telepresence could well supplant television as the standard for home entertainment. Combined with some of the technologies that we have already explored in this chapter, virtual reality could soon transport us to a Mediaworld unlike any we have ever known.

dium in its own right, not in the way they think of television, for example. McLuhan's oft-quoted line of the medium as message didn't originally apply to the PC—or did it? And if the answer to that question is *Yes*, then exactly what kind of medium is it?

Is the PC an expansive, open-ended, technologically sophisticated channel to the world—past, present, and future? Or is it limited by its complexity? Does the PC's graphical and oh-so-modern attractiveness to the video generation make it the equal of television and film? Or is the PC's access to and manipulation of information held prisoner by its reliance on such paraphernalia as keyboards, display terminals, and floppy disks?

Can the personal computer create a society of aware citizens, with instant access to necessary information? Or does PC technology spew noise into the channel, obscuring critical thought and debate? Can the PC bring people together as a community of insights and ideas? Or will the PC landscape remain the elite domain of the computer-literate? And, the ultimate query: Does the shape of PC technology influence our view of the world?

We often limit the PC's influence by calling it a *productivity tool*, a *learning environment*, or a *game machine*. The phrases fail to consider the personal computer's greatest attribute—that it can enhance, educate, and entertain, all from within the confines of its metal casing.

You hear a lot of talk about how multimedia is the next great wave of personal computing. You also hear a lot of talk about how multimedia is just another buzzword that hypes purposeless technology at the expense of purposeful engineering. Well, here's another earful. Multimedia isn't a product. Multimedia isn't hardware or software you can buy. It isn't TV pictures and stereo music on your computer. It's the essential interplay of multiple perspectives necessary for critical thinking and creative solutions.

The writer Walker Percy launched speculations by "sidling up alongside" ideas through language and the power of metaphor. If multimedia can separate PC use from the encumbrances of technology, then we have gained a valuable perspective on the roles computers play in our lives.

Issues and Answers: The Communications Future

About the time the semester winds down and we begin to discuss the future of Mediamerica and Mediaworld, I hear two major concerns about the new technologies from students. One involves the fear that machines will "take over" or somehow usurp the human experience and leave us emotionally bankrupt. The second, often mentioned in connection with video games and now virtual reality, is familiar because it has been put forth by the opponents of television for years: Are we increasingly escaping from reality into a world of fantasy made possible by the new technologies?

Both concerns are real, and arguments can be made on each side. On balance, it seems to me that both concerns are essentially unfounded.

Some years ago, *Channels* magazine argued convincingly for the acceptance of "technology without fear." There is no more reason to be put off by communications technology than by jet planes, automatic dishwashers, or old-fashioned radios.

To utilize the new technologies, we don't need to know everything about what makes them work, any more than we need to know how a motor works in order to drive a car or how a TV set works in order to watch it. Devices are becoming increasingly complex, but unless they are "user-friendly" — comprehensible to the average consumer without too much trouble — they will never be widely used or accepted.

Another quality that seems promising about the new technologies is that they allow the consumer to control more of what she or he sees, hears, and experiences. Cable TV and satellite delivery systems allow us to choose from dozens of entertainment and instructional channels, freeing us from the "tyranny" of the big three. Computers give us instant access to information in a way that is unprecedented. Home video technologies enable us to watch what we want when we want. In essence, the new technologies have delivered a means to put us in control of our own mediated reality as never before.

Mediated reality is best understood as another form of reality, not an escape from it. Back in Chapter 1 we discussed the crucial differences between real life and mediated reality. These are especially important in light of the proliferation of the new technologies, each

with its own mediated content. To turn on the screen or pick up the digitally transported version of the day's news is to still enter the world of mediated reality. Through media courses such as the one you're taking right now, we are all learning more about the nature of mediated reality as it exists and as it will exist in the future.

Although we should not embrace change for its own sake, neither should we reject it out of fear, anxiety, or lack of knowledge. The technological landscape of Mediamerica and Mediaworld is changing more rapidly than ever before. Never has there been a better time for you to develop your skills as a critical consumer of mass-mediated information. To do this, you will need to be open to change, because it is inevitable. It may be "the business of the future to be dangerous," but that future is still ours to create. Your increased awareness, knowledge, and sensitivity regarding the changes to come can only help enhance your experiences in Mediaworld as well as real life. Your understanding can be the key to making the Mediaworld of the future a more positive and meaningful one for all of us.

Queries and Concepts

1 As a research project, find out what is the impact of cable and the other new technologies in your community. Try to obtain data concerning the availability and success of these new program sources. Can you speculate as to what impact some of these new programs might be having in your area?

2 If you currently receive MTV or a similar program in your area, do a brief content analysis of the rock videos you find in the program. How many are straight concert footage, and how many involve some kind of storytelling? What percentage of

videos currently involve at least one black performer?

3 In one page, tell why you think signals coming from satellites should or should not be free to all those who have purchased the equipment to receive them. What are the economic implications of your conclusion?

4 You are about to buy your first computer. How many tasks that you do on a regular basis could possibly be accomplished more efficiently with a computer? You'll need to spend some time at your local

computer outlet to learn more about current computer capabilities.

5 Your boss has given you the task of dreaming up the most amazing virtual-reality game ever conceived. What is it like? What qualities does it have that will ensure universal success?

Readings and References

Wilson P. Dizard, Jr.
The Coming Information Age. 2d. ed. New York: Longman, 1984.

A highly regarded work in the field. Though dated in places, Dizard's insights still hit the target often. Highly recommended.

Linkups: The Foundation of the Communications Revolution

Statistical information in this section and throughout the chapter can be found in *Variety*'s special report on cable TV, November 15, 1991.

The Wired Nation: Cable TV

"Cable TV." *Consumer Reports,* Sept. 1987, pp. 547–555.

Morrie Gelman
"MTV, Power and the Kingdom." *Variety,* Nov. 18, 1991, p. m-1.

John Lippman
"Cable on (the) Defensive." *Los Angeles Times,* Nov. 23, 1991, p. d-1.

"MTV, The Channel That Ate the World." *Los Angeles Times/Calendar,* May 8, 1991, p. c-3.

Premium and Pay-Per-View: Cable and Information Services

Daniel Cerone
"If 75 Cable-TV Channels Just Aren't Enough, Try 150 . . ." *Los Angeles Times,* Dec. 17, 1991, p. f-1.

John Dempsey
"Comcast Taps into Cable Future." *Variety,* Feb. 24, 1992, p. 8.

David J. Fishman
"Two Way Television." *Discover,* May 1991, p. 37.

"Forging Cable's Technology Future." *Broadcasting,* May 4, 1992, p. 35.

Peter Lambert
"Technology Key to Bright Cable Future." *Broadcasting,* May 11, 1992, p. 4.

"Ushering in Smart Cable TV." *Broadcasting,* May 4, 1992, p. 64.

Cable at the Crossroads: Reregulation

Dennis Wharton
"Reregulation Threat Haunts, Sways NCTA." *Variety,* May 1, 1992, p. 13.

Fiber Optics

John Free
"Fiber Optics Head for Home." *Popular Science,* Mar. 1992, p. 64.

John Schwartz
"The Highway to the Future." *Newsweek,* Jan. 13, 1991, p. 56.

DBS: Direct-Broadcast Satellites

Graham Button
"Stan Hubbard's Giant Footprint." *Forbes,* Nov. 11, 1991.

Peter Lambert
"Hughes to Offer Cable Programmers Free DBS Ride." *Broadcasting,* April 27, 1992, p. 14.

Dennis Wharton
"Hughes Markets Dishes to Sticks." *Variety,* April 23, 1992, p. 1.

Commercial Satellite Applications

Frederick Williams
The Communications Revolution. New York: New American Library, 1983.

It comes as quite a shock to see how closely Williams' predictions have come to pass. Very accessible reading.

The New Communications. 3d ed. Belmont, Calif.: Wadsworth, 1992.

Williams takes his future show on the road for students. A breakthrough text. Highly recommended.

Technology and Communication Behavior. Belmont, Calif.: Wadsworth, 1987.

How the information revolution will enhance our ability to communicate.

HDTV: The Couch Potato's Dream

Harry A. Jessell
"1992: The Year of HDTV?" *Broadcasting,* May 23, 1992, p. 62.

Peter Lambert
"HDTV: A Game of Take and Give." *Broadcasting,* April 20, 1992, p. 6.

The Computer Revolution?

John Eckhouse
"Special Report: Personal Computers." *San Francisco Chronicle,* Jan. 11, 1988, p. 1.

"Jobs and Gates Together." *Fortune,* Aug. 26, 1991, p. 50.

Scott Leibs
"The Return of the Pen." *Compute,* April 1992, p. 76.

Kathy Robello
John Schneidawind
"A PC Anniversary." *USA Today,* Aug. 12, 1991, p. b-1.

Kenneth M. Sheldon
"You've Come a Long Way, PC." *Byte,* Aug. 1991, p. 336.

Jane Morril Tazelaar
"Visions of Tomorrow." *Byte,* Sept. 1991, p. 207.

Compact and Laser Discs

Chuck Phillips
"High Cost of Listening." *Los Angeles Times/Calendar,* May 3, 1992, p. 6.

Dialing the Future: New Telephone Technologies

William J. Cook
"Dialing the Future." *U.S. News & World Report,* Feb. 3, 1992, p. 49.

Debra Wishik Englander
"How to Be as Smart as Your Phone." *Money,* Jan. 1991, p. 123.

Janet Mann
"The Business of Phone Tag." *Datamation,* Sept. 1, 1991, p. 89.

"Not Just a Yuppie Toy." *Business Week,* Feb. 24, 1992, p. 36.

Judith Stone
"Dial S for Science." *Discover,* Dec. 1991, p. 76.

Wire to Wire: The Marriage of Cable and Phone Technologies

"AT&T to Offer New Types of Cable Services." *Los Angeles Times,* May 5, 1992, p. d-1.

John Lippman
"How the Line Between Cable, Phones May Blur." *Los Angeles Times,* Oct. 26, 1991, p. b-1.

Thomas McCarroll
"A Giant Tug-of-Wire." *Time,* Feb. 26, 1992, p. 36.

Multimedia Systems

Edward C. Baig
"A Marriage of the Media." *U.S. News & World Report,* Nov. 25, 1991, p. 83.

Edward Murray
"CDs Beyond Music." *C.D. Review,* June 1992, p. 16.

Evan I. Schwartz
"Multimedia Is Here, and It's Amazing." *Business Week,* Dec. 16, 1991, p. 130.

Virtual Reality

Brenda Laurel
"Strange New Worlds of Entertainment." *Compute,* Nov. 1991, p. 102.

Janet Wiscombe
"It's a Virtual Blast." *Long Beach Press-Telegram,* April 5, 1992, p. j-1.

Note: Students interested in the latest developments in the new technologies would do well to consult current copies of any of the magazines included in these references.

Index

Acknowledgments

We gratefully acknowledge permission to use material found on the following pages:

Pp. 1, 22: Archive Photos

P. 3: Lyrics by Stephen Stills, Columbia Pictures Industries, Inc. © 1966 Cotillion Music/Springalo Toones/Ten-East Music. All rights reserved

P. 29: Topham/The Image Works

Pp. 35–36: Copyright 1994 USA Today. Reprinted with permission.

P. 37: Reprinted by permission of *The Wall Street Journal,* © 1994 Dow Jones & Company, Inc. All rights reserved worldwide

Pp. 49, 95, 110, 111, 114, 121, 138, 155, 250, 252, 253: Historical Pictures Service, Inc.

Pp. 50–51: Excerpt from "The Shooting Script" by Herman J. Mankiewicz and Orson Welles, as published in *The Citizen Kane Book.* © 1971 by Bantam Books, Inc.

Pp. 51, 257: RKO General Pictures

Pp. 54, 304: CBS News

Pp. 58–59: KNT News Wire, Knight-Ridder, Inc.

P. 68: *National Enquirer*

P. 70: Ann Landers/Field Newspaper Syndicate

P. 77: Harte-Hanks Newspapers, Inc.

P. 86: FPG

P. 87: Audit Bureau of Circulations

P. 88 left: Copyright © 1983 by Triangle Publications, Inc., Radnor, Pennsylvania. Reprinted with permission from *TV Guide®* Magazine.

P. 88 right: *TV/Cable Week*

Pp. 96–97: *Journal of Popular Culture,* © 1975

Pp. 102–103: original essay by Amy Krakow. Used with permission.

P. 104: Mad Magazine is a trademark of EC Publications, Coppyright © 1992. All rights reserved. Reprinted with permission.

P. 106 magazine covers: (left) Reprinted with permission of *Bronze Thrills;* (center) © 1992 *Compressed Air Magazine;* (right) *Wine Spectator* © 1992 Skanken Communications

P. 123: Archive Photos

Pp. 124–125: Hubert Ellingsworth

P. 127: Spencer Grant/Stock, Boston

P. 128: Akos Szilvasi/Stock, Boston

P. 132: Courtesy KABL, San Francisco

P. 137: Edwin Ginn Library, Tufts University

P. 143: Stock, Boston

P. 154: *Scientific American,* December 22, 1877

Pp. 155, 158: FPG

P. 160: Topham/The Image Works

P. 161: Photoworld/FPG

P. 163: Courtesy A & M Records

P. 170: © 1992 BPI Communications. Used with permission of *Billboard,* Soundscan, Inc./Broadcast Data Systems, Inc.

P. 171: Photo by Ralph P. Fitzgerald/LGI © 1987. Used by permission of Lynn Goldsmith, Inc.

P. 180: UPI/Bettmann

P. 190: Arbitron Ratings, 1992. Used with permission for educational purposes only

P. 195: Children's Television Workshop

P. 199: Nicholas Johnson

P. 206: Photofest

P. 210: Bill Cosby

P. 213: Sullivan Productions

P. 214 top: Devillier Donnegan Enterprises

Pp. 214 bottom, **227:** Courtesy of the National Broadcasting Company, Inc.

P. 220: MTM Enterprises, Inc.

P. 221: Courtesy of Brocata & Kelman, Los Angeles

P. 222: Courtesy ABC Television

P. 229: Photograph courtesy of Pee-Wee Herman © Herman Toys, Inc.

P. 237: © 1992 CNN, Inc.

Pp. 246, 255: Viacom Enterprises

P. 260: Archive Photos

P. 262: Photofest

P. 264: Turner Broadcasting System, Inc.

P. 270: Guy Billant/Photofest

P. 283: Underwood Photo Archive

P. 286: Rick Smolan/Contact Press Images

P. 287: Radio Advertising Bureau

P. 290: Advertising Council

P. 294: Courtesy ARCO Marine, Inc.

P. 295: Reprinted with permission of Nike, Inc.

P. 296: Bruce Kliewe/Jeroboam

P. 297: Ralston Purina Company

P. 298: Luigi & Allesandra Maclean Manca

P. 299: Used by permission of New Republic Clothiers, New York, NY

P. 300: Seagram Distillers Company

P. 302: © 1990 by Ronald K. L. Collins, Michael F. Jacobson. Excerpted from *The Christian Science Monitor* (Sept. 19, 1990). Used with permission of the authors.

P. 313: Bruce Kliewe/Jeroboam

P. 318: Courtesy Honeywell Corp. (M. Suder Library)

P. 320: Beverly Beck Ellman

P. 326: Marshall Fishwick

P. 342: Courtesy of Radio-Television News Directors Association

P. 343: Lynne J. Weinstein/Woodfin Camp & Associates

P. 349: From *Newsweek,* October 21, 1991 © 1991 Newsweek, Inc. All rights reserved. Reprinted by permission

P. 353: Photo by Bob D'Amico. Copyright American Broadcasting Companies, Inc. Courtesy of Steven Bochco Productions and ABC, Inc.

Pp. 356–357: *Code of the Comics Magazine Association of America* reprinted with permission

P. 368: Photofest (M. Suder Library)

P. 371: M. Payer/Stock, Boston

P. 380: AP/Wide World Photos

P. 383: Courtesy of Laser Computer

P. 384: AP/Wide World Photos

P. 386: Warner/Amex Cable

P. 390: Reprinted by permission of Tokyo Broadcasting System, Los Angeles Bureau

P. 392: Photo by Flavio Bonetti. Reprinted by permission of *Mondo Uomo* Magazine

Pp. 392–393: © 1991 San Francisco Examiner

P. 395: J. Chiasson/Gamma-Liaison

P. 397: Tom Sobolik/Black Star

P. 420: Reprinted by permission of *Journalism Quarterly*

P. 463: US Satellite Broadcasting Company

P. 464: Courtesy U.S. Sprint/United Telecom (M. Suder Library)

P. 466: Photo by John Greenleigh. Courtesy of Apple Computer, Inc.

P. 467: Stock, Boston

P. 468: Courtesy IBM (M. Suder Library)

P. 469: Sony

P. 470: RCA

P. 472: Magnavox

P. 474: Courtesy U.S. Sprint/United Telecom (M. Suder Library)

P. 476: Courtesy IBM (M. Suder Library)

P. 477: Courtesy Autodesk, Inc. (M. Suder Library)

P. 478: Reprinted from *Compute,* June 1991. Copyright © 1991 Ziff-Davis Publishing Company, L.P. Reprinted with permission